A GLOSSARY OF LITERARY
AND CULTURAL THEORY

A Glossary of Literary and Cultural Theory provides researchers and students with an up-to-date guide through the vibrant and changing debates in Literary and Cultural Studies. In a field where meanings are frequently complex and ambiguous, this text is remarkable for its clarity and usefulness. This third edition includes 17 entirely new entries and updates to more than a dozen others which address key concepts and contemporary positions in both literary and cultural theory. New entries include:

- Actor Network Theory
- Anthropocene
- Ecocriticism
- Digital Humanities
- Postcapitalism
- World Literature.

Peter Brooker is Emeritus Professor of Literary and Cultural Studies at the University of Nottingham, UK. He is co-author of *A Reader's Guide to Contemporary Literary Theory*, 6th edition (Routledge, 2017) and author of the reissued *Bertolt Brecht: Dialectics, Poetry and Politics* ([1988] Routledge Revivals, 2016).

A GLOSSARY OF LITERARY AND CULTURAL THEORY

Third Edition

Peter Brooker

Routledge
Taylor & Francis Group

LONDON AND NEW YORK

Third edition published 2017
by Routledge
2 Park Square, Milton Park, Abingdon, Oxon OX14 4RN

and by Routledge
711 Third Avenue, New York, NY 10017

Routledge is an imprint of the Taylor & Francis Group, an informa business

© 2017 Peter Brooker

First edition published under the title *Cultural Theory: A Glossary* in 1999 by Hodder Education

Second edition published under the title *A Glossary of Cultural Theory* in 2002 by Arnold

British Library Cataloguing-in-Publication Data
A catalogue record for this book is available from the British Library

Library of Congress Cataloging-in-Publication Data
Names: Brooker, Peter, author.
Title: A glossary of literary and cultural theory / Peter Brooker.
Other titles: Cultural theory
Description: Third edition. | Abingdon, Oxon ; New York, NY : Routledge, 2017.
Identifiers: LCCN 2016026355 (print) | LCCN 2016044248 (ebook) |
ISBN 9781138955486 (pbk. : alk. paper) | ISBN 9781138955462 (hardback :
alk. paper) | ISBN 9781315666327 (ebk) | ISBN 9781315666327 (Master ebk) |
ISBN 9781317354772 (Web PDF) | ISBN 9781317354765 (ePUB) |
ISBN 9781317354758 (Mobi/Kindle)
Subjects: LCSH: Culture--Terminology. | Literature--Terminology.
Classification: LCC HM621 .B76 2017 (print) | LCC HM621 (ebook) |
DDC 306.01/4--dc23
LC record available at https://lccn.loc.gov/2016026355

ISBN: 978-1-138-95546-2 (hbk)
ISBN: 978-1-138-95548-6 (pbk)
ISBN: 978-1-315-66632-7 (ebk)

Typeset in Times New Roman
by Saxon Graphics Ltd, Derby

What is interesting is always interconnection,
not the primacy of this over that.
Michel Foucault

TABLE OF CONTENTS

PREFACE

Originally a Glossary of Cultural Theory, this book is now extended with revised and new entries to become a Glossary of Literary and Cultural Studies. This makes good the argument in the book's original introduction that the study of culture is an inclusive endeavour, and that theory provides a deep and wide resource which is pertinent to, and deployed across, the individual discipline or subject areas of Literary or Cultural Studies.

I should return briefly here, however, to the question of 'theory' itself. 'Theory', with its capital letter, entered into Literary and Cultural Studies and allied areas in a new way in the 1970s and in some quarters developed in an abstract and indulgent vein that many found abstruse and only fleetingly relevant to their own studies or day-to-day concerns. I have wanted to argue that this distressing use of theory should be distinguished from a better, enabling use which problematizes taken-for-granted attitudes and positions (on theory itself as much as anything else) and conceptualizes long-standing or new issues in a productive way. I prefer also to think of this as 'theorization' or 'living theory' active across a range of academic and social arenas. In practice, too, it is 'theories' in the plural, rather than 'Theory', which address key issues (on gender, globalization, power or pleasure, for example) in and across different disciplines or subject areas. Theories therefore commonly 'travel' and are rearticulated or refuted. Literary Studies, as one such particularly eclectic field, draws regularly in this way on concepts from psychoanalysis, philosophy, sociology or history. I hope that readers of this volume will themselves travel from one term to another or to a family of terms. Hence the tag 'see also' accompanying the individual entries. The 'Classification of Keywords' below suggests how certain concepts can be associated with a given domain of this type. However, as such a classification illustrates, repetitions and overlaps also frequently occur. And some 'areas' – Marxism, feminism, poststructuralism – are plainly not academic disciplines in the narrow sense, but traditions and movements of ideas and issues informing a range of intellectual work in more discrete subject areas. Terms associated with these traditions – ideology or textuality, for example – have no single 'discipline' home.

Concepts, it should be added, have a history, indeed, several intellectual histories according to how they are mobilized and according to the problems they address. The entries in the Glossary seek to present ideas in this way: in terms of their key twists and turns, the debates they have entailed, the contributors to these debates, and the fields and questions their work has helped define.

All of this implies how dynamic and strategic the use of theoretical concepts, or the activity of theorization, can or should be. Interestingly, one tendency in particular points this out. If the failings of an abstruse and limited 'Theory' have been duly recognized and surpassed, a particular manifestation of the 'Theory' era – what indeed passed as a code word of this phase – is thought most definitely to belong to the past: that is 'postmodernism'. As a description of a period style, of literary and artistic modes and or social trends, postmodernism held sway especially in the last decades of the twentieth century before being rejected as overextended, modish or, worse, complicit with the consumer society it sought to diagnose. But if 'postmodernism' is indeed history, the prefix 'post' itself has far from receded: for we speak now freely of 'postcapitalism', the 'posthuman', of 'post-theory', and 'postgender' positions and politics. This broad application to matters of subjective and sexual identity, to the movements of people, and national and world economies (no less, ironically, than the sweep of a full-blown, politicized postmodernism) speaks surely, and more emphatically than ever, of a period and sensibility in transition – so much so that the word 'transition' does the work of an active verb ('to transition') and 'trans' can serve as both adjective and noun. The experience of change this articulates can be accompanied by anxiety, anguish and division but will also involve a questioning of taken-for-granted assumptions, beliefs and static redundant models. As such, it shows how necessary a confident and flexible appraisal of ideas and attitudes is to a new-found stability. I hope that this Glossary can play a small part in encouraging the working 'living' theory that will assist its readers in finding or strengthening this confidence and in developing their own way forward.

A note on the text

Where individual terms referred to in one entry have an entry of their own they are included in capital letters. In addition, each entry directs readers to related concepts, under the rubric of 'See also...' The Bibliography includes all texts referred to. Each of these devices has the important function of directing readers to other keywords and to studies beyond the covers of this book. The descriptions 'Literary Studies' or 'Cultural Studies' are given capital letters (as are Media Studies or Sociology). This is to help distinguish these terms from the 'study of culture' or 'study of literature'.

A note on this edition

Updating this Glossary for a third edition has proved to be an at once formidable and exhilarating task – on both counts because of the continuing vitality of theoretical work. I hope this new edition helps others catch up and stay abreast of some of the main lines of development that feed into the study of literature and culture and the Humanities. It contains 17 new terms, and revises and expands on some 15 existing entries. Among the new terms are entries for Actor Network Theory, Affect, Animal Studies, Anthropocene, Ecocriticism, Establishment,

Homo Sacer, Postcapitalism, Robotics, Terrorism and World Literature – often themselves a sign of new perspectives amid present-day crises. Similarly, many of the revised and expanded terms, among them Class, Ecology, the Internet, Nature, Posthuman, Sexual Difference and Digital, register the new experiences and new thinking that mark the present era.

Thanks to the anonymous Readers for Routledge who prompted some of these changes.

CLASSIFICATION OF KEYWORDS ACCORDING TO MOVEMENTS AND FIELDS

FEMINISM

Androgyny; body; chora; compulsory heterosexuality; cyberfeminism; cyborg; desire; différance; difference; *écriture féminine*; essentialism; excess; fetishism; *flâneuse*; gaze; gender; gynesis; gynocriticism; ideology; imaginary; *jouissance*; masquerade; 'men in feminism'; nomadism; patriarchy; performativity; phallocentric; pleasure; posthuman; queer theory; reproduction; semiotic; sexual difference; sexuality; subject; symbolic; transgressive; utopia.

FILM, MEDIA, POPULAR CULTURE

Addresser/addressee; articulation; audience; code; communication; convergence; cult; cultural intermediaries; culture industries; flow; gatekeeping; gaze; genre; image; kitsch; mass; message; *mise-en-scène*; montage; narrative; negotiation; pop; popular; populism; reception; scheduling; suture.

FORM AND MODE

Aesthetic; affect; allegory; aura; author; autonomy; avant-garde; camp; canon; closure; defamiliarization; digital; ecocriticism; *écriture*; elite; estrangement; fantasy; formalism; genre; Gothic; hermeneutics; hyperreality; icon; image; interpretive community; kitsch; metafiction; modernism; montage; narrative; nature; popular; post-theory; readerly/writerly; reading; realism; rhizome; taste; textuality; trauma; utopia; value; world literature.

MARXISM

Agency; alienation; alienation effect; base and superstructure; capital; class; colonialism; commodity fetishism; conjuncture; consciousness; consumerism; critical theory; critique; dialectics; dominant; enlightenment; hegemony; historicism; humanism; ideological state apparatus; ideology; ideology critique; imperialism;

interpellation; *jetztzeit*; mass; materialism; nationalism; postcapitalism; post-Marxism; production; reification; relative autonomy; reproduction; totality; utopia; value.

POSTMODERNISM/POSTCOLONIALISM

City; deterritorialization; ethics; ethnicity; flow; globalization; hybridity; hyperreality; local; modernism; modernity; nationalism; nostalgia; orientalism; parody; pastiche; post-Fordism; posthuman; psychogeography; queer theory; race; simulation; space; spectacle; syncretism; thirdspace; totality; virtual reality.

PSYCHOANALYSIS

Condensation and displacement; desire; dreamwork; excess; fantasy; fetishism; gaze; imaginary; mirror-stage; misrecognition; *Nachträglichkeit*; Oedipal complex; other; phallus; schizoanalysis; sexuality; subject; suture; symbolic; transference; trauma; uncanny; unconscious.

SOCIETY, POLITICS

Actor network theory; animal studies; anthropocene; body; capitalism; citizenship; city; civil society; class; common culture; community; consumerism; cosmopolitanism/ cosmopolitics; counter-culture; cultural politics; culturalism; culture industries; diaspora; distinction; ecology; elite; establishment; ethics; ethnicity; ethnography; everyday life; field; *flâneur*; formation; globalization; governmentality; habitus; *homo sacer*; hybridity; identity; ideology; incorporation; intellectuals; liminality; local; modernity; multiculturalism; place; postcapitalism; public sphere; reflexive modernization; site; structure of feeling; subculture; symbolic violence; taste; terrorism; tourism.

STRUCTURALISM, POSTSTRUCTURALISM, DISCOURSE

Alterity; aporia; archaeology; archive; articulation; author; bricolage; closure; code; deconstruction; deterritorialization; diachronic/synchronic; dialogics; *différance*; difference; discourse; dissemination; *écriture*; *épistème*; ethics; excess; the event; genealogy; governmentality; heteroglossia; heterotopia; intertextuality; *jouissance*; langue; metanarrative; metaphysics of presence; *mise-en-abyme*; narrative; nomadism; parole; pleasure; power; readerly; rhizome; sign; subject; supplement; suture; synchronic; synergy; textuality; trace; translation.

TECHNOLOGY, CULTURE

Anthropocene; chaos; communication; cybernetics; cyberspace; cyborg, digital; digital humanities; hypertext; internet; message; network; robotics; thing theory.

ABJECTION

A term developed by Julia Kristeva (1982) to name the horror of being unable to distinguish between 'me' and 'not-me' of which the first, primary instance is the embryo's existence in the mother's body. The abject is what the subject seeks to expel in order to achieve an independent identity, but this is impossible since the body cannot cease both to take in and expel objects. The latter include tears, faeces, urine, vomit, mucus, which in the infant are the SITE of future erogenous zones as well as of cultural taboos. The abject is a troubled marker between the unclean and clean, and between the pre-Oedipal and Oedipal, the sign of an undecidable boundary line between the inside and the outside of the body, and therefore of a divided subject: it is, says Kristeva, the 'in-between, the ambiguous, the composite' (1982: 4).

Significant borderline states occur with menstruation and pregnancy, and Kristeva examines the latter in ICONS of the mother-figure, especially in religious discourse, which she sees as uniquely tolerating the mother, notably in the figure of the Virgin Mary. The abject is also related to Kristeva's concept of the SEMIOTIC, which is similarly associated with the domain of the maternal, the pre-signifying and pre-Oedipal. Although repressed, it is similarly never surpassed or silenced but intervenes to disrupt the SYMBOLIC order.

The concept of the abject has also been utilized in discussions of the GOTHIC and sci-fi horror genres. Barbara Creed, for example, discusses films such as *The Thing, Alien* and *Aliens* in these terms. Such films, she says, explore 'the "bodies" of female alien creatures whose reproductive systems both resemble the human and are coded as a source of abject horror and overpowering awe' (Brooker and Brooker [eds] 1997: 48). The monstrous or abject is the expelled but powerful feminine, even when, as in the film *Videodrome,* this metaphorically invades the male BODY. In further examples, the 'abject maternal' is explored by E. Ann Kaplan (1990) in a discussion of Alfred Hitchcock's *Marnie,* and Maud Ellman reads T.S. Eliot's *The Waste Land* as a text that reinscribes the personal, sexual, literary and social others (the waste) it tries to expel. *'The Waste Land,'* she says, 'is one of the most abject texts in English literature' (Fletcher and Benjamin [eds] 1990: 181).

See also PSYCHOANALYSIS; UNCANNY.

ACTOR NETWORK THEORY

Actor Network Theory (commonly abbreviated as ANT) derives from the work of Bruno Latour, Michel Callon and John Law in the 1980s and took its impetus from a challenge to the dominant understanding of the special status of science and scientific knowledge. ANT sees the production of scientific knowledge as not unlike the operation of other social processes, which it understands as dynamic and collective networks. It opposes any *a priori* assumptions regarding such networks and does not distinguish, or accept a hierarchy, between nature and society, agency and structure, micro-content or macro-level context, or, most markedly and controversially, between human and non-human, towards which it exercises a principle of 'generalized symmetry'.

As a method, ANT is therefore fundamentally deconstructive and relational. Networks are conceived as comprised of diverse participants and practices observed in process and interpreted by way of certain guiding terms. Thus 'actants' names participants whether human, animal, textual or technological, which enter into associations in which they exert agency and from which, in turn, forms of action, or definition or redefinition (both material and semiotic) are realised. Actants may indeed themselves comprise networks at the outset, that is to say, combinations of features or entities which then enter new assemblages. ANT is duly interested, therefore, in the forms and effects of association, carefully described as 'juxtaposition', 'translation' (the organization and conversion of entities), 'transportation' (the network's becoming useful), 'enrolment' (how others are enlisted), how roles or 'scripts' emerge or are bestowed, and the way these processes are involved in the building or 'stabilization' of a given network or cluster of networks.

'Translation', describing how entities are 'converted'; that is to say, brought through the process of dispute or dissension into alignment or agreement, appears as a core concept in this overall process since it establishes the convergence of the network and its influence or 'success'. If tightly focused or 'simplified', the network is described as 'puncturalized'. Even so, coherent and durable networks will need maintaining or reasserting by a 'spokesperson' in the face of outside competition.

ANT can provide a salutary realization that institutions, places of learning and work and cultural practices, such as a government or university department, a primary school or doctor's clinic, the making of a film or the publication of a book, are composed of multiple interacting activities, personnel, units and technologies. However, its patient analysis can be dauntingly precise in its use of terms and has been seen as limited to a *description* of network formation rather than providing a critical analysis of power relations inherent in such structures. There have also been long-standing reservations about the attribution of agency to non-human objects or entities (see Winner 1993), although it should be noted that ANT does not ascribe 'intentionality' to the non-human.

Bruno Latour famously rang the death knell on ANT in an address in the late 1990s when he announced 'that there are four things that do not work with actor-network theory; the word actor, the word network, the word theory and the hyphen! Four nails in the coffin' (Latour 1999). He has returned to its defence, however, in his *Reassembling the Social: An Introduction to Actor-Network-Theory* (2005). Here, Latour appears to be concerned above all to polemicize against Sociology's continued adherence to what he considers the *a priori*, static and homogenizing concept of 'the social' or 'social context', rather than his preferred notion of dynamic 'associations'. But he also directly addresses questions of power, inequality and a deteriorating environment. 'Critical Sociology', he contends, can, as presently constituted, have little purchase on such issues.

See also DETERRITORIALIZATION; RHIZOME; SPECULATIVE REALISM; THING THEORY.

ADDRESSER/ADDRESSEE

The participants in the standard model of COMMUNICATION between whom a MESSAGE is passed. Sometimes, particularly in earlier representations of this model, addresser and addressee are understood as equivalent to 'sender' and 'receiver'. However, it is important to maintain a distinction between an actual sender of a message, and the position or role of the addresser, as well as between an actual receiver and addressee. Thus, as is commonly recognized, a novelist as private citizen cannot be identified with the narrator of a novel; or even, straightforwardly, with the name on the cover of his/her book, since this bestows the public persona of 'AUTHOR' (involved in contracts, copyrights and so on) who is distinct from that person as a private individual, or in some other occupation (teacher, MP, actor). Also relevant here is the distinction first made in American literary criticism of the 1960s between the author, existing 'outside' the text, and the 'implied author' whose presence can be detected in the voice or presence working over and above the words of the narrator and characters 'in' the text. Furthermore, different individuals can occupy the same named role or office of addresser (as 'headteacher', 'broadcaster', 'prime minister', or in the common use of 'spokespeople').

A comparable distinction is necessary at the other end of the process of communication since the addressee, the person for whom the message is intended (an 'implied' or 'ideal reader', consumer or voter), may be quite different from the person who actually receives, decodes or interprets it. The actual recipient will be involved in a process of NEGOTIATION with the intended meaning of the message and the position of its ideal recipient or addressee. A further difference is that although senders may be a group or organization, there are often many, sometimes thousands or millions of actual receivers. This is clearest of all in MASS communications, and has led to attempts to theorize and empirically assess the range of responses and positions that actual viewers or listeners in an AUDIENCE might occupy. This does not rule out the usefulness of the concept of the addressee, however, since it is an indication of the ideological assumptions of programme makers about their audience and how this is inscribed in media texts. Actual audience members may also of course coincide with the constructed position of the addressee wholly or in part, whether on a given occasion or over a period of time.

See also *ÉNONCÉ/ÉNONCIATION*; READING; SCHEDULING.

AESTHETIC(S)

The term 'aesthetic' has both narrow and expanded uses. Thus, it can be used to name the formal or compositional aspect of a work of art as against its content, to refer to a coherent philosophy of art, or to the artistic dimension of culture as a whole. 'Aesthetics', meanwhile, embraces the study of any or all of these things. Traditionally, however, it has concerned itself with the nature, perception and judgement of beauty. The term was first used with this sense in the eighteenth century, and aesthetics has been a prominent part of German philosophy, most influentially in the work of Immanuel Kant. The tendency in this discussion has been to try to identify the transcendent and timeless aspects of beauty, and to discriminate against what is contingent and therefore not art. In this way, it has been allied to the discussion of cognate terms such as 'genius' and TASTE, and has operated in a similar fashion to the notion of the CANON.

Terry Eagleton's *The Ideology of the Aesthetic* (1990) has argued that while seeking an essentializing and transcendent definition of art, this tradition has in fact served to buttress particular ideas of subjectivity, freedom, autonomy and universality, which make it 'inseparable from the construction of the dominant ideological forms of modern class society' (1990: 3). Aesthetics, like art itself, therefore becomes an ideological and historically conditioned set of discourses.

This analysis does not seek to dispense with the realm of the aesthetic, but to provide it with a situated cultural history and more open, alternative political character. A more iconoclastic response to the bourgeois ideology of 'Art' and all it entailed was associated with the European AVANT-GARDE of the 1910s and 1920s. The American title of a later, seminal volume of essays on postmodernism, *The Anti-Aesthetic* (1983) edited by Hal Foster (English title, *Postmodern Culture*) would appear to suggest that this reaction has continued in the postmodern period. However, it would be rash to assume a consensus on art, non-art, anti-art, or the viability of aesthetics in the contemporary period, which is often seen as having witnessed a separation of art, ethics and political worlds. Some commentators (Eagleton among them) have sought to reconnect the symbolic or cultural and the political in the present. The discussion of 'feminist' and 'black' aesthetics, or of a 'geopolitical aesthetic' or 'postmodern political aesthetic' in the work of Fredric Jameson (1991, 1992) would share this broad aim. However, the image-driven world of the postmodern was seen as producing an entirely 'aestheticized' society (Connor 1989: Ch. 2). In which case, where all is seen as fashion, taste and style, there can be nothing for the aesthetic as a distinct realm and practice to detach itself from or connect with.

This state of affairs, and Eagleton's analysis of the ideological function of the category of aesthetics, suggest that the term is redundant or compromised. Recent works by Slavoj Žižek, Alain Badiou and Jacques Rancière would suggest otherwise. Noting this revival of the term 'in the last decade', in an era of what Slavoj Žižek (2004) terms 'today's "postmodern" post-politics', Steven Connor in his 'Doing without art' (2011) concludes – in spite of his own preference for abandoning the term – that its persistence must have to do with its function (not what it was but 'what it did'). Its persistence therefore suggests a changed function or a return to a pre-postmodern conception. Such is Badiou's notion in the *Handbook of Inaesthetics* (Badiou and Toscano 2005: 9) of art as a kind of autonomous authority whose truths 'are given nowhere else than in art': a position which Connor believes at once empties art of significance and saturates it with 'pregnancy and puissance' (2011: 55). Rancière develops a more explicitly politicized aesthetics of CRITIQUE, similarly indebted to a pre-postmodern PARADIGM. His *The Politics of Aesthetics* (2000: trans. 2004) views society as determined by boundaries which allocate the role and station of citizens (what he terms 'Distribution of the Sensible' – that is to say, the horizon of what can be perceived, thought and said). This regime is determined by the political order (what he terms 'The Police'). The 'Aesthetic Regime of Art' commencing in early nineteenth-century Romanticism and including the historical avant-gardes, frees art from any set role or responsibility in this regulated schema. In this new-found AUTONOMY, art challenges the consensual 'distribution of the sensible' of the status quo. In this broad application, therefore, aesthetics refers to more than art works and extends into the political domain. 'Politics' itself is characterized by acts of 'Dissensus', in which aesthetics participates in conjunction with subordinated groups and classes who assert themselves to claim a voice in society in the name of equality and democracy – a process Rancière refers to as the process of 'Political Subjectivization'.

Žižek (2004) comments that Rancière established 'the aesthetic dimension as INHERENT in any radical emancipatory politics' (76). While Connor comments on the 'implausibility' of any such proclamation on 'the political promise of the aesthetic' (2011, 54), Žižek finds in Rancière 'in our time of the disorientation of the left... one of the few consistent conceptualisations of *how we are to continue to resist*' (79).

AFFECT

'Affect' in literary and art criticism has conventionally referred to an individual or generalized emotional response to a text, art work or performance. The reliance on such an evidently subjective response was dismissed by the school of 'New Criticism' introduced in the United States in the 1920s (see Selden *et al.*, 2017, Chapter 1), most directly in the essay 'The Affective Fallacy' by Monroe C. Beardsley (in *The Verbal Icon: Studies in the Meaning of Poetry,* 1954) because it diverted attention from a literary text's 'objective' formal structure. A *volte face* occurred with the introduction of 'affective stylistics' and a direct concern with a reader's evolving response, sentence by sentence, or word by word in a text, developed by the American critic Stanley Fish (see Selden *et al.*, Ch. 3). In the so-called 'linguistic turn' inaugurated by structuralism, subjective response and affect was once more dismissed or ignored in favour of TEXTUALITY.

A much broader-based, cross-disciplinary, and closely considered analytical mode has come in recent decades to mark the 'turn to affect' and the advent of 'Affect Studies': a consolidated expression of which has been Gregg and Seigworth's collection, *The Affect Theory Reader* (2010). The editors describe affect as:

> found in those intensities that pass body to body (human, nonhuman, part-body, and otherwise), in those resonances that circulate about, between, and sometimes stick to bodies and worlds, *and* in the very passages or variations between these intensities and resonances themselves. Affect, at its most anthropomorphic, is the name we give to those forces—visceral forces beneath, alongside, or generally *other than* conscious knowing, vital forces insisting beyond emotion—that can serve to drive us toward movement, toward thought and extension' (1).

5

They add that 'There is no single, generalizable theory of affect: not yet, and (thankfully) there never will be' (3); thereby welcoming a study of affect which will be incremental, open and variegated, like affect itself, as it moves, in the editor's terms, through rhythmic contours, shifting modalities and encounters 'both into and out of the interstices of the inorganic and non-living, the intracellular divulgences of sinew, tissue, and gut economies, and the vaporous evanescence of the incorporeal (events, atmospheres, feeling-tones)'(2010, 2). For some, such a self-conscious vocabulary, which runs analytic method in synch with its object, betrays a double problem: at once privileging 'body' over 'mind' ('conscious knowing') and evading theory's rational, critical and conceptual discourse for a discourse that replicates the subtleties of its subject – affect, itself (See Reiser 2012 and 2009).

Gregg and Seigworth's answer to any quest for a 'generalizable theory' is to think rather of 'orientations'. Among them are sources in psychology, phenomenology, Cultural Studies, political philosophy, Postcolonial and Subaltern Studies, FEMINISM, QUEER THEORY, neuroscience, CYBERNETICS, and bioengineering: themselves sharing a common orientation away from the 'linguistic turn' of STRUCTURALISM and POSTSTRUCTURALISM and the humanist assumption of a privileged, individualized subject, in favour of the pluralist and fluid interactions of body to body, body and world, human and non-human.

In addition, the editors enlist certain key inspirations governing work in the field. Firstly, in psychology, Sylvan Tomkins's identification of innate human psychobiological reactions registered in the face and body (including, in a list of nine such types: smiling in an expression of joy; raised eyebrows; frowning, a clenched jaw and red face in an expression of anger) – further developed in the Humanities in Eve Sedgwick and Adam Frank's influential essay 'Shame in the Cybernetic Fold' (1995). Secondly, Gilles Deleuze's notion of affect's interiorized, 'crocheted' movement across complex assemblages of bodies and things, explored in Brian Massumi's early essay 'The Autonomy of Affect' (1995). Thirdly, Roland Barthes' evocation in a late 1978 lecture published as *The Neutral* (2005) of 'a hyperconsciousness of the affective minimum, of the microscopic fragment of emotion... [which implies] an extreme changeability of affective moments, a rapid modification, into shimmer' (2005, 101). And, fourthly, Lawrence Grossberg's insistence from within Cultural Studies on contextualizing affect in terms of 'affective alliances' in two seminal early essays 'Another boring day in paradise' (1984) and 'Is there rock after punk?' (1986) and across 'mattering maps' (what 'matters' in everyday life) in his *We Gotta Get Out of This Place* (1992).

Further suggestive theoretical discussion and analysis, as well as critique of the 'turn' to affect, appear in Leys (2007, 2011); Reiser (2009, 2012); del Rio (2008); and La Caze and Lloyd's 'Philosophy and the Affective Turn' (2011).

See also TRAUMA.

AGENCY

A term referring to the role of the human actor as an individual or group in directing or effectively intervening in the course of history. Liberal HUMANISM sees the individual or

SUBJECT as unified and self-determining. It therefore ascribes agency to this subject as a more or less unrestricted actor in shaping her/his own life and a more general social destiny. MARXISM and other theories recognizing the influence of social and economic DETERMINATIONS beyond the individual offer a more qualified and complex view. 'Men make their own history,' Karl Marx famously declared, but 'do not make it under circumstances chosen by themselves'. For Marx, the working CLASS was denied agency and would only assume its role as actor in the world through the revolutionary transformation of economic and social relations inspired by class CONSCIOUSNESS.

Critics of this view, within Marxism and POSTSTRUCTURALISM, see it as no more than a postponement of the humanist ideal. Non-humanist positions, developed, for example, by Louis Althusser and Michel Foucault, appear to deny agency altogether. For Foucault, for example, POWER is omnipresent and though exercised with aims and objectives has no presiding 'headquarters', no specific source in the decisions of groups or individuals (1979: 94–5). As Anthony Giddens comments, 'Foucault's history tends to have no active subjects at all. It is history with the agency removed' (1987: 98).

For some, the anti-humanism of poststructuralism comes unnervingly close to a belief such as Margaret Thatcher's that 'there is no such thing as society': a view that surrenders agency to market forces. Nevertheless, poststructuralist arguments have challenged the traditional Marxist emphasis upon CLASS and party as the agencies of radical change, and significantly influenced models of the operation of power and IDEOLOGY. They have proved relevant if problematic, too, for feminist and other oppositional theories interested in the strategies that would render women and other subjugated peoples the 'subjects' (i.e. agents) of their own, rather than the 'objects' of an imposed, history. Debating the implications of poststructuralist theory for political action, Michèle Barrett highlights the problem posed by DECONSTRUCTION: 'Feminists recognise that the "naming" of women and men occurs within an opposition that one would want to challenge and transform, yet political silencing can follow from rejecting these categories altogether' (1991: 166). To deconstruct existing relations of power, she implies, threatens to deconstruct the concept of agency itself and thus to undermine any counter-strategy.

Contributions to a 'post-Marxist' theory of agency, which have absorbed the lessons of poststructuralist critique, have been associated with thinkers such as Ernesto Laclau, Chantal Mouffe and Stuart Hall. As described by Lawrence Grossberg, Hall offers, 'a non-essentialist theory of agency'. He proposes 'a fragmented, decentred human agent, an agent who is both "subjected" by power and capable of acting against those powers'. 'It is a position,' Grossberg adds, 'of theoretical anti-humanism and political humanism, for without an articulated subject capable of acting, no resistance is possible' (Morley and Chen [eds] 1996: 156–7).

See also ARTICULATION; IDENTITY; IDEOLOGY CRITIQUE.

ALIENATION

In general, though the concept is articulated and explained differently in different traditions, alienation conveys the sense of a life determined by external 'alien' forces, and a consequent lack of control or authenticity and oneness with oneself. The concept has its source within classical philosophy and religious thought in the perceived duality of human existence: as false and unachieved in the known world but true and fully realized in another transcendent sphere.

In Hegel's philosophy man (*sic*) is seen to develop through alienation and its transcendence, realizing a spiritual essence in labour. This formulation was critiqued in the early writings of Karl Marx who saw labour itself as alienating and consequently developed the concept in one of its key modern directions. In the *Economic and Philosophical Manuscripts* (1844), Marx describes a condition of man's (*sic*) alienation from nature, from others and from the products of his labour. The latter, in particular, is induced by the exploitation of the worker under capitalism, enforcing an identification of the worker with the commodity VALUE of the products of labour. Ultimately this is seen to produce a profound alienation of man from himself.

Alienation in this sense has been taken up in much social commentary and as a widespread theme in literature and film (including novels by Émile Zola and George Gissing, for example, and films such as Charlie Chaplin's *Modern Times,* 1936).

Later observers than Marx saw alienation not so much as the effect of capitalism as the characteristic condition of urban living in the modern metropolis. The impersonality of modern technologies, the speed of new transport and the increased size of CITY crowds were seen to create a disorientating double effect of proximity and isolation (Simmel 1969 [1903]). Alienation in this urban context was the subject of much modernist literature (by Charles Baudelaire, T.S. Eliot, John Dos Passos). The related experience of anonymous systems of modern bureaucracy and political manipulation is close to the use of the concept in Max Weber and its development in later Sociology. This, too, has been explored in literature and film, from the writings of Franz Kafka to William Burroughs and in films such as *The Parallax View* (1974) and *JFK* (1982).

In another quite common sense, deriving from Sartre and existentialism, alienation is seen not as a specific historical mentality characteristic of capitalism, or of MODERNITY, but as a universal human condition.

See also ALIENATION EFFECT; REIFICATION.

ALIENATION EFFECT

A term derived from the theory and theatre practice of the German Marxist playwright and poet, Bertolt Brecht (1898–1956). Brecht sought to discover ways of dramatizing Marx's insights into the operation of capitalism and spoke, with this in mind, of creating a 'dialectical theatre' (Brooker 1988). He therefore employed a set of devices in staging, music, acting, and the telling of parable, to confound an audience's comfortable identification with characters and story as encouraged by conventional REALISM or Naturalism. Together, these techniques produced the 'alienation effect'. It would be an error to think that Brecht wished in this way to reinforce alienation in Marx's sense. His intentions were precisely the opposite: to induce a 'critical attitude' that would dispel the passivity necessary to the maintenance of the conditions producing alienation under capitalism. A measure of this difference appears in the term he used in German. Marx's word was *Entfremdung* while Brecht wrote of the *Verfremdungseffekt,* for which a better translation would be 'de-alienation' effect. As such, it is related to similar devices in modernist theory and art such as 'DEFAMILIARIZATION' and 'ESTRANGEMENT', though these have not always had the overtly politicizing intention of Brecht's method.

Brecht's ideas were taken up more widely, in association with FEMINISM, PSYCHOANALYSIS and the MARXISM of Louis Althusser, in the film theory of the 1970s associated with the journal *Screen* (see MacCabe 1974; Walsh 1981). Indeed, Brecht's concept is, to some degree, indebted to the theories of MONTAGE developed in Soviet cinema theory and practice of the 1920s, notably in the cinema of Sergei Eisenstein. Later examples in the 'Brechtian' tradition in theatre would be Heiner Müller, John Arden, Edward Bond and Dario Fo, among others, and in cinema, Jean-Luc Godard, Jean-Marie Straub and, more indirectly, Hal Hartley and Peter Greenaway. There are those, however, who think that the alienation effect is now everywhere and nowhere: that it is present in advertising and MASS television programming, as well as cinema and theatre, and that consequently such devices are no longer the province of a critical AVANT-GARDE. This scepticism derives from arguments about a loss of distinction between the IMAGE and the real in postmodern society and the frustrations therefore attending any form of artistic or theoretical IDEOLOGY CRITIQUE.

See also SCREEN THEORY.

ALLEGORY

A term derived in the first instance from classical rhetoric, and from religious art and interpretation. An allegorical tale or painting indirectly identifies a set of important figures or suggests a NARRATIVE behind or as an extension of its literal meaning, as, for example, in the stories of Adam and Eve in the Garden of Eden, or of Rama and Sita. Folk tales, fables and nursery rhymes can also in this sense be allegories and often carry a moral lesson. Allegory is therefore a way of encoding a broad world-view or complex MESSAGE in a more focused, accessible and entertaining narrative form. Often, from medieval morality plays to modern times, POPULAR GENRE forms have been employed to this end – though it would be a mistake to ascribe a directly didactic rather than artistic or commercial intention to this choice. John Ford's westerns are, in this way, commonly thought to be allegories of the making of the American nation while a film such as David Cronenberg's *Videodrome* can be read as an allegory of the postmodern condition. Allegory has also been a way for writers, artists and film-makers to express a satirical or critical intent in the face of censorship or official disapproval. Examples in the modern period would be works by Orwell, Brecht, Soyinka or an individual text such as Arthur Miller's *The Crucible.*

Within Cultural Theory, an important point of reference has been the writings of the German philosopher and critic, Walter Benjamin (1892–1940). In the early essay, 'Goethe's elective affinities' (1923), Benjamin determined that the truth of a work of art resided in its allegorical rather than symbolic structure. Later, he extended this belief to cultural objects generally and theorized that while the commodity form characteristic of MODERNITY reinforced ALIENATION, it nevertheless retained the allegorical germ of an alternative, collective social mode. Thus, the degraded, unfulfilled present gave access – precisely in its incompleteness – to the opposite UTOPIAN possibility of a fully achieved history. On similar grounds, Benjamin saw the modern CITY as simultaneously the scene of false history, forgetting and phantasmagoria, and the SITE of a radical transformation. Here, too, the awakening spark was produced in peripheral objects and figures, and moments of sudden, spontaneous memory or shock encounter. This view of things therefore not only proposed that objects and environments were in themselves allegorical, but required the observing historical materialist critic and philosopher to perceive them as such. Benjamin's cultural critic and historian – like Charles Baudelaire, the poet of nineteenth-century Paris he studied – was therefore himself necessarily an allegorist, but as a Marxist allegorist also a dialectician who saw the opening to a transformed future in the contradictions of the present.

Benjamin's understanding of allegory has been influential on later Marxist and Left cultural critics, particularly in relation to postmodern arts and culture. Thus, Craig Owens, in a direct debt to Benjamin, proposed that allegory be seen as the informing principle of an AVANT-GARDE art whose leading devices he defines as 'appropriation, site specificity, impermanence, accumulation, discursivity, hybridization' (1980: 75). Later citations and uses of allegorical method in this vein have sought to restore its more dialectical and political edge. Fredric Jameson's work provides a leading example of this. Jameson recasts Benjamin's thinking in his essay on 'Reification and utopia in mass culture' (1990c) and refers often to his own method of interpretation as allegorical or as 'allegorical transcoding'. As this suggests, Jameson seeks to read cultural texts – from literature, photography, video and cinema, avant-garde installation and architecture – as allegorical emblems of broader political and economic conditions. The world system of late capitalism is so complex, comments Jameson, that it can only be mapped and modelled, and therefore known, indirectly, 'by way of a simpler object that stands as its allegorical interpretant' (1991: 169). Unlike the biblical and traditional method of allegorical decoding, however, where X in a given text stood for Y in a realm of meaning outside it, the allegorical transcoding of the postmodern era is akin to scanning across related items in a text, or world of texts, and aims to 'transcode' these into a second CODE of AESTHETICS, theory or politics. This newer form of allegory, says Jameson, is 'horizontal rather than vertical' (1991: 168).

Perhaps the best and most sustained examples of this critical method at work appear in Jameson's studies of American and other films (1990b, 1992). The second volume includes a discussion of Jean-Luc Godard's *Passion*. Of this, says Jameson characteristically, the allegorical structure – could we but decode it – would provide a grasp of 'the structure of the modern age itself' (1992: 185).

See also COGNITIVE MAPPING; POSTMODERNISM.

ALTERITY

A term given currency by the emphasis upon DIFFERENCE in STRUCTURALISM and POSTSTRUCTURALISM and its impact upon discussions of the relations of the self and OTHER. While many philosophers and social thinkers from diverse traditions would respond to the poststructuralist challenge by arguing for forms of commonality in intellectual and social life (Rorty 1989; Benhabib 1992), others see a condition of radical uncertainty in which the SUBJECT is decentred and alienated. They consequently seek to theorize this condition or the terms of possible relations in what is, at a primary level, a world of non-relations. Lyotard's concept of the DIFFEREND is one such attempt to recognize incompatible positions or discourses. Probably the most influential example of such thinking, however, is the philosophy of Emmanuel Lévinas. Lévinas seeks to found an ethics on the perception of irreducible otherness. The other, he writes, is possessed by an:

> alterity that is not formal, is not the simple reverse of identity, and is not formed out of resistance to the same, but is prior to every initiative, to all imperialism of the same. It is other with an alterity constitutive of the very content of the other.
>
> (1969: 38)

The encounter with this radical other is the founding moment of the ego, of consciousness and of ethical responsibility.

Aside from the contrary arguments, indicated above, this theory is not without its own problems. For while alterity is proposed as a mark of otherness, it is also presented as a constitutive, neutral and common state. A theory of absolute difference and incommensurability cannot apparently escape the FOUNDATIONALISM it appears to reject. Furthermore, the implication of Lévinas' remarks above must be that an encounter with the other is an encounter not of one but of two or more (other) egos, simultaneously constituted – and that, as Jacques Derrida (1978) has pointed out in an essay on Lévinas, radical otherness depends in fact on a level of sameness (see also Tallack [ed.] 1995).

The concept has been transposed by Thomas Docherty (1996) to the realm of AESTHETICS and criticism. The dominant mode of criticism, he argues, employs various theoretical paradigms to 'unmask' the meanings of texts. In so doing, it finds consolation and self-assurance, but risks ignoring or circumventing 'a substantial alterity in the aesthetic' (1996: vii). Docherty posits art as 'a fundamentally different order of being' (1996: vii) and calls for a new 'humility' towards the 'specific difficulties and resistances' (1996: viii), which comprise its alterity.

See also DIFFEREND; HUMANISM.

ANDROCENTRIC

Meaning 'centred upon the male' (Gk 'andro') and used particularly in feminist theory and criticism of any DISCOURSE that reinforces PHALLOCENTRIC or patriarchal attitudes. Its literal opposite is 'gynocentric' (see GYNOCENTRICISM). A cognate term, 'anthropocentric' (centred upon the human), is employed in ecological arguments where it signifies an indifference to, or wilful exploitation of, the natural and animal world. This may also in effect be a criticism of androcentricism, in that relevant decision-making is in the hands of men and that 'NATURE' is coded in traditional fashion as 'feminine'. In their extended form, these criticisms may combine in a CRITIQUE of the ENLIGHTENMENT belief in the privileged position of the human species, represented by 'Man', and the regulation of nature for human ends.

See also PATRIARCHY.

ANDROGYNY

A term from the Greek 'andro' (male) and 'gyn' (female) describing the union of the sexes in one being. In the modern period, its most famous invocation is probably in Virginia Woolf's *A Room of One's Own* (1929). Woolf here exposes the inequalities of literary and general culture, and argues particularly for a woman writer's financial independence. She speculates on the ignominious career 'Shakespeare's sister' might have had, but nevertheless presents Shakespeare as the model of the great – because 'androgynous' – mind (1973: 97).

Woolf's discussion of the male and 'female sentence' anticipates later theorizations on women's writing, especially in French FEMINISM (see also Moi 1985). She concludes that 'it is fatal for anyone who writes to think of their sex', that, 'one must be woman-manly or man-womanly... The whole of the mind must lie wide open' (Woolf 1973: 102). This association of androgyny with writing occurs in Hélène Cixous's conception of bisexuality in writing as 'the presence – variously manifest... of both sexes, non-exclusion either of the difference or of one sex' (1981b: 254) and more indirectly in Julia Kristeva's idea of the SEMIOTIC. This denotes the pre-SYMBOLIC, non-PHALLOCENTRIC realm of expression realized in relations between mothers and children, and in forms of AVANT-GARDE or modernist writing. Thus, male writers such as Mallarmé, Genet and Joyce can be thought to express the 'feminine' semiotic. (However, this relation is not reversible, in the sense that women writing the 'masculine' is a desired option.) In the United States, androgyny in literary texts was directly explored by Carolyn Heilbrun (1964). However, the ruling opinion in later Anglo-American feminism has been that the idea of androgyny retains sexual dichotomies and so reinforces sexist attitudes.

The idea or pose of the androgyn has been explored in POPULAR CULTURE and performative notions of SEXUALITY. In the first case, this seems once more to be more an option for males (Mick Jagger, David Bowie) than for women. However, Martin Humphries reports that the early gay liberation movement aimed 'to break down distinctions between femininity and masculinity' so as to create 'an androgynous world... within which gender would no longer be relevant' (Metcalfe and Humphries 1985: 71). Lesbianism, cross-dressing and transsexuality also explore androgynous identities in dress styles, BODY alteration and sexual role-playing.

Further related examples of the CYBORG or 'angel' (Irigaray 1987: 126) suggest how the idea of androgyny, while tending to evoke a transcendent union of sexual opposites rather than their DECONSTRUCTION, nevertheless resonates with notions of HYBRIDITY and betweenness, 'the gap between man and woman' as Luce Irigaray puts it (1987: 124), and thus joins the postmodern challenge to centred identities and dualisms.

See also *ÉCRITURE*/WRITING; SEXUAL DIFFERENCE; QUEER THEORY.

ANIMAL STUDIES

'Animal Studies' is a new interdisciplinary academic area in which Anthropology, Sociology, medicine, museology, as well as Literary, Cultural and Film Studies are interested parties (see Twine and Taylor, eds, 2014). It shares a concern with the relation of humankind and the natural, which tends towards anthropomorphism (the humanization of animals) or zoomorphism (the animalistic characterization of humans), or posits some conception of reciprocal non-hierarchical identities which would attribute 'personhood' to animals. A vast field of potential study opens out: from folklore and fable, to centuries of the depiction of animals in poetry and written or visual narrative and documentary (see e.g. Kirkpatrick and Faragó [eds] 2015). Of interest, too, are near-future or alternate world scenarios of transformation, interbreeding, hybrid combinations, or reversals, of human and animal relations (from Jonathan Swift's *Gulliver's Travels* to Margaret Atwood's *Oryx and Crake* and rebooted films in the *Planet of the Apes, Terminator, Jurassic Park* franchises).

Animal Studies engages also with legal and moral issues concerning the treatment, well-being and survival of animals and with medical science or activist campaigns on the plight of endangered species. In this spirit, it seeks, in the terms of the Centre for Human Animal Studies (CfHAS) in the UK, to work in collaborative, cross-disciplinary ways: 'to examine how rethinking our relations with animals can create meaningful social, policy, environmental, ethical and cultural change… that challenges anthropocentric (human-centred) thinking and approaches and recognises the interests of animals.' To this, CfHAS adds that 'representational practices and cultural understanding' work alongside its other key themes of 'climate change and sustainability'; 'health and well-being', 'ecological conflicts', and 'intersectionality and social justice'.

The main effect in encouraging such 'rethinking' is twofold: firstly, to open out the totalizing concept of 'Nature' to internal differentiation in evoking the phenomenal variety and specialized faculties of animal species and subspecies; and, secondly, to critically examine the concept of the 'human' and the consequent categorization of the non-human. For centuries it has been thought that animals do not reason or suffer; that they are not sentient, and that they do not have language. These criteria are plainly self-servingly anthropocentric and roundly critiqued. But what, above all, undermines this hierarchical ladder descending from the human through animal species to plant life is the acknowledgement of human beings as themselves animals.

Prominent sources in critical theory for this rethinking have been Jacques Derrida's *The Animal that Therefore I Am* (2008) and Giorgio Agamben's *The Open. Man and Animal* (2004). Derrida's text – whose title plays upon, as it undermines, René Descartes's 'I think therefore I am' – questions the assumed boundary line distinguishing the human and animal in European philosophy, which in denying reason, ethics, the unconscious to animal life has laid down the bedrock of human attitudes and conduct. Derrida prefers the phrase 'that which we call animal' and proposes a 'limitrophy' (29) to explore the space between the boundary lines or limits of 'that which we call animal' and 'that which we call human'. 'Everything I'll say' he writes 'will consist, certainly not in effacing the limit, but in multiplying its figures, in complicating, thickening, delinearizing, folding, and dividing the line precisely by making it increase and multiply'(29).

Agamben offers an equally thoroughgoing critique of western philosophy. From Aristotle onwards, the human ('man') has been defined by the exclusion of the OTHER, including animals, from the polis. This absolute distinction of the political human being as citizen from the inhuman or animal laid the foundations of the modern bio-political system, or what Agamben calls 'the anthropological machine'(2004, 29). That the relation between humans and the higher apes is in fact ambiguous, and that the animal exists within the human, accounts for the violence with which the boundary line is imposed. Agamben finds an alternative to this order in two directions: in the work of biologist Jakob von Uexküll on the consonance of different species and their space-time environments in what are to human perception 'unknowable worlds', and in an opening illustration of a scene in a thirteenth-century Bible depicting the vison of Ezekiel of a banquet of the righteous at the end of time, who beneath their crowns are shown 'not with human faces, but with unmistakably animal heads' (2). The image of a return in Paradise to Eden when 'man himself will be reconciled with his animal nature' (3) prefigures Agamben's reflections on other imagined worlds and of a low-key, innocent coexistence within the human and with the non-human beyond the present.

Recent work in Animal Studies urges a further redefinition of the human, invoking the concepts of the transhuman or 'transitional human' to express humanity's relation with its others (See Blake, Molloy, Shakespeare [eds] 2012). Derrida and Agamben interiorize this relation. Their theorizing deepens the Animal Studies agenda in challenging us to reimagine the 'human animal' – the animal within the human – where the boundary lines are not effaced, but rendered more complicated, thickened and multiplied.

See also NATURE; POSTHUMAN; UTOPIA

ANTHROPOCENE

The term 'Anthropocene' designates a new geochemical and biological epoch, following the epoch of the Holocene, which itself followed the ice age some 11,500 years ago. The Anthropocene is marked by the decisive human impact upon the Earth's environment and biosphere. The term was coined in the 1980s, but its contemporary usage owes much to the Nobel Prize winning chemist Paul J. Crutzen. In 2000, Crutzen and Eugene F. Stoermer proposed that the onset of this epoch be identified as the latter part of the eighteenth century, since this showed the early signs of 'greenhouse gases' resulting from human activity: one example of which was the invention of the steam engine. A later paper in the journal *Science* in 2016 identified the mid twentieth century as the point of its distinctive onset. Here, Dr. Colin Waters, cited the telling effects on the environment and wildlife of the human production of plastic (300m metric tonnes annually) and concrete (of which more than half the amount ever produced was produced in the last 20 years). To this, we need to add, he suggests, the presence of isotopes from nuclear weapons testing in the 1950s and 1960s.

Some scientists would set alternative, much earlier start dates for the Anthropocene than the mid twentieth or the late eighteenth centuries. And some are sceptical about any single starting point. Also, in mid 2016, the term has yet to be formally ratified by the Stratigraphy Commission of the Geological Society of London. Nonetheless, 'anthropocene' is in regular use in scientific and journalistic circles and academia, including the Humanities. Examples of the latter include a special issue on 'Deconstruction and the Anthropocene' in the *Oxford Literary Review* (34: 2, 2012) and the newly established interdisciplinary journal *Anthropocene Review*. Bonneuil and Fressoz's *Shock of the Anthropocene* (2015) offers a rigorous analysis of relevant issues and posits alternatives for sustainable living in this new era (Bonneuil is also the editor of an Anthropocène series for Editions du Seuil, Paris). Other acknowledged key works which abut on trends in ECOLOGY and ECOCRITICISM are Gaia Vince's *Adventures in the Anthropocene* (2015), which tracks the impact of climate change on the world's poor, and Anna Tsing's *The Mushroom at the End of the World* (2016), which presents the story of the humble but supremely valued Matsutake mushroom as a lesson in multi-species cohabitation and survival. A vein of speculative fiction has also contributed to narrative scenarios of scarcity and survival which beset Planet Earth in the Anthropocene. One such postapocalyptic novel, Cormac McCarthy's *The Road* (2006, film 2009), is for Robert Macfarlane (2016) 'now almost an Anthropocene ur-text'.

APORIA

A term from the Greek, meaning 'without an opening' (*a* = without; *poria* = gate). In Classical and Renaissance handbooks of rhetoric 'aporia' is a figure of speech naming a state of doubt or a speaker's uncertainty about how to proceed with an argument. A celebrated example would be Hamlet's 'to be or not to be' speech. The term has been revived in poststructuralist thought to similarly name a paradox or moment of self-contradiction that cannot be resolved dialectically and where meaning therefore becomes undecidable. A deconstructive reading in particular seeks to disclose how a philosophy or literary or other text arrives through its own operation at such a moment. According to Christopher Norris, aporia is consequently, 'the nearest one can get to a label or conceptual cover-term for the effects of *différance*... What deconstruction persistently reveals is an ultimate impasse of thought' (1982: 49). A further connection is with the concept of the DIFFEREND employed by Jean-François Lyotard to describe the situation where two opposed arguments cannot be reconciled or judged from an 'objective' third position.

In NARRATIVE, an aporia may occur where there is no resolution of the traditional kind provided by a marriage, inheritance or the explanation of a mystery. This has become an accentuated feature of postmodern writing and film. In well-known examples such as Paul Auster's *New York Trilogy* (1985) or the film *The Usual Suspects* (1995), for instance, the suspense conventionally associated with detective and thriller stories is reinforced in a self-conscious way and remains unresolved. The reader or viewer is presented less with the explanation of a mystery than the black hole of aporia in which the unanswered questions are as much about writing or film-making as about the intrinsic events of the story.

ARCHAEOLOGY

A term associated explicitly with the earlier works of Michel Foucault (1926–84): *The Birth of the Clinic: An Archaeology of Medical Perception* (1973), *The Order of Things: An Archaeology of the Human Sciences* (1970) and *The Archaeology of Knowledge* (1972). Foucault was concerned in these works to make key assumptions, ways of knowing and establishing truth PROBLEMATIC, to ask how ideas and ways of speaking of 'madness' or 'illness', for example, came about and came to prevail. In so doing, he aimed to track and uncover the ARCHIVE, the rules by which the kind of statements or 'discursive practices' characterizing a domain of knowledge were assembled and modified. These DISCOURSES constituted what was accepted as knowledge within a discipline, a science or, collectively, an intellectual epoch, or *ÉPISTÈME*. It follows, too, that they play a major part in defining the terms comprising social and individual identities and directing people's lives.

Foucault's perception of the relations between knowledge and, later, power and discourse has affinities with both POSTSTRUCTURALISM and MARXISM, though he shares neither the first's emphasis on TEXTUALITY, nor the second's CLASS analysis and overt political orientation. The notion of archaeology owes less to these traditions, therefore, than to a traditional philosophical enquiry into the history of ideas, which Foucault understands as the dispersed discursive statements characterizing an era.

See also GENEALOGY.

ARCHI-WRITING

See *ÉCRITURE*/WRITING.

ARCHIVE

A term derived chiefly from Michel Foucault (1926–84) and identified by him in *The Archaeology of Knowledge* (1972 [1969]) as 'the *general system of the formation and transformation of statements*' (1972: 130, original italics). So defined, the archive is not simply a corpus but a level of practice, different from a tradition or a library of statements, which 'enables statements both to survive and to undergo regular modification' (1972: 130). The system of rules governing this process defines the 'discursive practices' and 'discursive formation' characterizing an era, or *ÉPISTÈME,* and this in turn is what distinguishes it from past and present eras.

The archive is an integral part of Foucault's 'archaeological' method, a practice employed in his own work in the study of reason and mental illness (*Madness and Civilisation,* 1967), medical understanding (*The Birth of the Clinic,* 1973) and the formation of the human sciences (*The Order of Things,* 1970). His later work was more concerned with relations of DISCOURSE, POWER and knowledge, and employed a 'genealogical' analysis to that end.

Jacques Derrida (1996) deconstructs the ambiguities of the notion of the archive, with special reference to Freud and the science of PSYCHOANALYSIS, as both repository and originary foundation (both 'place and law'), as public and intimate record, as full and repressed memory.

See also DECONSTRUCTION; GENEALOGY.

ARTICULATION

A term employed in STRUCTURALISM and MARXISM which has come to occupy a quite central place within Cultural Theory and analysis. Articulation suggests both something that is spoken or brought to expression, and describes a relation between otherwise unconnected parts. The most important sense of the term, however, is that this relation is understood as structured but flexible – articulated in the way that we speak of the moving parts of an articulated body or vehicle. In its later uses, this implication is taken to mean that relationships (in language, society and CULTURE) are open to rearticulation.

In structural linguistics, language is said to have a 'double articulation', comprising sound and thought or ideas. Thus, Ferdinand de Saussure writes of language as 'the domain of articulations... Each linguistic term is a member, an articulus in which an idea is fixed in a sound and a sound becomes the sign of an idea' (1966: 120). It is on the basis of this arbitrary, or conventional, relation that Saussure argues for the two-sidedness of the linguistic SIGN, composed of an acoustic or visual IMAGE (signifier) and concept (signified).

In a further use of the term, Roland Barthes described 'the structuralist activity' as involving 'two typical operations: dissection and articulation' (1972b: 216) and as therefore joining analysis with the motivated activity of producing 'something new' in the act of 'fabricating meanings' (1972b: 215, 218).

In the Marxist tradition, the term has been used to describe the coexistence of different economic modes of PRODUCTION and the way some traditional forms survive and are articulated with newer forms: feudal with late capitalist economies; the monarchy with democratic political forms. It is therefore part of the vocabulary of a periodizing analysis that seeks to account for the differential levels and uneven development within a given historical CONJUNCTURE.

The term has gained currency within Cultural Studies in reaction to reductionist or economistic positions in Marxism and to essentialist ideas of the unified individual SUBJECT. At the same time, this thinking has drawn upon the

Marxist tradition (in particular Marx, Gramsci, Althusser), as well as upon the leading concepts of structuralism and poststructuralist critique. Ernesto Laclau and Stuart Hall have in particular inspired this further elaboration of the term in the context of a changing agenda within Cultural Studies and CULTURAL POLITICS (see Slack 1996).

Two statements by Stuart Hall, from the early and mid 1980s, express the related relevance of the term to questions of theory, method and strategy, as well as an indebtedness to structuralist and Marxist uses:

> The unity formed by this combination or articulation, is always, necessarily, a 'complex structure': a structure in which things are related, as much through their differences as through their similarities... It also means – since the combination is a structure (an articulated combination) and not a random association – that there will be structured relations between its parts, i.e., relations of dominance and subordination.
>
> (Slack 1996: 115)

> The so-called 'unity' of a discourse is really the articulation of different, distinct elements which can be rearticulated in different ways because they have no necessary 'belongingness'. The 'unity' which matters is a linkage between the articulated discourse and the social forces with which it can, under certain historical conditions, but need not necessarily, be connected.
>
> (Morley and Chen [eds] 1996: 141)

Hall's work, in particular, has given the term wide currency, even to the point when it has seemed that articulation comprised 'the theory or method of cultural studies' (Slack 1996: 113). Its leading focus, however, has been upon relations of CLASS, GENDER, SEXUALITY, RACE and ETHNICITY in the world of REPRESENTATION, and in the development of non-essentialist notions of IDENTITY. Here, too, in an articulation of academic discourses that marks the field itself, theory and analysis have drawn upon a variety of concepts – DIFFERENCE, DIASPORA, HYBRIDITY – developed in FEMINISM, POSTSTRUCTURALISM and POSTCOLONIALISM. Thus, Pratibha Parma in a response to Hall's call for a 'politics of articulation' that will resist notions of absolute fixity, and in her own terms acknowledge factors not only of race but of class and sexuality in the discontinuous histories of black communities, writes of how, 'The concept of diaspora, which embraces the plurality of these different histories and cultural forms, allows access to the diversity of articulations around identity and cultural expression' (Rutherford [ed.] 1990b: 120).

The force of the term, in this and other formulations, is therefore to emphasize how the relations of social forces and the composition of cultural identities are neither immutable nor unified, but how one factor may become more determining than others in a given complex instance. 'Articulation' highlights the dynamic nature of social and cultural meanings, and the necessary provisionality of methods and strategies of analysis, expression and action.

See also AGENCY; ESSENTIALISM.

AUDIENCE

The object in general terms of all forms of COMMUNICATION, but used most often to refer to a group or MASS, and as such distinguished from a 'readership' or 'spectators' – the 'audiences', respectively, for forms of written communication and 'spectacles' such as sporting events. The term has its most direct association with theatre and concert-going, and is used consistently to refer to film and television viewers.

Theoretical and critical debates on audiences have been concerned with their social composition and the issue of 'effects' (see Marris and Thornham [eds] 1996). Initially, audiences were assumed by producers, advertisers and researchers to be uniform and predictable. Textually based studies also customarily assumed that the researcher or critic represented or could represent the understanding of audiences. (It has been common also for critics of written texts to invoke 'the' reader.) Some of these practices and assumptions persist. Nevertheless, it has become clear from both theoretical and ethnographic studies over the last 20 years that audiences must be understood as socially constituted and differentiated. Influential work in this field on television audiences, initially adopting a strong class-based analysis, has been conducted through the 1980s and 1990s by David Morley (see 1980, 1986). Further work on soap opera (Hobson 1982; Ang 1985) and the domestic use of video recordings (Gray 1992) has emphasized the importance of gender and the contextualized circumstances of viewing. This has been confirmed by Janice Radway's (1984) influential, empirically based study of women's romance, and theorizations of the male and female GAZE. Elsewhere, Marie Gillespie's (1995) study of Southall teenage viewers in 1992 has brought the necessary dimensions of ETHNICITY and generation to the contemporary picture of the TV audience. (See Seiter *et al.* [eds] 1989 for a review of research on television audiences.)

The debate on effects has followed a similar course. Early work in the 1950s and 1960s was based upon a largely American-based behaviourist approach (which assumed a given stimulus would be met with an equivalent response). Studies in this mould, influenced by Hans Eysenk's research on sex and violence in the media, tended to conclude that young audiences (the main object of concern) were either inclined to imitate what they saw on the screen, or to become desensitized. This has proved a particularly persistent view, endorsed by conservative pressure groups and a mainstay of public opinion on the media. Meanwhile, in academic work, the alternative model of a socially differentiated and contextualized audience gained force and was joined, following concentrated case studies in the 1970s, by a view of media effects as indirect and limited. 'Gratification' studies also saw audiences as using the media in more discriminating and positive ways rather than being passively used by them. The discipline base of this work remained in Social Psychology and assumed a symmetry of some kind between a given content and an audience response. The major break with this tradition came from within British Cultural Studies and a shift of attention from 'effects' to 'IDEOLOGY'. Its *locus classicus* is Stuart Hall's essay 'Encoding/decoding' (1997a [1974]), which drew on STRUCTURALISM and the idea of HEGEMONY to posit a range of possible audience responses to a coded ideological message (see CODE).

Later work has questioned the earlier emphasis on social CLASS and the continued viability of the concept of hegemony (Bennett 1990), and has looked instead to Michel Foucault's idea of the more dispersed operation of POWER and to Pierre Bourdieu's concept of TASTE (Fiske 1987, 1989). Fiske sees media audiences as operating within a relatively autonomous cultural FIELD, and as responding in discriminating and subversive ways that contradict the intended ideological meanings and effects of media products. In this model, the media can be appropriated at the level of signification for the making of alternative and resistant cultural identities.

In a direct response to Fiske and others, Jim McGuigan (1992) argues that this approach offers a partial and over-sanguine view that ignores questions of media ownership and PRODUCTION. What he terms 'cultural populism' invests too much in text-based readings at the expense of a study of political economy (see Storey 1993). A further view of media audiences appears in the writings of Jean Baudrillard. For Baudrillard, there is no distinction between the world of media, or other, images and the 'real world': the media have 'imploded' into the real, bringing a 'dissolution of TV in life, dissolution of life in TV' (1994: 30). In such a world, there can be no meaningful discussion of causes and effects, or of active and passive audiences. The only possible resistance to the ubiquitous, invasive power of the image is the non-response of the 'silent majority'.

See also ADDRESSER/ADDRESSEE; CONVERGENCE; CULTURE INDUSTRIES; RECEPTION.

AURA

A term used initially by Walter Benjamin (1970b) in the essay 'The work of art in the age of mechanical reproduction' to denote the uniqueness of a work of art, and the mystical value attached to it through its association with tradition and ritual. This quality, Benjamin argued, was endangered by the processes of mechanical REPRODUCTION. He did not see this as having entirely negative consequences, however, since the newer MASS arts of photography and especially cinema introduced a new radicalizing, collective dimension; an argument connected in his work with their allegorical rather than symbolic nature.

Theodor Adorno, Benjamin's contemporary, and a leading figure of the School of Social Research with which Benjamin was associated, shared an interest in technology and art but disagreed about the potential of the commercial arts of mass reproduction. In a direct reply to Benjamin's argument, he defended the AUTONOMY of art and was critical of Benjamin's attribution exclusively of the 'bourgeois' attributes of a magical or spiritual aura to it. This, said Adorno, ignored the internal, dialectical juxtaposition within autonomous art of both magical aura and a contrary 'mark of freedom' (1992: 52).

The AESTHETIC and cultural status of original works of art remains a matter of debate. In recent times, certainly, original works of art, especially paintings, have risen enormously in commercial VALUE (see Bourdieu 1984): thus, in a vulgarization of Benjamin's meaning, their 'aura' has increased, not diminished. At the same time, the expanded processes of technical reproduction have reinforced Benjamin's point. Fredric Jameson, for example, suggests that along with 'the ideology of the unique self', the original art work is a thing of the past (Brooker [ed.] 1992: 168). This loss of uniqueness, an attendant loss of distinction between high and mass or POPULAR CULTURE, and a resulting stylistic eclecticism are taken to be common features of POSTMODERNISM.

See also ALLEGORY; DIALECTICS.

AUTEUR

This French term for AUTHOR was given currency especially by discussions from the early 1950s of Hollywood cinema in the film review *Cahiers du Cinéma* and by the American critic Andrew Sarris who, responding to the work of the *Cahiers* critics, introduced the idea of 'auteur theory' to film study (Caughie [ed.] 1981). The *Cahiers* group was headed by André Bazin, later known for his celebrated defence of realist film AESTHETICS in *What is Cinema?* (1967), and numbered several future film-makers such as François Truffaut, Jean-Luc Godard and Claude Chabrol among its contributors. These figures came to prominence in the so-called French 'New Wave' in the late 1950s and early 1960s.

The *Cahiers* critics bestowed *auteur* status on American directors, such as Alfred Hitchcock, Howard Hawks, John Ford and Sam Fuller, who were otherwise known for their work in or across particular popular GENRES. In the films of these directors, the critics found signs of individual style, and a consistency of theme that gave their work an artistic integrity and personal signature over and above conventional genre formats and the constraints of the Hollywood studio system. *Auteur* criticism therefore valued a consistency of ideas and technique whether this was or was not coupled with the authorial badge of an original script (as was the case with Orson Welles or, later, Jean-Luc Godard). It therefore drew attention to matters of formal and thematic construction in POPULAR cinema, in reaction to the staid costume dramas and adaptations of contemporary French cinema. This gave American film an artistic respectability, but not so as to claim it for 'high art'. Arguably, the result was to be seen in the youthful, low-budget films with contemporary settings, novice actors and unstructured narratives of the French New Wave (Truffaut's *Les 400 Coups* 1959; Godard's *A Bout de Souffle* 1959). As a critical perspective, however, auteur theory emphasized individuality at the expense of the more conventional or collective features of Hollywood genre films and showed little sign of the kinds of psychoanalytic and sociohistorical approaches developed in later film criticism.

AUTHOR

The most sensational theory of the author derives from Roland Barthes' essay (1977a [1968]) announcing his death – 'his' because the figure of 'the Author' who is deposed (capitalized and in the masculine pronoun in Barthes' text) bears all the marks of symbolic maleness: the single origin and end of all meaning. Barthes writes:

> The image of literature is tyrannically centred on the Author, his person, his life, his tastes, his passions… The Author, when believed in, is always conceived of as the past of his own book… he exists before it, thinks, suffers, lives for it, is in the same relation of antecedence to his work as a father to his child.
>
> (1977a: 143, 145)

Barthes' essay shares a deconstructive and anti-humanist impulse with other tendencies in poststructuralist thought and shifted attention in its promotion of decentred and deferred meanings on to the figure of the active reader ('The birth of the reader must be at the cost of the death of the Author', Barthes ends his essay [1977a: 148]).

The reaction to Barthes' 'Death of the Author' has been vigorous and sustained, and frequently concerned to restore the authority of the author, along the COMMON SENSE lines of 'who else wrote *Bleak House* but Charles Dickens?' It is less often observed that, in Barthes' discussion, 'the Author-God' is replaced not simply by the reader but by the figure of the 'scriptor', or writer. The 'only power' this figure has 'is to mix writings, to counter the ones with the others, in such a way as never to rest on any one of them' (1977a: 46). The 'scriptor' is therefore an agent or medium, created in language rather than existing before or after it; a product of the 'tissue of signs' or of TEXTUALITY.

Michel Foucault's essay 'What is an author?' (1986b [1969]) followed shortly after Barthes' intervention. Foucault seeks not to displace the author (although he imagines a future CULTURE without such a figure) but to explain the 'conditions of being' that give some writers and forms of writing the authority of authorship in present societies. The proper name of an author, he adds, is not be identified with 'the real and external individual' bearing that name (1986b: 107). Thus 'Dickens' is only an 'author' by virtue of his writings and not because of other aspects of his life or personality. These are aspects of what Foucault calls the 'author-function', which he sees as having coincided historically with the advent of individualism and notions of private property with all this entailed in terms of copyright, contracts, authors' rights, and so on, and thus of the consequent possibility of transgression. In accordance with the rest of Foucault's work, the 'author-function' is therefore bound up with relations of POWER, DISCOURSE and knowledge, their maintenance through ideological, legal and other apparatuses, and the accompanying conceptualization of the SUBJECT.

A considered response to Barthes and Foucault appears in Sean Burke's *The Death and Return of the Author* (1992). His edited volume *Authorship* (1994) follows Foucault's lead in supplying a history of ideas of the author from Plato to Jorge Luis Borges.

See also *ÉCRITURE*/WRITING; HUMANISM; READING.

AUTONOMY

The question of the independence or autonomy of ideas, INTELLECTUALS, institutions and cultural works is a long-standing one. The common view is that art is by definition free of commercial values or ideological *partis pris*. The concept of autonomy is therefore invoked to reinforce a distinction between minority and

MASS art, or high and low CULTURE. In general terms, this is a liberal humanist view of art, but a defence of autonomy has been reiterated in the Marxist tradition by Theodor Adorno and other members of the Frankfurt School and by Left critics (in the American journal *Partisan Review* in the 1930s and 1940s, for example). In these arguments, autonomy is invariably granted to modern or modernist works as opposed to 'dependent' works, the latter seen as compromised by conventional forms, dogma or market values. A notorious example occurs in Adorno's approval of Schoenberg's 'new music' and dismissal of jazz (1955). However, it should be noted that Adorno elsewhere perceived a level of common contradiction that undercut such a stark opposition. Both autonomous and POPULAR, or mass art, he wrote (his example is the cinema), 'bear the stigma of capitalism, both contain elements of change' (1992: 53).

These same questions arise in discussions of fine art or film and in relation to CULTURE INDUSTRIES such as the press or broadcasting systems, or universities where autonomy, understood as freedom from financial or political control, is thought to safeguard integrity and worth.

Postmodern theories have taken arguments about autonomy in a further direction since in the contemporary 'IMAGE society', SIGNS and REPRESENTATIONS are seen to acquire an autonomy that detaches them from any stable referent. One further effect is that the traditional notion of the autonomy of the SUBJECT is undermined, since this is now seen as constructed in and by signification.

See also AESTHETICS; CRITICAL THEORY; SIMULATION; SPECULATIVE REALISM.

AVANT-GARDE

A term used to refer in French to the military corps sent ahead of the main body of an army (the 'vanguard') and adopted, by analogy, to describe experimental movements in the arts. In particular, the avant-garde has tended to mean the so-called 'historical' avant-garde of the early decades of the twentieth century; many of which announced themselves provocatively as new movements (Vorticism, futurism, dada, surrealism). Peter Bürger (1984) draws a significant distinction between these movements and MODERNISM. The latter is usually thought of as less libertarian or left-wing in its associated political ideologies (though if this is true of figures such as T.S. Eliot and Ezra Pound, it is a problematic description of Virginia Woolf or James Joyce) and seen as hostile towards POPULAR or MASS CULTURE (Huyssen 1986). The aim of the avant-garde was conversely, says Bürger, to destroy the institution of 'Art' and to return artistic practice to EVERYDAY LIFE. Again, however, if this is generally true, it is complicated by the wish of an influential commentator such as Clement Greenberg in 'Avant-garde and kitsch' (1939) and elsewhere, to preserve a distinction between, as he saw it, the serious, self-referential art of the avant-garde and commodified mass art or KITSCH.

Many would agree that – in one sense – the aim of the avant-garde has been achieved in POSTMODERNISM, well known for its eclecticism and blurring of distinctions between high and popular culture. This would appear to bring the avant-garde to an end. At the same time, the concept is now viewed as a dubious one for other reasons: the speed of acceptance of new art, the trivializing antics of its largely male personnel, the embarrassment of the original military metaphor. However, the question persists, in relation to postmodern if not avant-garde art, of whether it can retain the originality and critical, shocking force of the earlier movements, or is simply an index and accomplice of commodity culture. Eagleton (1986b) inclines to the latter view, while Jean-François Lyotard (1984) seeks to recast the experimental spirit of the historical avant-garde as the postmodern (see SUBLIME). Susan Rubin Suleiman (1990), meanwhile, proposes a feminist re-evaluation of earlier and postmodern artists, including among the latter, figures such as Hélène Cixous, Angela Carter, Jeanette Winterson and Cindy Sherman. A further important commentator on the contemporary avant-garde, who in poststructuralist terms favours repetition and reduplication rather than originality, is Rosalind Krauss (1985).

See also ELITE; CRITIQUE.

BASE AND SUPERSTRUCTURE

'Base and superstructure' is a key doctrine within the Marxist tradition, offering a model for the structure of human societies. In developing the theory of historical MATERIALISM, Marx and Engels considered economic activities, the PRODUCTION and continual REPRODUCTION of the means of life, to be fundamental in human history and to possess explanatory power over other areas of social activity. This primary economic sphere was described as the 'base' of society, while those other, secondary areas – including political, legal and religious institutions, as well as artistic production and intellectual work – were grouped together as the 'superstructure'. The best-known and most succinct formulation of this theory appears in Marx's 'Preface' to *A Contribution to the Critique of Political Economy* (1859). Marx here defines the 'economic structure' or 'real foundation' (what has come to be called the 'base') of society as the sum total of the prevailing 'relations of production' corresponding to the development of productive forces. On this foundation, Marx writes:

> rises a legal and political superstructure… to which correspond definite forms of social consciousness. The mode of production of material life conditions the social, political and intellectual life process in general. It is not the consciousness of men that determines their being, but on the contrary, their social being that determines consciousness.
>
> (Marx and Engels 1969: 503)

Simply put, this doctrine – and MARXISM as a whole – presents a form of economic determinism, presenting a society's level of economic development as the primary explanation for its other features, including all forms of CULTURE. On this basis, Marxist critics have not only described and analysed the culture of the past and present as bound and determined by its economic base, but have also argued that certain supposed or proposed future developments will not be possible without the fundamental changes in economic organization that would herald the transition to a socialist society. Thus, Fredric Jameson, for instance, has written that 'artists and writers who want to change their styles may well once again come to the conclusion that they must first change the world' (1988a: 71). Similarly, Terry Eagleton has frequently claimed that POSTSTRUCTURALISM's celebration of DIFFERENCE and indeterminacy is the 'premature' anticipation of a condition not yet possible.

The doctrine of base and superstructure has come in for heavy attack as contemporary theory has revised and questioned the fundamental tenets of Marxism. The most evident objection is that this model is too deterministic, that Marx's vocabulary of 'conditioning' and 'determining' fails to allow for human AGENCY, or for a two-way process between the respective spheres of activity. Marx and Engels themselves were in fact careful to offer such dialectical qualifications. In a letter of 1890, for instance, Engels insisted that:

> According to the materialist conception of history, the ultimately determining element in history is the production and reproduction of real life. More than this neither Marx nor I have ever asserted... The economic situation is the basis, but the various elements of the superstructure... also exercise their influence upon the course of the historical struggles and in many cases preponderate in determining their form.
>
> (Marx and Engels 1970: 487)

Much of the subsequent history of Marxist Cultural Theory has revolved around the attempt to rethink and revise the relations between base and superstructure. The question Colin MacCabe has asked – 'How exactly does economic organization cause effects at levels which cannot be directly related to it?' (1993: x) – has been tackled by such thinkers as Gramsci, Benjamin, Adorno, Althusser and Jameson through a series of innovative accounts of DETERMINATION, HEGEMONY, IDEOLOGY and MEDIATION.

At the same time, it has been argued that, however it is supplemented, the base-and-superstructure model is more of a hindrance than a help to cultural analysis. Raymond Williams, for example, argues that the terms 'base' and 'superstructure' are inherently limited by their misleading spatial metaphor and by their effective REIFICATION and separation of what are in reality dynamic, contradictory and closely linked aspects of society. 'What is fundamentally lacking', Williams contends, 'is any adequate recognition of the indissoluble connections between material production, political and cultural institutions and activity, and consciousness' (1977: 80; see also Eagleton 1983 on Williams).

The true contemporary opponent of classical or revised models of the base and superstructure, however, is the postmodern social theory of Jean Baudrillard. This would entirely invert the Marxist model by arguing that in late twentieth-century societies, supposedly 'superstructural' activities (leisure, CONSUMERISM, the media, advertising, IMAGE production) have become all-pervasive, entirely displacing an outdated model of 'material production'. In such a dispensation, CULTURAL POLITICS, so important a corollary of the Marxist tradition – if it has credibility at all – becomes a matter of REPRESENTATION and competing SIMULATIONS.

See also CAPITAL; CLASS; DIALECTICS.

BODY

The body has become a topic of intense interest in recent Cultural Theory. This is for a variety of reasons: its place on a changing feminist agenda, including a revised interest in women's bodies in relation to CONSUMERISM and medical health; a POPULAR concern with fitness; a wide interest inside and outside academic life in questions of SEXUALITY; the high-profile arguments of gay and lesbian groups on the issues surrounding AIDS; the influence of postcolonial theory upon conceptualizations of the racialized body, and current attention to biotechnologies and developments in genetic engineering.

Second-wave FEMINISM had been marked by differences between essentialist arguments, which evoked the female body as the site of authentic IDENTITY, and social-constructionist perspectives, which looked to GENDERed cultural categories. This tended to mean that the body was deemed 'natural' or was neglected. A further move, associated with French feminism in particular, had sought to rewrite normative definitions of SEXUAL DIFFERENCE by turning to the female body as inspiration for a counter-DISCOURSE (*ÉCRITURE FÉMININE*) and a female IMAGINARY (or SEMIOTIC) to contest the PHALLOCENTRIC narratives of Freudian and Lacanian PSYCHOANALYSIS. However, this thinking, too, is seen as PROBLEMATIC in granting AGENCY to a pre-linguistic, pre-cultural notion of the female body.

Further debates have concerned the REPRESENTATION of women in pornography, REPRODUCTION and abortion. Pornography was signalled as a key issue by Andrea Dworkin (1981) and the lobby for total censorship remains vocal, especially in the United States. These, and subsequent, highly charged debates over the 'right to life' of an unborn foetus and a woman's 'right to choose' abortion have revealed deep antagonisms between 'radical', 'liberal' and other alignments in contemporary feminism. Meanwhile, certain 'post-feminists', again especially in the United States, have relaxed the earlier feminist opposition to PATRIARCHY and distanced themselves from its 'prudery'. While accusing the cosmetics industry of inducing a conformity to the 'beauty myth', for example, Naomi Wolf claims a right to 'some romantic foolishness or unsanctioned sexual longing or "frivolous" concern about clothes' (1993: 68).

A somewhat clearer perspective, developing but not disowning earlier social-constructionist views, has recognized how the female body – far from being 'given' and 'natural' – is in fact altered under the pressure of fashion, consumerism and prevalent notions of the ideal sexual form. Fatness and slimming have therefore become feminist issues, as have the 'eating disorders' of anorexia and bulimia, body building, plastic surgery and skin treatments (Orbach 1978, 1993; see also Woodward [ed.] 1997). These issues, too, are understood as impacting upon gendered, ethnic and racial identities (Jordan and Weedon 1995).

On another front, gay, lesbian and other activist groups have drawn attention to the medical and physical facts concerning HIV and AIDS, and in a rare alliance, combined campaigning and care for sufferers with academic studies across different disciplines. Susan Sontag's study (1988), among others, explored the prevalence of metaphors of disease and war in discourses on AIDS, while others have tracked its misrepresentation, or sought to monitor and memorialize the effects upon patient and carers of physical change linked to suffering (Weeks and Holland [eds] 1996; Benson in Woodward [ed] 1997).

The complex importance of the body under colonialism was made evident by Frantz Fanon's seminal *Black Skin, White Masks* (1986 [1952]) and this has been much explored since. Postcolonial theory has alerted readers to a long history of visual and other representations enforcing racist attitudes. Invariably, this has been focused upon physical characteristics (facial features, the brute 'animal' strength of the black man) and upon the sexualized body: in myths of the black man's sexual potency and appetite, and the display, for example, in Europe in the 1800s, of Sarah Bartmann, the 'Hottentot Venus' (Jordan and Weedon, 1995, Part IV; Hall [ed] 1997b). In this century, a concentration upon physique (often internalized by its subjects) has all but naturalized an association of African-Americans with dance and sport. Meanwhile, other ethnic groups – West Indian and Indian males, for example – have been differently stereotyped by way of their bodily features.

In all of these examples, the body has been stigmatized by gendered, sexualized and racialized significations (sometimes crossed with representations of the poor and working class) in order to justify normative POWER structures. The prevailing issue (from slavery to abortion to bulimia) might be said to be one of control – the means whereby the SUBJECT is 'embodied' in society through agencies external to itself, or is in control of her/his own body and its representations. Prevalent theories in the field address this question in different ways: in terms of the historical emergence of the 'civilized body', marked by highly coded 'polite' manners and deportment (Elias 1978); of the discursive management of bodies in prisons, medicine, schools (Foucault 1986a) and the embodiment of class background in social bearing and marketable 'physical capital' (Bourdieu 1984; see also HABITUS).

Chris Shilling and Susan Benson usefully summarize and critique these theories (Woodward [ed] 1997). Shilling calls for a fuller recognition of 'the body as a material and physical phenomenon' (1997: 81); the 'matter' that is worked upon in social discourses and ideologies. This 'MATERIALISM', allied with a concern with self-determination in the face of widespread apparatuses of direct and implicit control, has also had recourse to the theories of Mikhail Bakhtin on the subversive and pointedly lewd deportment of the 'lower orders' at the time of CARNIVAL. Also relevant here is the development of new biotechnologies, which raise the question of the malleability of the physical body and human identity in newly accentuated ways (the singer Michael Jackson was only the most sensational example of this kind of alteration). The theme or metaphor of CYBORGS has been a way of reflecting on the technologies and ethics of 'POSTHUMAN' identities both in theoretical works (Haraway 1990, 1991) and a range of science-fiction novels and films.

See also ETHNICITY; RACE.

BRICOLAGE

This and the related term 'bricoleur' were used by the structural anthropologist Claude Lévi-Strauss (1908–1996) to describe the nature of MYTHIC thought in so-called 'primitive' societies. Mythic narratives, Lévi-Strauss argued, were assembled in 'a kind of intellectual bricolage' (1966: 7) from the existing stories, NARRATIVE remnants and other available scraps in a given culture.

Following Lévi-Strauss, and similarly influenced by the model of structuralist analysis, the linguist Gérard Genette proposed a distinction between the 'bricoleur' and the 'engineer'. While the engineer uses the appropriate tools and designated parts for the job, the bricoleur 'makes do', putting together the left-over, extracted and borrowed pieces at hand so as to compose a new whole. This 'typically structuralist' operation, says Genette, discovered by an ethnologist in the study of early civilizations, turns out to be a description of literary criticism (1982: 63). While the novelist who 'questions the universe' is equivalent to the engineer, the critic, like the bricoleur, 'addresses himself to a collection of oddments left over from human endeavours' (1982: 64). These leftovers are the themes, motifs, keywords, metaphors, quotations and so on comprising works of literature.

The kinds of distinction Lévi-Strauss and Genette draw between NATURE and CULTURE, and between the critic and writing were challenged by Jacques Derrida (1978) in an essay announcing the method of DECONSTRUCTION. 'If one calls bricolage the necessity of borrowing one's concepts from the text of a heritage which is more or less ruined,' he writes, 'it must be said that every discourse is bricoleur' (1978: 285). The figure of the engineer who constructs a totality supposedly 'out of nothing' emerges therefore as 'a myth produced by the bricoleur' (1978: 185). Lévi-Strauss is himself a bricoleur, says Derrida, whose 'book on myths is itself a kind of myth' (1978: 286). It follows also that deconstruction, 'which borrows from a heritage the resources necessary for the deconstruction of that heritage itself' (1978: 282), is also a kind of bricolage.

In another direction, bricolage has often been used interchangeably with terms such as collage and MONTAGE to describe the style of artistic composition of the early twentieth-century AVANT-GARDE in the arts and in the cinema. Though its later use retains something of this association, its application is more widespread than the arts. It has been used, for example, to describe the practice of self-conscious allusion to, or quotation from, other works characterizing a range of postmodernist forms (Hebdige 1988; Mercer 1994), to describe the ingenuity with which young women play upon 'the orthodox signs of femininity' (McRobbie 1994: 128), and even to describe the methodology, as a whole, of Cultural Studies. This, too, it has been said, 'could best be seen as a bricolage' (Grossberg, Nelson and Treichler [eds] 1992: 2).

See also STRUCTURALISM.

CAMP

In her essay 'Notes on camp' (1966), the critic Susan Sontag identified camp as 'the sensibility of failed seriousness, of the theatricalization of experience' (1966: 287).

This she distinguished from the 'seriousness' and intensity, respectively, of 'high culture' and 'AVANT-GARDE art'. Camp has been chiefly associated with an exaggerated gay style, with PARODY and self-dramatization, and Sontag's terms are clearly applicable to this. But although she recognized the association of camp taste with homosexual CULTURE and its importance as a 'gesture of self-legitimation' (1966: 290), she saw this in a broader context. 'Notes on camp' and other essays in the collection in which it appeared, *Against Interpretation* (1966), was part of Sontag's polemic against the liberal humanist defence of modernism and an associated hierarchy of high, middlebrow and MASS art on the part of a contemporary generation of New York INTELLECTUALS. Sontag associated camp with a 'new non-literary culture' of music, dance, films and architecture whose creativity needed to be recognized in a new critical vocabulary. Camp taste reached back, she argued, through aspects of surrealism to the 'history of snob taste', the mark of an 'aristocratic posture' in an age of affluence (1966: 291). Camp was not to be identified with mass or POPULAR culture, therefore, but was a way, for gays and others, of maintaining a distinctive, aestheticizing attitude in the midst of this culture; it was the answer, she said, to the question of 'how to be a dandy in the age of mass culture' (1966: 288).

Sontag's argument is an early positive response to the forms of mass and popular culture, and of the performative, ironic role-playing this promoted and seemed to require. Her remarks on this, even to an ambivalence on the social statement implied in the cultivation of style, anticipate later postmodern commentary on a world of ironic surfaces and SIMULATIONS. In fact, it might be said that Sontag was describing an early moment in this very culture.

See also KITSCH; QUEER THEORY.

CANON

A term derived from the Greek *kanon,* meaning measure or rule. Its early usage refers to the selected authoritative texts of the Bible and 'canonized' theologians. As John Guillory points out – establishing the leading feature of the term as it carried over into literary CULTURE – the canonizers of early Christianity operated on a principle of exclusion: 'They were concerned above all else with distinguishing the orthodox from the heretical' (1995: 233).

The canon has subsequently been understood as a list of 'great books', invariably drawn from the period of classical to modern European literature and identified with named authors: Homer, Dante, Milton, Shakespeare, T.S. Eliot. These works are defended as the embodiment of AESTHETIC and universal moral or 'human' VALUE. Although this clearly implies a process of judgement and discrimination, it is a circular and self-ratifying one, since the truly great are deemed unquestionably great and, in this respect, beyond judgement. Their canonic status is self-evident and you either recognize it or you don't. What such an orthodoxy depends upon of course is authority: the 'unspoken authority', as we say, of canonic texts and their expert interpreters.

Many have come to question this authority, particularly over the last 20 to 30 years. This criticism highlights the principles of selection and exclusion on which the canon depends. In fact, these soon become obvious. Certain works by a selected author are preferred to others (Shakespeare's *Hamlet* to his *King John*); a certain DISCOURSE (what counts as 'literature') is preferred to non-literature (POPULAR GENRE writings, other popular cultural forms, anonymous media texts); certain literary forms, the epic, poetry, or poetic drama, are preferred to the novel; tragedy is preferred to comedy. These hierarchies are also joined by other exclusions of CLASS, GENDER, RACE and ETHNICITY. The canon therefore emerges as the embodiment, not simply of aesthetic values, but of a selective humanist ideology whose representatives are white, male and European. It is on these grounds primarily that the authority of the concept and its contents have been questioned. The result has been an 'opening of the canon' to hitherto neglected authors and forms, or to the establishment of alternative canons, or 'counter-canons', from traditions of women's writing or Caribbean writing, for example, to canons of cultural theorists, lists of 'classic' movies and the hundred best pop singles. At the same time, this opening of the canon, along with the dissemination of popular and MASS culture and their academic study has provoked a defence of the 'western canon' in traditional terms (Bloom 1995).

A modified or alternative canon is also, it has to be said, a partial and contradictory response (since, strictly, there can only be one canon whose members are fixed absolutely). Guillory proposes instead an understanding of the canon's composition and role in cultural history. Such an approach illustrates, for example, how women or black writers have not simply been excluded, but included at certain times and in certain terms (women novelists in the nineteenth century; African-American and writers of colour in the late twentieth century). A major factor deciding this has been access to literacy and the means to write or produce (see Woolf 1929).

The canon (much like the looser notion of 'tradition') has therefore depended on a CONSTELLATION of aesthetic, moral, class-based and gendered values, and has been deployed in the promotion of an idea of culture, or sometimes to bolster an ethnic or national IDENTITY. It is only possible to maintain, or to CRITIQUE, this IDEOLOGY though the institutions that make its operation possible: publishing, the press, media and, principally, education. A study of the canon along these lines, says Guillory, will not dispense with the notion or its works, but provide a historicized understanding of canonized texts, the regulative constraints under which they are judged and our own positions as self-aware participants in this cultural process.

See also ELITE; EUROCENTRICISM; INTELLECTUALS.

CAPITALISM

'Capitalism' names an economic system founded on a concentration of ownership of the means of production and wage-labour which replaced the feudal system of aristocratic landowners and peasantry in the late eighteenth century to develop into the factory system of the nineteenth century analysed by Karl Marx and Frederick Engels. This period, described in terms of its economic system as 'industrial capitalism' and in social terms as 'bourgeois society', saw the rise to dominance of a middle-class of businessmen and owners (individual capitalists) and a subordinate working class. Its sphere of operation is a market economy based on supply and demand and free competition in the setting of prices, and its prime mechanism – the production of 'surplus value': the additional value, over and above the cost of production and the sum paid in wages, which was then realized as profit.

Successive stages of development have seen this system pass from the early twentieth century into what is termed 'monopoly capitalism' and thereafter 'late capitalism', or in the twenty-first century GLOBALIZATION, the latter ushering in the era of service industries and advanced consumerism radiating from the highly mediatized or networked economies of the major powers, namely the USA, Europe, Japan and China. In the course of this history, single, regional or national owners and companies have become enlarged and diversified and/or replaced by companies and conglomerates headed by super-rich individuals, families or multi-layered executive teams with interests across the world. In some cases of 'nationalization', businesses or industries have been brought under state ownership. The result might be termed 'state capitalism', but increasingly the older description of 'capitalist' and 'capitalism' has been replaced by the language of 'business' and 'free enterprise' or simply 'the market'.

Capitalism has been the subject of a vast library of debate and discussion, in political life, in academia and in journalism. A recent highly influential analysis has been Thomas Piketty's *Capital in the Twenty-First Century* (2014). Where politicians and economists have been preoccupied with questions of output and growth in the belief that this will benefit the whole of society, Piketty turns attention to changing patterns in the accumulation of income and wealth over the history of capitalist economies. Inherited wealth, Piketty argues, will in the natural course of capitalism's operation, always outstrip income (i.e. work). Aside from the exceptional periods of relative equality in the immediate postwar periods following 1914–18 and 1939–45, the accumulation of wealth from profits and investments, as well as inheritance, has produced wide and increasing disparities where currently half the world's wealth is in the hands of the super-rich one per cent (reported by Credit Suisse, Oct, 2015) while a mass of the world's population lives in poverty (see also Seabrook, 2007 and 2015). Piketty calls for a global tax on inherited wealth, plus an 80% tax on incomes over $500,000 to correct this imbalance. A related analysis of social class by Mike Savage (2015) confirms the increasing disparities of wealth in the UK in the twenty-first century where definitions of CLASS, he argues, are now reconfigured in terms of background, generation and geography. Thus, those with privileged backgrounds who belong to an older population and live and work in major cities are the most socially and financially advantaged (an elite of six per cent have a household income of £89,000, savings of £142,000 and property worth £325,000).

Novels and the visual arts have also regularly depicted the conditions of capitalism, sometimes directly, from the mid-Victorian examples of Elizabeth Gaskell's *North and South* (1854) and Charles Dickens' *Hard Times* (1854) to films of the postmodern or late capitalist period of finance capitalism and advanced consumerism such as *Wall Street* (1987) and *American Psycho* (novel 1998; film 2000). An interesting insight on present-day conditions is provided by John Lanchester's novel *Capital* (2013; TV 2016) – where 'Capital' is, in the first instance, the capital city of London. The novel sets out what is termed 'a moral fable about money' in its depiction of a cross-section of the inhabitants (Polish, Hungarian Zimbabwean, Pakistani and English) of a single south London street where house prices have risen dramatically and this guaranteed wealth, not income, defines its residents as 'rich'.

See also ELITE; ESTABLISHMENT; NETWORK; POSTCAPITALISM

CARNIVAL

The idea of the carnival or the 'carnivalesque' was developed by the Soviet theorist and critic Mikhail Bakhtin (1895–1975) in his study of the seventeenth-century prose satirist, François Rabelais, author of *Gargantua and Pantagruel* (Bakhtin 1963, 1965). The concept is derived from the practice of medieval carnival when, in an episode of permitted licence, the people would enjoy a holiday from their labours and in the process lampoon the authorities of church and state. Carnival therefore turned the world upside down and can be seen as an act of subversive nose-thumbing on the part of the lower orders who indulged themselves on the same occasion in the pleasures of the BODY in eating, drinking and promiscuous sexual activity. This EXCESS similarly affronted the decorums of polite society. Bakhtin argues that this social mode was adopted as a form of literary satire by Rabelais and employed what he identifies as the key features of 'decrowning activity', eccentricity, laughter, PARODY, profanation and 'doubling'.

The carnivalesque has been especially influential in Literary and Cultural Study in the last 20 years as the writings of the Bakhtin school came into circulation. Given that the full-bodied folk culture of carnival has receded in the west, the idea can only be applied metaphorically or by extension to other activities in discussions of contemporary popular culture (see Stallybrass and White 1986). Lynne Pearce, while seeking to appropriate Bakhtinian concepts for current literary analysis, is particularly scathing about those who, in 'gutting' Bakhtin's texts have turned such concepts into 'empty signifiers' (1994: 55, and see 80–111). The carnivalesque is a particular victim of this process. Nevertheless, it has proved a relevant, still socially referenced and creative motif in literary and cultural analysis. The film *Territories* (1984), for example, directed by Isaac Julien, bases its own carnivalesque AESTHETIC on the London Notting Hill Carnival and its West Indian roots, but does so in a self-reflexive film essay upon contemporary metropolitan DIASPORA culture. As Kobena Mercer comments, 'the text enacts or embodies the critical spirit of Carnival... itself carnivalizes codes and conventions' (1994: 59).

Robert Stam's discussion, also in a study of the application of Bakhtinian thought to film, explains the continuing appeal of the concept, especially for those seeking to identify a subversive, if temporary or problematic, critical power in popular culture. He both focuses Bakhtin's theory of DIALOGICS and confirms its radicalism, since in carnival, says Stamm, 'everything resulting from socio-hierarchical inequality or any other form of inequality among people is suspended' (1989: 21). Essays by John Fiske and Laura Kipnis (Grossberg *et al.* [eds] 1992) further suggest how Bakhtinian theory is put to work in this field. Elsewhere, Fiske (1987: 240–5) suggests how television in general, so often regarded as low and offensive, and at odds in its vernacular idioms with official IDEOLOGY, can be seen as having the force of the carnivalesque.

See also CHRONOTOPE; HETEROGLOSSIA.

CHAOS

Chaos theory (sometimes called 'complexity theory') is regarded as the twentieth century's third great revolution in the physical sciences, following the theories of relativity and quantum mechanics (Gleick 1988). The theory was developed in the mid 1970s on the basis of Benoit Mandelbrot's findings in fractal geometry. This explored rough and irregular shapes – a coastline, mountains, cloud formations, for example – and discovered that their complexity was patterned rather than random. Fractal geometry therefore provided a description and mathematical model for complex natural forms of a kind that had defeated Euclidean geometry. These forms, Mandelbrot – and, following him, Mitchell Feigenbaum – subjected to increasing degrees of magnification to discover an invariant recursive patterning or a 'statistical self-similarity': 'the essential quality of fractals in nature' (Barnsley *et al.* 1988: 21). The results have been best illustrated in computerized IMAGE-making, which can reproduce the complex patterned substructure of natural forms, or invent what are called 'fractal forgeries' from a simple initial equation, following their trajectory until predictability (or order) breaks down (into 'chaos'), which introduces a new complex system. The natural sciences, mathematics and computer programming collaborate in such exercises and the resulting images, if not the mathematics, have found their way on to popular magazine covers, posters and T-shirts.

Simply put, chaos theory, building on this basis in fractal geometry, perceives intricately patterned recursive structures in all manner of natural and human activity. In the words of one commentator, 'chaos theory depicts a universe that is deterministic, obeying the fundamental physical laws, but with a predisposition for disorder, complexity and unpredictability' (Hall, quoted in Hawkins 1995: 9). Its main concepts are the 'butterfly effect', 'complexity' and 'strange attractors'. The first suggests that unforeseeable effects may follow from very small causes (an earthquake or dramatic climate change from the movement of a butterfly's wings in a now popular image, or a decision to buy or sell on the stock market). The second suggests that chaos and order interact, and are always on the edge of the other, and the third that there are certain forces that trigger instability from the 'magnetic basins' at the heart of chaotic systems.

These concepts depend upon an exact mathematics (Prigogine and Stengers 1985; Gleick 1988) and the theory is keenly debated. One point of general contention is whether it represents a fact of NATURE or has the status of metaphor produced within the DISCOURSE of the science of mathematics (Hayles 1991). Potentially, however, the theory has profound implications for all of the sciences and for the study of CULTURE. Indeed, it is thought that many writers and theorists in the broad areas of POSTSTRUCTURALISM and POSTMODERNISM share a belief in indeterminacy and provisionality that chaos theory has arrived at by a different route (Strehle 1992: 220–1; Hayles 1990; Kuberski 1994). Its leading concepts have also been actively applied to the study of literature and artistic culture. A spirited example of the first is Harriet Hawkins' (1995) readings of high and POPULAR, past and present literature, and culture (from *Paradise Lost* and *The Tempest* to *Jurassic Park*).

A more polemical case is made by Charles Jencks (1993) for the adoption of the theories of complexity to architecture. The 'sciences of complexity', he says, illuminate 'the new Post-Modern paradigm' (1993: 9). Their findings are visibly expressed in the architectural projects of Peter Eisenman, Frank Gehry and others, in 'a language... close to nature, of twists and folds and undulations; of crystalline forms and fractured planes' (1993: 9). But Jencks views these as harbingers only of a necessary new CONSCIOUSNESS. To this end, he presents a general scheme of evolution emanating from a 'cosmic code' through a series of 'jumps' to eras of energy, matter, life and consciousness. Each jump and our present unique ability to partly understand this process is a mystery, says Jencks. His polemic, while based on a particular cultural discourse, is an interesting example of how such thinking is brought to an expansive, spiritual conclusion: to a belief, in spite of its poststructuralist scepticism towards stability and harmony, in 'a metanarrative of the universe and its creation' (1993: 7).

Other writings echo this profound tension between expressions of wonder at infinite complexity and the belief in an all-encompassing oneness: a tension, expressed in the very terms of the theory itself, between 'chaos' and 'order'.

CHORA

Derived from Plato's *Timaeus* where it is used to invoke a bridge or passage between mind and body, or the intelligible and sensible worlds. In recent theory it has been taken up in French FEMINISM, notably by Julia Kristeva and, more obliquely, by Jacques Derrida in association with architecture. Both Kristeva and Derrida draw out the term's reference to spatiality – to the notions of SITE, locale and region – and to women and femininity, the last in association with the GENDERed meanings of 'receptacle', 'nurse' and 'mother'. Kristeva (1984b) develops the latter meaning especially, seeing the chora as the undifferentiated womb-like PLACE shared by mother and child. In connection with her theorization of the SEMIOTIC, the chora posits a non-PHALLOCENTRIC place and relationship opposed to the dominant SYMBOLIC order. The DISCOURSE and mode of being of this place will be maternal, rhythmic, inchoate and pre-verbal.

Derrida (1993) is interested in the deconstructive potential of the idea and the way in which it might prompt a different conception of the relation between theory and practice or form and matter in the world of architectural design. Like other key terms in his writing, such as SUPPLEMENT or TRACE or the 'pharmakon', again from Plato, which designates both cure and poison, the indeterminate or intermediate spatial designation of chora has the potential to unhinge the unifying logics of texts and the conventional binary distinctions of architectural discourse.

Elizabeth Grosz's (1995) discussion of the term brings Derrida's indirect contribution to a re-conceptualization of space, beauty and function in architecture into a 'confrontation' with Luce Irigaray's sweeping CRITIQUE of the phallocentric foundations of western knowledge. Grosz aims to restore a connection between femininity and women's corporality so as to produce an embodied concept of women's autonomy 'in the domain of the dwelling', as she puts it, 'where and how to live, as whom and with whom?' (1995: 48). In particular, she would restore the conceptual and material importance of maternal SPACE: a 'primordial' space 'from which all subjects emerge', though this is ceaselessly usurped by masculine modes (1995: 55).

CHRONOTOPE

A compound of the Greek terms for time and PLACE. It is used by the Soviet linguist and critic Mikhail Bakhtin (1895–1975; see also DIALOGICS and HETEROGLOSSIA) to describe both the 'intrinsic connectedness of temporal and spatial relations that are artistically expressed in literature' (1981: 84) and the more specific conventions of GENRES and subcategories of the novel. His essay 'Forms of time and chronotope in the novel' presents a lengthy survey of varying chronotopes characterizing pre-novelistic forms such as the adventure NARRATIVE, the idyll, the chivalric romance, including some brief discussion of more contemporary forms such as GOTHIC fiction, the novel of the salon and parlour, and of provincial life, which emerged with nineteenth-century REALISM (1981: 245–8). An important example is the chronotope characterizing the earlier writings of Rabelais, otherwise a key example in Bakhtin's theory of CARNIVAL. Here, Bakhtin identifies a collectively experienced chronotope that had its source in the 'collective historical life' (1981: 208) shaped in its sense of time and place by a life of labour on the land. Subsequent chronotopes have been less collectively based.

In addition, Bakhtin identifies subcategories – one such is the life of the rogue, the clown and the fool in the early novel, who exist in 'their own special little world, their own chronotope' (1981: 159). This suggests the coexistence of different, even multiple chronotopes, as main and subplots within a given text and is consistent with the general theory of the dialogic interaction or friction of languages, registers and ideologies in the writings of the Bakhtin circle. Lynne Pearce (1994) coins the term 'polychronotopic' to describe this coexistence and suggests its applicability to modernist and postmodernist fiction. She presents a GENDEREd model of the chronotope along these lines in a reading of Jeanette Winterson's *Sexing the Cherry* and Toni Morrison's *Beloved.*

The idea of the chronotope also clearly retains its application to POPULAR GENRES. It provides a way of identifying how the conventions of the Gothic, the western, the gangster film, science fiction, situation comedy, soap opera and so on are contextualized in SPACE and time, but more interestingly of how the stock co-ordinates of a DOMINANT generic chronotope (police headquarters and gangster nightclub, apache encampment and cavalry fort, space station and alien lair) enter into a relation of dialogic opposition, mirroring, or mutual transformation. The concept suggests a way, that is to say, of analysing situated REPRESENTATIONS of self and OTHER.

See also CITY; HETEROTOPIA.

CITIZENSHIP

The most influential theory of citizenship in relation to postwar societies is associated with the sociological model of T.H. Marshall (1977, 1981). Marshall describes citizenship in terms of the accumulation of rights over the last three centuries, from the establishment of civil and legal rights to the successful struggle for the rights of political association and parliamentary democracy in the nineteenth century, to the institutionalized social rights of the welfare state of the mid twentieth century. In present societies of this type, citizenship is defined in terms of a system that balances state provision in the areas of employment, health and education against the ill effects of CAPITALISM. Social democracy is therefore seen to shield the citizen from the hazards of the market and CLASS conflict.

This PARADIGM is said now to have been seriously undermined, both ideologically and structurally, by changes in the political CULTURE and economies of western societies. Post-industrial societies have witnessed dramatic changes in employment and consumer patterns, the erosion of the model of the nuclear family, the casualization of labour and increased urban poverty (see POST-FORDISM). Traditional working-class organizations have declined and are ineffective against multinational corporate business interests. The welfare state has been 'rolled back' to make room for privatization. Meanwhile, the revolutions in the Soviet Union and Europe of the late 1980s, nationalist movements in Europe and elsewhere, and the increased movement of peoples have further unsettled the postwar certainties that defined citizenship in terms of CITY, state and nation. For many, being now a British, American, South African or German citizen has become a seriously fraught issue. At the same time, while traditional rights have been undermined, the activities of the 'social movements' (the women's movement, black, gay liberation and ecology movements) have brought a raft of further rights to public notice: human rights, animal rights, the right to work, the right to abortion, the right to life, children's rights, consumer rights and so on.

These compound changes have made citizenship a matter of widespread and topical debate. Within Sociology and political thought, there has been a consequent attempt to mark out the terms of a new paradigm. Roche (1992) sees a shift of emphasis and vocabulary from rights to 'duties and obligations', initiated by the New Right of the 1980s. Turner sees an 'expansion of abstract universal social rights devoid of particularistic or national foundations' (1993: 14). GLOBALIZATION, the complexities of contemporary cultural identities and ecological awareness suggest the need, he says, for 'a new discourse of human rights and animal rights', but one that 'must avoid the equation of citizenship with sameness', balancing postmodern PLURALISM with social solidarity (1993: 15, 16). Clarke envisions a newly defined 'deep citizenship'; a 'post-liberal' conception of an active, newly sensitized ethical and political sense exercised in relations between 'self and world, self and others, and self and cosmos' (1996: 125).

A further notable contribution to this paradigm shift is the work of Ernesto Laclau and Chantal Mouffe (1985). Here, in the context of a general project of 'liberal socialism', a movement away from the state, as above, is coupled with a critique of traditional class identities and of orthodox MARXISM. Citizenship is redefined 'as a form of political identity that is created through identification with the political principles of modern pluralist democracy' (Mouffe 1993: 82). This means reconceiving the individual of liberal democracy as a citizen comprised of a 'multiplicity of identities' (1993: 84) and rethinking COMMUNITY so that this is founded not on sameness but on a principle of 'equivalence' that respects the individual's diversity.

Finally, in this trend, ideas of a transformed citizenship are connected with debates on global democracy. Thus, David Held argues that the new citizen of the new millennium will need to be the citizen of a state and a 'cosmopolitan citizen', too. 'Citizenship in a democratic polity of the future', this means, will require us to take on a more mediating role, 'which encompasses dialogue with the traditions and discourses of others with the aim of expanding the horizons of one's own framework of meaning and prejudice' (2000: 425).

See also COSMOPOLITANISM; CIVIL SOCIETY; PUBLIC SPHERE.

CITY

The nineteenth- and turn-of-the-century city was seen as a key expression of MODERNITY. Here, commentators found the processes of increased rationalization in political and economic life, the technological developments bringing modernization in transport and communications (the car, the telephone, the typewriter, electricity) and the unprecedented accumulation and movement of people. The mentality of the city dweller in the anonymity of the city crowd became a particular object of study by sociologists as well as writers and artists (Williams 1973, 1992; Bowlby 1985). A key essay in a continuing tradition of Urban Sociology was Georg Simmel's 'The metropolis and mental life' (1903), which gave a lead to Louis Wirth, Robert Park and others in the Chicago school of the 1920s and 1930s. The concept of the 'mental map' developed by Kevin Lynch and the work of Richard Sennett have proved very influential in conceptualizing later developments in the period of postmodernity (see Le Gates and Stout [eds] 1996).

Changes in architectural style and the urban environment have indeed been one of the most visible SIGNS of POSTMODERNISM. Charles Jencks, architect and commentator, proposes, for example, that we can date postmodernism from the dynamiting of the modernist or 'international style' Pruitt-Igoe housing project in St Louis precisely at 3.32 pm on 15 July 1972. Others have associated the signs of postmodernism – an expanded consumer CULTURE, computerization, hands-on technology, changed social composition and employment patterns, the selective accumulation of wealth – directly with the city. Whereas the modern or modernist city was characterized by a planned grid, a functional transport system, high-rise buildings of glass and concrete, a clear demarcation of uptown and downtown, or of east and west ends – the latter harbouring a financial district – the postmodern city is seen as a place of leisure, CONSUMERISM and the 'tourist gaze'. Whereas the first gave material expression to a rationalist order and mentality, the second is experienced as a decentred, or multicentred, cosmopolis. Unlike the 'carbuncles' or stereotypical glass boxes of the modernist era, its buildings are eclectic, wittily decorated organic shapes.

Key examples of this style of postmodern city are Las Vegas and Los Angeles. As David Lyon writes of the second: 'the symbolic centrelessness of LA becomes a metaphor for postmodern consumer culture in general: all is fragmented, heterogeneous, dispersed, plural – and subject to consumer choices' (1994: 61). A different perspective, based more on an economic than a cultural analysis produces a different postmodernism and postmodern city. For Saskia Sassen (1991), for example, it is not Los Angeles, but London, New York and Tokyo – nodal points in the world's financial NETWORK – that are the postmodern 'global cities'.

Questions of the physical, social and economic nature of the postmodern city and its relation to global CAPITALISM continue to excite much discussion (Carter, Donald and Squires [eds] 1993; Watson and Gibson [eds] 1995; King [ed] 1996). The themes of this debate have come to embrace many of the major motifs in the contemporary study of culture: of SUBJECTIVITY and IDENTITY and their embodiment in PLACE, COMMUNITY and SPACE; the relevance of the modernist figure of the FLÂNEUR to contemporary urban identities organized around GENDER and ETHNICITY; the impact of postcolonial themes, subjects and concepts (HYBRIDITY, DIASPORA) upon the conceptualization of the cities of the First and Third World.

Much of this debate also naturally concerns the world of REPRESENTATIONS: in literature, film, photography, painting as well as the architecture referred to above. Key examples in this wide field remain Berman (1982) and Harvey (1989). Further works of interest include Timms and Kelley ([eds] 1985), Wilson (1991) and Kennedy (2000). Pacione ([ed] 2001) provides a comprehensive resource of major contributors on the city on a range of related topics. See also CITIZENSHIP; GLOBALIZATION; PLACE.

CIVIL SOCIETY

A concept introduced in seventeenth-century political philosophy to name the institutions of the modern state, but developed by Hegel, Marx and others in the Marxist tradition to distinguish the realm of social relationships, organizations and institutions from the state. In this tradition, civil society therefore appeared as an arena that functioned under the sway of the state but might be mobilized against it.

The most influential formulations of civil society – certainly upon British Cultural Studies – occur in the writings of the Italian Marxist, Antonio Gramsci

(1891–1937) (see 1971a: 'State and civil society'). Gramsci argued that modern capitalist societies are governed for the most part by consent and only rarely by coercion. This consent to the HEGEMONY of a ruling CLASS is exacted, said Gramsci, within the realm of civil society. Where Marx had come to view civil society as a social surface disguising real class antagonisms, Gramsci restored the substance of IDEOLOGY and ideological struggle to the concept. This was further emphasized in the distinction between 'repressive' and 'IDEOLOGICAL STATE APPARATUSes' developed by the French Marxist philosopher, Louis Althusser (1918–1990); the first referring to agencies of the state such as the army and police, and the second to social and cultural institutions such as the church, the media, education and the family.

Both formulations have been found wanting, however. Urry, for example, detects a number of inconsistencies in Gramsci's discussion (1981: 21) and feels that Althusser conflates civil society with the state. Neither thinker, in his view, escapes the limitations of the tiered model of BASE AND SUPERSTRUCTURE (or of the economy and state) that civil society is deemed to mediate between. Nor do they offer a model adequate to the diverse forms of 'contradictory and conflictual', social activity and association comprising this realm in late capitalist societies (1981: 24).

Urry is among those who shift the concept of civil society away from the more demarcated areas of ideological institutions and a concern primarily with social class to the heterogeneous arena of personal life and social REPRODUCTION. Civil society is similarly understood by Stuart Hall to have undergone dramatic change, encompassing patterns of consumption, 'a politics of the family, of health, of food, of sexuality, of the body' (Morley and Chen [eds] 1996: 234). The study of civil society, so conceived, becomes a study less of class ideologies than of 'a network of strategies and powers and their articulations' (1996: 234). The implication is that civil society has become, and is perceived as, more complex. While this departs from the categories of orthodox Marxism it confirms, in Hall's view, Gramsci's analysis of historical development and political action (1996: 427).

Others, by contrast, view this changed situation as arguing for a turn from Gramsci to Foucault's more dispersed notion of POWER and of civil society as a 'correlate' of government not as in a dichotomous relationship with it (Burchell, Gordon and Miller [eds] 1991; Bennett 1998: 72–6).

See also ARTICULATION; CITIZENSHIP; COMMUNITY; GOVERNMENTALITY.

CLASS

A key term in MARXISM, Sociology and the broad study of CULTURE. At its simplest, Marxism presents an economic definition of class, whereby class IDENTITY is established in 'objective' terms by the individual's position in the economic structure of society and its attendant social relations. Owning a factory and living off its profits decides one is a member of the bourgeoisie. Selling your labour for a wage at the same factory designates you as a member of the proletariat. This distinction is often exchanged for the more usual, but inconsistent, distinction between middle and lower, or working class – inconsistent because the first terms suggest a hierarchical ranking, topped by an upper class, whereas 'working' class implies a distinction between productivity and non-productivity.

Marx avoided this confusion in a distinction between 'wage-labourers, capitalists and landlords'. However, this introduces an additional distinction between kinds of ownership – of property and land as well as the more obvious industrial means of production – and brings a further 'class', the aristocracy, into view. Since the aristocracy is associated with an earlier 'feudal' system, this then suggests the further complexity of how elements of an earlier mode of production can survive in a later social and economic order. Nor in itself does the central relationship between workers and capitalists suggest where, for example, a manager in a factory – who is a wage-labourer (although traditionally 'salaried') but not a capitalist – is to be placed in class terms. Usually in such cases, a further distinction such as lower-middle class, or *petite bourgeoisie,* is used to refine the basic binary or tripartite distinction, and is then accompanied by the further elaboration of the attitudes and values, comprising the culture or IDEOLOGY associated with a class or class fraction. Further internal distinctions are similarly possible within the working class – between skilled and unskilled, or manual labour, for example.

An objective class identity, as this begins to suggest, does not bestow a 'class CONSCIOUSNESS', since this requires a knowledge of objective conditions and, in its politicized form for the working class at least, a political will and class organization (in the shape of trades unions or a political party) to remedy perceived inequalities. At this point, class clearly becomes more than an economic category.

The sociological definition of class emphasizes a further set of factors such as background, education, occupation, status and taste. A class identity can therefore once more reinforce, or cut across, the lines of a traditional Marxist definition. A low-paid teacher might, for example, be objectively working class but, in terms of values and aspirations, middle class. At the same time, this class position will not necessarily determine political attitude or belief. Modern British society can therefore present us with lower-upper middle-class socialists (the way George Orwell defined himself) or the phenomenon of a self-made working-class Tory millionaire.

Class is also defined by market researchers via a set of categories close to the sociological account. The emphasis here, however, is on people as consumers. Thus, we are defined as Class A i, ii or iii; B i, ii or iii, and so on, according to income, spending power and habits. This perspective would seem to be inimical to traditions within Cultural Studies. Richard Hoggart's founding study *The Uses of Literacy* (1957), for example, opposed a (regional British) working-class identity and culture to an encroaching (Americanized) consumer culture, and this has been a continuing emphasis. Nevertheless, studies on SUBCULTURES, in particular, have recognized the formative part consumer culture plays in the making of class and other identities. (see Hebdige on how the findings of 'commercial life style and psychographic' research can be usefully combined with the 'critical and diagnostic' work of academic study (1989, 53)).

A concern with social class has marked intellectual life in the UK across a range of disciplines in the Humanities and Social Sciences, and this has distinguished it from comparable work elsewhere, especially in the United States. Class has also itself changed in the UK, especially in the postwar period. The ways in which the British working class has been 'restructured and recomposed' in relation to culture and ideology, as well as the theoretical models and methods appropriate to its study, is the subject of the important volume, *Working Class Culture* (Clarke *et al.* 1979), produced at the Birmingham Centre for Contemporary Cultural Studies. In later work, however – again across a broad academic spectrum – class has been commonly considered in relation to, or has been replaced by, the role of GENDER, RACE, ETHNICITY and SEXUALITY in discussions of social and cultural identity. Some later discussion on unemployment, homelessness and disaffected youth has employed the category of an 'underclass' to describe those (usually male) who were felt to have dropped out of – or never joined – a labour market, nor to function as active consumers, and for whom both traditional and newer categories therefore appeared inadequate (Jencks and Peterson 1991; Mann 1992; Kelso 1995).

An additional newer term, the 'precariat' has been used to describe those on casual contracts who have limited economic power or social standing. Mike Savage (2015) sees social class in the UK as quite radically reconfigured away from its traditional categories and as composed at the top and bottom levels of the super-rich and the precariat and very poor. Class is defined now, he argues, more by wealth, CULTURAL CAPITAL accruing from family background and education at elite universities, and location – primarily in urban areas and above all in London. Even within top universities and within the same subject specialism, it appears that those from Oxford, the London School of Economics, Kings College, London and Imperial College will earn higher incomes that those from top-tier Russell Group Universities. The result is a 'class ceiling' limiting movement into the top echelons of business and the professions and a widening gap between the super-rich and 'the rest of us'.

See also CAPITALISM; ELITE; CONSUMERISM; ESTABLISHMENT; POSTCAPITALISM.

CLOSURE

A term that suggests not simply that texts come to a literal physical close but that their formal design or narrative movement constructs a position for the reader that reinforces a dominant view of the world or IDEOLOGY. The term has been used especially in accounts of nineteenth-century or so-called 'classic' REALISM. Thus, Catherine Belsey, drawing on Louis Althusser and structuralist theory, suggests that closure is one of the defining features of realism (1980, especially Ch. 3). The others are 'illusionism', the creation of an effect of real life, and a 'hierarchy of discourses' in which the invisible author assumes a position of privileged knowledge above an internal narrator, fictional characters and readers.

Realist narrative introduces an enigma or crisis in the world it depicts and brings this to a resolution at the point of closure when order is re-established. This movement, says Belsey, also produces a final convergence of DISCOURSES and an equivalence of knowledge (the reader knows what the author knows and what the detective finally reveals to the characters) which, she argues, affirms a humanist ideology of the unified, knowing and self-determining SUBJECT. It is in the interests of this ideology to appear 'natural' and 'simply the way things are' and thus, first, to conceal the role of language in its construction (the fictional structures it is necessary to efface if the illusionism of realism is to be successful) and, second, to suppress persistent internal contradictions that would trouble the desired impression of unity and order. 'Classic realism,' Belsey writes, 'cannot foreground contradiction. The logic of its structure... the movement towards closure... precludes the possibility of leaving the reader simply to confront the contradictions which the text may have defined' (1980: 82).

Closure is therefore associated with a particular ideology and fictional form, which is implicitly or directly contrasted with a more openly enigmatic or contradictory kind of text. This distinction is comparable to the distinction drawn by Roland Barthes (1976) between what he termed 'lisible' ('READERLY') and 'scriptable' ('WRITERLY') texts. Belsey terms the latter 'interrogative' texts. It is clear from her discussion that there can also be an interrogative reader of the realist or 'readerly' text; one who, following the lead of much poststructuralist thought, would read 'against the grain' or 'in the margins' of the text to reveal what has been suppressed.

See also _ÉCRITURE_/WRITING; HUMANISM.

CODE

Used to designate the rules and conventions by which an individual item is recognized as belonging to a common linguistic, visual or cultural system. Thus, the English language is a code and this comprises subcodes such as the languages of medicine, computer experts, rock journalists and darts enthusiasts. This gives rise to the view that a code is the arcane province of a select group of users and needs to be 'decoded' – though decoding in reality can only translate a less common into a more common code.

The use of the term 'code' in Literary and Cultural Studies is derived in the main from STRUCTURALISM and traditions in SEMIOLOGY. Structuralism proposed that all COMMUNICATION systems, from the simplest hand signals to the sophistication of film and fictional NARRATIVES can be understood by analogy with the primary system of language. An early influential model of communication in this tradition was proposed by the linguist, Roman Jakobson (see ADDRESSER/ADDRESSEE). Two further influences derived from the analysis of MYTH by the anthropologist, Claude Lévi-Strauss and the literary and cultural semiology of Roland Barthes. Lévi-Strauss saw myths as stories that encode and reconcile a general series of binary oppositions (life: afterlife; human: supernatural; home: exile). Individual tales function within a linked system of myths to ratify the traditions and so confirm the IDENTITY of the tribal COMMUNITY. This model was employed in Film Studies in the 1970s, especially in the analysis of POPULAR GENRES such as the western and gangster film, which were seen similarly to encode both general and specific cultural oppositions – between good and evil, the east and west, the system of the law and natural justice – in the narrative settings, character types and ICONOGRAPHY of individual films.

Roland Barthes' early essays on the IMAGE, on narrative and on fashion (see Barthes [ed] 1977b) have a firm place in the history of formal and ideological analysis, and illustrate the wide application to literature, written, visual and MASS cultural forms, which was one of the immediate attractions of this method. In 'Rhetoric of the image' (1977b), he identified three MESSAGES structuring the formal composition and meaning of the visual SIGN (his example is an advertising image): the 'linguistic', comprising the caption and printed text; the 'literal'; and the 'symbolic', identified as the over-layered aspects of the visual image. The literal message depends on objects in the image being recognized simply for what they are – a car, a book, a bottle of wine – and is, said Barthes, non-coded. The symbolic message builds on this to create coded symbolic, ideological or cultural meanings. In 'The introduction to the structural analysis of narrative' (1977b), Barthes identified the codes that organize and activate meaning in a narrative sequence. Chief among these were the 'nuclei', the 'hinge points' in the narrative, and 'catalysers', consecutive units, themselves of different types, that 'fill in the narrative space between nuclei' (1977b: 93). His later study *S/Z* (1975) extended this structuralist method to an analysis of the five codes (named the 'hermeneutic', 'semic', 'symbolic', 'proairetic' and 'cultural') in Balsac's story *Sarrasine*. In itself, this had little influence and was overtaken in Barthes' own work and elsewhere by poststructuralist approaches committed to more open, plural meanings.

A key essay directly employing the language of codes in Cultural Studies was Stuart Hall's many times reprinted 'The television discourse – encoding and decoding' (1997a [1974]). Here, an account of encoding and decoding the media message at the points of PRODUCTION and RECEPTION is allied with an interest in its ideological purposes and effects, for which Hall draws on the theory of HEGEMONY. A TV news bulletin, for example, is coded in a number of ways, from the choice of presenter and studio set to the use of stills, film, voice-over, report or interview, and the running order of items. These are decided according to both a 'professional code' and an implicit ideological agenda. However, Hall advances a model allowing for the way viewers may accept, negotiate or reject these coded assumptions. His discussion is informed by a class perspective, which on its own now seems somewhat restrictive, but it continues to offer an important and suggestive model.

The use of the terms 'code' and 'subcode', or the related 'subtext' to suggest a subordinate or underlying meaning has become common outside structuralism and academic life. However, in academic work itself, this vocabulary retreated in the 1980s and 1990s as the structuralist assumption of an ordered system of meaning has been challenged by the poststructuralist emphasis on decentred TEXTUALITY, and as the associated idea of scientific rigour is seen to imply a FORMALISM that represses both history and the question of VALUE. Umberto Eco is perhaps one of the few literary and cultural commentators able to sustain a more structuralist vocabulary in poststructuralist and postmodern times (see Eco 1986). A more curious and enigmatic use of the concept of code in this connection appears in the writings of Jean Baudrillard. In *The System of Objects* (1968) and early writings of the 1970s, Baudrillard argued that consumer societies had made

Marxist analysis in particular obsolete. The TV advertising system, not the economy or relations of production, imposed a code, said Baudrillard, of social standing, regulating status and aspirations. In a further elaboration, he came to see contemporary societies as entirely dominated by media SIMULATIONS, the resultant code inducing a mass uniformity to which the only resistance could be the passivity of the silent majority.

See also AUTHOR; DISCOURSE; NEGOTIATION.

COGNITIVE MAPPING

A term employed by Fredric Jameson in connection with the experience of new spatial relations in POSTMODERNISM. It is derived, says Jameson, from the concept of 'cognitive estrangement' used by the critic Darko Suvin to describe the defamiliarizing or estranging effects of science fiction (Grossberg *et al.* [eds] 1988: 348). Jameson introduces the concept of cognitive mapping in his account of the bewildering effects of the Bonaventure Hotel in Los Angeles. The experience of being unable to get one's bearings in the 'postmodern hyperspace' of the hotel leads him to conclude that this postmodern use of space 'has finally succeeded in transcending the capacities of the individual body to locate itself, to organise its immediate surroundings perceptually, and cognitively to map its position in a mappable external world' (1991: 44). This, he then generalizes as the problem of how we are to 'map' the expanse of global CAPITALISM and locate ourselves in relation to it.

Jameson looks consequently for 'an aesthetic of cognitive mapping – a pedagogical political culture which seeks to endow the individual subject with some new heightened sense of its place in the global system' (1991: 54). A critical form of art in postmodern culture will therefore seek to invent the enabling co-ordinates of such a global cognitive map. The idea can be understood first as an attempt to re-conceptualize the forms of CRITIQUE associated with an earlier oppositional MODERNISM in circumstances where a position of critical distance no longer appears available. Second, within Jameson's late Marxist framework, the concept is an attempt to re-conceptualize an oppositional proletarian CLASS CONSCIOUSNESS. As Jameson later comments:

> 'Cognitive mapping' was in reality nothing but a code word for 'class consciousness' – only it proposed the need for class consciousness of a new and hitherto undreamed of kind, while it also inflected the account in the direction of that new spatiality implicit in the postmodern.
>
> (1991:418)

See also ALIENATION EFFECT; ESTRANGEMENT; SPACE.

COLONIALISM

See ORIENTALISM; POSTCOLONIALISM.

COMMODITY FETISHISM

A key concept in Karl Marx's *Capital*. Marx sees capitalism as driven by the need to produce commodities for consumption in an ever-expanding market. In the process, the 'use-value' of the objects produced by human labour is replaced by their 'exchange-value', expressed generally in money terms. Understood in its prime function as a commodity under CAPITALISM, the resulting object becomes a 'fetish', substituting itself for the social relations it has occluded or repressed. The work of IDEOLOGY is to naturalize this state of things in society and its accompanying, supporting mentality. In being brought to consent to this condition, the worker under capitalism is a victim of ALIENATION, though Marx uses this specific term in his earlier work rather than in the mature work of *Capital*. In the latter, he speaks rather of REIFICATION, the conversion of the subject to an object. The extreme form of this process in Marx's analysis is the reification of the labour power which the worker has to exchange. Not only the products of labour, but the labourer too, becomes a commodity and is induced to see him/herself this way.

Marx of course looked for the supersession of this specific historical condition. Analyses of late capitalism in terms of increased 'commodification' would seem to suggest that the process has been exacerbated. From a classic Marxist point of view, this is indeed the case. However, MASS consumption has produced a re-conceptualization of the commodity as having positive and flexible social, cultural and personal meanings, indeed 'use-value', and not simply the exchange and money value that enforce reification (Appadurai [ed.] 1986). The idea of the commodification of labour power, along with other key Marxist concepts, has also been critiqued by 'post-Marxist' thinkers. Laclau and Mouffe (1985), for example, see it as a 'fiction' forced into being by the Marxist commitment to a theory of inflexible laws of economic necessity.

See also CONSUMERISM; FETISHISM; MARXISM; VALUE.

COMMON CULTURE

The idea of a common CULTURE has been regularly connected with the valued cultural life of a 'COMMUNITY' and with the commonness of its everyday meaningful activity – as in Raymond Williams' dictum that 'culture is ordinary' (Williams 1989a). In Williams' essay 'The idea of a common culture' (1989a [1968]), this was defined against the conservative tradition of T.S. Eliot and F.R. Leavis, and against MARXISM – the first because it is, says Williams, objectionable as well as inconceivable in practice, the second because it has tended to separate the realms of culture and the economy. As 'an alternative emphasis', Williams stresses 'that there is no special class, or group of men, who are involved in the creation of meanings and values, either in a general sense or in specific art and belief' (1989a: 34). 'In talking of a common culture', he writes:

> one was saying first that culture was the way of life of a people, as well as the vital and indispensable contributions of specially gifted and identifiable

persons, and one was using the idea of the common element of the culture – its community – as a way of criticising that divided and fragmented culture we actually have.

(1989a: 35)

The study of culture therefore saw a vital part of its task not as the preservation, but as the making, of a common culture in the face of an official or selective culture that served the interests of a ruling class or cultural minority. This commitment has been an integral part of the 'culturalist' tradition, which has maintained a belief in the productive human AGENCY of ordinary, working-class or 'common people'. While criticized for its romantic and populist cast, this perspective has proved a resilient influence in a range of later work on POPULAR, youth and SUBCULTURES, even where this is buttressed by other theoretical sources (Fiske 1989; Hebdige 1979, 1988).

The debt to Williams in this tradition is plain to see in Paul Willis' *Common Culture* (1990). The making of a common culture depends, says Willis, on 'symbolic creativity' and on a 'grounded aesthetics'. These terms describe the ways people attribute meanings to the symbols and practices of 'the received natural and social world', which define their lives and thus render this world 'controllable' in the light of their own situated needs (1990: 22). Whereas the engaged creation of meaning is usually associated with PRODUCTION, Willis sees consumption as a contemporary realm of creative symbolic activity. Cultural meanings, this implies, are not already given, or intrinsic to, objects or practices, but made in the process of consumption or use. A common culture therefore arises from the symbolic creativity of consumers in a world that, in its own terms, is driven by profit, but where this logic can be contradicted or diverted by the creative use of its abundant commodities for other purposes. An unprecedented flow of 'commercial cultural forms', in Willis' words, makes 'many more materials... available for necessary symbolic work'. The result is 'forms not dreamt of in the commercial imagination and certainly not in the official one – forms which make up common culture' (1990: 19).

Some find here an apparent resignation to the workings of a capitalist economy and an over-optimistic belief that commodification processes can be turned against themselves (McGuigan 1992; see also Storey 1993). It is instructive, too, to compare Willis' 'populist' view with Williams' own earlier thinking. Williams insisted on the 'vital and indispensable contribution' of minority works to the making of a common culture and on the necessary creation of 'an educated and participating democracy'. To bring a common culture into being required a programme of radical change in education and communications. Willis and others find a common culture more in the ways things are than how they might be.

See also CONSUMERISM; CULTURALISM; POPULISM.

COMMON SENSE

As defined in the influential writings of the Italian Marxist, Antonio Gramsci (1891–1937), 'common sense' is the embedded, incoherent and spontaneous beliefs and assumptions characterizing the conformist thinking of the MASS of people in a given social order. All people, and not only specialist professional intellectuals, are 'philosophers', writes Gramsci. However, while their 'spontaneous philosophy' contains an element of practical empirical knowledge termed 'good sense', which is the germ of an alternative world-view, it is in the main composed of superstition, folklore, simple religious beliefs and the deposits of previous philosophy (Gramsci 1971a: 323–6).

As Gramsci makes clear, common sense is established by a process of consent to ruling CLASS attitudes and interests, which are thereby accepted by society at large as being in its own general interests. What is specific and partial is therefore universalized and what is cultural is naturalized to the point of being taken for granted in a view of the world as simply 'the way things are'. In a connected and extremely influential concept in Gramsci's writings, this process is then understood as vital to the maintenance of economic and political HEGEMONY.

Common sense penetrates deeply within the mental life of a society, but it is not unchanging. It is the task of INTELLECTUALS, writes Gramsci (especially the proletariat's own 'organic' intellectuals), to criticize the 'chaotic aggregate of disparate conceptions' comprising common sense and so instil 'new popular beliefs... a new common sense and with it a new culture and a new philosophy' (1971a: 422, 424). This requires conscious political work and education to engender criticism of established common sense and so articulate a coherent philosophy that will be the foundation of an alternative hegemony. While 'going beyond common sense', criticism and philosophy (virtually synonymous terms and, along with the description 'philosophy of praxis', coded words in Gramsci's text for MARXISM) must work from within popular attitudes. As he writes, 'the starting point must always be that common sense which is the spontaneous philosophy of the multitude and which has to be made ideologically coherent' (1971a: 421).

Common sense and its cognate terms therefore represent a significant contribution from within the Marxist tradition to an understanding of the part played by CULTURE, CONSCIOUSNESS and IDEOLOGY, rather than political and economic structures alone, in shaping and transforming society. The term has been much used in conjunction with other non-Marxist concepts in different forms of cultural analysis. Also, while Gramsci's ideas derive from a developed political – rather than cultural or artistic – theory, there are affinities between the work of the political intellectual as described by him and the activities developed in the traditions of artistic MODERNISM, of DEFAMILIARIZATION and ESTRANGEMENT.

See also ALIENATION EFFECT; CRITIQUE.

COMMUNICATION

The standard reference for models of communication remains the technical model devised for the purpose of efficient telecommunications by C.E. Shannon and W. Weaver in the late 1940s. This named a sender or information source, MESSAGE, receiver and destination, and saw the main priority of communication as being the unimpeded transmission of a signal from one point to the other. This was adopted in early studies of MASS communications, though its limitations for such work were soon apparent. It conceives of communication in mechanistic terms as a one-way transmission, and does not allow therefore for 'feedback' or for the role of any contextual or extraneous features – viewed in the original model in a revealingly negative term, as 'noise'. Also, the term 'message' tends to draw attention to an intended content rather than unintended meanings or matters of form. Some of these weaknesses were addressed in the further elaboration of the model in linguistics that substituted the roles of ADDRESSER and ADDRESSEE for the sender and receiver, and supplemented the original model with a number of variable functions. This has had some influence in Literary Studies, stylistics and Media Studies, although the model remains skeletal and requires considerable amplification in any of these applications (see Dance and Larson 1976; McQuail 1987). One remaining problem is the common confusion between the actual senders and receivers of messages, and the positions of addresser and addressee; a conflation that oversimplifies the differentiated identities and complex NEGOTIATIONS involved in the PRODUCTION and interpretation of even the simplest messages.

These weaknesses have prompted more sophisticated readings of the semiotic and ideological construction of texts for their meanings rather than messages (including what they do not say) as well as ethnological studies of the flexible, socially marked and contextualized positions occupied by listeners and viewers. As some have pointed out, however, this development has tended to overload RECEPTION with a significance (where viewer response is credited with an autonomy, creativity and subversiveness) denied to the point of production and its complex settings (see AUDIENCE).

In one way, this difference of emphasis describes the contemporary differences between a largely text-reader-audience-based tradition in Cultural Studies of the media and a continuing interest in institutions, allied to questions of ownership and control, in the more Social-Science-based branches of Communications Studies. While this distinction persists, the work of Raymond Williams (1962, 1974) and James W. Carey has exemplified a broader study of communications in relation to COMMUNITY and CULTURE. 'A cultural science of communications', as Carey defines it, will be an interpretive study of 'the contradictions in our thought, action and social relations' reproduced across a broad range of media technologies (Carey 1992: 9). Deacon, Pickering, Golding and Murdock (1999) also offer a very useful practical guide to students conducting empirical research in both communication media and versions of cultural analysis.

See also CODE; CULTURE INDUSTRIES; SCHEDULING; TRANSLATION.

COMMUNITY

In *Keywords* (1976b) and elsewhere, Raymond Williams draws attention to an emphasis in the idea of community on 'certain kinds of direct and directly responsible relationships', and how these have been mobilized against 'a centre of power and display' embodied in the state or general society (1989a: 112). These combined associations of immediacy, locality and mutual obligation in community were developed, says Williams, in conjunction with the idea of neighbourhood in developing industrial societies where community described a rural community or a community of industrial workers.

A further use has described experiments in alternative living on non-materialist or non-competitive lines; a meaning that surfaced in the 1960s in the use of the term 'commune' for co-operative households or settlements associated with the 'hippy' movement. In more contemporary uses, the description 'community politics', though fading in the 1980s and 1990s, retains some of the radical sense of grass-roots organization based upon active campaigns responsive to the needs of specific localities.

In Raymond Williams' own work, the term has been used in discussions of 'writers and the community' (Williams 1980a) and in his repeated argument for access by independent groups of producers to democratically organized communications systems (see 'Communications and community', Williams 1989a). The stress, once more, in this formulation, upon LOCAL association and responsibility is vital, Williams argues, to the making of a democratic CULTURE. An increasingly complex metropolitan society makes it necessary, he writes, 'to go beyond the simple community', but does not invalidate the idea of a 'genuine community' or of 'community politics' (1989a: 117).

Williams comments further that 'community' is unusual in contemporary political vocabulary in never being used in a negative sense (1976b: 66; 1989a: 116). However, the connotations of 'local, face-to-face' relations have often now been found implausible and conservative in the face of radically altered metropolitan conditions. Iris Marion Young, for example, in an influential essay, argues that the ideal of community 'denies difference' is 'undesirably utopian' and 'totalizes and detemporalizes its conception of social life' (1990: 302). This view is now commonly adopted within the field of postmodern Cultural Geography (Patton 1995; Harvey 1996). The experience of a fractured heterogeneity in global metropolitan centres has, so it is argued, accentuated the actual and symbolic loss of earlier rural and industrial communities. Hence, the argument, in Young's terms, for a 'politics of difference' that values 'unassimilated otherness' over an impossible communal association (1990: 301).

Others, attempting in different ways to move beyond the polarities of this debate, seek an idea of community *within* a politics of difference. Doreen Massey, for example, argues that places have 'multiple identities'; communities, even in the CITY, have 'internal structures', a differentiated specificity 'constructed out of a particular constellation of social relations' integrating 'in a positive way the local and the global' (1993: 238, 239). Elsewhere, Jean-Luc Nancy (1991) theorizes community as 'being-in-common': a description fundamentally opposed to the idea of community as essence, which presupposes or anticipates a oneness of 'common being'. 'Being *in* common', writes Nancy, 'has nothing to do with communion, with fusion into a body, into a unique and ultimate identity' (1991: xxxviii). It means sharing a lack of 'substantial' identity, a singularity or 'finitude', which the individual communicates or 'exposes' to the other: 'finite existence exposed to finite existence' (xl). It is this relation that constitutes community and, so defined – where community means sharing 'a resistance to everything that would bring it to completion' (8) that it also constitutes a politics, in turn radically opposed to the idea of a unity of people or nation or destiny that Nancy associates with totalitarianism. (For some use of Nancy's ideas, see Donald 1999).

See also DIASPORA; IMAGINED COMMUNITY; TRANSLATION.

COMPETENCE

See READING.

COMPULSORY HETEROSEXUALITY

A term given general currency by Adrienne Rich's seminal essay of the late 1970s 'Compulsory heterosexuality and lesbian existence' (Rich 1987). Rich views compulsory heterosexuality as a pervasive IDEOLOGY that subjects all women to the pressures of normative SEXUALITY and brands lesbianism as 'unnatural'. To be combated, it needs first of all to be recognized (including by heterosexual feminists) as 'a *political institution*' (1987: 35). The use of 'physical brutality' and the 'control of consciousness' to enforce heterosexual norms takes many forms, says Rich (from chastity belts to the constraints of marriage, the exploitation of women's labour, the restriction of physical movement, the demotion of women's creativity and intellectual achievements) but this extensive repressive apparatus at the same time reveals the perceived threat and thus the subversive potential of 'lesbian existence'. The latter term, denoting women-to-women sexual relationships, Rich sees as a specific instance of a 'lesbian continuum', which denotes 'a range – through each woman's life and throughout history – of woman-identified experience' (1987: 51). This female bond she sees as the source of women's collective political power.

The essentialist assumptions of Rich's argument are critiqued in later postmodernist FEMINISM and QUEER THEORY, and some arguments against heteronormativity have drawn instead upon the thinking of Monique Wittig (1992) who invests lesbianism with an inherent political effect 'outside' the regime of heterosexuality with which feminism is complicit. Nevertheless, Rich's perception of heteronormativity as an ideological DISCOURSE, and of its operation through social and cultural institutions, has had a profound and lasting influence. Butler (1990) acknowledges the important interventions of both Rich and Wittig, but eschews their binary thinking of homo/heterosexuality; woman/lesbian to reveal how heteronormativity's monological discourse represses its own potentially unruly multiplicity and sexual diversity. Warner ([ed] 1997) argues further that the sexual must be seen as deeply embedded in the social and that heteronormativity can only be overcome through a 'new queer politics' with a wide 'transnational' application beyond sex-specific issues.

See also ESSENTIALISM; HEGEMONY; POWER.

CONDENSATION AND DISPLACEMENT

Terms used by Sigmund Freud in *The Interpretation of Dreams* (1974b [1900]) to describe the two mechanisms operating in dreams and the ways they therefore give expression to the UNCONSCIOUS. Thus, anxieties or desires can be condensed in complex symbols or displaced and expressed through association. The first are densely concentrated, or 'overdetermined', and pack a number of meanings together in a brief image or episode. Thus we might dream very directly of ourselves in a violent encounter with a figure who resembles a number of persons in our lives, or of uttering a repeated ambiguous phrase. On the other hand, if emotions of profound grief or desire, for example, cannot be directly expressed or are censored, they may be displaced in a dream IMAGE of a related object or in a NARRATIVE of looking for a name or destination, for example.

In Jacques Lacan's poststructuralist rereading of Freud, the similarity of these mechanisms to linguistic figures of speech is further brought out. Thus, Lacan associates condensation with metaphor and displacement with metonomy (Lacan 1977).

See also DREAMWORK; PSYCHOANALYSIS.

CONJUNCTURE

A term employed in Marxist analysis to denote the factors or DETERMINATIONS thought necessary to a proper understanding of the 'complex and differential temporality' of a given historical period or FORMATION (Anderson 1988: 322). Thus, Perry Anderson proposes a 'sociopolitical conjunctural analysis' of literary MODERNISM, which sets this cultural and artistic movement in a triangulated context of three co-ordinates, comprising the CLASS character, emergent technology and politics of the period. These he names as 'a still usable classical past, a still indeterminate technical present, and a still unpredictable political future' or, in other terms, 'a semi-aristocratic ruling order, a semi-industrialized capitalist economy, and semi-emergent, labour movement' (1988: 326).

A comparable analysis of POSTMODERNISM, specifically of Los Angeles, is advanced by Mike Davis (1988, see also Davis 1990, 2nd ed. 2006). Rejecting a flat equation of postmodernism with late CAPITALISM, Davis suggests a reinterpretation in terms, once more, of relevant co-ordinates: 'the rise of new international rentier circuits in the current crisis phase of capitalism'; the abandonment of the modernist ideal of urban reform; and, alongside this, 'the new class polarization taking place in the United States' (1988: 81). Callinicos (1989) presents a conjunctural analysis of both modernism and postmodernism.

See also ARTICULATION; MARXISM; MODERNITY.

CONNOTATION/DENOTATION

A distinction between levels of meaning associated especially with structuralist analysis. Thus, the denotative level of a SIGN, IMAGE or statement is its literal or directly referential meaning. A car is simply the vehicle we name as car or how it would be described in its most functional aspect (in practice, denotation is an analytical distinction only since the use of language is never entirely literal, objective or context-free). Connotation designates the secondary meanings produced through association by a word, sign or image. Thus, a car might suggest an economical or extravagant lifestyle, holidays, romance or status. If a foreign car, it might conjure up more specific cultural connotations: of 'Americanness' or 'Italianness', for example. If it is a Lincoln convertible, then it might suggest the assassination of President John F. Kennedy, and evoke references to this event and type of car in songs, novels and other commentary. Metaphorical or symbolic meanings are all of this connotative type. Connotation therefore operates in the realm of social, ideological or cultural values. For such meanings to be activated, readers, viewers or consumers require a cultural vocabulary and readiness to respond accordingly. They may also detect other connotations than those intended.

See also CODE; NEGOTIATION; STRUCTURALISM.

CONSCIOUSNESS

The set of attitudes, ideas and values characterizing the state of awareness and thus self-identity of an individual, group or social CLASS. The term is used sometimes in association with IDEOLOGY (defined as 'false consciousness') or in a more positive association, originally in MARXISM, with determining 'social being'. Class consciousness in Marx describes the conscious IDENTITY of either of the two major classes (bourgeoisie and proletariat) where the class's knowledge of its own conditions in relation to the overall structure of society is developed to the point where it can act in its own interest. The class has not only an objective identity as a class 'in itself' but becomes a class 'for itself'. The idea of class consciousness was developed particularly within the philosophy and criticism of Georg Lukács, in relation notably to the historical novel and European realism (1963, 1969).

Following Lukács, the Marxist philosopher and literary critic Lucien Goldmann drew a distinction between 'actual' and 'potential' consciousness to mark the distinction between types or stages of consciousness. Goldmann used this distinction to confirm the VALUE of a literary text, which developed the less formed 'actual' consciousness of the social group it represented to its most articulate maximum potential (Goldmann 1975; see also Williams 1980b).

Clearly, as employed by Goldmann, this distinction is an evaluative one. As such, it might be used to confirm the value of serious art works as against the symptomatic and mediocre status of POPULAR culture texts or, presumably, to reverse this distinction or mark distinctions within a form or GENRE. It might also be extended beyond social class. Did the Rolling Stones express the potential consciousness of a generation? Did 'punk' or Oasis or Blur? Did cyberpunk novels reflect the subcultural attitudes of a generation of predominantly male readers ('hackers' or 'nerds') in the 1980s, or articulate this average mentality to a point of transformative self-awareness (McCaffery [ed] 1991)?

The expression 'consciousness raising' was used to refer to the discussions of usually women-only groups in the early years of the Women's Liberation

Movement in the late 1960s and 1970s. It implies a process of coming to awareness in the formation of consciousness and thus suggests degrees of coherent and articulated consciousness as well as ways of producing this other than those associated with traditionally defined social classes.

The term 'stream-of-consciousness' has been used to describe attempts within modernist fiction (in James Joyce's *Ulysses* and the novels of Virginia Woolf, for example) to transcribe the content and rhythm of inner states of mind in the form of unedited interior monologue. This is sometimes likened to 'free association', employed by the artistic AVANT-GARDE and within PSYCHOANALYSIS; though in both these cases, its purpose is to trigger the expression of UNCONSCIOUS, and not conscious, thoughts and feelings.

The 'consciousness industry' is a term coined by the German writer and cultural critic, Hans Magnus Enzensberger (1970) to point up the ideological role of the CULTURE INDUSTRIES or MASS media.

See also COMMON SENSE; STRUCTURES OF FEELING.

CONSTELLATION

As employed by the Marxist critic and philosopher, Walter Benjamin (1892–1940), constellation describes the relation in a materialist analysis of history between the past and present. The term is important to Benjamin's defence of historical MATERIALISM against a 'historicist' approach that interprets history as a sequence of cause and effect along an evolutionary continuum. 'The past,' he writes, 'can be seized only as an image which flashes up at the instant when it can be recognised and is never seen again... a memory as it flashes up at a moment of danger' (1970b: 257). A historical materialist:

> stops telling the sequence of events like the beads of a rosary. Instead, he grasps the constellation which his own era has formed with a definite earlier one. Thus he establishes a conception of the present as 'the time of the now'.
> (1970b: 265)

See also CONJUNCTURE; HISTORICISM; *JETZTZEIT*.

CONSUMERISM

If the age of MODERNITY was an age of PRODUCTION, both in economic terms and as an emphasis in theoretical work and analysis upon cultural production, the era of POSTMODERNISM or POST-FORDISM and beyond is seen as an age of consumption. It has been 'the society of consumerism' in an influential title by the French philosopher, Jean Baudrillard (Poster [ed] 1988: 29–56; see also Lunt and Livingstone 1992: 20–22). This description is linked to a perceived AUTONOMY of the signifier, and the supposed 'loss of the real', or the advent of 'HYPERREALITY', producing in the new 'ambience' of the shopping mall an emblematic scene of contemporary mentality when consumers are seduced and stupefied all at once by the display of diversity.

There is little doubt that a shift towards increased commodification and MASS consumerism has taken place in contemporary western societies (see Miller 2001 for comprehensive historical documentation). This is confirmed by a number of increasingly familiar features in these societies: extended credit facilities, share ownership, segmented markets, volatile consumer preferences and the rise of consumer organizations, pressure groups and media 'watchdogs' organized around issues of consumer rights. These developments have in turn affected the nature of commodities and the policies of producers. However, this process has prompted different responses, in theory and analysis. For where Baudrillard greets a society homogenized by consumption patterns to the point where all life is 'massaged, climate controlled and domesticated into the simple activity of perpetual shopping' (1988: 34), others see only a baleful reflection in the realm of CULTURE of the untrammelled circulation of commodities in a now expanded world market.

A more active response has protested (through the use of boycott and direct action) against the unjust labour practices and contribution to environmental deterioration of major western corporations. The features of this economy are well known and much debated. One popular account, Naomi Klein's *No Logo* (2000) has given voice to the widespread frustration at the unaccountable operations of corporate power. Her case against high-profile brands such as Shell, Hilfiger and Nike (which, in 1992, paid Michael Jordan more in endorsements than its entire Indonesian workforce) has given protestors some ammunition and a direct target.

A further, somewhat contrary, approach – taken up particularly in work on youth and SUBCULTURES – sees the activities of consumption, shopping, the world of fashion and music, as playing a key part in the active construction of personal, gendered and group identities (Hebdige 1979; Lunt and Livingstone 1992; McRobbie 1994). In part, this work brings a populist emphasis to the theme of 'EVERYDAY LIFE' apparent in some work in Sociology and Social Psychology (Lefebvre 1991; see also Storey 1999). In part, also, it is informed by a feminist critique of the emphasis in classical MARXISM on the capitalist 'mode of production': a priority that relegated women's lives as consumers and the domestic sphere of the household to secondary features in the drama of male-governed CLASS struggle in the world of industrial production (Bowlby 1992; Nava 1992).

In a final extension, indicative of a general use of the description 'consumer culture', consumption has also been used in studies of the RECEPTION of media programmes (see Morley 1995) and in discussions of the 'consumption' of PLACES (Urry 1995, Mort 1996). In this usage, it is connected with theorizations of IDENTITY and PLEASURE, as above, and, in general terms, with accounts of POSTMODERNISM (Featherstone 1991) and GLOBALIZATION.

See also COMMODITY FETISHISM; COSMOPOLITANISM.

CONVERGENCE

A term employed, notably by Henry Jenkins (1998), to describe the coexistence of traditional and new media, and the appropriation and circulation of media images and narratives by means of new digital and recording technologies.

The term recognizes, first, how individuals, groups and families in advanced media societies have easy access to TV, radio, CD, audiotape, and vinyl record and play facilities, to mobile phones, PCs and laptops, and how frequently these technologies will be used at the same time, sometimes by the same individual in the same room. Not surprisingly, there is speculation about, if not the common reality of, a 'black box' incorporating different technologies in one piece of hardware (see Hartley 1996). Second, 'convergence' draws attention not only to the fact of the coexistence of media technologies, but to the 'new ways audiences are relating to media content, their increased skill at reading across different media and their desires for a more participatory and complex media culture' (1998:2–3). Here, a further distinction should be drawn. In what is termed 'media convergence', a production-led, multi-platform experience enables a viewer (of news, documentary or entertainment TV) to gather further information, pose queries, follow up subplots or character background, and to purchase related products through a dedicated INTERNET site. Conspicuous, structured, but, to some degree, interactive examples of this have been introduced to sustain viewer involvement in 'reality TV' programming in the UK and USA, such as *Big Brother* and *Survivor.*

Henry Jenkins is interested, by contrast, in forms of grass-roots interactive participation, best termed 'cultural convergence'. His prime examples are fans adept at interactive technologies and digital media, who use the internet to maintain a fan COMMUNITY sustained by its knowledge, respect for, and inventive re-inflection of the established archive. Major examples would be the net-based fan cultures of *The X-Files, Twin Peaks* or *Xena* (Gwenillian-Jones, in W. Brooker and Jermyn [eds] 2002) or of comic-book heroes, such as those in *Doctor Who, Star Trek* and *Star Wars* (see Jenkins and Tulloch 1995; Brooker 2000, 2002). Jenkins highlights how 'rejecting aesthetic distance, fans... attempt to integrate media representations into their own social experience', asserting 'their own rights to form interpretations, to offer evaluations and to construct cultural canons' (1998: 3). The 'fan' base use of digital media therefore foregrounds and arguably pioneers a different interactive way of reading culture, while 'audiences' meanwhile conform more to the structured interaction devised by producers.

Throughout, this distinction plays out some of the long-standing features in the relation between a grass-roots POPULAR CULTURE and the commercial entertainment corporations or CULTURE INDUSTRIES. The latter respond by endorsing or co-opting the 'appropriative aesthetic', which marks fandom, or by evoking legal powers to protect a corporation's products against the violation of copyright. Lucasfilms, as Jenkins shows, has done both, recruiting an independent film-maker whose film *Troops* explored marginal aspects of the *Star Wars* mythos, while blocking the production and circulation of readings and rewritings of the same narratives by fans with no career prospects or monetary gain in mind. The issue, therefore, is as much a matter of intellectual property as of methods of appropriative reading or 'textual poaching' (Jenkins 1992), and this entails, as do other uses of digital technology, the broader question of corporate ownership and control, and the alternative vision of a technologically advanced participatory culture.

See also AUDIENCE; CYBERSPACE; INCORPORATION; SUBCULTURES.

CO-OPTION

See INCORPORATION.

COSMOPOLITANISM/COSMOPOLITICS

The word 'cosmopolitan,' says Bruce Robbins, 'immediately evokes the image of a privileged person: someone who can claim to be a "citizen of the world" by virtue of independent means, high-tech tastes and globe-trotting mobility' (1992: 171). Traditionally, the term carries, as this suggests, the sense of not belonging to any particular state or nation. In the earlier modern period, the gentleman traveller, intellectual or artist exchanged this connection, of birth and upbringing, for an association with the culture of sophisticated metropolitan milieus, principally in the cities of Europe. By extension, these cities themselves, or those parts that supported bohemian or artistic life, were themselves seen as cosmopolitan. In this sense, the term refers to mixed ethnic and polyglot cultural settings of a kind mirrored in the eclectic internationalist aesthetic of modernist art. If this connotes mobility, of people and ideas, and detachment, the cosmopolitan life did not, for many artists at least, confer privilege or imply independent wealth. For their patrons and for upper-class tourists, it would be a different matter. We need, therefore, even in surveying earlier uses of this term, to distinguish between types of cosmopolitanism.

The associations of cosmopolitanism with privileged aloofness, have attached themselves, albeit controversially, to high-profile intellectuals and authors in the postmodern world (hence Robbins' 'high-tech taste' and 'globe-trotting mobility') especially in the context of debates on POSTCOLONIALISM. Thus, Edward Said and Salman Rushdie, among others, have been castigated for a rootless cosmopolitanism that sets them at a remove from the particular struggles of indigenous peoples (Clifford 1980; Brennan 1989). In one direction, this relates to arguments about migrancy and NOMADISM as both a metaphor and reality of postmodern times; in another, it raises questions about the privilege of ethnocentric perspectives, and about new configurations of POWER and influence brought about by GLOBALIZATION.

It is in this double context that there has been a revived interest in the meanings of cosmopolitanism. Jacques Derrida (2001), in an example of DECONSTRUCTION'S more explicit political interest, probes the ETHICS of cosmopolitanism with the issues of asylum and immigration in mind. He urges the implementation of the idea of 'cities of refuge', and an examination of the principles and practice of hospitality they might afford. Bruce Robbins is himself concerned to revalue the concept-word in the direction of a shared cosmopolitan perspective that would do away with hierarchical distinctions between the mobile western outsider and the local, non-western, subordinate 'other'. He borrows the concept of 'discrepant cosmopolitanisms' from the anthropologist James Clifford to this end. This concept helps us, says Clifford, avoid 'excessive localism' on the one hand and 'the overly global vision of a capitalist or technocratic monoculture' on the other (Clifford 1992: 108). In the comparative perspective this encourages, different cultures can be understood alike 'as sites of dwelling *and* travel' (1992: 105) while both travellers and local people can be understood as experiencing and sharing 'specific cosmopolitan viewpoints'.

This thinking is in line with the broader programmes outlined by social and political theorists for a 'cosmopolitan project' that would address the worst consequences of globalization. David Held and others call for a conception of cosmopolitanism that, as above, would bring a self-reflexive openness to cultural difference and in which citizens experience 'multiple citizenships' (2000: 426). This is one part only, however, of the highly ambitious project to make the long-cherished idea of global democracy a reality. In this view, the compromised authority of the state (as at once too big and too small), the potentially dire effects of volatile world financial markets, and the lack of transparency and accountability of transnational corporations call for a radical restructuring of international law, financial controls and systems of representation (see Archibugi and Held [eds] 1995; Linklater 1998; Held and McGrew [eds] 2000). Held believes these structures exist in embryo in, for example, the Maastricht Treaty, the European Union and United Nations (Held 2000). The Conservative Party's symbolic defence of national currency in the UK and the refusal of the USA to abide by international agreements suggest some of the difficulties this evolutionary perspective would face.

The kinds of deep political changes envisaged in a new cosmopolitanism have persuaded some that 'cosmopolites' is a more appropriate term for this project (Archibugi 2000; Cheah and Robbins [eds] 2000). The latter term is also used, with this political emphasis, to describe the growing movement of popular protest against the exploitation of labour and the environment by corporate powers and the indifference or ineffectuality of national governments. In a series of protests and ensuing confrontations with police, 'anti-capitalist' protesters have, since 1999, targeted meetings of the World Trade Organization, the International Monetary Fund, and G7 and G8 summits of world leaders, as well as high-profile corporations. Evidently, the issues raised by globalization have spilled from the academy on to the streets. It may therefore be, as Robbins suggests, that 'the term cosmopolitanism... describes the sensibility of our moment' (1992: 183). Nevertheless, the different ends and means employed – between forms of non-violent and anarchistic violent street protest, and between the more and less evolutionary proposals for global democracy – suggest, once more, how carefully distinctions within and between cosmopolitanisms need to be drawn.

See also CITIZENSHIP; CONSUMERISM; ECOLOGY; NATIONALISM.

COUNTER-CULTURE

This term is associated with the 1960s and early 1970s and was introduced into cultural debate in this connection by Theodore Roszak's study, *The Making of a Counter Culture* (1971). It refers to the loosely related organizations, networks, communes, music and drug scenes that arose in this period, primarily in the United States, in opposition to the Vietnam War, the power of the 'military-industrial complex' and, more generally, to the conservative morality of postwar middle

America. The counter-culture drew for inspiration simultaneously on the Beat movement of the earlier decade and on a new generation of cultural theorists, political activists and gurus as different as Herbert Marcuse, Marshall McLuhan, Susan Sontag, Mao Zedong, Che Guevara, Eldridge Cleaver and Timothy Leary. In its more militant political aspect, it numbered large, though never consistently MASS, groups such as Students for a Democratic Society as well as splinter groups such the anarchist Weathermen, and recruited literary luminaries such as Allen Ginsberg, Robert Lowell and Norman Mailer for the protest march on the Pentagon in 1968. Other groups, in the women's liberation and civil rights movements, were loosely affiliated to the political wing of the counter-culture, but focused their criticism and campaigning upon the more specific – and in the event more enduring – themes of sexual and racial oppression.

These latter movements, along with emerging campaigns for gay rights and the environment, are now customarily referred to as 'social movements' and have followed their own independent and sometimes overlapping histories (including periods of inner friction as between pacifist sections of the black community and the militant Black Panthers). Their active and sometimes aggressive campaigning for social and political transformation was distinct from the counter-cultural lifestyle of the 'hippies', whose philosophy of free love, free education and anti-MATERIALISM was premised on 'dropping out' of society, not on remaking it (see Hall 1969).

Folk and rock music (notably of Bob Dylan, Joan Baez, Jefferson Airplane, the Grateful Dead) was an important expression of counter-cultural lifestyle and, along with the earlier movement in British pop (which itself entered a 'hippy' phase in the late 1960s), helped shift the ground of cultural attitudes to the point where dress, length of hair and lifestyle came to count in more explicit and self-conscious terms than formerly as ways of making a political statement. Combined with the agendas of the social movements, this new orientation marked the onset of CULTURAL POLITICS.

The counter-culture was always a dispersed movement and was confounded by the dramatic expressions of social and political violence that characterized this same period in American life. Notable among such incidents were the assassinations of Martin Luther King, Malcolm X and the Kennedys; the violent confrontation between protestors and police at the Chicago Democratic Convention in 1968; the shooting of students by the National Guard at Kent State University in 1970; and race riots and deaths on the streets of Watts, Los Angeles, Washington DC and Detroit. Ugly scenes at a Rolling Stones concert at Altamont and the murder of Sharon Tate by the Charles Manson 'Family' in 1969 brought an end to the message of love and peace that had energized the counter-culture's earlier years. Moreover, the Vietnam War, which had prompted a long bout of anti-American and anti-establishment feeling, ended with the withdrawal of troops in 1973, leaving the movement without a unifying enemy or aim.

Many novels and films record and reflect on aspects of the 1960s counter-culture, among them Norman Mailer's *Armies of the Night* (1968), Marge Piercy's *Vida* (1980), Alice Walker's *Meridian* (1982) and the film *Easy Rider* (1969). Other contemporary writings include Richard Neville's *Play Power* (1970) and

Germaine Greer's very influential *Female Eunuch* (1970). Fredric Jameson's 'Periodizing the 60s' (1988c) analyses the intellectual and political tendencies of the decade from the perspective of a later postmodern moment.

See also COMMUNITY; CULT; POPULAR.

CRITICAL THEORY

Though sometimes understood as synonymous with contemporary theory, this term designates primarily the theoretical work of the so-called Frankfurt school. The school was established as the Institute for Social Research at the University of Frankfurt in 1923, resettled in New York in the 1930s and returned to Frankfurt in 1950. Its leading members were Theodor Adorno (1903–1969), Max Horkheimer, Leo Lowenthal and Herbert Marcuse (1898–1979). Walter Benjamin (1892–1940) also contributed to the Institute's *Journal for Social Research.*

The school was indebted throughout to Marxist theory, but adopted a less CLASS-based model in its work on fascism and contemporary MASS society in the 1930s and 1940s (Kellner 1989a). This distinguished it from the political inflection of some of Benjamin's writing, conceived in what Adorno thought to be too close an affinity with the political AESTHETIC of Bertolt Brecht. The school's major work is probably Adorno and Horkheimer's *The Dialectic of Enlightenment* (1979) first published in 1947, a critique of ENLIGHTENMENT rationalism, which is seen as complicit with totalitarianism and the 'administered' societies of late CAPITALISM. This work contained the much-reprinted joint study, 'The culture industry: enlightenment as mass deception', an unrelenting denunciation of what were perceived as the conformist banalities of a manipulative mass culture. This has remained a key point of reference in subsequent debates (see Adorno 1991; Storey 1993).

At his most challenging, Adorno maintained a scrupulously DIALECTICal analysis of the contradictions of contemporary society, but while in this respect indebted to MARXISM, he looked to the strenuous formal difficulty and AUTONOMY of modern literature and music (Beckett, Schoenberg) for a countervailing sensibility to capitalism rather than to the traditional AGENCY of the organized working class. The CULTURE INDUSTRIES, in particular, he and others of the school saw as eroding political consciousness and as threatening to absorb all but the most uncompromising of 'authentic' art. Herbert Marcuse shared this position, but adapted to American society more easily than other members of the school. His later works, *Eros and Civilisation* (1955) and *One Dimensional Man* (1964), in which he sought a *rapprochement* between Marxism and PSYCHOANALYSIS, became key texts for the COUNTER-CULTURE of the 1960s. Marcuse saw students and other contemporary protest movements as part of a new political configuration and introduced a utopian note quite at odds with Adorno's pessimism. His *The Aesthetic Dimension* (1978) similarly attributed an 'affirmative' critical role to art, though in terms other than those of orthodox Marxism (Kellner 1984).

Critical theory has exercised a wide influence upon subsequent Literary, Social and Cultural Theory, including the work in Germany of Jürgen Habermas.

Habermas would reject the association of rationality with totalitarianism or managerial capitalism of the kind made by Adorno and Horkheimer, and many have found their condemnation of a commercialized mass art simplistic and unhelpful. However, others have been convinced by the apparent neutralization of CRITIQUE and of class struggle in the present era of the appropriateness of Adorno's analysis (Jameson 1990a). A further development has been associated with the German social theorist, Ulrich Beck and cognate work by Anthony Giddens in British Sociology. Beck's idea of 'REFLEXIVE MODERNIZATION', by which the principles of modernity would be simultaneously critiqued and radicalized, has been welcomed as a model of the 'new critical theory' needed to respond to the 'transformed political culture… of GLOBALIZATION'. 'Such a theory,' write Lash and Wynne, 'must be reflexively critical and disruptive of the assumptions of the very project of the Enlightenment' (Beck 1992: 8).

See also POPULAR.

CRITIQUE

Critique, Terry Eagleton points out, is to be distinguished from criticism (1991: xiv). Whereas the latter assumes a disinterested vantage point outside the text or event, critique takes up a position within the object of study seeking to elicit its contradictory tendencies and to foreground its valid features. Richard Johnson has stressed the importance of critique in precisely this sense to the development of Cultural Studies. He writes:

> I mean critique in the fullest sense: not criticism merely, nor even polemic, but procedures by which other traditions are approached both for what they may yield and for what they inhibit. Critique involves stealing away the more useful elements and rejecting the rest. From this point of view Cultural Studies is a process, a kind of alchemy for producing useful knowledge.
>
> (Storey [ed] 1996: 75)

Johnson is interested in the ways in which Cultural Studies has appropriated the different methods of different academic disciplines, but critique applies equally and more broadly to the cultural study of social processes and literary and cultural texts. Thus constituted, the study of culture becomes a radicalizing, broadly political activity. It is not, however, as Johnson puts it, to be understood by that token, as 'a research programme for a particular party or tendency' (Storey [ed] 1996: 79). Its connection with such formal politics is loose and variable, but none the less 'a real one': characterized, he writes, by a 'constructive quarrel' with existing styles of political discourse and forms of action' (Storey [ed] 1996: 79). Critique is therefore a vital defining aspect of engaged intellectual work or CULTURAL POLITICS, which extends beyond a specific discipline or subject base to the many differently located forms of the study of culture.

See also DECONSTRUCTION; DIALECTICS; SYMPTOMATIC READING.

CULT

A term used to describe both selected cultural texts and personalities, and small communities or social movements, founded most often on esoteric religious beliefs. In the first sense, used, for example, of a film such as *Casablanca,* the TV series *Twin Peaks* or *The X-Files,* or of the following for a star such as James Dean or Madonna, the term cult connotes an enthusiasm for, and insider knowledge of, a generally POPULAR text or ICON. The paradox is that such texts and stars can have a simultaneously wide and specialist following, although cult tends usually to designate the latter. In practice, following a cult in this sense is close to being a fan, or to fan worship, when the proof or mutual reinforcement of cult membership and the cult status of the chosen object take the form of the imitation of a look or gesture, or the citation of favoured moments, dialogue or sayings. As described by Umberto Eco (1986) in the prelude to a shot-by-shot analysis of *Casablanca,* a cult text is characterized by its recycling of 'intertextual archetypes' already logged in the encyclopaedia of popular NARRATIVES (1986: 200). These provoke an 'intense emotion' of recognition and the desire for repetition, which is satisfied by re-viewings, the quotation of characters and episodes, the making up of 'quizzes... and trivia games' by which the adepts 'recognise through each other a shared expertise' (1986: 198). A perfect film, says Eco, 'remains in our memory as a whole', whereas a cult movie is imperfect and 'unhinged' and 'must live on, and because of, its glorious ricketiness' (1986: 198).

In this first sense, the term cult attaches first to the text or star and by extension to their following. In the second sense, the term attaches first to the following and is used now usually to describe eccentric and introverted religious communities who have split from mainstream faiths or from earlier sects. 'New Religious Movements', as such groups are also called, are defined by the presence of a charismatic leader, total commitment (of both time and money) on the part of its usually youthful members and, in recent forms, by coercion and violence, whether turned outwards or inwards upon members themselves.

Among the most well-known cults employing strong but non-violent persuasion are the Unification Church or 'Moonies', so called after its founder the Rev. Sun Myung Moon; the Scientologists or Modern Science of Mental Health founded by L. Ron Hubbard, which has a wide following (including celebrity members) in the USA and Europe; and Rajneeshism, founded in the 1970s by the late Bhagwan Shree Rajneesh in Oregon, USA. The latter is one of many later movements deriving their beliefs from eastern religions and is a subject of study, along with Jerry Falwell's Baptist Community in Lynchburg, Virginia, in Frances Fitzgerald's *Cities on a Hill* (1987).

The most marked feature of New Religious Movements in recent years has been their adoption of more coercive and authoritarian tactics, and their alleged involvement in murder, or more typically, collective suicide pacts. The most sensational event of this kind involved the deaths of 900 people in Jonestown, Guyana, in 1978. Other such cults have been the Order of the Solar Temple, which was responsible for deaths in 1994, 1995 and 1997 in Switzerland and Canada, and the San Diego-based group, Heaven's Gate, of which 39 members committed suicide in 1997 in the belief, so it is said, that they were angels returning to the planet Sirius.

All cults attach themselves to the extraordinary, even to the extraordinary in the ordinary. They are by that token a criticism of unrelieved banality, or of mainstream ideas, and this dissatisfaction has some social basis and explanation. Some examples would tend to suggest how present unrest finds a compensating interest or belief in the spiritual realm and the paranormal, expressed both through cultural texts and cult groups – linking the long-standing cult of UFOs with *The X-Files,* for example. Cults of both types can therefore help reveal a contemporary and sometimes common cultural mentality. Nevertheless, the difference between religious cults and the sense of the term as it applies to cultural texts and icons ought to be carefully observed.

See also TERRORISM.

CULTURAL CAPITAL

An expression introduced by the sociologist of culture and education, Pierre Bourdieu (1930–2002) to describe the possession of knowledge, accomplishments, formal and informal qualifications by which an individual may gain entry and secure a position in particular social circles, professions and organizations. It may therefore be seen as a more systematic way of accounting for what is entailed in loose descriptions of the 'cultured' individual or social type. Cultural capital marks and reinforces kinds of relative advantage and disadvantage in society, although, says Bourdieu, it may be held and not 'invested' at any given time and can overlap with, or diverge from, the distribution of 'economic' or 'social' capital (measured by income, wealth and power).

In Bourdieu's writings, the education system in particular serves as the filter and adjudicator of a cultural capital gained initially in the home, or from an already-established class background. This capital is likely to give 'a head start and credit' (1984: 70). However, it may or may not be sanctioned by the certifying procedures of the education system that would convert it into 'educational capital'.

Bourdieu's theory draws on extensive empirical studies of the education system, and other institutions and practices in France, and while cultural capital and other related concepts have a broad application, the differences in national educational and other systems suggest that what counts as 'currency' in this respect will be, in many ways, culturally specific.

See also FIELD; HABITUS.

CULTURAL INTERMEDIARIES

The category 'cultural intermediaries' was employed first by Pierre Bourdieu (1984), and is used primarily to describe workers in the areas of advertising, design and management consultancy. Later work saw a new interest in these groups in relation to changes in the production of goods and services, and the related circulation of images, especially as these are consequent upon GLOBALIZATION. One feature of this changed economy is a shift from MASS production to modes of more flexible specialist production and the related practice of 'niche marketing'. Cultural intermediaries perform in this market to bring together consumption and production in new, more adjustable and intimate ways, by styling or restyling brands to meet the practical or lifestyle choices of targeted consumer groups whose TASTE they may, in other ways, have already helped create (see Du Gay *et al.* [eds] 1997). Cultural intermediaries play an important part, therefore, in establishing the ICONS, idioms and look of EVERYDAY LIFE.

Workers of this type exist not only in advertising and marketing, but also in radio, television and print journalism as well as academic life (with some individuals crossing between the latter occupations). Bourdieu saw cultural intermediaries as belonging to a new CLASS fraction of the *petite bourgeoisie.* Subsequent studies are turning their attention to the role and influence of these figures in the workplace, in relation to owners and senior management, and to their educational backgrounds, tastes and cultural dispositions or common lifestyle. Bourdieu's term HABITUS is useful here, but needs, so later studies argue, to take more account of the gendered relations, sexual codes and dispositions of those who work together as teams (Nixon 1997; see also Nixon 2002). Research in these directions is at a comparatively early stage and new topics readily suggest themselves. A study of lifestyle magazines, for example, would raise intriguing questions about the relation between a shared professionalism, personal attitudes or habitus, and the promotion of sexualized lifestyle images. Again, a comparative study of cultural policy-makers, cultural commentators in journalism, academics, together with product designers and advertisers, would further open out the common and differentiated roles and attitudes of this new middle-class group.

See also CONSUMERISM; GATEKEEPING; INTELLECTUALS.

CULTURALISM

Culturalism describes a main position on relations between CULTURE and society. In Britain, especially, it shared an earlier emphasis (with Matthew Arnold and F.R. Leavis) on the vital, shaping influence of culture, but sought to extend this traditional and largely conservative conception beyond selected literary and artistic works to include the study of contemporary POPULAR culture, institutions and practices in society at large. This perspective informed the work of Richard Hoggart (1957), and the earlier writings of Raymond Williams (1961), and Hall and Whannel (1964), and was thus an important influence on sections of literary study and the emerging agenda of British Cultural Studies. The term itself was coined by Richard Johnson (1979a, 1979b) to suggest the common theoretical assumptions connecting the work of Hoggart and Williams and, in Johnson's assessment, the Marxist historian, E.P. Thompson. These figures share a belief, says Johnson, that the attitudes and values of a social COMMUNITY can be read through an examination of its lived cultural processes and the cultural texts the people of that community themselves produce and consume. As expressed in

Raymond Williams' *The Long Revolution* (1961), the analysis of culture is the attempt to discover the complex organization of 'elements in a whole way of life', to reveal the 'common elements' in 'a particular community of experience' (1961: 64), 'the actual life that the whole organisation is there to express' (1961: 65).

As formulations such as these suggest, culturalism is founded on a humanist belief in the expression and reconstitution, through appropriate analysis, of authentic and common lived experience. As such, as Stuart Hall points out in 'Cultural studies: two paradigms', culturalism stresses human AGENCY – the active production of cultural meanings rather than their passive consumption. This line of thinking, he confirms, has had a strong influence on studies keen to affirm the contradictory but positive role popular culture and subcultural practices have had in the construction of identities and social meanings. At the same time, Hall identifies a second major theoretical PARADIGM stemming from Structuralist Anthropology and the MARXISM of Louis Althusser. This first stresses the role of determinant linguistic and ideological conditions, and second, posits less a coherent social TOTALITY than a 'social FORMATION', whose 'relatively autonomous' parts are articulated in a unity of structured differences. As Hall observes:

> Whereas, in 'culturalism', experience was the ground – the terrain of 'the lived' – where consciousness and conditions intersected, structuralism insisted that 'experience' could not, by definition, be the ground of anything, since one could only 'live' and experience one's conditions in and through the categories, classifications and frameworks of the culture.
>
> (Storey [ed.] 1996: 41)

He adds:

> Structuralism represents an advance over culturalism in the conception it has of the necessary complexity of the unity of structure... the conceptual ability to think of unity, which is constructed through the differences between, rather than the homology of, practices.
>
> (Storey [ed] 1996: 44)

Hall does not adumbrate a synthesis of these two paradigms. The assumptions of both positions are in fact recognized as problematic and have undergone further revision in the encounter with new issues posed by different theoretical perspectives within Marxism, FEMINISM, POSTSTRUCTURALISM, and by studies of RACE and ETHNICITY.

See also HUMANISM; SUBCULTURES.

CULTURAL MATERIALISM

An approach developed in the 1970s and 1980s in British literary and critical studies, especially in the areas of Shakespeare and Renaissance Studies, and associated with the work of Jonathan Dollimore, Alan Sinfield, Graham Holderness, John Drakakis, Lisa Jardine and others (see Scott Wilson [ed] 1995; Brooker and Widdowson [eds] 1997: Ch. 1). The primary influences on this approach are Michel Foucault's theorizations of POWER, knowledge and DISCOURSE, and the work of Raymond Williams, from whom the term is derived (Williams 1977). The result is a committed, politicized analysis of INTERTEXTUALITY, focused in the first instance upon literary texts, understood in a changing general history of power relations. At its most polemical, this analysis is directed by a historical sense that emphasizes the construction of the past in accordance with a present agenda in CULTURAL POLITICS.

Behind Raymond Williams' use of the term and his sense of the 'inescapable materiality of works of art' (1977: 162), lies an echo of dialectical and historical MATERIALISM, and thus of MARXISM and theories of IDEOLOGY. The conjunction of 'culture' and 'materialism', however, suggests how the spheres of art or ideology, and material social and economic forces – sometimes held apart or in a REFLECTIONist, mechanical relationship in classical Marxism – are here understood as inextricably bound together, CULTURE is therefore to be read as embedded in society and as itself a set of material practices. For some, this risks over-identifying textual with non-textual forms and practices. Again, however, cultural materialism (as this description, rather than 'material culture', suggests) names an approach rather than an object of study. As such, it distinguishes itself from what is sometimes felt to be the more narrowly textualist approach associated with NEW HISTORICISM developed in the United States (see Veeser [ed] 1989). This difference can be exaggerated, however. New Historicism unquestionably extends the notion of the text and textuality beyond literature, and sees a range of discourses as implicated in relations of power, ideology and the making of history. The adoption of Foucault can give both approaches a pessimistic cast. However, a debt to the Marxist tradition and to Raymond Williams' distinction between DOMINANT, RESIDUAL and EMERGENT ideologies (see Sinfield 1992: 9) gives British cultural materialism a stronger political optimism.

There is no intrinsic reason, however, why cultural materialism should be limited to a debate with New Historicism over Renaissance texts, as New Historicist studies of Romanticism and American Studies, and Dollimore (1991) and Sinfield's (1994a, 1994b) work on gay writing and SEXUALITY have shown. It is best understood, in fact, as an intervention in contemporary cultural politics, as giving criticism a political role in relation to its own material, institutional settings and operational ideologies.

See also INTELLECTUALS; QUEER THEORY.

CULTURAL POLITICS

It is often argued that the study of culture and the academic discipline of Cultural Studies, in particular, are inescapably political because of the issues of VALUE, IDEOLOGY and POWER this study involves. It is worth pointing out the difference, however, between the political character and influence of cultural work or texts themselves; of cultural policy-makers, funding agencies or administrators who may be affiliated or in close contact with formal political parties; and the political aims of Cultural Theory and analysis. The first might be described in terms of 'the politics of culture'. Cultural politics comes into play in academic study in so far as it is openly committed to a CRITIQUE (or defence) of established or DOMINANT culture. If critical, this puts it in a position both outside and within given intellectual, social and economic structures, most immediately those of the education system and publishing. Given, also, the different forms of academic work, in higher education alone – from published monograph, editorial work, conference presentation, undergraduate seminars, administration, examining and so on – its cultural politics will be differentiated and often problematic in aim and effect.

The theory cultural politics draws upon is concerned principally with questions of ideology, power and SUBJECTIVITY, as this theory has been developed within MARXISM, FEMINISM, PSYCHOANALYSIS, POSTCOLONIALISM and in versions of POSTSTRUCTURALISM and POSTMODERNISM. In what became something of a mantra of such work in the 1980s, its themes are announced as 'race, class and gender'. If sometimes rhetorical, these topics have been investigated in considerable depth in specific textual and historical studies, and in connection with a range of CULTURE INDUSTRIES or institutions (language, the media, education, law, religion, the family) across a number of academic disciplines. Cultural politics is not therefore confined to work within a single designated area, assigned to the study of culture, for other areas – legal or theological studies, for example – may feel they are drawing upon its methods and agenda in developing a subject-specific cultural politics. The same might be true, though most likely in a less explicitly theoretical form, of those cultural INTELLECTUALS, in a more general sense of this term, who engage in a cultural politics specific to non-academic fields.

Within Cultural Studies itself, a declared cultural politics has been associated, most noticeably, with arguments on the productive social role of marginalized or subordinated POPULAR cultures and SUBCULTURES. This work has then sometimes extended to media and film, and to branches of the social sciences in studies of a textual, ethnographic and institutional kind. Within Literary Studies, one of the key debates has concerned the cultural role and ideological influence of CANONIC or traditional AUTHORS and texts. This led some in the early 1970s, for example, to call for a moratorium on the teaching of Shakespeare. In the event, Shakespeare and Renaissance Studies proved one of the most highly profiled examples of cultural politics. Another facet of this debate has been concerned with the reclamation of non-canonical writings (as well as art, philosophy, music, dance) of women, working-class, black and ethnic groups. This has been carried out, once more, across a wide front, involving education, theatre, publishing and other cultural organizations.

In one such strategy, Jordan and Weedon (1995) are directly concerned with how the dominant culture has positioned 'working class people, women, people of colour' and how they 'have attempted to reclaim and transform the dominant in their own interests' (1985: xi). In general terms, it is just this kind of double assumption that, first, in the words of these authors, 'social inequality is legitimated through culture' (1985: 5) and, second, that this inequality may be revealed and alleviated through cultural creation and criticism, which has tended to identify and inform cultural politics. McGuigan (1996) offers a cooler investigation of cultural policy and cultural politics from a more neglected social-science perspective.

See also CULTURALISM; CULTURAL MATERIALISM; IDEOLOGY CRITIQUE.

CULTURE

An indispensable but multi-accented term with a complex and still-open history, which in itself expresses the complexity of general human history. At its extremes, culture is used on the one hand, as in its early usage, to refer to organic cultivation, as of soil and crops, or to a biological 'culture' made in the laboratory and so by extension to individual human accomplishment (as in descriptions of a 'cultured gentleman'). On the other, it is used to refer to intellectual and artistic works or practices that, in their very forms and meanings, define human society as socially constructed rather than natural. Sometimes, this second meaning is then generalized to produce descriptions of the tenor or 'spirit' of a social group or whole society, period or nation. 'Culture' is therefore used to refer to individual style or character, to a stage of artistic or intellectual development, to the expressive life and traditions of a social group, to a social-historical moment or a broad epoch. We talk about a cultured left foot, about the culture of football, about film culture, African-American or Scottish culture, eighteenth-century or mod culture, or the culture of the 1960s or 1980s.

Perhaps the most profitable way of studying such a mutable term is along the lines of Raymond Williams' account of its European usage over the last three centuries (1976b). Williams suggests that in its 'most widespread use' culture has referred in the later nineteenth and twentieth centuries to the world of the arts (literature, music, painting, sculpture, theatre, film). In this sense, the term has nevertheless been understood and invariably valued in different ways. In a traditional perspective, it is seen as embodied in a selective CANON of works (comprising 'high culture') and valued above commercial or POPULAR artistic forms ('low' or 'MASS culture', to which some might wish to deny any genuine 'artistic' status).

Of underlying and fundamental importance to this view, as to other less traditional perspectives, is the attitude taken towards mass or industrial or, in the twentieth century, advanced consumer society. Debates about culture in this most familiar sense have indeed accompanied, and been prompted by, the social and economic developments of this period. Culture has, therefore, been defined in relation to this historical form of society, traditionally once more in terms that see one as opposed to the other. The resulting defence of culture as equivalent or necessary to authentic moral or spiritual values sets art works – pre-eminently a selective tradition of literary texts – against the mechanical and materialist order of industrial society.

So defined, as in the writings of Matthew Arnold, F.R. Leavis and T.S. Eliot, among others, culture is mobilized to serve a liberal or radical conservative

IDEOLOGY. However, a similar defence has also informed the opposition to mass society of Marxists such as Theodor Adorno and others associated with the Frankfurt school. In both traditions, the valued culture is that of a minority or an ELITE, though the authors, artists, genres and individual works may be as different as the Greek classics, the realist novel, and the contemporary AVANT-GARDE. In a reverse evaluation, the 'popular' culture of punk or jungle, or of commercial cinema might be preferred to any of the above. This comprises a radical, contemporary shift of definition and of the terms of valuation. Nevertheless, all these views share the assumption that culture can have an active, shaping influence upon ideas, attitudes and experience. As such, they contrast with the position that sees culture as secondary to, and as a reflex of, other processes in the society and economy, which are thought to be more fundamental and determining than culture itself. This latter view has been associated with an economistic or 'vulgar' MARXISM, but in more refined versions still draws on the Marxist model of (an economic) BASE AND (ideological/cultural) SUPERSTRUCTURE, which most commentators feel it necessary to address.

However complex, therefore, the definition of culture is vital to notions of the objects of study, the methods and aims of a range of academic disciplines (including Philosophy, Linguistics and Education, as well as the more obvious Anthropology, Sociology, Literary, Media and Cultural Studies). Its use and meanings in these contexts may be inconsistent and more or less descriptive or evaluative. However, the study of culture can never be free of assumptions of VALUE or an involvement in meaningful, value-making activity on the part of the researcher, or the works or social actors being studied. Perhaps the most influential conception of culture in this academic work, especially in the Humanities, has been Raymond Williams' own founding definition of culture as 'a whole way of life of a social group or whole society'.

Work along these lines has developed straightforwardly from neither the liberal-conservative nor Marxist traditions, but from a critical engagement with each. Writing in 1981, Williams sees a convergence of the idea of culture as 'a whole way of life' and its association with intellectual and artistic activity. What unites these emphases, he says, is the idea of culture as a signifying system, 'through which necessarily... a social order is communicated, reproduced, experienced and explored' (1981: 13). This thinking helped inspire a conception of creative work and cultural practice as constituting rather than 'expressing' a given social order, and stimulated new directions in Literary Studies, the Sociology of Culture and Cultural Studies as elsewhere. (For a rigorous revaluation of Williams' and Stuart Hall's role in the formation of Cultural Studies, see Mulhern 2000).

However, it would be false to suggest there is a consensual definition of culture in the contemporary period, or even that the idea of culture as a 'whole way of life' is universally accepted. In an early response to Williams, the Marxist historian E.P. Thompson proposed an alternative definition of culture not as a 'whole way of life', but as a 'whole way of struggle' (1961). In a later phase, the influence of contemporary feminist, poststructuralist, postmodern and postcolonial theory has led many to reiterate the critique of earlier notions of minority culture in terms now of their white, western and male-centred bias. In addition, many would raise doubts concerning the homogenizing conception of 'the whole' and unified, or the desire for this, in the realm of culture as in other fields. The variant meanings of culture are now more readily understood as the necessary expression of a range of signifying practices across different media and discourses. We are brought, therefore, to a pluralized and dialogic conception of cultures of dissonance, difference and diversity, and to the debates this in turn engenders (Hall in Morley and Chen [eds] 1996; Bhabha 1994).

See also COMMON CULTURE; COMMUNITY.

CULTURE INDUSTRIES

A description used to refer to commercially and state-owned organizations in the arts and media, committed to the direct PRODUCTION, sponsorship, display and distribution of cultural goods and services. These can range from exhibitions, sports events, books, newspapers and associated kinds of journalism, film, video and TV production, to all kinds of musical production from opera to POP. Louis Althusser includes these organizations in his account of IDEOLOGICAL STATE APPARATUSes but this category includes institutions (education, the family, the legal system) that are not cultural organizations in the present sense.

The changing histories of the major culture industries (especially the communications and entertainment industries) show an increasing commercialization, concentration of ownership and use of expanded world markets for the purposes of wider distribution and increased profit. This is accompanied by competition between industries, a heavy investment in advertising, and generally expanding consumption of the goods and services they provide. Communications and media industries also increasingly make use of advanced computer technologies and MASS-production techniques, and a flexible labour force, all of which characterize these industries as themselves products of developments in industrial and consumer CAPITALISM. What distinguishes the culture industries in this general picture of multinational and global capitalism is the nature of their product and its role in shaping attitudes and ideologies. Hence the description sometimes employed of 'consciousness industries' (Enzensberger 1970).

In one main tradition of analysis associated with Theodor Adorno, Max Horkheimer (1972) and members of the so-called Frankfurt school (see CRITICAL THEORY), the forms and effects of mass culture are seen to serve the ends of commodification and to duplicate the social relations of capitalism in the realm of IDEOLOGY. The culture industries (the term was first coined by Adorno) are therefore seen as manipulative and their audiences as passive consumers. They are then contrasted in both respects with the non-commercial forms of authentic art, thought of as a product of the lone artist of integrity. A perceived standardization of product and effect is therefore opposed to the supposed AUTONOMY, originality and critical force of art. This opposition is also often repeated in distinctions of VALUE and quality made within mass culture itself, between the 'serious' novel and POPULAR fiction; the novel and soap opera; or the art film and Hollywood blockbuster, even where it is recognized by critics and professionals alike that these forms are similarly commercially produced for specific markets.

Along these lines, the debate about the culture industries becomes difficult to disengage from debates about high and low culture that have shaped cultural analysis as a whole. There is some merit, therefore, in the Frankfurt school's attention less to specific texts or products than to general processes in a system of cultural production. In this approach, while the culture industries might be diagnosed as the uncomplicated symptom of capital accumulation, the focus of discussion is upon processes of production, control and the satisfaction of needs. The question therefore posed is less that of the merits of individual texts or GENRES than the more widely conceived nature and function of entertainment.

This broader perspective has been pursued especially with the Sociology of Media, where commentators (Garnham 1990; Collins 1990; Curran and Seaton 1991; but see also Williams 1976a and Hoggart 1970 in the tradition of British Cultural Studies) have been consistently concerned with questions of political economy and of ownership and control (see the readings in Marris and Thornham [eds] 1996). These issues are now raised not only in relation to the more traditional media industries, but in relation to information conglomerates and the operation of newer technologies, primarily the INTERNET. A further contemporary issue, of concern to a traditional mass cultural industry, such as TV, with the development of cable, satellite systems and DIGITAL imaging, has been that of 'deregulation'. This, once more, is a feature of transnational and globalized communication NETWORKS, which are increasingly able to operate beyond the borders of national governments.

In a final, unexpected but increasingly familiar sign of this same postmodern economy, traditional industries, such as mining and shipbuilding, have become a new type of culture industry, or 'industry for culture', in the shape of heritage sites run for educational interest or the purposes of TOURISM.

See also CANON; CONSUMERISM; GLOBALIZATION.

CYBERFEMINISM

Cyberfeminism has come to describe some of the issues raised by contemporary science and technology of special interest to women (see also ECOLOGY). Wakeford (2000), for example, and the wide-ranging contributions to Green and Adam ([eds] 2001) report, respectively, on women's creation of combined electronic and social networks, and the specifically gendered involvement of women users with new technologies.

In one example of this debate, Judith Squires takes issue with the 'cybernetic future' envisaged by Sadie Plant (1995). The latter's 'cyber feminism', Squires writes, 'is distinctly apolitical' (1996: 209). Plant's belief that CYBERNETICS is beyond questions of POWER and politics, that women's 'flashes of intuitive exchange' make them more attuned to new technologies, ignores how GENDERed and patriarchal structures remain 'embodied' in society. It returns FEMINISM to an earlier 'mystical maternalist feminism' (1996: 207) and the celebration of 'essential, though disembodied woman' (1996: 210). This, Squires contrasts with

Donna Haraway's feminist CYBORG, 'an "ironic political myth"… explicitly grounded in the political realities of contemporary society' (1996: 207).

Haraway's 'A manifesto for cyborgs' (1985) remains a seminal point of reference. Jenny Wolmark's *Cybersexualities* (1999), for example, acknowledges Haraway's contribution to a 'non-hierarchical and non-binary' construction of gendered subjectivity, and many have looked, following Haraway, to feminist science fiction in support of the imaginative-political force of the cyborg figure. Feminist readings of CYBERPUNK fiction and films, however, show how this discourse can remain oblivious to questions of gender, or employ 'cyber' narratives to project anxieties about masculinity, or a mixed attraction and fear of technology on to women's bodies in scenarios, especially of alien reproduction (see Creed 1993; Doane and Spinger in Wolmark [ed] 1999).

See also POSTHUMAN.

CYBERNETICS

The prefix 'cyber' is from the Greek meaning to steer, pilot or guide and is used in a number of combinations, among them CYBERPUNK, CYBORG, cyberia, cybersex, CYBERSPACE and CYBERFEMINISM. The term 'cybernetics' was introduced by the American Norbert Wiener in his *Cybernetics: or Control and Communication in the Animal and the Machine* (1949) to describe feedback and control mechanisms in systems using computers. It now has a wide provenance, covering the entire field of interactions between humans and advanced technologies: from the use of sophisticated prostheses and VIRTUAL REALITY helmets to 'cybernetic communities' in cities or worldwide financial or other NETWORKS (Robertson 1995; Dovey [ed] 1996; McBeath and Webb 1997).

The underlying question in these many applications concerns changing definitions of the human, as a brain and physical BODY, and in social, intellectual relations with others. Some argue that new technologies will take us into a brave new POSTHUMAN era of enhanced knowledge and well-being, and of fundamentally altered conceptions of relations between the human and the machine. Others remain more sceptical and see in this scenario a UTOPIAnism driven by a faith in technology as a benign and self-ordering instrument that ignores persistent inequalities of access, and the question of the selection and use of information (Wyatt, *et al.* [eds] 2000). The issue of the 'control' of technologies and its products implicit in the prefix 'cyber' remains, in short, a supremely important one.

See also HUMANISM; INTERNET.

CYBERPUNK

A term introduced in the early 1980s to identify a group of American and Canadian science-fiction writers, among them Lewis Shiner, Bruce Sterling, Pat Cadagan, Rudy Rucker and, above all, William Gibson. In an anthology of writings by these and other authors entitled *Mirrorshades* (Sterling 1988) – so-called after the matte-black and chrome sunglasses that were an icon of the movement – Bruce

Sterling associated this innovation in science fiction with a more general integration of science and the Humanities, 'the realm of high tech and the modern pop underground' (1988: ix). Cyberpunk, wrote Sterling, was the 'literary incarnation' (1988: x) of this movement and was especially alert to the new relation of contemporary microtechnologies and the human body (contact lenses, the walkman, mobile phones). In Gibson's fiction of the 1980s (*Neuromancer, Mona Lisa Overdrive, Count Zero* and *Burning Chrome*), the main characters (called 'console cowboys') 'jack into' cyberspace through a deck connected to a socket in their heads and are able to access information, though this is protected by artificial intelligences (AIS) servicing multinational corporations. Along with a related series of films (*Robocop, Terminator, Videodrome* and especially *Blade Runner*), cyberpunk is therefore seen as reflecting changing conceptions of 'the human' in relation to micro and advanced information technologies – a scenario leading Fredric Jameson to describe cyberpunk fiction as 'the supreme literary expression if not of postmodernism, then of late capitalism itself' (1991: 419n).

In general terms, cyberpunk can therefore be situated in three ways: as drawing upon earlier examples of more experimental writing within or bordering science fiction (William Burroughs, J.G. Ballard, Philip K. Dick); in relation, second, to the COUNTER-CULTURE of the 1960s and the punk phenomenon in pop music in the 1970s; and, third, as the literary expression of themes in POSTMODERNISM (McCaffery [ed] 1991; McHale 1993). In this last respect, cyberpunk echoes a range of questions in postmodern theory about CULTURE, technology, information and global CAPITALISM. While Sterling suggests it voices an anarchistic, streetwise dissent in relation to the contemporary world, others have seen it as a blatant marketing device and as complicit with the machinations of multinational corporations. Either way, cyberpunk is viewed as an ALLEGORY of the 1980s, but as having receded or mutated into another fictional form in the 1990s. Here, too, William Gibson's writing (*Virtual Light* 1993; *Idoru* 1997) provides the best examples of this development.

See also CYBORG; NETWORK; POSTHUMAN.

CYBERSPACE

A term invented by the science-fiction author William Gibson, introduced by him in the short story 'Burning Chrome' (1982) and expanded in the novel *Neuromancer* (1984). The inspiration for the term, says Gibson, came in the sight of the rapt intensity of teenagers in video arcades and the familiar sensation of 'actual space' behind the computer screen (McCaffery [ed] 1991: 272). In *Neuromancer*, accordingly, cyberspace (or 'the matrix') 'has its roots in primitive arcade games... in early graphics programs and military experimentation with cranial jacks' and is further defined as 'A consensual hallucination experienced daily by billions of legitimate operators, in every nation, by children being taught mathematical concepts... A graphic representation of data abstracted from the banks of every computer in the human system' (1984: 67).

'Cyberspace' has since become common usage in the worlds of business and information technology, and is used interchangeably, in these and popular contexts, with references to the web, INTERNET and VIRTUAL REALITY. The many uses of this new technology for leisure, communication, business, information storage and retrieval, now all on a global scale, raise ethical and political questions of an unprecedented kind. Reflections on the changing nature of the human; questions of access, control and democracy; along, increasingly, with mounting issues of data and identity theft, cybercrime, and the activities of national security agencies, dominate both academic and journalistic debate. For some representative titles: see Bell and Kennedy ([eds] 2000), Bell (2001), Brenner (2010), Davidoff and Ham (2012). See also, of the massive coverage on the case of Edward Snowden, who leaked classified information from NSA (the National Security Agency) in 2013, the documentary film *Citizenfour* (2014).

See also CYBORG; GLOBALIZATION; HYPERREALITY.

CYBORG

A contraction of the term 'cybernetic organism' introduced by Manfred E. Clynes in 1960 (see Gray *et al.* [eds] 1995: 29–53). The cyborg is an amalgam of the human and the machine, and as such distinct from the earlier, purely mechanical, robot or automaton. This development has been made possible by advances in microtechnology, genetic engineering and biomedical science. A number of science-fiction texts and films (see CYBERPUNK) include cyborg figures and explore the altered conceptions of 'being human' they provoke. However, replacement organs and prosthetic BODY parts have made 'cyborg' identities an everyday reality, as does, in a looser sense, the common use of contact lenses, MP3 players and mobile phones, or the interface of the human with the car, camera or computer (see Featherstone and Burrows [eds] 1995; Michael 2000).

To this extent, the development of cyborg identities is consistent with the description of media technologies as extensions of the human sensorium by Marshall McLuhan in the 1960s. Arguably, too, humans have always used tools, and augmented their capacities with mechanical aids and industrial machinery. However, there is a cultural-historical and psychic difference between using a hammer and driving a car, and between this and wearing an artificial limb, undergoing skin grafts or accepting an implant. The latter directly affect the surface, shape or internal functions of the body. Advanced biotechnology can now influence the ageing process, memory, mobility, athleticism, colour and gender of an individual. Nor are these practices confined to movie and pop stars in Californian clinics; new technologies are having a dramatic impact in surgery, healthcare and everyday medicine.

The cyborg therefore relates most importantly to the possibility of radically altered bodies and conceptions of IDENTITY. These implications have been explored with greatest originality by Donna Haraway. In her much-cited essay, 'A manifesto for cyborgs' (1985), she presents the cyborg as 'a condensed image of both imagination and material reality' (1990: 191); the ambiguous product of 'militarism and patriarchal capitalism' (1990: 193); but a resource and harbinger of transformed social relations 'that changes what counts as women's experience

73

in the late twentieth century' (1990: 191). 'The cyborg is a creature in a postgender world' and resists all 'seductions to organic wholeness' (1990: 192). Haraway's conception of a cyborg politics that exploits the possibilities of a decentred, borderline identity has affinities with the tactics of TRANSGRESSIVE reading and a commitment to HYBRIDITY elsewhere – 'Cyborg unities are monstrous and illegitimate' (1990: 196) – but she seeks to combine this poststructuralist orientation with a more traditional left feminism. As she puts it: 'What kind of politics could embrace partial, contradictory permanently unclosed constructions of personal and collective selves and still be faithful, effective – and ironically, socialist feminist?' (1990: 199).

See also CYBERNETICS; FEMINISM; POSTHUMAN; SEXUALITY; ROBOTICS.

DECONSTRUCTION

This philosophy or critical method is associated with the work of Jacques Derrida (1930–2004). Deconstruction has had a very wide influence upon a range of intellectual disciplines and the term has gained POPULAR currency in criticism and journalism. However, it is often used in these contexts with the sense simply of 'analysis' when, as Derrida's writings make clear, it has a more precise and challenging meaning. At the same time, these writings can be frustratingly evasive and opaque (though defenders would understand this as a sign of a necessary indeterminacy). Though deconstruction is referred to here as a 'method', for example, Derrida would have probably denied such a description. Also, although it draws for inspiration upon the philosophies of Nietzsche and Heidegger, deconstruction is not presented as a 'philosophy', nor beyond philosophy. Derrida writes, rather, that 'the passage beyond philosophy' does not mean 'turning the page of philosophy... but in continuing to read philosophers *in a certain way*' (1978: 288). Deconstruction therefore stands in relation to philosophy as a critical attitude or way of reading. As Derrida puts it, 'it is a question of explicitly and systematically posing the problem of a discourse which borrows from a heritage the resources necessary for the deconstruction of that heritage itself' (1978: 282).

Deconstruction therefore borrows from the systems it questions and vice versa. This form of immanent CRITIQUE Derrida directed in the first instance at western philosophy (including essays on Husserl, J.L. Austin, Michel Foucault). This he revealed to be invariably and contradictorily committed to a set of assumptions that centre and fix meaning. All of the familiar terms for fundamental, underlying principles '(essence, existence, substance, subject)... transcendability, consciousness, God, man and so forth' (1978: 280), assume, says Derrida, a moment of pure origin or a first cause; 'an invariable presence' (1978: 279) that constrains and betrays the movement of meaning. This tendency Derrida terms LOGOCENTRICISM. Deconstruction, it is important to realize, does not seek to eliminate or 'destroy' logocentric assumptions. Rather, it recognizes their inescapable function. We are bound therefore to give terms such as 'origin', 'essence' or 'truth' some credence, while being sceptical of their claims to authority or finality. Indeed, there would be no deconstructive scepticism without the fixed terms it seeks to undermine. The major stabilizing or centring terms of western philosophy and common thinking are therefore 'problematized', or, as Derrida puts it, placed 'under erasure': that is to say, written in and crossed out at the same time. Thus deconstruction makes 'a double play' that 'allows what it obliterates to be read' (1981a: 6).

Deconstruction made its first impact at a now celebrated conference on STRUCTURALISM at Johns Hopkins University in 1966, when Derrida read the paper 'Structure, sign and play in the human sciences' (quoted above). The following year saw its publication in *Writing and Difference* and the appearance of two other volumes, *Speech and Phenomena* and *Of Grammatology*. Derrida's essay critiqued the way the concept of 'structure', so important to the movement of structuralism, constrained the actual play of meaning. As suggested, however, Derrida worked from within, rather than simply against, structuralism, pursuing in particular the logic of its emphasis upon 'DIFFERENCE' as constituting meaning in language. Derrida's famous coinage *'DIFFÉRANCE'* combines this insight with the contention that meaning is always potentially in play across the interconnected discourses that comprise the weave of language. *'Différance'* therefore captures the double sense of how meaning is both constituted in 'difference' and permanently 'deferred'. In the course of his work, Derrida has employed a series of cognate terms such as 'TRACE', 'DISSEMINATION', or 'spacing' to further express this movement of meaning in language and the nature of TEXTUALITY.

Derrida's discussion in 'Structure, sign and play' of the work of the structural anthropologist Claude Lévi-Strauss (see BRICOLAGE, CODE, MYTH), and elsewhere of Jean-Jacques Rousseau (see SUPPLEMENT), Freud and Ferdinand de Saussure (see *ÉCRITURE*/WRITING), presented readers with examples of deconstructive method in practice. This consists of two moves: first the critique and inversion of the hierarchical binary oppositions (nature over culture; speech over writing) that structure these philosophies and make them examples of logocentrism and, second, the dispersal of meanings in accordance with the principle of *'différance'*.

These ideas and procedures, directing attention to what is demoted or marginalized, have been taken up especially in Literary Studies (for Derrida's views on literature, see Derrida 1992a), in FEMINISM (see especially Hélène Cixous' 'Sorties', 1981a) and postcolonial studies (see Spivak 1987; Bhabha 1994). Derrida's influence in these fields has been accompanied by the question of the relative formalism and quietist or affirmative political implications of deconstruction. Gayatri Spivak (1983), for example, examines Derrida's own method in terms of its relative complicity with PHALLOCENTRICISM and thus of its problematic value for feminism.

The more formalist or narrowly textualist side of Derrida's work has been especially taken up in the USA in the POSTSTRUCTURALISM of the so-called Yale school of critics (see Norris 1982; Eagleton 1990, Currie, 2013) but there is, according to Christopher Norris, a duality in Derrida's own writing. Norris (1987) prefers the earlier to the later work since he finds here a more evident commitment to the ENLIGHTENMENT principles of truth, rationality, justice and a more rigorous philosophical method compared with the more 'literary' later work (of, for example, *Glas* 1974). The aestheticist tendencies of the latter, Norris finds echoed in POSTMODERNISM. His response contrasts with that of Richard Rorty (1982) who prefers the way the later work undermines the pretensions of philosophy.

Derrida has himself commented that he is 'of course... "in favour" of the Enlightenment', adding that it is 'in the name of... a new Enlightenment that I deconstruct a given Enlightenment' (Papadakis [ed] 1989: 11). His later study *Spectres of Marx* (1994b) would seem, in a similar vein, to confirm his affinities with a 'spirit of Marxism'. 'Deconstruction', he writes in this connection, 'has never had any sense or interest, in my view at least, except as a radicalisation, which is to say also in the tradition of a certain Marxism' (1994a: 56). However, this position, too, has met with a mixed response from Marxist thinkers (Ahmad 1994; Jameson 1995).

DEFAMILIARIZATION

A term used interchangeably with ESTRANGEMENT and the less usual DISTANTIATION, and in association often with Bertolt Brecht's ALIENATION EFFECT. It can be said to have derived most directly from the concept of *ostranenie* ('making strange') developed by the Russian Formalists, particularly Victor Shklovsky. In 'Art as device' (1917), Shklovsky wrote that the technique of art was 'to make objects "unfamiliar", to make forms difficult, to increase the difficulty and length of perception because the process of perception is an aesthetic end in itself and must be prolonged' (Lodge [ed] 1988: 20).

As many commentators have suggested, thus conceived, defamiliarization is an aesthetic concept with limited formal effects and, as such, is to be distinguished from the more politicized function it was given by the Soviet AVANT-GARDE and by other European modernist movements. Osip Brik suggests how in these late movements the aesthetic device was put to use in the service of a 'social demand'. Stanley Mitchell, citing Brecht's theory of the 'alienation effect' (German *Verfremdungseffekt*) sums up the differences between the more formalist and political versions of defamiliarization:

> In both theories the proper role of art is seen as one of de-routinization, de-automatisation: art is the enemy of habit; it renews, refreshes our perceptions; by 'making strange', it defamiliarizes. But while Shklovsky's *ostranenie* was a purely aesthetic concept, concerned with renewal of perception, Brecht's *Verfremdung* had a social aim: if the world could be shown differently, i.e. as having different possibilities, could it not be differently made? Brecht wished to strike not merely at the perceptions, but at the consciousness of his spectators.
>
> (In Brooker [1988] 2016: 70)

The consensus in accounts of POSTMODERNISM is that such distinctions count now for little or nothing. In this view, the modernist device of defamiliarization or estrangement has been neutralized by the levelling effects of a CULTURE of IMAGES.

Either it is thought that the critical distance this device depends upon, or aims to produce, is no longer possible, or credible, or that examples are so ubiquitous in advertising and the media as to have lost all critical effect. As Fredric Jameson comments, drawing out (though not necessarily endorsing) this double implication, 'defamiliarization, the shock of otherness, is a mere aesthetic effect and a lie' (1991: 286).

See also CRITIQUE.

DESIRE

Following the Reformation and through the eighteenth to the twentieth centuries, modern discussions of desire have been concerned predominantly with the forms of human rather than divine love, or relations between these. In the contemporary period, the concept has been of importance to a number of broadly poststructuralist or postmodern and feminist theories, most often engaged in a debate with the findings of Freudian and Lacanian PSYCHOANALYSIS. In these accounts, desire is understood as a key – for some, a determining – activity in the making of the GENDERed and sexualized SUBJECT.

An important locus for these debates has been the theory of the French psychoanalyst, Jacques Lacan (1901–1981) who was in this respect much indebted to the nineteenth-century philosopher, G.W.F. Hegel, and has himself proved a problematic influence upon later feminist theory. Following Freud, Lacan situated desire in the UNCONSCIOUS, which develops simultaneously with the formation of the subject at the point of entry into the SYMBOLIC order. The subject's 'desire is for the desire of the Other' in Lacan's formulation (1977: 321). The subject, that is to say, seeks both the love or recognition of the OTHER (a desire to be desired by the Other) and to possess the Other (a desire for the Other). Bound up in this complex emotion is the wish also to be the Other, to find that the Other is not different but a self-reflection and hence the same: in which case, desire is in fact self-desire. The OEDIPAL COMPLEX determines that for the male child, who is the paradigm for this account, this Other is the mother (who appears as the desired object but also as a warning of castration). This desire is forbidden and thus repressed as the child accommodates himself to the symbolic authority of the father embodied in the PHALLUS. Desire is therefore founded on a primordial absence, yet committed to a necessarily futile quest for what is lacking. As such, for Lacan, the structure of desire determines the very nature of SEXUALITY. As Madan Sarup summarizes, whereas 'Need is satisfiable, desire is insatiable' (1992: 68). Accordingly, it can only find sublimated or oblique expression in FANTASY or FETISHISM.

The Unconscious, Lacan famously declared, is structured like a language. In so far as desire can be figured, in this understanding, as a permanently ungrounded signifier, Lacan's notion is comparable to the infinitely deferred play of meaning that Jacques Derrida assigns to language and TEXTUALITY. For Gilles Deleuze and Félix Guattari, authors of *Anti-Oedipus* (1984), desire is similarly decentred, dynamic and perpetual. Unlike Lacan, however, they see it for this very reason as an affirmative and revolutionary force; a FLOW of energies that seeks and establishes connections and 'free syntheses' (1984: 116), constantly frustrating the efforts of rational society whose purpose is to contain or 'territorialize' it. This is the basis of their critique of psychoanalysis (signalled in the title of their volume), since this too seeks to confine desire in the bourgeois narrative of the Oedipus story and the family. Instead, Deleuze and Guattari promote a 'SCHIZOANALYSIS' founded on the metaphor of schizophrenia as a 'potentially liberatory psychic condition' (Best and Kellner 1991: 90). In a deliberately improvisatory combination of Nietzsche and Marxist materialism, they polemicize for a new politics that will match and outwit CAPITALISM both in its macrostructures and its control over the 'molecular' interior life of the subject. Subjects become, in this scenario, 'desiring machines' whose liberated desire will depose the totalizing HEGEMONY of the 'capitalist machine'.

Feminist theories of desire have also developed from a debate with Freudian and Lacanian psychoanalysis. French feminists in particular – for example, Julia Kristeva, Hélène Cixous and Luce Irigaray (see Wright [ed] 1992) – have sought to rewrite Freud's endorsement of the traditional gendered distinction between active and passive sexuality, and the phallic character of the structure of desire in Lacan. Luce Irigaray, for example, has celebrated the plurality of forms of female sexuality and argued that female desire is founded on touch rather than sight or the GAZE. The latter she sees as having characterized western thought and as 'foreign to female eroticism' (1985b: 25–6). The 'multiplicity of female desire' expressed through touch, contact and sharing, means 'woman always remains several... the other... already within her and autoerotically familiar to her' (1985b: 30, 31). Here in 'a sort of expanding universe' without limits, Irigaray finds the basis for a 'female IMAGINARY' to contest the presumptions of phallocentricism and woman's standard role as 'use-value' and 'commodity' for men (1985b: 31).

In a summary account, the American feminist Judith Butler (1995) presents a further set of rejoinders to the long tradition from Plato to Lacan, which has represented desire as singular, phallic and an invariant search for a lost origin. She questions the negativity of these accounts – which set desire 'at an infinite distance from pleasure' (1995: 381) – and their complicity with heterosexual norms. She writes how feminist, gay and lesbian scholars have posed sexual difference differently, putting homo/heterosexual definitions in crisis. In a notable example, Eve Kosofsky Sedgwick (1985) has demonstrated how a triangular relation based primarily in homosocial desire between male protagonists and their rivals (for a woman) operates across a range of literary and other texts. Butler posits 'more variable and complex' scenarios, linking desire to PLEASURE, emerging from such studies and speculates too, opening the concept further, on 'a social or cultural unconscious to desire'. How, she asks, are we to describe 'the complex intertwining of those racial and gendered imaginaries by which desire acquires its political valence?' (1995: 385).

See also DETERRITORIALIZATION; FEMINISM; STRUCTURALISM.

DETERMINATION

A concept associated especially with the model of the BASE AND SUPERSTRUCTURE in Marxist theory. Marx proposed that the economic base determined the superstructural elements of a society (the latter including IDEOLOGY and CULTURE). As Raymond Williams writes, the idea of determination is vital to the 'essential content of the original Marxist proposition' (1980a: 36). He warns, however, that the possible meanings of the term have been narrowed to suggest a relation of 'prefiguration, prediction or control' between the levels of the Marxist model. Instead, Williams suggests, in an influential contribution, related to the adoption of the concept of HEGEMONY, that the idea of determination is revalued 'towards the setting of limits and the exertion of pressure and away from a predicted, prefigured and controlled content' (1980a: 34). This importantly distinguishes the meaning of 'determination' from 'determinism'. At the same time, Williams reintroduces the equally central Marxist proposition 'that social being determines consciousness'. This, he argues, restores the social content and 'the key emphasis' of social intention to the idea of determination. The process of determination, Williams comes to suggest, is expressed in the 'intentions by which we define the society, intentions which in all of our experiences have been the rule of a particular class' (1980a: 36).

See also MARXISM; OVERDETERMINATION.

DETERRITORIALIZATION

A key concept in the philosophy of Deleuze and Guatarri, and especially elaborated in their *Anti-Oedipus* (1984) and *A Thousand Plateaus* (1987). Their philosophy depends on a particular lexicon, including, in addition to the current term, RHIZOME, FLOWS, NOMADISM (and see PSYCHOANALYSIS), strata and assemblages. The concluding section of *A Thousand Plateaus* comprises a brief summation of some of these terms. Here 'assemblages' are described as always 'basically territorial' (1987: 503), composed of different contrary aspects: in the first instance they are both non-discursive bodies and discursive utterances ('content and expression'); in the second, they are defined by their constitution as 'territories' and by a counter 'deterritorializing' interior movement that agitates for change. Animal, social and political assemblages are therefore seen as dynamic combinations of reterritorializing forces that seek stability and the 'lines of flight', creative energy or DESIRE, that 'cut across' or deterritorialize a given assemblage and 'carry it away' (1987: 504).

The 'Conclusion' of *A Thousand Plateaus* further distinguishes in abstract fashion between 'relative' and 'absolute' types of deterritorialization (1987: 508–10). The first takes place in the actual world and can take a 'negative' form when the lines of flight are blocked, or 'positive' when the lines of flight escape the forces of repressive reterritorialization. 'Absolute' deterritorialization refers to a deeper movement in the 'virtual' order of things, acting on the 'molecular' rather than 'molar' plane of existence (Patton 2001: 210). 'Deterritorialisation is absolute', write Deleuze and Guattari, 'when… it brings about the creation of a new earth' (1987: 510). These more profound, qualitative transformations depend on a relative deterritorialization coming to a point of connection with other deterritorializations in other fields to produce a new natural, social or political 'assemblage'. This does not produce a new majority society or culture, but installs a continuing deterritorialization that generalizes a 'creative process of becoming-different or divergence from the majority' (Patton 2001: 213). This process is central to Deleuze and Guattari's conception of revolutionary politics.

See ACTOR NETWORK THEORY; PSYCHOGEOGRAPHY.

DIACHRONIC/SYNCHRONIC

See SIGN; STRUCTURALISM.

DIALECTICS

In classical thought, dialectics formed part of the trivium with rhetoric and grammar, and named a mode of reasoning through debate and disputation. In later medieval thought and in German idealist philosophy, it named both the art of reasoning, or logic, and the investigation of truth. Though these meanings survive, dialectics has subsequently been associated specifically with the detection of contradiction and its effects in the structuring or deformation of a whole. This sense has chiefly derived from MARXISM. However, the analysis of texts or social processes in terms of their internal contradictions, and the view that these expose limits or force change, are common in sociological and cultural study, and might be linked with the identification of subordinate or marginalized groups and meanings, with or without any direct reference to dialectics or to Marxism.

In the Marxist tradition, Friedrich Engels defined dialectics as:

> the science of the general laws of motion, both of the external world and of human thought – two sets of laws which are identical in their substance but differ in their expression… the dialectic of concepts itself became merely the conscious reflex of the dialectical motion of the real world.
>
> (Marx and Engels 1970: 619)

These laws, Engels named in *The Dialectics of Nature* as the transformation from quantity to quality, the identity of opposites, and the negation of the negation. This scheme derives from the German philosopher G.W.F. Hegel's formula of the dialectic as a movement from thesis and antithesis to a new higher unity or synthesis. Marx and Engels famously stood Hegel on his head, giving a materialist grounding to his idealist account of the dialectic as a movement operating primarily in thought and only secondarily in the world. Marx posited a dialectical movement in history, operating in the specific historical stage of CAPITALISM through the internal contradictions that would bring this economic system to an end. Thus, the factory system produces its opposite in the collective assembly of workers; the drive to maximize profit produces its opposite in over-competition, falling profit and economic crisis. This process, said Marx importantly, occurs independently of CONSCIOUSNESS. In the full working of the dialectic, however, and the supersession of capitalism, it is the proletariat that develops a knowledge, through the experience of CLASS struggle, of its own conditions and the nature of historical development.

Marx's analysis gave rise to the description of Marxism (by the Soviet philosopher G.V. Plekanov) as 'dialectical MATERIALISM', though this description is generally distinguished from the related 'historical materialism'. While the latter describes Marxism's stress upon the material basis of historical development, 'dialectical materialism' usually refers to its philosophical method and the attribution of a generative dynamic (or 'laws') to that historical process.

The history of Marxism has witnessed many reversals and revisions in dialectical theory and practice, though the concept remains central. Two elaborations might be identified here. The first is Lenin's identification of dialectical consciousness with the political party and his philosophical reflections on dialectical method. The latter confirm its central tenets: 'the splitting of a single whole and the cognition of its contradictory parts... is the essence of dialectics' (Marx *et al.* 1977: 381). Historical development he sees as proceeding 'in spirals, not in a straight line... by leaps, catastrophes and revolutions'; 'breaks in continuity' (1977: 374).

A second important re-emphasis occurred in Theodor Adorno's *Negative Dialectics* (1990), where he wrote that 'dialectics is the ontology of the wrong state of things' (1990: 11); that is to say, a dialectical understanding knows that what passes as the real is false. Adorno commits dialectics to a CRITIQUE of the real, to 'the seeming inevitability and thus legitimacy of whatever is' (1990: 268) or, in other words, to a critique of ideology, especially of COMMODITY FETISHISM and REIFICATION – the false identification of the human subject and object enforced by capitalism. Though pessimistic, Adorno's account commits the critical theorist, in Marxist terminology, to a belief in the 'use-value' of objects and the existence of a real subjectivity, repressed under the ubiquity of the 'exchange value' of the marketplace.

It is doubtful whether, in Adorno's view, this real subjectivity would ever be recovered. The force of his negative dialectics is that he sees the movement between thought and experience as in fact endless. As such, his theory is a rejection of the 'affirmative' dialectics of the thesis–antithesis–synthesis schema. This sequential model has informed 'historicist' versions of human progress, but has been critiqued by many key figures in Marxist philosophy and cultural criticism. Adorno's negative dialectics, so Fredric Jameson argues, provide a model of critical thought appropriate to POSTMODERNISM when his 'prophecies of the "total system" finally came true' (1990a: 5).

See also HISTORICISM; IDEOLOGY.

DIALOGICS

An influential concept developed by the Soviet linguist and critic, Mikhail Bakhtin (1895–1975) and the 'Bakhtin School', primarily in writings, later reissued or translated, from the late 1920s. The school includes the work of P.N. Medvedev and V.N. Vološhinov, who are sometimes regarded as independent authors, sometimes as Bakhtin's collaborators, and sometimes as pseudonyms for Bakhtin. The Bakhtinian theory of language (notably in Vološhinov's *Marxism and the Philosophy of Language,* 1986 [1929]) can be understood as both a contemporary critique of the dehistoricizing model developed by Ferdinand de Saussure and adopted in the STRUCTURALISM of the 1960s, and as anticipating later theories of DISCOURSE. In this model, linguistic utterances are seen as engaged in a simultaneously verbal and ideological dialogue and as thus implicated in the unequal distribution of POWER, caught in a pull towards unitary, official discourse and opinion.

Bakhtin wrote: 'Discourse lives on the boundary between its own context and another, alien context' (1981: 284). He saw the literary form of the novel, broadly understood, as especially exploiting this double life of interacting and contesting discourses (see HETEROGLOSSIA), and finds in Dostoevsky, in particular, an example of the 'polyphonic' novel, where the author's characters 'are capable of standing beside their creator, of disagreeing with him, and of even rebelling against him' (1963: 4). As this suggests, the thrust of dialogics is to open discourse to the alien and subordinated, and thus to unsettle and discountenance authority. This is achieved, above all, through the use of PARODY and satire for which Bakhtin finds a precedent in the serio-comic genre of the late Roman Mennippean satire and the ironic form of the Socratic dialogue where popular opinion is exposed to free investigation. But the anti-authoritarian impulse of satire, irony and parody is given its fullest reign, for Bakhtin, in Rabelais, where the world of the body and the vernacular of the lower orders are simultaneously liberated in a chorus of belly laughs at up-ended officialdom (1965). This dismantling of the hierarchies of social and linguistic convention (which in later and more sober terms has become familiar from DECONSTRUCTION) Bakhtin termed the 'carnivalesque' (see CARNIVAL).

There has been extensive discussion of dialogics and other aspects of Bakhtin's theory, including the question of the authorship of the published texts of the circle. This has been related to differences between more liberal and more Marxist readings of the theory, the first seeking in one way or another to distinguish or absolve Bakhtin from the more evident Marxism of the earlier texts by Medvedev and Vološhinov. For further explication and suggested applications in literary study, see Stallybrass and White (1986), Lodge (1990) and Pearce (1994). Dentith (1994) combines a very useful set of readings with commentary. For dialogics in relation to general questions in theory and broader textual study, particularly in relation to film, see Hirschkop and Shepherd (1989), and Stam (1988,1989).

See also CHRONOTOPE; INTERTEXTUALITY.

DIASPORA

A term used traditionally to describe the continuing cultural and religious connections between Jewish peoples, despite their common experience of exile. More recently, it has been used in Literary and Cultural Theory and especially in postcolonial studies, and studies of RACE and ETHNICITY to describe a similar range of cultural affiliations connecting other groups who have been dispersed, or who have migrated across national boundaries (Gilroy 1993; Hall 1996b). Thus Asian, Irish, African, Caribbean and other ethnic groups – including theoretically in a post-imperial age a dominant ethnic group such as the English – are connected in a diasporic network via family ties, morality, manners, sporting and artistic traditions to a homeland, or to an idea of a homeland. The symbolism associated with this sense of belongingness can produce strong nostalgic and separatist tendencies. In response, theoretical writings on this theme have proposed that the term be 'decoupled' from an actual or desired common homeland and understood instead, in more poststructuralist vein, to describe a dynamic NETWORK of communities without the stabilizing allusion to an original homeland or essential IDENTITY (Hall 1990, 1996b). Instead, there is the common shifting and unfinished history of displacement and settlement. Cultural identity, writes Stuart Hall, is constituted not as 'an essence but a positioning' (1990: 226). He is led to conclude that 'Diaspora identities are those which are constantly producing and reproducing themselves anew, through transformation and difference' (1990: 235). He connects this with the condition and experience of HYBRIDITY, as does Paul Gilroy. The concept of diaspora, Gilroy argues, helps critique essentialist notions of identity in the name of 'innovation and change'. The concept 'should be cherished,' Gilroy writes, 'for its ability to pose the relationship between ethnic sameness and differentiation: a changing same' (1993: x, xi).

The term is used more loosely to describe a dispersed intellectual FORMATION, or the spread and interanimation of ideas. Thus, the global development and variety of forms of Cultural Studies itself have been described as a 'diasporic story' (Morley and Kuan-Hsing Chen [eds] 1996: 10–13).

See also ESSENTIALISM; POSTCOLONIALISM.

DIEGESIS

See NARRATIVE.

DIFFERENCE/*DIFFÉRANCE*

The widely applied concept of 'difference' has its source in the structural linguistics of Ferdinand de Saussure (see STRUCTURALISM). Saussure was concerned to analyse the structural relations comprising the system of language. Relations between parts of the individual SIGN are arbitrary, or conventional, Saussure argued, while those between signs in sequence are marked by the processes of selection and combination. 'The man saw the film' is the meaningful statement it is because it is not 'The man ate the fish'. Meaning results from the selection of equivalent elements, which could be substituted for those in a given sequence, but are absent from it. Presence and absence are thus mutually defining. In language, Saussure wrote famously, summing up this principle, 'there are only differences *without positive terms*' (1966 [1915]: 121).

This theory informed the structuralist approach adopted in the 1960s and 1970s within Literary, Media and Cultural Studies. In the event, this analysis often focused upon relations of opposition (the starkest form of difference) structuring the form and meaning of a text. Symbolic and ideological meanings could be seen as founded, for example, on binary oppositions between types of heroine, such as the vamp and the housewife, or between domestic and urban locations, or between the lone individual and a faceless bureaucracy. A further implication, however, was that meanings depended on what was not present, on the 'not-said' of texts, or upon other disregarded, oppressed or silenced discourses. An awareness of 'difference' therefore encouraged a reading in terms of DOMINANT and marginalized or censored meanings, and of similarly structured relations of INTERTEXTUALITY in which certain texts were preferred and others were relegated to the periphery (see also SYMPTOMATIC READING).

Already in its inevitable concern with the meanings, or significations, and not simply the formal structural relations of specific texts, a structuralist approach had gone beyond Saussure's own agenda. The general force of the term difference was wider still, however, and impacted especially upon conceptions of IDENTITY. Here, it linked with theorizations of the SUBJECT in a CRITIQUE of essentialist notions of the social or sexual self.

These notions, whether in structuralist textual analysis or in conceptions of individual, social or cultural identity, were subject to a further theoretical critique inaugurated by Jacques Derrida's reading of Saussure (1976; see also ÉCRITURE/ WRITING). Derrida detected a hierarchy in Saussure's thinking that privileged speech over writing. Saussure assumed, that is to say (in a very traditional way), that speech has the immediacy and authenticity, or 'presence', of a moment of transparent and original articulation, while writing is its delayed and distorted representation in a further, impure, medium. Derrida argued that, on the contrary, there was no such prior and pure moment of presence. Speech was a variable medium that was itself distant from any supposed moment of pure origin. Speech, that is to say, shares the characteristics of writing. In this sense, therefore, 'writing' emerges not as the secondary and distorted rendering of speech but as its very precondition. Similar oppositions, which privileged the first term of a given binary pairing such as nature/culture, God/man, reality/appearance, man/woman or white/black, were similarly open to critique or DECONSTRUCTION. Under its scrutiny, the structured relations in a system of differences become unhinged. Instead of contained or 'centred' and hierarchically arranged differences, there is, says Derrida, *'différence'*. This term, which is Derrida's coinage and whose own difference from the French *'différence'* is only perceptible in writing, combines the notions of difference or 'differing' with 'deferral'. Rather than being prior to a given articulation or identical with it, signification, or presence, is always postponed. In other words, difference, and therefore meaning, are in a constant process of being constructed (see Derrida 1981a and Kamuf [ed] 1991).

Derrida's deconstructive critique had, in the first instance, a quite localized object, but widened to reveal a comparable 'metaphysics of presence' characterizing the whole of western philosophy, and went on to inform significant movements in FEMINISM and contemporary CULTURAL POLITICS (see Rutherford 1990b; Tallack [ed] 1995: Section 3).

See also SEXUAL DIFFERENCE; TEXTUALITY.

DIFFEREND

A concept [Fr. *différend*] introduced by Jean-François Lyotard in the work, *The Differend* (1983) to designate incommensurable differences. A differend, Lyotard writes, 'would be a case of conflict, between (at least) two parties, that cannot be equitably resolved for lack of a rule of judgement applicable to both arguments' (1983: xi). Both sides in a dispute may claim legitimacy according to the conventions of the 'genre of discourse' in which they operate, but cannot be fairly judged by a single rule of judgement since this belongs to only one, or to neither, of those GENRES. Lyotard's suggestion is that this is not an exceptional circumstance, but 'that a universal rule of judgement between heterogeneous genres is lacking in general' (1983: xi).

The significance of the concept is twofold. First, it questions the assumptions of a consensual social or political programme, based, as in the theory of Jürgen Habermas, on a belief in communicative interaction. It therefore reinforces, in an uncompromising way, the implications of Lyotard's view (1984) of postmodern society as dependent on discrete 'language games', along with his critique of the ENLIGHTENMENT 'grand narratives' of intellectual and social progress. Second, in its attention to the 'phrases in dispute' of its subtitle, Lyotard's volume shows the continued influence of the language PARADIGM in philosophy and social thought. As Lyotard puts it, the context of his thesis is:

> The 'linguistic turn' of western philosophy (Heidegger's later works, the penetration of Anglo-American philosophies into European thought, the development of language technologies); and correlatively, the decline of universalist discourses (the metaphysical doctrines of modern times; narratives of progress, of socialism, of abundance, of knowledge).
>
> (1983: xiii)

The important question is what, in ethical and political terms, can result from this philosophy? The answer might seem to be relativism rather than consensus. What qualifies this, however, is the search for new idioms, 'new rules for forming and linking phrases' (1983: 13) to express, testify to, but not resolve the condition of the differend.

See also ALTERITY; THE EVENT; ETHICS; OTHER.

DIGITAL

This is, first of all, a technical term describing a system of coding in binaries of one and zero or on/off signals, as against an analogue system, which transmits a signal in a flow of time. An audio or video cassette uses an analogue method, meaning we have to search for the required point along it. A CD is, by contrast, digitally coded and we can select the track we want without such a search, or reorder the sequence. Computers, tablets and smart phones are digitally coded and have made possible the expanding means of communication by social media. Some technologies use both systems. Thus, an analogue watch has hands moving around a segmented clock face, while a digital watch shows only numbers. Digital broadcasting was introduced worldwide around 2010 and has made possible transmission via the INTERNET and an increase in TV channels to a potentially unlimited number in high definition.

Different social and cultural scenarios are extrapolated from the advent of increased digitalization. So-called 'smart' or 'digital cities', for example, employing an intensive concentration of advanced computer and COMMUNICATIONS technologies, are thought in one description to provide 'the means to maximise the potential of human resources, revitalise the social and economic fabric of communities, reaffirm a sense of community and create a pathway to sustainable economic development' (*City*, 7, 1997: 167).

In the realm of theory, Jean Baudrillard saw the transition from a culture founded on analogy, or the resemblance of an image to its referent (or a signifier to its signified) to a digital culture as a PARADIGM shift, bringing us to a new order of SIMULATION. 'Digitality is among us', he announced (1993: 61). Darley (2000) considers the impact of – among other technologies – computer games, theme parks and simulation rides upon the visual culture of this new era. For his part, Baudrillard sees digitalization as existing in a pervasive binary form of question/ answer and as inscribed particularly in a culture of testing most evident in political polling. Opinion polls do not engender opinion, but report answers '*design-ated* in advance' (1993: 62); they 'refer only to a simulacrum of public opinion' (1993: 65). He concludes, 'We live in a referendum mode precisely because there is no longer any referential' (1993: 62).

Landow (1992: 20–1) feels Baudrillard is mistaken in his belief that digitality involves only binary opposition and in further attributing this to new media in general (as above, not all media employ digital technology). However, Baudrillard's critique of a digitalized cultural mentality chimes with those who see an apocalyptic tone in its promotion. He quotes the linguist Thomas Sebeok as detecting a common structure in genetic and verbal codes, making it 'possible to describe both language or living systems from a unifying cybernetic point of view' in 'a complete science of the dynamics of semiosis' (1992: 59). Baudrillard finds here 'the hallucination or illusion of a world reunited under a single principle', one resting in 'biological nature', but which has less to do with genetics than 'the ideal of a social order governed by a kind of genetic code' (1992: 59). In the name of science, the biological theory of the code has assisted in the transition to 'a neo-capitalist cybernetic order' (1992: 60). His comments focus an important debate: whether digitalized communications systems produce the difference, diversity and democracy they promise, or enforce sameness and the extended life of existing power structures (see Dovey [ed] 1996).

See also CYBERNETICS; CYBERSPACE; NETWORK; POSTCAPITALISM.

DIGITAL HUMANITIES

Digital Humanities has emerged as a defined field and methodological initiative in the decades since the 1990s and especially since the advent of the personal computer and the widespread use of the INTERNET and its cognate platforms. It offers to reconfigure the Humanities' constituent subject areas by engaging scholars and students in the interdisciplinary, computational, predominantly quantitative, analysis of texts or media, written and visual, of all kinds. (For representative collections of essays in the field, see Schreibman, Siemens and Unsworth [eds] (2004, 2016); Siemens and Schreibman [eds] (2013)).

A significant concern is raised by 'the normalising pressures of digital protocols' (e.g. HMTL and XML mark-up languages) which cannot tolerate ambiguities and 'exercise rhetorical and ideological force' in the interest of formal logic (Drucker, 2009:14). As such, computational methods are at odds with a traditional Humanities sensibility attuned to complexity and undecidability. At the same time, the pragmatic advantages of digitization in bibliographic research, editorial scholarship, or the analysis of recurrences and patterns across a corpus of written or media texts, are readily apparent. Similarly, textual analysis can be enhanced and contextualized with a hitherto unheard of immediacy by the accompanying scrutiny of relevant digitized archives, bibliographic, biographical, geographical and historical, or other specialist material as determined by the elected research questions. A corollary of this development is that the production of the results may or may not take, or may take more than, a conventional printed form; a potential summed up in the title of Jeffrey T. Schnapp and Matthew Battles' *The Library Beyond the Book* (2014).

An illustration of the advent of multiple forms of output is presented by the cognate emergence of the digital novel. One such is *The New World* (2015) first issued as an ebook and subsequently a print edition, written by Chris Adrian, in collaboration with Eli Horowitz. The digital version considerably extends the print version (the difference being in one instance that of a 14-line sonnet and 53 pages of repetition). Horowitz similarly co-authored the earlier *The Silent History* (2014) with Matthew Derby, Kevin Moffett and Russell Quinn, designed specifically for use on iPad and iPhone. The story tells of how a community responded to the advent of a generation of children born without the power of speech. The story develops through oral testimonies, initially issued one per week in serialized form, and additional site-specific interactive reports by readers of the testimonials – unlocked only, however, when present at the location of the testimonials by GPS-activated devices. The format opens up possibilities of immersive, non-linear reading, the latter a feature common to internet browsing. This and other features of a digitalized existence, shifting in and out of the moment, across networks of time and space, of repetition, simultaneity and randomness are an influence, arguably, too, on otherwise non-digital novels. Examples would be Ali Smith's *How to be Both* (2014) a novel in two parts, both numbered 'One', which can be read, and are printed, in opposite orders; Mark Danielewski's *Only Revolutions* (2006), which plays havoc with linear development, typography, font, footnotes, marginalia and layout; and Tom McCarthy's self-consciously experimental, late modernist *Satin Island* (2015). McCarthy comments on how two central inspirations of the book: Kafka's systems and bureaucracy, and Stéphane Mallarmé's dream of the all-inclusive 'book-to-come', 'anticipate digital culture. The way everything, all our kinship networks, belief systems and so on are mapped and notated every time we go on Amazon or Facebook... the "book" exists, it's writing itself all the time' (*Guardian Review*, 10.10.15, 3).

See DIGITAL; HYPERTEXT; WORLD LITERATURE.

DISAVOWAL

Used by Sigmund Freud (1856–1939) in association with the related concept of 'negation' to describe a patient's simultaneous affirmation and denial of a repressed experience or DESIRE. The concept has been of interest to feminists in accounting for the way women are brought to negotiate with the structures of SEXUALITY in patriarchal society. Elsewhere, it has been taken up by Homi Bhabha (1994) in conjunction with Freud's concept of FETISHISM to explain the nature of stereotyping in colonial and racist DISCOURSE. Fetishism supplies a substitute for the object of desire. It is founded, says Freud, on the revelation of the mother's lack of a penis; an experience that threatens the male child with the prospect of castration. A fetishized object acknowledges this loss or lack while allaying the fear and anxiety associated with it, since the object of desire is replaced by its selected, and more controllable, inanimate substitute. The fetish object masks absence or loss and indeed provides a compensatory pleasure. Fetishism therefore shares an ambiguous structure of affirmation and denial with disavowal. Bhabha sees this at work in the use of the colonial stereotype, since this too provides a way of acknowledging and denying DIFFERENCE. The stereotype distances and familiarizes the OTHER, expressing fear and contempt at the strangeness of the other, but normalizing this difference at the same time. Bhabha writes:

> The fetish or stereotype gives access to an 'identity' which is predicated as much on mastery and pleasure as it is on anxiety and defence, for it is a form of multiple and contradictory belief in its recognition of difference and disavowal of it.

> (1994: 75)

See also GAZE; POSTCOLONIALISM; PSYCHOANALYSIS.

DISCOURSE

A term which had its earliest uses in linguistics and literary study but which, by extension, and through the influence of developments in SEMIOTICS and POSTSTRUCTURALISM, and the work of Michel Foucault in particular, has come to have a wide application across the Humanities. In linguistics, discourse is used to refer to utterances beyond the unit of the sentence and to passages of dialogue. In literary study, the term was used in American New Criticism to distinguish between literary GENRES, and to affirm the superiority of 'poetic discourse' and an associated set of AESTHETIC and social VALUES. STRUCTURALISM, which challenged the evaluative assumptions of this PARADIGM at the same time as it influenced many other fields, argued that meaning or signification is created in and through language. The concept of discourse in its later uses derived from this source, but with a more precise and contextualizing force than in its previous structuralist uses.

Discourse is now generally used to designate the forms of REPRESENTATION, conventions and habits of language-use producing specific fields of culturally and historically located meanings. Michel Foucault's early writings ('The order of discourse', 1971, in Young [ed] 1981; *The Archaeology of Knowledge,* 1972) were especially influential in this. Foucault's work gave the terms 'discursive practices' and 'discursive formation' to the analysis of the kinds of statement associated with particular institutions and their ways of establishing orders of truth, or what is accepted as 'reality' in a given society. An established 'discursive formation' is in fact defined by the contradictory discourses it contains, and this tolerance Foucault understands as a sign of stability rather than – as it would be understood in MARXISM, for example – of conflict and potential change. Thus characterized, a given 'discursive formation' will give definition to a particular historical moment or ÉPISTÈME. 'Discursive formations' do nevertheless display a hierarchical arrangement and are understood as reinforcing certain already-established identities or subjectivities (in matters of SEXUALITY, status or CLASS, for example). These DOMINANT discourses are understood as in turn reinforced by existing systems of law, education and the media. Evidently, this is a generally pessimistic scenario, although some recognition is given to the role individuals and pressures within institutions themselves may have in modifying a pattern of dominant meanings.

The implication of Foucault's work is that members of a society, including its INTELLECTUALS, are implicated in discourse and in the discursive regimes or systems of POWER and regulation that give them their livelihoods and definition. There is no place to stand outside such systems. At the same time, since discourse and power are anonymous and without centre or single AGENCY, the political role of the critical intellectual is unclear. Foucault's own work offers a model of the intellectual as historian of modes of thought – as a self-effacing cultural analyst rather than prophet, judge or polemicist. This style of work has been influential upon NEW HISTORICISM. Nevertheless, Foucault's studies of how forms of knowledge come about, and come to govern truth and identities, can be seen as fundamentally questioning. In this guise, accompanied by the concepts of IDEOLOGY and HEGEMONY, his theory has been given a more interventionist turn in CULTURAL MATERIALISM, and in specific arguments on penal reform, healthcare and sexuality.

In its general use, the term discourse has gained a more dispersed currency than the above might suggest. Both in academic work and elsewhere, it can be used variously to denote the modes of thought and vocabularies characterizing institutions, domains of CULTURE or cultural practices (law, medicine, the BBC, information technology, cinema, *haute couture,* skateboarding, wine tasting); an intellectual mode or tendency (PSYCHOANALYSIS, POSTSTRUCTURALISM, POSTMODERNISM); to distinguish different fields of study (Theory, Philosophy, Sociology, Literary, Film or Media Study); or to identify the language of different social groups or occasions (the language of management and workers, interviews, weddings, a cup final).

See also ARCHAEOLOGY; DIALOGICS; MATERIALISM; QUEER THEORY.

DISPOSITIF

A term employed by the French philosopher Michel Foucault to name the apparatuses of POWER that regulate a society. Foucault employs the term in one instance when reflecting on the identity and role of 'the plebs' (the 'people', generally defined) who are the 'the permanent, ever silent target for apparatuses of power' (1980a: 137). The plebs, he says, are less 'a real sociological entity' than an inverse social energy. There is a diverse 'plebeian quality or aspect' in individuals and across social classes. This does not stand outside relations of power, but reveals power's limit, or other side: it is 'that which responds to every advance of power by a movement of disengagement. Hence it forms the motivation for every new development of networks of power' (1980a: 138). The term *dispositif* therefore carries the sense of how the apparatus or NETWORKS of power respond to this disengagement at a given LOCAL, historical moment, obviously so as to accommodate this reaction and renew or strengthen their hold.

Joseph Rouse usefully understands *dispositifs* as the 'alignments' of the heterogeneous agents and sources that, in Foucault's account, operate or 'dispose' power. These include 'not just agents but also the instruments of power (buildings, documents, tools, etc.) and the practices and rituals through which it is deployed' (1994: 106).

See also DISCOURSE; IDEOLOGY.

DISSEMINATION

A term used by Jacques Derrida and the title of his volume *Dissemination* (1981b). It refers to the play of meanings beyond a fixed point of origin or conceptual reductionism, and, like other cognate terms in the vocabulary of DECONSTRUCTION (see TRACE and DIFFERENCE/*DIFFÉRANCE*), confirms the lack of any pure identity or presence in language. Derrida's usage exploits the metaphor of the sowing of seeds (or of 'semes' – the basic unit of meaning identified by linguistics). Like seeds, signifiers are cast abroad, never to settle in one place of definitive meaning. The essay 'La dissémination', which closes the above volume, associates this dispersal of meaning particularly with 'literary' discourse in a discussion of the experimental novel, *Nombres,* by Philippe Sollers, a leading member of the *Tel Quel* group of French left intellectuals.

The postcolonial theorist and critic, Homi Bhabha (1994) puns further on Derrida's term in his coinage 'DissemiNation', used by him to describe the provisional commingling or 'gathering' of common experiences shaping the life of the contemporary migrant. The term evokes, says Bhabha, 'the scattering of the people that in other times and in other places, in the nations of others, becomes a time of gathering' (1994: 139).

DISTANTIATION

Used by the French Marxist philosopher, Louis Althusser (1918–1990) in his discussion of art's relation to IDEOLOGY in a sense closely related to the idea of ESTRANGEMENT or DEFAMILIARIZATION. Both terms describe the way art (sometimes extended to intellectual and other cultural practices) produces a critical distance upon conventional perceptions or attitudes and ideologies. Althusser, however, sees art as itself 'bathed' in ideology. The critical distance it possesses will therefore necessarily be an 'internal' distance upon the ideology that informs and directs it. Balzac and Solzhenitsyn, he writes:

> give us a 'view' of the ideology to which their work alludes and with which it is constantly fed, a view which presupposes a retreat, an *internal distantiation* from the very ideology from which their novels emerged. They make us 'perceive' (but not know) in some sense *from the inside,* by an *internal distance,* the very ideology in which they are held.
>
> (1971b: 204)

The 'knowledge' of ideology (if this is an appropriate term), which art in this way provides, will be of a different kind from the knowledge provided by 'science'; a name in effect, in Althusser, for Marxism. Althusser suggests that art and science differ 'in the *specific form* in which they give us the same object... art in the form of "seeing" and "perceiving" or "feeling", science in the form of *knowledge* (in the strict sense, by concepts)' (1971b: 205). However, given the status of Marxism in his writings, it is difficult to avoid the implication that Marxism is possessed of a greater distance upon ideology, that it can give us a knowledge of ideology from the outside.

Althusser's ideas were further developed in theory and literary analysis by Pierre Macherey (1978) and Terry Eagleton (1976).

See also ALIENATION EFFECT; IDEOLOGY CRITIQUE; RELATIVE AUTONOMY.

DISTINCTION

A term developed by the French sociologist of culture Pierre Bourdieu (1930–2002) and adopted as the title of his study *Distinction: A Social Critique of the Judgement of Taste* (1984). The force of Bourdieu's use of the term lies in his having appropriated and extended a concept conventionally used to distinguish high from MASS, or everyday, CULTURE. An expression of cultivated AESTHETIC taste limited to the world of the fine arts confers social distinction or status upon its bearer and exerts SYMBOLIC VIOLENCE upon those without it. In another of Bourdieu's leading concepts, TASTE is a form of CULTURAL CAPITAL whose implicit and compounded aesthetic and social hierarchies help legitimize relations of economic power in society. 'Taste classifies and it classifies the classifier', as Bourdieu puts it (1984: 6).

Bourdieu therefore proposes that we view 'distinction' as operating across all social activity:

> The science of taste and of cultural consumption begins with a transgression that is in no way aesthetic: it has to abolish the sacred frontier which makes legitimate culture a separate universe, in order to discover the intelligible relations which unite apparently incommensurable 'choices', such as preferences in music and food, painting and sport, literature and hairstyle.
>
> (1984: 6)

Bourdieu's evidence of such 'choices' is assembled from French society and is understood to reveal the subtle differentials primarily of social CLASS. In principle, the concept can clearly be extended to other cultures, however, as well as potentially to the markers of GENDER (see Moi 1991) and ETHNICITY.

See also HABITUS.

DOMINANT/RESIDUAL/EMERGENT

A distinction introduced by Raymond Williams (1977) in a critique of more generalizing epochal analyses of history and in a refinement of the theory of HEGEMONY associated with Antonio Gramsci. Williams' terms bring a dynamic and differential model to conceptions of the social order and cultural change. Thus, traditional and newer cultural tendencies are seen to coexist as residual traces or emergent signs within a given dominant order. Both can also run counter to the existing order, presenting an 'alternative' or 'oppositional' position in relation to it. The 'alternative' does not pose a challenge and is tolerated or incorporated, while the 'oppositional' (residual or emergent) urges radical change – of a conservative or progressive kind – which would unseat a prevailing orthodoxy. The hippies of the 1960s who 'dropped out' of mainstream American or western CULTURE, or notions of a rural idyll, would be examples of the first, as would some religious cults, whereas a militant political faction, whether of the left or right, would be examples of the latter. In addition, says Williams, there are those elements in a culture that are 'archaic, and wholly recognised as an element of the past' and the 'merely novel' (1977: 122, 123). He suggests, too, that we need to recognize the 'pre-emergent... active and pressing but not yet fully articulated' (1977: 126), which echoes his related concept of 'STRUCTURES OF FEELING'.

The most important implication of Williams' distinction for literary and cultural analysis is that these different tendencies are seen to exist within a single FORMATION or text. This is a valuable corrective to the reductive analysis, which would see certain cultural forms – organized religion or blockbuster films, for example – as unqualified expressions of dominant IDEOLOGY (of official morality, capitalist values, PATRIARCHY or racism), and see others as expressions of unalloyed progressive radicalism. The church, for example, is a varied and conflicted organization whose highlighting of poverty and inequality vies with a defence of traditional family values and coexists with less active, 'archaic' elements. Even highly commercial mainstream cultural texts have to, on a regular basis, acknowledge eccentric or deviant behaviours if only to reaffirm normative VALUES. Hence, in mainstream cinema and TV, the common opposition of the figures of the action hero and intellectual, or career woman, wife, mother and homemaker, and of plot lines contrasting normative heterosexual romance with iconoclastic SEXUALITY. Williams's terms give us a vocabulary for these contrasts, internal juxtapositions and uneasy tensions in literary texts and in MASS or other cultural forms, as these re-enact and debate the contradictions and changes in society as a whole.

In a broader context, this distinction impinges on conceptions of history and ideology, and has some problematic implications for the latter. Most often, ideology has been associated with the dominant ideology of a CLASS, group, nation or culture. If alternative and oppositional positions (in FEMINISM or socialism, for example) are also to be understood as 'ideologies', the term is set to include any association of ideas and values. It begins to appear as if there can be no position that is free of ideology. Nor, if everything is ideological, can this term be defined, as is usual with definitions, against what it is not. It is noticeable that Williams himself avoids the term 'ideology', preferring instead to speak of 'elements', 'practices' or 'cultures'.

See also INCORPORATION.

DOUBLE-CONSCIOUSNESS

See HYBRIDITY.

DREAMWORK

The term employed in PSYCHOANALYSIS to describe the transformation of the raw material of the UNCONSCIOUS, childhood or recent memories, including the previous day's events, into the 'manifest content' of dreams. The mechanisms by which this operation is achieved include CONDENSATION AND DISPLACEMENT, secondary revision which gives the dream some consistency and coherence, and the rendering of this in primarily visual images. The resulting 'manifest content' is fleeting and elliptical, and in an indirect and distorted relationship to its 'latent content'. The latter can only be discovered, says Freud, through interpretation (1974b [1900]). The meaning of the dream resides less at this 'deeper' level, however, than in the processes of transformation – the 'work' of the dream – by which its content finds form and expression.

See also FANTASY.

ECOCRITICISM

The term 'ecocriticism' is reported as first appearing in William Ruekeet's 1978 paper 'Literature and ecology: an experiment in ecocriticism'. It was promoted later, especially by Cheryll Glotfelty. Her co-edited *The Ecocriticism Reader* (1996) defines ecocriticism as taking 'an earth-centered approach to literary studies' (xviii). It asks how literary works represent NATURE, how 'science itself is open to literary analysis' and seeks 'cross-fertilization between literary studies and environmental discourse' (xix).

Lawrence Buell (2005) identifies two phases in ecocriticism: the first associated with nature writing, poetry and wilderness fiction; the second, described as 'social ecocriticism', concerned with issues of environmental justice and with urban and degraded landscapes. Examples of this approach would include Buell's own 'environmentally oriented study of literature' (Buell 2005) and the notable early example in the UK of Richard Mabey's *The Unofficial Countryside* (1973). Other relevant recent examples explore 'edge cities', shopping and entertainment developments outside former city boundaries (Garreau, 1992; Farley and Symonds, 2012) and 'edgelands', the unkempt no-man's land or forgotten natural life at the borders of the urban. Much of Patrick Keiller's film work and Iain Sinclair's writing belong to these same categories.

A broader distinction can also be drawn between eco*criticism*, concerned with literary works and nature writing, and the science and agenda of ecology where the latter has taken the public form of environmental movements such as Greenpeace, the Green Party, Gaia, the World Wildlife Organization, Friends of the Earth, the Animal Liberation Front and other libertarian and anti-capitalist networks.

Arguably, it is this latter work which has given ecocriticism in the academy its contemporary impetus. But inspiration also derives from the longer tradition of 'ecological' thinking, scientific advance and agitation on the use of the world's resources, on behalf of the environment, plant and animal life from figures such as Jean-Jacques Rousseau, Adam Smith and Thomas Malthus in the eighteenth century, the English Romantic poets, the American transcendentalists, the Victorian sages John Ruskin and William Morris, as well – of course –as Charles Darwin. An innovative landmark in this tradition in the twentieth century was Rachel Carson's *Silent Spring* (1962), an exposé of the toxic effects, especially on bird-life, of pesticides used in American agriculture. Carson's study also anticipates the hybrid genre of journal, autobiography and polemic which has come to characterize the 'new nature writing' and of which the multi-prize winning *H is for Hawk* (2014) by Helen Macdonald is a conspicuous recent example. (See also the writings of Kathleen Jamie, Robert Macfarlane and *Granta* 102, 2008). For a critique of such writings as personal stories, travel books or literary criticism rather than campaigning Environmental Studies, see Cocker 2015, and for a response, Macfarlane, 2015a.

The theoretical crux of ecocriticism lies in the perceived relation between 'CULTURE' and 'NATURE'; the first commonly designated as the domain of the 'human', classically accorded the faculty of reason, and as such opposed to 'animal', and an unthinking inert nature. This hierarchical understanding is further maintained by combinations of political, economic or ideological control over land, material resources, and technologies accruing to governments, corporations or individuals. What then comes into view is a history of the fate of nature in the successive eras of industrial CAPITALISM, market economies, agribusiness and globalization. And what, in this history, speaks for nature are the findings of ecological science, personal testimony, ethical protest and action, but also, in their own terms, the arts, notably landscape painting, film, photography and literature.

It is this last that ecocriticism principally draws attention to. Garrard's (2012) thoughtful survey of the field shows how ecocriticism can bring a historicizing and culturally aware literary critical perspective to diverse materials by examining the rhetorical strategies or tropes they employ: among them the tropes of pastoral, wilderness and apocalypse. We find too how these change over time and can merge one with the other.

Thus, the strength and originality of the Romantic pastoral has arguably declined historically into an all-too-easy convention, and while a notion of the healing solace of nature away from the hurly-burly of daily life remains firmly in place, it falls well below the agenda of the Greens or social ecocriticism. At points, too, the pastoral has merged with depictions of wild nature or the wilderness. One such example is presented by the mythology of the American west, familiar from literature and film, where the relation between culture and nature is played out in a 'pre-civilized', lawless realm between a normative white culture and the 'other' represented by the demonized native American or 'Indian' and an associated hostile landscape. What is of interest to ecocriticism is how these standard polarities are rendered problematic or internally critiqued. A continuing point of reference in this respect, as told in the book and film *Into the Wild* (1996, 2007) is Christopher John McCandless's lone pursuit of the wild places of America which took him, without proper preparation or a map, to Alaska and death by starvation.

Apocalyptic narratives, Garrard's third major trope, commonly pitch any hope of a new life in the future, in the midst of warnings against the ills or evils of present existence. To this belong utopian and dystopian narratives, of which More's *Utopia*, William Morris's *New from Nowhere* and Orwell's *1984* are touchstones, and all of which also include some positively conceived pastoral aspect. Late capitalist modernity has generated many apocalyptic scenarios, including the effects of global warming. Science or future fiction in literature, film and television have dramatized these issues in projections of future or other worlds where the advent of floods, famine, pollution, mass infection and so on are acted out and where (changed) relations between the human and technology – or the alien other and the natural or animal life – may be reimagined. In these worlds, galleries of robots, cyborgs, replicants, monstrous plants and animals in devastated landscapes challenge normative definitions of the human. As above, ecocriticism maintains an interest precisely in the deformations and reworkings of received concepts of the human, culture and nature.

See also ANIMAL STUDIES; CYBORG; POSTHUMAN.

ECOLOGY

Ecology derives from the Greek *oikos,* signifying the unity of NATURE (including human, animal and plant life) and science. Arguably, environmentalist and ecological movements are concerned to make good this original meaning in a condition of harmony and equivalence when nature in its different senses will be free of the alienation and exploitation wrought by the abuse of science and technology. At the same time, as Raymond Williams has said, ecological proposals are invariably proposals about different 'kinds of society' (1980a: 71). They can, therefore, occupy a wide spectrum of political positions and perspectives, whether this means looking to an ideal past or transformed future society. In the process, they accordingly set themselves against the anti-ecological interests governing the present.

We think of the ecological movement as in this way shaping a distinctly contemporary agenda, and certainly there has been increased public awareness during the 1990s and 2000s of issues such as acid rain, pollution, pesticides in the food chain, the extinction of species and, above all, global warming. Many (of otherwise different ages, social classes and political persuasions) have engaged in campaigns on these issues as well as others, such as road-building, the use of GM crops and animal rights. The environmentalist or ecology movement comes, therefore, to represent the kind of local or single-issue politics described in more theoretical contexts as belonging to the postmodern rather than the modern era (see POSTMODERNISM).

There has, however, been a long history of ecological thinking and agitation on behalf of the environment and animal or plant life. French Enlightenment philosophers, English Romantic poets and American transcendentalists have joined natural philosophers, geologists, botanists and social thinkers – including, most notably, Charles Darwin – in drawing attention to the integrity and complexity, as well as the ecological and spiritual benefits, of natural life. The twentieth century drew on and developed the arguments of these earlier figures in response to the increasingly global damage effected by advanced capitalist societies. Rachel Carson's *Silent Spring* (1962) was a key popular example, but arguably the more recent period has, as a matter of principle, seen the emergence of democratically organized groups, rather than of celebrated leaders or foundation textbooks. A leading inspiration in this respect was the sustained demonstration by women at Greenham Common in the 1970s against the stationing of cruise missiles in the UK. Other groups, once again across a spectrum of ideologies and tactics, have included Greenpeace, formed in 1971; the Green Party, formed in Germany in 1980; Gaia; the Animal Liberation Movement; and looser networks embracing 'ecofeminism' and sections of the 'anti-capitalist movement'.

Inspiration has also come from more individual initiatives, such as the proposal for 'rewilding' Britain (i.e. reintroducing wolves, the lynx, wild boar, the goshawk and eagle owl among other disappeared creatures). This has been associated notably with the eco-campaigner and journalist George Monbiot (2014), although July 2015 saw the formal launch of a national movement. A further initiative has been to restore the forgotten regional terminology for distinct natural features inaugurated by the landscape writer, walker and academic, Robert Macfarlane (2015b). Macfarlane gives as examples of dozens of such words, the Sussex 'smeuse', the gap made by a small animal in the base of a hedgerow; the Northamptonshire 'crizzle', a verb for the freezing of open water; and the Devon term 'zawn' for a chasm made by waves smashing against a sea cliff. The National Trust has, in response, introduced a campaign to restore this forgotten vocabulary to young people.

This entire tradition shares a disenchantment with the priorities of a society that seeks to master nature in the interests of increased growth, expanded markets and profit. It also shares, however, the difficulties of an appeal, which is prone to ESSENTIALISM (the nostalgic assumption of a pre-cultural origin in nature), to INCORPORATION by advertising and marketers, and the vested interests of those in POWER. Global corporations have shown themselves adept at adopting a green agenda, to the point of developing alternative sources of power, in the interests of maintaining or expanding market share. Governments, too, move slowly, or resist change, or backtrack on commitments to low carbon emissions or renewable sources of energy. In the international scene, the Paris Climate Change Conference of world nations, November/December 2015 agreed to avoid more than the critical figure of 2° C of warming above pre-industrial levels. This is to come into force in 2020. Meanwhile, several nations have conspicuously transgressed this agreement.

A fragmented project of disparate aims has, in these circumstances, become characteristic and the not-surprising complaint is that this has been too limited: 'the globalisation of corporate environmentalism', argued Neil Smith, requires 'a global response' (1996: 46). For an 'ecosocialist' such as David Harvey, conscious of the connections across ecological, economic and political orders, ecological crisis means discovering a language and strategy that will 'make radical ecology truly radical' (1996: 175). Meanwhile, the effects of climate change have been envisioned and debated in novels and film, as well as environmental campaigns, scientific papers and journalistic commentary. Notable examples have been, amongst novels: J.G. Ballard's, post-apocalypse novels, including *The Drought* (1965) and *The Drowned World* (1962), Ian McEwan's *Solar* (2011), Barbara Kingsolver's *Flight Behavior* (2012) and Margaret Atwood's trilogy: *Oryx and Crake* (2003), *The Year of the Flood* (2009) and *MaddAddam* (2013), while recent films have included *The Day After Tomorrow* (2004), *The Age of Stupid* (2009) and *The Colony* (2013). See also the critical study by Adam Trexler, *Anthropocene Fictions* (2015).

See also ANTHROPOCENE; ECOCRITICISM; GLOBALIZATION; UTOPIA.

ÉCRITURE/WRITING

An attention to *écriture* or 'writing' as a critical concept has different sources and points of reference, all in the first instance in French theory. In the major examples, the key theorists were associated with the journal *Tel Quel*, which in 1967 announced that 'a comprehensive theory... about the practice of writing cries out for elaboration'. Roland Barthes had already inaugurated such a theory in his *Writing Degree Zero* (1967 [1953]). Here, Barthes traced the simultaneous construction and demise of the concept of 'Literature' in French nineteenth-century writing in an early example of the later distinction he was to make between the closed and finished 'work' and the open 'text'. 'Writing' embraced both, but tended to be associated with the process of TEXTUALITY rather than the perfected object. As such, Barthes' study was an early contribution to a scaling down of the status of 'Literature'; a move continued in arguments made, among others, by Raymond Williams (1977), which critiqued the ideological privilege accruing to a selective literary tradition or CANON. Williams later pointedly titled a collection of essays *Writing in Society* (1984). This rethinking has had a wide impact on criticism and education, and can be seen in expanded literary syllabuses, in courses on a range of 'canonic' and POPULAR writing and on writing (including fiction, autobiography, diaries) by women.

The second significant use of the term appears in Jacques Derrida's critique (1976 [1967]) of the structural linguistics of Ferdinand de Saussure (see STRUCTURALISM). Derrida demonstrates how Saussure prioritizes speech over writing and understands the second as the mere execution of a prior spoken utterance. Speech is valorized for its 'presence' and authenticity in a hierarchy that, says Derrida, betrays a 'metaphysics of presence' typical of western philosophy. He shows how, in fact, speech bears the marks of writing. The effect, in a double move typical of his deconstructive procedure, is not simply to invert the original hierarchy but to overturn the very idea and dependency on hierarchy. It is not that writing is prior to speech, but that there is only 'writing'. In a related argument, following Freud, Derrida (1978) proposes the idea of an 'archi-writing'. Freud suggested that the wax slab of a child's 'magical writing pad', which takes the imprint of marks through transparent covering sheets, presents an analogy for the UNCONSCIOUS. Derrida wished to free this idea of the assumption of an underlying presence or LOGOCENTRICISM. Thus, an 'archi-writing' or 'archi-trace' is not an indelible original script, but, as with the marks on the writing pad, is there and not there, written and erased, present and absent. Derrida writes, 'It is this constitution of the present, as an "originary" and irreducibly nonsimple (and therefore *stricto sensu* nonoriginary) synthesis of marks or traces of retentions and protentions… that I propose to call archi-writing, archi-trace, or *différance*' (Kamuf [ed] 1991:66).

See also *ÉCRITURE FÉMININE*; TRACE.

ÉCRITURE FÉMININE

A coinage derived from the French journal *Psychanalyse et Politique,* and the feminist critics and writers, Hélène Cixous and Luce Irigaray in the 1970s. By this, they meant to name a 'feminine writing' that would challenge the discourse of the SYMBOLIC order in a counter-language appropriate to feminine DESIRE and DIFFERENCE. To this end, the theory drew upon the writings principally of Jacques Lacan and Jacques Derrida – although Cixous protests that since theory is PHALLOCENTRIC, *écriture féminine* will, by definition, escape theorization. The term 'feminine' here is somewhat ambiguous. It has the sense first of 'female', since the source of this writing lies, in Irigaray's view, in the biological female BODY and, second of 'feminist', since it is evidently antagonistic to the operations of PATRIARCHY inscribed in conventional writing. It therefore suggests, by turns, an essentialist and social-constructionist understanding of woman's IDENTITY. In reply, some see the body in the frequently evoked notion of 'writing the body' as metaphorical and polemical rather than anatomical. (Julia Kristeva's analogous concept of the SEMIOTIC, it should be noted, is not limited to women writers.)

In terms of its formal practice, *écriture féminine* would be experimental, subversive, spirited and playful, and excite something like the experience of *JOUISSANCE*. Cixous's own prose and drama (see Shiach 1991) might be its best, most immediate example, although earlier texts by other writers are open to a reading in these terms. The concept does raise a number of fraught questions, however: whether language, and literary language in particular, is GENDERED in any absolute or regular way; whether there can be a new language that departs entirely from the old; and whether a contemporary AVANT-GARDE, be it feminist or otherwise, can, on its own, have any significant political effect.

See also FEMINISM; INTERTEXTUALITY; SEXUAL DIFFERENCE.

ELITE

Used to describe both 'high culture' and a social, political or intellectual group or association. The case for an elite or minority CULTURE is traditionally made on the basis of the moral seriousness and AESTHETIC merit of a selected CANON of texts. This is thought to embody the qualities of a particular national culture, or to express universal artistic and civilized values. When the emphasis is upon formal experimentation in such works, then an elite culture might be equated with the AVANT-GARDE. This is most likely to be opposed to canonic or traditional art forms. An elite culture therefore serves as a measure of standards of excellence, or of art's true nature. Both seek a radical effect: the first in a conservative and the second in a progressive direction. However, elite culture can only acquire either function first, in a comparison with what it is not, i.e. POPULAR or MASS culture or traditional art, and second, through the adjudications and influence of an elite group of specialists able to exercise the appropriate discriminating judgement.

Examples of such social elites include, within English literary culture, S.T. Coleridge's 'clerisy', Matthew Arnold's 'remnant' and the group organized around the journal *Scrutiny,* edited from 1932 to 1953 by F.R. and Queenie Leavis. These are radical conservative elites. In political culture, the Party, particularly the Communist Party in the role ascribed to it by Lenin, has assumed the progressive role of an avant-garde elite.

In contemporary societies, it is said that distinctions between elite and high and popular culture have broken down (see POSTMODERNISM). This has provoked a reaction from the defenders of an elite canon (Bloom 1995). The advocates of 'political correctness', though opposed to the canon as the embodiment of male, white, western values, also aim in the manner of elites to give a lead and to set standards by which certain texts, attitudes and behaviours can be approved and others excluded. Social elites are, however, generally difficult to identify in contemporary societies. Most obviously, they comprise personalities from the worlds of fashion, pop music, media, sport or European royalty, united around wealth and lifestyle. Some figures from these ranks might also be recruited by a political or other organization in the form of social gatherings, think-tanks and task forces. Such groups may include writers, performers, media professionals and academics recruited as advisers from the fields of, for example, education, social policy or economics. Businessmen, also, are particularly key members of contemporary elites and, along with selected academics, are probably the most influential members of such groups. Social and cultural theorists are rarely so close to mainstream political power, though they may belong to pressure groups of one sort or another, and approximate therefore to a loose avant-garde. Academic life also produces its own internal, highly paid and mobile elites, as do other professions.

See also ESTABLISHMENT; INTELLECTUALS; PUBLIC SPHERE.

ENLIGHTENMENT

A philosophical and cultural movement begun in seventeenth-century English philosophy, but developed throughout Europe in the eighteenth century, and an immediate influence upon the American and French Revolutions. Enlightenment doctrine was consequently associated with a range of thinkers, among them John Locke, Tom Paine, David Hume, Denis Diderot, Voltaire, Goethe and Lessing. Its principal belief was in the power and authority of reason in intellectual and practical life, and a number of allied convictions stemmed from this: in man's (*sic*) goodness and perfectibility, in scientific and social progress, and tolerance and equality before the law. Its influence can be associated with the rise of the bourgeoisie and with improvements in print technology. The latter helped circulate key ideas, but also inspired the characteristic Enlightenment aim of the French encyclopaedists to compile a summation of human learning and its practical application in one publication (an eventual 17 volumes, with 11 of supplementary technical illustration assembled by Diderot and Jean D'Alembert in 1772).

The Enlightenment rejected the irrational and demoted the realms of feeling and the imagination, and there have been any number of reactions to this emphasis, from the Romantics to its wholesale rejection by Friedrich Nietzsche. The latter has, in turn, helped inspire a scepticism within POSTSTRUCTURALISM and POSTMODERNISM towards the claims of reason and the credibility of any supposed universal truths, such as equality and progress. Postcolonial criticism, in particular, has pointed to how these ideals are founded on a selective European model and thus bear the legacy of colonialism (see EUROCENTRICISM). On another front, from within MARXISM, it has been argued that contemporary MASS societies have distorted Enlightenment reason into the corrupted and impoverished form of 'instrumental reason' or rationalization (Adorno and Horkheimer 1979).

Contemporary debate can be examined in essays by Michel Foucault (1986a) and Jürgen Habermas (1992b). Habermas terms Foucault a 'neo-conservative' and opponent of reason (1992a: 137). However, it would be more accurate to say that Foucault endorses neither reason nor unreason. He similarly refuses the 'blackmail' of being for or against the Enlightenment, which he sees as neither an epoch nor body of doctrine, but an 'attitude' or critical consciousness. Foucault understands our connection with the Enlightenment as 'the permanent reactivation of an attitude – that is, of a philosophical ethos that could be described as a permanent critique of our historical era' (1986a: 42). Habermas, working within the tradition of the Frankfurt School of CRITICAL THEORY, and indebted to Adorno and Horkheimer, laments the contemporary fragmentation of AESTHETIC, ethical and political realms. The unified Enlightenment or 'modern project' can be rearticulated, he believes, through an intersubjective 'communicative reason', underpinned by a commitment to the goals of truth, right and sincerity.

See also FOUNDATIONALISM; INTELLECTUALS; LEGITIMATION; PUBLIC SPHERE.

ÉNONCÉ/ÉNONCIATION

Umberto Eco (1979b) usefully translates these French terms as 'sentence' and 'utterance'. This captures the force of the original distinction as employed in French STRUCTURALISM and SEMIOLOGY between a statement (what is 'enounced') and the act of making a statement (in English, an 'enunciation'). As glossed by Stephen Heath, the translator of essays by Roland Barthes, the first term 'signifies what is uttered (the statement or proposition), the second signifies the act of uttering (the act of speech, writing or whatever by which the statement is stated, the proposition proposed)' (Barthes 1977b: 8). Heath also draws attention to an important related distinction between the *sujet de l'énoncé* and the *sujet de l'énonciation* (the SUBJECT of the statement or sentence, and the subject who makes the statement). That these are not identical is plain when we make statements about ourselves: 'I was in France last year' is a statement made at a different time and place from the position of the 'I' being referred to (the subject of the *énoncé*). In Stephen Heath's example, 'In the utterance "I am lying"… it is evident that the subject of the proposition is not one with the subject of the enunciation of the proposition – the "I" cannot lie on both planes at once' (1977b: 8). This distinction confirms the view elsewhere in structuralist, poststructuralist and psychoanalytic thought that the human subject is split or 'decentred'.

See also DISCOURSE; POSTSTRUCTURALISM.

ÉPISTÈME

A term introduced by Michel Foucault (1970). It denotes a historical epoch or, more narrowly, an intellectual era, and the prevailing epistemology (ways of knowing) and criteria that characterize and give this era systematic form. In *The Order of Things* (1970), Foucault employs the term to describe the difference between the classical and modern order. The second, he argues, is founded on humanist assumptions, centred upon 'Man', which inform and are reinforced by the new sciences of Psychology, Sociology and the study of literature and MYTH emerging in this period. Most importantly, the humanist *épistème* shared by this ensemble of sciences governs what counts as knowledge or truth.

Foucault's concept is more specific than descriptions of the 'spirit' of an age, but more totalizing than uses of the term IDEOLOGY with which it is sometimes thought to have affinities. An *épistème* describes the regularities in forms of knowledge over a whole epoch (the 'classical' or 'modern', for example), whereas a description such as 'bourgeois ideology' names the DOMINANT ideology of a specifically capitalist social and economic order. Nor does the concept of *épistème,* so defined, suggest what internal dynamic – intellectual or otherwise – prompts a change from one epoch to another.

See also CONJUNCTURE; DISCOURSE; PARADIGM.

ESSENTIALISM

A term describing the assumption that human beings, objects or texts possess underlying essences that define their 'true nature'. An 'essence' is fixed and unchanging, but has a double existence: as both the inherent or innate property of an individual object or being, and the abstract, external essence governing the type to which all examples conform. From Aristotle onwards, there has been a long debate in European philosophy on the very existence of essences, their relation to appearances or natural forms, and the accessibility of this essence to human knowledge or perception. A common recourse – to a secular age, a last resort – has been the idea of the creator in whom the essence and knowledge of all things are seen to reside. The most thoroughgoing CRITIQUE of this tradition has been made by Jacques Derrida, who argues that western philosophy as a whole is founded on a 'metaphysics of presence' – that is to say, upon a belief in a transcendent first cause or point of pure origin. All such thought, he argues, is 'centred' upon 'an invariable presence... (essence, existence, substance, subject)... transcendentality, consciousness, God, man and so forth' (1978: 280). Derrida's method of DECONSTRUCTION has inspired a wide critique of the binary oppositions that invest a first term in a series – such as speech/writing, nature/culture, man/woman, God/human, the real/representation – with the authority of a governing fixed point.

In another – at some points connected – direction, essentialist versus social-constructionist arguments have characterized debates in FEMINISM, and discussions of GENDER and SEXUALITY. Feminists have appealed to an essential 'female' nature or experience in the analysis of literary and cultural texts (see GYNOCRITICISM), in arguments about pornography and violence against women. Men in such arguments are presented as essentially impersonal, abstract, aggressive, power-seeking and competitive. Women, conversely, as Lynne Segal puts it, are seen as 'more nurturant, maternal, co-operative and peaceful' (1987: ix). Segal sees this as a strong tendency in feminism of the 1980s, and responds from an alternative socialist-feminist perspective that emphasizes DIFFERENCE, change and a necessary alertness, from men and women, to the 'dangers of such essentialist thinking' (1987: xii).

Generally, it would seem that the social-constructionist arguments (by way of alignments with materialist or historicizing thought, debates with PSYCHOANALYSIS, deconstruction or POSTMODERNISM) have held sway: that indeed the BODY itself, so often invoked in forms of biological essentialism as the unqualified determinant of man or woman's NATURE, is understood as materially shaped by social ideologies and personal histories. Postmodernism, in particular, has impressed upon us that there is 'only culture' and that what counts as 'nature' is a variable perception from within CULTURE.

However, if essentialist arguments are thought to have little credibility in current academic life, they have a strong and vocal presence outside it: in popular notions of what is natural in boys and girls, as well as men and women, and in stereotypes of ethnic and racial types. The POPULAR appeal to family values is driven by an attempt to return men, women and children to their true 'natural' state, which is then deemed good for 'society'. Conservative 'men's groups', of the 1990s, meanwhile, renewed essentialist arguments in the invocation of a lost masculine essence: as, for example, in the idea of the natural, but now repressed, 'wild man' of Robert Bly's influential *Iron John: A Book About Men* (1991).

See also COMPULSORY HETEROSEXUALITY; MEN IN FEMINISM.

ESTABLISHMENT

'The establishment' refers to a controlling group in society. However, this narrow definition has a capacious application since it may refer to a leading, influential group in politics, the civil service, the church, the arts, intellectual or academic life, entertainment or business, or more broadly to a ruling social class comprising a wealthy ELITE, numbering members of the aristocracy, including in the UK, the monarchy and upper-class families with interests in other fields such as business or politics. In practice, therefore, 'the establishment' may refer to those at the top of the internal hierarchy in a given organization, institution or governing administration (the church, a political party, science, medicine or broadcasting), or to a configuration across these different groups or organizations. In this wider application, it is associated (in the UK, conspicuously) with a privileged sector who are members of select clubs or recruited from public schools and top-ranking universities (above all Oxford and Cambridge), who are also likely to mix socially. As this suggests, the composition of the establishment will be particular to individual nations (see Silk and Silk 1980; Hennessy 1986; Newman 1975–98) and may be centred in those nations even where leading figures, for example in banking, electronic media and academia, have global connections and influence.

The recent study by journalist Owen Jones (*The Establishment* 2014) is an exposé and CRITIQUE of the operation of the establishment that emerged in the UK in the 1970s and which triumphed in the 2000s. Its subtitle, *And how they get away with it*, refers in particular to the financial crash of 2008, for which Jones deems bankers and rogue financiers responsible. It is not they, however, he argues, but British tax-payers who have paid the price in the shape of government bailouts of failing banks and a programme of continuing cuts to the public sector and systems of tax relief. The reason being, says Owen, that banks and financiers are protected as institutions and individually by those in government and supporting think-tanks with whom they are allied ideologically and as members of the same elite. Thus, he writes, 'The state is the backbone of modern capitalism and sustains it: protecting big business, training its workers and subsidising their wages, bailing out its financial heart, directly topping up bank profits' (179–80). The establishment works, he argues, not as a conspiracy, but as 'an organic and dynamic system' (xvii) in which top civil servants and accountants shift to advisory roles in government, and those in business and politics exchange places. His polemic is directed, therefore, at the powerful who deflect blame and responsibility for the ills of society away from themselves, and his concern is less with the social composition of this group or network than their shared economic interests and a mentality that tells them that 'those at the top deserve even greater power and wealth'(xii). The answer to the self-serving culture of wealth and power, he suggests, is less a widening of the establishment's membership than a set of reforms including greater transparency and accountability, a limit of donations to political parties, a ban on second jobs for MPs, a tax system which will pursue massive tax evasion, and democratic public ownership. He presents these reforms as a modest proposal, but as a presage of a desired fuller 'democratic revolution'.

See also CAPITALISM; POSTCAPITALISM.

ESTRANGEMENT

Used sometimes to translate the German terms *Entäusserung* or *Entfremdung* in the texts of Hegel and the early Marx and Engels – though the more common translation is 'ALIENATION'. It refers in Hegel to the movement of the DIALECTIC from the condition of the object's identity with itself to that of self-estrangement, or objectification, when it enters a relationship with other things, before it is restored to itself in a new unity. Marx rewrote this idealist conception as a set of social conditions and processes. Thus, under capitalism, workers were seen as estranged or alienated from themselves and the products of their labour. A new order of things and the working out of the dialectic of history could only be achieved through revolutionary social change.

Bertolt Brecht employed the term *Verfremdung,* partly in acknowledgement of Marx, in his concept of the *Verfremdungseffekt,* usually translated as ALIENATION EFFECT. He was also influenced by what has become an overlapping concept of AESTHETIC estrangement or 'DEFAMILIARIZATION' theorized by Victor Shklovsky and the Formalist circle of critics in the Soviet Union of the 1920s. The Russian term was *ostranenie* (to 'make strange', 'defamiliarize' or 'estrange'). The Formalists defined literature by its difference from ordinary language. The devices of rhyme, rhythm, poetic form and narrative that distinguished literary DISCOURSE were felt to exert an estranging distance upon perceptions. The claim that art renews or enlivens perceptions, or makes us see things in a new way, is of course a common one. *Ostranenie* can therefore be seen as one way of conceptualizing a general truth. A distinction should be made, however, between this view of art and the strategies employed by Brecht and other modernist and AVANT-GARDE artists of the early decades of the century. In this art (including literature, theatre, painting, sculpture, photography, cinema, textiles, interior design, architecture), the aesthetic and perceptual effects identified by Shklovsky were radicalized, both in the sense that the languages and forms employed were more conspicuously 'estranged' than in previous art, and in the general intention to exert a profound psychological or ideological effect upon its readers or audiences.

Darko Suvin, a commentator on Bertolt Brecht and theorist of science fiction, employs the term 'cognitive estrangement' to refer to the latter (1979). This provides the formal framework of science fiction, he says, which is 'cognitive' by way of its affiliations with reason and science and 'estranging' in its presentation of 'other worlds' and all that this entails. We might think of other POPULAR GENRES – the fantastic, the GOTHIC – as exerting similar effects. However, Suvin's concept, as Patrick Parrinder points out, 'carries a strong bias towards social criticism' (1980: 72). As in MODERNISM, estrangement is seen to prompt changes in CONSCIOUSNESS and the world beyond the text. In Parrinder's view, the reverse is in fact more likely: 'The estrangement effect of the majority of SF stories is contained and neutralised by their conventionality in other respects. The result is the familiar reality is replaced by an all too familiar unreality' (1980: 74).

See also CRITIQUE; DISTANTIATION; IDEOLOGY.

ETHICS

Ethics names the concern to investigate the nature of right and wrong thought and action, and the terms of judgement upon these, in personal, social and political life. From the writings of Plato and Aristotle to the present day, this investigation has been conducted in the realm of moral philosophy. This tradition (including philosophers such as Hobbes, Kant, G.E. Moore, Sartre and, in more recent influential examples, John Rawls and Martha C. Nussbaum) has debated the role of pleasure, self-interest, duty, nature, religion and the law in establishing universal ethical precepts by which issues of justice, VALUE, rights, equality and freedom could be decided. As this suggests, all social and cultural activity has an ethical dimension. An influential example in literary criticism appeared in Wayne C. Booth's exploration of questions of moral responsibility connecting authors, narratives and readers in *The Company We Keep: An Ethics of Fiction*, 1988. And in Literary Studies, the 'turn to ethics' has, in the 2000s, become established as the subject of conferences, introductory readers and collections of essays (Garber, Hanssen, Walkowitz [eds] 2000; Davis and Womack [eds] 2001; George 2005). But ethics has naturally occupied a wider province across the Humanities and academic work in general, concerning, in addition, the ethics of research, subject-matter, method, pedagogy and professional conduct.

One of the problematic features of the broader ethical project, for all its internal differences, has been the assumption that universal ethical principles are ready-made or can be established. In this respect, it subscribes to a faith in reason, a belief in progress and in a common humanity characteristic of ENLIGHTENMENT thought. As in other areas, these assumptions have been subjected, point by point, to the profound scepticism generated by postmodern thought and DECONSTRUCTION. Objections have come from other quarters too, however. Thus, Frazer, Hornsby and Lovibond (1992) oppose the liberal humanist tradition in moral philosophy because of its normative assumptions of a universal male subject and consequent exclusion of 'issues of sexuality, the bodily self, moral connectedness, friendship, the emotions, psychological fluidity and finitude' (1992: 8) relevant to a feminist ethics. Whereas other specialisms modify ethics, say the authors, *'feminism...* transforms *ethics'* (1992: 3). To this end, they posit a combined ethical and political agenda targeted at the injustices of PATRIARCHY. Their feminism commits them, all the same (evident in descriptions of 'women's generic interests', 'men as such' and the 'avowedly female experience', 1992: 4, 914) to a still-universal and essentialized – if gendered – notion of the ethical subject.

These authors ignore the posthumanist emphasis on DIFFERENCE. Others, too, commonly suppose POSTMODERNISM and deconstruction to have surrendered questions of ethics for an indifferent textual irony. Zygmunt Bauman contends, rather, that 'The great issues of ethics... have lost nothing of their topicality' (1993: 4), but that the way of discussing them must alter. What principally creates this difference is the irresolvably ambiguous and contradictory nature of the present. 'Morality is incurably *aporetic',* Bauman concludes (1993: 11; see also APORIA). The humanist expectation of a universal ethical code therefore stands exposed as a false, partisan and impossible ideal. We must learn instead to face the radical indeterminacy of the postmodern – armed, however, Bauman surprisingly concludes, with a 'moral conscience' that alone can distinguish good from evil (1993: 249–50).

The ethics of deconstruction are explored by Critchley (1992) and, in connection with literary criticism, from different angles, by Hillis Miller (1989) and Eaglestone (1997). Critchley and Eaglestone, in what proved a common tendency, find an original and persuasive conception of ethics in the philosophy of Emmanuel Lévinas. Ethics, in Lévinas, consists in putting into question the ego, the knowing subject, or the 'Same' by the 'OTHER'. 'For me,' wrote Lévinas, 'the term ethics always signifies the fact of the encounter, of the relation of myself with the Other' (Critchley 1992: 17). This philosophy, Critchley aims to show, corresponds to the ethics of Jacques Derrida's deconstructive reading of texts. Thus, in attending to the 'CLOSURES' of a text, deconstruction at once reveals the limits that constrain *and* open this text to its exterior 'Other'.

This argument echoes the uncompromising deliberations on the nature of contemporary ethics by Jean-François Lyotard. Lyotard's key notion, in this respect, is the DIFFEREND, a term describing the relation of two statements or positions for which there is no superior court of appeal. Lyotard avoids the pessimistic relativism that might result from this perception since the figure of the judge 'is obligated to the idea of justice that he or she can never master' (Readings, 1991: 126). The just person must continue to seek a judgement without the aid of established criteria, testifying to the 'differend' and continually being judged in turn.

See also ALTERITY; *HOMO SACER*.

ETHNICITY

A concept often coupled and sometimes confused with the term RACE, but that ought to be distinguished from it. While 'race' is, in a basic definition, marked by phenotypical differences that are physical and visible (of body size, hair type and skin colour, for example), ethnicity describes different social and cultural identities, which may or may not be accompanied by such physical differences.

Moreover, biological definitions of race are often falsely linked to mental characteristics or used as the justification for social inequalities. Such thinking is 'racist'. Also, even when this link between biology and racial character and social position is not made, racial groups, so defined, are thought to have a genetic, and thus determined and unchangeable, basic IDENTITY (see also ESSENTIALISM). To dispute this is to dispute the whole concept of race, though not the existence of racism.

In some instances, a recognition of ethnicity has historically replaced the description of different peoples as 'races' (of Jews and blacks in the USA, for example). The Asian population in the UK is similarly referred to in official and public discourses as an 'ethnic minority' rather than as a 'race'. This does not prevent the terms being turned about, however. As John Rex points out, 'a group which has common cultural characteristics only (rather than common physical ones)' may well be 'termed a "race" by those who oppose, oppress and exploit them' (1986: 17).

Ethnicity is therefore a broader and more flexible cultural description than the biologically based or inflected categorization by race. Chiefly, ethnic identity implies a sense of belongingness, founded on an attachment to an actual or possible homeland, its cultural heritage, belief system, political history, language, characteristic MYTHS, customs, manners, food, sports, literature, art or architectural style. A corollary of this is that ethnic identity is based on perceived differences between a given identity and that of a neighbouring group or DOMINANT culture within which an ethnic group, or groups, may be positioned. This suggests an association between ethnicity and MARGINALITY, which might be reinforced by an ethnic group being in a numerical minority in a differentiated multi-ethnic society. However, this connection does not necessary follow (as, for example, in the case of the British in India). Nor does being a numerical majority (non-white populations in major American cities) secure social status and political POWER.

In academic work, the concept and definitions of ethnicity have been associated with American social science and ethnology (see Sollers [ed] 1996). In the study of CULTURE and REPRESENTATION, this discussion has joined critical study of the DISCOURSE of race and racism. This has attempted to give more prominence to the complex and mutable self-definition of individuals and groups in contemporary multi-ethnic societies (see Centre for Contemporary Cultural Studies 1982; Gilroy 1987; Gates 1988; Morrison 1992). The concept of ethnicity therefore emerges as consistent with a contemporary emphasis, derived in the main from poststructuralist and feminist theory, upon DIFFERENCE and the wider interest, in POSTCOLONIALISM and elsewhere, in the formation of migrant and 'borderline' or hybrid identities (see HYBRIDITY).

As some commentators (Rex 1986) have remarked, however, the association of ethnicity with cultural difference can overlook the advent of ethnic conflict. In such instances (hostility between Hassidic Jews, African and Caribbean Americans in New York City, or between Croats and Muslims in Bosnia), ethnic conflict comes, through the distortion cited above, to resemble racial conflict. It would be a mistake, also, to ignore the conservative or reactionary defence of ethnic identities that may exist in tension with a more progressive or transformative dialogue across cultures.

In the important essay 'New ethnicities' (1996b), Stuart Hall responds to these issues by identifying a shift of emphasis from a use of the collective term 'black' and a concern in the sphere of cultural production with 'relations of representation', to a use of the term 'ethnicity' and a concern with the 'politics of representation'; this announces, he says, 'a new cultural politics which engages rather than suppresses difference' (1996b: 446). He adds, however, that if this concept of new ethnicity is to be politically effective, it cannot endorse a notion of difference that entails 'an infinite sliding of the signifier', and that there is a need to decouple 'a non-coercive and a more diverse conception of ethnicity' from a dominant notion that connects it with the conservative discourses of NATIONALISM, IMPERIALISM, racism and the state (1996b: 447). Hall therefore posits a CULTURAL POLITICS in which meanings are contested 'inside the notion of ethnicity' (1996b: 447). Examples, cited by Hall, of an engagement with these theoretical issues are the films *Handsworth Songs, Passion of Remembrance, My Beautiful Laundrette* and the work in Great Britain of Isaac Julien and Hanif Kureishi (see also Mercer 1994; Morley and Chen [eds] 1996: Part V).

See also DIASPORA; MULTICULTURALISM; POSTSTRUCTURALISM.

ETHNOCENTRICISM

The use of this term has become quite complex. In general terms, however, it can be said to refer to the ways in which the language, beliefs or customs of a particular ethnic group are reinforced, defended or promoted, whether in intellectual work, a political or military campaign, or a cultural or educational programme.

Roger Brown (1965) defined ethnocentrism as 'the application of the norms of one's own culture to that of others' (1965: 183); Agnes Heller writes of how 'what is called "ethnocentricism" is the natural attitude of all cultures towards alien ones' (1984: 271). In such descriptions, ethnocentrism becomes a term for how the self or SUBJECT imposes itself upon, or constitutes, the OTHER as alien to itself, in a relation of active antagonism. Extreme cases of this have been seen in the ethnic conflict marking the history of Northern Ireland, the Middle East, Bosnia and Rwanda. More generally, ethnocentrism is used to refer to the assumed privilege of European ethnic groups and particularly white Europeans. As such, it can be employed as virtually synonymous with EUROCENTRICISM. Gayatri Spivak writes in this way (commenting on Jacques Derrida's treatment of this same topic) of 'the European intellectual's ethnocentric impulse' and problematic role in the west's constitution of its other (1988: 292). In this connection, in academic work, the term has been used especially to critique the assumption in more traditional forms of Anthropology and Ethnology that the ethnographer can stand outside and apart from an observed CULTURE. It therefore implies a complacent cultural superiority, or an implicit racism.

Ethnocentrism therefore reinforces or directly asserts a particular cultural IDENTITY. The ethnic identity in question might have a regional, subcultural or nationalist aspect, and this can be of the otherwise 'observed' culture as well as, or as a counter to, that of the anthropologist observer, outside critic, journalist or tourist. Obviously, this difference can be of considerable significance. However, whether the ethnocentrism in question is that of a DOMINANT or a marginalized culture, the term implies a selective or exclusive, 'centred' perspective and project. It should also be pointed out that, for Jacques Derrida, ethnocentrism is inevitable and inescapable. Ethnology, he writes, is

> primarily a European science employing traditional concepts, however much it may struggle against them. Consequently whether he wants to or not – and this does not depend on a decision on his part – the ethnologist accepts into his discourse the premises of ethnocentrism at the very moment when he denounces them. The necessity is irreducible; it is not a historical contingency.

(1978: 282)

Ethnocentricism, Derrida implies, cannot therefore simply be thrown off, but requires a vigilant 'critical rigour' and self-consciousness.

See also DECONSTRUCTION; ETHNOGRAPHY; POSTCOLONIALISM.

ETHNOGRAPHY

A practice of cultural investigation dependent on the methods of 'participant observation' where the researcher seeks to apprehend the immediately experienced meaning of an activity or event at first hand and from the inside. Most often, ethnographic studies will use interviews, group discussion, an informant or field assistants, or a combination of these to this end, together with other forms of information-gathering. These methods were developed particularly in Anthropology and Sociology, and have been adopted in the study of youth cultures (Willis 1979; Back 1996) and media audiences (Morley 1980, 1986; Gillespie 1995). The problems this method encounters derive in general terms from the position of the researcher as being simultaneously a part of, and apart from, a given CULTURE, SUBCULTURE or CONSCIOUSNESS. There are likely also to be varying degrees to which the researcher is a complete observer or complete participant, and this may be complicated by factors of gender, ethnic, generational and linguistic difference.

These questions have given rise to internal debates and divisions within ethnographic practice, which have in turn often been mapped on to traditional distinctions between scientific or interpretive or qualitative PARADIGMS. The empirical orientation of ethnographic study is also sometimes opposed to more purely textual or theoretical approaches, a distinction that echoes the competing claims made at an earlier date between CULTURALISM and STRUCTURALISM, and identified by Stuart Hall (1996a) as constructing the two major paradigms shaping the study of culture.

Clifford's (1988) reflections on the situatedness of the ethnographer within the field of study have been influential in addressing these issues across a broad range of study. Also, arguments by Geertz (1975), Clifford and Marcus ([eds] 1986) and others on the interpretive and, more precisely, NARRATIVE forms inevitably taken by ethnographic study have suggested some significant common ground between this empirically based tradition and semiotic analyses of forms of REPRESENTATION. Both methods, it can be said, share the assumption that subjective and social meanings are 'textually constructed', if this occurs in different situations and according to different protocols, and by way of different, spoken or written, discursive conventions. At the same time, it might even be said that all cultural research, and not only that with a basis in the social sciences, involves some form of 'participant observation', since the social cannot be studied without our being a part of it. At this point, the debate joins the broad discussion of the question of VALUE and the role of the valuer in the study of human culture, whether the material studied is what young people do and say on a Saturday night or the text of a Shakespeare play.

See also POSITIVISM.

EUROCENTRICISM

A term describing the way a particular cultural model, 'centred' upon European intellectual traditions and sociopolitical systems, has been generalized so as to apply to the world at large. The bias in this geo-cultural and largely white, male perspective upon human history and world affairs has been especially exposed in postcolonial studies. Other contemporary critical theories have contributed to this decentring CRITIQUE, but have not themselves been exempt from perpetuating some aspect of Euro- or ETHNOCENTRICISM. Thus, Anglo-American and French FEMINISM of the 1970s and 1980s, while significantly diverged on other topics, consistently ignored the conditions and claims of African-American women and Third World women of colour. DECONSTRUCTION and postmodern theory also, while profoundly critical of the assumptions of western philosophy and of MODERNITY, remain in many ways the product of western cultures and sensibilities.

It might be said that this is true also of western postcolonial theory. Homi Bhabha responds directly to the charge 'that the place of the academic critic is inevitably within the Eurocentric archives of an imperialist or neo-colonial West' (1994: 19). He proposes theorizing the concepts of NEGOTIATION and cultural DIFFERENCE as a way of moving beyond the divisive polarities of theory and activism, centre and periphery, self and OTHER on which Eurocentricism is founded.

Stam and Shohat's *Unthinking Eurocentricism* (1996) seeks to critique Eurocentricism by way of a strategy linking MULTICULTURALISM with the methodologies of Media and Cultural Studies. Essays in the volume offer to consider topics such as REALISM, spectatorship, stereotyping, Hollywood and Third World cinemas in new non-Eurocentric ways.

See also CANON; ENLIGHTENMENT; ETHNICITY.

EVERYDAY LIFE

This expression means what it says: the routine practices of daily existence. Often, in academic study, as elsewhere, it is taken for granted or evoked as a generality, and sometimes again, somewhat oddly, distinguished in references to 'the media and everyday life' or 'consumption and everyday life' from other key terms and activities it might be thought to include. Its use does have a general purpose and more precise provenance, however. In general, references to 'everyday life' can be taken to express an emphasis upon the forms and meanings of a common or POPULAR CULTURE and to assume, with Raymond Williams, that 'culture is ordinary' rather than the exclusive province of an elite. This in turn invariably signals a broadly political perspective on cultural production and consumption, and a belief that the routine or banal in daily life is in fact a complex field of contested cultural meanings.

Highmore (2001) presents a historical introduction to twentieth-century theories of everyday life. Two key reference points can be cited here. One is Michel de Certeau's *The Practice of Everyday Life* (1988). As if to confirm the above, de Certeau addresses his book 'To the ordinary man' and titles the first section 'A very ordinary culture'. He is concerned throughout to foreground the 'ways of operating' in daily life and to distinguish in particular between cultural 'strategies' imposed from above and the 'tactics' by which people – as consumers and users of the city, media or language – deflect or subvert these intentions so as to produce their own meanings. Everyday life is therefore characterized as a creative practice of 'making do', in a kind of habitual demonstration of the artistic practice of BRICOLAGE. Further, de Certeau's insights have been taken up in Cultural Geography (Harvey 1989), in the study of audiences and fans (Henry Jenkins (1992) in particular develops de Certeau's concept of 'textual poaching') and in relation to cultural consumption (Storey 1999).

The second, more directly theorized, treatment of everyday life is associated with Henri Lefebvre, whose *Critique of Everyday Life* (1991a [1947]) is credited with introducing the concept to western Marxism. Here, Lefebvre extends the concept of ALIENATION in the early writings of Marx and Engels to all aspects of experience in postwar capitalist societies. The profound emptiness of such societies Lefebvre sees as only further 'mystified' by the false consolations of consumerism. Offsetting this experience are what Lefebvre terms 'moments' – fleeting instants or episodes in personal or political life that confer a sense of presence and fulfilment (see Shields 1999). (Lefebvre's idea is likened to the politicized understanding of 'situation' developed by the libertarian-anarchist 'Situationist International' with which he collaborated in the 1960s in Paris – see PSYCHOGEOGRAPHY.) Lefebvre further explored this thinking in the study of urban life (1991b), and his insights in this area have significantly shaped the postmodern interest in SPACE and the CITY. Here, Lefebvre distinguished between the 'perceived space' of everyday social life, the 'conceived space' of planners and speculators, and a third sphere of 'lived space'. The latter he associates with a symbolic reimagining of urban space that reconfigures the banality of the first. Art and literature, he believes, have helped keep such alternatives alive. Everyday life under capitalism can therefore be redeemed and, as above, given new social meanings through the creative reappropriation of its given products and structures.

EXCESS

An important term in the thought of the French philosopher, ethnographer and fiction writer Georges Bataille (1897–1962) where it is associated with the free and joyful expenditure or waste of energy in sex or acts of sacrifice. Bataille found a prime example of this principle in the description by the French anthropologist Marcel Mauss of the practice of 'potlach', the celebratory destruction of goods in a show of prestige by natives of the American north-west. This he extended to an emphasis on obscenity and horror, which he saw as characterizing both art and the erotic. The beautiful was thus linked in his thinking to the base: pleasure bound up with loss, mutilation and death. These ideas were elaborated in his pornographic tale *The Story of the Eye* (1928), which shows the affinities he shared also with French surrealism. Bataille drew, in addition, upon the irrationalist philosophy of Friedrich Nietzsche whose work he helped introduce to French intellectual life. His own emphasis upon the dysfunctional, the prodigal and the grotesque itself had a wide influence upon a number of French poststructuralist and postmodern theorists, including Foucault, Deleuze and Guatarri, Lyotard and Derrida (1978). In these thinkers, and in Lacanian psychoanalytic thought, excess is invoked to designate the unconstrained play of meaning and that which lies outside the normative SYMBOLIC order. In this guise, in both Lacan and Derrida, excess is associated furthermore with the 'feminine'. This association has in turn been taken up within FEMINISM, especially by French feminists who see here a way in which the sign 'woman' can exert a disruptive potential within and upon PATRIARCHY.

Excess comes, therefore, to signal a range of activities and meanings opposed to the constraints of western rationality, to PHALLOGOCENTRICism, the priorities of capitalist production and normative ideas of the human SUBJECT.

EXCHANGE VALUE

See COMMODITY FETISHISM; VALUE

FALSE CONSCIOUSNESS

See IDEOLOGY.

FANTASY

In its more general use, this term describes a non-realistic mode of fiction or storytelling in any medium and across a number of different GENRES (melodrama, romance, fairy tale, ghost story, science fiction, UTOPIAn fiction). In particular, it involves magical or supernatural happenings, and this degree of improbability defines its relation to realistic conventions and the probabilities of everyday life (see REALISM). Fantasy is frequently regarded as escapist, in a dismissive association with 'children's literature', POPULAR genres, such as those above, or modes such as the GOTHIC, with which it is frequently linked. The question, however, must be what it is an escape from and to. Like other cognate popular forms, fantasy can be said to stage an encounter between the norms of this world and its OTHERS, thereby challenging stable conceptions of the real and its accompanying perspectives on order and illegality, moderation and EXCESS, and so on. The invention of alternative social worlds that are critical of the present have made fantasy of interest to feminist and other writers and readers who see here a way of exploring the possibilities of TRANSGRESSIVE GENDER and sexual roles, or of entire alternative worlds (Cranny-Francis 1990). These may work as conscious allegories of present society or through a compulsive extrapolation upon its ideas of the monstrous or perverse (Creed 1993).

The NARRATIVE conventions of 'the fantastic' as a genre were analysed by the structuralist critic, Tzvetan Todorov (1973). Todorov detected an unresolved 'hesitation' at the heart of the 'pure' fantastic between the 'marvellous' and the 'UNCANNY' – the first producing a supernatural, and the second a natural, explanation of fantastic events. An important study of fantasy as a broadly conceived subversive 'mode', as indicated above, remains Rosemary Jackson's *Fantasy: The Literature of Subversion* (1981). See also Easthope (1989), Donald ([ed] 1989), in relation to film, and Burgin *et al.* ([eds] 1986). Jackson also outlines its place within PSYCHOANALYSIS (where the preferred translation of Freud's term is 'phantasy'). Psychoanalysis aligns fantasy to reverie, dreams and to the UNCONSCIOUS, positing it as the narrative exploration of repressed anxieties or desires. In these scenarios, a mental image of the object of DESIRE is set in a rudimentary context (more disordered in nocturnal dream than in daydream) and presents the SUBJECT with a shifting position as witness and/or participant. Art similarly gives indirect expression to a cultural unconscious, in both fantasy texts, or where fantasy is an undercurrent in otherwise realistic dramas. Often, this concerns aspects of SEXUALITY: an anxiety about reproduction, for example, including its appropriation by men (*Frankenstein, Alien*); the fear of active female sexuality (*Dracula, Fatal Attraction, Basic Instinct*); or, for Freud, the apparently universal fantasy of witnessing sexual intercourse between parents.

These, and other fears and desires, can be seen as the symbolic re-enactment of 'primal fantasies' in early childhood and, like dream or reverie, open to explanation in terms of the mechanisms identified by Freud of CONDENSATION and DISPLACEMENT. Psychoanalysis therefore confirms the centrality of fantasy *in* the 'real world' and not to one side of it, revealing 'the supposedly marginal operations of fantasy to be constitutive of our identity' (Burgin in Wright [ed] 1992: 87).

Fantasy as understood by Freud and Jacques Lacan plays an important part in the writings of the philosopher Slavoj Žižek (see Žižek, 1997, and Butler, 2014). Žižek shares Lacan's view that 'desire is the essence of reality' and that fantasy orchestrates a subject's DESIRE, providing the physical object which embodies or focuses that desire. The object thus stands in an anticipatory and metonymic relation with the wished-for satisfaction. However, such is the structure of desire, that this satisfaction remains elusive. This is because desire is predicated on a feeling of lack and a search for unity, which is never assuaged. Žižek gives this a political application to the subject in society for whom fantasy presents the desired 'object' of freedom and well-being, lacking in present social reality. The experience of lack and dissatisfaction felt by the subject is projected onto an OTHER who does experience this better state, producing also, says Žižek, hatred, violence against, or prejudice towards the Other. At the same time, fantasy can invoke objects of desire which act as a distraction, thereby defusing political dissatisfaction, quelling the feeling of lack and reconciling the subject to a given ruling ideology.

See also GAZE; IMAGINARY/SYMBOLIC.

FEMINISM

The beginnings of the feminist movement are generally set in the late eighteenth century and associated with the writings in social theory, polemics and fiction of Mary Wollstonecraft Godwin, author of *A Vindication of the Rights of Women* (1792) and *Maria or the Wrongs of Women* (1797). The movement grew in strength and organization in the second half of the nineteenth century in Great Britain and the United States when it was mobilized, particularly around the question of female suffrage. This gave rise to the reformist campaigns of the suffragists and the militant action of the suffragettes before the delivery of the vote in the first two decades of the twentieth century. The development of the women's movement and of feminism (the latter becoming the more common usage) in the later twentieth century occurred in what are described as 'second' and 'third-wave' feminism.

'Second-wave' feminism, most often styled 'the women's liberation movement', occurred in the late 1960s and 1970s in association with the contemporary civil rights movement and the New Left student protest movement, the latter mobilized chiefly around anti-Vietnam War protests. The women's liberation movement therefore participated in a dynamic moment of profound social and cultural change (including changed definitions of CULTURE and politics), most obviously witnessed in the advent of a new phase of rock 'n' roll and its associated changes in lifestyle. Key works of the period were Kate Millett's *Sexual Politics* (1971), Germaine Greer's *The Female Eunuch* (1971), Sheila Rowbotham's *Woman's Consciousness, Man's World* (1973) and Juliet Mitchell's *Woman's Estate* (1975). Simone de Beauvoir's earlier *The Second Sex* (1949) and Betty Friedan's *The Feminine Mystique* (1963) were also important influences. Second-wave feminism was prompted by an awareness that formal political equality had not brought social and cultural equality. It inaugurated a critique of PATRIARCHY, of taken-for-granted sexist attitudes and ideologies in institutions, literary and cultural texts, and personal behaviour, including that of the male revolutionary left. It also initiated an entirely new mode of democratic discussion in women-only groups and networks committed to 'CONSCIOUSNESS raising' and to campaigning on issues of women's health, childcare, and equality at work. Above all, through the slogan 'the personal is the political', it raised to general awareness the invidious distinction between woman's supposed domestic sphere of home and family and the male-defined public sphere (see Morgan [ed] 1970). Feminist journals and publishing houses, and innumerable studies across the gamut of academic disciplines followed the inspiration of these early texts and initiatives, radically transforming women's self-perceptions, and the methods and objects of study.

The 'third wave' is characterized by this intervention in the academies of western societies. It marks the more rigorous pursuit of feminist theory in an ongoing engagement with MARXISM, PSYCHOANALYSIS, STRUCTURALISM and POSTSTRUCTURALISM, and consequently of debates on questions of language and writing (see ÉCRITURE FÉMININE), CLASS, SEXUALITY, the BODY and SEXUAL DIFFERENCE. Within Literary and Cultural Studies, feminism was concerned chiefly with issues of GENDER and REPRESENTATION across a range of texts and cultural forms. This diversity was accompanied by new alliances, but also by divisions – between French and Anglo-American feminism (Moi 1985), between essentialist and social-constructionist perspectives, between lesbian and radical and liberal positions, by debates over the role of theory, and the relevance of academic feminism to the lives of ordinary women (Gallop 1992). These debates were, and are, still played out most conspicuously in relation to issues such as pornography, mothering and the family (Segal and McIntosh 1992; Coward 1992).

In the 1980s and 1990s, the feminist engagement with POSTMODERNISM and POSTCOLONIALISM raised further questions about women's role in relation to the new technologies and changed conditions of advanced consumer societies (Nava 1992; Plant 1995) and its political debt to universalizing 'METANARRATIVES' of the ENLIGHTENMENT project (Nicholson [ed] 1990; Benhabib 1992), and it has exposed tensions between the agendas of white middle-class western feminists, African-American feminists or 'womanists', and Third World women of colour (hooks 1981; Spivak 1987; see also Parma 1990). The 1990s also saw a striking development of new agendas within lesbian studies and QUEER THEORY (see Abelove *et al.* [eds] 1993). In addition, a 'backlash' against earlier feminism (Faludi 1992) on the part of right-wing politicians, the media and 'post-feminist' authors (Wolf 1990; Paglia 1992; Roiphe 1994) exacerbated the sense of fragmentation, and hence frustration, of an earlier generation, while convincing others that feminism had entered, or must enter, a new phase.

Commenting on this fractious scene, Imelda Whelehan believes feminism has been the victim of media stereotyping and draws strength from its diversity and 'chameleon-like organisation' (1995: 21). Indeed, the broader history of the movement suggests that differences are neither new nor disabling. Whelehan appeals to feminists to resist the distortions of the media and 'male-oriented knowledge' (1995: 19), and to remain united in their opposition to patriarchy and male domination. 'The existence of active debate,' she writes, 'confirms the richness of feminist discourse, which is constantly diversifying and shifting ground in an effort to undercut the hegemony of male discourse' (1995: 20–1).

See also DESIRE; GYNOCRITICISM; 'MEN IN FEMINISM'.

FETISHISM

In Freudian psychoanalytic theory, the male child must pass through the OEDIPAL COMPLEX in order to be socialized. In so doing, he must negotiate the threat of castration and submit to the authority of the father, who represents the power of the PHALLUS and the SYMBOLIC order. The mother, who appears not to have a penis, reinforces the threat of castration. The child must therefore transfer his affection for the mother to an allegiance with the father. This is accomplished by supplying the IMAGE of the mother with a fetish that represents the missing phallus. The threat of castration the woman represents is therefore allayed or 'disavowed' in the construction of the image of a woman who is 'masculinized', but remains female.

This theory has been applied, via Lacan's reading of Freud, to the operation of the male GAZE in cinema. Thus, re-enacting the Oedipal narrative in which the young male had experienced the mother's lack of a penis as a threat of castration to himself, the male viewer of active – rather than passive and compliant – women on screen (the 'femme fatale' of *film noir*) is deemed to feel similarly threatened. There are two ways, it is said, in which the male viewer can counter such a threat: either through the controlling gaze of voyeurism in which the woman is surveyed, but cannot look back, or through a fetishistic gaze in which part of the woman's body or clothing is over-invested with sexual meaning. Hence, the focused attention to BODY parts, or on high heels, evening gloves or stockings. The woman is commodified in phallic style, thus creating, once more, a masculinized image of woman who can act at the same time as a consolation for lack and an object of DESIRE. The films of Alfred Hitchcock are often cited as examples of voyeurism, especially *Psycho* (1960). A film that explores fetishism is Michael Powell's *Peeping Tom* (1960).

The postcolonial theorist and critic Homi Bhabha suggests that the concept of fetishism can be used to understand racist stereotypes (1994: 73–5). In this case, the anxiety concerns not the OTHER's (the mother's) lack of a penis, but the racial or ethnic other's lack of the same skin colour. In the stereotype, which like the fetish fixes an object (its representation, writes Bhabha, is not false but simplified in an 'arrested fixated form'; 1994: 75), there is the same combined recognition of DIFFERENCE and its DISAVOWAL: an experience of mastery and pleasure as well as self-defensive anxiety. Kobena Mercer (1994) takes up the question of racial fetishism in a study of the photography of Robert Mapplethorpe. See also Hall ([ed] 1997b: 264–77) in the context of issues of REPRESENTATION.

FIELD

In the work of the French sociologist of CULTURE and education, Pierre Bourdieu (1930–2002), a field is a NETWORK of relationships and a SITE of struggle, the context in which individuals, in key terms in Bourdieu's theory, invest their CULTURAL CAPITAL and exercise their HABITUS – the latter defining the open set of attitudes and dispositions by which they conduct their way in the world (1984). Bourdieu views the struggle referred to as a struggle for dominance. Each such field is viewed as comprising a network of individuals, institutions and influences, homologous with other competing fields, but with its own logic and structure. The field of education, for example, contains a jockeying for power specific to itself, but is in conflict with other fields such as the field of commerce or politics. The number of fields is infinite, and individuals bring their distinctive 'habitus' and competing economic and cultural capital to them in mixed and uneven ways. Thus, workers in the educational and cultural field are high in cultural capital, says Bourdieu, but low in economic capital when compared with workers in the field of commerce or business. These differences then establish the terms of struggle for dominance. If power is achieved in one field, an individual or group may then seek to transpose it to another: from the realm of culture to politics, for example.

See also CULTURE INDUSTRIES; DOMINANT/RESIDUAL/EMERGENT; IDEOLOGICAL STATE APPARATUS.

FLÂNEUR

A concept employed by the Marxist critic and theorist, Walter Benjamin (1892–1940) in his reading of the nineteenth-century French poet, Charles Baudelaire.

The flâneur is the stroller or window-shopper, and came into existence with the building of the Paris arcades in the period of the Second Empire in the 1840s. The arcades were glass-covered, gas-lit passageways lined with elegant shops, miniature worlds, says Benjamin, where the boulevard had been made into an interior and the *flâneur* found a particular dwelling place. Benjamin adopted the arcades as his lifetime project and the centre of his study of Baudelaire (1973b). He saw versions of *the flâneur* in the prostitute, the dandy, the *apache* and rag-picker, and in them allegories for the figure of the poet who could thus be 'in' but not 'of' the urban crowd, a spectator pursuing his/her own nonchalant course through the city's peoples and environments; 'botanising on the asphalt', as Benjamin puts it (1973b: 36).

Equivalent figures, set in the streets of the emerging metropolis, appeared in writings by Edgar Allen Poe, Stephen Crane, Virginia Woolf, James Joyce and other modernist authors, as well as in Baudelaire's poetry. A further contemporary example is the new figure of the detective, a parallel Benjamin himself drew with Edgar Allen Poe's stories – including his 'The man of the crowd' – very much in mind (1973b: 40–52).

The concept has been re-examined by Janet Wolff in terms of women's place in the nineteenth-century CITY and the construction of MODERNITY. The latter, she argues, has concerned itself with the PUBLIC SPHERE of the factory, the office, politics and city life. While men and women shared the experience of increased rationalization, anonymity and fragmentation, which came to characterize this public domain, women were confined to the suburbs and the domestic sphere. The consequence, she writes, is that, 'The dandy, the *flâneur,* the hero, the stranger – all figures invoked to epitomise the experience of modern life – are invariably male figures' (1994: 206).

While the figure of a female *flâneuse* was, in Wolff's view, a non-existent possibility, the different ways in which women did occupy the public sphere need, she argues, to be recognized. One such arena was the department store of the 1880s, which allowed for the legitimate public appearance of middle-class women. Both these themes are taken up in later writing. Elizabeth Wilson, for example, contests Wolff's account. 'Unattended-unowned-women', writes Wilson, including the symbolic figure of the prostitute, although chaperoned and regulated, came increasingly to occupy 'the public sphere of pavements, cafes and theatres' (1995: 61). Rachel Bowlby (1985) further explores the ways of the *flâneur/flâneuse* in relation to shopping at the onset of contemporary consumer society. But Wilson also suggests a different reading of *the flâneur.* She sees 'a figure to be deconstructed, a shifting projection of angst rather than a solid embodiment of male power', the expression of an unstable, attenuated and self-effacing masculinity, become indeed 'passive, feminine' (1985: 74, 75). See also the collection of essays in Tester ([ed] 1994).

The idea of the *flâneur* might also be cross-referenced to the distinction made by Michel de Certeau (1988) between a rationalist discourse in the city, which he associates with an aerial view, and the practice of EVERYDAY LIFE lived at street level. De Certeau's emphasis on the latter has influenced the 'populist' tradition in Cultural Studies and is acknowledged, for example, in the work of John Fiske (1989). In postmodern discourse, the idea of *the flâneur* has been expanded into an aesthetics and politics of 'NOMADISM', connected with the migrancy and border-crossing thought to characterize this era (Chambers 1993; Braidotti 1994). Brooker (1999) examines the use of the term in modern and postmodern contexts.

See also GAZE; MODERNISM; PSYCHOGEOGRAPHY; TOURISM.

FLÂNEUSE

See FLÂNEUR.

FLOW

This term has three independent uses in Cultural Theory. First, Raymond Williams (1974) introduced it to describe the scheduling and experience of an evening's TV viewing. In this sense, the term emerges from a quite specific discussion of television in the 1970s and in the context, in particular, of a comparison running through Williams's study, between British and American programming. Williams was struck by the frequency of advertising and of trailers on American TV and, while he suggested ways in which this flow could be analysed in terms of its measurable units and techniques, his principal response is to observe the disruption it creates in the viewer's sense of the integrity and coherence of discrete programmes or issues. Thus, he writes:

> I still cannot be sure what I took from that whole flow. I believe I registered some incidents as happening in the wrong film, and some characters in the commercials as involved in the film episodes, in what came to seem – for all the occasional bizarre disparities – a single irresponsible flow of images and feelings.
>
> (1974:92)

Second, the term 'flow', or more usually 'flows', is used by the poststructuralist philosophers Gilles Deleuze and Félix Guatarri (1984) to refer to the libidinal energies channelled in restrictive ways by the authoritarian structures of bourgeois society. Their analytic and political strategies of 'DETERRITORIALIZATION' and 'SCHIZOANALYSIS' – the latter founded specifically in a CRITIQUE of the accommodations with capitalist priorities made by PSYCHOANALYSIS – are intended to release these repressed flows in a subversive, lateral and non-hierarchical movement (see RHIZOME).

Third, 'flows' is used by the social and urban theorist, Manuel Castells, to refer to the systems of electronic communication underpinning the financial, information, media and servicing NETWORKS characterizing contemporary global societies. Whereas many commentators feel SPACE is a causality of this development, Castells sees in this new technological PARADIGM the challenge 'to reconceptualise new forms of spatial arrangements' (1997: 13). The 'space of flows', as he terms it, appears to have an autonomous life above the wishes of capitalists and workers, regions or states. Thus, he speaks of 'uncontrollable financial flows' and of 'the flows of wealth, information and crime' across the borders of nation-states (1997: 15). Castells sees an opposition, however, between the 'space of flows' and an alternative 'place of space' (a physically contained cultural locale). The latter, he says, is 'the predominant space of experience, of everyday life, and of social and political control' (1997: 14) and can, along with other forms of resistance (social movements, local governments), penetrate and subvert the powerful space of flows.

See also GLOBALIZATION; LOCAL; PLACE.

FORDISM

See POST-FORDISM.

FORMALISM

The Formalist movement appeared in the Soviet Union in the 1910s and 1920s. Its leading theorists were Victor Shklovsky, Boris Eikenbaum and Jan Murakofsky. Though it was contemporary with highly politicized movements in agitprop and constructivism, and a volatile general culture of Marxist-influenced ideas, the movement's attentions were deliberately focused on the formal specificity of literary works. It sought to define their distinctive 'literariness' and found this in the devices that distinguished literary from ordinary language. This was conceptualized in the influential concepts of *ostranenie* (or 'making strange') and, later, 'foregrounding': rule-breaking innovations that created and exploited literature's linguistic difference. A further enduring distinction introduced in the field of NARRATIVE theory was between 'plot' (*sjuzet*), the simple linear ingredients of a tale, and 'story' (*fabula*), its organization as structured narrative. In addition, in a model of COMMUNICATION developed by the Prague linguist, Roman Jakobson, after the original movement had been forced to quit the Soviet Union in the 1930s, literature was distinguished by the 'poetic function', defined as 'the set towards the message as such' (1988: 37). The 'poetic function' named the self-consciousness that structured a poem, or other utterance, in its conspicuously sonic and rhythmic patterns, or was responsible, by extension, for narrative design.

Jakobson was a transitional figure who linked the Russian and Prague Schools and, in turn, linked these with the STRUCTURALISM of the 1960s. All three movements (as well as, for example, the school of American 'New Criticism') have been described in derogatory fashion as 'formalist'. The term is taken to imply a limitation since the approach ignores questions of social and cultural context or IDEOLOGY. This difference is registered in the fuller concepts of DIALOGICS and HETEROGLOSSIA developed by Mikhail Bakhtin and associates in the Soviet Union from the late 1920s, and in the more politicized meaning given to the idea of 'making strange' in Bertolt Brecht's concept of the ALIENATION EFFECT.

The derogatory sense of formalism generally remains the current meaning (but see POST-THEORY). The above comparisons are telling in this respect, but perhaps this criticism itself assumes an over-simplified division between 'form' and 'content'. It is worth noting Roland Barthes's remark, for example, that 'a little formalism turns one away from history... a lot brings one back to it' (Easthope 1991: 177).

See also ESTRANGEMENT; DEFAMILIARIZATION; MESSAGE.

FORMATION

A term introduced by Raymond Williams (1980a) to describe the terms of association of significant cultural groups, artistic movements or tendencies. His examples are William Godwin and his associates in the late eighteenth century, the Pre-Raphaelite Brotherhood and, principally, the Bloomsbury Group, including Virginia and Leonard Woolf, Clive and Vanessa Bell, Lytton Strachey, Maynard Keynes and Roger Fry, among several others. Such groups are an assembly of individuals held together by an AESTHETIC and political IDEOLOGY, CLASS position and, in the case of the Bloomsbury Group, quite markedly, by personal friendship, marriage or partnership, and a shared 'social conscience'. The term therefore provides an analytical perspective upon the supporting personal, social and ideological structures by which artists, intellectuals and others in a cultural circle or movement relate to each other and a wider social world. As Williams points out, social histories and Sociology generally ignore such groups. An attention to such formations, however, promises to develop a 'modern cultural sociology'. Most importantly, this analysis requires a double focus that acknowledges 'the terms in which they saw themselves and would wish to be presented, and at the same time enable[s] us to analyse these terms and their general social and cultural significance' (1980a: 152).

Examples other than those Williams cites could obviously be found. We might think, for example, of the postwar academic left in Great Britain, for example, including figures such as E.P. Thompson, Richard Hoggart, Stuart Hall and Williams himself, or the generation of post-1968 French intellectuals, including Derrida, Baudrillard, Foucault and Barthes (see Callinicos 1989: 162–74, on the latter in something like these terms). In this sense, the term is usefully considered in relation to Williams's concept of shared STRUCTURES OF FEELING. Elsewhere, he employs the term more broadly to identify 'conscious movements and tendencies (literary, artistic, philosophical or scientific)' that can be thought of more directly in relation to dominant, alternative and oppositional ideological formations (1977: 119; see also DOMINANT/RESIDUAL/EMERGENT).

The term 'social formation' was given a further interpretation in the tradition of structural MARXISM. Louis Althusser, in particular, employed the term as a way of distinguishing between a proposed 'scientific' model of Marxism and the tradition of humanist Marxism, which stressed the role of human AGENCY in social change. A 'social formation' Althusser saw as comprised of a structured hierarchy of relatively autonomous institutions and practices determined 'in the last instance' by the economic infrastructure.

See also AUTONOMY; CONJUNCTURE; HUMANISM.

FORT-DA GAME

See SUTURE.

FOUNDATIONALISM

A term used to refer to the universalizing beliefs, inaugurated by eighteenth-century ENLIGHTENMENT philosophy, in justice, human rights, scientific knowledge and human mastery of the natural world. Though these beliefs may inform a world-view, they should be distinguished from 'fundamentalist' beliefs in which the acceptance of religious and civil laws or political dogma determines the smallest details of an individual's or a community's conduct. Foundationalist beliefs of the kind described have become associated with the IDEOLOGY of liberal HUMANISM governing western societies over the last two centuries and have consequently been subjected, along with this ideology, to the three-way CRITIQUE of POSTSTRUCTURALISM, POSTMODERNISM and POSTCOLONIALISM. Under this scrutiny, the would-be universal tenets of foundationalist belief have been exposed as partial and based upon the privileged world-view of a dominant CLASS in dominant European nations. They have served, so the indictment runs, to support colonial and imperialist political systems, a falsely totalizing philosophical tradition and the mythical unified SUBJECT of bourgeois capitalism.

This devastating critique has produced the experience of an absence of grounded foundations and thence, so it is said, of any credible universal political programme in postmodern societies. However, there are those who, while viewing claims for transcendent moral or political foundations as dubious and untenable, are loath to abandon the philosophical and ethical belief in ideals of truth, justice, equality or democracy. The task for such a philosophy is to reconcile these principles with a commitment to PLURALISM. Much of the most compelling of relevant theory (by Jürgen Habermas, John Rawls, Ernesto Laclau and Chantal Mouffe, Seyla Benhabib, and Cornell West) has contributed to this debate (see Bernstein 1991; Fairlamb 1994). Tallack ([ed] 1995: 357–68) sees this 'renaissance' in ethico-political discussion as involving an exchange between traditions in moral and political philosophy and critical theory. He presents such thought, appropriately, as 'post-foundational'.

See also ETHNOCENTRICISM; EUROCENTRICISM; FUNDAMENTALISM.

FRACTALS

See CHAOS.

FRANKFURT SCHOOL

See CRITICAL THEORY; CULTURE INDUSTRIES.

FUNDAMENTALISM

The belief in a first cause, principle or set of principles to the extent that this determines all aspects of a life. Deeply held religious views may therefore be referred to as fundamentalist, as may some CULTS; indeed, these may overlap, although a cult is generally distinguished from the major fundamentalist faiths by being more esoteric, isolated and limited in its membership. Fundamentalism has recently been associated particularly with Islamic sects, but Islam is a world movement composed of different versions of Islam and is of centuries' duration. In more strictly fundamentalist Islamic societies – such as Iran and Saudi Arabia – politics and CIVIL SOCIETY are governed by a strict adherence to religious law (Halliday 1996). The terrorist incidents in the United States of 11 September 2001 confused this distinction and brought the relations between world faiths – along with their accompanying cultural and political ideologies, and the disparities between rich and poor nations – to a shuddering crisis.

Among the many issues this ongoing conflict has raised are the possible terms of coexistence of differently ordered societies in a 'new world order'. One way in which this has been posed is in terms of the relation of fundamentalism to western POSTMODERNISM (Ahmed 1992; Gellner 1992). We should note, too, however, that there has been a rise of fundamentalist Christian groups or sects in the recent history of advanced western capitalist societies, noticeably in the United States. These can be understood, moreover, as belonging to a long tradition of such movements begun with the seventeenth-century Puritans. Such groups tend to be non-conformist or conservative in their moral and political orientation, to endorse extreme individualism and, on occasion, to combine this with nationalistic, anti-government attitudes (Melling 1999). In some cases, such groups are organized as militia and view themselves as engaged in, or preparing for, a war to defend their beliefs.

The social theorist, Manuel Castells, while recognizing the conservatism of both Islamic fundamentalism and fundamentalist groups in the United States, views both as a mark of resistance to the spread of global capitalism (1997: 151–2). Certainly, their respective beliefs in founding universal laws and exclusive 'tribalism', as Castells terms it, distinguish them from the PLURALISM and HYBRIDITY that characterize much of contemporary culture.

There can also be fundamentalist political, rather than religious, beliefs and movements, though, as above, these may again overlap, as in the example of fundamentalist Loyalist-Protestant, Catholic-Republican groups in Northern Ireland. A more exclusively political fundamentalism occurred in communist China under Mao Zedong. In this usage, the term suggests dogma and intransigence, and would be unlikely to be accepted by the individuals, groups, or regimes themselves.

See also ESSENTIALISM; FOUNDATIONALISM; TERRORISM.

GATEKEEPING

A term employed within media PRODUCTION and especially journalism to describe the role of intermediary personnel, such as editors or others occupying a strategic decision-making role between the points of production and RECEPTION. The term is derived from American-based Social Psychology and assumes a one-way transmission of COMMUNICATION that passes through various filters. It draws attention to the importance of professional CODES (of public service, impartiality, what is deemed newsworthy, comic, in good or bad taste and so on, and may involve questions of law and copyright, as in the use of 'leaked' information). It therefore implies or constructs an understanding of an AUDIENCE or readership and of cultural and ethical values alongside professional practice, of whom competitors are also an important part. In a study of the role of gatekeepers in British television in the 1970s, Stuart Hood maintained that this process reinforces a 'middle-class consensus politics', which places the tradition of impartiality on the side of the establishment (1972: 418). This, he relates to the selective recruitment patterns of the broadcasting media – in effect, another 'gate' through which some pass and others do not.

There are limitations to the concept itself, however, and to the model to which it belongs, since they do not allow for the production of meaning or of VALUE through interaction, dialogue or NEGOTIATION. Studies of the media in the 1980s and 1990s have tended to shift attention to these processes and to the consumption rather than the production of media MESSAGES.

See also CULTURAL INTERMEDIARIES; FLOW; SCHEDULING.

GAZE

There are two uses of the concept of the gaze relevant to the study of literary and cultural forms, one deriving from the work of Michel Foucault (1926–1984), the other associated with film theory; both are, in the end, concerned with relations of POWER.

Foucault argued that we should understand perception as governed by the modes of DISCOURSE characterizing particular social and intellectual regimes and not as a literal index of a way of seeing things. His work is commonly seen to belong to an 'anti-ocular' movement in French thought that polemicizes against the primacy that sight has had in western culture (an everyday example of this would be the use of the expression 'I see' to mean 'I understand'). Foucault employs the concept of the gaze in this connection in describing his *The Birth of the Clinic* (1973). This is a study of the new forms of medical practice that emerged with the introduction of the clinic as a site for diagnosis and teaching in the late eighteenth century, and highlights in particular changed perspectives on anatomy in the treatment of illness and disease. It is a book, says Foucault, about space, language and death, and 'about the act of seeing, the gaze' (Hoy [ed] 1986: 191). His use of this term carries the sense of being objectified, subordinated or threatened by the look of another, and points to the role of medical practice in securing a dominant discourse of seeing. Foucault also deals directly with the conditions and effects of the gaze in the concept of 'panoptic surveillance' in the later study *Discipline and Punish* (1977). His example is the 'Panopticon', a model prison designed by Jeremy Bentham, which would comprise a circular building of prison cells, an open yard and a central tower. From this tower, the prison-keeper could observe all the inmates in the prison without himself being observed. The Panopticon would therefore ensure the effects of constant surveillance through an invisible and not necessarily actual observer. It is a dramatic instance, therefore, of the association of power and the gaze Foucault is concerned to identify.

The second use of the concept of the gaze derives from the radical film theory of the 1970s associated especially with the UK journal *Screen* (see SCREEN THEORY). Contributors to the journal sought to absorb the leading concepts of PSYCHOANALYSIS and SEMIOLOGY, and to mobilize these in a politicized reading of film that was at the same time indebted to the modernist MARXISM of Bertolt Brecht and to FEMINISM. A specific theory of the 'male gaze' was elaborated by Laura Mulvey in her extremely influential essay 'Visual pleasure and narrative cinema' (first published in *Screen* 16:3 Autumn 1975 and reprinted many times). Mulvey drew on Freud's concept of 'scopophilia' (a translation of Freud's German *Schaulust*) to designate the PLEASURE of watching screen IMAGES, and on Lacan's concept of the 'MIRROR-PHASE'. The latter describes the moment when, in the formation of the ego, a young baby sees its perfect, unified image in a mirror and thenceforth experiences IDENTITY as always 'reflected back' – its unity always desired rather than realized. Viewing images in a darkened cinema is likened to 'voyeuristic phantasy' and can be understood, Mulvey argues, as an expression both of 'active scopophilia' or the looking at an object separated from the self, and 'narcissism' or self-love, involving the contrary movement of identification with a fuller, more perfect image presented on screen. Mulvey draws out the implicit GENDER imbalance in the psychoanalytic theorization of these concepts and argues that in DOMINANT or mainstream cinema, the gaze in question is male, and that it is men who are invited to view and DESIRE women on screen as objects. Scopophilia thus means 'taking other people as objects, subjecting them to a controlling and curious gaze'. Men look while women are positioned as sexual objects who can only exhibit 'to-be-looked-at-ness' (1989b: 16, 19).

The male gaze, Mulvey adds, can take either a direct or indirect form. The first corresponds to the moments in cinema of 'SPECTACLE' (from the performance of a song to a striptease) when the narrative is suspended and the woman as 'star' performs, as it were, directly for the viewer. The second occurs in narrative action when the male gaze of the viewer is mediated through an identification with the leading male protagonist ('the bearer of the look') on screen. At the same time, women are thought to represent a threat – in Freudian psychoanalytic theory, the threat of castration, since women are seen to lack the PHALLUS. In conventional Hollywood GENRE film, this is overcome, Mulvey argues, in a narrative that either victimizes or fetishizes women (the fetish standing in as a FANTASY object for the threatened loss). The male gaze is therefore active and the expression of a drive for mastery, whereas the 'female gaze' is necessarily subordinated and passive, limited to an identification with the woman being looked at.

Mulvey's aim in the essay is to polemicize against this positioning of women and the way popular film reinforces the structures of PATRIARCHY. She argues that this calls for no less than the 'destruction of pleasure' associated with conventional cinema and for a new non-illusionist AVANT-GARDE cinema, along Brechtian lines, which encourages active critical participation. Her arguments have aroused much debate and frequent rejoinders. In her own 'Afterthoughts on "Visual pleasure and narrative cinema"'(1989c), Mulvey explains that she is not endorsing the position of the male as the representative spectator but that, with Freud, she understands SEXUALITY as comprising both masculine and feminine attributes. The gaze is therefore 'masculinized' but, though repressive, may reactivate the female spectator's early 'fantasy of action' (1989: 37). This suggests that, although identification is gendered, this is psychically and culturally, but not permanently, organized in terms of the binary pairs of male/female, active/passive. Cinema shows how SEXUAL DIFFERENCE is 'unstable, oscillating' (1989: 30).

Elsewhere, the idea of more mobile subject positions, for women as well as for male viewers, has been developed as a critique of the seemingly fixed positions described by Mulvey. For these arguments in relation to 'the woman's film', melodrama and television, see, for example, Pribram ([ed] 1988), Gamman and Marshment ([eds] 1988) and Stacey (1994). A set of relevant essays and extracts on this theme, including Mulvey's essay, is contained in Easthope ([ed] 1993).

See also FETISHISM; NEGOTIATION.

GENDER

A term for the social, cultural and historical construction of SEXUAL DIFFERENCE. As such, gender is to be distinguished from essentialist conceptions of sexual IDENTITY or SUBJECTIVITY founded on a natural 'core' of biological sex or the BODY. This now commonly accepted definition and distinction was introduced by feminist theory and criticism of the 1970s, although feminist debates of this period were themselves marked by the respective claims of essentializing definitions of 'woman' or 'woman's experience' and social-constructionist arguments (see GYNOCRITICISM).

The elision of sex with gender equates male and female with masculine and feminine. This then 'naturalizes' the standard traits of sexual difference established in society (men are physically strong and therefore associated with the world of labour, sport and physical combat, and are active in the public domain; women are physically weak and therefore passive, their sphere is the home, and their bodies determine their roles as mothers and objects of male DESIRE). This dualism not only reinforces male authority over women, but also perpetuates the norm of male heterosexuality as the model of natural sexual identity. Adrienne Rich termed this the 'COMPULSORY HETEROSEXUALITY' of western societies (1980). The hierarchical binary opposition of male/female, in other words, reinforces PATRIARCHY and sexual privilege to the disadvantage of women, lesbians and gay men. The study of gender is therefore motivated by a CRITIQUE of such polarities and their associated terms. If gender is understood as socially and culturally defined, then it can be 'undefined' or deconstructed. Feminists and others have therefore understood the analysis of gender as necessary to the defeat of sexism and important to general social change.

This analysis has been conducted across a range of academic disciplines and, especially, within Literary Studies and forms of Cultural Studies, in the sphere of textual REPRESENTATIONS. An important aspect of such study has been an analysis of the composition and influence of stereotypes. It should be understood, however, that many cultural texts and DISCOURSES both comply with and themselves subvert such stereotypes. The use of an all-male cast of boys to play women, and the frequent use of disguise and cross-dressing in Shakespeare's plays, for example, serve to reveal that normative assumptions about sexual identity are in fact cultural-historical and not simply 'natural'. Films such as *Tootsie* and *The Crying Game* may be said to operate in a basically similar way. They may of course return us to the familiar world where sexual and other norms are affirmed (see hooks 1994, on *The Crying Game*), but they may also work as examples of ESTRANGEMENT. That is to say, like criticism and theory, they may make us aware that what is 'familiar' and 'natural' is a matter of social convention.

The association of 'gender studies' with FEMINISM has tended to focus attention on the representation of women. But gender is also, obviously, and increasingly, important in conceptions of masculinity. This has been pursued inside and outside the academy in 'men's groups', which have taken liberal, socialist and conservative forms and met with a mixed response from feminists. The agenda signalled by the subtitle of Boone and Cadden's edited collection of largely Literary Studies, *Engendering Men: The Question of Male Feminist Criticism* (1990) proved to be a provocative one for those it implied were 'women feminists'. Elsewhere, Eve Kosofsky Sedgwick's study of 'homosocial' relations shaping literary and film texts (1985) has proved a more productive intervention, as have the challenges to normative CODES of masculinity and heterosexuality within gay studies and QUEER THEORY. Meanwhile, studies by, for example, Connell (1987, 1995) and Seidler (1989, 1992) have brought historical and sociological perspectives to the study of masculinity.

Probably the most influential example of 'gender theory' emerging from an intersection of queer theory, feminism and POSTMODERNISM has been the work of Judith Butler. She sees 'compulsory heterosexuality' as reinforcing a 'gender coherence' (1993: 37; see also Segal 1997). Gender roles, she says, in *Gender Trouble,* 'congeal over time to produce the appearance of substance, of a natural sort of being' (1990: 33). Butler seeks to 'trouble' this coherence and draws attention to the performative aspect of SEXUALITY in the adopted personae of, for example, butch lesbian, femme lesbian and drag queen, who imitate or PARODY set categories and therefore expose their contingency. Eve Kosofsky Sedgwick, once more, and Jonathan Dollimore (1991) show, in related studies, how heterosexuality is already internally unstable or incoherent and that it is shadowed by its 'other', 'homosociality' or homosexuality, as a necessary, desired and feared aspect of itself.

Some believe that Butler's argument and the postmodern take on gender in queer theory (in which the body becomes a pluralized floating signifier without the anchor of settled reference) risks ignoring the force of material social circumstances and the physical matter of the body. As Chris Shilling, following Connell (1987), writes:

> gendered categories and practices operate as material forces which help to shape and form women's and men's bodies in ways that reinforce particular images of femininity and masculinity... Gendered practices and images of the body exert an influence which does not, then, remain at the level of consciousness or discourse. They become embodied and can affect people for life.
>
> (1997: 83–4)

The body too, therefore, Shilling and others understand, is itself constructed according to various social ideologies, activities and eventualities, including work, sport, dieting, illness and the process of ageing.

As this account suggests, the study of gender inevitably involves a consideration of sexual difference and sexuality. In addition, few – in theory at least – would separate these questions from the other overlapping or contradictory ways in which cultural identities are constructed: by CLASS or ETHNICITY, for example. Studies of the interwoven relations of gender, sexuality and ethnicity have occurred in African-American theory and criticism, and in postcolonial studies, often by women writers (Spivak 1987; Trinh 1989; hooks 1990a). In Film Studies, examples occur in Dyer (1990, 1993b); Mercer (1994) and Young (1995).

See also ANDROGYNY; ESSENTIALISM; TRANSGRESSIVE.

GENEALOGY

A term associated with the later work of Michel Foucault, particularly the study *Discipline and Punish* (1977) on the relations of knowledge and POWER. Genealogy identifies the complexities of historical processes and points to the 'discontinuous, illegitimate knowledges' that counter the 'centralizing powers' operating to stabilize contemporary society (1980a: 83–4). It is therefore less totalizing and more supportive of interventionist oppositional discourses than Foucault's earlier concept of ARCHAEOLOGY. Genealogy tracks how objects of study (the human SUBJECT, the poor, the POPULAR, a GENRE) are identified; how DISCOURSES, second, constitute and evaluate these objects; and, third, how general propositions emerge from this process and are dispersed to uphold a particular 'discursive formation'. In this way, definitions and COMMON SENSE notions of truth, about, say, the 'individual', 'woman', 'the media' and so on, are maintained in society. Genealogy does not therefore directly analyse or interpret a particular text or kinds of text, but shows how it is constituted; how – to suggest an example that is not Foucault's own – 'melodrama' might be popularly identified as a 'woman's' genre, associated with romance, sentiment and hysteria in a discourse that reinforces GENDER stereotypes and the rule of PATRIARCHY, as well as distinctions between low and high CULTURE. A genealogical analysis will therefore seek to unmask the process by which this kind of association between cultural forms and relations of power comes about.

See also HEGEMONY.

GENRE

The term for a type of literary, artistic or cultural composition characterized by a set of recognizable conventions of character, ICONOGRAPHY and NARRATIVE. For the most part, the term is used in accounts of 'POPULAR genres' (science fiction, detective fiction, the musical, the western, soap opera, sitcom). A broader application includes both discrete traditional forms (the elegy, the ode) or more dispersed modes (romance, pastoral). Other conventional forms – the novel, or realist novel, election broadcasts, news bulletins, lectures – might also feasibly be described as genres.

The contemporary analysis of the familiar 'popular genres' has drawn upon structuralist models (identifying the binary oppositions governing looks, locations, cultural themes in the gangster film or western, for example) and theories of IDEOLOGY (see, on film, Cook [ed] 1985: 58–112). The view of genres as CODEd systems, comparable in their structure and operation to other linguistic and artistic forms was an effective early reply to the dismissal of popular genres as the formulaic products of the MASS-production entertainment industries. In fact, a structuralist analysis, however textual or 'scientific' in intention, could not itself avoid the issue of cultural VALUE, nor the debate on high or minority versus popular or mass culture in which popular genres have been a regular participant (Hawkins 1990).

A greater problem for genre analysis, however, has been, not in countering cultural elitism, but in responding to the poststructuralist CRITIQUE of the assumption that texts or groups of texts could be viewed as 'centred' and classifiable systems of meaning. In 'The law of genre' (1992b), Jacques Derrida writes that while the notion of genre designates a norm that repels 'impurity, anomaly or monstrosity', there is 'lodged within the heart of the law itself, a law of impurity or a principle of contamination' (1992a: 225). Under this 'law of the law of genre', as Derrida terms it, 'Every text participates in one of several genres, there is no genreless text … yet such participation never amounts to belonging' (1992a: 230). This at once opens the concept of genre to include all texts and unsettles the classificatory approach that seeks to distinguish one genre absolutely from another. If we accept this 'law' we have, henceforth, to think of intertextual relations within and across genres, of mixed modes rather than pure models. Many familiar novels and films (*Raiders of the Lost Ark,* the *Star Wars* franchise, *Strange Days*) in fact proceed from this looser sense of belongingness, mixing, in these cases, adventure with the war film, the western with space opera, and science fiction with the porn thriller (Collins 1993). A spate of so-called 'Scandinavian' TV detective dramas, and an example such as the ongoing series *The Fall*, similarly cross detective fiction with the thriller or horror genres.

At the same time, the study of historically earlier, now 'recycled' modes in cinema, such as *film noir,* romance and melodrama, have given a lead to a differently oriented analysis of popular genre forms, concerned with the circumstances of

PRODUCTION and RECEPTION in a changing CULTURE of popular images and attitudes (see Gledhill 1987, 1997).

GLOBALIZATION

A term introduced in the 1980s and used principally to describe the world expansion of economic markets in the late twentieth century. In many ways, this process follows the underlying logic of industrial CAPITALISM in the west as it enters the information age and the reign of multinational corporations. However, some significant changes have also accompanied this development (see Held and McGrew [eds] 2000 on both views). Among the latter, the saturation of markets and costly overheads in the western world has stimulated the re-siting of companies in the so-called Second and Third Worlds. These offer new markets, but also, and primarily, present a pool of cheap labour. While western products and CULTURE (music, films, TV, in so-called 'mediascapes') find consumers in distant continents, these countries also serve to produce the products that are sold in the west. A major producer such as Japan has also shifted the axis of major capitalist nations from the west to the Pacific Rim, a development reinforced by the appearance of other vigorous economies and financial centres in the region, such as Malaysia and Singapore.

Capitalism has, in these terms, become a world system operating across national borders, but one characterized by 'FLOWS' of finance and information, rather than by centralized economic or political control. This development in interlinked world economies underlies many descriptions of POSTMODERNISM. This is then variously understood as a synonym for advanced global capitalism or as its cultural reflex or, less often, as a heterogeneous and critical response to that system. What prompts this last perspective is the paradoxical evidence of fluid and hybrid cultures, combining east and west, in a world of increased uniformities at an economic level: a world of Salman Rushdie, Hindipop, African-American cinema alongside McDonald's or Rupert Murdoch's communications empire.

Debates on globalization have been taken up especially in Cultural Geography and social theory. The nation-state is commonly thought to be in crisis and this gives rise to a range of possible scenarios, from the triumph of so-called 'third cultures' – anonymous transnational systems comprised of financial, legal and information NETWORKS – to intensified nationalist competition and conflict. A major contributor to these debates is Manual Castells (1996, 1997) who questions the uniformity and comprehensiveness of globalization. 'There is', he insists, 'no such thing as a global single society' (1997: 155).

A further important theme in these debates is the relation of the LOCAL and the global (Massey 1993) or what is styled as 'glocalization' (Robertson 1995). Does this involve a reassertion of western HEGEMONY or do the 'flows' of people, information, images and money bring about new cross-cultural encounters and a recognition of diversity? (Featherstone 1991; Featherstone et al. [eds] 1995). Often this question is taken up in relation to specific localities and especially in relation to the contemporary 'global' CITY (Sassen 1991).

See also COSMOPOLITANISM; NATIONALISM; POST-FORDISM.

GOTHIC

The word 'Gothic' or 'Goth' originally referred to northern European tribes of the fourth, fifth and sixth centuries. Later, with the pejorative connotations of uncouth, ugly, archaic or barbaric, derived from this association, the term was applied by Renaissance critics to thirteenth-century architectural styles. It came thence to denote anything vast, gloomy or medieval in architecture, or to describe signs of decay and wildness in buildings or landscapes. In all such applications – whether in relation to architecture, literature or art – there is the implication of an alternative AESTHETIC idiom that counters or offends mainstream classical styles, along with their attendant middle-class norms of taste and morality. In developed and self-conscious examples, the Gothic is thereby linked with notions of repression, taboo and terror. At its starkest, the 'barbaric' is invoked against a conception of 'civilization' and against normative conceptions of 'the real'.

'Gothic literature' dates from the late eighteenth and early nineteenth centuries (Horace Walpole's *Castle of Otranto* (1764) and Ann Radcliffe's *Mysteries of Udolpho* (1794) are notable founding texts, followed by innumerable others, including the stories of Edgar Allen Poe and the novels of the Brontë sisters). This GENRE has presented NARRATIVES of a 'darker' psychic reality often linked to particular locations. It might be said that the Gothic mode therefore presents an example of the CHRONOTOPE, conjoining a particular time or times – the Middle Ages and the period of the late eighteenth and nineteenth centuries, when the key Gothic texts first appeared – with a repertoire of familiar 'Gothic' places. The latter include deserted moors, remote and ruined castles, abbeys and country houses, the ghettos and alleys of industrial cities, or the interiors of chapels, vaults, cellars, crypts, secret passages, corridors and so on, complete with creaking doors and staircases. These landscapes are also typically peopled by a gallery of marginal and TRANSGRESSIVE types: mad scientists, evil monks or nuns, rapacious aristocrats, outlaws, monsters, or the undead – doubles of one kind or another releasing a contrary side to the rational world of progress, stability and respectability.

On these grounds, the Gothic can be understood as giving narrative form to the social and psychic OTHER of bourgeois MODERNITY. In addition, there is an evident association between the form's standard ICONOGRAPHY and especially its locations with the realm of the UNCONSCIOUS. Not surprisingly, the Gothic mode is often approached through a psychoanalytic, as well as an ideological, perspective (Punter 1997) and seen to give expression to the suppressed fears and desires of a particular social class or social order. However, as Botting (1996) argues, the Gothic is ambivalent in its aims and effects, and can be understood as a 'safety valve' that gives expression to these subliminal emotions only so as to reaffirm the norms that have been unsettled. Major examples such as *Frankenstein* and *Dracula* would be cases in point. Also, since the conventions sketched above are now so easily imitated, the Gothic has arguably become clichéd beyond redemption and subject only to comedy or self-parody. Linda Bayer-Berenbaum is one commentator who believes that the Gothic's essential features – 'an intensification of consciousness, an expansion of reality and a confrontation with evil' (1982: 16)

– persist even in examples of modern PASTICHE. Even where there is laughter, this is combined with the Gothic's 'principal effect', she says, which is 'terror'. These, she links in the modern period to an awareness of the horrors of war, of the Holocaust and the destructive powers of technology (1982: 13).

In contemporary culture, the Gothic or 'Gothicism' has a very wide provenance that overlaps with 'horror' genres and the grotesque, and has become a familiar category in academic life, publishing and the entertainment industries. In the late 1970s (and for some years beyond), it also embraced the subcultural style of 'Goths', known by a shared dress code and appearance (black clothes, white face, heavy make-up), a preference for certain bands (Bauhaus, the Cure) and places – for example, Whitby in North Yorkshire, where Dracula first landed in Bram Stoker's late nineteenth-century tale. Once more, these developments ask the question whether Gothic is, or has become, a marketable, easily incorporated and eventually conformist cultural style, or expresses an alternative philosophical orientation opposed to the social and economic status quo.

See also EXCESS; SUBCULTURES; UNCANNY.

GOVERNMENTALITY

Michel Foucault (1926–1984) has been a pervasive influence upon Cultural Theory (see ARCHAEOLOGY, ARCHIVE, DISCOURSE, ÉPISTÈME, GENEALOGY, POWER). Attention has been drawn more recently, also, in the idea of governmentality, to a perspective upon the state and social and political relations, which some commentators have found particularly apposite to modern times. What, in *The Foucault Effect* (Burchell, Gordon and Miller [eds] 1991), is described as the 'activity or art called *government*' (1991: ix), or what Foucault terms 'governmentality', has characterized the ensemble of institutions and procedures by which the modern liberal state has sought to manage the economy and administer to its population (1991: 87–105). The concept extends in Foucault's thinking beyond a conventional political emphasis and direct state governance, however, to include diverse practices such as the organization of health and welfare, the use of social statistics, the introduction of insurance, conceptions of criminology, poverty and work. It also depends on the accredited experts who command the discourse of such fields or related institutions.

The effect of rational governance across these many spheres is therefore to restrain, while administering to the being and actions of individuals, families, communities and populations. Government entails an 'economy' that polices subjects through statistics, surveillance and the law while also conscripting them through internalized programmes of self-management. However, all such discourses and institutions are bounded by the very limits that define them. Accordingly, so Foucault argues, systems of governmentality always, in practice, reveal their own limitations despite their pretensions to coherence. While they exclude other possible orders of being, they simultaneously disclose them as what they prohibit. The state is, in consequence, characterized by an anxiety at the fragility of the 'thresholds' it inevitably sets in defining its regimes of power, for if there are thresholds there is the possibility of transformation and an alternative beyond them. While Foucault is often seen to present a pessimistic political scenario, the logic of governmentality confers upon people the 'ability to know "beyond" governmental knowledge' (Gordon in Burchell, Gordon and Miller [eds] 1991: 18) and thus CRITIQUE the present order of things.

Governmentality has become a visible topic of discussion in social and political thought (see Miller and Rose 1990; Dean 1999). Tony Bennett (1998) is one cultural critic who has taken up Foucault's notion. What attracts him is that Foucault describes a system that sponsors a critique of its limitations in the terms of its own supposed provisions. To view governmentality this way thus gives 'rise to an active, disputatious and, above all, demanding relationship to cultural power' (1998: 178). It has an advantage, therefore, over a bipolar model of unrelenting power and unrelieved subjection, and over postmodern notions of transgressive but, at root, ineffectual resistance. For Bennett, this has a further significant implication. To accept Foucault's view of the increasing governmentalization of social relations, means that the study of culture must reflect less on its Marxist or libertarian heritage than on more practical 'reformist' strategies, which exploit the logic of rationality's internal limitations (Bennett 1998: 61–2). More polemically still, this means that such study must recognize how its own location within academic institutions places it, too, 'within the realm of government' (1998: 6).

See also CIVIL SOCIETY.

GYNESIS

A concept formulated by Alice Jardine in her study *Gynesis: Configurations of Woman and Modernity* (1985). It signifies, she writes, the 'putting into discourse of "woman" or the "feminine" as problematic' (1985: 236), occupying the 'spaces' in the master or male-centred DISCOURSE where the feminine is represented. Barbara Creed (1997) uses this notion in her analysis of the hybrid genre of sci-fi horror films, following Jardine's suggestion that in American, unlike European, POPULAR CULTURE, gynesis appears less at a level of theory than of REPRESENTATION. Film texts such as the *Alien* trilogy, *The Fly* and *Videodrome,* Creed argues, are invaded by 'woman' – in symbolic representations of the processes of REPRODUCTION and female BODY parts. The male body is thereby transformed into what is conceived as the 'monstrous feminine': giving birth, metamorphosing, growing a vagina-like wound, for example, in NARRATIVES that enact a loss of controlled male IDENTITY. In this way, such texts expose their own 'non-knowledge', putting notions of the SUBJECT, the body, the UNCONSCIOUS in crisis, using the figure of the woman as 'OTHER' to explore the unknown, 'uncertain future' (1997: 47).

Jardine believes that gynesis can occur as a disruptive force in both male- and female-authored texts, not unlike Julia Kristeva's notion of the SEMIOTIC 'chora' to which both Jardine and Creed allude. The 'CHORA' is the womb-like space in which mother and child are united. Jardine reflects on how all space has been traditionally CODED feminine, and Creed sees in the operation of gynesis in the texts she examines 'a quest for the mother' (1997: 50). She examines the complexity of this search for – and destruction of – the mother alien creature, and rescue of her daughter by the androgynous Ripley in *Aliens*. Creed is suspicious, however, of the benefits of such postmodern role-play for women.

See also ABJECTION; FEMINISM.

GYNOCRITICISM

A term introduced into the field of Literary Study by the American feminist critic, Elaine Showalter (1941–). The term appeared first in her essay 'Towards a feminist poetics' (1979 in Showalter [ed] 1986) and helped to theorize the practice of her earlier and extremely influential *A Literature of their Own* (1977). This had brought an extended tradition of British women novelists of the nineteenth and twentieth centuries to serious critical attention and stimulated both academic work and the publishing of women's writing. In the later essay, Showalter distinguishes gynocriticism from the criticism by women of male authors. Its object, she says, is to draw a historical map of women's writing (such as her own work had done), to analyse female creativity, and to study and promote the work of women authors.

Gynocriticism therefore names a committedly 'woman-centred' approach. This has been criticized, however, from within FEMINISM for its latent ESSENTIALISM – the belief that there is a distinct and autonomous female writing derived from an unproblematized, commonly recognized 'female experience'. Toril Moi (1985) argues that this reinforces a liberal humanist notion of the unified SUBJECT, and commits writers and critics to a realist mode since this is deemed to reproduce the valued experience most successfully. Moi contrasts Showalter's emphasis on 'female writing' with the interest of French feminists in 'feminine writing' or *ÉCRITURE FÉMININE*. She makes her case particularly through a reading of the fiction and theory of Virginia Woolf, whom Showalter sees as narrow, elusive and as repressing her woman's experience. Moi also responds to the distinction Showalter makes between epochs of women's writing: from, as Showalter sees it, the 'feminine' in the period 1840–80; the 'feminist' in the period 1880–1920; and the 'female' from 1920 to the present. The term 'female', Moi responds, is biologically based, 'feminine' is culturally constructed, while 'feminist' is an elected political category.

See also CANON; REALISM.

HABITUS

Appropriated by the French sociologist of culture and education, Pierre Bourdieu (1930–2002) from, in his own account, the tradition of Aristotle, Aquinas and figures in European philosophy, including Hegel and Durkheim. Bourdieu defines habitus as 'a durable, transposable system of definitions' acquired initially by the young child in the home as a result of the conscious and unconscious practices of her/his family (1990: 134). This comprises the 'primary habitus'. Subsequently, this is transformed into a secondary, tertiary or further habitus by the child's passage through different social institutions, principally schooling. This developed habitus contains within it, however, as Bourdieu makes clear, the characteristics of early socialization in the home and family, which persist as 'the basis of all subsequent experiences... from restructuring to restructuring' (1992: 134).

Bourdieu's notion of structure implies a flexible idea of DETERMINATION. The habitus is both structured and structuring. It is the consequence of an individual's family, CLASS position, status, education, IDEOLOGY and distinctive tastes (derived from the individual histories of its contributing members), and might also be more broadly derived from a common historically produced set of dispositions on the part of a particular social or ethnic group. As Bourdieu writes, 'The habitus – embodied history, internalized as second nature and so forgotten as history – is the active presence of the whole past of which it is the product' (1990: 56).

At the same time, this acquired configuration is open to creative variation as the individual meshes with a relatively stable common habitus and conducts this forward. The individual's habitus therefore emerges from a dialogue with a family, ethnic, class-based or gendered collective habitus in an evolving process of structuration and restructuration that shapes individual and social mobility.

The habitus is therefore a generative rather than a fixed system: a basis from which endless improvisations can derive; a 'practical mastery' of skills, routines, aptitudes and assumptions, which leaves the individual free to make (albeit limited) choices in the encounter with new environments or FIELDS. As in a sport or jazz, in Bourdieu's favoured analogies, mastery of the rules or an instrument gives a 'feel for the game', which enables individuals to improvise in response to the circumstances of the moment. As in these cases, habitus, in an important emphasis, is also 'embodied', articulated in BODY language and gesture across an entire range of concrete behaviours, from patterns of consumption to decisions as to how to use one's time.

See also ETHNICITY; CULTURAL INTERMEDIARIES; IDENTITY; TASTE.

HEGEMONY

A term meaning, in Greek, 'rule' or 'leadership', whose influence in Literary and Cultural Studies derives from its use in the writings of the Italian communist activist and philosopher Antonio Gramsci (1891–1937) to describe the operation of IDEOLOGY in modern capitalist societies (1971a). In classical MARXISM, the dominant ideology of a given society is identified with the interests of the dominant economic CLASS. 'The ideas of the ruling class are in every epoch the ruling ideas,' Marx wrote in *The Communist Manifesto*. Thus, the class in control of 'material PRODUCTION' is seen also to control the realm of ideas and 'mental production' or, by extension, the domain of CULTURE.

Gramsci developed this notion to account for the way a ruling class maintains itself in power, or secures and sustains its hegemony. It does this, he argued, not simply through a direct expression of its economic authority, but by actively exercising its intellectual, moral and ideological influence in the realm of CIVIL SOCIETY – a term for the social realm between the economy and state. Thus, it aims to persuade the majority of the population of its economic and cultural legitimacy as a ruling class. In capitalist societies, it is in the interest of the ruling class to have society as a whole accept the rule of property and the workings of a market economy, and thus a range of attendant inequalities of wealth, status and opportunity. Since the advantages of this system for all, rather than some, of the population are not immediately obvious, the ruling class must win consent to its legitimacy, even to the point of making it appear inevitable and simply 'the way things are'.

This is Gramsci's key insight. For a ruling class to maintain its hegemonic position, the institutions, hierarchies, ideas and allied social practices that serve its fundamental economic interests must be accepted spontaneously as the 'natural' order of things. Hegemony therefore seeks to articulate and renew the prevailing 'COMMON SENSE' mentality in society as a whole.

Although, as this suggests, hegemony is secured for the most part in Gramsci's view by consent, there are also moments of crisis, or flash-points, in a society when a given consensus and hegemonic order are challenged. At such times (when dissatisfaction or opposition are expressed in a demonstration, strike or riot, in their most evident public forms), it may be necessary to re-secure the social and political order by 'coercion' rather than 'consent'. This calls for the exercise of the rule of law or an explicit show of force. This has led some commentators to see a distinction in Gramsci's thought between hegemony, which is won by consent, and ideology, which may be imposed by violence. If so, at the same time, as Terry Eagleton notes, hegemony appears to be 'a broader category than ideology: it includes ideology, but is not reducible to it' (1991: 112). A ruling class can maintain its hegemony, that is to say, through a variety of means, including the directly ideological, across the broad spheres of political, economic and cultural activity.

The distinction between consent and coercion in Gramsci's discussion was further developed by the French Marxist philosopher, Louis Althusser (1918–1990), particularly in his influential essay, 'Ideology and ideological state apparatuses' (1971a). Here, Althusser distinguished between 'repressive' state and 'IDEOLOGICAL' STATE APPARATUSes – the first referring to the government, courts, army and police, the second to political parties, the church, media, family and, above all, for Althusser, education. This, too, has had an influence, especially on British Cultural Studies – though a figure such as Raymond Williams has shown an evident preference for the Gramscian model (see Williams 1977). This work-characteristically sought to employ the idea of hegemony in combination with the concepts of POWER and DISCOURSE in the study of the media, popular and youth cultures, or of the SIGN systems defining mainstream and subcultural forms (Storey [ed] 1994: Part 4).

Gramsci had suggested that a particular hegemonic regime was not a permanent order of things, but had to win consent to a negotiated ideological settlement with subordinated groups. The general importance of this for the broad study of culture was, first, that it confirmed that MASS and POPULAR forms 'mattered' and had a significant ideological function, and, second, revealed how culture was the site of contradiction, since artistic and cultural forms comprised both consensual and potentially alternative and oppositional meanings. Thus, it could be seen how cultural expression endorsed, but simultaneously extended or challenged an ideological consensus. This set of ideas gave a vocabulary and legitimacy to a radical academic perspective, and helped describe the role of INTELLECTUALS committed to the CRITIQUE of 'COMMON SENSE' and the building of a 'counter-hegemonic' culture.

For a variety of reasons, the class perspective of this position became less insistent in the 1980s and 1990s. Nevertheless, the idea of hegemony has directed the attention of a generation or more of academics and students to the ways in which conventional and alternative or dissident meanings can coexist in the popular press, soap operas, a pop song, football chant, style of clothing or dance, or a whole other range of social forms and behaviours. It therefore remains a central and productive concept in the study of culture, open to further elaboration and practical work.

See also DOMINANT/RESIDUAL/EMERGENT; ESTABLISHMENT; HABITUS; NEGOTIATION.

HERMENEUTICS

A term often used interchangeably with 'interpretation', but referring more strictly to the theory of interpretation and the issues, techniques and procedures this entails. It is associated particularly with the German philosophical tradition, including contributions from Martin Heidegger and Hans-Georg Gadamer on the nature of the truth 'disclosed' in the work of art, compared with the propositional statements of natural science. Two kinds of general question posed within hermeneutics have concerned the existence of stable meaning in texts and the role of individual authors, readers and historical context in establishing this meaning. The tension identified in this way between text and SUBJECT in an already circulating world of interpretations was early encapsulated in the idea of the 'hermeneutic circle' proposed by Wilhelm Dilthey. These issues have been taken up notably in RECEPTION theory.

In the modern period, the issues of concern to the hermeneutic tradition have been queried within both traditional literary criticism and POSTSTRUCTURALISM. Doubts about the authority of the AUTHOR over the meaning of texts were sounded, for example, in the idea of the 'Intentional Fallacy' introduced by the American critics W.K. Wimsatt and Monroe Beardsley in the mid 1940s and further undermined by Roland Barthes's famous polemic on 'The death of the author' (1977a [1968]). An even more dramatic move 'against interpretation' was announced by the American critic Susan Sontag in a book of that title (1966). Meanwhile, theories of IDEOLOGY, DISCOURSE and INTERTEXTUALITY have shifted attention away from the interpretation of individual texts, and thus from the theory governing such interpretation, to the network of textual relations and institutional contexts within which texts are produced and consumed.

To examine textual meanings in these latter terms means reading or viewing are no longer understood as a penetration of textual surfaces in the search for determinate meanings, or as an exercise in evaluation. The emphasis in 'reception theory' on relations between texts and readers means that it has come to share some, but not all, of the assumptions of poststructuralist theory. At the same time, the sense of interpretation as the discovery of implicit authorial intentions, the expectation of CLOSURE and of an allied quest for stable meaning have a strong residual force, particularly within literary culture where new author-based readings of single CANONIC texts remain common.

See also REALISM; REPRESENTATION; VALUE.

HETEROGLOSSIA

A term from Greek meaning 'other languages', and a central concept in the theories first developed in the 1920s and 1930s by Mikhail Bakhtin and his associates (see DIALOGICS, CARNIVAL, CHRONOTOPE).

Mikhail Bakhtin (1981 [1934–41]) distinguished between monoglot, polyglot and heteroglot language situations, marked in turn by their shared or centralized values, the coexistence of differences, and the union of diverse voices and perspectives. Earlier, V.N. Vološhinov (1986 [1929]) had theorized that language was multi-accented, socially situated and, as such, involved in the operation of IDEOLOGY and relations of POWER in society. A decentralizing impulse towards multiplicity and dissent (heteroglossia) was seen to exist in tension with a reverse, centripetal movement in language and society towards the stability of a common or official (monoglot) DISCOURSE. This offered a sociological theory of language and CLASS power but also a focused SEMIOLOGY since 'differently oriented accents' were seen to 'intersect in every ideological sign' (1986:23). This interaction and struggle over meanings were seen as internalized in individual signs and speech acts, and as enacted across the wide spectrum of social situations in a fluctuating tussle between containment and the full expression of heteroglossia at times of social crisis.

The merits of the theory in steering between a narrow FORMALISM and the crude REFLECTIONISM of socialist REALISM in the contemporary Soviet Union were welcomed in the period of its later publication when the non-historicized theories of language in STRUCTURALISM and POSTSTRUCTURALISM held sway and a more flexible theory of MARXISM also seemed called for (see Raymond Williams 1977 and Bennett 1979, both instrumental in introducing the theory to Anglo-American readers). The concepts of the Bakhtin circle, especially as formulated in Vološhinov's text, have also helped inspire the development of a more linguistically based 'social semiotics' (Hodge and Kress 1988).

Bakhtin saw heteroglossia as developed especially in the novel and pre-eminently in the work of Dostoevsky, where a range of voices, perspectives and meanings produces a 'polyphony' that denies single authorial control (Bakhtin 1963). Lyric poetry, he saw as more private and in that sense, monoglossic. This narrowing of the concept to a particular literary GENRE, though this is widely conceived in Bakhtin, is, however, questionable, given its inspiration in a broad social theory of language. Its subsequent use has extended its application beyond the novel genre and beyond literature (some might think thereby diluting the original concept). Robert Stam's definition of heteroglossia as the 'interanimation of the diverse languages generated by sexual, racial, economic and generational difference'

(1989: 17) is an example of its broader contemporary usage – one that brings it in line with a contemporary left agenda in CULTURAL POLITICS.

See also COMMUNICATION; INTERTEXTUALITY; PLURALISM.

HETEROTOPIA

A term meaning 'many places', derived from Michel Foucault's posthumously published essay 'Of other spaces' (1997 [1986]). Foucault here defined heterotopias as social SPACES, combining different or opposite functions: a 'single real place' in which different, incompatible 'spaces and locations' are juxtaposed (in Leach [ed] 1997: 354). An earlier usage in Foucault's *The Order of Things* (1980) defines a heterotopia as a linguistic–discursive SITE whose incongruous parts fail to coexist in any coherently grounded system. In 'Of other spaces', Foucault presents heterotopias as 'a sort of counter-arrangement, of effectively realized utopia, in which... all the other real arrangements that can be found within society are at one and the same time represented, challenged and overturned' (1997: 352). He cites a number of possible examples: boarding schools, psychiatric hospitals, prisons, cemeteries, museums, libraries, festival sites, vacation villages and honeymoon hotels.

A problem arises in the suggestion that heterotopias exist both outside of other spaces and are, as 'counter-sites', radically different from them, but exist at the same time, as the above examples suggest, within a general socio-economic order. As Genocchio (1995) concludes, perhaps it is better therefore to think of heterotopias as 'more of an idea about space than any actual place' (1995: 43); an idea which insists that the ordering of space is arbitrary and regards space as always transient, polysemous and contested.

In spite of this problem, the term was actively taken up within Cultural Geography to describe the discontinuities and decentred heterogeneity of postmodern urban places as, for example, in Edward W. Soja's studies of Los Angeles (1989, 1995).

See also CITY; HETEROGLOSSIA; UTOPIA.

HISTORICISM

Most often, this term is understood simply to imply a historical approach that sets a text or texts in an appropriate past historical context. As such, even when the appropriate historical context is thought to be the present rather than a past time of writing, the description 'historicist' would apply to a wide range of approaches across different disciplines.

However, historicism has also acquired a set of more precise and more contentious meanings, particularly within Marxist thought. Thus, while there is a strong historicizing tradition within MARXISM ('To think everything historically; that is Marxism,' writes Pierre Vilar 1994), including such otherwise diverse figures as Georg Lukács, Antonio Gramsci and Jean-Paul Sartre, historicism has also been given an influential derogatory connotation.

The Marxist philosopher and critic Walter Benjamin (1882–1940), for example, in the essay 'Thesis on the philosophy of history' (1970 [1940]), sees historicism as marked by a double falsehood: in its acceptance, first, of the past as given and thus as unmediated by the present; and, second, in its evolutionist notion of progress. The latter, Benjamin sees as encouraging the mere chronological relation of historical events as a sequence culminating in the present. For Benjamin, history, properly understood, is discontinuous, catastrophic and always in crisis. The doctrine of progress therefore disguises or ignores the reality of a contradictory experience of POWER and exploitation, and the technological dominance of the natural world. To promulgate such a partial view therefore makes historicism the accomplice of ruling CLASS interests. By contrast, a materialist view of history, or historical MATERIALISM, seeks, in a recurrent idiom in Benjamin's writing, to 'explode' the myth of its bland continuity, to 'blast' past and present into a revolutionary CONSTELLATION, fully aware of the history of the oppressed and open to radical transformation.

Louis Althusser's 'Marxism is not an historicism' (1979) shares some of Benjamin's general polemic, but is informed by a more thoroughgoing CRITIQUE of earlier Marxisms. These are seen as mistaken in deriving history from the economic system (see BASE AND SUPERSTRUCTURE) or from human AGENCY. Historicism, for Althusser, therefore takes the two main forms of economism and HUMANISM. His posited alternative to this 'centred' notion of historical development is an analysis of the structure of its characteristic 'mode of production'. This is understood as comprised of relatively autonomous subsystems, including the economy, which is seen to play an ultimately determining role. Althusser finds the sanction for this structuralist (some would say poststructuralist) model in Marx's *Capital*. Unlike Marx's own earlier works, in Althusser's view, *Capital* in particular produces a 'scientific', that is to say anti-humanist and non-historicist, knowledge.

Althusser's reading has, in turn, been critiqued from within Marxism and seen as itself de-historicizing and as depoliticizing the methods of Marxist analysis. A notable criticism along these lines was advanced by the Marxist historian, E.P. Thompson (1978; see also Anderson 1984).

A further contribution from Fredric Jameson, 'Marxism and historicism' (1988b) seeks to reconcile Marxism and the poststructuralist positions deriving from Althusser, including, notably, the decentred historicism of Michel Foucault. Jameson's argument rests on the importance to Marxist historiography of the concept, or 'master code', of the 'mode of production' (here echoing Althusser), coupled with Marxism's interest in the transition from one mode to another (principally the transition from feudalism to CAPITALISM). Thus, in its analysis of a given mode of production, suggests Jameson, Marxist historicism offers a knowledge of history that sees the present as a composite of past and future – the first existing in residual traces and the second in anticipations of a transformed future from within this present mode.

Jameson's model is therefore both synchronic and historicist, and as such a 'structural historicism', but it does not entirely resolve the outstanding issue of this debate. For throughout it all, the difficulty remains for Marxism, in particular, of producing a knowledge of history, whether 'transcendent' or 'scientific', when this knowledge is itself necessarily produced 'in' history. Such a knowledge must therefore strive to recognize its own historicity, seeking simultaneously to be 'in' and 'of' history, though not beyond or outside it.

See also CONJUNCTURE; DIALECTICS; IDEOLOGY.

HISTORIOGRAPHIC METAFICTION

See METAFICTION.

HOMOLOGY

'Homology' means 'the same kind or structure' and was introduced into Marxist Literary Studies, in particular, as a way of expressing the perceived relations of correspondence between the form or social content of a literary work and its social context. It is therefore an example of the way Marxist criticism attempted to insert a mediating term between society and art or, in the traditional model, between the economic BASE AND ideological SUPERSTRUCTURE. Raymond Williams draws attention to the source of the term in the life sciences and detects a range of senses from resemblance to analogy, embracing forms of 'general', 'serial' and 'specific' homology. It can, he suggests, bring a sophistication to the understanding of social relations. Chiefly, however, Williams points to the severe limitations of the concept for literary and cultural analysis, where it is used to identify correspondences or homologies between a pre-established social or ideological order and a given text or cultural object. He concludes that none of the dualist theories (those assuming a distinction between art and society in need of some bridging concept), neither those employing concepts of reflection, MEDIATION, correspondence or homology 'can be fully carried through to contemporary practice, since in different ways they all depend on a known history, a known structure, known products. Analytic relations can be handled in this way but practical relations hardly at all' (1977: 106–7). The alternative Williams points to is the concept of HEGEMONY.

See also IDEOLOGY.

HOMO SACER

An influential concept introduced by the Italian philosopher Giorgio Agamben in *Homo Sacer: Sovereign Power and Bare Life* (1998) and further developed by him in a series of related philosophical, ethical, aesthetic and political contexts, including *The State of Exception* (2005). Agamben begins with a distinction drawn by Aristotle between life at birth ('zoé') and the social and political life ('bios') we later enter. The first simple or animal life is a prerequisite for our enjoying the 'good life' as citizens. It is, however, excluded from the political realm. Secondly, he derives the inaugural concept of '*homo sacer*' ('sacred man') from a Roman law which judged that for certain crimes the convicted person could be sentenced to death, but, although condemned by the law, could not be legally executed. Nor, because at the same time designated as sacred ('sacer'), could the criminal be sacrificed. The condemned man could, however, be killed by fellow citizens.

Agamben deploys the implications of this joint 'exclusion and inclusion', by which the individual is paradoxically placed both outside and inside (judged by) the law and the state, to the relations of the human BODY and POWER (termed 'biopolitics') as they continue in modern-day political societies. High-profile examples of those caught between belonging and exclusion to the point of a purgatorial interregnum between life and death are: the death-row inmate, the suspected terrorist held without trial, and – in an especially conspicuous current example – the refugee, prohibited entry and free transit. Human life, reduced to the body (bare life) in such instances, is exposed to the whim or will of the authorities. Agamben comments 'the production of a bio-political body is the original activity of sovereign power' (1998, 6).

Agamben finds here a broader application, arguing that instances of '*homo sacer*' culminate in the modern 'state of exception' of which the death camps and the iconic example of Auschwitz are the pre-eminent symbol (see Agamben, 2002). One result of the ongoing 'refugee crisis' across Europe is, of course, the emergence of camps as holding places in a kind of no-man's land, exposing migrants to the exercise of sovereign power over and above the rule of law, or on the basis of a new law, in the supposed name of the public good. We meet this scenario in what is referred to as a 'state of emergency'. Agamben draws on Carl Schmitt's use of this concept and has in mind too Walter Benjamin's riposte in his 'On the concept of history' ([1940] 2003) that the state of emergency is permanent: 'the tradition of the oppressed' Benjamin wrote, teaches us that the state of emergency in which we live is not the exception but the rule' (392).

An example in recent times has been the American President, George W. Bush's introduction, after the attack on the World Trade Centre, of a state of emergency, enabling the arrest and detention of suspected terrorists. Agamben warns that in allowing the exception to become the rule, liberal democracies act as totalitarian states. His *State of Exception* (2005) examines this tendency in twentieth-century European societies and in the USA.

Agamben's account of the operation of biopolitical power is daunting, not least because of the immense difficulties of conceiving an alternative politics which would articulate human life outside the reach of power and the dialectical conundrum of inclusion and exclusion. His statement here, 'Politics is now literally the decision concerning the unpolitical' (2005: 173) expresses this difficulty. It is Walter Benjamin, to whom Agamben turns once more in *The State of Exception*, who provides the most uncompromising solution to this problem. In answer to Schmitt, Benjamin had declared that 'it is our task to bring about a real state of emergency'; that is to say, political revolution (Benjamin, 2003: 392), ousting the 'fictitious' or 'political' state of emergency in which we live (Agamben 2007: 58–9). It defies the legitimacy of sovereign power and the law, and is itself 'a human action which has shed every relation to law' (ibid). And finally, it opens onto 'a state of the world in which the world appears as a good that absolutely cannot be appropriated or made juridical' (ibid. 64).

See also ETHICS; TERRORISM.

HORIZON OF EXPECTATION

See RECEPTION.

HUMANISM

The term for a general philosophical view that places the human at the centre of the world, or, more specifically, sees inner being or the individual mind as the determinate source of meaning and action. Its beginnings are commonly set in the Renaissance and associated with the rise over two centuries of a secular humanism that made man and reason, not God, the centre of the universe. This was theorized most famously prior to its full realization in the eighteenth and nineteenth centuries in René Descartes's theory of the *cogito* ('I think therefore I am'). This unequivocal confirmation of individual human CONSCIOUSNESS as the guarantee of existence and IDENTITY, when translated into 'I can be what I want', fuelled the triumph of the middle CLASS in nineteenth-century industrial societies. As a result, what is most often meant by humanism is the compound of individualism and class interests known as 'liberal humanism'. Catherine Belsey (1980) argues that 'classic REALISM' reinforced the idea of a coherent, unified human SUBJECT necessary to this class ideology. In the radical criticism of the 1970s and 1980s, it became commonplace to view traditional criticism as performing the same ideological role. Belsey sees Wolfgang Iser's theory of reading as an 'excellent theoretical account of what... most liberal humanist readers in the second half of the twentieth century actually do when they read', but adds 'it is no more than that' (1980: 36).

The structuralist and poststructuralist revolutions in the Humanities, which influenced Belsey, inspired a widespread anti-humanist self-CRITIQUE, evident in arguments about the death of the AUTHOR, the indeterminacy of textually generated meanings, and the dispersal of knowledge and POWER through decentred discursive formations. An earlier assault on the humanist conception of the unified individual had occurred with Freud's discovery of the UNCONSCIOUS. As Jacques Lacan commented, 'The very centre of the human being was no longer to be found at the place assigned to it by a whole humanist tradition' (1977: 114). Much the same might be said, from another perspective, of Marx's theory of ALIENATION and of the DETERMINATION of individuals and social life by IDEOLOGY and the mechanisms of a capitalist economy.

At the same time, there has been a strong tradition of socialist (as of feminist) humanism, which sees the human collectivity of the working class (or women) as self-determining agents of change. This view, too, has been critiqued from positions within poststructuralist theory. Louis Althusser, for example, contrasted the humanism of Marx's early work with what he understood as the true Marxist science of the later anti-humanist *Das Kapital*. His aim was to expunge from Marxism the myth of 'Man' as author and actor of the drama of history. This reading of Marx was in turn refuted by, among others, the socialist historian, E.P. Thompson (1978).

In the present period, Fredric Jameson confirms that individualism has been buried under the avalanche of postmodernism (1991: 167–8). Others, however –

for example, Jürgen Habermas, Noam Chomsky and Christopher Norris – would seek to defend the claims of rationality and truth associated with the humanist tradition. At this point, where these discussions engage questions of ETHICS and politics, they join debates on the continued legitimacy of ENLIGHTENMENT ideals. Chambers (2001) takes up these issues in an examination of examples from fiction, philosophy, architecture and music to pose a 'post-humanist' perspective upon postmodern culture.

See also ESSENTIALISM; FOUNDATIONALISM; HISTORICISM; POSTHUMAN.

HYBRIDITY

A hybrid combines unlike parts and is the result, in botanical or animal life, of the cross-breeding of different species or varieties, or, in another application, of the cross-fertilization of different languages. In the realm of theory, these meanings have been extended to refer to the mixed or hyphenated identities of persons or ethnic communities, or of texts that express and explore this condition, sometimes themselves employing mixed written and visual discourses. In its more textual reference, hybridity is therefore close to the meanings of 'collage' and 'BRICOLAGE', derived from the AESTHETICS of MODERNISM. In relation to the theme of IDENTITY, examples of hybridity would include: 'creole' (of someone born in the West Indies or southern parts of the USA but of French descent); 'mulatto' (someone of mixed black and white blood); and 'mestizo'/'mestiza' (someone of mixed Spanish and Native American descent). The term also has a more metaphorical application in the discussion of non-essentialist sexual identities and role-play (see Epstein and Straub [eds] 1991; see also ANDROGYNY), or to new relations between the human and technology, as in the literature of CYBORGS.

Probably the most common use of the term, however, occurs in postcolonial theory and studies of RACE and ETHNICITY. In these contexts, it is used to describe the newly composed, mixed or contradictory identities resulting from immigration, exile and migrancy (in relation to Asian-American, Black-British or Turko-German communities, for example). A precedent for this occurred in the description by the black scholar W.E.B. Du Bois (1903) of the 'double-consciousness' or 'twoness' of the American negro. Du Bois saw this hybrid condition as resulting from the experience of slavery and the continued HEGEMONY of white CULTURE. As such, it was the source of suffering and ALIENATION. In later studies, however, the tendency has been to treat this experience more positively in the process of critiquing essentialist notions of the SUBJECT, COMMUNITY or nation. Paul Gilroy, for example, describes his study, *The Black Atlantic: Modernity and Double Consciousness* (1993), as an attempt 'to repudiate the dangerous obsessions with "racial" purity'; as 'an essay about the inescapable hybridity and intermixture of ideas' and 'the instability and mutability of identities which are always unfinished, always being made' (1993: xi).

An indication of the increased popular awareness of hybridity, and of the complexities of identity beyond the binary distinction of 'black' and 'white', was shown in the remarks of Tiger Woods, 1997 winner of the United States Masters

Golf Tournament. Woods was the first non-white to win the competition. He rejected the description of himself as 'black', however. He was, he said, in a word of his own coinage, 'Cablinasian': a combination, that is to say, of Caucasian, black, American Indian and Asian.

In academic discussion, hybridity is often used alongside other cognate terms such as LIMINALITY (moving between categories or stages) and SYNCRETISM (a combination of kinds or styles) or the language of 'thresholds', 'betweenness', 'intervals' and 'borders' (see Chambers 1993; Bhabha 1994; Humm 1991; Bromley 2000).

See also DIASPORA; ESSENTIALISM; MULTICULTURALISM; POSTCOLONIALISM; SEXUALITY.

HYPERREALITY

A term associated with the effects of MASS PRODUCTION and REPRODUCTION, and suggesting that an object, event, experience so reproduced replaces or is preferred to its original: that the copy is 'more real than real'. In the writings of the French social philosopher and commentator on POSTMODERNISM, Jean Baudrillard (1929–2007), and of the Italian semiologist, Umberto Eco (1932–2016), hyperreality is associated especially with cultural tendencies and a prevailing sensibility in contemporary American society.

In Baudrillard's discussion, hyperreality is synonymous with the most developed form of SIMULATION: the autonomous simulacra that is free from all reference to the real. In the essay, 'The precession of simulacra', Baudrillard writes of Disneyland as 'a perfect model of all the entangled orders of simulation' (1988: 171). Its function is less the ideological expression of an idealized America than to disguise the fact that 'all of Los Angeles and the America surrounding it are no longer real, but of the order of the hyperreal and simulation' (1988: 172). Baudrillard therefore sees the hyperreal of selective imitation and IMAGE-making presented by Disneyland as the rule rather than the exception. The resulting 'society of the image', prompts a panic-stricken attempt to shore up the real that has been eroded. This, so Baudrillard believes, is futile, since the attempt to produce meaning and save 'the reality principle' in a media-saturated society can only produce its opposite, an exacerbated experience of hyperreality.

Umberto Eco's theme, in his essay 'Travels in hyperreality' (1986) is 'faith in fakes' (the American title of the volume containing this essay). He goes 'in search of instances where the American imagination demands the real thing and, to attain it, must fabricate the absolute fake' (1986: 8). His travels take him to the Lyndon B. Johnson Library – where he finds proof that in America, 'the past must be preserved and celebrated in full-scale authentic copy' (1986: 6), to heritage villages, the Madonna Inn, seven wax versions of Leonardo da Vinci's *Last Supper,* William Randolph Hearst's museum-castle (the Xanadu of Orson Welles's film *Citizen Kane*) and Disneyland, the home of the 'total fake' (1986: 43). Unlike Baudrillard, Eco does not suggest the real is supplanted or erased, but that imitations – because newer and more complete – are preferred to their ancient or unavailable originals. He is therefore more critical than Baudrillard (Baudrillard would say in an outmoded fashion). Thus, 'the Absolute Fake,' writes Eco, derives from the vacuum 'of a present without depth' (1986: 31), and he sees Disneyland as the 'quintessence of consumer ideology' (1986: 43). Moreover, Eco detects a different, more modernist culture and attitude in New York and New Orleans. In the latter, he finds that 'history still exists and is tangible' (1986: 29), concluding that, 'The sense of history allows an escape from the temptations of hyperreality' (1986: 30).

See also CONSUMERISM; SPECTACLE; SPECULATIVE REALISM; VIRTUAL REALITY.

HYPERTEXT

Hypertext refers to the use of technology to produce 'more text', in a more immediately accessible and interactive way than is possible in the conventional reading of the printed text, in standard teaching practice, or through the use of traditional libraries. In studying a novel (or any written, audio or visual text) in hypertext, one would potentially have available on screen, not only an initial primary text, but related texts (related novels, letters, biographies, reviews, criticism, socio-economic cultural background materials) to consult, annotate and reorder. As the student-researcher follows a particular trail in hypertext, any of this 'secondary' material might become the 'primary' text, or suggest another. Indeed, the concept of a 'primary' text might give way to a lateral exploration across textual surfaces.

The idea is derived from the American engineer, Vannevar Bush and was initially conceived in the mid 1940s in response to the information overload experienced by academics. Bush proposed a mechanized device called a 'memex' – 'an enlarged intimate supplement' to an individual's memory – in which would be stored books, records and communications available for speedy access (Landow 1992: 15). In the 1960s, Ted Nelson, following Bush, coined the term 'hypertext' to refer to a form of electronic text made available on an interactive screen, which would consist of non-linear chunks of text with links and pathways so that it 'branches and allows choices to the reader' (Landow 1992: 4).

Computer technology has, it is argued, made it possible to realize these earlier ideas. In addition, George P. Landow perceives a close connection between this material technological advance and ideas in modern literary theory. Hypertext, he argues, is consonant with Mikhail Bakhtin's notion of the 'poly-vocal' text, with Roland Barthes's distinction between the 'WRITERLY' as against the 'READERLY' text, with ideas of decentred TEXTUALITY or INTERTEXTUALITY, and the new active role of the reader theorized by Barthes, Michel Foucault and Jacques Derrida. This affinity is confirmed, he reasons, by a shared vocabulary of 'links', 'network', 'web', 'path', 'matrix', 'interweaving' and so on (1992: 17, 25). Hypertext, Landow concludes, emerges as the 'literal embodiment' of key poststructuralist concepts (1992: 34).

Hypertext can therefore be seen as an example of SYNERGY between disciplines in the broadly defined area of CYBERNETICS. Questions about its realization and relation to theory raise matters of control and the scale of change that are relevant to this whole field. Can a library sufficient for the free, in-depth, and independent study of Joyce's *Ulysses* (Landow's example) actually (rather than potentially) exist in a hypertext package? And if it is acknowledged that hypertext materials are selective, who is to make this selection? Landow sees hypertext as leading a PARADIGM shift equal to the earlier transition to print. Does this mean it would eliminate or combine with the materials of print culture and more traditional forms of face-to-face learning?

It might be noted in this connection that Derrida's DECONSTRUCTION does not entail the end of reading books as such. Rather, it would inaugurate the practice of reading them, as Derrida puts it, *'in a certain way'* (1978: 288).

See also DIGITAL; DIGITAL HUMANITIES.

ICON/ICONOGRAPHY

Terms derived from the vocabulary of religious painting and art criticism. In this context, an icon is a saint or sacred subject, and this status is often transferred to the REPRESENTATION itself. In its secular usage, the term is used to refer to a 'star' of media, entertainment or sport, worshipped by fans and admirers for a combination of physical looks, talent and unobtainability (Marilyn Monroe, Prince, David Beckham). A culture's POPULAR icons are therefore a clue to its ideas of beauty and worthiness. Princess Diana was, in the 1990s, a striking contemporary example of this type (see Steinberg and Kear [eds] 1999). In what now seem distinctly outmoded examples within political culture, Soviet society, communist China and countries of the eastern bloc made icons of Lenin, Stalin, Mao Zedong and other leaders. The IMAGES made of such figures (Andy Warhol's screen prints of Monroe and Mao; posters of Che Guevara) can also be seen as evidence of how meanings change or are neutralized in changed artistic and cultural contexts.

An iconic SIGN, as identified by the American semiologist, Charles Sanders Peirce, is one in which an image resembles, but does not seek to exactly reproduce the object it represents (in cartoons or road signs of deer or cattle, for example). All visual images are commonly regarded as iconic. Iconography is consequently used to refer to a system of visual imagery or of serial motifs in painting, photography, cinema or TV. It is of use, therefore, in GENRE criticism to describe the CODEd use of familiar objects, costumes, interiors, urban settings or landscapes characterizing the musical or western, for example, as well as examining how these change.

IDEALISM

The belief that the world exists only as it is perceived and that 'reality' is consequently to be understood as a mental or subjective construction (as 'ideas' in the mind). As a philosophical system, idealism is associated in its more extreme, subjectivist version with the eighteenth-century British philosophers, Bishop Berkeley (1685–1753) and David Hume (1711–1776). A moderated version, which sought to distinguish between the subjective or ideal and the objective existence of 'things-in-themselves' derives from Immanuel Kant (1724–1804).

The first position is termed subjective idealism and the second, transcendental idealism. One early answer to subjective idealism was delivered by Samuel Johnson's famous kick at a stone accompanied by the remark, 'I refute it thus!' A more extended rebuff of these and later versions of idealism has appeared in the traditions of MATERIALISM from Thomas Hobbes (1588–1679) to Marx and Engels, and latter-day materialists working in the Marxist tradition, or those who acknowledge some indebtedness to it.

Terry Eagleton criticizes certain tendencies in POSTSTRUCTURALISM and POSTMODERNISM as comprising a 'new idealism' (1996: 4, 48) and this has been a quite common charge. The view that the world is known through its textual or media REPRESENTATIONS, that history – in a debate triggered especially by postmodernism – is known through the available narrativized accounts of the past, are, without doubt, prone to idealism. So, too, are examples of METAFICTION. However, a view of the world as linguistically or semiotically CODED or as only made intelligible through TEXTUALITY does not mean that knowledge of this world is viewed as subjective and confined to ideas or individual consciousness. Nor does it necessarily entail a rejection of non-textual material conditions.

See also CULTURAL MATERIALISM; DECONSTRUCTION; ESSENTIALISM.

IDENTITY

Identity is an especially topical issue in the contemporary study of CULTURE, with many ramifications for the study of ETHNICITY, CLASS, GENDER, RACE, SEXUALITY and SUBCULTURES. Paradoxically, this is itself a sign that the concept is in crisis, since identity becomes an issue, as Kobena Mercer puts it, 'when something assumed to be fixed, coherent and stable is displaced by the experience of doubt and uncertainty' (1994: 259).

In broad terms, this uncertainty can be explained by two key major social and economic developments. First, the events in Europe of 1989 undermined received identities just as they undermined geographical and political borders within European states and between former communist and western social democratic regimes. Second, GLOBALIZATION has increased the experience of migrancy, altering relations between western and other cultures, and the sense of identity of individuals whose lives have taken them across the borders between First, Second, and Third Worlds, or across, in effect, pre-modern and postmodern societies.

At the same time, these developments are themselves ambiguous and incomplete. For, while they have promoted a relaxation of fixed and coherent identities, this has been accompanied by contrary tendencies: the revival in eastern Europe of traditional ethnic identities (of Bosnian Serbs and Croats in the former Yugoslavia, for example), and a more emphatic construction of individuals as consumers for the ever-expanding markets that characterize globalization.

Contemporary identities can therefore be fluid or consciously delimited. Any number of factors are likely to be under NEGOTIATION in either case – whether of religion, nation, language, political IDEOLOGY or cultural expression. Islam, for example, is a religious faith that shapes the social, economic and political character of entire regimes, and can reach into the detailed social and sexual lives of its adherents. In Northern Ireland, religious faith combines with political belief in the continued enmity between Catholic and Protestant communities. Often, too, such identities are reinforced in further relations beyond their immediate definition, as in the divided allegiances of Northern Ireland communities to the implications of Britishness – itself a source of ambivalent identity and a topic of dispute on the mainland (see Storry and Childs 1997). Identities of these and other kinds – of generation and sexual orientation, for example – are also expressed in symbolic cultural forms: in the adoption of national dress or musical styles (from rap to the marching bands of the Irish Apprentice Boys); in a certain diet (kosher, vegan, junk food); in the symbolic coding of hairstyles or footwear; or in the exposure or concealment of body parts, and so on.

Developments in theory have accompanied the general social processes indicated above and have played their part in underlining, and providing a vocabulary for, a changing awareness of the many subtleties of identity. An early influential development within poststructuralist FEMINISM and latterly, the study of RACE, was the CRITIQUE of essentialist notions of identity (of being a 'woman' or a 'black man') and of the allied affirmation of a given identity in relation to its supposed binary opposite. As Henrietta Moore remarks, 'the assertion of the non-universal status of the category "woman" is by now almost a commonplace' (in Woodward [ed] 1997: 60). This critique has been consolidated in a recognition of the overlapping and inconsistent alignment of additional factors of class, race, ethnicity, sexuality, age and so on. Being a black, lesbian, mother born in New York and living in Paris, for example, suggests a fluid personal, ethnic, linguistic and cultural identity, where no one factor predominates. Where one factor *does* predominate, or is chosen as a description governing an individual or group's actions (i.e. being a woman, being Serbian, Palestinian, black or gay), this is termed 'identity politics' (see Hobsbawm 1996).

There can be little doubt that contemporary Literary and Cultural Theory has sought to challenge or deconstruct essentialist, universalizing or fundamentalist identities. This has given currency to concepts of DIFFERENCE, HYBRIDITY, migrancy and the DIASPORA (Gilroy 1993; Bhabha 1994; Morley and Chen [eds] 1996) and a preference for these terms over conceptions of settled ethnic, national or geographical identities. Obviously, this is not simply a theoretical preference, but an aspect of contemporary CULTURAL POLITICS, presented in the name of a better – because more open – pluralist and tolerant world.

A politics of this kind should be distinguished from the sectional exclusivity of 'identity politics' of a group or nation and from a traditional left politics based on a universalizing, class-based identity. It must be said, all the same, that traditional or essentialist identities cannot be wished or written away. They similarly answer to real needs, and often to fears of subjection and the loss of identity: precisely, in their own terms, to the 'experience of doubt and uncertainty' Kobena Mercer describes above. It is this complexity of response that makes identity a topical and important issue.

See also NATIONALISM; POSTHUMAN.

IDEOLOGICAL STATE APPARATUS

A description introduced by the French Marxist philosopher, Louis Althusser (1918–1990) in an important essay in his *Lenin and Philosophy* (1971a). The concept develops Antonio Gramsci's emphasis on the operation of IDEOLOGY in CIVIL SOCIETY, and has been extremely influential on a range of work within Literary, Film and Cultural Studies (Easthope 1988; Mulhern 1995).

Althusser distinguishes between two kinds of state apparatus: repressive state apparatuses (or RSAs – for example, the penal system, police and army) and ideological state apparatuses (ISAs – including religion, the legal system, education, the family, CULTURE and COMMUNICATION). The first are coercive in their operation, while the second function to unify society through ideology and reproduce a regime through consent. The latter are relatively independent of the state, though they serve to ratify and legitimize it, and to function, says Althusser, 'beneath the ruling ideology which is the ideology of "the ruling class"' (1971a: 139).

Althusser's concept is an important aspect of his CRITIQUE of traditional MARXISM and his rereading of Marx (Althusser 1969, 1971a). It impacts in this way upon other key concepts such as HISTORICISM and MATERIALISM. Althusser proposes a thoroughly anti-idealist and anti-humanist Marxism, which would suggest that everything is 'material', including ideas. Thus, 'the "ideas" or "representations"', etc., which seem to make up ideology do not have an ideal (*idéale* or *idéelle*) or spiritual existence, but a material existence' (1971a: 155). Ideological state apparatuses therefore simultaneously comprise ideas and material forms. This perception was welcomed since it appeared to rearticulate Marx's classic distinction between the economic BASE AND the ideological SUPERSTRUCTURE, so as to free it from a mechanistic and deterministic interpretation. In Althusser's view of 'the social FORMATION', ideas and ideological forms (the 'REPRESENTATIONS', above) have a 'RELATIVE AUTONOMY' and the economy, while determining, is determining 'in the last instance'. This formulation was seen to acknowledge the specificity and critical ideological potential of culture.

IDEOLOGY

The theory of ideology dates from the eighteenth-century ENLIGHTENMENT, but is derived principally from the writings of Karl Marx and Friedrich Engels, and employed in a crucial analytic role, often in a critical dialogue with the Marxist tradition, across a range of disciplines.

One of the main points of reference for the debated uses of the term is Marx and Engels's *The German Ideology* (in *Selected Works,* 1969, Vol. 1). This contains three key – but problematic – statements, presenting ideology as a CLASS ideology, as a distortion of reality and as a distant echo of a deeper reality. These are presented below, together with a sketch of the term's developing uses.

In the first definition, Marx and Engels state that 'The ideas of the ruling class are in every epoch the ruling ideas... The class which has the means of material production at its disposal, has control at the same time over the means of mental production' (1969: 47). This class definition suggests already that ideology can be understood in two ways: both as a fixed set of ideas and as a process whereby the partial views of a ruling class come to hold sway over the whole of a society. The first meaning is close to a traditional, and still common, view of ideology as a set of well-formed and explicit doctrines or dogma (employed by 'ideologues'). In this sense, ideology has come to be associated less with a class than with a political party, extremist faction or 'fundamentalist' movement. In MARXISM, too, however, the association of ideology with the well-formed ideas of a ruling class has been rejected as too narrow.

This first proposition has attracted two further, and now common, reservations. The first is with regard to the implication that a subordinated working class is simply subjected to a dominant class or its ideas, without qualification or resistance or any recognition of ideology's persuasive rhetorical force. The second is with regard to an exclusive concern with social class as a category of analysis, agency of control and thus of social change.

There are consequently two revisions to the basic premise. The first derives from the idea of HEGEMONY, as formulated by the Marxist philosopher, Antonio Gramsci (1881–1937). This suggests that, for the most part, control in modern societies is won and maintained by 'consent' to ruling ideas, rather than through their direct imposition or the pure force of domination. Gramsci's theory consequently also expanded the first sense of ideology to include both formal ideas and 'COMMON SENSE', the latter operating at the level of habitual and unexamined attitudes, and itself comprised of both assimilated ruling-class ideas and a progressive practical consciousness. Thus, ideology is seen to 'naturalize' an existing social order at a very deep level of everyday thoughts and action, but as being neither simply imposed nor irresistible. These ideas have had a profound influence within academic study, especially in the study of POPULAR and SUBCULTURES (see also DOMINANT/RESIDUAL/EMERGENT).

Second, the importance of social class has been questioned both by those who argue that changed social and technological developments and patterns of work have altered, if not eroded, traditional class identities, and by those who argue for the importance of language, GENDER, generation, RACE, ETHNICITY, SEXUALITY and nation. These arguments derive from FEMINISM, PSYCHOANALYSIS, anti-racist, postcolonial, gay and lesbian positions, as well as from the study of youth and popular cultures, and the general influence of POSTSTRUCTURALISM. They have directed attention, therefore, to the ideologies of PATRIARCHY and colonialism rather than, or in addition to, class; or to relations between POWER and DISCOURSE, rather than capital and labour. While the first perspective might share with traditional Marxism the view that these ideologies help maintain relations between rulers and ruled, and derive similarly from material conditions, the second is more likely to express a conscious departure from Marxism. Here, ideology tends to denote the large world of SIGNS, REPRESENTATIONS and VALUES that helps support a dominant social order.

In the second statement in *The German Ideology*, Marx and Engels write:

> If in all ideology men and their circumstances appear upside down as in a camera obscura, this phenomenon arises just as much from their historical life-process as the inversion of objects on the retina does from their physical life-process.
>
> (1969: 25)

This view – that we see the real world in an inverted but correctable IMAGE – emphasizes how ideology masks real relations and so naturalizes the condition of ALIENATION. It has given rise also to the understanding of ideology as 'false CONSCIOUSNESS' and thus in turn to the idea of an opposing 'proletarian consciousness' (Lukács 1971). Marxism's claim to a monopoly on the truth was critiqued by Karl Mannheim in *Ideology and Utopia* (1929), and many have since resisted the idea of 'false consciousness' on the grounds that it implies that the MASS of people, with the exception of Marxists who are possessed of a 'correct analysis', are deluded and living a false existence. A further reservation concerns the analogy between a technological and a human physical process (the camera and the image on the retina), which reinforces the sense that the transformation of a false – into a true – vision is a simple, if not automatic, one.

A later, more refined version of this distinction between a correct and a false understanding appears in Louis Althusser's rereading of Marxism as a 'science' capable of presenting a theoretical knowledge of the capitalist mode of production. Ideology is here seen less as a set of false perceptions than a limited but 'lived' form of practical knowledge. Althusser's Marxism has been much debated, and the invocation of 'science' (an issue, as indicated above, in earlier descriptions of Marxism as 'scientific socialism' or 'proletarian science'), strongly disputed (see Thompson 1978; Elliott [ed] 1994).

In the third statement, Marx and Engels draw a distinction between ideology and 'real life-processes'. They write:

> [We] do not set out from what men say, imagine, conceive, nor from men as narrated, thought of, imagined, conceived, in order to arrive at men in the flesh. We set out from real, active men, and on the basis of their real life-process we demonstrate the development of the ideological reflexes and echoes of this life-process.
>
> (1969: 25)

The priorities here follow from the determining role Marxism gives to the economic structure of society – comprising, with its associated social relations, says Marx, 'the real foundations'. (See BASE AND SUPERSTRUCTURE.) The terms in which this is expressed, however, relegate ideology – in a catch-all that would include the ideas, narratives and imaginings that, for many, constitute CULTURE – to a secondary role where it echoes or reflects an established reality. Few would accept this formulation or the mechanical MATERIALISM to which it gives rise. The model has been revised, therefore, by the identification of MEDIATIONS between 'real life' and ideological forms (such as class, tradition, artistic movement, GENRE, medium) and by an attention to the institutions of church, family, media organizations and education. The latter emphasis is derived from Gramsci's analysis of 'CIVIL SOCIETY' and was especially developed in Louis Althusser's notion of the IDEOLOGICAL STATE APPARATUS. Althusser's theory of ideology (following both Gramsci and Freud) as the 'imaginary' realm of 'lived experience' granted ideological forms a 'RELATIVE AUTONOMY' in their relation to social reality.

It therefore qualified Marxism's economic determinism (since the economy was seen as determining 'in the last instance') and the view of ideology as a passive reflection, thus giving ideas and cultural forms an active influence in society. In this respect, Althusser's theory was extremely influential: upon feminism (Mitchell 1974), literary criticism (Eagleton 1976) and the film theory developed in the journal *Screen* in the 1970s (see SCREEN THEORY).

An important source for this more dialectical understanding in Marx is the association he makes in the 'Preface' to *A Contribution to the Critique of Political Economy* (1969) of a range of 'ideological forms' ('legal, political, religious, artistic or philosophic') with forms of consciousness. Social reality is seen as subject to contradictory and transformative forces and ideology as the domain in which 'men become conscious of this conflict and fight it out'. This social consciousness, Marx adds, must be explained from the contradictions of material life. Ideology, here, is no longer to be understood as false consciousness, nor as an inversion, nor passive reflection, but as a site of conscious struggle and a shaping influence upon 'social being'.

The idea of social and cultural practices and of theory participating in ideological contestation across different domains (legal, political, religious, etc.) has been an influential and fruitful one. Allied to the revisions indicated above, this would comprise a working theory of ideology in the Marxist or post-Marxist tradition. Where the emphasis upon social class or the determining influence of the economy are rejected rather than revised, then the theory of ideology has proceeded in a non-Marxist direction, as in Mannheim's critique from within the 'sociology of knowledge', or from positions within psychoanalysis, feminism or liberal pluralism. In the latter, and in more conservative positions, ideology is viewed pejoratively as a fixed set of opinions or prejudices, or the systematic dogma of a religious order, political party or theory, such as Marxism itself. Where any notion of a material reality is rejected, as in some anti-Marxist positions in postmodern theory, then it is likely that the theory of ideology and ideological analysis will be rejected too. A harbinger of this view appeared in Daniel Bell's *The End of Ideology* (1965) and has been resumed at the end of the Cold War under the theoretical influence of poststructuralist scepticism and nihilist versions of postmodernism. A particularly firm response to this position argues for a return to the conception of ideology as presenting a false or deceptive picture of material relations (including now the ideologies of postmodernism) (Eagleton 1991; Hawkes 1996).

In a further move, the Slovene philosopher Slovoj Žižek has once more questioned any distinction between ideology as a set of false ideas and a true, real world. He sees ideology as thoroughly material. Nevertheless, it is the material world itself, he argues, that is false and distorted. Thus 'Ideology is not simply a "false consciousness", an illusory representation of reality, it is rather this reality itself which is already to be conceived as "ideological"' (1989: 21). As David Hawkes implies, this is tantamount to the view that we are really 'living a lie' (1996: 176–81).

See also DETERMINATION; HISTORICISM; HUMANISM.

IDEOLOGY CRITIQUE

'Ideology critique' names the committed and systematic study of the operations of ideology at the levels of both theory and concrete analysis. As *Ideologiekritik*, this was associated with the work of members of the German language and Marxist-based Frankfurt School (including Theodor Adorno, Max Horkheimer, Herbert Marcuse), but has acquired an extended application to other, more recent, forms of criticism and theory, including feminist and postcolonial studies.

IDEOLOGY has a highly varied set of meanings, even within these overlapping and broadly compatible forms of work. Much depends, therefore, on the theoretical understanding adopted of this term. Its analysis is also determined by the objects of study, and whether this is empirically or textually based. A number of possible issues may thus be of concern in ideological analysis: ownership and control; the structure of institutions; conditions of work and leisure; professional CODES; the semiotics of IMAGES and REPRESENTATIONS; the construction of AUDIENCES; the conventions of RECEPTION and READING, and so on.

For all these differences of focus, however, ideology critique is concerned to reveal and unmask the workings of dominant ideologies. In the textual analysis of MASS media texts, especially, this can be all too easily reduced to the identification of capitalist or bourgeois or patriarchal ideology *tout court,* and to the citation of supporting forms, conventions and stereotypes. The value of theories of ideology is that they point to the contradictory processes involved in the maintenance of dominant ideology (see HEGEMONY). At its best, ideology critique will understand these contradictions and ambiguities as differently embedded at each level or stage in the circuit of texts of all kinds, or the operation of CULTURE INDUSTRIES, from their economic to their formal structure, reception and use. The term 'CRITIQUE' itself in fact suggests just such a contradictory positioning.

Whereas 'criticism', as Terry Eagleton writes, assumes an:

> external, perhaps 'transcendental' vantage point, 'critique' is that form of discourse which seeks to inhabit the experience of the subject from the inside, in order to elicit those valid features of that experience which point beyond the subject's present condition.
>
> (1991: xiv)

Critique therefore assumes that dominant ideology harbours an alternative to itself.

A further question concerns, not only the dialectical subtlety of theory and analysis, but how the critic/observer is positioned in relation to ideology: the question, in short, of the perspective and role of the critical intellectual in contemporary society. Traditionally, and within the modern period, such a figure stands 'outside', at a distance from the object of study: the representative of objectivity, science, or truth. Under the influence of POSTSTRUCTURALISM and POSTMODERNISM, however, these concepts have been seriously questioned. If we conclude that the critic is inescapably positioned within ideology, then there can be no grounds for critique in these terms. The authority of the critical intellectual and ideology critique is undermined, or has to be differently posed. At the very least, it now seems that an awareness of such questions has to be built self-reflexively into analysis.

See also CRITICAL THEORY; DIALECTICS; INTELLECTUALS.

IMAGE

Commonly understood as the mental or visual REPRESENTATION of an object or event as depicted in the mind, a painting, photograph or film. In film-making and Film Studies, 'image' is also synonymous with a single shot in an edited sequence. The term has a further long-standing usage in literary discourse, especially in connection with poetic language, where it refers to the indirect comparison of one object or experience with another (through metaphor, metonymy, analogy), or is used, along with the term 'imagery', to refer to any figure of speech or, collectively, to figurative language.

In AESTHETICS and philosophical debate, image therefore becomes part of the discussion of the problematics of REPRESENTATION (in the concern with how far an image faithfully or falsely represents reality) and is thereby bound up with questions of perception, knowledge and CONSCIOUSNESS. In so far as an image is thought to misrepresent an original reality, or to represent it superficially, it is linked to IDEOLOGY – to the degree that this term is thought to describe a false or selective view of the world. With what is called the 'crisis of representation' brought about by POSTSTRUCTURALISM and POSTMODERNISM, however, it is often questioned whether an image can be thought to simply represent, or misrepresent, a supposedly prior or external, image-free, reality. Reality is seen rather as always subject to, or as the product of, modes of representation. In this view, we inescapably inhabit a world of images or representations, not a 'real world' and true or false images of it.

In a further move, associated with postmodernism and the writings particularly of Jean Baudrillard, we are thought to exist in a world of HYPERREALITY, in which images are self-generating and entirely detached from any supposed reality. This accords with a common view of contemporary entertainment and politics as being all a matter of 'image' or appearance, rather than of substantial content. In this sense, image is associated with the world of publicity, advertising and fashion. This would seem to reinforce the contemporary association of image with superficiality. However, it suggests at the same time how image-making is connected with business and profit-making, and the making of identities. In this connection, it may connote an imposed stereotype, or an alternative subjective or cultural IDENTITY.

The latter retains a strong and persistent interest in the Humanities. In a sometimes related perspective, deriving from feminist psychoanalytic theory, the 'visual' and thus the 'culture of the image' is associated with the male GAZE and thus the workings of the patriarchal UNCONSCIOUS in modern and advanced consumer societies. The study of 'images of women' or 'women's images' sees this field as one in which stereotypes of women can be reinforced, parodied, or actively contested through critical analysis, alternative histories, or creative work in writing and the media committed to the production of positive counter-images.

See also MIRROR-PHASE; SEMIOLOGY; SIGN.

IMAGINARY/SYMBOLIC/REAL

Distinctions developed by the French psychoanalyst, Jacques Lacan (1901–1981) to describe the phases in the constitution of the psychic SUBJECT. The 'Imaginary' order is defined as the undifferentiated realm of pre-verbal images and fantasies, comprising 'mirror images, identifications and reciprocities' (Bowie 1991: 92) experienced by the infant in its close association with the mother. It inaugurates an entrapment in illusion and is closely related to the experience of the MIRROR-PHASE, which the child must negotiate in the process of socialization. In the mirror-phase, the infant sees itself (or sees itself being seen) as unified and whole (as in a mirror) and learns to distinguish this image from its present incompleteness. The subject is therefore constituted in an experience of division and loss, as being in lack. The 'Symbolic' order is the realm of language (of symbolization). Entry into this realm coincides with the resolution of the OEDIPAL COMPLEX in the child's submission to the prohibitive 'law of the father'. It is also the moment of the formation of the UNCONSCIOUS, the arena of repressed desires associated with the unity of the Imaginary order. The Symbolic therefore confirms the subject in a quest for the unobtainable lost object (the breast or the bottle), which offers apparent fullness of being, setting the individual on a course governed by the experience of irremedial lack and unfulfilled DESIRE. In so doing it mediates between the Imaginary and a third realm named as the 'Real', which is beyond language and abstractly defined in Lacan as a realm of the impossible – all that cannot be represented in the Imaginary and Symbolic.

Lacan's schema has been much debated, critiqued and re-inflected, particularly within feminist theory and thus within areas of feminist Literary and Cultural Studies. In French feminist theory, Julia Kristeva has stressed the association in the Imaginary with the mother and the body, but prefers to name this pre-verbal realm of oneness as the SEMIOTIC. The desire and unity associated with this realm are not entirely repressed, she argues, and continue – as evidenced, for example, in AVANT-GARDE art and writing – as a subversive influence within and upon the Symbolic.

Second, Luce Irigaray has urged the need for a GENDERed reformulation of the concept of the Imaginary in the interests of a 'female/feminist' Symbolic, which will be free of the restrictions of male rationality. Her notion of a 'female imaginary' is founded on a critique of the Oedipal narrative and in particular of its exclusion of the female infant other than in terms, in Lacan as in Freud, of the defining example of the male child. She sees 'the morphological marks of the female body' as 'characterised by plurality, non-linearity, fluid identity' (Whitford [ed] 1991: 54). On this basis, and in her altered view of the constitutive role of touch, Irigaray envisions a new type of sexual IDENTITY and differently gendered Symbolic order. This, it is suggested, informs a new aesthetic founded on a different mode of viewing, since 'the flat mirror [of orthodox theory] does not reflect the sexual organs and the sexual specificity of the woman' (Whitford [ed] 1991: 65).

The importance of the look in Lacan's theory (in the reflection of the self and (m)other in the mirror-phase) has made his writings of interest to theories of the GAZE developed particularly within Film Studies. However, the masculinized bias and emphasis upon the power of the PHALLUS in Lacanian theory have meant women are positioned within the Symbolic order as an object rather than subject, as desired rather than desiring. The problem for feminist film theory and cinema, therefore, has been to avoid duplicating the scenario that confirms the male viewer in a controlling position. In a seminal, but contentious, contribution to this debate, Laura Mulvey (1989b) argues that the cinematic codes of 'illusionist narrative film' that reinforce the authority of the male gaze and the structures of PATRIARCHY must be broken down. The 'first blow' against these conventions, she writes, 'is to free the look of the camera into its materiality in time and space and the look of the audience into dialectics and passionate detachment' (1989b: 26). Women, she concludes 'cannot view the decline of the traditional film form with anything much more than sentimental regret' (1989b: 26).

See also FANTASY; *JOUISSANCE*; PSYCHOANALYSIS.

IMAGINED COMMUNITY

A concept introduced by Benedict Anderson (1983) to describe the nature of national IDENTITY in modern societies. Developments in literacy and communications have meant that a national identity, and the bonding in solidarity with others this implies, can exist over and above the territorial existence of a nation-state. Such an abstract and symbolic identity, founded on a conception of 'the people' as a collectivity, exists, Anderson suggests, in the 'homogenous empty time' of social modernity. This he sees as embodied especially in the print technologies of the novel and newspaper. The result, and the hallmark of the modern nation, is a 'remarkable confidence of community in anonymity' (1983: 40).

The concept has been adopted, and also adapted, in discussions of NATIONALISM and the changing status of the nation-state. James Donald, in a discussion of 'Englishness' and POPULAR cultural forms, for example, suggests that in addition to 'a communality figured as a narrative of nationhood', which is equivalent to Anderson's 'imagined community', we need to distinguish 'nationalist ideologies' and the apparatuses, institutions and discourses that produce the 'national culture' (1993: 166–7). Easthope (1998) examines the long historical continuities in the constructed national identity of 'Englishness' (see also Colls and Dodds, eds, [1986] 2014).

An 'imagined community' would seem to be related to the experience of a diasporic identity conceptualized especially within postcolonial thought. Here, too, a 'belongingness' is felt by those removed from a territorial 'home'. However, Homi Bhabha argues that the notion of an 'imagined community' is inadequate to the contemporary experience of MASS migration and settlement. This, he argues, has produced both deep anxieties and different kinds of international identification ('around issues of sexuality, race, feminism') beyond or in the MARGINS of the national culture (1994: 6, 157–61). The important idea of 'home' in connection with family, community and nation, and the destabilizing impact of postmodern culture is examined by Morley (2000).

See also COMMUNITY; DIASPORA.

IMPERIALISM

Imperialism is the process of conquest, and exploitation of the resources of one nation by another, and has a long and continuing history from the period of Roman conquest to the present century. The most prominent period of imperialism, involving several European nations, occurred from the late eighteenth and through the nineteenth century, including the 'scramble for Africa' in the 1880s and 1890s. The result was that, by 1914, Europe controlled 85 per cent of the globe. This most blatant expression of empire was driven historically by the need of competing western economies for raw material, expanded markets and cheap labour. However, imperialism in this period was fuelled just as importantly by an ideological project founded on a belief in the cultural and political superiority of the imperializing nation. This consolidated ideological, economic and bureaucratic system – exercised on a global scale – is what distinguished imperialism from colonialism, 'the early, amateur form of imperialism', as Seamus Deane describes it (1995: 355). It maintained this systematic HEGEMONY in diverse ways: from slavery to the promotion of a 'civilizing' or 'modernizing' project in the realm of political and civic administration, law, religion, health and education. In the period since the Second World War, imperialism has acquired new forms marked less by European rivalries, military conquest or occupation than by an economic relation between 'First World' capitalist powers and dependent Third World nations. The aftermath of colonialism in this phase has become the object of studies in POSTCOLONIALISM.

Aside from official rationales of the earlier classical stage of imperialism (dependent on ideas of duty, historical destiny and racist ideologies), most studies have been critical of this history and frequently indebted to traditions in MARXISM (Brewer 1980). Much academic study has also been concerned with the ways in which Christianity, Anthropology, literature, art and CULTURE have participated in the imperialist process as reinforcement and conscience, drawing in this respect on political and economic history and theories of IDEOLOGY. This work treats, not only episodes of imperialist history, but the articulation of relations between the self and OTHER, the CANONic status of specific texts, and the role of culture in disseminating notions of a liberal, civilizing education and/or racist ideologies. A text to which many commentators return with these questions in mind has been Joseph Conrad's *Heart of Darkness* (see Brooker and Widdowson [eds] 1996: Ch. 6). Other early European writers of interest are Rudyard Kipling, E.M. Forster and Albert Camus. A summative study in this tradition of commentary, which considers these and other authors is Edward Said's *Culture and Imperialism* (1993a). Here, Said calls for a 'contrapuntal' reading of the different literatures of different nations, which will set examples from the colonizing centre and colonized periphery together:

Camus and André Gide alongside Frantz Fanon and Racine on Algeria, for example; Jane Austen's *Mansfield Park* alongside C.L.R. James (1993a: 313).

Elsewhere, an original study in the realm of art history of the 'cultural colonialism' of the Parisian painters Gauguin, Van Gogh and Émile Bernard is Griselda Pollock's *Avant-Garde Gambits: 1888–1893* (1992).

See also EUROCENTRICISM; GLOBALIZATION; NATIONALISM; ORIENTALISM.

IMPLIED READER

See RECEPTION.

INCORPORATION

This term, or the synonymous 'co-option', refers to the process by which resistant or innovative artistic or cultural forms (in fashion, music styles, alternative comedy, the AVANT-GARDE, forms of political protest and so on) are taken up and commodified by the CULTURE INDUSTRIES or political authorities. A much-cited example in POPULAR culture would be 'punk' – a street-inspired phenomenon that rapidly became a tourist attraction. In a pessimistic view, this co-option of alternative and oppositional voices is seen as proof of the absorptive powers of late CAPITALISM and the ineffectiveness of any strategy for change. Contemporary society is seen as immune to shock and any protest is rapidly defused. Negus's (1999) case studies on rap, country music and salsa suggest a more complex relation between the music industry, musicians and fans as do McRobbie's (1999) studies of new British artists, music and the fashion industry. Also, the public reaction to the work of certain artists – to Robert Mapplethorpe's photographs or Marcus Harvey's painting of Myra Hindley, or the censorship of films such as *Crash* and *Intimacy* – would suggest that the view of an unshockable, all-powerful commercial culture is an over-simplified one. Politically, too, terrorist attacks, while perhaps a contemporary sign of despair at immovable dominant cultures, cannot be said to be absorbed by them. It is possible also to see the rapid turnover and absorption of ideas as an ameliorative and energizing process; one that modifies rather than simply confirms the status quo (an example might be attitudes towards the environment, where both official policy and public awareness have changed in response to committed protest). The terms 'co-option' or 'recuperation' are generally used when this process is understood as working in the reverse direction, when the authorities are seen to make limited concessions in their own interests. Herbert Marcuse (1965) termed this same strategy 'repressive tolerance'.

In theoretical terms, incorporation can best be understood in relation to the workings of IDEOLOGY, to the relations of POWER and DISCOURSE, or the shifting relations of what Raymond Williams identified as a mesh of DOMINANT, RESIDUAL and EMERGENT ideological tendencies. Above all, it can be understood as an instance in the operation of HEGEMONY, the negotiated play of social, ideological and discursive forces by which power is, by turns, maintained and contested.

See also COUNTER-CULTURE; NEGOTIATION; SUBCULTURES.

INSTRUMENTAL REASON

See ENLIGHTENMENT.

INTELLECTUALS

'Intellectual' is a term of recent, twentieth-century origin and has been applied retrospectively to earlier centuries as well as in contemporary contexts. In its earlier usage, it describes those of different occupations in the professions, sciences and arts who claim, or are credited with, the right to speak over and above particular interests on matters of general philosophical, ethical and AESTHETIC import. What gives intellectuals this role is their own expertise and the authority of reason and truth guiding their DISCOURSE. As such, intellectuals are the inheritors of a faith in ENLIGHTENMENT reason and a product of MODERNITY, while they are, at the same time, critical of the social and political effects of this inheritance (Bauman 1987).

There are two main contemporary contributions to a theory of intellectuals and considerable discussion on their changed role in present-day society. The first theory derives from Antonio Gramsci's distinction between 'traditional' and 'organic' intellectuals (1971b: 3–23). As above, 'traditional' intellectuals are thought to be disinterested and to rise in the name of reason and truth above sectarian or topical interests. 'Organic' intellectuals, on the other hand, speak for the interests of a specific CLASS. Moreover, traditional intellectuals are bound to the institutions of the previous hegemonic order, while organic intellectuals seek to win consent to counter-hegemonic ideas and ambitions. Gramsci is interested in the formation of intellectuals who will be organic to the interests of the working class (and who therefore find their place within the revolutionary party). If traditional intellectuals are thought to be, in fact, 'interested' on behalf of a class, then the distinction as framed disappears, and intellectuals of both types can be seen as the rival representatives (the mobilizers, internal critics) of sectional interests in a class society.

The second, later, contribution to a theory of intellectuals is made from a non-Marxist position by Michel Foucault (1980a: 126–33). Foucault identifies a newer type of 'specific' intellectual identified by profession, conditions of life and work, and relation to the 'politics of truth'. This argument follows from Foucault's belief in the dispersed nature and operation of POWER in contemporary societies, and the way this is implicated in discourse and knowledge. The types of discourse and institutional mechanisms by which certain statements of truth are obtained and sanctioned in society constitutes its 'regime of truth'. It is the function of intellectuals, says Foucault, to reveal this and the terms, therefore, of an alternative regime, detaching the power of truth from its present hegemonic forms. In some ways – in his discussions of the task of 'critical interrogation on the present and on ourselves' (1987a: 49–50, and see 249) – Foucault is indebted to the modern tradition. However, he neither views the intellectual as the disinterested voice of reason outside the mechanisms of truth and power, nor suggests he/she will occupy the role of a representative of a class along the lines of Gramsci's organic intellectual.

The problems Foucault and others confront in considering the contemporary role of the intellectual are twofold: the availability or non-availability of a position of 'critical distance' and the question of representativeness. Gilles Deleuze, in conversation with Foucault, is convinced that 'a theorising intellectual... is no longer... a representing or representative consciousness' and Foucault concurs: 'The intellectual's role is no longer to place himself "somewhat ahead and to the side" in order to express the stifled truth of the collectivity'; theory is 'an activity conducted alongside those who struggle for power and not their illumination' (1977a: 206, 208). The 'specific intellectual' will therefore work in alignment with others in specific, local, institutional struggles.

This thinking is a symptom of the altered, more modest and diversified role ascribed to the intellectual under the conditions of postmodernity. It follows from Foucault's own theorization of power and from arguments made elsewhere on the erosion of the METANARRATIVE of progress, a loss of faith in reason and a general scepticism towards any position of supposed universal authority. This scenario leads Zygmunt Bauman (1987) to suggest the contemporary role of the intellectual is that of an 'interpreter' in the conversation across discourses, rather than a traditional 'legislator' who arbitrates on their respective value. Many would agree with Bauman that the traditional conception is an expression of EUROCENTRICISM. However, key contemporary intellectuals, such as Noam Chomsky (see 1969, 1991) and Edward Said (1993b), take a more vigorous, dissenting and public role than the idea of 'interpreter' suggests. Nor, elsewhere, is there a consistent postmodern alternative to, or rejection of, the role of representative critic.

An influential postmodern text such as Jean-François Lyotard's *The Postmodern Condition* (1979) is, as Steven Connor points out, something of an allegory of this very condition. Lyotard talks of the decline of modernity, of educational institutions, and of the 'authority required for intellectuals to get a hearing when they mount the rostrum' (Connor 1989: 42). Nevertheless, he gives a commanding role to experimental method in science and to those who would follow its avant-gardist example. He 'ends up', says Connor, 'not only giving the intellectual a central place in the struggle to bring about micropolitical multiplicity, but also... giving the illusion of analytic dominion over it' (1989: 42).

Elsewhere, scepticism about the universal intellectual has opened other possibilities for 'specific' intellectuals who might be viewed as 'organic', not to a traditional working class, but in their association with feminist, gay and black or more heterogeneous political groupings. One such is Julia Kristeva's (1986b) account of a new type of 'dissident intellectual'. This figure (the political rebel, the psychoanalyst, the writer and the woman who 'always feels exiled' 1986b: 296) would be politically engaged in a way Bauman's interpreter would not; employing theory (or 'thought') 'as an "analytic position" that affirms dissolution and works through differences. It is an analytic position in the face of conceptual subjective, sexual and linguistic identity' (1986b: 299). Meaghan Morris seeks to broaden the role of Foucault's 'specific intellectual' beyond the academy to join with a '"mixed" public... at events organised on thematic or political rather than purely professional principles' (1988: 11). bell hooks, also, while aware of the issue of the 'representativeness' of black intellectuals in postmodern times, affirms the connection of the black academic beyond a specific institutional location with a broader black community. Their work, she writes, 'is primarily directed towards the enhancement of black critical consciousness and the strengthening of our collective capacity to engage in meaningful resistance struggle' (1990b: 31).

Related questions have arisen in this same period, finally, in connection with the intellectual and POPULAR or MASS culture (sometimes comparable to notions of the 'people' or a 'mass' working class). Lawrence Grossberg, in one contribution, sees the emergence of a new type of 'critical fan': both fan and intellectual 'simultaneously on the terrain but not entirely of it' (1988: 68). He views the loss of critical distance and authority as 'a concrete historical dilemma' (1988: 67); a perspective that enables a correspondingly 'historically specific form of critical distance' (1988: 68). See also Ross (1989).

See also CANON; CULTURAL INTERMEDIARIES; ELITE; HEGEMONY; PUBLIC SPHERE.

INTERNET

The internet, which includes the World Wide Web, is the most unprecedentedly dispersed COMMUNICATIONS NETWORK ever devised. It was begun as a network connecting computers to radio and satellite systems in the 1960s by the US Defense Department and is now a global system (reaching 40% of the world's population in 2014) circulating a massive range of information, as well as generating huge personal fortunes and profits for companies such as Google, Amazon and Facebook. For example, the Facebook site founded in 2004 by Harvard College students recorded 1.18 billion users in August 2015 and has reached a market value of nearly $250 billion. The YouTube website, founded in 2005, was bought the following year by Google for $1.65 billion.

The 'net' has been welcomed by educationalists, academics, professions and businesses of all kinds, and also by campaigners, advertisers, media organisations and politicians, for offering instant communication, unprecedentedly wide contact, and open access to news and knowledge. It has extended its reach to include TV and radio transmission, provided a platform for new social media (YouTube, Facebook, Twitter, Instagram, etc.) and has been adopted by young and old alike as a device for play, documentation, storage, access and interpersonal communication. The language of computing (interface, virus, bug, boot, blog, hacking, browsing, social media, trolls) has become common currency and the experience has changed a gamut of everyday habits and professional practices, from shopping to dating, from reading, listening and viewing to the conventions of research, forms of writing and authorship, and the publication of word, sound or image. Distinctions between the workplace and home are fundamentally altered as 'working from home' has become a reality.

The impact of the internet has, in short, been revolutionary. However, its operation and occasional failures, its susceptibility to hostile attacks – or, in certain nations, the exercise of censorship – highlight issues of privacy, power and control which are of mounting concern. For individuals, the benefits of communicating across the world by Skype are matched by the threat of identity theft; the fun of Twitter is met with vile abuse, and pornography becomes commonplace. And while nations fear the loss of top-secret data, opponents fear the loss of individual freedoms and access to the truth.

For discussions of VIRTUAL REALITY and IDENTITY see Jones (1977) and Holmes (1997), and for wider current debate, Coombs and Collister (2015). Scott (2015) argues that the dissolution online of the distance between space and time opens human existence to the fourth dimension imagined in Gothic and other literature.

See also CONVERGENCE; CYBERSPACE; DIGITAL; TERRORISM.

INTERPELLATION

A term employed by the French Marxist philosopher, Louis Althusser (1918–1990) to name the process by which a human subject is 'hailed', or addressed, and thus positioned in relation to IDEOLOGY (1971a: 160–70). In an illustration from Althusser, when a policeman calls out '"Hey, you there!" One individual (nine times out of ten, it is the right one) turns round, believing/suspecting/knowing that it is for him' (1971a: 163). In turning round, recognizing the call is for himself, the individual becomes in that moment a 'SUBJECT', positioned in relation to the general ideological CODES of law and criminality (or more accurately 're-positioned', since for Althusser, *'individuals are always-already subjects'* (1971a: 164)).

The idea of interpellation was very influential, along with other aspects of Althusser's theory, in Literary, Film and Cultural Studies in the 1970s, but has been criticized since for its abstractness, particularly as regards the AGENCY which, or who, interpellated subjects. It was employed in this earlier period, notably in discussions of the forms and ideological work of 'classic realism' in film and literature (MacCabe 1974; Belsey 1980). These arguments suggested that the conventions of REALISM (named as 'a hierarchy of discourses', 'illusionism' and 'closure' by Belsey) interpellate the reader into a position that reinforces the ideology of liberal HUMANISM.

This general indictment of realism has, in turn, been much debated (Easthope 1988; Lodge 1990). Meanwhile, if the term itself is less used, an attention to the process of ideological positioning has been retained. Belsey had noted that the reader might refuse the position into which they are interpellated by a realist text and points towards an 'interrogative' critical reading (1980: 84). Along these lines, the concept comes close to the distinction developed elsewhere (Hall 1997a [1974]) between preferred, negotiated and oppositional decodings of a media MESSAGE.

See CODE; NEGOTIATION.

INTERPRETIVE COMMUNITY

A description introduced by the American literary theorist and critic, Stanley Fish (1938–). Fish (1980) argues that the meanings of texts are produced by interpretive (or 'interpretative') communities who share certain ground rules about literary and, by implication, other kinds of texts, and about ways of READING and assessing these. Readers interpret texts by exercising acknowledged 'interpretive strategies,' says Fish, and the stability of an interpretation is established by the resulting consensus within a self-defining COMMUNITY of readers. Meaning therefore depends, not on the texts themselves, but on the make-up of a community, and its differences or disagreements with others.

Fish's concept clearly undermines any assumption of inherent textual meaning, or the idea of a purely individualized interpretation. However, the internal dynamics within communities and across them, as well as the terms on which these are constituted, may be very complex. It is fairly clear, too, that the same readers might agree about one text and disagree about another, or shift between communities to the point of undermining any permanent distinction between them. In itself and without refinement, therefore, the concept can appear limited.

See also AUDIENCE; HERMENEUTICS; RECEPTION.

INTERTEXTUALITY

A term implying that individual texts are inescapably related to other texts, and that their meanings are correspondingly provisional and plural according to how these relations are discerned and highlighted. The term is associated with the 'linguistic turn' to STRUCTURALISM, and with the insights of Derrida's DECONSTRUCTION. A further brief theorization occurs in an early essay by Julia Kristeva who saw in Mikhail Bakhtin's concepts of DIALOGICS and CARNIVAL, the logic that 'any text is constructed as a mosaic of quotations; any text is the absorption and transformation of another' (1986a: 37).

Intertextuality implies, as here, a method of composition, but essentially it has determined a way of READING; one that is neither confined to the supposedly immanent meaning of a given text, nor seeks this meaning in an 'external' source. Instead, intertextuality promotes a lateral reading across the surface of different interwoven texts. As Roland Barthes wrote in 'The death of the author' (1977a [1968]), which helped inaugurate this new orientation:

> We know that a text is not a line of words releasing a single 'theological' meaning... but a multi-dimensional space in which a variety of writings, none of them original, blend and clash. The text is a tissue of quotations drawn from the innumerable centres of culture.
>
> (1977a: 146)

It follows that:

> In the multiplicity of writing, everything is to be disentangled, nothing deciphered; the structure can be followed, 'run'... at every point and at every level, but there is nothing beneath: the space of writing is to be ranged over, not pierced.
>
> (1977a: 147)

Just how this 'multiplicity' of writing from 'innumerable' cultural discourses is understood will determine the kind of intertextual reading practised. Whether this proceeds according to a reading along designated dimensions or CODES – or in a less regimented, but still precise, manner – marks the difference between a structuralist and poststructuralist understanding of intertextuality. The latter has been the more influential. There are significant differences, all the same, between poststructuralist models of intertextuality. Thus, where intertextuality is understood as the very condition of language and the production of meaning, there is, in principle, no restraint on the writings 'ranged' over and made relevant. The version of poststructuralism adopted by the Yale school of literary critics in the United States is frequently cited as having taken this route, and is charged in English commentary particularly with the production of errant and self-indulgent readings (Norris 1982; Eagleton 1983b). A more focused, and it might be said 'centred', intertextual reading will follow the references, echoes and allusions of a given text situating it, for example, in a tissue of contemporary writings. Such is the approach characteristically adopted within NEW HISTORICISM. A third reading, still concerned with a given text, might detect and foreground marginal, self-contradictory, or repressed textual and ideological meanings. At this point, an intertextual reading will join with other psychoanalytic, feminist, Marxist or postcolonial approaches.

See also AUTHOR; HYPERTEXT; TEXTUALITY.

JETZTZEIT

A concept used by the German-Jewish Marxist philosopher and critic, Walter Benjamin (1892–1940) in elaborating the methods of historical MATERIALISM and translated as 'the presence of the now', 'the time of the now' or literally as 'now time'. Benjamin contrasts historical materialism with HISTORICISM. The latter, he says, sees history as a linear narrative or continuum; in his 'Theses on the philosophy of history', he writes: 'its method is additive; it musters a mass of data to fill homogenous, empty time' and 'contents itself with establishing a causal connection between various moments in history' (1970 [1940]: 263, 265). By contrast, the materialist historian sees history as 'time filled by the presence of the now' [*Jetztzeit*] (1970: 263) and aims 'to blast open the continuum of history' (1970: 264) to realize this, arresting time and thought so as to produce a configuration of the past and the present in an instantaneous, crystallized moment (the now). This moment, Benjamin envisions as pregnant with tension and a revolutionary potential cognate, in the theological discourse that informs his MARXISM, with the experience of redemption and messianic revelation. Thus, he writes in 'Thesis XVIII' that a materialist historian:

> stops telling the sequence of events like the beads of a rosary. Instead he grasps the constellation which his own era has formed with a definite earlier one. Thus he establishes a conception of the present as 'the time of the now' [*Jetztzeit*] which is shot through with chips of messianic time.
>
> (1970: 265)

See also HISTORICISM.

JOUISSANCE

A French term (once used in a related but obsolete sense in English), employed in psychoanalytic theory by Freud and Jacques Lacan, and in literary theory by Roland Barthes to denote an extreme, unsettling experience of enjoyment, delight or jubilation. In French, the term, from *jouir,* has the sense of ownership as in 'enjoying a right', of playfulness, and is associated with sexual orgasm, the latter meaning rendered in English by terms such as 'bliss' or 'ecstasy'.

In psychoanalytic theory, *jouissance* is contrasted with the experience of 'lack'. *Jouissance* is pre-Oedipal and in the sense of sexual pleasure, the province and right of the father. The competitive DESIRE for this *jouissance* on the part of the father's sons is denied, under the threat of castration, but subsequently transferred to the site of 'woman' as the locus of legitimate male desire. In so far as this desire is not fulfilled (i.e. does not find expression in sexual enjoyment), the male experiences lack, though this is compensated for by the possession of phallic power.

Following Lacan, French feminist theory has sought to define a non-paternal *jouissance;* one that contravenes Oedipal laws and the rule of language. In Lacanian theory, the *jouissance* of woman consists in what exceeds the totalizing phallic FANTASY of the male. Julia Kristeva sees the *jouissance* of woman as existing within the Oedipal system (woman is positioned in, but is not of, this order), but at the same time as something that cannot be articulated there. Women (especially, for Kristeva, the figure of the mother) and *jouissance* are therefore closely associated. Thus, *jouissance* represents 'a maternal function... beyond discourse, beyond narrative, beyond psychology... beyond figuration' (1984b: 247). It is a space of fundamental 'unrepresentability' beyond the Symbolic order, towards which all converges: 'a primal scene where genitality dissolves sexual identification' (1984b: 249). The corollary is that woman and *jouissance* are associated with the BODY and the 'IMAGINARY' (a pre-Oedipal and pre-Symbolic realm in Lacanian theory) – desired, but dangerous and unobtainable; seen, but not spoken or speaking. In these terms, *jouissance* provides a subtle concept for the investigation of the complex REPRESENTATION of woman in a range of texts, particularly film and other visual cultural forms.

Both Lacan and Roland Barthes distinguish *jouissance* from *plaisir* ('PLEASURE'), the latter denoting a more comfortable sense of satisfaction and settled identity. In his *The Pleasure of the Text* (1976), Barthes associates *plaisir* with an agreeable reading experience and the closed forms of REALISM and *jouissance* (translated as 'bliss') with the unsettling challenge of more open, modernist or AVANT-GARDE texts, though both pleasure and *jouissance* can be experienced at different moments of the same text. Barthes's examples are literary, but the implications of the concept extend beyond literary texts to an association with non-conventional modes of representation, and thus, as above, with the 'inexpressible'. As such, it is related to the concept of 'the SUBLIME' as defined in relation to POSTMODERNISM by Jean-François Lyotard (1984).

See also GAZE; PHALLUS; READERLY/WRITERLY.

KITSCH

A cultural object or ICON of conspicuously 'poor' or no taste (an ornament, song, picture, verse or cheap paperback) or the self-conscious and provocative preference for such an object in defiance of the conventions of 'good taste' or of 'high art'. Tretiakov's *Girl* or plaster 'flying' wall ducks would be common examples. Kitsch values objects that are 'so bad they are good' and can be close in this respect to the meaning of CAMP. It therefore challenges received distinctions between art and MASS merchandise, though it is likely to bestow VALUE on one-time POPULAR objects, rather than presently mass-produced items, or upon selected, eccentric examples of the latter (a Mona Lisa fridge magnet, for example, rather than an average fridge magnet). In another direction, kitsch objects may be amateurishly crafted items that display some incongruity of design or purpose, a table lamp in the shape of a lighthouse or superhero, for example, giving a utilitarian object an extra decorative function. It prizes the eccentric and the AESTHETIC, therefore, in a world of low-grade, disposable junk.

In an essay of 1939, 'Avant-garde and kitsch', the art critic, Clement Greenberg sought to rally artists to the cause of the AVANT-GARDE in the face of an encroaching commercial CULTURE and degraded sensibility. Kitsch objects are the opposite of high art, but their appreciation as kitsch in fact requires a sophisticated sensibility – on the part of the observer or collector, rather than of their producer or original user. As such, it owes something to the playful spirit of dada and surrealism, and is not at an opposite extreme from the avant-garde. Arguably too, as if to confirm this, POP art of the 1960s by Roy Lichtenstein, Peter Blake and others made 'art' out of 'kitsch'.

LANGUE AND PAROLE

See SIGN; STRUCTURALISM.

LEAVISISM

See TEXTUALITY.

LEGITIMATION

The question of legitimation has become an issue in relation to the credibility of the founding doctrines of the ENLIGHTENMENT and the continued 'project of MODERNITY'. The Enlightenment beliefs in reason and equality were proposed in the name of universal emancipation and progress. However, it has, in the event, proved suspect on each of these counts: its legitimizing universals are a disguise for the colonialist projection, so it is said, of a specific cultural model upon the world at large and the instrument in the history of nineteenth-and twentieth-century western societies of totalitarian oppression and the inequalities of capitalism. This charge is made most directly, but with the claims of science and scientific knowledge first of all in mind, in Lyotard (1984).

Many, however, would seek to defend or redefine, and so legitimize, the ideals of truth and justice (see Tallack [ed] 1995: Section 5). Directions in poststructuralist and postmodernist thought, broadly defined, would propose an alternative theoretical perspective based on the principles of diversity and DIFFERENCE, or Lyotard's 'mini-narratives' without transcendent legitimation. In some forms, however, this alternative itself stands accused of totalizing arrogance (bestowing universal value upon intellectual and cultural developments specific to the advanced capitalist, or 'postmodern', nations of the west) or of an empty relativism.

Interestingly, Jacques Derrida, otherwise a celebrated champion of difference, had suggested in the early key essay, 'Structure, sign and play in the human sciences', that DECONSTRUCTION must acquit itself of 'a critical responsibility' in its borrowings from a heritage that it seeks at the same time to deconstruct (1978: 282). The European heritage is, by implication, inescapable. So, too, therefore, are the dilemmas of legitimation across a range of philosophical and political positions.

See also EUROCENTRICISM; FOUNDATIONALISM; METANARRATIVE.

LIMINALITY

A concept developed by the Franco-Dutch folklorist Arnold Van Gennep (1960) and anthropologist Victor Turner (1969), and adopted especially within postcolonial studies and studies of RACE and ETHNICITY. Liminality refers to a state or stage of transition, as between childhood and a more social or public IDENTITY. While this suggests the putting on or acquisition of a role, liminal phases and states can also mean the 'renunciation of roles, the demolishing of structures' (Turner, in Back 1996: 244). Les Back (1996) takes up this latter meaning to describe the shift into new roles and communal identities in youth cultures in south London. In this context, a liminal space is the local public realm or 'alternative public sphere' (1996: 244) where African-Caribbean and white youth engage together on non-racist terms, having renounced the divisive racism of mainstream society. The liminal space is one where multiracial peer groups can remake the cultural signs and symbols by which identity is defined, rejecting the prejudice of racism for an acceptance of different ethnicities. As Back's study shows, this often occurs in an exchange and cross-over of musical styles and idioms.

See also HYBRIDITY; PUBLIC SPHERE.

LOCAL

A term that has entered the vocabulary of accounts of POSTMODERNISM in relation to ideas of COMMUNITY and the global or GLOBALIZATION. The local is viewed variously, either as the subject of reactionary nostalgia (Young 1990), as the site of a new cosmopolitanism (Massey 1993), or, in major cities, as the place of the disaffected, policed and disadvantaged. Mike Davis (1988), for example, describes the Los Angeles experienced by Hispanics and Asians as the 'bad edge of post-modernity', a nowhere strung between the local and global (Lyon 1994: 60).

Elspeth Probyn (1990) seeks a sense of the local that will be of use to feminist theory. To this end, she distinguishes it from 'locale' and 'location'. The first is composed of a PLACE and event – the home and the tensions of marriage and family life, for example. The second she understands as a term for how knowledge is ordered – sited and sequenced – from the position, for example, of a western or male subject. The local she sees as a co-ordination of time and place, and as used to demean women, since 'women's practices and experiences have been historically dismissed as local' (1990: 178). There is a complex exchange and interdependence between these discourses and practices. Thus, it is through the 'process of location, of fixing statements… that the knowledges produced in locale are denigrated as local, subaltern and other' (1990: 185). Probyn argues, not for abandoning the local, however, but for working 'more deeply in and against it' (1990: 186), loosening its meanings and ideological hold.

See also SPACE; SUBALTERN.

LOGOCENTRICISM

A term derived from the Greek *logos* meaning 'word', 'law', 'sense' or 'meaning', and introduced by the French philosopher, Jacques Derrida (1976) to characterize those systems of thought that evoke or assume the existence of a single organizing centre, first principle or underlying cause. This centre, however, as Derrida points out, exists paradoxically both inside and outside of a given system of ideas: what is thought of as an informing influence is also felt to be prior to, and outside of, a given system. It is simultaneously a 'presence' and an 'absence'. The idea of God as at once a transcendent, absent being or force and as existing within all things is a prime example of such thinking. In the biblical text, 'In the beginning was the Word', there is the belief that one cause was prior to, and responsible for, all creation. God is a 'transcendent signifier', in Derrida's terms, whose spoken word is credited with full meaning or presence: 'the Word was with God', the text continues, 'and the Word was God'. This form of logocentrism, which invests authority in an originating moment of speech, Derrida terms 'phonocentrism'.

There are many similar examples of what Derrida calls this 'metaphysics of presence'; the belief, that is to say, in a validating outside principle that guarantees meaning in the here and now. In fact, Derrida claims that the entire tradition of western philosophy is logocentric: it has 'always assigned the origin of truth in general to the logos', he announces in *Of Grammatology,* 'the history of truth, of the truth of truth has always been… the debasement of writing and its repression outside "full" speech' (1976: 3). As this implies, logocentricism is also, says Derrida, fundamentally idealist: 'It is the matrix of idealism. Idealism is its most direct representation' (1981a: 51).

Philosophy – and POPULAR thought – therefore assumes, in an idealist fashion, the existence of transcendent but informing notions of essence, origin, truth, reality and so on. Derrida means to show how these ideas 'centre' thought, and give it unity and identity, but at the price of denying the fact of DIFFERENCE. Since the individual must employ a system of REPRESENTATION independent of subjective

CONSCIOUSNESS, the idea of a pure self-consciousness when the subject is fully present to him/herself is an illusion. There is, instead, difference and self-division, coupled with the quest or DESIRE for unity.

In the STRUCTURALISM of Ferdinand de Saussure, and its stress on difference, Derrida finds a powerful critique of logocentricism, but he detects also in Saussure a characteristic privileging of the spoken over the written word that affirms it. In Lacanian psychoanalysis, he similarly discovers a joint privileging of the PHALLUS and logos that makes it PHALLOGOCENTRIC. Derrida's critique of these systems of thought gives rise to the form of POSTSTRUCTURALISM or, more precisely, the method of DECONSTRUCTION associated with his work.

See also *ÉCRITURE*/WRITING; IDEALISM.

MARGIN(ALITY)

Margin(ality) refers to the place of repressed or subordinated textual meanings, but also to the position of dissident intellectuals and social groups (women, lesbians, gays, blacks) who see themselves at a remove from the normative assumptions and oppressive power structures of mainstream society. While to be 'on the margins' can suggest a negative experience of ALIENATION, the term is used in academic debate and activist politics to suggest a position of advantage from which the dominant society can be critiqued and disrupted. The difficulties here are that not all such individuals or groups have the resources to 'speak from the margins' and that the position may be a precarious one prone to INCORPORATION.

Theoretically, the concept derives from the combined influences of PSYCHOANALYSIS, theories of IDEOLOGY, and DECONSTRUCTION, which have alerted critics to suppressed or subordinated meanings, and provided the critical means to elicit these. The term also embodies a spatial metaphor (as does the related distinction between 'the centre and periphery'), which owes something to studies in Cultural Geography and POSTCOLONIALISM. As these perspectives point out, marginalized groups, whether or not in association with textual meanings, reside in the suburbs, ghettos, on the edge of cities or in 'Third World' cultures made marginal to the First World. In this broader context, western intellectuals who deem themselves marginal are revealed as centred. Postcolonial critics argue, of course, for ways to transform this situation, by strategically reversing it – 'Try to behave as if you are part of the margin, try to unlearn your privilege', Gayatri Spivak recommends to the western theoretical establishment (1990: 30); by revealing the interanimation of categories – 'The centre itself is marginal', proclaims Trinh T. Minh-ha (in Ashcroft *et al.* [eds] 1995); or by moving beyond the binary of centre and margin by means of concepts such as HYBRIDITY and the DIASPORA.

See also ETHNICITY; PLACE.

MARXISM

The *Collected Works* of Karl Marx and Friedrich Engels comprises some 50 volumes. Arguably, however, the most influential texts for cultural study have been the shortest: the three-page 'Theses on Feuerbach' and the five-page 1859 'Preface' to *A Contribution to the Critique of Political Economy* (see BASE AND SUPERSTRUCTURE). Further important texts have been Marx's *Economic and Philosophic Manuscripts* of 1844, *The Eighteenth Brumaire of Louis Bonaparte* and *Capital* (Vol. 1), Engels' *Condition of the Working Class in England* and the co-authored, *The German Ideology*. 'Marxism' includes these works as part of the original corpus and the subsequent writings of numerous authors, including major political leaders (Lenin, Stalin, Mao Zedong, Che Guevara), activists and academics in a number of disciplines. The term embraces overlapping and antagonistic traditions in Existential Marxism (Sartre), Hegelian Marxism (Georg Lukács, Fredric Jameson), Marxist HUMANISM (E.P. Thompson, Raymond Williams), revolutionary Marxism (Trotsky, Callinicos, Eagleton), scientific or structural Marxism (Althusser, Macherey) and Marxist-FEMINISM (Mitchell 1974; Barrett 1980, 1988). Later developments have also produced debates between DECONSTRUCTION and Marxism (Ryan 1982; Derrida 1994b) and POSTCOLONIALISM (Ahmad 1992), as well as developments in POST-MARXISM (Laclau and Mouffe 1985; Mouzelis 1990; Giddens 1990; Docherty 1990; Barrett 1991).

It is possible to track Marxism, not only through these traditions and debates (see Anderson 1979, 1984), but through its degrees of influence as a model of explanation in the different intellectual and political histories of various cultures and through the fortunes of particular key concepts. Thus, in Britain, Marxism was an influence, primarily upon Literary Studies, in the 1930s and then across a wider academic spectrum in the late 1960s and 1970s when it coincided with the formation of an influential model of Cultural Studies. Reflecting on this moment, Angela McRobbie describes Marxism as 'a major point of reference for the whole Cultural Studies project in the UK' (1992: 719). Important initiatives in this period were inspired by the work of Antonio Gramsci – in particular, his theory of HEGEMONY – and by forms of structuralist and feminist Marxism which, in conjunction with PSYCHOANALYSIS, informed so-called SCREEN THEORY and key essays on REALISM and the male GAZE by, respectively, Colin MacCabe and Laura Mulvey. The main Marxist influence on this work in film, but extending to Literary and Cultural Studies in general, was the structural or scientific Marxism of Louis Althusser, especially Althusser's theorizations of IDEOLOGY (see Eagleton 1976; Easthope 1988). By the 1980s, however, as Francis Mulhern writes, this wind had blown itself out. He sees 'a milieu increasingly indifferent to Marxism and ever more ignorant of it', in which Althusser's name 'survived as little more than a souvenir' (1995: 168, 169).

Mulhern's analysis is focused upon Literary Studies, but applies across a broader front. Nicos Mouzelis, for example, comments from within Sociology and Political Science on 'the general anti-Marxist climate of the 1980s' (1990: 20), following the revival of interest just a decade earlier, while Colin Sparks writing in the mid 1990s feels – in what he believes is a regressive tendency – that it is 'possible to claim that almost nobody today active in the field of Cultural Studies identifies themselves with the theoretical framework of what was once Marxist Cultural Studies' (1996: 96).

During the 1980s, the earlier Marxist impetus was overtaken by feminism and by the agendas associated with postcolonial and post-Marxist theory. Underlying this development, there has been a reassessment of the importance of the category of social CLASS, and thus of notions of 'the dictatorship of the proletariat', the importance of the political party, and the role of activists and INTELLECTUALS in programmes of political action. Though the traditional concept of class has been defended (Sandler, Blair and Diskin 1995; Sparks 1996), the general consequence of this fraught set of debates has been to place class alongside, or to displace it by, considerations of GENDER, RACE and ETHNICITY.

A further challenge to Marxism and its 'grand narrative' of intellectual and social progress has derived in this period from versions of POSTMODERNISM, especially in the attack upon the ENLIGHTENMENT project associated with Jean-François Lyotard. This too, however, has been negotiated into a variety of post-Marxist positions (Nicholson and Seidman [eds] 1995; Morley and Chen [eds] 1996) or disputed (Callinicos 1989; Harvey 1993; Eagleton 1996).

These debates on changed intellectual methods and political strategies have been widespread, and in their specific relation to Marxism have taken different forms, finally, according to the histories of specific cultures. The United States, where Marxism has been weaker in the postwar period than in Great Britain, has followed a similar general course (see Aronowitz 1989), though questions of race and ethnicity have been foregrounded there from an earlier date (see hooks and West 1991). Meanwhile, other theoretical movements within the general orbit of poststructuralism, at points in a dialogue with Marxism, have inspired a new liberal pragmatism (Rorty 1989). The Marxist model has undergone comparable but complex changes of emphasis elsewhere, in Australia and the Third World. In Europe, it has followed at least three routes: the philosophical orientation, signalling a distancing from class politics, identified by Perry Anderson (1979, 1984) as characterizing 'Western Marxism'; the continuing currency, shown in the work of Jürgen Habermas, of the traditions of the Frankfurt School; and, in France, a dialogue with Marxism that has produced in erstwhile Marxist intellectuals, such as Baudrillard and Lyotard, a range of poststructuralist and postmodern positions, which are non- or anti-Marxist, as well as the *rapprochement* between deconstruction and a 'spirit' of Marxism announced by Jacques Derrida (1994b).

See also ALIENATION; DIALECTICS; HISTORICISM; MATERIALISM.

MASQUERADE

A term current in contemporary FEMINISM and QUEER THEORY, which derives from an influential article 'Womanliness as a masquerade' (1929) by Joan Riviere, psychoanalyst, translator and colleague of Sigmund Freud. Riviere argued how women adopt a public mask of 'womanliness' or 'femininity' to satisfy the desires of, and allay the fear of, challenge and competition to men. Women are therefore seen to perform according to man's image of what a woman should be, and in so doing, to confirm the stereotypes of PATRIARCHY. This performance is seen, at the same time, to allay the woman's anxiety and fear, especially of parental retribution.

Judith Butler (1990) has argued for a more positive appropriation of masquerade in the spirit of mimicry and PARODY. Rather than confirming woman's stereotypical social or fixed psychic role, masquerade is understood in this view to CRITIQUE essentialist assumptions of sexual IDENTITY (Riviere had said there was no 'genuine womanliness' behind the mask). Indeed, along with the related concept of PERFORMATIVITY, masquerade in Butler's writing serves to emphasize how all identities are constructed, and open to play and transformation.

MASS

A term used in accounts of the mass media or systems of mass COMMUNICATION and of mass society. In its limited, technical usage the term designates the advent of forms of mass PRODUCTION, and the requisite technologies and distribution techniques characterizing the operation of these systems. Since these systems are themselves a feature of advanced industrial or capitalist societies, however, the term cannot easily be separated from a broader reference to their supporting and consequent social and economic forms. The description of the mass media as CULTURE INDUSTRIES acknowledges this connection. References to 'mass society' take their lead from these systems, but extend beyond a technical description and beyond these industries to consider the accompanying appearance of a 'mass' population of largely urban dwellers; the workers who are the producers and consumers of the goods and services of this society, including the products of the mass communication systems. Often, such accounts have been centrally motivated by a concern with the effects of these developments upon cultural sensibilities. The description 'mass society' therefore seeks to conceptualize broad social, economic and ideological forms of which the mass media are a SIGN, symptom and possible cause.

'Mass society theory' along these lines began to appear, particularly in the United States, from the mid 1930s within the strengthening discipline of Sociology. Notable contributors to this debate were Daniel Bell, Paul Lazarsfeld, C. Wright Mills and Dwight Macdonald (Brookeman 1984). However, its governing perspective extended beyond academic work to 'mass observation' surveys and federally supported work in writing and photography in the widespread contemporary documentary movement. Academic commentators were invariably critical of what they saw as the meretricious forms and standardizing effects of mass cultural products, which they contrasted one way with the AVANT-GARDE or 'high CULTURE', and another with a supposedly authentic folk culture. Mass culture theory therefore inaugurated some of the leading positions in the continuing debate on POPULAR culture.

The Marxist school of social or CRITICAL THEORY, associated with Theodor Adorno, Max Horkheimer and others, shared the AESTHETIC IDEOLOGY informing this CRITIQUE, but sought to retain a belief in the contradictory potential for social progress in an otherwise conformist industrial society.

From within a less theorized – but in some ways, comparable, tradition in England – the literary and social critic, F.R. Leavis (1895–1975) had similarly defended the values of a 'minority culture' embodied in a selective literary tradition against the debasing effects of a standardized mass 'civilization'. Founding figures in the emerging field of British Cultural Studies, such as Richard Hoggart (1918–) and Raymond Williams (1921–1988) developed their own more complex views of contemporary culture in a debate with this position. Hoggart's *The Uses of Literacy* (1957) sought to defend the cultural forms of an indigenous, authentic working-class culture against a perceived 'Americanization' of British life at the hands of the vulgarizing, new mass entertainment industries. In a seminal early essay 'Culture is ordinary' (1958), which shared this defence of 'ordinary people' against 'commercial culture', Raymond Williams countered both the Leavisite tradition and an available Marxist vocabulary to warn against the use of the term 'masses'. He wrote in an influential statement:

> I don't believe that the ordinary people in fact resemble the normal description of the masses, low and trivial in taste and habit. I put it another way: that there are in fact no masses, but only ways of seeing people as masses.
>
> (Williams 1989a: 11)

The French philosopher of postmodern HYPERREALITY, Jean Baudrillard (1929–) has offered to fundamentally shift the ground of the above debate. To think of the 'silence of the masses' in the traditional terms of ALIENATION and passivity is beside the point, he argues, for this very silence presents 'an original strategy' of resistance, at once 'ironic and antagonistic' (1988: 208). The mass media (Baudrillard's example is opinion polls) produce an excess of information and the reverse of certitude. They do not bolster, but destabilize, social and political reality. This is the basis of their appeal – a source of pleasure 'to the ironic unconscious of the masses… whose deepest drive remains the symbolic murder of the political class, the symbolic murder of political reality' (1988: 212). Our addiction to the media is founded on a desire for 'this perversion of truth and falsehood… the desire for simulation'. In the masses' blank non-participation, Baudrillard concludes, resides a strategy of 'spontaneous total resistance to the ultimatum of historical and political reason' (1988: 217).

For relevant essays by F.R. Leavis, Dwight Macdonald and Adorno, see Storey ([ed] 1994).

See also AURA; ELITE; SIMULATION.

MATERIALISM

Simply put, materialism names the belief that matter has causal primacy over 'spirit' or the 'ideal', and that these are determined by the material world rather than vice versa. This definition is deceptive, however, and the word contains a number of inflections and ambiguities, including the POPULAR sense derived from the above association with matter and the world of objects that connects it with the acquisition of possessions and the accumulation of capital.

Beyond this, there are variant meanings in philosophy and political theory and 'any serious materialism' in these realms, as Raymond Williams remarks, brings 'inevitable problems' (1980a: 103). We can first of all distinguish 'mechanical materialism' or 'vulgar materialism'. Dr. Johnson's famous rebuttal of idealist philosophy by kicking a very material stone to prove its existence is of this type, but generally these terms have a pejorative meaning and are used to denote an unsophisticated belief in the primacy of material objects. Even so, the most basic forms of materialism will generally be associated with science and the rational search for laws in nature as against any assertion of a higher reality associated with religion or metaphysical being.

'Dialectical materialism' is, second, used to denote a more complex form of materialism that notes the dynamism and mobile, relational quality of matter, and allows for the action of human subjects on the world (see DIALECTICS). This is often said to be the philosophical stance of MARXISM, but although Karl Marx and Friedrich Engels certainly sought to define and employ a dialectical mode of analysis, they themselves never actually used the phrase 'dialectical materialism' to describe Marxism. A further term, 'historical materialism', coined by Engels, has instead effectively become synonymous with Marxism, though a 'structural Marxist' such as Louis Althusser criticized traditional Marxists, including Antonio Gramsci, for too hastily collapsing dialectical into historical materialism. As this suggests, at this level, materialism is concerned less with abstract questions of matter and spirit than with models of historical knowledge and questions of causality and AGENCY, and thus comes to influence debate on forms of political action.

A key reference point in these varied and long-standing issues is Marx's distinction between a society's material economic BASE and its SUPERSTRUCTURE. This suggests that economic factors, rather than ideas, politics, artistic or cultural production, give a decisive direction to human history. This can be interpreted as the proposition that ideas and CULTURE are explained as the 'ideal' reflexes and reflections of this more profound 'material' level. But if this is accepted, the model inclines towards a 'vulgar', non-dialectical Marxism at odds with the intentions of its founders.

In its most uncompromising form this materialism equates with 'economism' (the belief that the economic level of society is not only ultimately, but utterly, determining). This position has shaped the social and cultural life of a number of socialist regimes in the postwar period and has been indirectly discredited along with the political regimes themselves. An overly economistic or reductively deterministic materialism has also come under fire in philosophy and criticism, not just from traditional idealists, but from within Marxism and from many thinkers involved in the explosion of cultural and literary theory.

One of the most cogent revisions of historical materialism along these lines has been the CULTURAL MATERIALISM first theorized by Raymond Williams in *Marxism and Literature* (1977). Williams argues, not for culture's autonomous status from the material world but, on the contrary, for the recognition of the materiality of culture itself: for 'the material character of the production of a cultural order' (1977: 93). Williams thus proposes a 'rematerialization' of art and culture, arguing that, 'The inescapable materiality of works of art is then the irreplaceable materialization of kinds of experience' (1977: 162).

In a further challenge, influenced initially by Louis Althusser's theory of IDEOLOGY, 'materialism' often seems to assert, not just the primacy of the material over the ideal, but that everything is material. Thus, claims have been made for the materiality of language and REPRESENTATIONS (Coward and Ellis 1977) of the BODY, and literary and cultural texts themselves, either as physically produced historical artefacts, or in the ways that modernist and postmodernist texts have foregrounded their own material status (Easthope 1983).

This 'pan-materialism' may seem to be the result of a rigorously materialist standpoint, but it brings with it a logical problem: if there is nothing 'immaterial', then the adjective 'material' loses all descriptive force, applying to everything and thus to nothing. Louis Althusser responded to this implication by acknowledging that 'Of course, the material existence of the ideology... does not have the same modality as the material existence of a paving-stone or a rifle.' Matter, he says, has different senses and 'exists in different modalities, all rooted in the last instance in "physical" matter' (1971a: 156). All the same, even a differentiated materialism sits oddly with the contrary argument from within POSTSTRUCTURALISM and POSTMODERNISM, that contemporary media societies are dominated by detached, freely circulating IMAGES and information FLOWS, that our bodies are mobile signifiers and our sexual identities malleable rather than material (Butler 1990, 1993).

In practice, contemporary criticism and theory often leave the precise meaning or extent of their 'materialism' ambiguous. In general, in a direct or distant debt to Marxism, materialism tends to indicate a commitment to the social and historical reading of texts, and the explanatory power of historical and economic factors in literary and cultural analysis. As suggested, however, other movements than Marxism, notably FEMINISM and PSYCHOANALYSIS, may also lay claim to the term. None are free, however, of the ambiguities or challenges sketched above.

See also HISTORICISM; IDEALISM; IDEOLOGY; POSTCAPITALISM; SPECULATIVE REALISM.

MEDIATION

This term has two senses. The first refers to the intermediary structures, forces or apparatuses thought simultaneously to help construct and contextualize individual literary, artistic or cultural works. Examples would be the conventions of GENRE, the chosen or available means of PRODUCTION (the written word, film or cartoon), the mode of production (determining the limited edition or mass production of a text) and considerations of GENDER, CLASS and IDEOLOGY. The Marxist critic, Walter Benjamin, drew attention to the effects of technology on the status of an artistic work (see AURA), but questions of production and the role of the market have long been the mainstay of sociological approaches to literary and other texts (see Altick 1963; Sutherland 1978). A literary critic who sought to read texts in terms of the mediating structures of class ideology in particular was Lucien Goldmann (1975). Raymond Williams (1980b) discusses the general features of Goldmann's work and the role of mediation in Marxist Literary Studies in his *Marxism and Literature* (1977).

The second understanding of the term is that all meaning is 'mediated', and has, that is to say, to pass through the editorial and interpretive screens of books, TV, newspapers and other forms of communication before it is received. In its radical form, the concept can therefore come to question the original and authentic status (as 'factually' or self-evidently 'true') of any statement or text. As such, it is consistent with the scepticism that characterizes much poststructuralist and postmodern thought.

See also BASE AND SUPERSTRUCTURE; HOMOLOGY.

'MEN IN FEMINISM'

Imelda Whelehan views the internal diversity and debate of contemporary FEMINISM in terms of a common strategy to dislodge 'the hegemony of male discourse' (1995: 21). This not uncommon perspective raises the question of men's relation to feminism and to PATRIARCHY. Opinion here is much divided, both among feminists and men. The latter's response can be said to have taken three directions. First, 'men's groups' were formed in an analogy with 'consciousness raising' women's groups in the 1970s. These sought to investigate the themes of patriarchy and sexism, and to adopt the methods introduced by feminist research, most usefully in relation to the construction of masculinities and on occasion in an alliance with cognate developments within gay studies. A notable publication that has pursued this agenda is the long-running magazine *Achilles Heel*. In *Recreating Sexual Politics* (1991 [2009]) Victor Seidler offers a frank commentary on the issues this development has raised, arguing for the need to reconstruct, rather than disown, masculinity and to integrate the 'personal' in a continuing dialogue with male socialist and left traditions.

A second development has seen the publication of academic texts composed of dialogues between feminist and male theorists, and of commentaries on issues within feminist debate or on GENDER. The theme of 'men in feminism' – after the title of one such collection (Jardine and Smith [eds] 1987) – has, however, been disparaged by feminists who feel it is an overbearing or trivializing distraction, or who have detected it as a cynical career move (Whelehan 1995: 184–9). Whelehan is especially unconvinced by the appropriation by male critics, such as Boone and Cadden (1990), of the description 'feminist'.

Third, 'the men's movement' has distanced itself from, or has directly opposed, feminism in the belief that it has emasculated traditional masculinity and undermined the male role in sexual relations, the family and society. An example is the movement inspired in the United States by Robert Bly's *Iron John: A Book About Men* (1991), which urges men to reclaim their repressed 'wildness'. Much of this thinking has entered popular journalism and culture. Related signs have been the appearance in the UK of a CULT of 'laddishness' in association with sport and pop music and, alongside it, the promotion of the 'new man' and the idea of man's search for the 'feminine' in himself. The most convincing study of such reactions to women and feminism has been concerned with the linked changes in the family and male employment, and the emergence of an underclass of directionless male teenagers and unemployed adults (Coward 1992; Mann 1992). This issue arose once more in the late 1990s in relation to the evidence of male under-achievement in schools.

See also CLASS; QUEER THEORY; SEXUAL DIFFERENCE.

MESSAGE

A widely used term in COMMUNICATION and Media Studies. In the technical and linguistic model from which it is derived, a message is the coded content transmitted from an ADDRESSER (or speaker) to an ADDRESSEE (or listener). As formulated by the eminent Soviet-born linguist, Roman Jakobson (1896–1982) the message then fulfils certain 'functions': maintaining an open channel of communication (the phatic function), or effecting an orientation of different kinds towards the speaker or listener (the emotive and conative functions, respectively, as in 'I feel good' or 'Hey you!'), an orientation towards the message itself (the poetic function), or towards the CODE, ensuring that this is shared (the metalingual function) (Lodge [ed] 1988).

None of this, of course, guarantees that a message is unambiguously transmitted or understood. Think of how many jokes misfire. Tone of voice or gesture, even in the simplest acts of communication, may obscure a message and confuse a listener. The need to interpret (and the possibilities for misinterpretation) in a specific context are therefore an inescapable part of any message.

Probably the most celebrated use of this term occurs in the writings of the one-time literary critic turned cultural commentator, Marshall McLuhan (1911–1980). McLuhan detected the beginnings of the global influence of electronic media (bringing the world together in a 'global village'). The forms of these media, he argued, shaped their content (the 'way' of communicating determining the 'what' that is communicated). He summed this up in the phrase 'the medium is the message', which rapidly became a slogan of the late 1960s. It forms the title of the first chapter of his *Understanding Media* (1964). McLuhan's appended pun 'the medium is the massage' – the title of an innovative text of aphorisms, cartoons and photographs, published in 1967 – further conveyed the sense of the involving, wraparound effects of the new media. Television, in particular, he saw as a totally new technology, demanding quite new sensory responses to its speed, elliptical editing and broken narratives – as evident above all in the new 'commercials'. 'Television demands participation and involvement in depth of the whole being. It will not work as background. It engages you... images are projected at you. You are the screen' (McLuhan and Fiore 1967: 125).

McLuhan's arguments look back to Walter Benjamin's reflections on the loss of artistic AURA resulting from the new mechanical means of production earlier in the century, and forward to the findings of the French philosopher of an age of SIMULATION, Jean Baudrillard. At this economic-cultural juncture, so Baudrillard asserts, the conflation of human and IMAGE is complete; there is no longer any medium or message as such to speak of:

> The medium itself is no longer identifiable... and the confusion of the medium and the message (McLuhan) is the first great formula of the new era. There is no longer a medium in the literal sense; it is now intangible, diffused, and diffracted in the real.
>
> (Baudrillard 1994 [1981]: 30)

See also AUDIENCE; METALANGUAGE.

METAFICTION

A term describing fiction that is about itself, which takes the processes and conventions of fiction writing – the creation of an illusory fictional world, the structure of narrative or the role of the narrator or author, for example – as its prime subject. Fiction of this kind will therefore be non-representational or non-realist, as this is customarily defined, since it purposely reveals and interrogates the conventions upon which realist fiction depends if it is to persuade its readers or viewers that it is a faithful, transparent depiction of the world. It is the deceitful paradox of a conventional form which denies its own mechanisms that metafiction sets out to expose, either, as in the case of a writer such as the American novelist John Barth, in the name of a conception of the world as composed of a tissue of stories, or in the case of the German playwright Bertolt Brecht or a writer such as John Berger, in the name of a new and truer REALISM. Metafiction is most often associated with the self-conscious INTERTEXTUALITY of POSTMODERNISM, but as Brecht's and Berger's names imply, it also has a modernist heritage. Earlier and much-celebrated examples would be Laurence Sterne's eighteenth-century novel, *Tristram Shandy* and Cervantes' *Don Quixote*. Writers commonly thought of as authors of metafiction (where the motivation might nevertheless be quite different) are B.S. Johnson, John Fowles, Angela Carter, Peter Ackroyd and Alisdair Gray in the UK; the Italian writers, Umberto Eco and Italo Calvino; and the American novelists, Vladimir Nabokov, Joanna Russ, Paul Auster and, more recently, Mark Z. Danielewksi. Perhaps the most cited example is the Argentinean writer, Jorge Luis Borges (see Hutcheon 1980; Waugh 1984). Linda Hutcheon has especially developed the concept of 'historiographic metafiction' in relation to the self-conscious narrative reconstruction of history (1989). Where many see postmodern 'paratextuality' as a sign of indulgence or mere play, Hutcheon views its frankness on the constructedness of history and 'the real' as a way of intervening in the politics of REPRESENTATION.

In cinema, Alfred Hitchcock's *Rear Window,* François Truffaut's *Day for Night* and Quentin Tarantino's *Pulp Fiction,* among many others, would be examples of 'metafiction film'. If the concept of fiction is extended to other NARRATIVE forms in other media, then television would provide numerous examples, especially in comedy, of metafictional television.

See also PARODY; PASTICHE; TEXTUALITY.

METALANGUAGE

A language about a language (meta = above, over). In linguistics, the 'metalingual function', as identified by the linguist Roman Jakobson (1896–1982; see Lodge [ed] 1988), is a statement about a CODE, as when we seek clarification about the meaning or definition of a term (as in 'What does "glossary" mean?'). More generally, a metalanguage is a critical or analytical DISCOURSE about another discourse. Linguistics is therefore a metalanguage about language itself. The structuralist theorist of NARRATIVE, Gérard Genette, citing Roland Barthes and the French poet, Paul Valéry in the following remarks, suggests that since literary criticism 'speaks the same language as its object' (unlike art or music criticism) it 'is a metalanguage, "discourse upon a discourse". It can therefore be a metaliterature, that is to say, "a literature of which literature itself is the imposed object"' (Lodge [ed] 1988: 63).

On this reckoning, 'Theory' is a metalanguage about the literary and cultural forms and processes that are its object, as well as the more empirical or textual analyses of these. Any theory can also produce a meta-metalanguage in an act of self-criticism or commentary upon itself. Poststructuralist thought would endorse this notion of a serial discourse talking about discourse, but challenge the assumption of a metalanguage that defines and fixes the terms of another discourse in any absolute sense. The implication of Jean-François Lyotard's notion of DIFFEREND, for example, is that there can be no 'objective' metalanguage that arbitrates upon others.

METANARRATIVE

A 'super' NARRATIVE about, or embracing, other narratives. The term is used interchangeably with 'grand narrative' (*grand récit*) by the French philosopher Jean-François Lyotard (1924–1998) and in subsequent discussions of POSTMODERNISM. 'Simplifying to the extreme,' writes Lyotard, 'I define postmodern as incredulity toward metanarratives' (1984: xxiv).

These narratives are those that have governed the pursuit of knowledge and freedom from the period of the ENLIGHTENMENT, and have therefore come to characterize MODERNITY. This epoch has legitimized itself, says Lyotard, through 'an explicit appeal to some grand narrative, such as the dialectics of Spirit, the hermeneutics of meaning, the emancipation of the rational or working subject, or the creation of wealth' (1984: xxiii). The self-deceiving and failed ambition of the two main narratives to achieve this 'universal' knowledge and 'universal' freedom have cost them their legitimacy. 'Neither economic nor political liberalism, nor the various Marxisms,' writes Lyotard, 'emerge from the sanguinary last two centuries free from the suspicion of crimes against mankind' (1986: 6). In the place of metanarratives, postmodern narratives will be *petits récits,* the mini-narratives, or 'language games' of social and cultural life whose variety and difference can make no claim to universality.

Some read metanarratives as gendered 'master narratives' (Owens in Foster [ed] 1983). Patricia Waugh, for example, ponders, 'As postmodernists register a sense of the collapse of the legitimacy of the grand meta-narratives of the West, are they not talking euphemistically of the loss of the legitimacy of patriarchal discourse?' (Wright [ed] 1992: 344).

METAPHYSICS OF PRESENCE

See ESSENTIALISM; LOGOCENTRICISM.

MIRROR-PHASE

According to the French psychoanalyst, Jacques Lacan (1901–1981), the infant acquires an IDENTITY by passing – in the period between 6 and 18 months – through the IMAGINARY and *en route* to the SYMBOLIC order. This passage is termed the 'mirror-phase'. In the Imaginary order, the child initially experiences a oneness in its close association with the mother. At the mirror-stage when the child encounters its own self-image (not necessarily literally in a mirror but in the mirror of others' eyes, especially in knowing itself viewed by the mother), this early unity is disrupted. It sees a unified, independent self in the mirror, but perceives this self as separate from its own viewing self and the observing parent. The self in the mirror is coherent and 'free-standing' at a time when the child's own motor activity is undeveloped. The image in the mirror comes, therefore, to represent a desired unity with which the child identifies, but presently experiences itself as lacking. The subject is caught in a dynamic of 'insufficiency' and 'anticipation', in Lacan's terms, moving 'from a fragmented body-image to a form of its totality that I shall call orthopaedic' (1977: 4).

This experience introduces a formative combination, argues Lacan, of recognition with MISRECOGNITION, which is characteristic of the ego and persists through the further passage into the Symbolic order. The ego, so formed, should be distinguished, as Madan Sarup points out, from the 'SUBJECT'. It is the ego, misunderstanding signals from the UNCONSCIOUS, that directs the subject in its futile search for unity (Sarup 1992: 83–4).

The concept of the mirror-phase is the most well-known and influential of Lacan's contributions to psychoanalytic theory. It was first presented in a paper in 1936 and published in a revised version in 1949, before its translation as 'The mirror stage as formative of the function of the I as revealed in psychoanalytic experience' (1977). This short technical discussion has since had a remarkable impact on theories of SUBJECTIVITY within the general field of cultural study. It was given currency primarily through French FEMINISM (see Mitchell and Rose 1982; Grosz 1990) and in the application of poststructuralist psychoanalytic perspectives to literary and cultural texts (Easthope 1988; Macey 1988). A notable application occurred in the study of the cinema, where the idea of the mirror-phase informed important early discussions of the male GAZE.

See also OTHER; PSYCHOANALYSIS; SEXUAL DIFFERENCE.

MISE-EN-ABYME

A French term 'to put into the abyss' said to have originated in heraldry and used to suggest a bottomless series of reflections or repetitions, most graphically of the kind where a picture (or shield) contains a miniature of itself, which then repeats this image in ever smaller copies. The term was adopted by André Gide to describe an internal reduplication within a literary work. In his novel *Les Faux Monnayeurs* (*The Counterfeiters* 1926), the hero is a novelist writing a novel of the same title. A similar device is used by the fictional writers Jorge Luis Borges and Umberto Eco, and is commonly associated with POSTMODERNISM's assumption of the instability of identity, and blurred distinctions between author and character. The term is also frequently employed in Jacques Derrida's theory of DECONSTRUCTION to suggest the effect of infinite regress produced by the operation of *DIFFÉRANCE* in language.

MISE-EN-SCÈNE

See NARRATIVE.

MISREADING (MISPRISION)

See READING.

MISRECOGNITION (*MÉCONNAISSANCE*)

Associated in psychoanalytic theory with the activity of the ego, which, as Freud discovered in treating patients in a state of post-hypnosis, was likely to make false connections, filling in gaps in understanding. Thus, a patient who put his fingers in his mouth following instructions issued during hypnosis to do so, explained this act by saying he had bitten his tongue. Freud reasoned that the ego looks for an acceptable explanation, though this may be a distortion or false interpretation of relations of cause and effect. Following Freud, the French psychoanalyst Jacques Lacan (1901–1981) suggested that the formative experience of the MIRROR-PHASE confirmed that this kind of misunderstanding was the central function of the ego. The mirror-phase described how the infant simultaneously recognized and misrecognized itself in the mirror, seeing a developed and unified reflection of its own undeveloped and fragmentary self. The ego subsequently directed the subject in a lifelong quest for this illusory and permanently elusive unity.

The idea was taken up by the French Marxist philosopher, Louis Althusser and incorporated into his theory of IDEOLOGY. Thus, ideology is characterized by a double recognition and misrecognition. Ideology constructs or 'interpellates' individuals as SUBJECTS, and succeeds when we accept the world and ourselves as unchangeable and simply 'the way things are'. In an illustration given by Althusser, someone knocks on the door and we say, 'Who's there?' They answer, 'It's me.' We recognize it's 'him' or 'her', open the door and confirm that this is true. At this level of obviousness, it can't fail to be true, just as 'we cannot *fail to recognise*' ourselves in ideology (1971a: 161). Thus, in ideology we recognize ourselves as free, ethical, unified and so on, but as we do so, we misrecognize or ignore the reality that contradicts this. The latter is 'the reality which... is indeed, in the last resort, the reproduction of the relations of production and the relations deriving from them' (1971a: 170).

The concept has been employed in a comparable, but independent, way by the French sociologist, Pierre Bourdieu. Thus, Bourdieu sees the social order as similarly striving to 'naturalize' itself and so legitimize its arbitrariness. It succeeds in so far as we are persuaded there is a match between our subjective expectations and objective social conditions, yet this recognition of legitimacy is, on its reverse side, says Bourdieu, a 'misrecognition of the truth of the legitimate culture as the dominant cultural arbitrary, whose reproduction contributes towards reproducing the power relations' arbitrariness' (Bourdieu and Passeron 1977: 31).

MODERNISM

'Modernism' covers an extremely unstable and diverse range of artistic and cultural objects or tendencies. The main use of the term in Literary and Cultural Theory is to denote the artistic production of a period whose parameters are contested, but whose point of greatest intensity is usually set in the early twentieth century. The widest definitions of the term (Berman 1982) would make it coterminous with MODERNITY, stretching from the eighteenth century, or even earlier, to the present day. The consensus, however, is for a narrower periodization, located somewhere between the 1880s and the 1930s (see Bradbury and McFarlane [eds] 1976). Thus, 1922 (the year of publication of T.S. Eliot's *The Waste Land* and James Joyce's *Ulysses*) is usually recognized as modernism's *annus mirabilis,* while a few anomalous examples (such as the later Samuel Beckett) are allowed to fall outside this range.

If Modernism can be roughly periodized, however, its definition remains problematic. In general, in the more standard view, the term denotes artistic experiment and novelty, a radical overhaul of existing forms of REPRESENTATION and available traditions and, as such, is seen to set itself against the emerging MASS or POPULAR culture of the same period. A further distinction is then often made between modernism and the AVANT-GARDE (Bürger 1984). However, as the different arts – in literature, drama, painting, sculpture, music, the new media of photography and film – produced different modernisms at different times, and as novelty was crucial to their definition as modern, there can be no convincing description of the essence of modernism. The roll-call of movements in Naturalism, Impressionism, Symbolism, Decadence, Cubism, Expressionism, Futurism, Imagism, Vorticism, Dadaism and Surrealism all have a claim to be 'modernist', and a single writer like James Joyce might well be said to have employed several of these styles and strategies. Modernism is therefore better understood in the plural, as a range of 'modernisms' (Nicholls 1995; Brooker *et al.* 2010).

In addition, many see these varied experiments in form as the response to a specific moment in the history of MODERNITY, an attempt to register the accelerated pace and disorienting rhythms of specifically urban life and its attendant STRUCTURES OF FEELING in the late nineteenth and early twentieth centuries. To this end, modernism introduced new contemporary subject-matter into 'high' art (provoking long-term censorship in the case of Joyce's sometimes scatological *Ulysses*), but above all sought to innovate in matters of artistic form. Among the new techniques employed were ESTRANGEMENT, MONTAGE, collage, demotic or everyday language, 'stream-of-consciousness' or interior monologue, PARODY and PASTICHE, and, pervading all these, a heightened self-consciousness towards the technical means of art itself.

However, the modernist attitude towards modernity was an ambiguous one. Some examples (Italian Futurism, Soviet Constructivism) can be said to have embraced technological change and modernization wholeheartedly. Yet, a distaste for the modern age – described by W.B. Yeats as a 'filthy modern tide' and by T.S. Eliot as an 'immense panorama of futility and anarchy' – is equally detectable. The central paradox of modernism is revealed here: in the yoking of daring formal innovation and new content with, on the one hand, radical or revolutionary political positions, or, on the other, with conservative or outright reactionary political attitudes. Bertolt Brecht's Marxist modernism is matched in this sense by Ezra Pound's fascism. At the same time, both these modernisms combined fragmented content, montage and estrangement with a quest for artistic, metaphysical or social order. This complex, double character, it might be said, was anticipated by the French poet, Charles Baudelaire in his famous early definition of modernity. It consisted, he wrote, of two halves: 'the ephemeral, the fugitive, the contingent' accompanied by its other half, 'the eternal and the immutable' (1982: 23).

It is important, even so, to stress that the overarching term 'modernism' was largely retrospective (Brooker [ed] 1992). The word only became widespread from the mid twentieth century, especially in American literary and cultural criticism, when it began to be agreed that a cultural period was over or ending. At this point, as Raymond Williams comments, '"modern" shifts its reference from "now" to "just now" or even "then"' (1989b: 32). Academic respectability has brought extensive reinterpretation to some favoured writers, while FEMINISM, postcolonial and African-American criticism (Baker 1987; Gilroy 1993; Radford 1997) has pressed the claims of other, neglected figures and movements. A series of Marxist critics, also, from Lukács and Adorno to Fredric Jameson (Bloch 1977), Perry Anderson (Nelson and Grossberg [eds] 1988), and Terry Eagleton (1986b) have sought to outline the historical causes and conditions of modernism.

A further reaction to the orthodoxy of modernism coupled with a sense that the postwar years were now 'new' ushered in the phase of POSTMODERNISM and its attendant debates. For many, this means that the shock and novelty of modernism have evaporated or been absorbed into mainstream CULTURE. A broader view has linked artistic or cultural modernism with contemporary movements in philosophy, from Henri Bergson's new theories of time to Friedrich Nietzsche's iconoclastic post-Christianity and Freudian PSYCHOANALYSIS. Along these lines, MARXISM, the original theories of STRUCTURALISM and DIALOGICS might also be thought of as 'modernist' (Culler 1976; Berman 1982). Furthermore, its radical energies might be said to continue in the transposed realm of theory (Huyssen 1986). Indeed, Jean-François Lyotard, philosopher of the postmodern, suggests that, properly understood, modernism continues as the defining impetus in the postmodern. 'Postmodernism is not modernism at its end but in its nascent state, and this state is constant' (1984: 79).

See also CITY.

MODERNITY

Often conflated with MODERNISM and modernization, though all three terms should be distinguished. Modernity describes the long period of evolving 'modern' social, economic and political forms, and is most often sited in the two centuries from the eighteenth-century ENLIGHTENMENT and French Revolution of 1789 to the twentieth-century postwar period. Modernization names the supporting scientific and technical development in these societies, and is evident in improved medicine and healthcare, transport, COMMUNICATION, MASS production and domestic appliances. Modernism, third, is a development in literature and the arts set in most accounts in the period of the 1880s to the 1930s. A reason for the confusion of terms is the use of the term 'modernity' by the French poet Charles Baudelaire to describe the art of the mid nineteenth-century illustrator, Constantin Guys. Modernity, wrote Baudelaire (1863) was marked by 'the ephemeral, the fugitive, the contingent' (1982: 23). This is a consistent perception in later modernist works and often associated with the new experience of the CITY. We can say, therefore, that modernism gives form and symbolic expression to the consciousness of modernity.

Accounts of modernity as a category of sociological and political thought understandably differ. Some detect its beginnings at an earlier date than suggested (Berman 1982), and some (Callinicos 1989; Giddens 1990; Habermas 1992a) would prefer to understand the present as a continuation and intensification of modernity, where others see the advent of postmodernity. The 'modern' with its associated sense of 'the new' (from Latin, *modernus, modo*) has a longer usage, from the sense the Renaissance had of its newness contrasted with the Middle Ages. It is clear, however, that modernity centrally names the processes of increasing rationalization in social and political life, along with the associated technological development and accumulation of people in cities that combined to produce the emerging new society of the late nineteenth and twentieth centuries. In other words, it describes the processes of industrialization and bureaucratization associated with capitalist development. However, an exclusively economic account omits the 'philosophy' of modernity: namely, a belief in scientific and social progress, human rights, justice and democracy, which inspired the American and French Revolutions as well as much later social, economic and political theory, including Marxism.

Advocates of POSTMODERNISM would argue that 'the modern project' that embodies this philosophy has failed or was fundamentally misconceived. The implication of the above distinction, however, is that modernity is itself contradictory: that its economic forms and allied social effects, and its tradition of social and political thought are at odds. This is the basis of arguments for its defence or redefinition; hence, in one major instance, Jürgen Habermas's conception of modernity as an 'incomplete project' (Brooker [ed] 1992: 125–38). Others would seek to relativize modernity and to recognize its specific, non-synchronous or contesting cultural histories. Thus, Paul Gilroy (1993) writes of the hybrid African, American, Caribbean and British culture comprising what he terms the 'Black Atlantic' as a 'counterculture of modernity'. In a further provocative contribution, Bruno Latour (1993) sees modernity as poised contradictorily between an official ideology that separates NATURE and CULTURE and a day-to-day reality in which science, technology, nature and discourse prove inseparable. He calls for an explicit proliferation of hybrid linkages of biology and society, the global and the local, the archaic and modern in a 'third estate' he terms a 'Nonmodern constitution'.

See also LEGITIMATION; METANARRATIVE; PUBLIC SPHERE.

MONTAGE

A term used especially in connection with MODERNISM to refer to the newer techniques of artistic composition and editing, which combined disparate images, IMAGE and text, or different media in the making of a new work. In general terms, it is often used synonymously with 'collage' and BRICOLAGE. A more specific association is suggested by the meaning of the term in German to refer to the technology of the assembly-line introduced in this same period. Its use in relation to artistic practice was therefore a way of declaring a positive connection between art and industry and the MASS PRODUCTION-techniques of the modern world. Its main association was, accordingly, with the use of the new technologies of photography and cinema, and the development in the European AVANT-GARDE of the 1910s–1930s of the techniques of photomontage and film composition. The leading proponents of montage in these fields were the Soviet Constructivists, El Lissitsky and Alexander Rodchenko, the film-makers Dziga Vertov and Sergei Eisenstein (who first theorized its use in cinema), and the Berlin dadaiste George Grosz, Hannah Hoch and, above all, John Heartfield (Willett 1978; Ades 1986). Heartfield's satirical photomontages fearlessly exposed the pretensions of Hitler's Nazism and the inequities of CAPITALISM, and are an example of how montage was employed to radical political effect. According to the Soviet critic, Sergei Tretiakov, photomontage:

> begins whenever there is a conscious alteration of the obvious first sense of a photograph – by combining two or more images, by joining drawing and graphic shapes to the photograph, by adding a significant spot of colour, or by adding a written text. All of these techniques serve to divert the photography from what it 'naturally' seems to say, and to underscore the need for the viewer's active 'reading' of the image.
>
> (Teitelbaum [ed] 1992: 28)

Tretiakov had John Heartfield's work in mind, but his description could be widely applied to the use of montage in the European artistic movements of the period. It was a major device, therefore, in effecting the modernist aim of ESTRANGEMENT or DEFAMILIARIZATION. At the same time, montage had been used for the purposes of comedy and caricature in POPULAR and professional photography from at least the mid nineteenth century, and to shock and surprise in the new commercial advertising and newspaper composition at the turn of the century. This emphasized the connection with the modern world and with urban life in the metropolis, but was a sign, too, of how the technique could be compromised by the very forces in mass society its more radical forms were meant to attack.

For contemporary European artists, the leading examples of the modern industrial and metropolitan life were to be found in the United States (Tower [ed] 1990).

Although montage was adopted in American art and writing with something of its earlier radical political aims (in the fiction of John Dos Passos and in the poster art and murals sponsored by the New Deal in the 1930s), it was here, too, that it was taken up in commercial art and design, with results that contemporary observers found banal (Teitelbaum [ed] 1992: 35). The more pessimistic implications of this development (prefiguring some commentaries on POSTMODERNISM) were expressed by Theodor Adorno:

> The principle of montage was supposed to shock people into realising just how dubious any organic unity was. Now that the shock has lost its punch, the products of montage revert to being indifferent stuff or substance. The method of montage no longer succeeds in triggering a communicative spark between the aesthetic and the extra-aesthetic; the interest in montage has therefore been neutralized.
>
> (Teitelbaum [ed] 1992: 35)

MORAL PANIC

A term introduced in the Sociology of Media and Youth Cultures (Cohen 1987) but now in general use to describe the way a particular incident or apparent trend becomes a national issue, of concern to a MASS of the population. What is particular about this public response is its 'moral' dimension, where this term alludes to the way the behaviour of certain groups is understood as deviant or a threat to an accepted morality and way of life, or where highly profiled events and tendencies are seen as the symptom of a general social malaise. Questions of morality therefore embrace general social values, and may extend to issues of law and order and appropriate government action. Examples would include the concern aroused by the reported increase in the UK of mugging in the 1970s (Hall *et al.* [eds] 1979), of 'joy-riding' and car theft by young teenagers in the early 1990s, the carrying of knives or offensive weapons, and of drug-related violent crime in the later 1990s. One incident that especially focused some of these concerns was the killing of two-year-old Jamie Bulger in 1993. More recent examples would include 'binge drinking', online abuse, and 'sexting' by schoolchildren.

Examples such as these have provoked concern about the level of youth crime, violence and drug abuse (Hall and Jefferson [eds] 1976; Young 1981); about parenting, education, the influence of media REPRESENTATIONS of sex and violence, or about cultural forms and technologies (house music, raves, the use of Twitter, the online availability of pornography) associated with these trends. Other kinds of moral panic have arisen in relation to AIDS, and in the UK to 'road rage' or food-poison scares.

All these and other cases evidently involve extensive press and TV coverage. The concept of moral panic therefore provides a useful double framework: both highlighting consistent or changing features in POPULAR attitudes, and revealing the role and operation of the media in reflecting or producing public opinion (Cohen and Young [eds] 1981).

See also SUBCULTURES.

MULTICULTURALISM

Multiculturalism has become an issue in education, cultural policy, and arts funding organizations as these institutions and agencies have sought to respond to the evident multi-ethnic nature of contemporary western societies. Its announced aims are to introduce children in schools and all sections of the community to the different belief systems, customs, crafts and arts of the nation's heterogeneous population. It is founded, therefore, on ideas of tolerance and a respect for DIFFERENCE. Critics claim, however, that this policy is at best partially enacted and characteristically disguises an assumption of the centrality of predominantly white ethnic groups, or of the dominant CULTURE (of English culture in relation to Scotland, Wales and Ireland, for example).

This argument is presented by, among others, Jordan and Weedon (1995), with particular reference to the status and funding of Welsh language and culture. The underlying values and idea of PLURALISM informing multiculturalism, they suggest, are those of liberal HUMANISM, and result in practice in the 'containment and domestication' (1995: 51) of ethnic difference. In part, this is achieved through the cultivation of what are commonly referred to as 'ethnic arts', a description that assumes an exclusive connection between certain forms of artistic practice and production, and particular ethnic groups. This, it is said, has the double effect of ghettoizing these arts and of leaving the supposed authority of the hegemonic culture undisturbed.

Jordan and Weedon point to a newer discourse of 'cultural diversity' in education and cultural policy but warn that this, too, is open to compromise. In response, they set out five criteria (1995: 485–6) for a 'genuine multiculturalism'. In brief these are:

1. a non-hierarchical understanding of cultures and traditions
2. 'genuine dialogue between cultures', premised on the exchange and intermixture of languages and artistic skills rather than their separation
3. a 'thoroughly anti-racist' approach, which would 'rigorously avoid conflating "race" with culture'
4. an approach that 'would not privilege "traditional" culture over popular culture, "high Culture" over the new cultural technologies'
5. the requirement of 'full multiethnic (and multiracial) participation throughout all the structures of the cultural institutions'.

This model, they add, is based on the fundamental belief that contemporary cultures are heterogeneous and differentiated, the 'TRUTH', as they put it, that 'THERE ARE NO PURE CULTURES, ALL ARE HYBRID' (1995: 487).

A similar argument against multiculturalism is made by Homi Bhabha: 'Multiculturalism represented an attempt both to respond to and control the dynamic process of the articulation of cultural difference, administering a consensus based on a norm that propagates cultural diversity' (1990: 208–9). Bhabha does not choose to redefine the term, however. Instead, he proposes a model, based on the recognition of HYBRIDITY and DIFFERENCE, but also possible dissent: a cultural politics 'based on unequal, uneven, multiple and potentially antagonistic political identities', which are articulated 'in challenging ways... often conflictually, sometimes even incommensurably' (1990: 208).

See also ETHNICITY; EUROCENTRICISM; PUBLIC SPHERE.

MYTH

Traditionally, myth is an anonymous tale relating heroic adventures, including encounters with the supernatural, which explain the world in allegorical form and thus ratify a society's beliefs and customs. 'Classical' myths, as one such set of stories, have continued to shape literary and other contemporary NARRATIVES in the west and have come to comprise a general cultural knowledge. Though this knowledge has receded in the present century, some names (Diana, Hercules, Bacchus) and stories from this tradition have continuing currency, if in abbreviated or transposed form. The story of Oedipus, derived from the Greek dramatist Sophocles and employed by Sigmund Freud to name the OEDIPAL COMPLEX, is a prominent example of this. Meanwhile, in what might be seen as a reaction to the centrality of Graeco-Roman mythologies, other traditional myths, from Irish, Caribbean, African-American and Indian cultures, have been newly mobilized in the twentieth century in the affirmation or remaking of national identities.

In some POPULAR uses, the term has a very broad application, as in references to 'the myth of the American West', for example, or 'the myth of the Orient'. In such cases, myth can imply a romanticized, distorted or false set of attitudes and is therefore close to the sense of 'stereotype' or, in a sometimes lighter vein, suggests a superstition or make-believe story. The 'myths' of black male SEXUALITY or of female passivity would be examples of the first type, while the 'myth of the Loch Ness monster' would be an example of the second.

In the realm of theory and criticism, myth was given importance through the work, principally, of the structural anthropologist, Claude Lévi-Strauss (1908–1996) and the literary critic and semiotician, Roland Barthes (1915–1980). Lévi-Strauss saw myths as setting basic, universal themes in narratives that themselves follow universal structures. A 'mytheme' is the unit of this universal structure and can be differently articulated in individual myths. Structural Anthropology in this tradition reads myths as the expressions of a narrative system and sees this as having the function, not simply of reflecting a society back to itself, but of resolving a dilemma or contradiction endemic to that society. The term 'mythology' is used to describe the system of such myths. Lévi-Strauss was led to conclude that myths were structured or CODED in this systematic way, according to a universal human mental disposition, and as answering a collective human need. However, the term 'mythology' has also been used to describe an individual and esoteric system of coded symbols or symbolic narratives – as in descriptions, for example, of the thought of William Blake or William Butler Yeats.

In the work of Roland Barthes, myth is virtually synonymous with IDEOLOGY and designates a level of symbolic or cultural CONNOTATION, active in a visual IMAGE or social narrative. Barthes developed this understanding of the term especially in the essays entitled *Mythologies* (1972a [1957]), a study of the activities and events of contemporary French cultural life, such as wrestling, striptease, a new Citroën motor car, films and advertising. This has proved an influential model for the study of popular CULTURE. Though the term 'myth' might not itself be used in this connection (but see Masterman [ed] 1983), the task of the cultural critic, following Barthes, is thought to be to 'de-mythologize' the embedded meanings of activities and REPRESENTATIONS as they shape and structure daily life, showing how their implicit CLASS and cultural attitudes have become 'naturalized'.

See also IDEOLOGY; INTELLECTUALS.

NACHTRÄGLICHKEIT ('DEFERRED ACTION')

A concept introduced by Sigmund Freud in his case study of the so-called 'Wolf Man' (1974, Vol. 17: 3–122) and especially emphasized by his commentator Jean Laplanche (1989). The 'Wolf Man' is said to witness an act of sexual intercourse between his parents at the age of one-and-a-half, but the traumatic shock of this incident is deferred until he is capable of bringing some mature sexual understanding to it. The implication of Freud's concept is that, as Laplanche puts it:

> nothing can be inscribed in the human unconscious except in relation to at least two events which are separated from one another in time by a moment of maturation that allows the subject to react in two ways to an initial experience or to the memory of that experience.
>
> (1989: 112)

In other words, an event has two occurrences: an original happening and a later interpretive construction of it. The subject is at more than one place (or time) at the moments of understanding that give the trauma its form and expression.

In a still more radical gloss on this concept, an event only acquires significance in so far as it is remembered. There is no first event other than its construction at a later stage, since meaning is always the retrospective result of a process of 'working through'. This suggests a radically non-linear notion of memory and individual history; positing, in effect, that a memory at a later date is the 'cause' rather than the 'effect' of the supposed earlier, original, incident. This suggests an unexpected affinity between Freud and later poststructuralist concepts of 'belatedness' and 'deferral'. This possibility has become of interest in relation to the writing and study of autobiographies and historical fictions in the light of problematized notions of history in POSTMODERNISM. An example of a study that follows through these implications with reference to Freud's concept is Peter Nicholls' reading of Toni Morrison's *Beloved* (Vice [ed] 1995: 50–63).

See also DIFFERENCE/*DIFFÉRANCE*; DISAVOWAL.

NARRATIVE

Narrative is a recounted tale or story, whether of fictional or non-fictional material. In the formal study of narrative (termed 'narratology'), a distinction is regularly made between 'story' (or sometimes 'plot'), used to refer to a sequence of events, and the 'narration' of these events. Narration is understood as the organizing of the linear sequence of events into a structured narrative and as ascribing a cause or motivation to it. Thus, a simple story sequence might be: 'Jack woke up, then he went to work, then he met Jill.' Introducing a plot would produce, 'After work, Jack met Jill as planned' and, constructing a narrative, 'I noticed Jack always met Jill after work.' As this suggests, narrative requires two things: an actual or implied narrator who brings a point of view, style or tone to the narration, and an AUDIENCE of readers or spectators, depending on the medium of narration.

One tendency has suggested that all human activity and COMMUNICATION can be viewed as narrative or as governed by it (Nash [ed] 1990). In extreme form, this can imply that all accounts of the world are equally fictional. Distinctions are possible – and perhaps necessary – however, between 'factual' and 'fictional' narratives and between kinds of each mode. Thus, if all narratives are seen as constructions of the raw material of a sequence of events, and in this way thought to help create – rather than report on – reality, their purposes, participants (authors, characters, readers or spectators), rhetoric and protocols can be quite different. It is possible, that is to say, to distinguish between the DISCOURSES that produce the narratives of science, economics, law, politics, advertising or journalism, and to distinguish these from the discourses of film, literature and drama. Often, of course, these narrative forms in turn call for further internal distinctions.

The academic analysis of narrative has derived from related traditions in FORMALISM (Propp 1968) and STRUCTURALISM (from, for example, Greimas, Todorov, Genette and Barthes). Propp's attempt to derive a universal system or grammar of narrative from the repeated basic structures of folk tales influenced the later approach in structuralist narratology and this accordingly combines abstract, universalizing description and close technical analysis (see Rimmon-Kenan 1983; Cohan and Shires 1988). One of the most sophisticated and influential models in this tradition has been proposed by Gérard Genette (1980, 1982). Genette distinguishes between *histoire,* or 'story', the chronology of events as they occur; *récit,* the order of events in a narrative; and 'narration', the act of storytelling or of 'enunciation'. A further common term associated with the middle level of *récit* is 'diegesis'. This denotes the fictional content of a narrative world: all that is given as the reality of a story. It includes dialogue, setting, and in the case of film and visual narratives, sound and *mise-en-scène* (the staging of a shot by means of setting, costume lighting and movement within the frame). Genette's analysis pays close attention to the position and point of view of the narrator, to the duration and frequency of events and to the composition of the diegesis. Some features of a narrative will also be 'extra-' or 'non-diegetic'. A film soundtrack, for example, which does not belong to the internal world of the story, as opposed to a song sung by one of the characters will be 'extra-diegetic'; a direct address to camera or, in written fiction, a direct authorial intervention will be 'non-diegetic'. In addition, a voice-over, or the internal monologue of a character, is described as 'intra-diegetic'.

This vocabulary, along with the language of CODES, subtexts and narrative functions is in quite common use and has been absorbed into the discussion of all kinds of written narratives, film and media texts (Metz 1974; Heath 1981; Hartley 1982). The study of still or single IMAGES is also understood as being implicated in narrative. Thus, a news photograph may represent a key moment in the changing course of history, a family snapshot belongs to a changing personal history, and an advertising image may depict the moment of delight in a before-and-after sequence.

Although the study of narrative and the use of a formalist and structuralist vocabulary are widespread, later developments in POSTSTRUCTURALISM have suggested that the structuralist aim to produce a scientific, universal grammar of narrative is deluded, and that the approach is also limited in its relative indifference to the reader or spectator and the processes of READING and RECEPTION. Roland Barthes presents an interesting transition in this respect; from his early structuralist account ('Introduction to the structural analysis of narrative', 1977b [1966]) to the later, more poststructuralist *S/Z* (1975), a study of the short story *Sarrasine* by Balzac. Here, Barthes's greater attention to the role of the reader, and to the intertextual relations comprising the story, suggests a more open and provisional conception of narrative structure.

In the Marxist tradition, the philosopher and critic, Walter Benjamin (1892–1940) drew a distinction between 'story' and the novel, and between the second and MASS-produced media forms. His essay 'The storyteller' (1970) suggests that the latter will make storytelling redundant, although it is clear that Benjamin values this more collective, participatory and pre-bourgeois form. The Marxist critic Fredric Jameson (1934–) has made particular use of the structuralist narrative theory of A.J. Greimas, but has sought to combine this with an ideological analysis and with PSYCHOANALYSIS. Thus, he detects a 'political unconscious' in the novel which, though repressed, works to contradict a text's formal narrative closure (1981).

See also ADDRESSER/ADDRESSEE; *ÉCRITURE*/WRITING; MYTH.

NATIONALISM

'Nationalism,' writes Madan Sarup, 'is a deeply contradictory enterprise' (1996: 149). This is because it is politically ambiguous and may be mobilized through symbolic cultural texts, IMAGES, MYTHS and history, either for conservative or progressive ends. In either form, it is likely to invoke the authenticity of an essentialist definition of national IDENTITY and to employ this in distinguishing the absolute boundaries of one nation from another. This boundary may be marked literally by territory, or by language, political traditions and the varied cultural SIGNS marking an ethnic or racial identity (see Ashcroft *et al.* [eds] 1995: Part V).

Always, as this suggests, nationalism arises in one nation's dealings with another, rather than in isolation, whether between states, or within them, since states and nations are not identical (the British state consists of England, Scotland, Wales and Northern Ireland). Where this relationship is oppressive, as in the history of IMPERIALISM, the conquering nation will impose its identity as the model of civilization upon another whose own identity is thereby suppressed. In the reverse situation, in moments of national liberation, a colonized nation reasserts its history, language and customs in the act of expelling its former rulers. One of the ensuing contradictions is that nationalist struggles are often led by a native bourgeois intelligentsia formed by the colonial power, which comes to occupy the institutions and role of the former colonizers. The result is that instead of decolonization 'one simply gets old colonial structures in new national terms' (Sarup 1996: 149). It is unlikely, Sarup adds, that any nationalism can escape the shared PARADIGM of colonizer and colonized that brought it into being.

This applies also on a global scale. For most nations of the world, to escape the profound experience of imperialism would be, in fact, to escape their own actual history: a resented past that, paradoxically, constitutes national identity. A purist or essentialist national identity, one can conclude, will always be backward-looking and always a selective, imagined construction (an implication explored by Benedict Anderson 1983). Much postcolonial theory and criticism is concerned with the issues involved here and commonly argues for a mixed and hybridized notion of individual and national identity. However, to argue that national identities are discursive constructions that idealize an actual complex intermixture does not resolve issues of POWER and subjection, as a contemporary example such as Ireland demonstrates (see Eagleton *et al.* 1990; Deane 1995: 363–8). In turning to a mythologized past, Ireland's 'romantic nationalism', as Eagleton (2015) has put it, has effectively squeezed out the colonial past, constructing 'a conjuncture of the very old and the unimaginably new, like the two interleaved texts, one modern and the other Homeric, of *Ulysses*' (37). As this suggests, literature and the arts will play their own distinctive parts in forming or reforming national identities.

Essentialist ideas of the nation have been further undermined by developments in information technologies and the expansion of global markets. GLOBALIZATION has meant that much of the world's business and communication proceeds over and above the lines drawn by national frontiers and beyond the jurisdiction and political authority of nation-states. Arguably, this continues the earlier process of imperialism by other means. By the same token, it does not rule out a defensive counter-assertion of discrete national identities. Nor does the internationalization of communication NETWORKS spell the end of a sense of national unity.

Witness, for example, the role of the print and visual media in mobilizing national sentiment at times of widespread public distress (the death of Princess Diana in the UK in 1997; terrorist attacks in New York 2001, London 2005, and Paris 2015) and, also, at times of joyous celebration (such as the staging of the World Olympics, where a display of selected national histories and iconography is broadcast to global audiences).

That national identity and independence remain a critical issue in the 2000s – in ways that combine cultural, economic and political factors – is seen also, for example, in: the implications of the UK's withdrawal from the European Union; the rise of nationalist parties of both right-wing and progressive inclinations across Europe; the complex issues bound into the fate of Ukraine, and potentially other former members of the Soviet bloc, in their relation with Russia. In such cases, Russia's own ambition for a 'Greater Russia' and the involvement of NATO and the USA mean that regional national disputes are played out on the world stage.

See also ETHNICITY; IMAGINED COMMUNITY; POSTCOLONIALISM.

NATION-STATE

See COSMOPOLITANISM; GLOBALIZATION; NATIONALISM.

NATURE

'If human beings,' write Beck, Giddens and Lash, 'once knew what "nature" was, they do so no longer' (1994: vii). This is not to say that nature was simple and is now complex. Rather, that it appeared self-evident when viewed through the lens of a range of ideologies which, until recently, have been accepted at a deep and enduring level. Evocations of nature and 'the natural' have echoed through theory, literature, media REPRESENTATIONS and everyday speech, reinforcing cultural norms at the expense of what is deemed deviant and 'unnatural'. In general, this thinking has depended on an opposition of human society and CULTURE (or 'Man') to an external nature. Nature, in turn, has been viewed in contrasting ways: as a malign or benign influence, obstacle or protector. As the symbol of unsullied purity, source of pleasure and sustenance, or untamed wildness, nature has been set in a frequently GENDERed, racial and western model against its supposed opposite: the (male) public world of urban life in industrial society.

As the terms of this latter configuration have come into question, so too has the accompanying conception of nature. The same might be said of the essentialist view of a unified and transcendent 'human nature' at the core of liberal humanist IDEOLOGY. Contemporary theory and debate – from PSYCHOANALYSIS to DECONSTRUCTION, from Anthropology to ANIMAL STUDIES and ECOCRITICISM – have argued that these ideologies are no longer credible. The idea of 'human nature' has been critiqued in terms of an alternative conception of divided, mobile, hybrid or CYBORG identities, while the historically established view of nature as the object of human domination, material use and abuse is deemed unacceptable. Bruno Latour (1993) argues that human societies – as against, for example, simian societies – are distinguished by their having allocated certain activities to 'non-human' technologies. A proliferation of such hybrid associations, he suggests, presents a way beyond the rigid dichotomies of MODERNITY (see also Michael 2000).

Contemporary academic discussion, journalism and forms of POPULAR action have arguably moved on, therefore, from the ramifications of the 'nature/culture' distinction to an awareness of HYBRIDITY and a concern with the interconnected ecological issues facing human, animal and plant life (Ellen and Fukui [eds] 1996, Huggan and Tiffin [eds] 2010), Monbiot (2013). However, as the opening quotation above suggests, a new uncertainty now surrounds the term: an ambiguity where there was once secure reference and meaning. For, if it is accepted that the old ideologies are at an end, this has not yielded a new consensus.

Kate Soper (1996) had outlined the new differences in perspective:

> while the ecologists tend to invoke 'nature' as an independent domain of intrinsic value, truth or authenticity, postmodernist cultural theory and

criticism emphasizes its discursive status, inviting us to view the order of 'nature' as existing only in the chain of the signifier.

(1996: 22)

This dichotomy remains evident, if posed somewhat differently. Thus, the end of the nature/culture distinction has produced, on the one hand, as in 'deep ecology', an insistence of the primacy of an all-embracing nature to which the human should defer, and on the other, the conviction of an irreversible cultural and symbolic order, exacerbated by the unprecedented advance of electronic media – the latter fuelling theories of a new POSTHUMAN and POSTCAPITALIST order. Soper had reasoned that if 'ecological realities' are to be addressed, some strategic distinction between the autonomy of human culture and the constraints of the natural world upon the human must be restored. The increasingly acute issues concerning climate change make such arguments more pertinent than ever.

See also ANTHROPOCENE; HUMANISM; SPECULATVE REALISM; THING THEORY;

NEGOTIATION

In his seminal essay on the processes entailed in the encoding and decoding of television DISCOURSE (1997a; see also CODE), Stuart Hall suggests that any structured MESSAGE will present a 'preferred meaning' or reading. This is the 'intended' meaning the producers of the message wish its listeners or viewers to accept and perhaps act on. If the recipient of the message does so respond, then she/he is operating inside what Hall terms the 'hegemonic' or 'DOMINANT code', COMMUNICATION between producer and receiver in such a case is seemingly transparent.

The process rarely proceeds so smoothly, however. Given the many possible meanings (or 'polysemy') of a message, says Hall, 'There can never be only one single univocal and determined meaning... no law to ensure that the receiver will take the preferred or dominant meaning... in precisely the way in which it has been encoded by the producer' (1997a: 30). A reader or viewer who neither straightforwardly accepts nor opposes an encoded hegemonic meaning will operate within what Hall terms a 'negotiated code'. This, he says:

> contains a mixture of adaptive and oppositional elements: it acknowledges the legitimacy of the hegemonic definitions... while, at a more restricted, situational level, it makes its own ground-rules... reserving the right to make a more negotiated application to 'local conditions'.

(1997a: 33)

In an example Hall gives, therefore, a worker may at one level accept the official explanation that a wage freeze is in 'the national interest', but at the situated or corporate level of personal and trades union interests, reject this hegemonic definition in favour of strike action.

The idea of a negotiated response to texts, messages and discourses of various kinds has commonly been adopted in Cultural Studies. Hall adds that the way people operate or occupy 'negotiated codes' proceeds from the logic of the particular situation they are in 'and from their differential and unequal position in relation to power' (1997a: 33). This important emphasis on the specificity of the situation from which a reader or viewer can effect a transactional meaning has been developed especially in feminist Film Studies in conjunction with theories of GENDER and in relation to the theory of the supposed HEGEMONY of the 'male GAZE'. Taking account of the specificities of negotiated meanings has helped question the authority of a fixed male gaze developed in the influential, psychoanalytically based model of film spectatorship. Instead, it has posited a variety of possible positions for women as TV or film spectators. Christine Gledhill (1994) argues, in relation particularly to the popular female cop show of the 1980s, *Cagney and Lacey,* for the appreciation of a series of negotiated meanings produced within institutions, texts and audiences, including those between feminist film critics and non-academic viewers. There is a need, first, to understand the range of negotiated meanings between 'the "feminine spectator", constructed by the text, and the female audience, constructed by the social-historical categories of gender, class, race' (1994: 243). This in turn suggests the need for a new kind of cultural history, Gledhill argues, which will itself be engaged in negotiating between the findings of textual analysis and 'the researches of the anthropologist or ethnographer' upon historical audiences (1994: 249).

See also CONSUMERISM; GENRE; RECEPTION.

NETWORK

A term designating channels of COMMUNICATION connecting people at a physical distance. It is used for different kinds and levels of system, including broadcasting, but is most commonly associated in contemporary culture with computer-driven information and entertainment networks. These may be comparatively small-scale, connecting members of an academic community or business or CITY, or pass beyond these in national and international communication and information-retrieval systems. At the same time, this usage may vie with another sense of the term 'networking', which implies face-to-face contact with friends and associates (from academic conferences to a *Star Trek* convention). An earlier meaning along these lines was associated with the non-hierarchical and decentred forms of communication adopted by the women's movement in the 1960s and 1970s. This is now invoked, sometimes in defence of, sometimes in opposition to, computer-based communication systems, especially with respect to the INTERNET. The staggering uses and effects of this revolutionary system are, as yet, unevenly absorbed. The arguments it has generated, however, over open, democratized access, ownership, censorship and centralized control have highlighted a series of issues relevant to the 'information society' as a whole.

These themes are taken up especially in the work of the influential social theorist Manuel Castells (1996, 1997). What Castells terms 'the network society' is characteristic of 'informational capitalism'. He sees this as having emerged from the revolution in information technologies in the 1970s, combined with a restructuring of capitalism and the contrary influence of the social movements of the 1960s (especially FEMINISM and ECOLOGY). His theory of the present operation of the network or information society is comprehensive and searching. Its main constituent features are:

1. the development of a dynamic, post-industrial economy dependent on information technologies for productivity and competitiveness, but prone to the logic of the market
2. the advent of a global economy whose networked markets, services and media systems operate on a planetary scale and determine national, regional and local employment but to the exclusion of unskilled labour and poor markets
3. a form of operation called 'network enterprise', by which multinational and subsidiary companies and suppliers throughout the world unite in strategic but provisional economic projects.

These features have a number of social, economic, political and cultural effects. The 'network society' alters employment patterns, enforces flexible working, weakens labour unions, exacerbates disparities between the rich and poor, concentrates media power, creates a media-influenced political discourse, and even seeks in its ever-accelerated communications to eliminate biological and clock time. Such a society follows, in short, the instrumental economic logic of capitalism. Yet, says Castells, it also 'opens up a new realm of contradiction and conflict' (1997: 16). He sees these contrary effects in a struggle over the definition of time, the richness and diversity of global media networks and music cultures, and the appropriation of the information networks by disadvantaged groups for their own ends.

See also CONVERGENCE; CYBERSPACE; GLOBALIZATION.

NEW HISTORICISM

HISTORICISM has a complex and specific set of meanings within MARXISM. Elsewhere, it has been associated with a pessimistic view of history viewed as a set of determining processes that deny human agency; with a commitment to a supposedly objective and value-free historical method; and with a valorization of past traditions over the present. A partial break with these assumptions, coinciding with an awareness of the limits of STRUCTURALISM and formalist critical method, occurred in the United States in a movement termed 'New Historicism' in the 1980s, and associated with, among others, the critics Stephen Greenblatt, Louis Montrose and Jonathan Goldberg in the area of Renaissance Studies, and Jerome McGann and Marjorie Levinson in studies of the Romantic period. The University of California-based journal *Representations* helped make connections between this work and other area studies, including the work of anthropologists and historians such as Hayden White (see Veeser [ed] 1989; Scott Wilson [ed] 1995; Hamilton 1996).

Following Michel Foucault's 'archaeological' method, New Historicism rejects the traditional historicist notions of continuity, progress and underlying historical unity. Instead, it seeks to read literary texts alongside or against other generally neglected contemporary documentary or imaginative texts (for example, to read Shakespeare's *Hamlet* in terms of contemporary law on divorce and inheritance, or records of suicide in young women, or, in an example from Greenblatt (1990), to read *The Tempest* in conjunction with Cicero's then widely known treatise on rhetoric, *De Oratore*). New Historicist method therefore not only CRITIQUES earlier influential, ahistorical critical PARADIGMS, while at the same time departing from a history based on continuity and the unified SUBJECT, but unsettles received distinctions between CANONIC literary and other kinds of less or differently valued texts. In this way, it draws attention to diverse production processes and the role of a range of DISCOURSES in the creation of social and historical meanings.

In spite of this new orientation, New Historicism is often thought to be academicist and merely contemplative in its view of the past and past texts. This is the advertised view especially of those associated with the related, but more overtly activist, British-based movement termed CULTURAL MATERIALISM. Following Foucault, Stephen Greenblatt, for example, sees the 'social energies' of a variety of DISCOURSES drawn into, but contained by, the mechanisms and modes of theatre. This self-cancelling 'subversion and containment' is then viewed from the unsettled retrospect of the present (in an echo of traditional historicism), or as reiterated in a later historical moment – discontinuous with, but in broad terms no advance on, the first. New Historicism therefore presents a decentred history open to cultural diversity, but tends also to inherit Foucault's more pessimistic idiom, as well as the eschewal in the body of his work of questions of AGENCY and the forces of change.

See also ARCHAEOLOGY; INTERTEXTUALITY; MATERIALISM.

NOMADISM

The figure of the nomad and the science of nomadism or nomadology was introduced by the French philosophers Gilles Deleuze (1925–1995) and Félix Guattari (1930–1992) in their *A Thousand Plateaus* (1987). The nomad is the embodiment – although the idea has perhaps primarily a symbolic or metaphorical force – of the philosophy of DESIRE advanced in their *Anti-Oedipus* (1984). Here, they argue against any fixed representation of desire (such as the OEDIPAL COMPLEX) that would confine the creative force and intensity of desire. The containment of desire within the model of the family in Freudian psychoanalytic theory assists in maintaining the capitalist social machine. To this, they oppose a strategy of 'schizoanalysis', which will undo this repressive representation and release schizoid revolutionary 'assemblages' of desire. The transformation of libidinal energy is accomplished – in a term combining the Marxist emphasis on production and Freud's concept of libido – by 'desire-machines'.

In *A Thousand Plateaus,* this theory of desire is expanded in a variety of social, linguistic and intellectual directions. Here, processes of liberatory DETERRITORIALIZATION and destratification are contrasted with the will to territorialize, unify and stratify. The book is organized, moreover, around the concept of assemblages and a distinction between extensive 'molar' (totalizing, unifiable) types of assemblage and intensive, 'molecular' assemblages, which are not unifiable or totalizable. In this scheme, nomadic assemblages are opposed to apparatuses of capture. In particular, Deleuze and Guattari see the state as attempting to regulate and channel the itinerant movement of nomadic workers – the masons, carpenters and smiths who built France's cathedrals. More loosely the term is associated with those nomadic tribes – 'war machines' as Deleuze terms them – who have looted and raided settled communities, and with AVANT-GARDE movements opposed to the institution of art. Both types, though in quite different senses, have employed violence against the establishment. A contemporary real-life example suggests itself in the confrontation of world powers and 'anti-capitalist' protesters in the late 1990s and 2000s over the effects of GLOBALIZATION. Here, too, the issue of political violence the philosophy entertains has been raised in a very acute way.

In academic work, the idea of the nomad has been taken up in Literary and Cultural Geography (see Chambers 1993; Soja 1996) where it has joined a vocabulary of migrants, FLÂNEURS, other travellers, or figures on the MARGIN as part of a general poststructuralist suspicion of stability and unity. 'Mobility is the order of the day,' complains Tim Cresswell (1997: 360). He critiques the 'romanticisation of the figure of the nomad as the geographic figure *par excellence* of postmodernity' (1997: 360), and joins with Ang (1994), Wolff (1993) and others in exposing how abstract and decontextualized these terms are. 'As well as travel metaphors being predominantly masculine, they are also profoundly Eurocentric,' Cresswell argues (379). His call for a more self-reflexive, contextualizing account of metaphors of movement will be, for many, a telling one. Adherents to nomadism might all the same see in this iconic identity a way to mobilize precisely against the fixities of PATRIARCHY and EUROCENTRISM. One such is Rosi Braidotti (1994) who adopts the idea of the nomad as an empowering 'political fiction', one that refers not necessarily or literally to travel, but to a 'style of thinking', 'a creative sort of becoming' and 'critical consciousness' (1994: 1, 6, 5), whose fluency across different idioms and disciplines she views as especially productive for postmodern FEMINISM.

See also DIASPORA; FLOW; PSYCHOGEOGRAPHY; RHIZOME.

NOSTALGIA

Nostalgia has attracted critical attention in relation to POSTMODERNISM and the supposed loss of a sense of authentic history. Fredric Jameson has introduced the category of the 'nostalgia mode' (a rendering of the French *la mode rétro*) to describe the way contemporary postmodern culture pastiches the past, re-presenting it at the level of cultural style. He cites the work of the American historical novelist, E.L. Doctorow as evidence of how 'real history' can only be presented now 'by way of our own pop images and simulacra of that history' (1991: 25). Films such as *American Graffiti, Star Wars* and *Body Heat,* Jameson sees as exhibiting three types of the nostalgia mode: the first 'historical reconstruction' recaptures the 'lost' period style of the 1950s; the second evokes an earlier experience of teenage movie-going, while the third presents the past so selectively that it blurs all contemporary or specific historical reference, as if 'it were set in some eternal 1930s, beyond real historical time' (1991: 21). Linda Hutcheon, in particular, has responded to Jameson on this theme. She argues that postmodern texts, including films, represent the past in a self-conscious, parodic and critical way, revealing its construction as narrative rather than a self-evident 'History' or unmediated 'truth' (1989; see also Brooker and Brooker [eds] 1997).

Elsewhere, nostalgia is related to the theme of memory and reminiscence. The African-American cultural critic, bell hooks, writes of nostalgia as 'that longing for something to be as once it was, a kind of useless act' and as such to be distinguished, she says, from 'that remembering that serves to illuminate and transform the present' (1990a: 147). Elizabeth Wilson argues that nostalgia can aid what hooks calls this 'politicisation of memory'. She points to its complexity and ambivalence; neither the 'pure sense of loss, nor… the emotional self-indulgence of mere sentimentality' of standard descriptions (1997: 138). The sense of loss, she suggests, can help us 'measure the distance we have come' and appreciate 'the reality of change', for if 'nostalgia is itself a rather passive emotion, yet it can lead us toward a more active responsibility both for the past and for the future' (1997: 138, 139).

See also PARODY; PASTICHE.

NOSTALGIA MODE

See HISTORICISM; NOSTALGIA.

OEDIPAL COMPLEX

Freud's theory of the Oedipal complex derives from the Greek myth of Oedipus and its early dramatization in Sophocles's *Oedipus Rex*. In this story, an oracle declares at the birth of Oedipus that he will kill his own father and marry his mother. When this occurs, and Oedipus realizes what he has done, he blinds himself. Freud extrapolated from this a universal drama of the psyche in which, as he saw it, the UNCONSCIOUS wish of every (male) child was to have sex with its mother and to eliminate its father. The father represses this desire by threatening castration, and the child comes thus to accept the authority of the PHALLUS invested in the father. This is simultaneously the moment of the creation of the Unconscious as the domain of the repressed and of the child's entry into society or, for Jacques Lacan, the entry into language and the SYMBOLIC order.

The Oedipal story is one of the founding NARRATIVES in Freud's psychoanalytic theory, and the SITE of frequent debate and dissension. Feminists have often (though not universally – see Mitchell 1974), criticized the GENDER bias of the Oedipal narrative, which leaves the little girl out of account, or sees her as an already castrated heterosexual boy experiencing 'penis envy'. The work of Melanie Klein, among early critics of Freud, helped identify a pre-Oedipal stage and a contrary emphasis upon mother–daughter relationships. Latterly, French feminists have particularly sought to theorize alternative scenarios to the centrality of the Oedipal complex and its apparent reinforcement of PATRIARCHY. One such is Julia Kristeva's

(1984b) notion, drawn from Plato's *Timaeus,* of the CHORA: a cave or space of undifferentiated mother–daughter symbiosis linked to her idea of the SEMIOTIC.

Freud draws on the ideas of the Oedipal complex elsewhere: in his reading of E.T.A. Hoffman's story of 'The Sandman', which forms part of his discussion of the UNCANNY, and in his scattered comments on Shakespeare's *Hamlet.* More developed readings of *Hamlet* along these same lines appear in the work of his followers, including Jacques Lacan (see Felman 1982; Brooker and Widdowson [eds] 1996). These readings would seem to suggest an affinity between PSYCHOANALYSIS and literary criticism – as if the mythic content of literary texts corresponded to the Unconscious and their reading to the interpretive work of psychoanalysis. A further, more radical, implication is that psychoanalysis is itself a narrative and storytelling practice (Brooks 1994; Bowie 1987). But if this is the case, then so too, it would seem, is criticism.

See also DESIRE; MIRROR-PHASE; SUBJECT.

ORALITY

The dimension of speech or oral COMMUNICATION, usually considered in its relation to literacy. No human society is without speech, but some cultures, or cultures at a certain stage of their development, give this a primacy over the written word. Such cultures have, on this basis, been patronized as 'primitive' or 'underdeveloped', but it is common too, in a reverse assumption, for speech to be valued as more immediate and authentic than writing. The second belief was the subject of Jacques Derrida's (1976) deconstructive CRITIQUE of structural linguistics and the Anthropology of Claude Lévi-Strauss. The implication, in this respect, of DECONSTRUCTION is that speech and writing are similarly structured forms of REPRESENTATION, rather than the first being a source of original meaning and the second its delayed, secondary expression in another medium. This has implications for our view of types of society. To question a hierarchical ordering of societies, however, does not rule out the observation of differences between them, in terms of their respective modes of organization and internal values or practices (the use of ritual, magic and MYTH, for example, in 'oral cultures' compared with a reliance on the written or printed text, the historical record and the associated use of libraries and museums in 'literate cultures').

We can also acknowledge how an emphasis on orality persists in a variety of cases, however this is valued, outside of predominantly oral cultures: in the life of the human infant in all societies, in particular cultural forms such as song, live poetry readings, conferences, teaching, or in the use of telephone and radio in societies characterized by highly developed forms of written, printed and technologically aided literacy. Walter Ong (1982) proposes the term 'secondary orality' to describe the skills and competencies required to respond to the adapted oral or mixed systems of communication employed in the modern MASS media.

ORIENTALISM

The contemporary understanding of 'Orientalism' is derived from Edward Said's study *Orientalism* (1978), a formative influence on debates in POSTCOLONIALISM.

The term, says Said, has three applications: it refers to the centuries of relations between Europe and Asia; to nineteenth-century specialists and teachers in oriental languages and CULTURE; and to the MYTHS and stereotypes produced by generations of writers, artists and administrators in the west of the orient and the oriental as exotic, indolent, devious and untrustworthy. The force of Said's study is to show how no representation of the east has been free of this ideological construction of the orient as the OTHER to its own self-image as the model of rationality and civilization. This, he argues, continues in contemporary representations of Islam. Said rejects the EUROCENTRICISM of this perspective, but rejects, too, any assumption of a free or neutral place outside POWER and DISCOURSE for the cultural observer and critic.

Said's study has been criticized for reinforcing the binary opposition between the occident and orient, and for the vagueness of the terms of his own position as critic of this constructed IDEOLOGY. If no western scholar is exempt from misrepresenting the orient as 'Other', then how is Said himself an exception (Young 1990; Sarup 1996: 152)? As Said himself puts it, the real issue is whether there can be a true representation of anything (1978: 272). The issue, as he presents it in the essay 'Orientalism reconsidered' is 'how knowledge that is non-dominative and non-coercive can be produced in a setting that is deeply inscribed with the politics, the considerations, the positions and the strategies of power' (Barker *et al.* [eds] 1986: 212; see also Williams and Chrisman [eds] 1993: Part 2).

Said's arguments on orientalism should also be considered in relation to the wider concerns of his later *Culture and Imperialism* (1993a). Here, Orientalism is seen as a specific outcome and effect of IMPERIALISM, itself understood as a pervasive influence on the present world. Said's proposed 'contrapuntal' method of reading texts from the metropolitan centre and colonized periphery together confirms his distance from any binary opposition, including that of the critic and the object of study. Said sees 'the intellectual and artist' as positioned 'between domains, between forms, between homes, and between languages' (1993a: 403). This self-conscious deconstructive orientation is common to much postcolonial criticism. At the same time, if the critic and artist are displaced, Said stresses, as above, that there can be no position of neutrality. His work therefore poses, in a particularly acute way, the dilemma of the contemporary intellectual who is both politically committed and a figure of exile.

See also IDEOLOGY; INTELLECTUALS; NATIONALISM.

OTHER

Used invariably in conjunction with descriptions of 'the self' or SUBJECT with which the 'other' is contrasted and which it therefore defines. A main theoretical source for the term lies in the philosophy of G.W.F. Hegel and his commentary on the mutually defining relations of master and slave, and thence in PSYCHOANALYSIS and the writings (much indebted in this respect to Hegel) of the French psychoanalyst, Jacques Lacan (1901–1981). In Lacan's theory, the child simultaneously identifies with, and differentiates itself from, a non-self (the mother and an idealized self) in the MIRROR-PHASE. The 'other' is the image of a unified and co-ordinated self the child sees and also, by extension, other children with whom it is in a relation of recognition, rivalry and competition. As the child is formed as a subject at the point of the entry into the SYMBOLIC order (when it enters language and submits to the authority of the father and symbolic PHALLUS), the Other, becoming capitalized in Lacan's theory, is the Other of the UNCONSCIOUS. The Unconscious, Lacan writes, is 'articulated like a discourse'; and this discourse is 'the discourse of the Other' (1977: 193). The Other is not a direct interlocutor but the symbolic place, the site upon which the subject is constituted; the something it lacks but must seek. It therefore directs the subject's DESIRE and destiny.

In Sociology and Symbolic Interactionism, the transitions mapped by psychoanalysis are understood in terms of early relations with 'significant others' and later, more mature relations with 'generalized others'. In theories of IDEOLOGY, the Other is construed as the non-self who departs from, and simultaneously defines, the norms of a dominant social order, whether by SEXUALITY, RACE or ETHNICITY. Racism, as one such construction, names the Other as for the most part non-white and, in a series of extrapolated correlations, as thereby inferior. ETHNOCENTRICISM, in a further version of relations between the self and Other, has reinforced the political and cultural centrality of the west by conceiving of other regions (notably the east) as devious and exotic. Edward Said (1978) has theorized this set of attitudes and practices as 'ORIENTALISM'.

REPRESENTATIONS of the Other occur across a wide variety of literary and cultural texts, perhaps most commonly of all in jokes and comedy where some 'other' is necessarily exploited or stereotyped as the butt of humour. The degree to which this is tolerated, or made tolerable through humour, is a revealing sign of a CULTURE'S sense of boundaries between itself and perceived others. Further examples occur in crime, or GOTHIC and science fiction, where the Other as murderer, monster or alien is a central agent in the narrative, but has to be expelled to preserve psychic and social norms. Again, these forms serve a revealing analytic or possible critical function, showing the Other to be an expression of an interior, if feared and repressed, self.

POSTCOLONIALISM has shown the colonial subject as similarly contradictorily imagined – as simultaneously demonized and exoticized, demeaned and ennobled – in ways that clearly reflect upon internal divisions within the colonizer. The polarities of subject and Other in this, as in other contexts, are shown as evidently unstable and the assumptions of pure origins and authenticity upon which they rest to be untenable. In one example, Margery Fee reports how Maori writers are often of mixed ancestry, are raised in ignorance of their birth and have English as their first language. A white European, it might be said, cannot write or speak for a Maori. But neither, Fee points out, can it be supposed that a Maori with '"pure" ancestry automatically will write as a Maori... the oppressed Other who "supposedly speaks authentically and unproblematically as a unified subject... might be playing textual games"' (Ashcroft *et al.* [eds] 1995: 244). Neither, Fee adds, can it be assumed that 'even a politicised Other will have freed itself from the dominant ideology' (1995: 244). Subject and Other, colonizer and colonized are revealed here and elsewhere as thoroughly intermingled and interdependent, sharing a conflicted history and consciousness. The invocation of a separated, external Other, with all its possible concomitant associations of a lesser being, or of absolute difference, is shown as a thoroughly ideological construction on the part of – and simultaneously a part of – the subject.

See also ABJECTION; ALTERITY; DIFFEREND; *HOMO SACER*; SUBALTERN; TERRORISM.

OVERDETERMINATION

A concept employed by Freud in his discussion of the processes of CONDENSATION and DISPLACEMENT characterizing DREAMWORK. Thus, multiple dream-thoughts may be condensed in one IMAGE, bringing different meanings to a point of convergence. The interpretation of the image will therefore seek to track down its different determinations (or a potent thought deflected into a minor image). The concept was adopted by the French Marxist philosopher, Louis Althusser, in further elucidating Marx's observations on the DETERMINATION of certain structures of production, and in an attempt to resolve what he saw as a common theoretical problem in MARXISM and PSYCHOANALYSIS – namely, 'with what concept are we to think the determination of either an element or a structure by a structure' (1979: 188). In the essay 'Contradiction and overdetermination' (1969), Althusser suggests how the concept may be used to describe the relations of what are variously described as the 'elements', 'structures' or 'practices' comprising the levels of the social FORMATION. Thus, each element is understood as comprised of contradictions that affect the whole structure and are acted upon in turn by the whole. Each contradiction is shaped by the complex whole, and further internalizes the effect of the contradictions in other practices that go to comprise that whole. Hence, overdetermination is a process of mutual determination or conditioning between parts and whole. This then defines the overall structure of dominance and subordination characterizing a social formation at a given historical moment.

See also IDEOLOGICAL STATE APPARATUS; IDEOLOGY.

PARADIGM

This term has two uses. In the first, it is employed in the structural linguistics of Ferdinand de Saussure, and thus in STRUCTURALISM and SEMIOLOGY, to denote a class or set of equivalent units. Saussure argued that language operates along two axes: a 'horizontal' paradigmatic axis, composed of a pool of equivalent units (the class of nouns, verbs, prepositions, etc.) and a 'linear' or syntagmatic axis in which elements chosen from an appropriate paradigm are combined in an acceptable sequence (of speech or 'parole'). By extension, we can be said to choose from a paradigm or class of objects (cars, shoes, shirts, drinks) in making up our appearance or the sequence of a day's actions.

The second use of the term derives from the American philosopher of science, Thomas Kuhn (1922–1996) who introduced it in *The Structure of Scientific Revolutions* (1962) to describe the general informing laws, theoretical models and methods shared by a given scientific COMMUNITY. Under this ruling set of assumptions and practices, scientists pursue what Kuhn called 'normal science'. The interest of the term, however, lies as much in how science changes as in how it routinely proceeds – in how, under the pressure of new questions and problems, a community comes to an awareness of the limits of a prevailing configuration. This marks the transition to a new paradigm and is the moment of 'scientific revolution'. Thus, Galileo and Einstein are associated with 'paradigm shifts'.

Kuhn wished to restrict the term to specialist innovations in natural science, but the concept has regularly been given a wider application to new models of explanation in science, and broader symptomatic changes in institutions, cultural style and ways of thinking. In some uses, it therefore comes to correspond to the description of a ruling or dominant IDEOLOGY.

Kuhn suggested that paradigms were radically incompatible, one with the other. If we accept this, it makes it easier to judge the paradigms of 'normal science' and its equivalents in other areas than to identify paradigm shifts. Is it feasible, for example, to talk of the movement from MODERNITY to postmodernity as a paradigm shift when the terms themselves suggest that something (modernity) is shared between these modes or periods? Is a change in fashion too trivial, or a change in national mood too vague, to be described in this way? In the event, the more limited but more absolute and spectacular examples from scientific thought – the acceptance of the big bang theory of the creation of the universe, for example – remain the most persuasive candidates for paradigm shifts. See, however, the confident description of a 'Great Paradigm Shift' in the realm of theory (Easthope and Thompson [eds] 1991: viii) and Stuart Hall's 'Cultural studies: two paradigms' (1996a).

See also *ÉPISTÈME*; HEGEMONY; PROBLEMATIC.

PARADIGMATIC/SYNTAGMATIC

See SIGN; STRUCTURALISM.

PARODY

Parody is founded on the imitation of another object or text. This means that, unlike related modes such as satire and burlesque, it incorporates part of the object or text into itself. Consequently, as Margaret Rose writes, 'most parody worthy of the name is ambivalent towards its target. This ambivalence may entail, not only a mixture of criticism and sympathy for the parodied text, but also the creative expansion of it into something new' (1983: 51). Examples from literature would be Cervantes' *Don Quixote,* which parodies contemporary romance – as does, in another era, Jane Austen's *Northanger Abbey* – and James Joyce's *Ulysses,* where in the 'Oxen of the Sun' section especially, Joyce parodies a sequence of styles from the history of English literature.

The term acquired new interest because of Fredric Jameson's distinction in his discussion of POSTMODERNISM between parody and PASTICHE. Parody, says Jameson, requires a norm whose eccentricities parody points up. In the postmodern era, a proliferation of artistic, cultural and social styles has undermined any such norms; Jameson writes, 'the norm itself is eclipsed, reduced to a neutral and reified media speech... In this situation, parody finds itself without a vocation' (1991: 17). Parody mimics so as to mock an original, but this purpose, too, is lost. Instead, says Jameson, there is the superficial, empty mimicry of pastiche. This is 'without any of parody's ulterior motives'; it is 'blank parody' (1991: 17) and is ubiquitous in postmodern culture. As such, this neutral or neutralized cultural style is, for Jameson, a symptom of a broader loss of authenticity and originality. It leads him to ask whether postmodern art and culture can have any of the critical or dissenting edge of MODERNISM when parody was still a possibility.

Unlike Jameson, Linda Hutcheon (1989) believes postmodern arts do employ parody, not as an exception but as a rule. She examines a number of texts in fiction, film and photography that, in her terms, are 'double-coded' – that is to say, install in the same gesture as they CRITIQUE the parodied object. One well-known text commonly cited in these discussions is John Fowles's *The French Lieutenant's Woman*. This uses the forms of nineteenth-century REALISM, but does so in a conspicuously self-conscious way, making readers aware that they are reading a fabricated twentieth-century narrative. Hutcheon speaks of 'its intense self-reflexivity of narration and its dense parodic intertextuality' (1989: 112). These features make it, for her, an example of 'historiographic METAFICTION'. Where Jameson sees the eclipse of both parody and a sense of history, Hutcheon views such works as instructing us in the NARRATIVE construction of history and SUBJECTIVITY. The norms they critique are the 'doxa' or consensus views on the nature of REPRESENTATION, which deny the role of narrative and INTERTEXTUALITY.

PAROLE

See SIGN; STRUCTURALISM.

PASTICHE

An imitation or copy of the style of an original object or text. Following Fredric Jameson (1984, 1991), pastiche is taken to be a governing feature of POSTMODERNISM (though Jameson does not argue that this should as a whole be understood as simply a matter of style). Pastiche can appear across a range of cultural forms: in architecture, painting, film, literature, POP music, or fashion. Thus, David Hockney's paintings in the style of Picasso, Irish theme pubs with 'authentic' fixtures and fittings, heritage parks and imitation Tudor houses are all examples of pastiche. As defined by Jameson, it has replaced the earlier practice of PARODY:

> Pastiche is, like parody, the imitation of a peculiar or unique, idiosyncratic style, the wearing of a linguistic mask, speech in a dead language. But it is a neutral practice of such mimicry, without any of parody's ulterior motives, amputated of the satiric impulse, devoid of laughter and of any conviction.
>
> (1991: 17)

Jameson sees pastiche as a sign of the failure of originality and the loss of historical sense. Unlike parody, it has no satirical or ironical intent. We might wonder, then, what point or purpose it has. If pastiche is openly self-knowing and self-referential, and thus strictly 'unoriginal', and is without evident comic or satirical humour, does this mean it is entirely derivative and empty? Woody Allen's film *Radio Days* pastiched an earlier period through its popular music, but does so with affection. And are not 'tribute bands' – surely a product of postmodernism – conceived, as the very name suggests, in the spirit of admiration and flattery? Examples such as this suggest that pastiche might in fact convey a distinctive emotional and humorous, if not satiric, content.

See also SIMULATION; SPECTACLE.

PATRIARCHY

A form of society ruled by men through the figure of the father (the patriarch), to whom all others, including younger males, are subordinate. The term has a wide, and some would say too generalized, usage. It is used synonymously with 'sexism' to indicate prevalent attitudes towards women, to refer to kinship systems and the organization of the family, to refer to systematic inequalities in employment opportunities, recruitment patterns and pay, to poor social, health and childcare provision for women, and to the supporting evidence in the worlds of literature, art and media REPRESENTATIONS, which reinforces some of the above.

The evidence of male domination led Virginia Woolf to declare in 1929 that 'England is under the rule of a patriarchy' (1973: 35), but the term gained its widest currency some 40 years later as a rallying cry for second-wave Anglo-American 'radical feminists', inspired by the polemics of early works by, in particular, Kate Millett (1970), Shulamith Firestone (1970), Eva Figes (1970) and Germaine Greer (1971). These and later writers found evidence of patriarchy in literature and criticism, in western philosophy, PSYCHOANALYSIS, medicine, Christianity, language, fine art, the family, domestic life and sexual relations. This all-encompassing CRITIQUE of the dispersed forms of male domination was linked with the strategy of 'consciousness-raising' in women-only groups and a separatist tendency that gave, and still gives, FEMINISM its main media image.

The strengths of the concept, it seems now, lie more in its unifying force for contemporary feminists than in its analytic or explanatory sophistication. In short, it names an enemy. The problems in its more uncompromising use – as detailed by later feminists – are that it is unhistorical and reductive, that it pays little heed to the specific forms of capitalist societies and thus to relations between CLASS and patriarchal ideologies, that it too readily equates the personal with the political and rides roughshod over differences between individual men and women, that it ignores the changing form of the family and cannot provide a model for the specificities of sexual relations (Coward 1983; Whelehan 1995). Later feminists of colour and from within postcolonial studies have further critiqued the concept for the way it ascribes a common IDENTITY and condition to all women, and ignores the specificities of nationality, RACE and ETHNICITY, as well as the quite different family and kinship structures of different cultures.

Throughout these discussions, the problem is that, as a description of the way things are, patriarchy cannot explain how such a system or IDEOLOGY came into being, or how, given its supposed immemorial character, this can be changed. In naming male domination as cause and effect, it is finally circular and in danger of consolidating the very order of society it seeks to displace. More positively, it might be said that patriarchy is not simply a problematic concept, but has helped problematize the series of issues named above: that it has provoked theoretical debate between feminism, MARXISM and psychoanalysis, and given a significant direction to contemporary feminism. The theoretical and political question that now arises is whether this most universalizing of feminist positions can survive the scepticism of POSTSTRUCTURALISM and POSTMODERNISM towards all such 'METANARRATIVES'.

See also CLASS; GENDER; SEXUAL DIFFERENCE.

PERFORMATIVITY

A concept that draws on professional theatre and performance studies as well as a general metaphor of theatricality to emphasize the social constructedness of IDENTITY. It has been taken up in this respect, especially in theories of SEXUALITY and the making or reinvention of gay and lesbian identities, particularly in association with the innovative writings of Judith Butler (1990, 1993). In this and other contexts, it has shifted the long-standing debate on ESSENTIALISM to a recognition of degrees and forms of constructedness. In its more provocative versions, however, a performative view of SEXUAL DIFFERENCE abandons, not only essentialist notions of identity and the allied evocation of a universal woman's or gay person's 'experience', but dismisses the controlling force of given social identities and the constraints upon the free play of subjective invention and reinvention. It posits a 'deconstructive' view of SEXUALITY, which implies that the adoption of a settled sexual role may be permanently deferred. While liberating, this can be seen to theorize sexual identity as superficial, even illusory. In querying ideas of fixed identity, it has at the same time problematized ideas of collective identity and thus of any common social-sexual AGENCY for change.

See also AUTONOMY; MASQUERADE; QUEER THEORY.

PHALLOCENTRIC

Used in the first instance of the psychoanalytic theories of Sigmund Freud and Jacques Lacan, which make the PHALLUS central to psychological development and especially the establishment of SEXUAL DIFFERENCE. More broadly, the term is used of any theory, textual REPRESENTATION, DISCOURSE or social system that, explicitly or implicitly, endorses the privileged symbolic power of the male over the female, and thus reinforces the cultural and material inequalities of PATRIARCHY.

PHALLOGOCENTRIC

A portmanteau word coined by Jacques Derrida (see Kamuf [ed] 1991), which combines the meanings of PHALLOCENTRICISM with LOGOCENTRICISM. Whereas the first asserts the primacy of the PHALLUS, the second assumes the spoken word is the source of a transcendent truth. 'Phallogocentric' is used therefore of a theory that makes the phallus central in the also privileged symbolic system of language. Jacques Lacan's theory of the child's simultaneous entry into the SYMBOLIC order of language and acceptance of 'the law of the father' symbolized by the phallus is such a theory. It is this that occasions Derrida's introduction of the term.

PHALLUS

A term in psychoanalytic theory for the authority invested in the male. Freud employs the term 'phallic' more regularly than phallus, and uses this to mean the penis. An answer to the biologism of Freud's usage is supplied by Jacques Lacan's association of sexual IDENTITY and the UNCONSCIOUS with the SYMBOLIC system of language the child enters, having negotiated the Oedipal phase. The child becomes at this point subject to 'the law of the father'. The phallus is the symbol of this power, an imaginary object, associated with the father but not identical with the male penis. It is rather the signifier of sexual difference in general (Lacan 1977: 281–91).

If Lacan's theory emphasizes the symbolic construction of SEXUAL DIFFERENCE, his account, like Freud's, gives girls little positive identity. They are, in effect, castrated boys and associated with lack or absence. This, and the associated attribution of 'penis envy' to girls and women, has occasioned much debate, especially within FEMINISM. While some feminists have defended Freud and Lacan as offering a description or analysis of psychic development and sexual difference, but not as endorsing its implications (Mitchell 1974), others see the inevitable association of the phallus with the penis as confirming the theory's complicity with the dominant patriarchal order. As Luce Irigaray writes:

> we might suspect the *phallus* (Phallus) of being the *contemporary figure of a god jealous of his prerogatives...* of claiming on this basis, to be the ultimate meaning of all discourse... in particular as regards sex, the signifier and/or the ultimate signified of all desire, in addition to continuing, as emblem and agent of the patriarchal system, to shore up the name of the father (Father).

> (1985b: 67)

See also DESIRE; GENDER; PSYCHOANALYSIS.

PHONOCENTRICISM

See LOGOCENTRICISM.

PLACE

There has long been an interest, in literary, film and art criticism, in 'a sense of place'. The concept informs D.H. Lawrence's *Studies in Classic American Literature* (1923), for example, and has been important to a major tradition of American writers, including William Carlos Williams, Charles Olson and Jack Kerouac. American GENRE films (for example, the western, the gangster movie and the road movie) have also clearly developed their themes and mythologies within specific landscapes and urban environments. The same might be said of much South African, Indian and Australian as well as British literature and painting.

Place is therefore an inevitable cultural condition, if not as always consciously recognized as others. However, the concept has been rearticulated in relation to the co-ordinated themes of POSTMODERNISM, POSTCOLONIALISM and the developing interests of the newer area of Social or Cultural Geography. The familiar features of this epoch – the global reach of capitalism, new information technologies, modern transport, enforced or voluntary social mobility, migrancy, precarious patterns of employment and so on – have, so it is argued, radically altered the common experience and symbolic associations of place. Thus, the editors of one of several relevant volumes write of how the 'presumed certainties of cultural identity, firmly located in a particular place which housed stable cohesive communities of shared tradition and perspective... were increasingly disrupted and displaced' (Carter *et al.* [eds] 1993: vii). The same volume also presents a useful distinction between place and the concept of SPACE. 'Spaces become places,' the editors point out, 'by being named... Place is space to which meaning has been ascribed' (1993: xii). It is places, therefore, that ground our sense of IDENTITY in sets of symbolic and psychical associations – what, or where, we mean by 'home', for example (see Sarup 1996).

Other commentators have suggested that this connection between space and place, which in the past physically situated social relations, habits, rituals and traditions, has weakened in contemporary societies. Among others, Manuel Castells, for example, referring to the now dominant 'FLOWS' of capital and information, believes that 'social meaning evaporates from places, and therefore from society, and becomes diluted and diffused in the reconstructed logic of a space of flows' (1989: 349; see also Massey and Jess [eds] 1995: 45–85). This would confirm the view most strongly put by Iris Marion Young that an attachment to the notion of place as entailing face-to-face contacts and an authentic sense of COMMUNITY is at best utopian and at worst conservative or reactionary. She argues instead for a conception of urban life open to 'unassimilated otherness' and founded on an ethic of DIFFERENCE (1990: 301).

In a response to this position, Doreen Massey argues that a sense of place can provide a necessary rootedness and stability. She sees communities as complex and mobile, extending in networks of friends, relatives and those with similar beliefs beyond a single physical place, which will itself be the site in contemporary societies of intersecting relations, languages, ethnicities and cultures. This kind of concentrated intermixture leads Massey to propose 'a global sense of the local, a global sense of place' (Gray and McGuigan [eds] 1997: 240).

Carter *et al.* [eds] (1993) investigate these questions in theoretical terms and in essays on popular and postcolonial literatures, travel and the media. Other useful volumes similarly combine theoretical discussion and concrete case studies (Keith and Pile [eds] 1993; Ashcroft *et al.* [eds] 1995: Part XII; Westwood and Williams [eds] 1997).

See also CITY; DIASPORA; LOCAL; NETWORK.

PLEASURE

Freud's notion of the 'pleasure principle', or libido, depicted pleasure as a set of instinctual drives, careless of social or moral constraints, or the need for self-preservation. Its untrammelled energies were contained in the psychic development of the individual, however, by the 'reality principle', representing the requirements of the superego, and accompanied, too, Freud later theorized, by a 'death drive' that sought pain and distress. Whereas the 'pleasure principle' found gratification in the release of tension, the 'death drive' sought to reduce this tension to zero.

Discussions of sexual pleasure have been especially taken up in feminist, gay and lesbian theory and politics. This has been marked by an ambivalence, however – already evident in Freud – between a tolerance of the free expression of minority sexual practices (the use of pornography, sadomasochism, pederasty) and a belief that sexual pleasure is inextricably connected to relations of POWER and hence that what are deemed liberatory practices can reinforce the inequalities characteristic of heterosexuality and PATRIARCHY (Jackson and Scott [eds] 1996: 224–37).

In literary and other textual discussion, pleasure is a common but little explored feature of the reader or viewer's response and judgement. Critics and teachers reply with impatience to the apparently simple question, 'Did you enjoy it?', preferring to discuss what is 'interesting', thus, reinforcing a distinction between theory and academic analysis and POPULAR response that marks the whole debate. Laura Mulvey's much-cited essay, 'Visual pleasure and narrative cinema' (1989b), which opened discussion on the nature of the male GAZE served, nevertheless, to underline this dichotomy in an uncompromising way. Mulvey drew on Freud's concepts of 'scopophilia' (the pleasure of looking) and voyeurism to describe the nature of the ruling male gaze and the position of woman as spectacle on screen. NARRATIVE cinema reinforced the terms of PATRIARCHY and Mulvey saw her task as overthrowing the second by dismissing the first. 'It is said that analysing pleasure, or beauty, destroys it. That is the intention of this article' (1989b: 16). This is undertaken not in the name 'of a reconstructed new pleasure', but to promote the 'dialectics' and 'passionate detachment' of an anti-illusionist cinema. The same strategy therefore set FEMINISM against popular pleasure and the AVANT-GARDE against Hollywood.

A major, roughly contemporary, theorization of pleasure was offered by Roland Barthes in *The Pleasure of the Text* (1976). Here, Barthes distinguished between texts of *plaisir* (pleasure) and JOUISSANCE (bliss). The first 'comes from culture and does not break with it, is linked to a comfortable practice of reading', whereas the text of bliss 'imposes a state of loss, the text that discomforts (perhaps to the point of boredom) unsettles the reader's historical, cultural, psychological assumptions' (1976: 14). The text of bliss that 'defamiliarizes' a reader so thoroughly is most likely to be (as with Mulvey) a modernist or avant-garde text. Barthes's discussion associates the latter kind of text with a state of extreme and inexpressible emotion (whether momentary or painfully prolonged) but, like Mulvey (who talks of the 'thrill' of transcending oppression), he too demotes the 'ordinary', because normative, experience of 'pleasure'.

The contrary side of this discussion has appeared in the more recent history of the study of POPULAR culture where it has been, for some, *de rigueur* to belong as a fan or enthusiast to a popular audience, to spontaneously enjoy reading comics, watching soaps, playing football or going shopping. 'EVERYDAY LIFE' comes, therefore, to determine the stance and idiom of academic analysis (what Meagan Morris calls a style of 'anti-academic pop-theory writing', in Storey [ed] 1996: 159). This mode is frequently evidenced by the work of John Fiske and Iain Chambers. For all its streetwise, democraticizing intent, this approach is seen by its detractors as complicit with consumerist CULTURE or as a 'populist' betrayal of the political task of the public INTELLECTUAL (see Webster, in Storey [ed] 1996).

These debates therefore continue to place popular pleasure on one side, and theoretical rigour and political purpose on the other. This problem is addressed by Terry Eagleton in a discussion of the pleasures and displeasures of the line 'a terrible beauty is born' in W.B. Yeats's poem 'Easter 1916' (an example, he says, that can extend to any DISCOURSE). Eagleton identifies a somatic level of response to sound, rhythm and closure, and an ideological and political level. Both may give pleasure (of different kinds), or one may produce pleasure and the other displeasure, with friction or trade-offs between the two. The issue of pleasure is rephrased in terms of its AESTHETIC and historically grounded complexities, and governed by a political project interested in points of connection: when 'what people like, and why' expresses itself in 'the pleasurable anxieties of difference' and 'political engagement' (1986c: 180).

See also DESIRE; SUBLIME; VALUE.

PLURALISM

A widely employed term describing less a single theorized position than the ideological tenor of much academic work in a liberal or more radical vein. Pluralism implies the acceptance of DIFFERENCE and diversity across a very broad possible range in a number of disciplines and areas of cultural and political activity: from the adoption of an open curriculum, the recognition of different intellectual perspectives or combination of different methodological approaches, to the affirmation of sexual and ethnic difference, or arguments for diversity in the composition of the political or PUBLIC SPHERE.

Explanations for the currency of pluralism are themselves – appropriately – of different kinds. It can be seen as a response to the declining belief in objective or 'scientific' method (see POSITIVISM); the dispersed fall-out from the combined poststructuralist and postmodern attack on fixed and universal meanings or totalizing explanations; the affirmative side of the CRITIQUE in postcolonialist and multiculturalist arguments of racial oppression or ethnic advantage; or the consequence of the end of Cold War ideologies. Other figures and movements, too – Michel Foucault, for example or, in a longer history, strands in MARXISM, FEMINISM and liberal HUMANISM – might be said to have contributed to the critique of privilege and POWER, and thus to the making of contemporary pluralism.

At the same time, it would be a mistake to think that the reign of pluralism is unquestioned or unproblematic. An openness to all kinds of texts can imply the abandonment of criteria of aesthetic or cultural VALUE, and methodological pluralism or postmodern 'language games' can be viewed as a recipe for a relativism that views everything as different but equal. Christopher Norris (1985) finds Richard Rorty's neo-PRAGMATISM, and POSTMODERNISM, generally wanting in this way: as having jettisoned the means to discriminate on questions of value, morality and truth. Others seeking 'post-foundationalist' positions similarly view pluralism with some scepticism (Tallack [ed] 1995). Arguments for MULTICULTURALISM, too, as Louis Menand (1995) points out, can be caught in the paradox that the diversity this project espouses comes in fact to mean conformity in a society where respect for diverse literatures and SUBCULTURES becomes the norm. In another direction, the rise of NATIONALISM and the advance of FUNDAMENTALISM contradict any account of pluralism as a dominant mode. Such movements might in fact imply quite the opposite: that at certain points there is no tolerance or NEGOTIATION, and that some beliefs and cultures are starkly incommensurate.

See also DIFFEREND; FOUNDATIONALISM.

POLITICAL CORRECTNESS

See CULTURAL POLITICS; ELITE.

POP

The 'pop art' movement appeared in the early 1950s in the UK when it was associated with the work of the artists Richard Hamilton, Eduardo Paolozzi and others connected with the Independent Group, and then later in association with the work of, for example, Peter Blake, David Hockney and the American artists Andy Warhol, Claes Oldenburg and Roy Lichtenstein. These artists appropriated the graphic styles of comics, advertising, films and the new consumer objects of EVERYDAY LIFE (American cars, TVs, phones, fridges), sometimes with evident affection, sometimes in a deadpan eclecticism. The combination of terms in the description 'pop art' joined the otherwise antagonistic realms of high and MASS culture, gallery art and advertising. The movement might therefore be said to announce one of the characteristic features of POSTMODERNISM.

Pop is also, of course, used – from much the same period – to refer to 'pop music'. However, this is as difficult to define as the related (but not synonymous) term POPULAR. Sometimes 'pop music' is used interchangeably with 'rock' or 'rock and roll', or as a generic category for a range of styles, but sometimes, too, is used more selectively to refer to ephemeral, blatantly commercial music issued as singles, played on mainstream radio stations and entered in the pop charts. This would suggest that 'pop' is less a single type or GENRE than a combination of type of lyric, musical form and performer in a market-led package. Even this common definition is difficult to sustain, however. Were the Spice Girls pop? Are Robbie Williams, Bryan Ferry, or the later – crooning – Bob Dylan equally pop? Was the U2 album called *Pop* pop in the same sense? Or does this last convey an ironic self-consciousness that challenges the hierarchical categories of 'serious art' and 'entertainment' like the earlier art movements? One thing we can be sure of is that, with or without such sophistication, in both art and music, the term 'pop' retains an inescapable reference to the materials and processes of consumer CULTURE. But this does not at all rule out complexity and creativity in its production, as Toynbee (2000) shows, nor diminish the role it has in the making of personal, social and sexual identities (see Whiteley 2000).

See also CONSUMERISM; KITSCH.

POPULAR

A key but ambiguous term in literary and cultural analysis. Popular CULTURE can designate the culture of the 'people' or working class (or sometimes 'working people'); folk culture; youth or SUBCULTURES; or popular GENRES in fiction and film. Often the term has been accompanied by a judgement of VALUE that views these cultural forms as authentic or as banal and conformist. Furthermore, such *qualitative* judgements may be contrasted or supported by a *quantitative* description that measures the popular by how conspicuous it is or by its commercial success. This is the most common underlying definition, equating the popular (and popular attitudes and TASTE) with the products of MASS-production processes and the mass media. In another important distinction, the popular in this latter sense is produced 'for' and not 'by' the mass or the people, who are consequently defined as consumers. There are some continuing paradoxes, however. Thus, what is thought to be popular in the sense of being 'of the people' might be a minority pursuit or PLEASURE, associated with a folk culture (morris dancing) or class culture (pigeon fancying). Again, 'popular' in this sense might be opposed to a commercialized mass culture, but far from quaint or backward-looking. Examples of this more 'progressive' kind occur in the realm of youth cultures, where fashions or music styles (punk, house, jungle) are seen as created 'on the streets', in clubs, regions or in some 'independent' way before being taken up by the mass CULTURE INDUSTRIES.

The study of popular culture is therefore confronted with a range of questions concerning definition and value, the role of the culture industries, and the reception and use of popular forms and genres. This last issue also involves the important question of the relative passivity or active discrimination of consumers. Work in this field has consequently employed a number of explanatory concepts from theories of IDEOLOGY (especially of HEGEMONY), GENDER, RECEPTION, and the construction of the SUBJECT. Much of the study along these lines (Fiske, Hebdige, McRobbie) has sought to view the popular, whether in relation to the mass media or youth cultures, as the positive expression of cultural meanings, as a subversive or CARNIVALesque rebuff to the homogenizing intent of DOMINANT ideology (Docker 1994). This has suggested affinities with some of the more pluralist definitions of POSTMODERNISM (Strinati 1995).

This approach cannot be said to define a consensus, however, and its construction of the politics of popular culture has been challenged as limited and uncritical by those drawing on different theoretical vocabularies. Where the first approach emphasizes the consumption of popular culture texts, the second emphasizes the processes of PRODUCTION, the role of institutions, cultural policy, and the governing mechanisms of capitalist economies. A fuller, integrated approach would seem the obvious resolution of these differences. However, what this debate suggests is that these approaches can only be joined in a model which appreciates that the processes of production and consumption, the operation of the culture industries and the reading of texts will often exist in a contradictory tension (see Ross 1989; Storey 1999).

See also AUDIENCE; CONSUMERISM; INCORPORATION.

POPULISM

An IDEOLOGY that gave its name to a political movement and organized party in the USA in the late nineteenth century and 1930s. Politically, its characteristic stand against bureaucracy, big business and government on behalf of the 'people' or 'little man' was ambiguous and the movement mobilized those it represented for both liberal or right-wing causes. Both the 'New Deal' and fascism – in the USA as in Europe – activated populist sentiment.

Something of this ambiguity, highlighted by present political trends in the USA and Western Europe, appears in the earlier accounts by Stuart Hall and Martin Jacques (1983), and by Hall (1988), of the period of Thatcherism in the UK as an era of 'authoritarian populism' or 'popular authoritarianism'. This analysis was presented in the context of a project for what was called 'New Times' launched from within the journal *Marxism Today* and is a clear instance of academic theory informing an active CULTURAL POLITICS (see McRobbie in Morley and Chen [eds] 1996). Hall's argument, drawing on Antonio Gramsci's theory of HEGEMONY, the concept of INTERPELLATION, and the idea of the ARTICULATION of cultural and political meanings, was that POWER could only be won and maintained through consent. Thatcher had achieved this by speaking to and making POPULAR a range of attitudes, primarily in the symbolic realm of individual and national IDENTITY. (A criticism was that Hall did not investigate the CLASS structure or material economic basis of the Thatcherite project; see Sparks in Morley and Chen [eds] 1996: 95.) This ideology was installed as a belligerent COMMON SENSE, which was most evident at the time of the Falklands crisis. It followed, Hall argued, that any effective reply to this regime would itself have to win popular consent to a series of counter-hegemonic positions.

In a third usage, the description 'cultural populism' is used by Jim McGuigan (1992) to describe what he takes to be a limited and overly sanguine view, in the work of John Fiske, Paul Willis and others, of the consumer's creative production of meaning and the making of a COMMON CULTURE in the face of a blatantly capitalist market. To claim capitalism produces an unprecedented abundance – an excess Willis sees as material for its CRITIQUE and supersession – is, for McGuigan, simply to endorse the self-serving mechanisms of the free market. He calls, therefore, for a dual critical analysis of both symbolic meanings and the economy (see Storey [ed] 1994: Part 7).

See also POSTCAPITALISM.

POSITIVISM

Positivism was introduced by the French thinker, Auguste Comte (1798–1857), the founder of Sociology, in an account of the evolution of human thought from its early theological and metaphysical modes to its perceived present stage of positive or scientific knowledge. The latter comprises laws of observable phenomena, and all else is rejected as of little or no account. The later form of so-called 'logical positivism', developed in the twentieth century, offered to distinguish science from non-science in a more philosophically sophisticated way. In so doing, it established a widespread notion of scientific method as characterized by an exclusive emphasis on observable, 'factual' evidence, a belief in 'objective' method and the production of verifiable results. This was extended in a long-lasting influence from its primary model in physics and the natural sciences to the social sciences, including economics, psychology, branches of history and allied disciplines.

In fact, however, positivist assumptions and procedures had been discounted in science itself since the first impact early in the century of the theory of relativity, and subsequent revolutions in scientific understanding have only further distanced it from this model. Nor, at the end of the century, does positivism hold sway in the social sciences (though empirical work is sometimes loosely termed positivist). It is now common for researchers in the human, social and natural sciences to recognize that the researcher will inevitably influence the object of study, that processes of selection and evaluation are inescapable, and that the progress of knowledge depends on hypotheses and theoretical speculation: in short, on ideas that exist in a running dialogue with empirical evidence and other ideas, rather than a growing mountain of autonomous facts.

Denzin and Lincoln (1994) describe the transition from positivism to 'post-positivism' in the social sciences and ethnography as one where quantitative methods employing statistical evidence and modes of verification have been superseded by a qualitative, 'multimethod' and self-reflexive approach in which the researcher as 'bricoleur understands that research is an interactive process shaped by his or her personal history, biography, gender, social class, race and ethnicity and those of the people involved in the setting' (1994: 3). Bruce Caldwell (1994) confirms the decline of the positivist model in economics, or, more precisely, in the interaction of the philosophy of science and economic method. He attributes this to the influence of the 'growth of knowledge' philosophies (associated with Thomas Kuhn, Imre Lakatos and others). Their findings, he argues, demonstrate the futility of 'the quest for a single, universal, prescriptive scientific methodology' and emphasize instead that 'science is a dynamic, growing enterprise' involving 'both constancy and flux, both bold conjectures and rigorous criticism, both normal science and revolutionary crisis'. 'The positivist fixation on the objective side of science,' he concludes, 'missed half of a beautiful and complex tale' and this can only be met in the present 'post-positivist environment' by a 'methodological pluralism' (1994: 244).

The fortunes of positivism might be paralleled with the movements in Naturalism or the documentary mode in the arts where it has similarly been claimed that the observer can stand outside of and above the evidence of the social facts depicted. In their naïve or unself-reflexive form, these modes have also been surpassed.

See also CHAOS; PLURALISM; VALUE.

POSTCAPITALISM

Theories of 'postcapitalism' (or, as sometimes, with a hyphen, 'post-capitalism') in the sense of a world 'after capitalism' have traditionally derived from models of a future communist, socialist, or anarcho-syndicalist society. Radical transformations of this kind are seen to depend on spontaneous, widespread popular revolt, the formation of workers' councils, or the agency of an organized revolutionary working class, acting in concert with an avant-gardist political party, which will abolish the state in favour of new democratic systems of government, common ownership, and social and economic equality. As such, projections of a world after capitalism have sprung from an opposition to the very conditions, namely a concentration of ownership and a system of wage-labour, which characterized its beginnings in the late eighteenth and early nineteenth centuries (see MARXISM and UTOPIA).

Recent arguments on postcapitalism tend to argue less for the abolition of CAPITALISM's fundamental mechanisms than for their radical reform. Michael Albert's *Parecon: Life After Capitalism* (2003), for example – its title is an abbreviation of the central tenet of '**Par**ticipatory **Econ**omics'– outlines a new social order based on anarchist principles of solidarity, equality, decentralized participatory decision-making, diversity and self-determination, while Harry Shutt's *Beyond the Profits System: Possibilities for a Post-Capitalist Era* (2010) proposes a change of priorities from growth and work to greater effective control over taxation, an increase in non-profit and state-owned enterprises, reduced working hours, and a citizen's income in a postcapitalism guided by cooperation, creativeness, equality and greater democracy. A further high-profile scenario of postcapitalism is set out in the political commentator and economist Paul Mason's *Postcapitalism: A Guide to Our Future* (2015).

Mason argues that capitalism in the twenty-first century has already entered a new phase of radical, but internally generated, transformation quite different from the anticipated revolutionary change in the classic sense. This change is said to have been prompted especially by the unprecedented advance of electronic media and automation working from within capitalism to produce a new economic and social order which will surpass and superannuate the old, including the traditional working class. What new NETWORKed technologies produce, above all, is information, and Mason points to two main effects of this accelerating process: firstly, distinctions between work and home, and work and free-time become blurred, thereby unsettling the relation between work and wages – at a time when trades unions are weakened; secondly, the freely available capacity for electronic reproduction (of words, music and images) means that the market cannot fix prices, which tend then, Mason argues, towards zero.

Moreover, the new networked technologies produce information of such an abundance that while global, super-rich, super-tech companies such as Google, Apple and Amazon aim to capture it, they cannot. The drive to global monopoly characteristic of late capitalist market economies is rivalled by the drive to freedom. Hence the appearance, Mason observes, of an expanding source of free information run on non-market lines in Wikipedia. Here, he finds a harbinger of a desired 'non-market, information-centred, low labour, post-capitalist world' (http://p2pfoundation.net/PostCapitalism).

Curiously, some other features of this transitional phase receive only a passing or no mention: the information-gathering activities of the intelligence services, for example. Mason sees the controversy between WikiLeaks and the NSA (the US National Security Agency) as 'the latest phase of a war over who can own and store information' (2015: 24), but not does comment on the cases of the whistle-blower, Edward Snowden, or of Julian Assange, the founder of WikiLeaks, and what these mean for the complex issues of national defence, surveillance, and the prospects of freedom and transparency of information in a postcapitalist society. Again, while he sees the advent of the terrorist movement, ISIS, along with civil war in Ukraine and the paralysis of NATO, as signs that the 'neo-liberal order has failed' (xii), he does not comment on ISIS's use of electronic media for the purposes of propaganda and recruitment in a very real war against western styled postcapitalism. Both examples paint a more faceted and sinister picture of the extent and purpose of information-gathering than that practised by networked citizens and global conglomerates.

It is the first of these, however, which is at the centre of Mason's attention. Thus, he finds everyday signs of a burgeoning new order in local cooperatives, parallel currencies and exchange systems, shared housing, carpools, food co-ops and free kindergartens brought on by the constraints of austerity programmes in western societies. Ingredients of what is styled 'a shared economy' run alongside, but counter the traditional capitalist market economy. People have been pushed to find these alternatives, but are also enabled in entirely new ways by the technologies of social media, such as Twitter and Facebook, which encourage networked self-determination. These same media have also served to mobilize protest movements, national and global petitions, and the appearance of left-wing political parties in European societies, notably Greece and Spain, and anti-austerity positions in Scotland and England in 2015, allied variously with green, or socialist or anarchist positions. But, again, while recognizing the advent of popular leftist tendencies, Mason looks rather to the 'networked citizen', a new type of 'educated and connected human being' (xvii) as the springboard to a new postcapitalist era.

See also ESTABLISHMENT; POST-MARXISM.

POSTCOLONIALISM

Postcolonialism is often linked with POSTSTRUCTURALISM and POSTMODERNISM. These movements can indeed be said to share a critical orientation and theoretical vocabulary – a recognition of DIFFERENCE and a common anti-essentialist notion of IDENTITY and cultural meaning, and, in the case of postmodernism, a shared critique of the hierarchies, universalism and EUROCENTRICISM of western MODERNITY. The prefix 'post', moreover, suggests a common attempt to describe a process of change, involving both continuity and new departures.

However, the focus of attention, and the intellectual and political objectives of each movement, are different, as the substantive terms in each case – STRUCTURALISM, MODERNISM, colonialism – illustrate, and are in certain respects even opposed. Postcolonialism is therefore the study of the ideological and cultural impact of western colonialism and in particular of its aftermath – whether as a continuing influence (neocolonialism) or in the emergence of newly articulated, independent national and individual identities. Characteristically, the experience being described involves both of these processes. Hence, the emergence of concepts describing a double, conflicted and transitional condition such as HYBRIDITY, syncretism, the concept of the DIASPORA, and of metaphors of migrancy, crossings and borders. This thinking has been brought to bear particularly on the question of identity and thus on conceptualizations of RACE and ETHNICITY.

As the number of individual studies, collections and readers in the field suggests (Williams and Chrisman [eds] 1993; Aschroft *et al.* [eds] 1995), postcolonialism itself embraces a range of overlapping and sometimes contesting arguments. Intellectually, it has been shaped by a long legacy of the study of IMPERIALISM and subsequently by the work, principally, of Edward Said, Homi Bhabha and Gayatri Spivak (see ORIENTALISM, HYBRIDITY and SUBALTERN; and see also Childs and Williams 1997 for introductory commentary on these figures). This theoretical work is directly political in its concerns (unlike much poststructuralism) and by inclination anti-western (and thus opposed to western postmodernism). However, postcolonial theory is also marked by its own internal political debates and differences. Thus, the key theorists named above, based in western universities and well versed as they are in European CULTURE, are seen by some as implicated in the history of western colonialism they seek to account for and CRITIQUE (R. Young 1990).

A related reservation is that these thinkers construe colonial history in terms of DISCOURSE and TEXTUALITY, and in this way bring western poststructuralist PARADIGMS to non-western experience (Parry, in Ashcroft *et al.* [eds] 1995). These are important issues and much debated (see Loomba in Williams and Chrisman [eds] 1993). Whatever else, however, Said, Spivak and Bhabha are themselves far from unaware of the role of western scholarship in constructing notions of the colonial 'OTHER'. Indeed, this centrally informs Said's theorization (1978) of REPRESENTATIONS of the 'Orient' and Spivak's critique of the stereotype of the 'Third World' and 'Third World Woman' (1987, 1990).

These questions of the relation of self and OTHER, and the ambiguous position of western INTELLECTUALS, are marked features of postcolonial study. An alternative perspective claims that colonialism or neocolonialism remains the decisive condition and experience (McClintock in Williams and Chrisman [eds] 1993). For some, also, this calls for an *anti*-colonialist or *anti*-imperialist analysis and strategy. An important influence on these varied tendencies has been Frantz Fanon (1925–1961), the Martinique-born psychiatrist and revolutionary. In *Black Skin, White Masks* (1952), Fanon presents the complex psychological effects of colonialism that induce the black man to adopt white ways, and draws attention especially to the role of the colonizer's language in enforcing an internalized sense of inferiority and in suppressing native traditions and history. From 1957 to 1961, Fanon worked for the Algerian National Liberation Front and in *Wretched of the Earth* (1961) presented his political conclusions and thoughts on the role of intellectuals and writers. He detected three phases in colonialism:

1. an assimilation of the cultural model introduced by the colonizer
2. an internal self-questioning of this response and the quest for authentic national roots
3. a commitment to liberation struggles on behalf of the masses through violent revolutionary action.

Independence could only result, Fanon argued, from a process of 'decolonization' attendant on the violent overthrow of the colonial heritage.

Fanon distinguishes between liberation and NATIONALISM, and this has influenced the thought, among others, of Edward Said (1993a). Elsewhere, Benita Parry (in Ashcroft *et al.* [eds] 1995) endorses his commitment to oppositional political struggle. Otherwise, Fanon's influence on postcolonial theory lies in the anti-essentialist notion developed in both above-mentioned texts of black and white as locked in mutually defining identities.

A further feature of the work alluded to here is its different geographical focus – upon the Middle East, India and Algeria – which present different economic and political histories and different conceptual issues. Furthermore, major questions in the field concerning race and ethnicity are quite differently articulated in different countries. Nor are these consistently or directly connected with histories of colonialism (witness the situation of blacks and European ethnic groups in the USA). The field is, therefore, in an important sense differentiated by the geographical and historical location of the cultural sphere under study, as well as by the perspective and participation of its commentators within these histories. This specificity and self-consciousness again distinguish work in postcolonialism and its cognate areas from poststructuralism or postmodernism.

See also COSMOPOLITANISM; ENLIGHTENMENT; MULTICULTURALISM.

POST-FORDISM

The term 'Fordism' was derived from the assembly-line production of the Model-T Ford automobile first built by Henry Ford in Detroit in the 1910s. This came to symbolize the MASS-production processes, associated forms of labour and labour relations of the 'second' industrial revolution. The term was first used in the 1930s by the Italian Marxist Antonio Gramsci (1891–1937) who saw how this new industrial system was connected to the creation of a new type of worker and social mentality (1971a: 277–318). A related term, 'Taylorism', after Frederick Taylor, author of early time-and-motion studies, influenced the principles of 'scientific management', which Ford introduced in the workplace and sought to extend to the home environments of his workers. American society became an example to the world of what it was 'to be modern', and the twentieth century was hailed as 'the American century'.

After the economic collapse (the 'Great Crash') of 1929, the Depression of the 1930s and the Second World War, a restructured Fordism proceeded in most western nations, as well as in Japan, in tandem with economic policies predicated on the expectation of full employment, high wage levels, state welfare provision and stable markets. This successful period of post-1945 Fordism proceeded until the economic recession of the early 1970s (Harvey 1989).

Post-Fordism emerged out of this economic downturn. Though its significance and the degree to which it departed from earlier systems are debated, some features are commonly recognized. Thus, the 1970s and 1980s are marked by the government implementation of 'monetarist' policies; the decline of traditional industries (mining, shipbuilding) and the rise of service industries (clothes, food outlets); the use of new technologies and the advent of the computerized 'information age', along with its associated 'hi-tech' industries in new, non-urban locations; the diversification of markets opened up by expanding multinational corporations; the GLOBALIZATION of financial markets operating beyond the boundaries of nation-states, including powerful markets in Tokyo and Singapore; the use of a flexible and decentralized labour force; the greater employment of women and 'Third World' labour on a 'flexi', part-time or provisional, contract basis; and the decline of (male-dominated) trades union power (Hall in Morley and Chen [eds] 1996: 224–5).

Two general features might be noted in this complex of changes. The first is a radical alteration of 'time-space' relations discussed by David Harvey. This denotes the experience of 'time-space compression' resulting from the speeding up of PRODUCTION, distribution and consumption, the rapid passage of money and information via new communications NETWORKS and the passage of people by means of advanced transport systems, and because of altered labour relations between the 'First' and 'Third Worlds' (Harvey 1989: especially Part III). Second, post-Fordism has meant an emphasis on CONSUMERISM over PRODUCTION, an unprecedented commodification of social life and an accompanying accent upon design and 'lifestyle' identities over the 'use-value' and CLASS identities of a Marxist PARADIGM.

Post-Fordism is frequently discussed in relation to POSTMODERNISM. According to Charles Jencks, the latter was announced by the blowing up of the Pruitt-Igoe housing complex in St Louis, Missouri, at a time (15 July 1972, at 3.32 pm, says Jencks, playfully) that synchronized with the end of Fordism. The 'enterprise zones' and corporate towers of the new era suggest a continuing parallel, but the chronologies across CULTURE and the arts make this a more uneven match than at first appears. In terms of a general emphasis, post-Fordism describes economic changes and postmodernism cultural changes. However, one of the most marked and profoundly challenging features of contemporary western societies is that this distinction has become less easy to make.

See also BASE AND SUPERSTRUCTURE; CAPITALISM; FLOWS; REFLEXIVE MODERNIZATION; SIMULATION.

POST-FOUNDATIONALISM

See ETHICS; FOUNDATIONALISM.

POSTHUMAN

Sometimes this term, which has its own divergent meanings, is blurred with the idea of the 'transhuman'. This latter concept is more prevalent on the INTERNET (including a 'Transhumanist Declaration' by the 'World Transhumanist Association') than in academic publications (but see, for example, Blake, Molly and Shakespeare, *Beyond Human* 2012), and is used to refer to a desired future sensibility and evolutionary next stage of the human when science and technology will ensure physical and intellectual enhancement, longevity and even immortality. As defined by Cary Wolfe (2010), 'posthumanism' is not 'post human' in the sense of being 'after' the human, but 'names the embodiment and embeddedness of the human being in not just its biological but also its technological world'(xv). An early inspiration for this theoretical and political turn was Donna Haraway's 'A cyborg manifesto' (1991), which welcomed the human–technology interface of advanced late twentieth century societies as destabilizing the taken-for-granted tenets of western capitalism and patriarchy. Developments in medical technologies (conspicuously of prosthetic limbs and implants, as well as everyday advances in hearing aids and lenses), the technologies of the gym and professional sports, communication devices worn as body-augmentation have made the figure of the cyborg more the norm than the exception.

The posthuman therefore refers, firstly, to an ongoing present condition rather than to an anticipated future. Second, it distances itself from normative ideas of the 'human' on which the 'transhuman' still depends. As elsewhere, therefore, the prefix 'post-' signals an attempt to problematize the substantive term it qualifies, here, the dominant conception of the human encoded in liberal HUMANISM. Discourses on the posthuman seek therefore at once to CRITIQUE the assumptions of unity and autonomous AGENCY conferred upon the humanist SUBJECT and the dualities of normal/abnormal, mind/body, human/machine in which it has been set. Differences of focus emerge from the different PARADIGMS adopted to reveal the counter-truths of the posthuman condition. Hayles' *How We Became Posthuman* (1999), and Halberstam and Livingstone's *Posthuman Bodies* (1995) give an idea of these different emphases.

Hayles draws upon CYBERNETICS to argue for a conception of the human defined, not by consciousness, but as a type of information system. Normative conceptions of the human are bedevilled, she says, by a hierarchy of the mind over the BODY, and by a dream of the disembodied human (persisting, in the realm of artificial intelligence, in the ideal of a computer on which an evolving human consciousness is downloaded). To become posthuman does not mean becoming a machine, Hayles insists, but understanding machines (tools, cars, computers) as a prosthetic extension of the human rather than its OTHER. More radically, Hayles asks us to view the human body and consciousness as a particular, but historically accidental, realization of informational codes. Indeed, in the idea of 'the computational universe', a universal informational code is seen to underlie all existing things. The posthuman (so understood) therefore reconfigures the human, setting it in a relation of equivalence and difference with other robotic or computer intelligences. The concept of artificial life (AL) as opposed to artificial intelligence (AI) confers the language of 'life' ('emergent', 'evolving', 'interactive' behaviour) on all such information-processing entities.

In Hayles' account, biologically unaltered humans become posthuman in their use of prosthetic computer technologies. Halberstam and Livingstone want, instead, to subvert essentialist conceptions of the human precisely by foregrounding the disfigured or transfigured bodies marginalized under humanist norms. Thus, they enlist the body as 'projected image', a 'body under the sign of AIDS', a 'contaminated body', a 'deadly body', a 'techno-body' and a 'queer body' (1995: 3) into the realm of the posthuman. Elsewhere, their volume associates the embodied signs of performative, CYBORG and 'alien' identity with the advent of the postmodern and contemporary forms of the fantastic, the GOTHIC and the grotesque. Arguments for the posthuman find their place, therefore, in a wide critique of the assumed stability of cognitive, social, sexual and cultural identities, and the allied dualisms of self and other.

For all their differences, these examples share a biotechnological emphasis. Gray (2001) notes how, not only the human body, but medicine, food, voting procedures and military conflicts, have become 'cyborged'. She therefore urges a broader debate that will address the issues confronting a 'posthuman politics'.

See also ETHICS; PERFORMATIVITY; SEXUALITY; TRANSGRESSIVE.

POST-MARXISM

As the preposition here (and in other contexts) suggests, post-Marxism sees itself as 'going beyond', but not annulling, the insights of classical MARXISM. An important influence on this thinking has been the writing of Laclau and Mouffe (1985) and Laclau (1990). In *Hegemony and Socialist Strategy* (1985), they argued against what they saw as a dependency in classical Marxism upon essentializing laws of economic necessity, Marxism's *a priori* privileging of the working CLASS, and the over-predictive ascription of counter-hegemonic activity to this class. Instead, they introduced a distinction between 'power blocs' and 'the people', seeing the latter as brought into contingent alliances in an indeterminate, discursive political climate. As this suggests, their vocabulary was indebted to POSTSTRUCTURALISM and was close to, though more optimistic than, the discussion of POWER and DISCOURSE in Michel Foucault. At the same time, the title of this volume indicates a debt to the theories of HEGEMONY developed by the Italian Marxist revolutionary Antonio Gramsci. These ideas are mobilized in the interests of a 'radical democratic politics'. Within Cultural Studies and the British Left, the influence of this model can be detected in Stuart Hall's analysis of Thatcherism and the counter-scenario of 'New Times' (1988; see also Morley and Chen [eds] 1996).

It would be a mistake to think that 'post-Marxism' signals an outright rejection of Marxism, or that it has comprised a new and unchallenged orthodoxy. A flexible and non-reductionist Marxism was defended by Norman Geras (1987, 1988), as has the concept of class (Sandler and Diskin 1995). Mouzelis (1990) does not argue for Marxism's wholesale rejection or retention, but for the value of its holistic approach and concern with human AGENCY in conceptualizing processes of social transformation. Within Literary Studies, Terry Eagleton's commitment to Marxism has strengthened while, within Cultural Studies, Angela McRobbie has expressed dismay at the loss of political urgency in post-Marxism and calls for an engagement with 'real existing identities' beyond its poststructuralist textualism (1992: 720, 730).

See also CAPITALISM; POSTCAPITALISM.

POSTMODERNISM

'Postmodernism' was first used in individual, idiosyncratic contexts in the late nineteenth and early twentieth centuries. It then gained its more familiar cultural meanings in American criticism in the 1950s and 1960s, and especially in the early 1980s, with the appearance of what have become, oddly enough, 'classic' texts such as Fredric Jameson's 'Postmodernism or the cultural logic of late capitalism' (1984) and the film *Blade Runner* (1981). From the earlier postwar uses onwards, however, the term has proved elastic and, for some, annoyingly elusive in its range of reference and attributions, whether in academic debate or across the arts, literature and culture. The difficulties of definition, if real, can be exaggerated, however, and are most interestingly seen as a symptom of the very mood or condition of indeterminacy the term is meant to describe. Beyond this, there are three useful distinctions that can be made: between the terms 'postmodernity' and 'postmodernism' and 'postmodern theory' – the last being the body of commentary upon the first two developments.

'Postmodernity' is commonly used to refer to a historical and cultural period, primarily in the advanced information and consumer societies of the west. The precise dating of this period is a matter of debate. (Jameson sees its beginnings in the 1950s and 1960s, David Harvey (1989), the economic slump of the 1970s. Others point to the 1980s.) Some, moreover, view this transition as a radical break with an earlier phase of 'MODERNITY', while others see an intensification and acceleration of existing processes. Such are the understandings of the prefix 'post-'. It is clear, all the same, that what is being discussed are the compound changes that have taken western capitalism into a new phase (whether continuous or radically distinct from a previous order) and are otherwise commonly described as 'late', 'multi-' or 'global' capitalism.

The term 'postmodernism', second, is used to refer to particular cultural texts and the sensibility or condition, referred to above, of the period of postmodernity. This aims to describe a prevailing postmodern AESTHETIC, evident in literary texts, films, TV, music, buildings, environments, street fashion and so on. This has been identified, notably by Jameson once more, as the conspicuous display of a formal self-consciousness, a borrowing from other texts and styles across GENRES in such a way that distinctions between high and low CULTURE, western and other cultures, or the past and present are broken down. The result is a self-ironic eclecticism and knowingness, experienced by media-wise audiences and readers, along with the postmodern artist, all well versed in the use of the key postmodernist devices of PASTICHE, PARODY, recycling and sampling. Postmodernism in this light is playful and allusive; its works are self-referential and intertextual METAFICTIONS – or meta-architecture or meta-film – exploiting a bank of past texts and diverse cultural forms, made available in the here and now, of a seeming 'perpetual present' by computerization and new media technologies. Jean-François Lyotard describes the experience of living what he calls this 'degree zero of contemporary general culture': 'one listens to reggae, watches a western, eats McDonald's food for lunch and local cuisine for dinner, wears Paris perfume in Tokyo and "retro" clothes in Hong Kong: knowledge is a matter of TV games' (1984: 76).

At its broadest therefore, this AESTHETIC, or lifestyle, is an expression of a general scepticism towards previous distinctions and certainties, not only in artistic or media culture, but in intellectual, political and EVERYDAY LIFE. These developments raise a number of questions (about the loss of originality and true historical sense, of authentic identity, values and standards in art and morality), and there are a range of responses to them: from those who deplore postmodernism's recycled emptiness and superficiality, to those who see it as a release from hidebound assumptions and elitist hierarchies.

Various contemporary theories within the wide orbit of POSTSTRUCTURALISM contribute to this debate and these, too, might be seen as a product of postmodernity, broadly conceived. Postmodern theory, however, refers in the first instance to a more precise set of arguments. Two are particularly influential and associated, respectively, with the French philosophers, Jean-François Lyotard and Jean Baudrillard. For Lyotard, the 'grand narratives' of human progress and liberation, rooted in ENLIGHTENMENT thought, have lost credibility as they have run aground in their opposites: totalitarian regimes and the arrogance of an assumed universal knowledge. 'Let us make war on totality,' he concludes in his *The Postmodern Condition* (1984; see also his 'Note on the meaning of "post-"', in Docherty [ed] 1993; and see METANARRATIVES). For Baudrillard, the logic of a media-saturated consumer society has detached the signifier from its signified in the terms of the structuralist SIGN. In a world of floating images and copies without originals, SIMULATIONS come to stand in for the 'real world' (Baudrillard 1988). These are evidently challenging arguments. Their combined effect is to present a double crisis, of legitimacy (since there are no founding principles), and of REPRESENTATION (since there is no reality for an IMAGE to represent).

Postmodernism and postmodernity are furthermore 'relational' terms. They imply a relation, first of all, with an earlier MODERNISM and MODERNITY. But there is also the question of the relation between what they themselves represent (in the respective spheres, crudely, of culture and society). Fredric Jameson's main contribution is to consider this relation. The main terms in play for him are suggested by his repeated gloss on postmodernism as 'the cultural logic' of 'late capitalism'. The main question his work poses is whether capitalism in this all-embracing, global phase allows for a critical theory and culture that are opposed to its effects (see COGNITIVE MAPPING). Other commentators are similarly concerned, in the realms of ethical and political discussion, to defend or redefine a critical standpoint on questions of truth, justice and democracy – terms deriving from the tradition of modernity, which postmodern arguments would seem to have undermined (Benhabib 1992; Nicholson and Seidman [eds] 1995).

The best general guides to postmodernism are Connor (1989 [rev. 1997]) and Bertens (1995). Anthologies of essays, with commentary, are contained in Brooker (1992) and Docherty (1993). For arguments opposed to postmodernism on moral and political grounds, or as mere intellectual fashion, see Callinicos (1989), Norris (1992), Eagleton (1996). More positive views are found in Huyssen (1986) and Hutcheon (1989). For its relation to FEMINISM, see Morris (1988), Nicholson ([ed] 1990). The question of black culture and postmodernism is examined by West (in Brooker 1992) and hooks (1990b). For some thinking on the movement 'beyond' postmodernism in visual media, see Brooker and Brooker ([eds] 1997).

The final implication of these many positions is that there can be no single authoritative account, still less a dictionary definition of postmodernism. More than any other term of contemporary theory – many of which argue to the same effect – it makes clear that there is a plurality of possible meanings: postmodernisms rather than one postmodernism.

See also GLOBALIZATION; POSTCAPITALISM; POST-FORDISM.

POSTSTRUCTURALISM

Like the other movements to which the prefix 'post-' has been attached (POSTCOLONIALISM, POSTMODERNISM), poststructuralism relates as both continuation and CRITIQUE to an earlier movement of ideas. Thus it shares with STRUCTURALISM a belief that meanings are produced within language or other encoded modes of signification analogous to language, but critiques the structuralist assumption that these meanings are ordered or 'centred' within a closed linguistic or cultural system. The most obvious example of poststructuralism in this sense is the DECONSTRUCTION of Jacques Derrida (see LOGOCENTRICISM, DIFFERENCE/*DIFFÉRANCE*). Other figures and theories have also been associated with poststructuralism. Perhaps the most instructive example is Roland Barthes (1915–1980) whose own work shows a transition from the systematic and would-be scientific procedures of structuralism to the playful and 'WRITERLY' features of poststructuralism. Other figures (Lacan, Foucault, Althusser) are more ambiguously related to poststructuralism, though they are frequently discussed as examples of it (Sturrock

1979; Sarup 1993). They can be said to have brought the terms of the poststructuralist critique of ESSENTIALISM and HUMANISM to different fields, namely PSYCHOANALYSIS, the history of ideas and MARXISM, and to have introduced a range of very influential concepts (IDEOLOGICAL STATE APPARATUS, INTERPELLATION, the IMAGINARY, the MIRROR-PHASE, DISCOURSE and POWER) now generally associated with poststructuralist practice.

It will be noticed that the figures named above are French. Some would interpret poststructuralism and its attendant (difficult) theorizations as a symptom of the displaced position of specifically French intellectuals in the period of the 1970s and 1980s. Callinicos (1989), for example, argues that after the failure of the radical social movements of the 1960s, signalled by the 'events' in Paris of May 1968, erstwhile politically committed INTELLECTUALS moved into the realm of theory or 'theoretical' as opposed to 'political' practice. Other figures, associated with postmodernism (Lyotard, Baudrillard), emerging from this same CONJUNCTURE arguably confirm this tendency.

Poststructuralism has, of course, had an extensive influence beyond France (see Easthope 1988; and SCREEN THEORY). However, it has also met with frustration and resistance from those committed to contrary positions in other intellectual and political cultures. The poststructuralist critique of the authority of the AUTHOR and the assumption of fixed meaning and notions of the unified SUBJECT, for example, as well as its apparent undermining of notions of 'the real', have met with scepticism or rejection from those committed to traditional AESTHETICS, and to versions of HUMANISM and MATERIALISM. The response of the British socialist historian E.P. Thompson (1978) to the work of Louis Althusser was a prominent case in point. At the same time, a counter-tendency, emerging from what Callinicos, after Edward Said, identifies as the '"worldly" poststructuralism' of Michel Foucault (1989: 68), emerged in the politically engaged project of CULTURAL MATERIALISM.

See also INTERTEXTUALITY; NARRATIVE; TEXTUALITY.

POST-THEORY

'Post-theory' has been primarily a movement in literary theory and criticism, though it has ramifications across the Arts and Humanities. 'Theory', with its commanding capital letter and associated star names – especially the cast of (mostly) French intellectuals associated with varieties of STRUCTURALISM, POSTSTRUCTURALISM and POSTMODERNISM (Barthes, Althusser, Foucault, Lacan, Derrida, Baudrillard, Lyotard, Kristeva, Cixous, Spivak, Bhabha and Fredric Jameson) had dominated thinking in the 1970s and 1980s and took deep root in Departments of English and related areas of study. The enthusiasm for 'high theory', so-called, had been attended by anxiety and frustration from the outset because of its perceived 'difficulty' and its relevance to the traditional study of literary texts 'as literature' (rather than philosophy or psychoanalysis or Sociology).

A number of studies on the cusp of, and into, the new millennium suggested that we had arrived at the 'end of theory', or more ambiguously at the moment of 'after' or 'post' theory. Among such works were Valentine Cunningham's *Reading After Theory* (2002), Jean-Michel Rabaté's *The Future of Theory* (2002) and Terry Eagleton's *After Theory* (2003), as well as the collections, *Post-Theory: New Directions in Criticism* (1999), *What's Left of Theory?* (2000) and *Life. After. Theory* (2003). In the event, what, by common consent, was thought to be over was the age of 'Theory', with its list of 'isms' and the need (or was it a fashion?) to pursue the latest title from Paris. This spelled less the 'end of theory' than a readiness to think of theor*ies* in the plural and of theoretical activity as a sceptical questioning of taken-for-granted attitudes and positions: 'a pugnacious critique of common-sense notions' which 'offers not a set of solutions but the prospect of further thought'. In this respect, theory is 'endless' (Culler 1997, 4, 15,120).

This common understanding was joined by a desire to return to the proper study of literary texts and thus to the question of 'how to read'. One response was a return to the activity of 'close reading'. As Valentine Cunningham (2002) put it, agreeing that 'We all – all of us readers – come after theory', the primary activity of studying literature called for 'tact': the 'gentle' 'caring', 'loving touch' of an 'unmanipulative reading' in 'close-up, hands-on-textual encounters' (3, 122). A more emphatic commitment to the priority of the literary opposed to the grander, 'political activism by another name' of Theory-led criticism called for the adoption of 'surface reading' (see Best and Marcus [eds] 2009, 2; and Love, 2010). Others, meanwhile, have wished to retain the political edge of theory's questioning attitude; the 'systematic reflection on our guiding assumptions', which Eagleton deemed 'indispensable' (2003). The collection *Theory after 'Theory'* (2011) edited by Attridge and Elliot, for example, confirms at once theory's diversity and the vibrancy of its contributions to broader debates in aesthetics, biopolitics, neoliberalism, and ETHICS (See also Eagleton, 2013, and Selden, *et al.*, 2017, Chapter 12).

Currently, after over a decade of 'post-theory', a 'turn' or 'return' to the *literary* would seem to coexist with continuing theorizing under its banner; a situation, that is to say, where there is not so much 'more theory' as 'more *about* theory', and where the automatic deference paid to charismatic figures of the recent past has receded. Potts and Stouts's edited collection *Theory Aside* (2014), for example, does not put theory to one side so much as pointedly look away from the canonic names of 'Theory' to neglected or forgotten thinkers (the psychiatrist and behavioural economist George Ainslie; the sociologist Erving Goffman; the 'new critic' I.A. Richards) who belong to unknown or rejected histories and can be recruited anew in the present.

Other works 'about theory' of the middle 2010s include accounts of theory's long history (Rodowick 2014); its reception (Currie, on Derrida in the USA, 2013); the strenuous pleasure of an encounter with its 'strangeness' (Thomas 2013); or its place within a globalized world (Leitch 2014 and Rabaté 2014). On the latter question, Leitch sees theory as now embedded and diversified, 'fractalised', across a range of topics (Animal Studies, ecocriticism, Affect Studies, Subaltern or Trauma Studies), and as such, in tune with postmodern pluralism and with the expanded, marketizing aims of the corporate university (see also Brown and Carasso, 2013). Rabaté, on the other hand, sees in theory's alertness to difference and the untranslatable an ethical and political critique of the homogenizing tendencies under GLOBALIZATION. These views share a degree of binary thinking – or in Currie's case (2013) inspect this – seeing a unified past, a steady state or original ('school' or commanding position in theory) and its disaggregated or deformed appropriation in the age of postmodern pluralism. On the other hand, globalization is seen as homogenizing, and theory a source of difference and diversity. (See Winters's (2015) survey of these works and on this tendency).

The simple truth is that social and economic conditions, historically or in the present, are neither unified nor fractalized, but both. And this, as Attridge and Elliott and Potts and Stout, in their different ways, demonstrate, is true also of theory itself. Somewhat newer names, (Georgio Agamben, Alan Badiou and Jacques Rancière) have currency, as in Attridge and Elliott; and forgotten thinkers can be recalled. And even the 'big names' of the past: Athusser, Barthes, Derrida, Foucault, Jameson are open to new understandings, whether of familiar or hitherto unpublished material; the latter appearing, moreover, in the changed circumstances of a new present (Winters 2015, 49).

See also AESTHETIC(S); DIGITAL HUMANITIES; SPECULATIVE REALISM; WORLD LITERATURE.

POWER

The most influential theorizations of power in contemporary theory have derived from the writings of the French philosopher, Michel Foucault (1926–1984). Foucault (1979, 1980a) understands power as associated, not with repression or inhibition, or straightforward domination, but as working through institutionalized and accustomed DISCOURSES that open up delimited forms of action, knowledge and being. In this way, the exercise of power constitutes, as it simultaneously controls, individual SUBJECTS. Institutionalized discourses have authority and legitimacy by definition, by virtue of being so institutionalized. The language of a specific discourse within a given system and society will therefore play a vital part in constituting subjective and social identities. Small changes will also have their effect, as one can see in the official language used to describe the unemployed as being not 'on the dole' as in an older language, but in receipt of 'benefit' or 'Jobseeker's Allowance', or as gaining 'work experience' in 'training' and 'retraining schemes'. One might think, too, of how 'students' are constituted by the discursive practices of governments, education authorities, and FE and HE institutions. These, again, produce an enabling, but regulatory, set of discourses that make it possible, within the terms and conditions established, to be a student, but deny this identity to those outside these structures.

In Foucault's understanding, power is dispersed and without a specific source or AGENCY, and this clearly affects forms of resistance to it. To see power as anonymous in this way is likely to promote a pessimistic or sceptical attitude (as in some poststructuralist intellectual circles), but does not recommend any collective or direct form of political action. If there is nothing outside of discourse, there can be no appeal to an autonomous or essential self or idea of absolute freedom; DOMINANT discourse must therefore be contested in discourse, by an alternative language that challenges and reforms it from within. The implication of Foucault's work is that such resistance and contestation will be conducted in local arenas and struggles over single issues: in the realm of 'micro-politics'. For this reason, his thinking is often contrasted with notions of power and opposition within MARXISM and some traditions of FEMINISM, both of which have appealed to collective identities (of CLASS or of women) on universal rather than simply local or specific issues. However, such universalist or 'metaphysical' assumptions are challenged, not only by Foucault's work, but by much poststructuralist and postmodern theory.

Definitions of power therefore affect our ideas of the individual and society, the object of study, and the scope of the intellectual or cultural critic's work and influence. It might be noted on this last issue that while viewing power as constitutive and inescapable, Foucault writes unambiguously 'that the analysis, elaboration, and bringing into question of power relations... [are] a permanent political task in all social relations' (1983: 223).

See also HEGEMONY; IDEOLOGY; INTELLECTUALS.

PRAGMATISM

The belief that an idea acquires meaning, VALUE or truth by dint of its successful adoption in the changing world of practical affairs. The pragmatist tradition in Europe and especially in the United States has followed somewhat different emphases, seeking to establish a measure of impersonal efficiency of individual and social benefit, a guide to principled but flexible action, or a method of inquiry, but is consistently oriented towards practical consequences rather than universal CODES or laws. It has come to more recent attention through the work of the American philosopher, Richard Rorty (1931–), who has interpreted poststructuralist indeterminacy, and the work of Jacques Derrida in particular, in a way that makes it compatible with American traditions of pragmatist philosophy. Early thinkers in this movement were Charles Sanders Peirce (see also SEMIOLOGY), William James, and John Dewey, and they have received renewed attention in recent American academic life.

Rorty's position (1980, 1982) is an attractive one in so far as he has absorbed the scepticism of continental poststructuralist theory, yet believes a sense of social conscience and purpose can be retained in ways appropriate to a world of postmodern contingency. His deflation of the traditional claims of philosophy – which can no longer offer to arbitrate, he contends, on abstract matters of truth, or appearance and reality – means that he writes and speaks in an accessible, conversational manner. At the same time, his reading of Derrida has been seen to encourage a mistaken relativism (Norris 1985), his style has been thought folksy, and his general position criticized for the bland assumption that he and American liberalism can stand as the model for political culture worldwide.

See also DECONSTRUCTION; PLURALISM.

PREFERRED MEANING

See CODE; NEGOTIATION.

PROBLEMATIC

Aside from its general use to indicate a set of problems, or in the verb form 'problematize', meaning to make or reveal as questionable, this term refers more specifically to a set of simultaneously enabling and restricting conditions. Louis Althusser employs the term in this sense, so as, as he writes, 'to designate the particular unity of a theoretical formation' (1969: 32). The problematic, it might be said, is the set of questions a theory or argument answers, the framework that gives a term or concept its meaning. Insofar as this framework presents a unity, it functions as an IDEOLOGY, reconciling contradictions, but setting limits to what is thinkable, given its particular starting point.

The problematic informing liberal HUMANISM, for example, is comprised quite centrally of a belief in the freedom of the individual. The assumed model of this individual is likely also to be white, male and European. To consider instead the social collective, or women of colour, as a priority means shifting to a different problematic – one that questions the coherence of the first and shows it as, in fact, founded on a limited application of the concept of freedom. In the terms of Althusser's translator, 'a problematic is *not* a world-view... it is centred on the *absence* of problems and concepts within the problematic as much as their presence' (1969: 253–4). A stricter meaning of 'to problematize', therefore, would be to disclose the contradictions and what is not said or thought within the unifying framework of a given problematic. In Althusser's terms, this requires a SYMPTOMATIC READING.

See also PARADIGM.

PRODUCTION

An emphasis on production is associated with MODERNITY and with MARXISM, as is evident in the identification of the proletariat as the productive CLASS and the agent of social and political change in a system of industrial production. The term has been mostly employed consequently in political economy and social theory, though it has been adopted more broadly. The changed nature of post-industrial production and corresponding changes in patterns of consumption is commonly understood in the context of GLOBALIZATION.

An analogy between art and industrial labour was vigorously asserted in Soviet art of the revolutionary period and in the 'machine aesthetic' of European Futurist movements. Walter Benjamin's influential notion of 'the author as producer' (1973a) inherited this usage and implied a re-conceptualization of the figure of the AUTHOR from lone genius to that of artistic or cultural worker engaged in contemporary modes of production.

In a related – but less polemical – direction, an emphasis on production has been evident in the more recent work of COMMUNITY groups seeking to employ contemporary means of production (printing, photography, video, the INTERNET) for their own ends. This emphasis has long been evident in writing groups, and in spheres of art and drama. However, although this latter work is often directly associated with questions of pedagogy, its connection with the agendas of mainstream academic theory is less certain.

In broader terms, a concern with production within the various forms of critical or cultural study has signalled a turning away from the perceived limitations of textual analysis to a study of the ideologies and institutions of production, or to work within policy studies, where there is a close engagement between academic 'think-tanks' – or specialist centres – and agencies in business and government.

See also CAPITALISM; CONSUMERISM; CULTURE INDUSTRIES.

PSYCHOANALYSIS

Psychoanalysis was founded by Sigmund Freud (1836–1939) as a study of mental processes and the therapeutic treatment of neurosis. In particular, Freud's theory of the UNCONSCIOUS established a basis of explanation for psychic processes in SEXUALITY. In the 1920s, Freud introduced the well-known distinction between the id, the ego and the superego. This model suggested that the untrammelled instinctual drives (the id) and the constraining mores of society (superego) could be brought to a point of reconciliation in the ego or social individual. The implication that the purpose of psychoanalysis was to heal a perceived psychic division and so 'normalize' the patient was taken up especially by 'ego-psychology' in the United States. This was rejected by the radical French psychoanalyst, Jacques Lacan (1901–1981) who maintained that Freud's major discovery had been the Unconscious and that this revealed how the subject was irremediably split. This emphasis, along with Lacan's appropriation of a structuralist linguistic model, aligned psychoanalysis with other trends in poststructuralist thought opposed to the humanist assumption of the unified, coherent SUBJECT.

Lacan's semiotic reading of Freud also confirmed the rhetorical and NARRATIVE nature of psychoanalysis itself. This is evident, not only in the description of psychoanalytic practice as the 'talking cure', in which a patient (the 'analysand') tells their story to the analyst who then interprets and shapes this, much like a text (Bowie 1987; Brooks 1994), but also in the derivation from literature and figurative construction of leading concepts. Many of these have, in turn, had a wide influence on literary and cultural criticism, and across the Humanities (Wright 1984; Donald [ed] 1991). In addition to the theory of the Unconscious and the general notion of the repressed, the most influential are probably the OEDIPAL COMPLEX, the UNCANNY, TRANSFERENCE, *NACHTRÄGLICHKEIT* (principally from Freud); the MIRROR-PHASE and the IMAGINARY/SYMBOLIC/REAL (principally from Lacan). These have been employed chiefly in the discussion of SUBJECTIVITY, SEXUALITY and SEXUAL DIFFERENCE, but in relation also to particular modes or GENRES: the GOTHIC and fantastic, or the uses of memory in autobiography and historical fictions, for example. Psychoanalytic approaches have often been combined in such readings with feminist and poststructuralist strategies, although this engagement has been marked as much by debate and revisions to major premises, especially concerning the Oedipal complex, as by their adoption.

An alternative tradition in psychoanalysis has been associated with Melanie Klein (1882–1960) and her psychoanalysis of children. The child is seen to feel love and hatred for the object of the mother, alternating between a 'persecutory anxiety' and a 'depressive anxiety', which respectively describe the fear of attack from the hated object and a wish to restore a loving relationship. Although Klein was not herself a feminist, her work has been welcomed by feminist scholars as eliciting a pre-Oedipal relationship between women and the mother (Mitchell [ed] 1986; *Woman: A Cultural Review* 1990; Rose 1993). For further commentary on the influence of psychoanalytic theory on feminism see Wright [ed] (1992).

A strikingly polemical challenge to the perceived political implications of the Oedipal complex has been advanced by Gilles Deleuze and Félix Guatarli (1984). They view the emphasis on lack and unfulfilled DESIRE in the Freudian notion of the Unconscious as complicit with the deprivations of capitalism, and instead propose a liberating 'schizoanalysis' in which a released libidinal energy will escape or 'deterritorialize' the repressive constraints of bourgeois society.

Finally, the scientific credentials of Freud's methods and findings have also been criticized. He has been charged, for example, by Frederick Crews (1997) with having manipulated both patients and evidence (a view that in part accords with the feminist critique of Freud's authoritarian treatment of woman patients in particular – see Hélène Cixous's restaging of one of Freud's most famous case histories, *Portrait of Dora,* 1976). Crews' criticism also has implications for the topical issue of 'false memory' syndrome and the question of child sexual abuse (see also King 2000).

See also RHIZOME.

PSYCHOGEOGRAPHY

A term associated particularly with Guy Debord (1931–1994), political theorist, activist and film-maker, and co-founder in 1957 of the *Situationist International.* Debord and colleagues proposed a set of cultural strategies to undermine the commodification of EVERYDAY LIFE under contemporary capitalism. This, Debord theorized in *Society of the Spectacle* (1967) and *Comments on the Society of the Spectacle* (1998). Psychogeography draws attention to the emotional or psychic aspects of urban experience, and to the spontaneous encounter with and reflection on this experience. Thus, in a brief table of definitions published in the *Situationist International* (No. 1 1958), it is defined as: 'The study of the specific effects of the geographical environment, consciously organised or not, on the emotions and behaviour of individuals' (Knabb [ed] 1981:45).

Debord further associates two key strategies with this practice: 'dérive' and 'détournement'. His 'Theory of the dérive' was first published in 1956. Its literal translation is 'drifting' but it entails a more active and purposefully disorienting strategy than this suggests. Debord defines it as 'An experimental mode of behaviour linked to the conditions of urban society: a technique of transient passage through varied ambiances' (Knabb [ed] 1981: 45). This, the Situationists practised in groups over sustained periods of time using false or new maps. 'Détournement' (in English 'diversion' or 'rerouting') is a more general category. Thus, Debord writes of the 'détournement of preexisting aesthetic elements' and their combination through the 'situationist use' of past means or media into a new form or 'superior construction of a milieu' superseding the previous work and its assumed meaning. Détournement therefore resembles the ideas of DEFAMILIARIZATION and ESTRANGEMENT first developed in MODERNISM, though the Situationists meant to give it a more politically combative than aesthetic accent. Also, 'détournement' is thought to have a wide potential application, to architectural styles and the built environment and to everyday situations, with their associated gestures, manners and rituals. The combined effect of the 'dérive' and 'détournement', therefore, is that an urban environment is encountered as an EVENT or 'situation' in all its limitations, risks and possibilities as if by an acutely observant stranger (see THE EVENT). It is newly experienced and perceived, and thus in effect destabilized, as is the urban mentality of the psychogeographer.

Situationist tactics influenced the strikes and student demonstrations of 'the events' in May 1968 in Paris, in which Debord was active, and have subsequently inspired many subcultural anarchistic artistic and political movements, notably the punks of the 1970s. Debord's thinking also finds echoes in other areas of contemporary theory and cultural practice. His account of the 'society of the SPECTACLE', for example, informs the later emphasis on 'SIMULATION' in the writings of the postmodern philosopher, Jean Baudrillard, while the idea of psychogeography belongs in a history of related notions in modernist and postmodern cultural aesthetics. The figure of the psychogeographer has obvious affinities, for example, with the earlier idea of the urban FLÂNEUR and draws also on the ideas of the surrealists on the modern city, as explored, notably, in Louis Aragon's *Paris Peasant* (1926) and André Breton's *Nadja* (1928), both set in Paris. In recent years, the idea of psychogeography and its associated strategies has attracted renewed interest in the study of the CITY and urban SPACE by scholars in the fields of Cultural and Literary Geography. There are affinities here, for example, with the idea of the 'mental map' developed by the urban geographer, Kevin Lynch, and with Fredric Jameson's concept of COGNITIVE MAPPING (see also Saddler 1998). A contemporary writer to whom these ideas are particularly relevant is the British novelist Iain Sinclair (see Brooker 2002).

See also DETERRITORIALIZATION; EVERYDAY LIFE; NOMADISM.

PUBLIC SPHERE

A concept developed notably by the German social theorist, Jürgen Habermas (1929–). Habermas (1989) is concerned in particular with the composition of the bourgeois public sphere in the eighteenth century. This was a COMMUNITY of lawyers, diplomats, doctors, pastors, scientists, scholars, schoolteachers, merchants and manufacturers, as well as writers: the new class, in short, of an emerging society who were united by a faith in ENLIGHTENMENT reason and an attendant rational DISCOURSE on science, politics, literature and manners. This discourse circulated in the clubs and coffee houses of the period (of which, there were reputedly over 3,000 in London) and in a new type of political journal such as, in England, the *Tatler* and *Spectator*. These publications helped establish a consensual public opinion, critical of both state and aristocracy. Habermas sees a subsequent loss of this unity across political, aesthetic and moral spheres, and looks for a revitalized public sphere in the present, founded on 'communicative reason' and a belief in the rules guiding discussion to consensus and truth.

Terry Eagleton (1984) points out how modern criticism has also derived from the eighteenth-century public sphere. However, he detects an ideological contradiction between its belief in transcendent rational discourse and the CLASS position of its members, and points also, as have others, to its blatant GENDER bias. While claiming universality, the public sphere was revealed as partial in its distinction, on the one hand, from the 'private sphere' of women and the family and, on the other, from the proletarian sphere of working-class publications and discussion. If contemporary criticism is therefore impotent or sidelined, as Eagleton argues, it cannot look to the earlier bourgeois public sphere for the model of a new interventionist role. He believes Raymond Williams was brought to work in isolation because of the lack of a supportive 'counterpublic sphere' of active socialist opinion, but sees an alternative example and inspiration in the women's movement and contemporary FEMINISM (1984: 118–19).

Others have similarly sketched alternative forms of a 'counterpublic sphere'. Carter *et al.* ([eds] 1993) introduce the idea of a heterogeneous public, physically and culturally located in the CITY. This conception, they oppose to both liberal and communitarian versions of the public sphere: 'the site of contestation between groups of distinct located... identities' (1993: xiv). Elsewhere, Homi Bhabha (1991) considers a hybridized, postmodern, 'public sphere, posited as a feminised body of memory and imagination', a conception, he says, that will make new kinds of social affiliation possible – 'those which come through pleasure, eroticism, friendship and a profound rearticulation of private values and public virtues' (1991: 65).

Eagleton's 'counterpublic' (or 'proletarian') public sphere would need, he says, to engage with the 'culture industry', to resist the influence of the 'mass-mediated public sphere' that dominates the construction of SUBJECTIVITY in the form of commodity production (1984: 123). A somewhat different view is taken elsewhere. John Thompson argues, in a discussion of Habermas, that we will not successfully understand the nature of modern public life if we 'interpret the evergrowing role of mediated communication as a historical fall from grace' (1994: 98). COMMUNICATION media, from print to electronic global systems, have created a new form of 'publicness', he suggests, to the point where individuals are networked across radically different spatial–temporal locales. A more developed notion of the role of the media has been proposed by John Hartley (1996). Following the Russian cultural semiotician Yuri Lotman's notion of a 'semiosphere', he proposes we recognize a 'mediasphere' operating as a two-way mediation between an inner political–economic–public sphere and an outer textual–cultural semiosphere. He goes on to identify 'a newly privatized, feminized, suburban, consumerized public sphere' as the dispersed 'image saturated space' where major contemporary issues on the environment, ethnic, sexual and youth movements are generated and debated (1996: 156–7).

See also CONVERGENCE; ELITE; INTELLECTUALS; NETWORK.

QUEER THEORY

Queer theory is a development of the 1990s, drawing on the earlier work of gay studies and gay activism (especially the protest groups ActUp and Outrage) from the early 1980s and the more recent high-profile developments in lesbian theory and criticism from the late 1980s. Further influences are the study of GENDER within FEMINISM and the iconoclastic impulses of POSTMODERNISM. The term 'queer' is a provocative description that appropriates an earlier, generally offensive, description of gay life and turns it to advantage. To 'be queer' is to openly adopt a non-'straight' life, while 'to queer' is to estrange or defamiliarize identities, texts and attitudes that are taken for granted and assumed to have fixed meanings. Such meanings are understood to endorse heterosexuality as a social-sexual norm. Queer theory is not, therefore, a separatist movement claiming an essence of gayness; rather, it emphasizes the constructedness, plurality and ambivalence of sexual identities. This makes heterosexuality one identity among others. It follows that sexual identities are malleable and a matter of choice or personal style.

In academic work, a major influence on queer theory, illustrating its intersection with feminist theory, has been the notion of performative SEXUALITY developed by Judith Butler (1990, 1993). Butler argues for the cancelling of all sexual IDENTITY *per se,* including the identification of 'lesbian' as a positive term. 'I would like to have it permanently unclear what precisely that sign means' (1990). In this very vagueness lies a strategy of disruption, built upon a concept of identity as improvised, discontinuous and in a process of becoming. Elsewhere, Jonathan Dollimore and Alan Sinfield in the UK have developed a more materialist version of queer studies in re-readings of Shakespeare, Renaissance and other literary texts. The respective theoretical sources for this thinking are Michel Foucault on DISCOURSE and sexuality, and the cultural materialist tradition inspired by Raymond Williams.

The orientation of both traditions, however, is towards diversity and resistance (Weeks 1985). A further consequence of the postmodern 'query' of boundaries is that academic boundaries – between Literary and Cultural Studies, Sociology, History, Philosophy – are also unsettled. Are transsexuality or cross-dressing topics for SEMIOLOGY, PSYCHOANALYSIS, feminism, gender, men's or Theatre Studies? Queer theory is therefore a fittingly eclectic and thoroughgoing critique of all essentializing intellectual and socio-sexual assumptions. Reservations about this somewhat apocalyptic rendering of the world as unrestrained discourse would qualify the indiscriminate celebration of 'deviance' (Grosz 1996) and return us in a more pessimistic reading of Foucault to the material constraints upon PERFORMATIVITY and to the very physicality of the BODY as limiting the idea that it is a text available for deviant embodiment; AIDS, as a case in point, has, for many, provided very material evidence of how conceptions of the body and sexual identity are controlled by social ideologies (Benson 1997: 152–60).

See also COMPULSORY HETEROSEXUALITY; ESSENTIALISM; POSTHUMAN; SEXUAL DIFFERENCE.

RACE

Race is a problematic category. The anthropological description of human races (note that we speak also of 'the human race') as Caucasian, Negroid and Mongoloid is based on identifiable genetic or phenotypical differences, but, given the possible genetic variation within races and the effects of migration, resettlement and intermarriage, the existence of races, as such, is itself often disputed (Miles 1989; Donald and Rattansi [eds] 1992). This accounts for the frequent use of the term in inverted commas; the implication being that it is a social and ideological construction and not a fact of biological nature.

If we do accept phenotypical differences as evidence of racial identities, the complication arises that the idea of an invariant racial nature or type can be used to justify social inequalities and an assumed, biologically given, hierarchy of intellectual abilities. A biological definition becomes appropriated within the realm of CULTURE for the purposes of asserting racial superiority. The result is one form of racism. Also, once this kind of connection is made, the term 'race' can be used to refer, in a process of 'racialization', to those who might otherwise claim an 'ethnic' IDENTITY (Jews in Nazi Germany, African-Americans in the USA, or Asians in the UK). A racialized description is used to brand such groups with the stereotypes that mark them as the inferior 'OTHER'.

The study of race, therefore, frequently develops as a study of racism and racist IDEOLOGY. There are three basic active forms this ideology might take: violent assault; institutionalized racism (exercised, for example, through poor provision in education, healthcare, housing, and/or discrimination and unequal pay in the workplace); and, third, through the expression of 'COMMON SENSE' attitudes based on unexamined and prejudiced assumptions (even of the kind that appear to make a positive statement, as in 'blacks are good dancers'). Sections of the media and forms of POPULAR entertainment, such as sitcoms and stand-up comics, can also play a part in reinforcing such taken-for-granted attitudes by naturalizing or making them permissible. We should note, too, that these forms and expressions of racism have changed historically as the objects of racism have also changed: from the slave trade, through colonization to twentieth-century patterns of immigration, making in the UK, for example, Jews, West Indians and Pakistanis the object of racist attitudes.

These issues are complicated, yet again, by the fact that some groups – notably blacks in the USA – have wanted at times in their history to claim a racial identity for themselves and in the process to present a positive association of being black with certain cultural activities (jazz, sport and entertainment, including dance). In this thinking, race is understood as combining certain physical characteristics – above all, skin colour – with a history and cultural tradition, and perhaps country or place of origin, or high achievement (Africa, the southern states, New Orleans,

Harlem). Race, that is to say, is expanded beyond biology to embrace a set of cultural and historical associations normally associated with descriptions of ETHNICITY. An affirmation of identity along these lines can also take an essentialist or separatist form, however, which militates against change or syncretism, and is, when aggressively maintained, similar – in form at least – to defences of white American or Aryan racial purity.

A number of academic disciplines and areas of intellectual work – including Sociology, education, FEMINISM and Literary, Media and Cultural Studies – are concerned with the theoretical issues outlined above, as well as with the social forms and textual REPRESENTATIONS taken by expressions of race and racism. Within British Cultural Studies, the collection, *The Empire Writes Back* (1982) and the subsequent writings in the UK and the USA of Paul Gilroy, Hazel Carby, bell hooks, Cornell West and others, have drawn attention to the exclusion of questions of race and ethnicity from a hitherto ethnocentric Cultural Studies agenda (see ETHNOCENTRICISM). Gilroy (1987, 1993), in particular, has stressed the need for a historical, rather than sociological, perspective on these questions and for a newly theorized consideration of race, CLASS and national identity in the context of wider social and economic relations. At the same time, this thinking has provided a full and subtle context for the study of black representations and cultural production in the media, film and writing. Further work in this field has also sought to include considerations of GENDER and SEXUALITY within this fuller sense of identity. Many would agree that this work has been inspired by women of colour, often writing in response to their own experience of the combined effects of racism, sexism and class prejudice (see hooks 1981, 1990a; Carby 1987; Spivak 1987; Trinh 1989; Parma 1990; Anzaldúa 1990).

See also DIASPORA; ESSENTIALISM; HYBRIDITY; MULTICULTURALISM; POSTCOLONIALISM.

READERLY/WRITERLY

A distinction between *lisible* ('readerly') and *scriptable* ('writerly') texts was drawn by the theorist and critic Roland Barthes (1915–1980) in *S/Z* (1975), a study of Honoré de Balzac's short story 'Sarrasine'. Barthes's premise is that readerly texts employ the conventions of traditional nineteenth-century realism, while writerly texts employ the disruptive AESTHETICS of MODERNISM or of the AVANT-GARDE. The first console readers in fulfilling expectations of structure and meaning, and confirm them in a position of satisfied passivity. The writerly text, on the other hand, is more disturbing and the reader necessarily more active: the writerly text is 'ourselves writing', says Barthes. It resists closure, presenting instead a 'plurality of entrances, the opening of networks, the infinity of languages' (1975: 5). In fact, Barthes' analysis of Balzac's story complicates this distinction, since, although *Sarrasine* is a putatively realist text, his extensive analysis of its several CODES opens it to multiple meanings. This would suggest that the nature and meaning of texts are decided by readers rather than their intrinsic form. Barthes's subsequent study, *The Pleasure of the Text* (1976), transposes the distinction between kinds of texts to the respective sensations of the reader, perhaps in recognition of this. Here, he describes the experience associated with the 'readerly text' as PLEASURE and the experience of the 'writerly text' as JOUISSANCE ('ecstasy' or 'bliss').

Barthes's discussion derives in both respects from earlier essays (1977b), on the distinction between the open 'text' and closed 'work', and from his emphasis, in the celebrated 'The death of the author', upon the active role of the reader in producing the meanings of texts (see AUTHOR). A comparable distinction between 'open' and 'closed' texts is inflected in different ways by Umberto Eco (1979b) and by Catherine Belsey (1980). Eco views texts such as *Finnegans Wake* and atonal music as 'open', and comics and popular genre forms as 'closed', while Belsey, in a more rigorously politicized project, seeks to distinguish between the attempted ideological CLOSURE effected by the texts of 'classic REALISM' and more open, 'interrogative', non-realist texts. Her concern is with literature's complicity in the construction of the liberal humanist SUBJECT and with alternatives to this.

See also ÉCRITURE/WRITING; TEXTUALITY.

READING

'Reading' is one of the most expansive of terms in the study of CULTURE, and frequently used synonymously with the practice of interpretation and the analysis of texts and DISCOURSES. These terms are themselves used to refer beyond the literally textual to social processes and institutions that, if not seen as texts themselves, are understood to be accessible only through semiotic or textual material. The use of the term 'reading' in such studies therefore enforces the sense, especially common in poststructuralist-influenced academic work, that the social and cultural world is constructed, rather than given, and that its textual or SIGN systems must therefore be 'read' if they are to produce social meanings.

Studies of reading are as pervasive as its practice and occur across the human sciences in empirical and theoretical forms in psychology and education, where 'standards' of reading and the evaluation of these are a matter of major debate, as well as in literary and cultural study. In the latter, these are generally subsumed under AUDIENCE studies. Attention is given here to developments in Literary Studies – although studies of the reading of POPULAR fiction are generally felt to cross this disciplinary divide (see Radway 1984 and RECEPTION).

Within more traditional Literary Studies, so-called 'reader-response theory' is often compared with the parallel movement in European-based 'reception theory' (Holub 1984; Freund 1987). There are differences of emphasis between these tendencies: the first is less concerned with AESTHETIC value or the process of reading, for example, than with the PRODUCTION of meaning. Also, in terms of their general philosophical orientation, reception theory belongs to a tradition of HERMENEUTICS (the philosophy and practice of interpretation) while reader-response theory is more indebted to STRUCTURALISM and POSTSTRUCTURALISM. For all this, they are fundamentally alike in considering the activity of reading in terms of what can be called 'notional' rather than actual, empirical readers (but see again

Radway 1984). The two kinds of reader are sometimes confused, but this is an important and necessary distinction (comparable to the distinction between the ADDRESSEE and actual receiver of MESSAGES in the model of COMMUNICATION).

Work in both fields has consequently theorized a range of types of notional reader or reading position: among them the 'narratee', the 'implied', 'ideal', 'mock', 'model', or 'informed' reader. One such reader is theorized within reader-response criticism by Jonathan Culler (1982) in terms of the idea of 'competence' – a concept borrowed from the linguist Noam Chomsky's idea of the linguistic competence necessary to the effective user of a language. Culler uses the idea to describe what is in effect an informed or educated reader's assumptions about the language, form and types of meaning produced by kinds of literary works (the use of NARRATIVE conventions in a prose novel; of stanzaic form, free verse, metaphor and ambiguity in poetry; the expectation of an overall formal and semantic coherence).

In a sense this, and the sometimes very similar categories named above (of the 'ideal', 'implied', 'model' reader), all describe the way the CODES that constitute a work also constitute its readers and inscribe these readers or 'reading positions' within the text. These approaches also tend to think of readers as seeking and occupying these positions (a 'mock reader' would do so provisionally), and tend therefore also to endorse the conventions they mean to describe. Though many readers and readings may in this sense be conventional, there are also dissatisfied and dissenting, but still competent readers, and non-conformist reading positions. Stanley Fish's notion of an 'INTERPRETIVE COMMUNITY' approaches this recognition in that Fish sees readers as determining the meanings of texts rather than being determined by them (or the position they appear to construct). Nevertheless, the emphasis in Fish's notion is on the consensus of reading strategies established within the interpretive community rather than on dissent.

A recognition of more critical, dissenting – or what might be termed more 'eccentric' – reading strategies has occurred in the more consciously politicized agendas of MARXISM and FEMINISM, and in the cultivation of the MARGINal and parenthetical aspects of texts encouraged by poststructuralism. An example of the first occurs in the practice of SYMPTOMATIC READING, which assumes that works are symptoms of ideological meanings of which they are not fully conscious or in control. These more unwitting meanings are seen to cross the grain of formal conventions, and encode or structure works in contradictory rather than coherent ways. Psychoanalytic readings similarly look for the 'unsaid' and repressed in texts, often in a theoretical alliance with a poststructuralist or feminist perspective.

The eminent American critic, Harold Bloom (1930–), to some degree influenced by Derrida and poststructuralism and PSYCHOANALYSIS, could be said to be interested in eccentric, non-conformist readings. In *The Anxiety of Influence* (1973), he discusses how a 'strong poet' resists the authority of his (*sic*) precursor – a relationship Bloom considers as equivalent to the Oedipal relationship between patriarch and son. The new 'strong poet' will absorb, and in some ways throw off, the early model in order to assert his own literary IDENTITY. Bloom extends this notion to the general practice of reading. Such strong and creative readings by readers rather than poets, are, as he terms them, 'misreadings' or acts of 'misprision', which turn the text in a new direction.

See also CONVERGENCE; DECONSTRUCTION; INTERTEXTUALITY; POST-THEORY.

REALISM

Traditional theories of realism are based on a binary model of art and the world. This REFLECTIONist or mimetic view is characteristic of the nineteenth-century novel and theatre, and has carried over into documentary literature and photography, mainstream film and much contemporary television. Conventional realism of this type is commonly seen to support an organicist AESTHETIC that values the coherent and well-formed work of art, and to bolster a humanist IDEOLOGY of the unified self-determining human SUBJECT (Belsey 1980). In 'socialist realism', associated especially with the Soviet Union, but evident elsewhere, as in the Marxist-influenced art of the USA in the 1930s and 1940s, a putatively reflectionist model was put to the service of party dogma. Critics saw this mode as representing less the truth of the world than a desired or disguised version of it (see Williams 1961). The related idea of 'critical realism' developed by the Hungarian Marxist critic, Georg Lukács, urged the depiction, not of a favoured reality, but of the 'social TOTALITY' in the belief that this would represent society's contradictory, and thus its progressive, aspects in spite of a conservative authorial or intervening ideology. This model of realism is close to the stated views of Marx and Lenin (Baxandall and Morawski [eds] 1973).

Conventional forms of realism assume a transparent relation of likeness, resemblance or analogy between reality and its REPRESENTATION. Roland Barthes finds an alternative to this tradition of 'analogic realism' (Moriarty 1994) in the epic theatre of Bertolt Brecht, which seeks 'not so much to express reality as to signify it', thereby introducing a 'certain distance between signifier and signified' (Barthes 1972b: 74–5). This critical and self-conscious distance – by which, art drew attention to its own construction and thus the construction of 'reality' – was integral to the techniques of ESTRANGEMENT or DEFAMILIARIZATION employed in the anti-illusionist arts of MODERNISM. In a celebrated debate in the 1930s, Brecht attacked Lukács's notion of realism as 'formalist' (that is to say, in Brecht's eyes, it adhered to a given literary form, rather than to a changing social content). Brecht's intention, by contrast, was to use any means possible to reveal the workings of the world and put 'living reality in the hands of living people in such a way that it can be mastered... for reality alters; to represent it the means of representation must alter too' (Brooker [ed] 1992: 42–3). In such terms, Brecht proposed a flexible, modernist and non-dogmatic 'socialist realism'.

In a study of contemporary theory and fiction, Susan Strehle (1992) sees a persistent and inadequate distinction between mimetic realism, on the one hand, and METAFICTION on the other: fiction is thought to be either about the world or about itself. Meanwhile, she argues, changes in our understanding of the 'real world' point a way beyond this simplistic binary. At their most fundamental, these changes are associated with the theories of relativity, quantum mechanics and CHAOS theory. The new science has taken physics beyond the assumptions of absolute space, time and motion, solid matter and objective method characterizing the 'Newtonian/realistic paradigm'; it has, as she puts it, 'reimagined reality' (1992: 13). Poststructuralist theory and contemporary fiction, she argues (her examples include Thomas Pynchon, John Barth, Margaret Atwood and Donald Barthelme), share with the new physics an emphasis on relativism and indeterminacy. Together, they participate in a new orientation that can be summed up in the key words 'discontinuous, statistical, energetic, relative, subjective, uncertain' (1992: 8).

Strehle's term for this fiction addressing a new reality is 'actualism' rather than 'realism'. The merits of the term, she writes, are twofold: that it has 'its roots not in things but in acts, relations and motions', and that it conveys the double sense of 'to make' and 'to fake' appropriate to a fiction that has abandoned 'the old mechanistic reality' for self-conscious artistry 'without losing interest in the external world' (1992: 14).

See also INTERPELLATION; SPECULATIVE REALISM.

RECEPTION

'Reception theory' is associated with the work of the literary critics and scholars Hans Robert Jauss (1921–1997), Wolfgang Iser (1926–2007) and others at the University of Konstanz, West Germany (Holub 1984). The German name, *Rezeptionaesthetik,* given to this work indicates its concern with AESTHETIC VALUE and experience; an emphasis that distinguishes it from the parallel, largely Anglo-American, movement in 'reader-response theory'.

There are two leading concepts associated with this theory. The first, formulated by Jauss (1982), is that of a so-called 'horizon of expectation' influencing writers and readers in the composition and READING of works. This describes the conventions of a mode, tradition, GENRE or literary idiom to which a particular work relates, and which a reader, having internalized such features from the experience of reading, brings to a new work. This interactive system of conventions and expectations comprises a PARADIGM, but individual works (those valued by Jauss in earlier writings) might break against the reader's disposition to receive them in its terms and thus initiate a new horizon. Alternatively, a reader may read a past work according to a changed paradigm – choosing to follow a queer reading of a Shakespeare text, for example – rather than to trace its structure of imagery. The concept of a 'horizon of expectations' therefore allows for historicized readings. However, it cannot overcome the problem this raises that there may be more than one way of reading a given text at a given time. In the terms of Jauss's chosen metaphor, there can only be one horizon, but this is inadequate to a situation where there are different and contending reading expectations and strategies.

The second main concept, introduced by Iser (1974, 1978) is that of the 'implied reader', conceived less as a possible historicized or otherwise situated reader than as a generalized position. Iser is interested in describing the 'act' of reading. This, he sees as a process by which the reader traverses the text, both in initial and successive readings, closing 'gaps' and filling 'blanks' so as to make the work consistent. The reader anticipates the text, and reading is therefore seen as projective and creative, but not to the degree (as in some 'reader-response' criticism and poststructuralist thought) that the reader 'produces' its meaning. Iser grants the text an existence prior to the reading process, which 'concretizes' its meaning and brings text and reader to a point of convergence, though (in a residual contradiction in Iser's position) this may never be fully accomplished.

A further form of reception study is empirically based research on actual recipients and the processes of reception of utterances or instruction. This is common in psychology and education and, in less technical forms, in AUDIENCE studies. A much-cited, but still significant example in Literary Studies is Janice Radway's *Reading the Romance* (1984), a study of 42 mostly married women readers of women's romance in Smithton, USA. The study is the ethnographic equivalent of Stanley Fish's notion developed within 'reader-response theory' of an 'INTERPRETIVE COMMUNITY', though Radway's concern is with non-academic readers who would not be 'informed' readers in Fish's sense. The women of Smithton were united as a COMMUNITY of readers around a published neighbourhood newsletter, who graded and recommended certain stories. The stories they favoured were those featuring bright, independent career women who were drawn into a difficult relationship with an arrogant and possibly violent male, but where the man was brought eventually to fulfil a 'maternal', caring role. Radway is led, through the theoretical work of Nancy Chodorow's *The Reproduction of Mothering* (1978), to suggest that the women find in these reformed males a figure that both recalls their own relationship with their mothers and affirms their present lives.

Radway approaches her research as a feminist interested in opposing PATRIARCHY. Though she avoids definitive conclusions on the IDEOLOGY of reading romance, she is inclined to see the women's very 'act' of reading (in preference to domestic tasks) as more of a protest against the patriarchal order of the household than their reading of the stories along the above lines, since the latter provides a way of reconciling the women to their assigned roles within patriarchy. Radway introduces both a social specificity and considerations of GENDER and ideology lacking in European reception theory (see also Fetterly 1978). Commentators have objected, however, to the distinction her approach enforces between the feminist scholar and other 'ordinary' women, and to the moralizing view she implies towards the role of PLEASURE or FANTASY in the reading experience (see Ang 1988; Storey 1993). In the 'Introduction' to the book's later issue in England (1987), Radway explains its rationale and reflects on her perspective in relation to trends in British Cultural Studies.

RECUPERATION

See INCORPORATION.

REFLECTION(ISM)

The concept of 'reflection' is employed in traditional AESTHETICS and criticism to describe art's relation to society: art, it is said, 'holds a mirror up to nature'. It is derived from the theory of 'mimesis', the Greek term for imitation, used by Plato and explored by Aristotle in his *Poetics,* and has been most influential in the discussion and practice of REALISM. The idea that art transparently reflects, or faithfully imitates, life has continued to influence conventional prose fiction, and has been transposed to documentary writing, photography and film, along with the non-artistic discourses of journalism and TV news broadcasts where the ruling criterion is that they present a 'window on the world'.

Notions of 'correspondence' and HOMOLOGY have developed the assumed relations in this model further, but do not question the basic premise of a given society and an artistic or cultural text that echoes it back. This assumption influenced some earlier Marxist versions of relations between the economic and cultural or superstructural levels of a society, but this understanding is generally discredited. The model allows for no dialectical or dialogic interchange between artistic, media or cultural texts and the other levels or DISCOURSES of society. It presumes, in other words, that there is a passive mirror-like reflection without active, cognitive reflection. The metaphor of reflection as intended is anyway PROBLEMATIC since a reflection is already a reversed, rather than a transparent and 'true', IMAGE. These objections have given rise to a disparaging use of the term 'reflectionist'.

See also DIALECTICS.

REFLEXIVE MODERNIZATION

A concept associated with the German social theorist Ulrich Beck's theory of the 'risk society' and with allied work by the British sociologist Antony Giddens (Beck 1992; Giddens 1990; Beck *et al.* 1994). The theory of the risk society has two aspects. First, it sees the faith in progress associated with scientific reason and technological advance at the heart of industrial MODERNITY as having produced the hazards of global warming, nuclear waste, genetic research, the use of herbicides in farming and so on. Second, unlike the traditions of CRITICAL THEORY, it argues for a positive response to these outcomes; one that will radicalize rather than reject the founding principles of modernity. This double-sided self-critique is expressed in the concept of 'reflexive modernization'.

Risk society, for Beck, is the result of an internal, 'unreflected quasi-autonomous' dynamic in modernity. He therefore reasons that the concept of reflexive modernization 'does not imply (as the adjective "reflexive" might suggest) reflection, but (first) self-confrontation... of the bases of modernization with the consequences of modernization' (1994: 5–6). 'Reflection' in the sense of increased social awareness can then follow from this, in a second stage, and is already occurring in everyday life and public debate, in the fields of work, the environment, the structure of the family and attitudes towards SEXUALITY. Beck sees in an increasingly sceptical and individualized society (though this brings its own insecurities), the harbinger of a greater self-determination, freeing people from institutions of social control and the scientific experts who presently legitimize while they monitor risks. A reflexive, or 'reflective', interrogative mentality is a necessary foundation for this more responsible future society. This will be a society of modernity still, but of another, new modernity, 'beyond its classical industrial design'. Beck therefore declares, 'Reflexive modernisation means not less but more modernity' (1992: 10, 4).

Beck *et al.* (1994) develop the idea of reflexivity and cognate terms in a more direct relation to the political and cultural realms, including debates on COMMUNITY and ECOLOGY. At the centre of their discussion is the question of who or what the agencies and medium of reflexive modernization are: whether these are more 'structural' and social, as in Beck and Giddens, or more 'cultural' as Lash maintains.

See also AGENCY; COSMOPOLITANISM; PUBLIC SPHERE.

REIFICATION

From the Latin *res and facere* and meaning 'to make into a thing'. The term is used to describe the process by which a human subject or dynamic set of social relationships are regarded as objects (or are 'objectified'), resulting in the experience of ALIENATION. In Marxist theory, this process is attributed to the exploitation of the worker by capital. The term is therefore related to Marx's concept of COMMODITY FETISHISM, which names the process by which the goods produced by human labour become commodities with an exchange or money value, and this is substituted for social relations of exchange. Under reification, people are regarded as things: workers are identified with the objects they produce for consumption and so lose their full humanity. IDEOLOGY works to ensure this identification. Though reification is associated especially with CAPITALISM, certain thinkers, including a Marxist philosopher and cultural critic such as Theodor Adorno, see it as a permanent feature of the human condition.

More generally, reification is used to refer to ways of treating language, texts and relationships as fixed and static.

RELATIVE AUTONOMY

The concept of relative autonomy was proposed notably by Louis Althusser (1971b; see also 1969). In Althusser's structural model of the social FORMATION, three different levels – the political, the economic and ideological (or superstructural) – are seen to exist in a relationship of mutual relative autonomy. The latter realm or level, comprised of ideological institutions or apparatuses (including education, media and communications), therefore enjoys a relative autonomy in relation to the state and the economy. Art is, at the same time, seen as having a relative autonomy in relation to IDEOLOGY. Of art, for example, Althusser writes, it 'makes us see… the ideology from which it detaches itself as art, and to which it alludes' (1971b: 204). Art, by definition, has 'an internal distance' upon ideology. This was taken up in Literary Studies by Macherey (1978) and Eagleton (1976) and in film theory in the journal *Screen*.

It should be added, however, that Althusser retains a distinction between 'authentic art', which has the relative autonomy and function he describes, and 'works of an average or mediocre level' (1971b: 204). It might be supposed from this, that mass art or media culture are without any autonomy and do not enable us to 'see' the ideology that conditions them. Many would reject this implication and extend a relative autonomy to artistic and cultural works in general. However, this then means that the question of VALUE, which necessarily distinguishes one thing from another – here, the autonomous or relatively autonomous from the dependent or mediocre – must be differently posed. Althusser's theory raises the further question of the critical distance or autonomy of theory; namely, in this instance, of Marxism. Certainly the 'scientific' knowledge Althusser attributes to Marxism would suggest that, for him, it operates at a greater distance from ideology than either 'authentic' or 'mediocre' art. However, the implication that theory or science, or Marxism, can lay claim to absolute autonomy has proved a highly contentious one (see Elliott [ed] 1994).

See also BASE AND SUPERSTRUCTURE; DISTANTIATION; IDEOLOGICAL STATE APPARATUS.

RELATIVISM

See PLURALISM; POSTMODERNISM.

REPRESENTATION

Without exception, the human, cultural and social sciences are concerned with the PRODUCTION and consumption of meaning and thus with the modes and media of representation in which this is articulated. How we understand representation is therefore bound up with the objects of study (texts, events, social processes), the preferred conceptual armature (DISCOURSE, IDEOLOGY, institutions, economy) and the methods of investigation that map out these changing fields. Representations and the term itself are therefore ubiquitous. However, it also carries a series of more specific and PROBLEMATIC implications: first, that objects, events, processes and such-like exist in an unmediated reality prior to representation and meaning; second, that a pure and authentic meaning inheres in an object prior to its being expressed, in which case representation comes to mean re-presentation and thus to entail the likely distortion of the authentic original; and, third, that one form of representation (though not recognized as such, for example, direct speech, a photograph, documentary film, newscast, biography, historical record) is more true to an original than other forms of representation, or is indeed identical with it. These assumptions and the binary distinction they depend upon of unmediated authenticity and secondary or unauthentic representation have been critiqued most directly by DECONSTRUCTION. If we take the force of this critique, the implication is that there is *only* representation (or 'writing') – only modes of signification, rather than a pure original, which is then represented (or misrepresented) in a secondary discursive medium. This argument is reinforced by other tendencies in POSTSTRUCTURALISM and POSTMODERNISM, which similarly question the existence of a fixed *a priori* meaning or pre-existent reality.

Stuart Hall (1997b) identifies two of the positions outlined above as, respectively, 'the reflective approach' (in which it is thought that representations 'reflect the true meaning as it already exists in the world') and 'the intentional approach' (in which it is assumed that 'words mean what the author intends them to mean') (1997b: 24–5). Both approaches are flawed, says Hall. The alternative – which is an alternative also to the extreme poststructuralist belief in the unreferenced play of SIGNS – is a 'constructionist approach'. 'Things don't *mean*,' writes Hall, 'we *construct* meaning, using representational systems – concepts and signs' (1997b: 25). In this view, there is no relation of reflection, imitation or one-to-one correspondence between signifying practices and the real world. Nevertheless, signs are used 'to symbolise, stand for or reference objects, people and events in the so-called "real world" – as well as emotions, imagined and abstract ideas which have no material form' (1997b: 28).

The constructionist view therefore understands representation as a symbolic practice by which meaning is given to the world. More emphatically, representations are seen to construct that very world; they are, writes Christine Gledhill, 'major sites for conflict and negotiation, a central goal of which is the definition of what is taken as "real"' (Hall [ed] 1997b: 348). Essays in the same volume develop these constructionist arguments through case studies on national IDENTITY, masculinity and the figure of the 'new man', and GENDER and soap opera.

See also NARRATIVE; REALISM.

REPRODUCTION

Biological reproduction was raised as an issue in the women's liberation movements of the 1970s (Chodorow 1978) and has remained of importance for contemporary feminists in relation to questions of healthcare, employment practices and benefits, as well as women's control of their own bodies.

In forms of literary and cultural study, reproduction has had two main senses. First, it has been connected with the role of IDEOLOGY and the reproduction, or otherwise, of dominant attitudes and values. Second, the advent of processes of mechanical – and latterly, electronic – reproduction characterizing MASS societies has challenged traditional conceptions of the unique and original work of art (Benjamin 1970b; see also AURA). A corollary of this is that conceptions of meaning and ways of 'READING' have also altered. Meaning is seen less as an inherent property of a given text than as a range of possible meanings produced in an ongoing dialogue of producers, readers/viewers in different contexts, cultures and historical periods. Familiar examples would be the texts of *Frankenstein* and *Dracula,* and the texts of Shakespeare's plays, all of which have acquired meanings as they have been differently interpreted, filmed or staged – that is to say, reproduced. In taking account of such situated meanings, therefore, criticism is brought to consider the conventions of different media and, logically also, the empirical study of AUDIENCES and readerships (Radway 1987; Holderness 1988; Gelder 1994).

See also BODY; REPRESENTATION.

RHIZOME

A term introduced by French philosopher Gilles Deleuze (1925–1995) and psychoanalyst Félix Guattari (1930–1992) in their co-authored *A Thousand Plateaus* (1987), following the earlier *Anti-Oedipus: Capitalism and Schizophrenia* (1984). In the later text, according to Best and Kellner, the authors 'have by and large settled their score with modernity and psychoanalysis to embark upon an affirmative voyage, a sustained celebration of difference and multiplicity which can be read as a new type of postmodern text, theory, and politics' (1991: 97). This project is based on the concept of the 'rhizome' – the botanical form of growth seen, for example, in an iris and which, unlike a single root form, produces different points of equal growth across a lateral path. Strictly speaking, there are few forms of rhizomatic growth, but Deleuze and Guattari list bulbs and tubers, the orchid, potato, couch-grass and, beyond this, packs of animals, rats, ants, burrows, language, maps, forms of writing, thinking and political action. *A Thousand Plateaus* accordingly announces a decentred intellectual and political scenario, working across a diversity of topics or 'plateaus' – including PSYCHOANALYSIS, the state, SUBJECTIVITY, DESIRE and DIFFERENCE – in a perspectival and non-logical, non-NARRATIVE structure whose form enacts its own content. Throughout, the governing principles of multiplicity and FLOW, or 'lines of flight' are opposed to the tyranny of the One and the Same evident in the 'arborescent' model of western thought:

> In contrast to centred (even polycentric) systems with hierarchical modes of communication and pre-established paths, the rhizome is an acentred, non-hierarchical, nonsignifying system without a General and without an organizing memory or central automaton... What is at question... is a relation to sexuality – but also to the animal, the vegetal, the world, politics, the book, things natural and artificial – that is totally different from an arborescent relation: all manner of 'becomings'... A rhizome has no beginning or end; it is always in the middle, between things, interbeing, intermezzo.
>
> (1987: 21, 25)

Rhizomatics therefore shares a CRITIQUE of the centred systems and hierarchical binary oppositions of western philosophy with Jacques Derrida's DECONSTRUCTION. It differs on two counts, however – first, in that Deleuze and Guattari draw on a generalized model or metaphor from the natural world and, second, because they put this to work in a more evidently politicized cultural project. In this respect, they associate rhizomatics or 'deterritorialized' thought with pre-modern and contemporary 'nomadic' social groups – feminists, gays, people of colour – who seek to escape from the totalizing rigidities of the social system. To this degree, their programme shares some of the more positive implications of Michel Foucault's

247

analysis of the role of micropolitical activity in unsettling hegemonic relations of knowledge and POWER. Thus, the rhizomatic path of *A Thousand Plateaus* connects aspects of Derrida with aspects of Foucault (a one-time close collaborator with Deleuze), transforming both in the spirit of its own unreserved libertarianism.

See also DETERRITORIALIZATION; NOMADISM.

RISK SOCIETY

See REFLEXIVE MODERNIZATION.

ROBOTICS

The term 'robot' was coined in 1917 by Czech writer Karel Kapec, author of the drama *RUR* ('Rossum's Universal Robots', 1920). Robot means 'serf' in Czech and the factory RUR mass-produce robots for use across the world as cheap labour (see Wollen, 1993, Ch. 2 'Modern Times'). In the play, a woman visitor from the Humanity League urges the factory to improve the conditions of the robots. However, their new-found self-consciousness leads them to revolt, with the result that they take over and destroy the factory and the whole world. The fear they embody is of revolution from below. But the connection the play makes between the subservient 'robotic' workforce – which would be unemotional, tireless, and uncomplaining – and the needs of new forms of mass production is also plain to see. Its predominant expression was 'Fordism' the name given to the mode of production developed in the making of the basic, identical motorcar, the Model-T Ford (which famously could be 'any colour', said Ford, 'so long as it is black'). The Fordist production line and allied industrial relations became the symbol of early twentieth-century Americanism.

The production line is exposed as anti-human by Charlie Chaplin in his *Modern Times* (1936) in which Chaplin's comic-melancholy persona of the tramp cum 'little man', becomes demented by the repetitive action of the production line, extending the worker's action of tightening bolts to all aspects of his life. Fritz Lang's earlier film *Metropolis* (1926) finds an accommodation with the machine and the Fordist mode of production. The film pits the 'False' against the 'True Maria'. The first is the robotic simulacrum of the 'True Maria' and the creation of mad scientist-magus, Rotwang. She is a vamp whose nominal purpose to motivate the workers to a higher pitch of production is subverted by Rotwang's own desire for power. The 'False Maria's' 'anarcho-hysteric flood of female sexuality' (Wollen: 46) produces an unwanted excess in the form of a self-destructive overproduction. She must be destroyed therefore (and is burned as a witch) in a counter-revolt led by the factory owner's son and the 'True Maria', who represents an acceptable feminine sexuality as his betrothed and a mother-figure to the workers. A model family and lineage emerges; owners and workers can be reconciled, and industrial progress through technology can proceed.

In the essay 'The mass ornament' (1927), Siegfried Kracauer saw the high-stepping chorus line, the Tiller Girls, as an expression of the rationality of the assembly-line transposed into the world of entertainment: 'The hands of the factory correspond to the legs of the Tiller Girls... The mass ornament is the aesthetic reflex of the rationality aspired to by the prevailing economic system' (1995: 79). American-style Fordism and its allied economic system held sway until the economic crisis of the 1970s. The following era of POST-FORDISM has tended to increase fears of automation and thus of job losses, accompanied by social and environmental devastation of once-thriving areas. In the event, and at the same time, automation has long been familiar and accepted in certain major industries (in automobile and aircraft manufacture, for example); finance and medicine depend on advanced technologies; every workplace is computerized; and microtechnologies have become indispensable to everyday life. But the extension of technology and artificial intelligences into new spheres of work has sparked renewed anxiety. Studies by Martin Ford (*Rise of the Robots* 2015) and Jerry Kaplan (*Humans Need Not Apply* 2015), for example, warn of how technologies will come to replace human workers in areas such as accountancy, law and journalism. No occupation is now immune. In itself, relief from humdrum routine appears to guarantee an often-promised better, freer society, but not if it is accompanied by poverty and destitution. Historically, mechanization leading to unemployment has seen the mixed results of misery, heightened social division, upheaval and revolt. The answer, say Ford and Kaplan, will be found in the introduction of a universal basic income. This would both allay such fears and preserve the dynamism of present-day CAPITALISM. Labour-saving technological advance leads inevitably, therefore, to larger questions of a more or less desirable social, economic and political order.

See CYBORG; POSTCAPITALISM; POSTHUMAN.

SCHEDULING

Scheduling refers to the arrangement of a sequence of programmes in broadcast media. It is therefore one of the ways in which the ADDRESSER relates to the ADDRESSEE in the model of COMMUNICATION. A number of factors may determine this: from the traditions associated with a particular channel or frequency to notions of public service, appropriate intellectual level, definitions of entertainment, assumptions about the AUDIENCE including special interest groups, topicality, ratings and, of course, financial constraints. An example of these factors in operation occurred in July 1997 in the most radical change to programming for 30 years on BBC Radio 4. The Controller in the role of 'addresser' cut a dozen programmes, and adjusted the formats and start times of a number of others. Among the reasons given for this was the need to modernize and clarify programming: thus the changes were described as a 'move away from a medieval town plan of a schedule... away from historic half-timbered programming to strategic scheduling that is clear, persuasive and satisfying' (*Guardian,* 31 July 1997: 3). This was combined with an eye to peak listening times, the need to halt a drop in ratings outside these times, to retain an audience of 4 million, which listened for only 15 minutes a week, and an assurance that standards would not fall.

As this illustrates, scheduling does not take place only at one end of the communication process but in NEGOTIATION with a perceived audience. John Hartley (1992) suggests that the audience's role is more active and decisive than this, and that new recording technologies, particularly, make it possible for audiences to construct their own schedules within and across services and media in a 'new regime of watching' in which people control not 'just their own equipment but... the act of looking too' (1992: 213, 215). Along these lines, it is possible for members of audiences to combine recorded broadcasts, video film, music and text from a range of sources and times in an entirely individual sequence.

See also CONVERGENCE; HYPERTEXT.

SCHIZOANALYSIS

See OEDIPAL COMPLEX; PSYCHOANALYSIS.

SCREEN THEORY

The film journal *Screen* played a significant role in the 1970s (in conjunction, notably, with *New Left Review* and the associated New Left Books) in introducing new European theory to an English academic readership. In particular, under its pointedly collective editorship, it presented an amalgam of PSYCHOANALYSIS and FEMINISM, indebted to the post-Freudian theories of Jacques Lacan, and the 'scientific', anti-humanist MARXISM of Louis Althusser. The result was a mode of left-modernist theorizing that echoed the political AESTHETIC of Bertolt Brecht and looked to the revolutionary Soviet cinema of Sergei Eisenstein and contemporary AVANT-GARDE film-makers, notably Jean-Luc Godard, working in a similar tradition. Key essays produced in this period were Colin MacCabe's 'Realism and the cinema: notes on some Brechtian theses' and Laura Mulvey's 'Visual pleasure and narrative cinema'. Both were opposed to the illusionism and CLOSURE of conventional NARRATIVE forms, including in MacCabe's account, the dominant literary form of 'classic realism' exemplified by George Eliot. REALISM and Hollywood cinema were seen as complicit in the construction of the bourgeois SUBJECT and the reinforcement of PATRIARCHY.

Both the air of political commitment and *Screen's* characteristic mode of abstract theorizing, allied to a dismissal of POPULAR forms, provoked heated debate within Film Studies. Also, the influence of a later generation of non- or anti-Marxist, poststructuralist thinkers, and a radical alteration in the political climate in education and British society from the late 1970s, took debate in another direction. However, there can be little question that the specific contributions and general orientation of the journal helped articulate and disseminate a distinctive style of CULTURAL POLITICS. With other, allied forms of work and intellectual association in Literary, Cultural Studies and Philosophy, *Screen* joined in producing the cultural and intellectual FORMATION that Antony Easthope characterized as comprising 'British Post-Structuralism' (1988).

See also IDEOLOGY; INTELLECTUALS; POSTSTRUCTURALISM.

SEMIOLOGY/SEMIOTICS

In a brief reference in his *Course in General Linguistics* (1915), the Swiss linguist, Ferdinand de Saussure anticipated the advent of a science of semiology 'that studies the signs within society'. This would be a part of Social Psychology and include the study of language within its broader framework. However, the idea of such a new science was not taken up until the early writings of Roland Barthes (*Elements of Semiology* 1977 [1965]) and *Mythologies* 1972a [1957]). In particular, Barthes developed the aspect of signification, or the referential function of the SIGN, which had been less important to Saussure. To this end, he introduced a distinction between CONNOTATION and DENOTATION. Denotation is the literal 'uncoded' meaning of a sign; the way in which the image of a bicycle is literally the mechanism itself (the denotative level is more an analytic convenience than an actual level of meaning, but we can imagine someone's first sight of a bicycle being of this type). At the level of connotation, the sign acquires social and cultural meanings according to how it is depicted. Thus, a bicycle can connote health, fitness or, in a broader set of associations, the countryside, in opposition to the car and town. In a more particular cultural association, say with the Tour de France, a bicycle can be brought to stand for the nation as a whole, or for 'Frenchness'. Barthes termed this last kind of connotation MYTH. This does not mean a mythological or false meaning, but as in Anthropology, a common way of thinking or perceiving in a CULTURE, akin to a cultural stereotype. Fiske and Hartley (1978) expound Barthes's ideas and suggest that connotation and myth, taken together, comprise a third level of ideological signification.

This revised model understands signs as contributing to systems of social meaning and has been used especially in the analysis of POPULAR visual media: of advertising, comics, photography, television and cinema (Eco 1979a; Blonsky [ed] 1985). Fiske and Hartley (1978) extend Barthes's model to an analysis of the television IMAGE, while Christian Metz (1974) proposed an ambitious semiology of the cinema, employing structuralist and psychoanalytic models.

A further foundational figure in the general science of semiotics was the American philosopher, Charles Sanders Peirce. Peirce proposed a tripartite division between indexical, iconic and symbolic signs, and this schema, rather than Saussure's, was used in an early and influential introduction to the semiology of the cinema by Peter Wollen (1969 [rev. 1972]). Wollen shows how a valorization of the indexical sign, founded on a causal or proximate relation of sign to object, was at the heart of theories of REALISM (he cites especially the writings of André Bazin and also Metz above), and demonstrates how the cinema can be equally iconic or self-consciously pictorial (in the films of Joseph Von Sternberg) and, indeed, employ all three types of sign. This interpenetration Wollen discovered in the cinema of Jean-Luc Godard – though he later preferred to think less in terms of a full use of the range of signs than of an antagonistic use of CODES as marking the AVANT-GARDE's relation to Hollywood ('Conclusion' 1972: 173–4).

A further source for semiotics lay in the model of language presented by the Bakhtin School and especially in V.N. Vološinov's *Marxism and the Philosophy of Language* (1973 [1929]), which offered a direct CRITIQUE of Saussure. Vološhinov emphasized the social and ideological determination of language as utterance and is cited by Hodge and Kress (1988) as an inspiration in their attempt to theorize what they term a 'social semiotics'. They outline (1988: 18) the following minimum components of study as necessary to such a programme:

1. culture, society and politics as intrinsic to semiotics
2. other semiotic systems alongside verbal language
3. parole, the act of speaking, and concrete signifying practices in other codes
4. diachrony, time, history, process and change
5. the processes of signification, the transactions between signifying systems and structures of reference
6. structures of the signified
7. the material nature of signs.

See also DIALOGICS; IDEOLOGY; STRUCTURALISM.

SEMIOTIC

A term used in association with theories of the SIGN (see SEMIOLOGY), but which has been employed in a particular sense by the French feminist, Julia Kristeva to name the pre-linguistic drives and impulses associated with the pre-Oedipal experience of the infant. In this sense, the semiotic is akin to what in Lacanian psychoanalytic theory is termed the realm of the 'IMAGINARY' and similarly opposed to the 'SYMBOLIC order', although Kristeva wishes particularly to emphasize an association of the semiotic with the mother. By extension, the semiotic is also associated in her *Revolution in Poetic Language* (1984a [1974]) with the experimental forms and language of the literary AVANT-GARDE. Kristeva cites works by the modernist writers, Stéphane Mallarmé, Antonin Artaud and James Joyce, for example, as evidence of the way the semiotic questions and destabilizes dominant literary modes. This has two implications. Although, first, the semiotic is pre-verbal, it necessarily finds expression within the Symbolic order. Second, although it is anti-patriarchal and important to the making of a feminist project, the semiotic is not governed by the biological identity of artists or writers.

See CHORA; OEDIPAL COMPLEX; PATRIARCHY.

SEXUAL DIFFERENCE

A term employed to express an often polemical awareness of GENDER and sexual orientation within FEMINISM and gay and lesbian CULTURAL POLITICS and thus to counter PATRIARCHY and the normative assumptions of heterosexuality.

Within feminism, sexual difference has implied at least three perspectives. First of all, an insistence on sexual separateness as an absolute DIFFERENCE determined by biology and associated for the most part with the earlier polemics of the women's liberation movement, which wished both to distinguish women as a collectivity from men and to present motherhood in an affirmative way (Chodorow 1978). This essentialist position – so named because it assumed an underlying common essence to being a woman – has subsequently been critiqued by a second view, which distinguishes between anatomical sex and gender, and sees the latter as constructed in relations of socially determined differences. This has in turn been associated with so-called 'identity politics', where IDENTITY (often extended in this description to include racial, ethnic, gay and lesbian – or the more inclusive nomination of LBGT – identities. See below) is understood as socially constructed but felt by that very token to be grounded in a common experience. However, 'the language of "authentic subjective experience", whether of racism or sexual exploitation, as Pratibha Parma (1990) and others have pointed out, can give rise to an invidious 'hierarchy of oppression' used to 'guilt-trip' the less oppressed and result in a limited 'political practice which takes as its starting point only the personal and experiential modes of being' (1990: 107).

In part, the emphasis on difference derives from social and ideological changes, and the need to respond to and intervene in these. In part, too, it derives from the theoretical influence respectively of PSYCHOANALYSIS and STRUCTURALISM. In the first, sexual difference is established at the point of entry into the SYMBOLIC order associated with the father. Identity is at that point established as no longer unified, but as divided between the conscious and UNCONSCIOUS, with boys and girls subjected in unequal ways to the power of society – internalized as the 'super-ego' in Freud – or of the PHALLUS, symbolizing what Jacques Lacan, following Freud, called 'the law of the father'. The second source of this emphasis, and itself an influence upon Lacan, was Ferdinand de Saussure's structuralist theory of language as composed of relations of difference. Thus we might recast the non-essentialist position above along the lines of Saussure's theory of the SIGN by positing a signifier of gender attached by convention to its social signified, and as belonging to a 'language' or system of gendered relations represented in the symbolic systems of society.

What, above all, this perspective tends to inherit from structuralism, however, is an emphasis on binary oppositions of culture/nature, reason/emotion, active/passive, public/private and so on, and to see these as inscribed in and reinforcing hierarchical binary oppositions between men and women, since women are associated with the second 'weaker' term. This binary opposition is reinforced in the privileged association of men with language and the power of the Symbolic order in psychoanalytic theory.

Certain key structuralist assumptions were, however, critiqued by Jacques Derrida (1976) and taken up especially in French feminism, notably in Hélène Cixous's essay 'Sorties' (1981a). Derrida showed how meaning can convincingly be viewed as neither stabilized in a settled one-to-one relation of signifier and signified, nor in a centred system of relations, nor a series of hierarchical oppositions. Instead of 'difference', he proposed the term *'DIFFÉRANCE'* to suggest how meanings both depended on difference and were endlessly deferred. An awareness that sexual differences exceed gender categories and that identity is complicated by other shifting allegiances made it likely that this discussion would follow the logic of Derrida's critique to posit more mobile or entirely performative conceptions of identity – seen as in a process of becoming, rather than as a state of being. Thus, the signifiers of sexual difference can be said to relate, not to fixed or conventional signifieds, but to other similarly detached signifiers. Identity (sexual and otherwise) becomes a chain of possible significations whose point of 'presence' or self-knowledge is infinitely deferred (Butler 1990).

An awareness and active promulgation of a plurality of differently accented sexual identities has become increasingly pronounced since the 1990s and into the 2000s. In the process, lesbian, gay, bisexual and transsexual identities have become familiarly represented in the designation LGBT. More recently, other initials: Q for queer or questioning and I for intersexual are added to this initializing to give LGBTQI. Further possible additions, among them, U for unsure, C for curious, T for transvestite, TS for two-spirit, P for polyamorous, are a sign of the intense, heightened awareness of forms of sexual difference across contemporary cultures, although some individual groups object to the assumption of an all-encompassing common aim (see Stryker 2008; and Brooks 2015).

Signs of changed attitudes and agendas include the establishment of new journals (e.g. *GLQ: A Journal of Gay & Lesbian Studies* and *TSQ: Transgender Studies Quarterly*) and a more confident recognition of LGBT issues in literary and film cultures. The example of a pop icon such as David Bowie (see Brooker, 2017) has also eased public attitudes. In writing, examples deploying the dominant mode of the memoir pioneered by Jan Morris's *Conundrum* (1974) have included Leslie Feinberg, *Stone Butch Blues* (1993), Jayne County, *Man Enough to be a Woman* (1995), Janet Mock, *Redefining Realness* (2014) and Juliet Jacques, *Trans* (2015). In film, an innovative British Film Institute (BFI) poll of 2016 asked eminent critics to nominate the top 30 films of all time depicting GLBT relations. The poll was topped by *Carol* (2015), directed by Todd Haynes, and included in its top ten Wong Kar-Wei's *Happy Together* (1997*),* Stephen Frears's *My Beautiful Laundrette* (1985) and Jean Genet's *Un Chant d'Amour* (1950). A further film of note starred Eddie Redmayne as Lili Elbe who underwent sex reassignment surgery in 1930. Her posthumously published autobiography, *Man into Woman* appeared in 1933.

A further small, but significant sign of change on the public stage, is the proposal in government in the UK to remove the designations of gender (M and F) on passports (already introduced in Australia).

SEXUALITY

A major theme in contemporary reflections on IDENTITY, informed especially by PSYCHOANALYSIS, FEMINISM and QUEER THEORY. The term is related to, but distinct from, 'sex' (used to refer both to the physical distinction between men and women, and sexual intercourse) and 'GENDER' (the social and cultural distinctions between men and women). Sexuality is used, rather, say Jackson and Scott, to refer to 'erotic desires, practices and identities' or 'aspects of personal and social life which have erotic significance' (1996: 2). This suggests a highly varied set of meanings. Nevertheless, sexuality has long been defined in relation to POPULAR stereotypes and the normative DISCOURSES of law, medicine and religion, as well as theory, which seek to generalize or confine its forms and meanings. Debates on sexuality in the recent period are marked above all by an increased awareness of this tension; between an acceptance or affirmation of diversity, on the one hand, and a defence of established norms, on the other.

This discussion has been shaped by the continuing issue of whether sexual identity is a biological given, determined by genes or anatomy, or is constructed in society and CULTURE. These alternatives define, respectively, essentialist and social-constructionist positions. Fairly evidently, in viewing sexuality as given by nature, and as thus fixed and unalterable, an essentialist view will reinforce heterosexual norms. The still deterministic perspective, which views sexuality as in effect 'given' by society if not by biology, such that an aggressive masculine sexuality is accepted as the way things are or should be, will have the same effect. Nevertheless, essentialist arguments have been evoked by feminists who feel it is necessary to argue for the autonomy and fundamental DIFFERENCE of women from men (MacKinnon 1987), or by lesbian feminists who wish to mark their difference from both heterosexual men and women.

The constructionist perspective has been influential within the social sciences in advancing the view of sexuality as 'socially scripted behaviour' (Gagnon and Simon 1973) and within Literary and Cultural Studies in presenting sexuality as similarly 'inscribed' within a range of social, historical texts. The first perspective has given a direction especially to critical studies of male sexual aggression and violence against women (Ungar and Crawford 1992). In broader terms, the constructionist view understands sexuality as shaped by the socializing regimes of parenting, early play and schooling, and the host of cultural forms, practices and institutions encountered by individuals and social-sexual groups. Stereotypical divisions can in that way be reinforced, or modified, by anything from toys to dress CODES, demarcated areas of the home and workplace, the sexualized imagery of sport, the languages of the press and media, and the official, institutionalized discourses of the law or religious creeds.

The study of sexuality therefore necessarily involves considerations of IDEOLOGY and REPRESENTATION. Within Literary and Cultural Studies, this has taken many specific forms, both textual and ethnographic – from studies of Shakespeare and Oscar Wilde (Dollimore 1991; Sinfield 1994a), or of heterosexuality, gay and lesbian images in the 'woman's film', mainstream and independent cinema (Johnston 1976; Lauretis 1987; Dyer 1977, 1990), to studies of advertising, photography, body image and online media (Atkins, 1998; Pullen, 2010). Work of this kind is characteristically interested less in recording society's standard script of sexuality than in the contradictory and destabilizing encodings between normative and dissident sexualities. This has revealed varied representations of women, of maleness and positive images of homosexuality, but has also foregrounded the fraught connections between sexuality, CLASS and RACE. White sexuality, for example, has been shown to depend on stereotypical representations of the black male as the symbol of a threatening or rival sexual potency, and of the black female as exotic or maternal, and both images to assume a persistent association with slave or servant status (hooks 1992; Hall 1997c; Young 1995).

In more directly theoretical terms, this work in literary and cultural analysis has been influenced by psychoanalysis and the work of Michel Foucault. Freud's contribution, breaking decisively with the physiologically oriented accounts of sexuality in the nineteenth-century science of sexology, was to link sexuality with the UNCONSCIOUS and thus the whole realm of feelings and FANTASY. Freud argued, notably in the 'Three essays on sexuality' (1905a, in Freud 1974c) that the Unconscious does not recognize a biological or gendered sexual distinction and is characterized by only one kind of sexuality, named the phallic. Not surprisingly, those who feel the PHALLUS is to all intents and purposes the male penis, think that this account privileges male sexuality. However, defenders of Freud read the undifferentiated – or at least bisexuality – Freud points to as the argument for a primary ANDROGYNY, or polymorphous sexuality.

Beyond this point in infancy, sexual identity derives, for Freud, from the experience of the OEDIPAL COMPLEX, which transforms a common phallic sexuality into a male sexuality determined by the fear of castration and a female sexuality determined by supposed 'penis envy'. For Jacques Lacan, the phallus has a symbolic function. It symbolizes a 'lack' that is articulated not in relation to anatomy (which would equate the phallus with the male penis) but in relation to language and DESIRE. This lack implies, moreover, that there is no whole sexual object, but always only a partial object, and thus an unfulfilled object of desire. This Lacan sees in fact as the very structure of desire whose mode, accordingly, is fantasy.

The abstractness and universalizing tendencies of psychoanalysis as well as its apparent complicity with a privileged heterosexuality, have prompted a deconstructive rereading of Freud and Lacan by French feminists (see on Irigaray in Wright [ed] 1992: 178–83). Others, including, especially, gay critics and theorists, have turned to the work of Michel Foucault. This has brought a historical understanding to constructions of sexuality and thus relativized persistent social and theoretical norms. Foucault adopted a thoroughly anti-essentialist notion of sexual drives and identity, and saw sexuality as being organized along the binaries of 'normal' and 'deviant' behaviours through the regulative discourses of modern societies. His belief that 'sexuality... is a name that can be given to a historical construct' (1979: 105) encouraged the view that sexuality can be redefined or reconstructed. It follows from Foucault's belief in the ubiquity of POWER, however, that there can be no simple liberation from the regulative structures of medicine, psychiatry and criminology that put sexuality, in these normative terms, at the core of questions of identity. This basic pessimism, allied to Foucault's external treatment of the specificities of GENDER and the pleasures of the BODY, and his eschewal of questions of individual and collective agency, have led some to a more materialist approach or to a combined discursive, psychological and social analysis (Weeks 1985; Vance 1989; Connell 1995).

A further development is associated with poststructuralist and postmodern positions, which affirm that sexuality is open to reconstruction and reinvention. This view reduces the emphasis on determining conditions or ideologies of an earlier left CULTURAL POLITICS to construe sexual subjects in terms of preference and self-determination. This more 'performative' theory (Butler 1990, 1993) has given rise to a popular emphasis in queer and lesbian theorizing upon diversity and a fluidity of sexual roles. To this end, it has been employed along with the concept of MASQUERADE in studies of bisexuality, cross-dressing and transvestism (see Garber 1992). In a wide-ranging example extending to film and popular culture texts, Garber (1997) explores the question of whether bisexuality is a 'third kind' of sexual identity or unsettles any kind of settled sexual difference.

The idea of a free-floating postmodern sexuality, where sexual identity is thought of in terms of PASTICHE and PARODY, has met with reservations from those who call for a stronger awareness of the material determinations of the body and oppressive social circumstances (Segal 1997). There remains, too, as Lynne Segal has pointed out, the intractable norms of a well-defended heterosexuality, making sexuality 'as complex and contested a terrain as it ever has been' (1997: 224).

See also COMPULSORY HETEROSEXUALITY; PATRIARCHY; PERFORMATIVITY; POSTHUMAN.

SIGN

The sign was identified by Ferdinand de Saussure, the founder of structural linguistics, as the main unit of language and COMMUNICATION. Each sign is composed of a 'signifier' (the acoustic image, or sound; Fr. *signifiant*) and 'signified' (the mental concept; Fr. *signifié*). The relation between these parts of the sign, says Saussure, is arbitrary – that is to say, conventional within the terms of a given language. Thus, in English, 'chair' is composed of a sound and the concept of chair as the object we sit on. In French and German, the concept, or signified, remains the same but the sound, or signifier, associated with it is different: *chaise* and *Stuhl,* respectively.

Sometimes Saussure's 'signified' is understood to refer to the object or material reality itself. In fact, Saussure termed this referential aspect of a sign its 'signification', though it was not the aim of structural linguistics to explore this. He was concerned, rather, to explain the systematic relations of language as a structure. The central insight for this analysis was that everything in language only functions as it does because of its relation to some other item which it is not, or for which it can be substituted. Hence, Saussure's much-quoted statement 'in language there are only differences *without positive terms'* (1966 [1915]: 121). Thus, an initial sound change in the word 'cat' to 'mat' changes the meaning (where, as here, a different sound creates a different meaning, it is called a 'phoneme'). The same applies to the combination of linguistic signs in a sequence, or 'syntagm', operating along a 'syntagmatic' or horizontal axis. The substitution of an equivalent but different item from the same class (verb, noun, adverb and so on), operating along a vertical or paradigmatic axis, produces a different meaning. We see these processes at work in the sentences: 'The boy chased the cat', 'The boy shook the cat' (substituting a different verb), 'The boy shook the mat' and 'The boy shot the man' (substituting a different verb and noun, and where 'cat', 'mat' and 'man' are marked by a single phonemic difference). These combinations and substitutions are made possible within the CODED system of English and it was Saussure's aim to understand the rules of such a system or *langue,* as he termed it. This, he distinguished from *parole,* the level of speech or individual language-use. It was at this level that the choices between items and their combinations were activated.

This model was taken up in STRUCTURALISM and SEMIOLOGY where it was extended to a variety of DISCOURSES including visual cultural forms. A further model of the sign employed in discussions of visual imagery in particular was developed by the American linguist, Charles Sanders Peirce. Peirce proposed a tripartite distinction between indexical, iconic and symbolic signs. In the first type, there is a physical connection of nearness or causality between sign and object: smoke, for example, is an indication of fire; a skin rash the sign of an ailment (Peirce cites a sailor with a rolling gait, a sun dial, weathercock and barometer). An iconic sign resembles the object (as in a painting or cartoon drawing) and the symbolic sign is, for Peirce, the arbitrary linguistic sign identified by Saussure (not, it should be noted, a 'symbol' in the conventional sense, such as the scales of justice, or the use of the colour black to symbolize death). This last usage gives rise to some confusion, and one commentator has suggested we think of Peirce's symbolic sign as having 'conceptual content' as a way of resolving it (Wollen 1972: 152). This difficulty aside, Peirce's schema suggests how he incorporated the sign's reference to an object and possible kinds of meaning, or signification, into his typology in ways Saussure did not.

SIGNIFIER/SIGNIFIED

See SIGN; STRUCTURALISM.

SIMULATION

A term derived from Greek philosophy and in common use in descriptions of computer programming and modelling. In contemporary theory it was adopted noticeably by the French philosopher of POSTMODERNISM, Jean Baudrillard (1929–2007) to describe changed relations of the IMAGE to its real-life referent, or – in Baudrillard's structuralist-derived vocabulary – of the signifier and signified. Thus, in Baudrillard's schematic cultural history of the SIGN, the signifier or image first reflected a basic reality; in a second phase, it 'masks and perverts a basic reality'; in a third, it 'masks the absence of a basic reality'; and, fourth, entering the realm of the pure simulacrum, 'it bears no relation to any reality whatever' (1988: 170). This suggests that there are distinct orders of simulation, but the term is used by Baudrillard and his commentators particularly to denote the last. This phase or cultural condition of pure simulacrum makes obsolete earlier forms of IDEOLOGY CRITIQUE, keen to unmask 'false CONSCIOUSNESS' or to demystify IDEOLOGY so as to disclose an obscured reality. Concepts of authenticity, depth, REPRESENTATION, exchange and PRODUCTION are similarly made redundant; as indeed are conventional notions of social activity, political analysis and action. These are replaced, in a vocabulary appropriate to a view of present society where all categories have imploded, by a new emphasis on consumption, REPRODUCTION and reduplication, and an accompanying fatalism. As an example, Baudrillard points to the replica of the caves of Lascaux which, he says, undermines distinctions between the original and its copy, making both artificial. Further examples include Disneyland and Watergate, Nixon's bombing of Hanoi and the Gulf War. The latter Baudrillard described as a 'virtual', media war that could not and did not 'really' take place (Brooker and Brooker [eds] 1997: 165–71).

Baudrillard's ideas appear provocative and overstated, and the reaction to them from those committed to a modernist PARADIGM, to rationality and norms of ethical conduct (and to the supposedly redundant terms cited above) is not surprising (Norris 1992). Nevertheless, Baudrillard may have prompted a necessary re-conceptualization of the forms of contemporary media society, of the place within it of consumption and the prevalence, consequently, of simulation (Kellner 1989b; Rojek and Turner [eds] 1993).

See also CONSUMERISM; HYPERREALITY; SPECTACLE.

SITE

A term used to suggest that meaning is produced by an interaction or conflict of forces focused at a particular point. Thus, the individual or human SUBJECT, a text, artistic movement or epoch might be regarded as the site on which AESTHETIC, philosophical, social, economic or cultural tensions, or some combination of these, is both decipherable and played out. Alternatively, a social theme or category itself, such as CLASS, RACE, GENDER or SEXUALITY, might be the site where other meanings, especially those influencing relations of POWER, are enacted. The corollary of this usage is that the initial terms or points of reference in each case (individual, text, gender) are seen as neither self-determining, nor complete in themselves. Instead, they are viewed as shaped by forces in a wider context, beyond, but also internal to, themselves.

Although any contextualizing or historicizing theory or critical method is bound to view things in this way, the use of this term coincides with the influence of STRUCTURALISM and POSTSTRUCTURALISM with which it shares an implicit physical metaphor. In particular, it can be said to aid the poststructuralist CRITIQUE of the assumed 'centredness' or harmonized totalities of texts, identities, artistic, cultural and social FORMATIONS. More broadly, it participates in a critique of the assumptions of humanist ideology, which regards individuals as self-determining agencies.

A further use of the term, and a comparable term like 'domain' – which again refers, not to a physical location in the material world, but a 'virtual' site – occurs in the language of computer communications, especially on the INTERNET where a multitude of such 'sites' are set up and connected.

See also HUMANISM.

SOCIAL FORMATION

See FORMATION.

SOCIAL MOVEMENTS

See COUNTER-CULTURE.

SPACE

As Edward W. Soja reports, the discipline of geography had, until recently, occupied a lowly rung in the regime of the human sciences where history and HISTORICISM have assumed a hegemonic role (1989:10–11). Geography received an important injection of credibility and fresh thinking, he argues, through, first, Henri Lefebvre's concept of 'living space', which viewed space as neither a void, nor a physical object, but 'another space... actually lived and socially created spatiality' (1989: 17–18), and, second, Michel Foucault's underlying commitment to a spatialized history. 'A whole history remains to be written of spaces,' Foucault had said, 'which would at the same time be the history of powers' (1986a: 149; Soja 1989: 21). Some commentators have felt this history substantially existed in the implicitly spatialized description of DISCOURSE and structures of POWER in Foucault's own work (see Foucault 1980c; 1986c). It is on this basis, at least, that Soja sees an emerging 'post-historicist and postmodern critical human geography' (1989: 19).

A further contributor to this debate and to a postmodern perspective on space has been the American Marxist commentator on the postmodern, Fredric Jameson. Jameson suggests that the passage from MODERNISM to POSTMODERNISM can be described as a waning of the modernist themes of time and temporality. Both our theoretical PARADIGMS and 'our daily life, our psychic experience, our cultural languages,' he writes, 'are today dominated by categories of space rather than by categories of time, as in the preceding period of high modernism' (1991: 16). As an example, Jameson cites the disorienting experience of the Bonaventure Hotel in Los Angeles. Its escalators and elevators, its lobby, its lack of obvious entrances and exits create a sense of 'bewildering immersion' in empty hyperspace, a 'milling confusion' where 'it is quite impossible to get your bearings' (1991: 43). He concludes that this decentred 'postmodern hyperspace' has out-manoeuvred the body's capacity 'to organise its immediate surroundings perceptually, and cognitively to map its position in a mappable external world'. The building and experience stand, then, for Jameson 'as the symbol and analogon' of the wider contemporary dilemma that is our incapacity 'to map the great global multinational and decentred communicational network in which we find ourselves caught as individual subjects' (1991: 44).

Others have interpreted the Bonaventura Hotel differently from Jameson (Davis 1988). Nevertheless, his description remains a *locus classicus* of the theme of postmodern spatiality and highlights some of the key aspects in its discussion. Three leading issues are: how space is 'embodied' for the individual in an immediate environment, including the implications this has for a spatialized conception of SUBJECTIVITY; the relation of postmodern architectural style to the social and economic composition of urban environments; the impact upon both IDENTITY and urban life of the processes of GLOBALIZATION.

An influential account of these themes is offered by David Harvey (1989). Like Soja and Jameson, Harvey sees a new era distinguished by a dramatically altered conception of space. Where modernist urban design aimed for an integrated conception of space (of building and environment in a co-ordinated social project), postmodern space displays an aesthetic AUTONOMY; design overrules function to produce an architecture of eclectic, unintegrated styles. However, Harvey remains committed to a materialist, historical analysis (to a modernist paradigm, it might be said). Where Jameson and others see the waning of a sense of time and history in the transition to postmodernity, Harvey argues that the effect of global CAPITALISM and communications has been to accelerate the production and consumption of goods, and the passage of information. The movement of people and modes of employment have also been radically affected by these new 'post-Fordist' modes of 'flexible accumulation' (part-time, casual labour, weakened trades unions, subcontracting, diversification). Thus, postmodern life is characterized throughout by the experience of what Harvey terms 'time-space compression'.

Manuel Castells, a major theorist of the 'information society' or NETWORK argues even more dramatically that capitalism works through new information technologies, effectively 'to annihilate time' (1997:12) as it seeks a rhythm of ever more rapid turnover and obsolescence. The result is 'timeless time' governed by the 'space of flows' (the global transactions of finance, the circulation of 'wealth, information and crime'; 1997: 15). This approximates once more to the loss of a historical sense and 'fragmentation of time into a series of perpetual presents', which Jameson sees as affecting EVERYDAY LIFE, art and culture in 'the world space of multinational capital' (Brooker [ed] 1992: 179). As these statements suggest, a new awareness of space, prompting the emergence of a new cultural or postmodern geography, has been accompanied by arguments on a transformed sense of time.

In contemporary thinking, space has become more evidently linked to themes associated with the CITY and ECOLOGY. Thus, Shaw and Humm's (2016) multidisciplinary collection debates new ways to inhabit space, evidenced by environmental camps, PSYCHOGEOGRAPHY, urban interventions and mappings of the extra-terrestrial upon everyday life. Film critic, David Thomson (*Guardian* 18 February 2016), meanwhile, speculates that popular, award-winning Hollywood films, above all *The Martian* and *The Revenant*, present spatialized scenarios which set the human (and, vicariously, the viewer) in testing wilderness or alien environments. Along with a will to survive, such films exhibit a newly alerted sense of the environmental sublime as a scene of both dread and wonder. This cinematic wilderness, Thomson suggests, stands in for the threats of global warming and social destitution: 'an end-of-days mood in both the natural and political world'.

See also COGNITIVE MAPPING; PLACE; THIRDSPACE.

SPECTACLE

The idea of the 'society of the spectacle' derives from Guy Debord's book of that title. Debord was a leading member of the Situationists group, a loose collective of radical political theorists and activists influenced by the Dadaist and Surrealist movements, which had a considerable influence upon the student and workers' revolt in France in May 1968, as well as upon similar events in Europe and beyond. Debord was the editor from 1957 to 1969 of the group's journal, whose use of collage and innovative graphics was itself an influence on the underground press of the 1960s and 1970s, on punk and a generation of fanzines. Debord's *Society of the Spectacle* was published in 1967 as a text of 221 paragraphs on unnumbered pages. His argument was that the mode of commodity production analysed by Marx as characteristic of CAPITALISM had been extended in the world of MASS communications and electronic media beyond commodities to include human relations. These, too, were now the subject of exchange VALUE. As he writes in the book's first paragraph, 'in societies where modern conditions of production prevail, all of life presents itself as an immense accumulation of spectacles.'

Debord's insights on the penetration of the commodity form, the ideological role of the new media, the absorption of 'real life' by its REPRESENTATIONS, the way history was becoming 'forgotten within culture' anticipate some of the key themes of POSTMODERNISM. Jean Baudrillard's ideas on HYPERREALITY and the society of the IMAGE particularly echo Debord's findings. There is a significant difference, however. Whereas Debord and the Situationists felt that the media and the form of the spectacle could be turned back against consumer capitalism, Baudrillard sees only a loss of distinction between the real and its SIMULATION, and the resulting passivity and indifference of a desensitized mass, no longer even in any clear sense the spectators a spectacle requires. His example of a fake hold-up helps illustrate this. Whereas a real hold-up threatens the right to property, a fake or simulated hold-up threatens the very principle of reality on which the established order depends. It poses the more profound challenge, therefore, but is bound to fall victim to the real, says Baudrillard, whose function 'is precisely to devour any attempt at simulation' on behalf of the established order (1994: 20). The kind of theatrical political tactic the Situationists favoured has already been anticipated in a world where 'all the holdups, airplane hijackings, etc. are now in some sense simulation holdups in that they are already inscribed in the decoding and orchestration rituals of the media'. Indeed, according to Baudrillard, TV, the principal postmodern medium:

> is no longer a spectacular medium. We are no longer in the society of the spectacle of which the situationists spoke, nor in the specific kinds of alienation and repression that it implied. The medium itself is no longer identifiable as such and the confusion of the medium and the message... is the first great formula of this new era. There is no longer a medium in the literal sense: it is now intangible, diffused, and diffracted in the real.
>
> (1994: 30)

See also PSYCHOGEOGRAPHY.

SPECULATIVE REALISM

'Speculative Realism' and the related thinking in so-called 'Object-Oriented Ontology' (commonly styled 'OOO') are often understood as examples of a PARADIGM shift in philosophy and Media Studies termed the 'New Materialism'. This in turn stretches to encompass those intellectual positions which broadly share the idea that non-human matter comprising the physical world can exercise agency and communicate independently of human consciousness or knowledge (see Shaviro 2014). A key text in this philosophical matrix has been Quentin Meillassoux's *After Finitude: An Essay on the Necessity of Contingency* (2006 [trans. Ray Brassier] 2009). Here, Meillassoux contests the received 'common sense' idea associated with Emmanuel Kant and named 'Kantian correlationism' that thought cannot conceive of 'the world itself' independently of our thinking about the world. Human consciousness and the cognitive-linguistic representation of the physical world are seen to be held in a coextensive relation: 'We cannot represent the "in itself" without it becoming "for us"', as Meillassoux summarizes (2006: 4). However, he critiques this belief by means of his opening example of 'ancestrality', namely that a fossil belonging to an 'ancestral realm' is evidence of existence prior to, and independent of, human cognition, indeed prior to the arrival of human beings.

The limitation expressed in Kant's 'correlationism' (that we cannot know the world beyond ourselves) may therefore be recast so as to affirm – speculating beyond the limits of the Kantian model – a world or worlds (realities) beyond human cognition. That this world is knowable only through speculative reason means accepting that objectivity and truth may well lie beyond the scope of human knowledge. This leads Meillassoux to affirm that events in the world are entirely contingent, and thus to question the explanatory status of scientific laws of the physical world, since, in the face of such radical contingency, any laws are themselves subject to random change and unforeseen transmutation.

If the first proposition has been widely accepted as a breakthrough in western philosophy, the second has been received with some caution. Thus, Christopher Norris (2013) feels Meillassoux's argument is 'broken-backed'; that its 'scientific-realist outlook' runs into 'a speculative bent that leans so far in a "radical" (self-consciously heterodox) direction as to lose touch with any workable variety of scientific realism' (187). The insistence, consequently, on the necessity of a radical contingency which, in Norris's view, ignores 'a whole range of significant ideas and developments within analytic philosophy of science' (194) in fact weakens its realist credentials.

There is little doubt, however, that Meillassoux's *After Finitude* stands as a founding text of 'speculative realism'. The use of this term has been associated especially with a conference held under this title at Goldsmiths, University of London in 2007, attended by Meillassoux and others, including Graham Harman, Ray Brassier and Iain Hamilton Grant, who have themselves become prominent in the field (see, for an introductory selection of essays, Bryant, Srnicek, Harman [eds] 2011 and for a comprehensive critical review, Gratton, 2014). This event, along with a second conference in Bristol, England in 2012, a flurry of blogs, dedicated journals (*Collapse* and *Speculative Philosophy*) and new book series have helped consolidate the impression of a new, highly active 'movement'. Brassier, however, has made a point of denying any common group identity. Rather, these philosophers can be seen as pursuing different lines of research, variously indebted to such figures as Alain Badiou, Slavoj Žižek, Alfred North Whitehead, Gilles Deleuze and Bruno Latour. If they join in a shared critique of anthropocentricism and a belief in the autonomy of reality, these realities are differently conceived: as a world of mutually autonomous objects, irreducible to their elements or relations (Harman 2002, 2005), in terms of an endlessly productive and capacious nature (Grant 2006), or a universe characterized by an unbounded nihilism (Brassier 2007).

At the same time, too, this work is markedly collaborative and dialogic. In one such strand, 'object-oriented philosophy' developed by Graham Harman in his exploration of the autonomy of human tools in his *Tool-Being* (2002), was further developed by Levi Bryant as 'Object-Oriented Ontology', or 'Onticology', in his *The Democracy of Objects* (2011). This similarly questions Kantian correlationism to emphasize the existence of non-human objects beyond human consciousness. Charlie Gere (2015), in turn, sees this emphasis on non-human communication as particularly germane to a newly conceived Media Studies whose expanded province appears as a 'cosmos in which communication is the prime means by which things emerge and find themselves in relation to each other' (279).

Elsewhere, in a broad application to the Arts and Humanities, N. Katherine Hayles (2014), known for her work on the POSTHUMAN, digital media and electronic literature (2008, 2012), has sought to respond to the challenge Harman's Object-Oriented Ontology poses to aesthetics, traditionally founded on a human (often a privileged, subjective) sensibility. Hayles looks, among others, to Jane Bennett's *Vibrant Matter* (2010) to argue for the importance, first, of viewing objects (biological, animate, inanimate) *in relation*, and, second, to the role, taking us beyond anthropocentricism, of the human capacity for an 'imaginative projection into the worldviews of other objects and beings' (2014: 178). Thus, by means of scientific evidence, metaphor and analogy, we come to an apprehension of 'their way of being in the world' (172). These positions combined provide the theoretical basis, Hayles submits, of a 'speculative aesthetics'.

See also MATERIALISM; THING THEORY.

STRUCTURALISM

Structuralism was derived from the theory of structural linguistics developed by Ferdinand de Saussure in a series of lectures given in 1909–11 and published posthumously in his *Course in General Linguistics* (1915). Saussure's theory and its influence rested on three key distinctions: between the parts of the linguistic SIGN, named the 'signifier' and 'signified'; between the collective language system (*langue*) and the individual language-user's operation of that system, or 'speech', named *parole;* and between language's historical dimension and present contemporary state, comprising in turn its 'diachronic' and 'synchronic' axis.

Saussure's emphasis was on the synchronic aspect of the *langue* and the structural relations comprising this.

This model was taken up in the 1960s when it seemed to offer a rigorous, non-subjective model for the analysis of literary and other cultural forms; one that would be free of the customary privileging of literary above POPULAR forms and would extend across written and visual, as across 'high' art and 'MASS' COMMUNICATION systems. The assumption was that literature, film or advertising – as well as, in some instances, more obviously social and non-textual systems like sport or fashion, or MYTH and ritual in the field of Structural Anthropology – could be understood and analysed as themselves comprising a language.

However, there are limitations in these fields to the analogy with natural language and thus to the model proposed by structural linguistics. First, the analysis of cultural forms generally is concerned with meaning or 'signification', as well as the structural relations that were a priority for Saussure. Where literary and other forms of cultural analysis adopted this model on the grounds of its 'scientific' credentials, they were therefore in danger of committing themselves to a formalist approach. Even where this restriction has been accepted as in much influential work on NARRATIVE, the dependence on Saussurean categories can seem forced – as in Gérard Genette's suggestion that 'story' be considered the equivalent of 'signified or narrative content' and 'narrative' the equivalent of 'signifier, statement, discourse or narrative text' (1980: 27). Second, Saussure saw the relation between parts of the sign (signifier and signified), and between signs, as governed by the entire system of the language (*langue*). It is fairly clear, however, that in particular cultural discourses these relations are defined, not by a whole culture, which would be the equivalent to '*langue*', but by the conventions of a SUBCULTURE or GENRE and that they are, moreover, motivated rather than arbitrary.

There are further problems, along these lines, in the analysis of visual media. An illustration would be the conventional shots of a private detective's office in American movies of the 1940s and 1950s: the reverse lettering on a door of the office, the shadow of the blinds, the flickering neon light from a store outside. These are signs, not only of the idea of door, blind or office, but of a style of life associated with a romanticized lone male figure caught in the complex underground world of crime, and law and order. They are parts of a coded narrative sequence that draws on, and might confirm or extend, the established codes of a type of Hollywood film. The use, drawing on other work within structural linguistics, of a concept such as CODE was fruitful in describing these fuller cultural meanings. Otherwise, such analysis was conducted under the auspices of SEMIOLOGY, rather than in the terms of the original Saussurean model.

Structural linguistics, and hence structuralism, were also subjected to two further critiques. The first was made by the Soviet scholar, V.N. Vološhinov, associated with the Bakhtin School of the 1920s. His *Marxism and the Philosophy of Language* (1973 [1929]) emphasized the social, ideological and historical aspects of language, and directly criticized Saussure's theory for ignoring these. The second critique was inspired especially by Jacques Derrida's DECONSTRUCTION of the fundamental, but unsustainable, premises of Saussurean linguistics, especially of Saussure's privileging of speech over writing. Derrida's early essay 'Structure, sign, and play in the discourses of human sciences' (1978 [presented 1966]) had shown how the very idea of structure rested on the assumption of a coherent system, but set the holding centre of this structure paradoxically both within and outside the system. This essay proved to be one of the founding texts of POSTSTRUCTURALISM and thus of a move, in one direction, beyond structuralism.

See also DIALOGICS.

STRUCTURES OF FEELING

A much-used term, first coined by Raymond Williams in the early study *Preface to Film* (1954), and developed by him in *The Long Revolution* (1961) and *Marxism and Literature* (1977). Williams employs it, he says, 'as an analytic procedure' in the study of written and artistic works and, by extension, to describe the way such works articulate a more general CONSCIOUSNESS for which there is 'no external counterpoint' in the material life, social organization or dominant ideas of a period (Williams 1979: 159). In *The Long Revolution*, the phrase names the thoughts and feelings of a representative generation – the writers of the 1840s are Williams's main example – who express what is 'a very deep and wide possession' (1961: 65) and its coming to formed consciousness. It follows for Williams, that a new generation will shape its response to changed circumstances in a changed structure of feeling.

Williams's concept is, therefore, neither to be identified with a CLASS outlook, nor with the whole society, nor confused with the adjacent, but distinct, term IDEOLOGY. Williams's *Marxism and Literature* (1977) contains chapters on both these and other related terms (notably HEGEMONY). His discussion here confirms that the advantage of the concept lies, for him, in its flexible conjunction of the two realms of 'objective' structure and 'subjective' feeling, suggesting how personal emotions and experience ('meanings and values as they are actively lived and felt', 1977: 132) are shaped in thought and consciousness, and take a social form in observable texts and practices. It differs in intention, therefore, from the abstract and reductive Marxist vocabulary of an earlier era and from Marxism's later, poststructuralist and anti-humanist mode. It differs also, in content, from a term such as ideology, since a 'structure of feeling' presents the immediate world of feelings and impulses, brought to a new point of articulation in successive generations, and does this in terms that are pre-ideological, or in tension with the dominant ideology's more systematic formulations. Throughout, Williams's emphasis is on describing 'forming and formative processes' as against 'fixed explicit forms': 'structures of feeling can be described as social experiences in solution,' he says (1977: 128, 133). It is with this sense, therefore, that he speaks of 'the structure of feeling of an emergent productive class' (1979: 173).

The concept is used particularly in literary and textual studies, not least in Williams's own, where selected texts are taken to give the tone to a period or generation, or, more precisely, to identify the shaping consciousness of particular social groups, from white middle-class male professionals (Pfeil 1988) to CYBERPUNKS (Suvin, in McCaffery [ed] 1991).

SUBALTERN

The Italian Marxist, Antonio Gramsci, spoke of 'subaltern classes' to designate the politically unco-ordinated popular MASS. The concept was further developed by the 'subaltern studies' collective of Indian researchers, headed by Ranajit Guha. In their writings (1982–94), the group seek to assemble a counter-history of POPULAR forms of action and CULTURE to contest both colonial and nationalist accounts. Gayatri Chakravorty Spivak (1942–) has written supportively, but with reservations, on the work of the group (1987, 1988). She brings a combined deconstructive, Marxist and feminist perspective to reflections on the way the west and western INTELLECTUALS perceive the subaltern as the OTHER and to the position of women, both western and Asian, in these relationships; 'Can the subaltern speak?' she asks. In so far as this invokes a unified, true and unmediated voice, her answer is 'no'. The colonized subaltern subject is, she says, 'irretrievably heterogeneous' (1988: 284) and, in a world of western and Indian textual and other REPRESENTATIONS, can neither 'know or speak itself' (1988: 285). Subaltern historiography therefore trails an essentialist category of 'the people'. But if, in Spivak's argument, the subaltern male is effaced, the woman is 'doubly effaced' in colonialist and subaltern history, 'even more deeply in shadow... as mute as ever' (1988: 287, 295).

The questions raised here of the role of western theory and DISCOURSE, of the intellectual's alignment with the subaltern and of the political AGENCY of oppressed, 'silenced' groups, are continuing issues in postcolonial studies.

See also ESSENTIALISM; MARGIN(ALITY); POSTCOLONIALISM.

SUBCULTURES

Subcultures are defined in the first instance in terms of their relation to the mainstream or dominant CULTURE of which they form an antagonistic, or eccentric, but supportive part. They are comprised, in close or loosely affiliated groupings, of those who share a set of common interests, values, tastes and often a specialist knowledge and argot; who pursue common, ritualistic practices or pastimes; who may display their unity in material objects, accoutrements, dress or a common 'look'; and who may be known through an association with a particular physical region, urban SPACE or venue. Hell's Angels, mods, punks or new age travellers therefore comprise subcultures, but so, too, do *Star Trek* fans, skateboarders and scientologists, as well as intensely committed networks of computer hackers, pigeon-fanciers and ballroom dancers.

An early, more journalistic than theorized study of postwar American subcultures appeared in Thomas Wolfe's *The Kandy-Kolored Tangerine-Flake Streamline Baby* (1965). Writings on the 'Beats', on pop and rock music (such as Greil Marcus's *Lipstick Traces* 1989), and on sport (Nick Hornby's *Fever Pitch* 1995), provide similar examples, which borrow indirectly from the sociological practice of 'participant observation' employed in a work such as William Whyte's classic *Street Corner Society* (1955). Documentary film and TV programmes (from *We Are the Lambeth Boys* 1959, to numerous contemporary examples) also offer invaluable studies in their own terms of the social composition, styles and attitudes of contemporary subcultures.

In academic work, the theoretical study of subcultures, in the UK especially, has been overwhelmingly concerned with the interconnected worlds of music, fashion and youth in the postwar period (Hebdige 1979; McRobbie 1991, 1994) or with youth and work (Willis 1979). Such subcultures are understood as being 'subordinate', but more subversive than 'subordinated' in their relation to mainstream culture. To this end, Subcultural Theory has drawn on Marxist notions of IDEOLOGY, on the Gramscian conception of HEGEMONY, particularly as elaborated in Raymond Williams' distinctions between DOMINANT, oppositional, alternative and RESIDUAL and EMERGENT tendencies in society (Hebdige 1979). At the same time, subcultures have been mapped on to distinctions of social CLASS and, latterly, GENDER, as well as personal and generational style. Studies of this kind therefore seek to report on the symbolic cultural meanings of apparently superficial or delinquent postures and practices, and how these actively constitute subjective and collective identities. Such identities are seen as a way of negotiating or resisting the established identities and pathways sanctioned by the conventions of a 'parent' society.

As this suggests, Subcultural Studies have tended towards a combined ethnographic and textual, or social-semiotic approach, internal to, and sympathetic towards, the groups they study. For some, this has posed problems of approach and method, particularly concerning the position and authority of the researcher. The more 'textualist' approach of Hebdige, for example, is seen to fall short of reading cultural style as an expression of class position (Sparks 1996) and, along with similar studies, to present an overly positive and 'populist' understanding that minimizes the constraining and assimilative powers of the dominant culture and its supporting economic structure (McGuigan 1992). A further problem of emphasis (on white working-class male and non-conformist rather than conservative subcultures) also remains.

Reservations such as these effectively stalled Subcultural Studies in the later 1980s. Following the general trajectory of Cultural Studies, however, later work concerned with gender, RACE and ETHNICITY (Mercer 1994; Back 1996) brought a new vigour and theoretical framework to this area. For a survey of the field see Thornton and Gelder (1996).

See also COMMON CULTURE; COUNTER-CULTURE; CULT; ETHNOGRAPHY.

SUBJECT

A term for the self, individual or human being (the 'human subject') adopted especially by those influenced by structuralist and poststructuralist PARADIGMS. Unlike 'individual', the term 'subject' draws attention to the double sense of AGENCY (as in the grammatical subject of an utterance) and of being subjected or subordinated to non-subjective DETERMINATIONS. Already, therefore, the term implies a divided rather than unified IDENTITY and, as such, critiques earlier conceptions – notably the dominant 'individualism' of the nineteenth and early twentieth centuries or, in philosophy, the conception of the individual presented by Descartes. This is commonly thought now to be superseded or 'dead'. The trope of the 'death of the subject' was notably introduced by Roland Barthes' essay on 'The death of the author' (1968), in a polemical case for a poststructuralist, rather than liberal humanist, approach to the reading of literary texts. Within humanist ideology and the various artistic and other DISCOURSES which endorse this – including, Barthes would suggest, the realist novel and traditional criticism – the individual is perceived as whole and stable, and as the origin of discourse and meaning. It is this view – whether regarded as true of an earlier era, or as an ideological construction – that is thought to be untenable (Belsey 1980).

The CRITIQUE of the liberal humanist view of the subject has a longer history than this suggests, however, and occurred notably in Marx and in Freud. The idea of the harmonious and self-determining individual is, for Marx, the bourgeoisie's idealized view of itself and is contradicted by the experience of ALIENATION from one's labour and one's self produced by the economic and social relations of capitalist society. Freud's later identification of the dimensions of the conscious and UNCONSCIOUS similarly questions assumptions of the unified individual. According to both thinkers, therefore, neither the social nor individual subject were whole or self-determining, since their actions and thoughts were determined by circumstances and drives beyond their control or knowledge. This should not be understood as a denial of all freedom, however. Marxism, for example, sees CAPITALISM as oppressive, but envisions the restoration of a full humanity beyond CLASS societies. Even Theodor Adorno, noted for his pessimism, identified two subjects: the false objective subject of capitalism, produced by and for the mechanisms of money and labour exchange, and a true repressed subject. Together, this gives rise to an internalized antagonism of two subjects, 'the subject as the subject's foe', as Adorno puts it (1990: 10).

Both Marxist and Freudian notions have been extremely influential and are echoed in contemporary theory, even where this critiques Marxist and Freudian orthodoxies, as in the work of Louis Althusser and Jacques Lacan, for example. A further inspiration to the anti-humanism of certain poststructuralist positions has also been found in Nietzsche. All three nineteenth-century thinkers clearly pointed to the double, contradictory sense of identity implicit in current usage. The difference in later discussions lies not in this perception, therefore, but in the kinds of determination that are seen to construct and shape the individual. Thus within poststructuralism, the subject is seen as constructed within language or TEXTUALITY, or discursive practices, or elsewhere as shaped by controlling structures and ideologies of nation, GENDER, RACE, ETHNICITY, the BODY and SEXUALITY, rather than by class or the psyche alone.

There can be significant differences of theoretical orientation across this range (as between poststructuralism, FEMINISM and postcolonial studies). Nevertheless, it is commonly accepted that the individual subject, so situated, is 'decentred'. This is in keeping with a common opposition to essentialist notions (that there is a prior or underlying essence, not only of the individual, but of the female or black subject, or of truth). However, while this theory clearly critiques the humanist subject, it does not escape the question of its fundamental unifying role or the desirability of self-determination. Is the decentred subject of poststructuralist and postmodern times a description of the way things are in language, identity and society, to the point of being virtually 'natural' and unalterable, or are there grounds for anticipating a newly centred individual?

See also HUMANISM; INTERPELLATION; MIRROR-PHASE.

SUBJECTIVITY

In PSYCHOANALYSIS, the individual is thought to acquire the IDENTITY of a human SUBJECT at the point of entry into language or the SYMBOLIC order. In more materialist theories, this process is viewed in terms of the individual's construction in social and ideological relations. Subjectivity is best understood as naming the interior experience of being a particular subject, rather than becoming a subject. Subjectivity might, therefore, contradict the way an individual comes to be positioned in the Symbolic or social order. Female subjectivity, for example, has consistently been theorized within FEMINISM in ways that define, or seek to define, an identity that contests the subordinated position of women in the normative scenarios of psychoanalysis or institutionalized power relations.

An equivalent tension can occur for others in marginalized social positions. Thus, an African-Caribbean teenager might be positioned as a 'black youth' and viewed in terms of a stereotypical identity that predicts his/her cultural tastes, character, low educational and job prospects, involvement in drugs, petty crime and so on. The term INTERPELLATION, employed by Louis Althusser, describes how an individual may be addressed or 'hailed' into a particular subject position according to such presuppositions. However, an individual might have a view of themselves that competes internally with the stereotypical view. The stereotype may therefore form part of the individual's subjectivity, but this will also provide a resistant alternative sense of self. This counter-identification may consequently allude to a residual core of self (as when someone 'feels working class' or 'feels Irish' in spite of social and material factors that occlude this identity) and thus have a nostalgic or essentialist aspect. Alternatively, a resistant counter-subjectivity may inspire a mobility (not so much a DESIRE for authenticity as 'to be somebody else'), which contrasts with the fixity of a given identity as human subject.

See also BODY; SEXUALITY; TRANSGRESSIVE.

SUBLIME

A first-century Greek treatise 'On the sublime', attributed to Longinus, associates the sublime with the experience of elevated thoughts and feelings prompted by terrifyingly beautiful prospects in nature. In the eighteenth century, Edmund Burke (1729–97), better known as a conservative political theorist, drew on these earlier ideas to make a comparison between the sublime and the beautiful in an account of landscape, art and social passions (*A Philosophical Enquiry into the Origin of Our Ideas on the Sublime and the Beautiful* 1759). Burke associated the sublime with terror, pain and danger. The eighteenth-century preference had been for an orderly landscape and society, which would express the authority of reason in physical as in human nature. The early nineteenth-century Romantic preference, which Burke here anticipated, was for the wild and remote, the untutored and grotesque. Most importantly, the sublime inspired an overpowering, inexpressible feeling of awe, often associated with the presence of the divine or some transcendental spirit or force, producing an emotion that was literally beyond words. Examples occurred in the paintings of Caspar David Friedrich and in William Wordsworth's *The Prelude* (1855). In social thought, its logical form was revolution.

The concept has returned to critical currency by way of the French philosopher, Jean-François Lyotard's account of POSTMODERNISM. Lyotard associates the postmodern with an experimental, AVANT-GARDE mode that interrogates and pushes beyond the 'modern', defining a present status quo. Its domain (Lyotard consciously draws on Burke, but also on Immanuel Kant's understanding of the concept as designating the monstrous and formless) is therefore the hitherto unexpressed, or that which is presently beyond intelligibility. The 'real sublime sentiment,' Lyotard writes, 'is an intrinsic combination of pleasure and pain: the pleasure that reason should exceed all presentation, the pain that imagination or sensibility should not be equal to the concept' (1984: 81). There follows Lyotard's much-cited definition of the postmodern – clearly informed by the above:

> The postmodern would be that which, in the modern puts forward the unpresentable in presentation itself; that which denies itself the solace of good forms, the consensus of a taste which would make it possible to share collectively the nostalgia for the unobtainable; that which searches for new presentations, not in order to enjoy them but in order to impart a stronger sense of the unpresentable.
>
> (1984: 81)

Elsewhere, commenting on the important feature of a lack of consensus of taste or judgement in the postmodern, Lyotard writes:

> With the sublime, there is no criterion for assessing the role of taste, and so everybody is alone when it comes to judging. The question then becomes: how can we share with others a feeling which is so deep and unexchangeable? …this community is yet to be. It is not yet realised.
>
> (1986:11)

In this way, in Lyotard's postmodern, the fundamentally AESTHETIC criterion of the sublime (as the unpresentable and unrealized) comes also to inform a social and political view.

See also DIFFEREND; GOTHIC.

SUPPLEMENT

A term given particular meaning in the writings of Jacques Derrida. In French, *supplément* has the sense of both a surplus and a substitution. The first meaning supposes that a given text is already complete and is supplemented by something extra to it (in which case it was not complete); the second supposes that something can be substituted for the original (in which case it was not unique or definitive). Derrida found this 'logic of supplementarity' at work in a number of writings, but especially in the writings of the eighteenth-century French thinker, Jean-Jacques Rousseau, to whom he devotes some critical discussion in *Of Grammatology* (1976 [1967]). Rousseau proposed that education supplements nature, implying simultaneously and contradictorily that nature is complete in itself and requires an addition for it to be made complete. What seems extra and external is in fact necessary and internal to that which it supplements.

Rousseau himself employed the term *supplément* and spoke also of masturbation as a 'dangerous supplement'. A similar logic applies to this example, since masturbation is thought of both as a perverse extra to SEXUALITY and as a substitute for it. But if masturbation takes the place of sexual activity, it must share something with it and cannot be as abnormal as supposed. 'Normal' and 'perverse' sexual activity can therefore be seen as different expressions of a common sexuality.

The strategy of reading that identifies 'the logic of the supplement' is characteristic of Derrida's deconstructive method. An opposition such as speech/writing, nature/society, normal/abnormal, in which the first term is privileged, is shown in fact to comprise a relation of DIFFERENCE not of hierarchical distinction. The double meanings of the term 'supplement' serve to unlock the tropes of philosophy and everyday thinking that seal things in their common place. Similar terms figure in Derrida's writing to the same effect: a 'pharmacon' is both poison and cure; the 'hymen' is both consummation and virginity (1981b [1972]; see also Kamuf [ed] 1991: 112–39, 169–99). Such terms confirm the differential nature of writing and meaning. The completeness of a given text, or the supposed plenitude of an object or idea are invaded by incompleteness and insufficiency, so questioning the assumptions that elevate one term and relegate another.

See also DECONSTRUCTION; *ÉCRITURE*/WRITING; TRACE.

SUTURE

A term from surgery meaning 'stitching' and employed especially in film theory to describe the way the viewer is 'stitched' as a SUBJECT into NARRATIVE DISCOURSE.

This meaning derives especially from psychoanalytic theory. In observing his grandson, Sigmund Freud had identified what he called the '*fort-da*' game. The child threw a cotton reel on a string from his cot and then pulled it back into view. It was thrown away (the German *fort*) and made to reappear (*da* = 'there'). Freud reasoned that this was the child's way of enacting the mother's departure, which pained and puzzled him, and of finding consolation for this loss by contriving her symbolic return. The episode is marked by presence and absence, and this the psychoanalytic theorist, Jacques Lacan, following Freud, saw as fundamental to language and the structure of DESIRE. Desire only comes into existence because of the experience of lack.

Similarly, meaning in the structuralist model of language adopted by Lacan, is dependent on simultaneous presence and absence, or in other words 'DIFFERENCE', such that a present term, for example, 'cat', only acquires meaning through its relation with another absent term, 'cap'. Lacan saw the *fort-da* game as prefiguring the child's inauguration (or being 'sutured') into the system of presences and absences comprising the SYMBOLIC order of language.

A further aspect of Lacanian theory is also alluded to in this discussion. In the MIRROR-PHASE, the child sees a whole and unified image of itself in a mirror, while at the same time realizing that this is not itself. The subject is split between a present and absent ideal image. The application of both of these ideas to film theory can best be illustrated by the editing technique of shot/reverse shot. The viewer is presented with the shot of a street scene, for example, and then with the shot of a spectator who, by cinematic and psychoanalytic convention, is understood to be the person looking upon the street as it has just been shown. As Madan Sarup notes:

> According to suture theory, the viewer experiences shot 1 as an imaginary plenitude, unbounded by any gaze, and unmarked by difference. It is thus the site of a jouissance akin to that of the mirror phase prior to the child's discovery of its separation from the ideal image which it has discovered in the reflecting glass.
>
> (1992: 155)

This plenitude is accompanied, however, by an immediate sense of deprivation as the viewer realizes s/he can see only a selected part of a possible wider panorama. The viewing position which authorizes the part that is seen is the position of the camera, and this is attributed in psychoanalytic terms to 'the "Absent One" or the "Other" [who] has all the attributes of the symbolic father' (Sarup 1992: 155). This (invisible) figure has everything the actual viewer lacks. The role of the reverse shot is therefore to resolve the discomfort created by this tension between plenitude (presence) and lack (absence). It does so by substituting the GAZE of the fictional character on screen for the controlling gaze outside the fiction. In this way, it presents a perspective with which the cinema-goer can identify, and so offers a consolation for the sense of loss. The illusionism of the realist film depends for its success on the willingness of the viewer to accept this stand-in for the unseen OTHER. This point of acceptance is the point of being 'sutured' into the set of cinematic conventions just as, in the psychic development of the subject, the individual is 'sutured' into the Symbolic order.

See also MISRECOGNITION (*MÉCONNAISSANCE*).

SYMBOLIC

See IMAGINARY.

SYMBOLIC VIOLENCE

A concept employed by the French sociologist of culture, Pierre Bourdieu (1930–2002) to refer to the ways in which dominant classes or CLASS fractions impose ruling ideologies upon dominated groups. Essentially, this is seen as being secured – as in the operation of Antonio Gramsci's related concept of HEGEMONY – by legitimizing class interests and beliefs as natural and right. Dominated or subordinated groups in society therefore consent to their own subjugation or minority status, accepting that a given but implicitly defended and stratified social order is the natural order. Bourdieu's concept therefore draws attention to 'the recognition by the dominated of the legitimacy of domination' (Bourdieu and Passeron 1977: 5). The result is a set of 'doxa', comprising the taken-for-granted knowledge of 'how the world is', which constitutes an individual and social group's uncritical practical experience.

See also HABITUS; INTERPELLATION; MISRECOGNITION (*MÉCONNAISSANCE*).

SYMPTOMATIC READING

A mode of analysis proposed by the French Marxist philosopher, Louis Althusser (1918–90) in association with other related terms, principally PROBLEMATIC. A symptomatic reading aims to elicit what is not said, or not sayable, within the terms of a given theory or ideological position. Althusser is concerned with developments in Marxist theory and suggests that a symptomatic reading of Marx's own texts is necessary to reveal the transition from IDEOLOGY to the scientific knowledge of Marx's *Capital*.

The practice of symptomatic reading was applied within literary study by Pierre Macherey in his influential *A Theory of Literary Production* (1978) and may be extended to the analysis of any argument or NARRATIVE. Any philosophical, literary or cultural text, thus, can be said to be informed, in Althusser's terms, by a 'problematic' comprising a set of governing assumptions that simultaneously give those texts their coherence while determining their limitations. This practice is to be distinguished, therefore, first from a style of interpretation that seeks to make supposedly conscious but implicit intentions explicit and, second, from a related criterion of evaluation that views the lack of unity as a disabling flaw. Moreover, a symptomatic reading does not simply cite what is beyond the terms of a given ideology, but what is in some way acknowledged but subordinated and repressed within it. Thus, a symptomatic reading of a western will seek to disclose the limits of its controlling and unifying ideas of masculinity, law and COMMUNITY, but will at its most productive note, not only what is evidently excluded (gay men, anarchism, the contemporary city), but what is contained or expelled within the terms of its governing problematic (drunkenness, gambling, prostitution, native Americans).

A symptomatic reading is, in these terms, close to the practice of CRITIQUE – though this looks for the more positive, progressive side of a contradictory set of ideas – and close also to the first stage of a deconstructive reading which seeks to identify the binary opposites that reinforce a hierarchy of relations and values. It might be said that, unlike DECONSTRUCTION, however, a symptomatic reading, for Althusser at least, does not seek to disperse such a governing hierarchy into relations of difference so much as reveal its ideology in the interests of a fuller (Marxist) knowledge.

SYNCHRONIC

See SIGN; STRUCTURALISM.

SYNCRETISM

The combination of different or supposedly opposite things. The term is used, for example, in cultural ETHNOGRAPHY to describe the sharing of speech and musical styles between black and white, or Asian and African-Caribbean adolescents, particularly in inner-city areas (Hewitt 1986; Back 1996). Examples in the UK would be the bhangra styles of music (joi bhangra, house bhangra, bhangra beat, northern rock bhangra – each with a particular regional association), which combine a song and dance GENRE of the Punjab with the western forms and techniques of sound sampling, drum machines, rap and hip-hop. Syncretism of this type can produce a cultural affiliation over and above caste, CLASS, religion or nationality, and is welcomed as an expression of non- or anti-racist attitudes. However, the optimism researchers have brought to the evidence of such cross-cultural exchange has been qualified by the realization that informal 'popular racism' (evident in jokes or name-calling, for example) or the direct use of the racist discourses of the far right can coexist in complex ways with the egalitarianism of syncretic cultural behaviours (Billig *et al.* 1988; Back 1996).

See also ETHNICITY; HYBRIDITY.

SYNERGY

A term for the confluence of ideas or different spheres. Examples would be interdisciplinary academic work, the blurring of traditional distinctions between critical and creative DISCOURSES encouraged by arguments in POSTSTRUCTURALISM, and the eclectic cross-over between POPULAR and high culture characteristic of POSTMODERNISM. It is therefore cognate with other current theoretical terms such as SYNCRETISM, HYBRIDITY, or Deleuze and Guattari's idea of the RHIZOME, which similarly describe or urge an erosion of fixed identities and settled boundaries. Since the 1980s, a particular application in the broad field of CYBERNETICS has pointed to the variety of connections between human and machine made possible by developments in computer-mediated communications systems, biotechnology and genetic engineering, and thus to the mixing of science, the media and popular culture in CYBERPUNK fiction and the cultures of the INTERNET.

The term 'synergetics' is employed by Klaus Mainzer to define 'an interdisciplinary methodology to explain the emergence of certain macroscopic phenomena via the non-linear interactions of microscopic elements in complex systems' (1994: 11). Sadie Plant (1996) glosses this idea, or what she terms 'connectionism', as implying that all manner of systems – whether 'natural' or 'artificial' – 'economies, organisms and ecosystems can equally be studied, defined and researched as self-organising systems' since 'there are processes of growth, evolution and learning which are common to them all' (1996: 210). She sees an interdisciplinary synergy or connectionism of this kind occurring between economics and the biological sciences, which both employ computer technologies in the investigation of self-organizing assemblages at interconnecting micro and molar levels. Plant views human learning processes and advanced computer technologies as examples of such self-organizing systems, alike in their operation and complexity and as 'leaking' into and 'cross-infecting' one another: 'machines learn, and learning is a mechanic process' (1996: 214). Such a conclusion challenges humanist ideas of knowledge, AGENCY and pedagogy, as well as the familiar separation of academic disciplines, including, Plant believes, the narrow interdisciplinarity of Cultural Studies. Its sense of 'purpose, autonomy and unified direction' ties it to a humanist model, she argues, which is at odds with the connectionist approach that sees CULTURE – 'all thinking, writing, dancing, engineering, creativity, social organisation, biological processing, economic interaction and communication of every kind' – as a self-organizing synergetic matrix (1996: 212).

See CHAOS; POSTHUMAN; VIRTUAL REALITY.

TASTE

In colloquial use, 'taste' is viewed as the expression of subjective judgement across all areas of social life (the arts, entertainment, fashion, lifestyle, even sexual partner) and, as such, is often understood as an unalterable sign of individual personality. In some ways, this echoes its theorization in classical AESTHETICS, where, as in the philosophy of Immanuel Kant, it is assumed that taste is the expression of transcendent, disinterested and thus unchanging criteria of judgement. The significant difference is that the latter is concerned to distinguish 'art' from the kind of 'non-artistic' discriminations made in the course of EVERYDAY LIFE. Contemporary social and cultural discussion of taste in relation both to high art and COMMON CULTURE is especially indebted to the work of Pierre Bourdieu (1930–) and in particular to the findings of his study *Distinction* (1984) based on an empirical investigation of patterns of consumption and lifestyle among French subjects in Bordeaux and Paris in the early and late 1960s. In direct refutation of the Kantian position, Bourdieu concludes that taste is an expression and reinforcement of social status and CLASS position, derived from the influence of family, education and employment. Thus, in his view, the acquired CULTURAL CAPITAL of the dominant middle class grants it access to 'legitimate' culture; this in turn unites this class and helps sustain its dominance. As in other matters, the upper class can 'disguise what they have *learned* as what they are *born* with' (Jenkins 1992: 139). The working class, Bourdieu sees as 'dominated', excluded from 'legitimate' culture and without independent aesthetic judgement, while the lower-middle class (the *petite bourgeoisie*) are caught between an untutored reverence for legitimate art and the immediacy of POPULAR culture. This class, he associates with the postmodern crossing of traditional cultural boundaries. For Bourdieu, the result is more mediocrity and 'unnaturalness' than a challenging new cultural aesthetic.

Many would have little difficulty in accepting Bourdieu's view of taste as a matter of social construction. However, commentators have queried several aspects of his theory, among them, his neglect of the role of the CULTURE INDUSTRIES (Garnham 1986) and his assumption that French society can serve as a model for the composition of social classes and consumer habits in other cultures (Jenkins 1992: 148). Most often, however, doubts are raised about Bourdieu's seemingly over-deterministic view of the role of social class, his condescension towards the working class, and dismissal of popular culture. Many would view popular culture as contradictorily inserted in hegemonic culture, as profoundly involved in aesthetic discriminations for producers and consumers, and as constitutive of flexible identities in which factors of GENDER, ETHNICITY and generation, as well as social class, play an important part (see Frith 1996 on popular music in this respect). In reply, Bourdieu argues that his critics have mistaken 'a reference to values' for the sociologist's 'judgement of value' and that 'populist exaltations of "popular culture"' offer no more than a 'sham inversion of dominant values' that in truth confirm the status quo (Bourdieu and Wacquant 1992: 83).

See also DISTINCTION; HABITUS.

TERRORISM

Though it may be thought to be a contemporary phenomenon, terrorism has a very long history. Randall D. Law (2009) begins his chronology of terrorism at 647 BCE, citing the terrorization of the city of Susa by an Assyrian Emperor. Key events through the next centuries include the Gunpowder Plot of 1605 and the reign of terror introduced by the new Constitution of the French Revolution. The latter saw the first use of the term 'terrorisme', which passed into English in Edmund Burke's *Letters on a Regicide Peace* (1795–96). 'The whole of their Government, in its origination, in its continuance, in all its actions, and in all its resources, is force; and nothing but force.' observed Burke (1939: 65). Thus, as Terry Eagleton notes, 'terrorism and the modern democratic state were twinned at birth' (2005: 1). Further examples of 'state terrorism' would include the show trials, mass imprisonment and disappearances of Stalin's Russia and the German Democratic Public, ruled by the activities of the secret police, a defining mechanism by which fear (terror) of betrayal or reprisals was instilled in the populace.

Until the present period, terrorist activities have otherwise been carried out by lone individuals, small clandestine groups or underground organisations which have targeted political enemies in the name of freedom and independence. Such have been the anarchist cells of the 1890s (the subject of Joseph Conrad's *The Secret Agent*, 1907), the 'Easter Rising' in Dublin of 1916, the anarchist-inspired Baader-Meinhof Gang/Red Army Faction in West Germany in the 1970s, the Angry Brigade and Weathermen in the same period in the UK and USA, respectively, and the IRA (Irish Republican Army), Basque separatists ETA (*Euskadi Ta Askatasuna*), and the Palestinian PLO (Palestine Liberation Organization).

In each case, the declared goal is freedom and the methods violent – a seeming contradiction justified in naming the enemy as the oppressor. In turn, the oppressive state will justify its own violence. Thus, as Slavoj Žižek (2002) comments when the Israeli Army 'attacks the Palestinian police and sets about systematically destroying the Palestinian infrastructure, Palestinian resistance is cited as proof that we are dealing with terrorists' (2).

This structure of denigration, expulsion or elimination of the OTHER is a consistent feature of terrorism and its opponents, locked in a narrative of 'war' and defeat until and unless 'peaceful' political solutions are found. Nowhere is this more the case than in the 'War on Terror' initiated in response to the bombing by al Qaeda of the New York twin towers on September 11, 2001, an EVENT which has led to protracted, highly complex wars, themselves giving rise to an exponential increase in diplomatic, journalistic and academic debate and analysis, as well as prompting direct and indirect terrorist scenarios in film (*United 93, Fahrenheit 9/11*), TV (the series *Spooks* and *Homeland*) and the graphic novel (Art Spiegelman, *In the Shadow of No Towers* 2004; see also Brooker 2005).

A striking immediate theoretical response to 9/11, pointing to a feature applicable to the later ISIS and plethora of groups operating in Iraq and Syria, appeared in Jean Baudrillard's *The Spirit of Terrorism: And Requiem for the Twin Towers* (2002). The 9/11 attacks, said Baudrillard, presented a new kind of terrorism which, in using airplanes and computer networks, took a 'form of action which plays the game… solely with the aim of disrupting it. …they have taken over all the weapons of the dominant power' (13). This has become more evident in the sophisticated use of the INTERNET and social media for propaganda purposes by ISIS, producing a bizarre collocation of modern communications media and (especially to western eyes) barbaric, medieval forms of torture and execution. This in itself has prompted an escalation of fear and a consequent increase in surveillance in threatened nations.

Terrorism Studies (see Horgan and Braddock 2011 and see the journal *Terrorism and Violence. Studies in Conflict and Terrorism*) continues to concern itself with the changing forms and meaning of terrorism over time, with the problem of definition – given changes in the forms, methods and reach of terrorism, extending in 2015 and 2016 to devastating guerrilla attacks in European cities – and with the tactics and goals of counter-terrorism. In one influential insight, Shiraz Maher of the International Centre for the Study of Radicalization at King's College London, argues (2016 and elsewhere) that the absolutist binary world-view of Islamic State explains not only their brutality towards 'infidels', but their intention to 'destroy the grey zone' of hybrid or fluent identities, such as that of British or French Muslims, or Muslim migrants who are seen to desert the caliphate IS claims to have established.

In all this, unlike the earlier more straightforwardly 'politically' motivated campaigns of earlier terrorist groups and movements, both al Qaeda and ISIS and their affiliates are engaged in a jihad (holy war) in the name of an Islamic order which dismisses western notions of democracy and freedom. At stake at this juncture, as is often said, is no less than an ideologically and religiously grounded war of 'ways of life'.

TEXT/TEXTUALITY

Within Literary Studies, the text has been the presiding unit of pedagogy and of academic criticism, particularly in the twentieth century. The most influential models have been those of Practical Criticism and New Criticism developed, respectively, by I.A. Richards and William Empson in England, and John Crowe Ransom, Cleanth Brooks and others in the United States. In addition, a moralizing, socially concerned criticism, which depended similarly on the 'close reading' and citation of literary texts, was associated with the critic F.R. Leavis and the journal *Scrutiny* that he co-edited from 1932 until 1953. Leavis or 'Leavisism' was opposed to the forms and cultural effects of modern industrial society (see Leavis's *Culture and Environment* 1932). However, this approach was developed in a more progressive direction by critics such as David Craig, Richard Hoggart and the early Raymond Williams. It therefore influenced early forms of British Cultural Studies – of which Hall and Whannel's *The Popular Arts* (1964) was a notable, text-based, Left or 'post-Leavisite' example.

A further influence on conceptions of the text and textual criticism within both Literary and Cultural Studies derived from the dissemination of structuralist theory in the 1960s and 1970s. Texts were thought to be formally and semantically CODEd in a systematic way and were correspondingly decoded by the reader. Roland Barthes' essay 'From work to text' (1977b) introduced a further influential distinction between the closed and representational, or realist, 'work' of more traditional understanding, and the more open, non-representational and modernist 'text'. The latter corresponded to what Barthes termed a 'scriptable' or 'WRITERLY' text as opposed to the 'lisible' or 'READERLY' work, and gave the reader a more active role in the production of meaning.

As Literary and Cultural Studies drew upon the assumptions and procedures of STRUCTURALISM, including a work such as Barthes' *Mythologies* (1972 [1957]), it treated a variety of non-linguistic cultural forms – from photography, film and fashion, to music, sport, the urban environment and architecture – as 'texts'. While this approach followed developments in structuralism, a parallel approach, indebted principally to Raymond Williams and drawing upon Sociology and Ethnography, brought a more social-materialist, or so-called 'culturalist', analysis to the study of youth and SUBCULTURES, cultural institutions and audiences.

From the mid 1970s onwards, work within this second PARADIGM has had to meet the further challenge of poststructuralist arguments on the inescapability of NARRATIVE and DISCOURSE – as indeed have the disciplines of history, Sociology and political economy in their own right. At the extremes of this encounter, a positivist belief in the self-evident existence and truth of facts confronted an unshakeable scepticism towards any non-linguistic, non-subjective reality. There are, of course, many intermediary positions and differences on either side of these positions (Callinicos 1989 draws a distinction between a 'wordly' and formalist textualism, for example). In this respect, POSTSTRUCTURALISM brought a new idiom to a traditional quarrel between MATERIALISM and IDEALISM.

At the core of this debate has been Jacques Derrida's statement that 'there is nothing outside the text' (1976: 163). Derrida's French is '*Il n'y a pas de hors-texte*' and it is possible to understand this in different ways: as countenancing a narrow formalism that sees nothing – neither a 'real world' nor 'context' – outside of the (single) text, or as affirming the play of meaning across interconnected texts. Derrida's writings would suggest the second: an understanding of the inevitable interweaving of textual threads across the borders of single texts and of the textual REPRESENTATION of all thought. His concept of the TRACE, among others, expresses this movement. 'This interweaving is the text produced only in the transformation of another text' (1981a: 26). 'The text,' as Roland A. Champagne comments, 'is thus always a palimpsest, that is, partly written over by another text which is partly visible' (1995: 30).

Thus conceived, textuality evidently implies relations of INTERTEXTUALITY and undermines – though it does not eliminate – all traditional (Derrida would say 'metaphysical') distinctions between a pre-existent material world and its textual echo or representation. It is in this respect that notions of textuality and the textual construction of meaning pose a challenge to those academic disciplines named above. In particular, the concept challenges those traditions of political thought indebted to MARXISM, FEMINISM or anti-racism that are committed to radical change, and see material social and economic conditions alone, rather than textuality or discourse, as an obstacle to it.

See also *ÉCRITURE*/WRITING; HYPERTEXT.

THE EVENT

This term occupies a key place in the philosophies of both Jean-François Lyotard (1924-98) and Alain Badiou (1937–). Their thinking displays similarities of reference and at times of cultural-political import – both theorize the 'event' in relation to radical political change – but they are best considered independently.

Lyotard's use of this term especially informs his conception of postmodernism. The event is 'a caesura in space time' (quoted in Readings 1991: xxi), which exerts a disruptive effect, after which, nothing will be the same. Whereas others view the postmodern as a style or historical epoch, Lyotard sees it as an experimental impulse that goes beyond existing rationalist PARADIGMS: as he puts it, the postmodern is 'that which... puts forward the unpresentable in presentation itself' (Lyotard 1984: 81). The event, therefore, is an instance of the postmodern SUBLIME; it is 'beyond words', and awaits a new vocabulary and set of criteria. Lyotard's interest, however, is in the moment of fundamental disruption before the event is recuperated and explained, if indeed it is, in terms of a scheme of history or ETHICS. The latter characterizes the modernist as against the postmodern mode and sensibility. Examples of the event indicated by Lyotard are the French Revolution, Auschwitz, the revolutionary '*événements*' of May 1968 in Paris (in which he was himself active). Others with a similar dramatic import and singularity might be the assassination of President John F. Kennedy, the building – and later fall – of the Berlin Wall, the release of Nelson Mandela. As Bill Readings says, it is not clear whether events happen all the time and we do not notice them, or only occasionally (Readings 1991: xxxi). Lyotard further associates postmodernism with experimentalism, and it is clear that for him, the art of the AVANT-GARDE – which challenges the institutionalized status of art – and notably of Marcel Duchamp (Lyotard 1990), is analogous to the social or political event.

As employed by Alain Badiou, the 'event' designates an unexpected (a 'purely haphazard') happening or punctual moment in which a hitherto 'supernumerary' or invisible 'part' breaks through the normative fabric of a situation or social order, where this intervention could not be 'inferred from the situation' itself (Badiou, 2006: 215). The transformation introduces an entirely new arrangement, idea, belief, or mode in society, science or the arts. The status quo experiences this as a traumatic disturbance, but for the newly emerged part, it can be profoundly emancipatory, a 'genuine "novelty in being"... a chance to begin again' (Hallward, 2003: 114). The idea or possibility of beginning again, *ex nihilo*, recalls the aspirations of the AVANT-GARDE (as it does in Lyotard), but Badiou would distance himself from the linkage of avant-garde innovation and the destruction of the old. For Badiou, the new beginning entails a conviction or faith in the – once established – absolute invariant 'truth' that the event produces. As Hallward comments: 'truth is a process and not an illumination. It takes much time and much effort. To be sustained it requires "conviction" (or faith), "love" (or charity), and "certainty" (or hope). It does not require, however, proof in the form of confirmed knowledge or corroboration' (2003: 110).

Badiou's examples range from 'falling in love'; St. Paul's conversion to Christianity as proclaimed in the resurrection; and, in the arts, the Symbolist poet Stéphane Mallamé's *Un Coup de Dés* (*Un Coup de Dés Jamais N'Abolira Le Hasard – A Throw of the Dice will Never Abolish Chance*) of 1897. In science we might propose, at the time of writing, the discovery of the new human-like species, '*Homo naledi*' in South Africa.

Perhaps the most conspicuous examples, however, are those of political revolt or revolution in which the agents appear dramatically – unscripted – from the wings, as it were, to occupy centre-stage and to change the plot. Badiou points in this respect, in a series not unlike Lyotard's, to the Paris Commune of the 1880s; the Russian Revolution when the worker or organized proletariat appeared as an iconic actor and agent of change; the Maoist Cultural Revolution of 1966–76; and the unprecedented alliance of students and workers as revolutionary political actors in the 1968 Paris 'Événements'. Examples could, once again, be feasibly multiplied from the late twentieth and twenty-first centuries of insurrectionary or insurgent movements across the world, most recently in the Middle East. Badiou has, in fact, cited the Arab Spring with reference to events in Egypt and Tunisia (*Le Monde* 18 February 2011). In general, however, he views events as exceptional occurrences.

See also PSYCHOGEOGRAPHY; TERRORISM.

THING THEORY

'Thing theory' shares a contemporary re-evaluation of the relation of the human and the world of physical matter and objects (broadly conceived and including tools and machines) conducted by those working in the fields of SPECULATIVE REALISM, and versions of the POSTHUMAN.

Though interdisciplinary in its purview and application, thing theory has found a recent illustrative home in a much-expanded Literary Studies, notably in the work of Bill Brown (2001, 2003). Brown's question about 'how inanimate objects enable human subjects (individually and collectively) to form and transform themselves' (University of Chicago, English Faculty webpage) embraces the activities of consumerism and collecting; kitsch and fetishism; the formation and consolidation or transformations of gender, sexual, ethnic and national identities. Thing theory therefore proposes a materialist methodology which, says Brown, 'takes objects for granted only in order to grant them their potency – to show how they organize our private and public affection' (Brown [ed] 2001: 7). Examples in the collection *Things* are playful and original, including the life of a coin, the role of gloves in Renaissance portraiture, the history of Italian coffee makers and the role of aluminium in fascist Italy.

To some degree, this shares the joyous itemizing of autonomous objects in work by Graham Harman and Ian Bogost in the field of speculative realism. Debates in this field, at the same time, raise the important question of how, on what terms, and with what effect independent objects can enter relational frameworks. For his part, Brown views the above examples as determinedly situated in the circuits of production, circulation and meaning, and as opening onto a wider history. In this respect, he writes importantly of how this new materialism 'will investigate how the literary helps to identify the cultural illogic that exposes history's noninevitability' (1996: 18), thereby departing from some of the organizing tenets of NEW HISTORICISM.

In addition, Brown proposes a key distinction between functioning 'objects' and 'things', the latter understood as objects that stop working, are laid aside, fall into obsolescence or acquire more than their first function (a book used as a doorstop, an old phone used as a toy). As an example, he cites Claes Oldenburg's giant 'Typewriter Eraser' as a bewildering object – now 'thing' – which has passed out of any recognized function into art. He brings this distinction to literature to ask of the pre-modernist American literature of the 1890s (Frank Norris, Sarah Orne Jewett, Mark Twain, Henry James) what it 'does with objects', how it addressed 'the question of things and their thingness' (2001: 12–13). This offers a new perspective on the philosophies of Naturalism and Realism, and intriguingly, in the case of Henry James especially, draws attention to the ineffability of 'things' – a regular term in James's lexicon – which signify a something beyond the world of physical objects. James, (Brown's leading example is James's *The American Scene*, 1907) 'gives voice to objects' which crucially speak 'not of their exchange value [as commodities] but of a value that is irreducible to exchange or use' (2003: 178). Things thereby acquire a ghostly agency, returning us to a pre-modern world where things 'had a personality and inherent power' and anticipating our own times when consciousness is dispersed beyond the independent subject 'throughout the material world' (187).

It is at this juncture – in the attribution of sentience and agency to the physical environment – that debates in new materialist thinking and on the posthuman become most challenging. Once more, this is linked to positions on the autonomy of objects and, conversely, their having their being in relational frameworks. 'What is it like to be a thing?' asks Ian Bogost (2012). In answer, in one exchange, the materialist feminist Stacy Alaimo (2014) – wary of the depoliticization of Bogost's all-inclusive lists of autonomous objects – turns to Karen Barad's (2007) notion of 'agential realism' and of the environment as 'entanglements of phenomena' not of independent objects. Viewing the world as made up of inseparable 'intra-acting agencies' rather than distinct objects, comments Alaimo, is 'counter-intuitive' and 'dizzying', but enabling in that it facilitates 'ethical and political modes that do not separate the human from the material world' (2014: 15).

See also AGENCY; ANIMAL STUDIES; CYBORG; ECOCRITICISM; ROBOTICS.

THIRDSPACE

A concept introduced by the postmodern cultural geographer Edward W. Soja, most thoroughly in his volume *ThirdSpace* (1996). Soja aims, by way of this term, to move intellectual and political life beyond what he sees as a persistent and limiting recourse to dualistic thinking, and in particular to establish the discussion of spatiality within a critical Cultural Studies. To this end, he outlines three guiding objectives: to release the discussion of urban space from its subordination to the hegemonic assumptions of history and Sociology; to critically review the supposed antinomies of modernism and postmodernism with a view to combining their most relevant features; and to combine and simultaneously move beyond the 'Firstspace' perception of the 'real' physical world and the 'Secondspace' perspective that interprets this 'real' through 'imagined' spatial representations. Soja's study as a whole, and this last objective, most evidently, is deeply indebted to the thinking of the libertarian Marxist thinker, Henri Lefebvre and especially to his founding text *The Production of Space* (1991b [1974]). Lefebvre had distinguished between a practical realm of 'perceived' space, the controlled and planned realm of 'conceived' space, and a third domain of the 'lived' 'spaces of representation'. This last corresponds to Soja's 'Thirdspace'. The movement through these terms is not, he argues, the movement through opposites toward a synthesis, as in classical DIALECTICS, but a movement towards a third position that, in a 'cumulative *trialectics*' embraces the first two terms and provides a conceptual perspective upon 'the multiplicity of *real-and-imagined* spaces'. Above all, 'Thirdspace' underpins a postmodern cultural politics whose principal strategy Soja terms 'thirding-as-Othering'; the determination to inject 'an-Other set of choices', which will disrupt the confinement of intellectual and political life in binary pairings.

The principal object of study in Soja's work has been the 'postmetropolitan' CITY of Los Angeles, but the affinities he sees between the 'radical openness' of Thirdspace and the work of theorists and activists in FEMINISM and postcolonial studies gives his work the broader base in the critical study of culture he seeks. One such thinker is Homi Bhabha whose own concept of 'Third Space' Soja also explores. Bhabha deploys this concept in a similar strategic move 'beyond' binary thinking, especially the entrenched hierarchies of colonial ideology. His 'Third Space' is less the 'real-and-imagined' urban space of Soja, however, than the 'in-between' space of literary and cultural meaning and IDENTITY that he and others have theorized as HYBRIDITY.

See also SPACE; POSTCOLONIALISM; PSYCHOGEOGRAPHY.

TOTALITY

A concept derived principally from the German philosopher, G.W.F. Hegel (1770–1831) and developed especially within a strand of the western Marxist tradition, though it has come to signal broader contemporary debates, of which MARXISM is a part. Key figures in this tradition are the Hungarian literary critic, Georg Lukács (1885–1971) and the American critic and cultural theorist, Fredric Jameson (1934–). Lukács emphasized the inexorable movement of the dialectic in Hegel towards a transcendent oneness: of mind (in Hegel) and of social unity (in Lukács). He argued that the great novels of European REALISM (Balzac, Thomas Mann) exemplified this movement, revealing the internal dynamic of the social totality over and above a condition of present ALIENATION and regardless of their authors' announced personal politics.

Lukács has been chastised for his IDEALISM, his undialectical HISTORICISM and (notably by Bertolt Brecht) for his 'formalist' preference for the realist form of the novel and blindness to the political merits of MODERNISM. The idea of the totality has consequently fallen out of favour; by association, first, with Lukács, in internal Marxist debates but, second, by association with Marxism in general. The emphasis within POSTSTRUCTURALISM and POSTMODERNISM upon DIFFERENCE, heterogeneity and PLURALISM suggests, for example, that present society is anything but a totality. For some, this has inspired an opposition to ideas of order, unity and wholeness in which the ENLIGHTENMENT tradition, Marxism and 'totalitarianism' stand equally condemned. It is in this spirit, for example, that Jean-François Lyotard closes his *The Postmodern Condition* with the words 'Let us wage a war on totality' (1984: 82).

Fredric Jameson, by contrast, though himself a major commentator on contemporary postmodern culture has remained committed to the idea of the social totality. The concept lies at the centre of tensions within his own work, but is a sign, beyond it, of an important rift in contemporary theoretical debate. Jameson draws a distinction between 'totality' and 'totalization' (1991: 331–3, 399–418). The first is the term for the social whole – now, says Jameson, more homogenous beneath its apparent abundant difference than ever. He means by the totality, he says, 'the mode of production' – that is to say, the economic mode of production of contemporary or late capitalism. In this globalizing phase, capitalism aspires to be a 'total system'. The dilemma for Jameson is that its unprecedented reach makes it 'unimaginable' and 'incomprehensible' (1991: 413). The second 'totalizing' activity by which this total system will be represented, comprehended and surpassed in political theory and art remains, however, so Jameson reasons, more vital than ever. This will express the system's 'unity in difference' ('a unified theory of differentiation' 1991: 343), a project he describes also as COGNITIVE MAPPING.

On the one hand, therefore, in Jameson and others, the idea of totality is thought to represent the residual, arrogant mastery of a Eurocentric intellectual, economic and political tradition. On the other, it is the means to understanding and liberation from this system. (See also Raymond Williams 1980a: 19–22, 35–7.)

See also DIALECTICS.

TOURISM

From its humble beginnings in trips to seaside resorts in the nineteenth century, tourism has grown to become a MASS industry and vital player in the operation of global capitalism: the third highest category of consumer spending in the UK at the end of the 1980s and growing worldwide at 5–6 per cent per annum (Urry 1990). In the UK, the total economic output from tourism has continued to grow; from £49 billion in 2008 to £56 billion in 2013, amounting to a 14% increase (Rhodes 2016). Tourism has therefore emerged as an important topic in the History and Sociology of Leisure, as well as for adjacent areas in Cultural Geography and Postcolonial Studies interested in the themes of social mobility, cultural IDENTITY and changed relations between 'First' and 'Third Worlds'. At the centre of such studies is the perspective of the advantaged traveller upon foreign cultures and thus of relations between the metropolitan or western observer and his/her perceived OTHERS. Unlike the anthropologist or permanent exile (though much pleasure derives in museums and commentary from early ethnographers and travel writers), the tourist seeks a SPECTACLE (seeing the sights), the scene of an older, less urbanized, less industrialized haven; a past time and CULTURE displayed in buildings, peoples and artefacts. Essentially, therefore, the tourist GAZE – or gazes since this 'varies by society, social group and historical period' (Urry 1990: 1) – is founded on a series of contrasts: of the present with the past, the CITY with the country, home with abroad, normal routine with exotic spectacle and, centrally, of work with leisure (MacCannell 1989). Tourism consequently provides the ambiguous PLEASURES of difference or the confirmation of stereotypes.

Two essays develop these themes in relation to the visual arts. First, following MacCannell, Griselda Pollock sees tourism as a prime vehicle of MODERNISM's 'totalizing idea'; a mentality that sets the countryside and foreign cultures as the mythologized other to the western metropolis (1992: 60–7). Pollock pursues these questions in a study of the relation of the Parisian AVANT-GARDE painters, Vincent van Gogh, Émile Bernard and Paul Gauguin, to Provence, Brittany and

Tahiti. In Tahiti, she argues, Gauguin imposed a sexist and ethnocentric FANTASY upon his subjects (notably in the 1892 painting of his Tahitian wife, Manao Tupapua). This encoded colonial stereotyping 'at the heart of capitalism's imperialist process' has been ignored, Pollock maintains, by a collusive art history establishment (1992: 72).

Peter Wollen, second, writes of how in the later postmodern or post-Fordist era, an expanded tourist industry, made possible by jet travel, computerized booking facilities, increased middle-class leisure and so on, is the expression not only of a changed global economy, but of a change in the nature and circulation of art. He sees the development consequently of a 'tourist art', with its accompanying new art market of souvenirs, craft and exhibition centres, but detects, too, an emerging 'para-tourist' gallery art of new 'originality and complexity' (1993: 196). GLOBALIZATION has reconfigured the boundaries between the First World metropolitan core and the, now frequently postcolonial, peripheries. From this, Wollen shows, with abundant citation, has come an inventive dialogue, 'a new hybrid aesthetic' (1993: 209) within and across cultures.

See also ETHNOCENTRICISM; HYBRIDITY; POSTCOLONIALISM; POST-FORDISM.

TRACE

A term derived from the writings of Emmanuel Lévinas and employed by the French philosopher, Jacques Derrida as a cognate term with others in the vocabulary of DECONSTRUCTION such as SUPPLEMENT, DISSEMINATION, spacing, displacement and, above all, DIFFÉRANCE.

Deconstruction challenges the assumption of fixed or stable meanings, positing instead a play of differences whereby, Derrida writes:

> no element can function as a sign without reference to another element which is not simply present. This interweaving results in each element... being constituted on the basis of the trace within it of the other elements of the chain or system... Nothing, neither among the elements nor within the system, is anywhere ever simply present or absent. There are only everywhere, differences and traces of traces.
>
> (1981a: 26)

'Différance', the term by which Derrida names this general condition, is 'the systematic play of differences, of the traces of differences, of the spacing by means of which elements are related to each other' (1981a: 27).

This linked chain of terms in Derrida's own writing describes, while it enacts, the project of deconstruction. They are themselves difficult to stabilize and so confirm deconstruction's belief in the indeterminacy of meaning. If we think of 'concepts' as stabilizing meanings, then the terms of deconstruction, including 'trace', are not concepts, but rather, as Derrida prefers, 'semi- or quasi-concepts' (Kamuf [ed] 1991: 5). Principally, and most productively, they activate a mode of reading that is sceptical of received or apparently self-evident meanings.

TRANSCODING

See ALLEGORY.

TRANSFERENCE

A term employed in psychoanalytic theory to describe the process by which, in analysis, the patient or 'analysand' projects infantile wishes upon the analyst. This usually implies an identification of the analyst with a figure of authority in the patient's childhood. Transference is therefore understood as 'actualiz[ing] the past in its symbolic form so that it can be repeated, replayed, worked through to another outcome' (Brooks 1984: 12). 'Counter-transference' describes the analyst's own unconscious reaction to the individual analysand and specifically to this experience. Freud theorized this process in papers between 1912 and 1915 (1974e, 97–100; 1974f, 97–108, 145–56, 157–74), but had earlier felt that the analysis of the patient known as 'Dora' had failed because he had not accounted for its effects (1974d, Vol. 7: 1–122). He continued to see transference as the patient's way of displacing, rather than confronting, a psychic disorder and as an obstacle to successful analysis, but recognized, nevertheless, that this was the only way it could be manifested.

Transference and counter-transference are relevant, outside psychoanalysis, to other exchanges involving relations of POWER and authority. Transference can occur whenever a person in a subordinate position, woman to man, student to teacher, employee to employer, black to white, concedes that their interlocutor has the authority of knowledge and is, in a phrase from Jacques Lacan, the one 'who is supposed to know' (1977: 253). Shoshana Felman (1987) and Michèle Le Doeuff (1989) have considered the implications of this in studies of pedagogic relations between teacher and pupil, and of female to male students.

See also PSYCHOANALYSIS.

TRANSGRESSIVE

To 'transgress' is, in Christian parlance, 'to sin'. In a secular idiom, it is also to 'cross the path' and go against social norms. These negative, moralizing ascriptions have been appropriated and reversed within radical criticism and politics in the promotion of transgressive texts, ways of reading, or sexual-cultural activities (Stallybrass and White 1986). A transgressive reading of Shakespeare's Hamlet, for example, might read its marginalized homosocial or homosexual meanings across the surface of the text; a transgressive reading of magazines for teenage girls might counter their commodification of women with a decoding of an implicit lesbianism.

Most often, however, the term is used in relation to direct expressions of transgressive SEXUALITY. The Marquis de Sade had reasoned that PLEASURE and subversion existed in wicked acts and this remains the problematic basis of theories and politics of sexual transgression. Is pornography – since it is illicit and 'wrong' – inherently transgressive? Is it, by that token, subversive of normative sexuality? These questions are explored especially in relation to QUEER THEORY, which seeks to disrupt essentialized sexual or GENDERed identities though dress, sexual performance or new alliances. Thus, heterosexual activity might be mimicked by a gay or lesbian couple. Whether all such 'transgressive' acts are subversive is debated by Elizabeth Wilson (1993). Jackson and Scott, editors of the collection *Feminism and Sexuality,* also expressed reservations about transgressive 'style': 'We ourselves doubt whether wearing a tutu with Doc Martens will bring patriarchy to its knees' (1996: 16). They question, too, whether all transgressive or 'outlaw sexualities' deserve protection and opprobrium regardless of questions of power, domination and the social derivation of DESIRE: 'there is a world of difference between a street prostitute and a millionaire pornographer or between a man who has sex with a child and that child' (1996: 19). Commentators such as these have called in the past, therefore, for a more discriminating and politically considered use of the term. However, a shifting agenda and attitudes into the 2000s make it clear that, in its increasingly widespread use, in dedicated academic journals, memoirs, novels, and film, the notion and experience of transgression has become of critical importance to those seeking sexual well-being (see Styker, 2008, Brooks 2015).

See also BODY; SEXUAL DIFFERENCE.

TRANSLATION

The practice of translation has long confirmed the major insight of structuralism on the arbitrariness of the linguistic SIGN (that the signifier has only a conventional – not a necessary – relation with its signified). The belief that an equivalent and correct translation of a 'foreign' text can be found has nevertheless proved a persistent one. However, in the more extended-uses of the term 'translation', this assumption of an underlying sameness across languages and cultures – concealing the superiority of the first, which dictates the terms of translation – has been questioned. This has been linked with the experience of cultural difference, inequality and exchange, and with their implications for subjective and national identities.

Salman Rushdie in *Imaginary Homelands* (1992) proposes we view the migrant or 'translated' person who straddles different cultures as the quintessential figure of the twentieth century. Homi Bhabha (1994) develops this idea, partly in relation to Rushdie's *Satanic Verses,* to draw attention to the resistant element, the residue that cannot be translated in this transaction. This, he likens to the condition of HYBRIDITY: an 'in-between' position that is neither singular and unified, nor multiform and pluralist, neither located in one place, nor homeless. This indeterminate place of translation describes the migrant individual and a transitional, ambivalent culture 'caught in-between a "nativist", even nationalist, atavism and a postcolonial metropolitan assimilation' (1994: 224).

Elsewhere, in terms that echo Bhabha, the implications of 'translation' for subjective and national identity and for the production of knowledge in and about non-western societies have been taken up especially in discussions of Asia and East Asia's relation to the west and GLOBALIZATION. The work of Yoshino Kosaku (1992) and Naoki Sakai (1997), for example, shows how modern Japan is haunted by the image of a unified and hegemonic west in both the national cultural and geopolitical spheres. The result is a schizophrenic identity of Japan as both distinct from the west and its mirror image in the east.

Naoki Sakai in particular explores these issues in the context of translation. He understands communication as a connection between incommensurable partners, rather than a mediation between the binary 'cofiguration' of West and East. And he advances the idea of translation as a 'heterolingual' mode of address (for both English- and Japanese-speaking readers, for example), which significantly produces a mixed or 'nonaggregate', rather than unified, community of scholars. Foreigners together, 'we' share in what Meaghan Morris calls 'the grit of incomprehension' (Sakai 1997: xiv). Translation becomes a model for negotiating with the linguistic and cultural OTHER on terms of fluctuating knowledge and ignorance. Sakai thereby posits what Morris terms a 'working model for transnational studies in culture' (1997: xiii); one that is founded, however, not on its universal applicability, but in directing attention to 'context… contingency… limitation' (1997: xxi).

These issues are also pursued in the journal, *Traces: A Multilingual Journal of Cultural Theory and Translation,* which appears significantly in English-language, Japanese, Korean and Chinese versions.

See also COMMUNITY; INTELLECTUALS; NATIONALISM.

TRAUMA

The word 'trauma' is from the Greek meaning 'wound' or 'injury'. The OED entry for 'trauma' has, in the past, given psychological descriptions such as emotional shock following a stressful event or distressing experience as the first meaning, and any physical wound or injury as the second. (The 2016 edition of OED, however, reverses this order.) Earlier uses from the eighteenth and nineteenth centuries had similarly given a physical designation first and an emotional or psychological meaning second. This was the case also in the first, more public uses of the term during the Great War (1914–18) in official army and medical diagnoses of shell shock. The symptoms were interpreted initially as a physical condition only, and frequently branded as cowardice and thus as liable to the death penalty. Increasingly, however, the effects were understood as a psychological condition, or as both physical and psychological. Psychological manifestations could include memory loss, flashbacks, nightmare, anxiety and confusion. There might also be a repetitive return to, and retelling of, the originary event, or a contrary avoidance, forgetting or repression of this. These have become the commonly recognized features of trauma. Early treatment involved electric shock, occasional hypnosis, and on the part of more enlightened figures (notably W.H.R. Rivers), the 'talking cure', associated with Sigmund Freud, but introduced independently by Rivers (and see Pat Barker's novel sequence *Regeneration*, 1991, 1993, 1995).

Freud's understanding of trauma evolved over his career and was summed up by Jean Laplanche (1967, rept. 1988) as 'An event in the subject's life, defined by its intensity, by the subject's incapacity to respond adequately to it and by the upheaval and long-lasting effects that it brings about in the psychical organization' (465). Key early texts by Freud include (with Josef Breuer) 'On the Psychical Mechanism of Hysterical Phenomena' (1893 [1974k]) and 'Remembering. Repeating and Working-Through' (1914 [1974f]). Traumatic events were seen to produce a profoundly disabling, altered state of consciousness or 'dissociation'. Treatment involved hypnosis, the aim of which was to bring the symptoms to fully conscious remembering, verbalization and narrative coherence (the process of 'working through' in the 'talking cure'). If this failed, the condition was deemed pathological.

Bringing a narrative construction to a traumatic event and its psychic effects, which precisely frustrate narrative reconstruction, is critical in all accounts. In modern times, Roger Luckurst (2008) speaks of the 1990s as characterized by a 'memoir boom' prompted by the struggle to articulate the collective traumas of post World War Two in narrative form. The symbol for this difficulty is the 'unspeakable' horror posed by Auschwitz. 'Holocaust Studies' have consequently become a major interdisciplinary subset of 'Trauma Studies' (see, among a wealth of literature, the journal *Holocaust Studies: A Journal of Culture and History*). The later twentieth and the twenty-first century, when instances of trauma have included the experience of sustained military combat, terrorist attack, natural disaster, sexual or racial abuse, and disclosures of paedophilia, have accentuated the difficulties of bringing diverse traumatic experience into coherent narrative form. Two especially high-profile examples where there has been a widespread public expression of grief and mourning to totally unexpected events have been, in the UK, the death of Princess Diana on 31 August 1997, and in the USA, the horror of 9/11 (the attack on New York's Twin Towers on 11 September 2001). (See Brooker 2005 and Tanguay 2013.)

In responding to such phenomena, Trauma Studies has tended, following Alain Badiou, to view the traumatic EVENT as an unforeseen, 'purely haphazard', occurrence whose effect is radically transformative (Badiou 2006: 215) and to explore the innovations in narrative form which seek to respond to the paradoxically unrepresentable nature of this event. This is a task for which an uncomplicated traditional realism – which assumes the double anterior existence of a unified individual subject and a known, directly accessible external or inner world – proves inadequate.

Trauma narratives in literature, film or other arts consequently assume diverse hybrid forms of narration or 'presentation' rather than 'representation', marked by the symptoms of forgetting or repression, flashbacks, displacement and compulsive or deferred intermittent retelling (see NACHTRÄGLICHKEIT). Equally, to this end, they may variously combine testimony, autobiography, history and fiction, and deploy established 'serious', mainstream or 'popular' modes such as melodrama, fantasy or romance. Trauma Studies explores this extensive field with a concern for the complex ETHICS of narrative and the possibilities of survival and healing (see Onega and Ganteau 2014; Nadal and Calvo 2014).

See also TERRORISM.

UNCANNY

The key theoretical source for this concept is Sigmund Freud's essay, 'The uncanny' (1919). Freud explores the etymologies of the German terms *unheimlich* (uncanny, unfamiliar, frightening) and *heimlich* (homely, familiar) to discover that at a certain point the meanings of these opposite terms are very close, since the sense of *heimlich* as 'belonging to the house' produces also the associated meanings of being concealed, made secret, or kept from sight. '"Unheimlich",,' Freud comments, 'is in some way or another a subspecies of "heimlich"' (1974h, Vol. 17: 226).

Freud further relates the uncanny, first, to the survival in the UNCONSCIOUS of a 'primitive' and subsequently repressed animistic mythological and mystic view of the world and, second, to the occurrence of repetitions, coincidences and doubles. This latter form he understands as the result of repressed experiences in infancy. The 'unheimlich,' he concludes, 'is what was once "heimisch", familiar; the prefix 'un' [un-] is the token of repression' (1974h, vol. 17: 245).

The uncanny has an obvious relevance, therefore, for an understanding of fictional NARRATIVES, especially of science fiction, horror, FANTASTIC and GOTHIC genres (Jackson 1981; Botting 1996) where the figure of the alien, or OTHER, proves to be the projection of a repressed inner self and unsettles notions of a unified personality. Freud's main illustration in his essay is indeed a literary one: the tale of 'The sandman' by the German Romantic writer, E.T.A. Hoffman. In this story a student fears losing his eyes. The source of his fear is the visits to his childhood home of a family lawyer. At these times, his father sent him to bed, threatening that the sandman would pull out his eyes if he disobeyed. The boy associates the lawyer and subsequently other men (an oculist, an eyeglass salesman) with the sandman and goes to his death fearing he has been trapped by this figure. Freud reads this story in terms of the OEDIPAL COMPLEX, seeing the boy's fear of the loss of his eyes as a displaced expression of the fear of castration. The boy and the reader therefore experience the repressed but familiar anxiety over castration as a now displaced, uncanny fear of the loss of eyes.

Freud's reading of this tale has been seen as a reductive and selective one. Hélène Cixous (1976) responded by pointing to the figure of a doll in the story, ignored by Freud, who is brought to life and is therefore a further example of the uncanny. (Angela Carter's story, 'The loves of Lady Purple' is the story of just such an animated vampiric doll). Jane Marie Todd (1986) probes the connection between the fear of castration and the male sight of the female body. Such re-readings and rewritings question the assumed male norms of Freud's theory and serve to introduce more woman-centred versions of the uncanny (see Wright 1989).

An interesting example of the use of Freud's term, drawing on Cixous, in relation to POPULAR culture is James Donald's reading of the subversive, destabilizing potential of vampire films (1992b).

See also ABJECTION; TRANSGRESSIVE.

UNCONSCIOUS

Although thinkers, writers and artists had long recognized the existence of repressed fears and desires, especially in the late nineteenth century, when the use of the term 'Unconscious' was quite common (witness also the publication of such texts as *Jekyll and Hyde* (1886), and Bram Stoker's *Dracula* (1897)), the Unconscious was defined as such – as a noun and with a capital letter – by Sigmund Freud. In his early writings, *The Interpretation of Dreams* (1900) and papers on the Unconscious in 1912 and 1915, Freud theorized its construction as one of three distinct psychic domains, the others being the preconscious and the conscious. He found evidence for its existence in obsessions, symptoms, word association, everyday slips of the tongue and, above all, dreams. These revealed gaps in conscious life whose missing content psychoanalytic practice showed was disguised or covered over – and thus only indirectly expressed – through such mechanisms as CONDENSATION and DISPLACEMENT characteristic of dreams. This repressed or censored content of the Unconscious comprised both, first, early memories of the individual and of general humanity originating in primal fantasies or scenes involving forbidden sexual knowledge, the fear of castration or seduction, and, second, instinctual drives or wishes that recognize no constraint and seek only fulfilment. These wishes or drives correspond to what Freud termed 'the primary process', and are censored and brought to a distorted expression, as in dream once more, by a controlling 'secondary process'. The combined operation of these two processes is often seen as analogous to artistic creativity, the implication being that a deep and primary motivation commonly receives oblique and not direct expression. From the 1920s onwards, Freud tended to associate the instinctual drives with the 'id' and saw this as controlled by the agency of the 'superego' (the voice of society internalized as a conscience) in the production of the social self or ego. At this time, he also theorized the existence in the Unconscious of a death drive.

Freud's 'discovery' was acknowledged and further developed by the French psychoanalyst, Jacques Lacan. Drawing on the STRUCTURALISM of Ferdinand de Saussure, Roman Jakobson and Claude Lévi-Strauss, Lacan reconceptualized the Unconscious in linguistic terms. It was, he wrote, a 'censored chapter' in the history of the subject (1977: 50), traces of which could nevertheless be read in the 'documents' of neurosis, surviving childhood memories, personal vocabulary, traditions, legends and dreams. The Unconscious, he declared famously, is 'articulated like a discourse' (1977: 193): to be understood as a symbolic system that was only detectable through language, and that itself worked through a chain of signifiers and figurative modes. Chief among the latter were metaphor and metonymy, which Lacan posited as corresponding to the mechanisms of condensation and displacement associated by Freud with the DREAMWORK. The Unconscious comes into being, moreover, at the point of the child's transition into the SYMBOLIC order, which is the point of the acquisition of language and the acceptance by the child of the symbolic authority of the figure of the father.

These formulations have had a significant influence on theories of the SUBJECT, SUBJECTIVITY and IDENTITY. They have also alerted readers to the role of unconscious, repressed DESIRES and anxieties, and the ways these find distorted or indirect expression in social behaviour, and all manner of literary and cultural forms of REPRESENTATION. In particular, theories of the Unconscious have been influential within feminist theory and criticism, in conjunction with a more materialist CULTURAL POLITICS (Mitchell 1974) or poststructuralist strategies (Kristeva 1984b; Irigaray 1985a, 1985b). At the same time, the latter work in particular has wanted to resist the perceived masculinized bias in both Freud and Lacan. It has sought therefore to re-conceptualize models of the Unconscious so as to articulate a female or feminist DISCOURSE as repressed, but unsilenced and TRANSGRESSIVE.

Within Marxist criticism, Fredric Jameson has sought in *The Political Unconscious* (1981) to rethink the Unconscious in social and collective, rather than individual and abstract, terms. In a study of a range of literary narratives, he sees the Unconscious as the repository of a repressed political CONSCIOUSNESS of a unifying history.

See also PHALLUS; PSYCHOANALYSIS.

UNDER ERASURE

See DECONSTRUCTION; TRACE.

USE VALUE

See MARXISM; VALUE.

UTOPIA

'Utopia' is derived from the Greek meaning, ambiguously, 'no place' (*ou topos*) and 'good place' (*eu topos*). The first meaning is echoed in William Morris's late nineteenth-century utopian fiction *News From Nowhere* (1896), one of the handful of key texts in the western tradition of utopian or dystopian texts (from the Greek *dys topos* – 'bad place'), including Thomas More's *Utopia* (1516), and in the twentieth century, Aldous Huxley's *Brave New World* (1932) and George Orwell's *1984* (1949).

More's Utopia is located elsewhere in space rather than time (often where this is the case the place is in the west, an association we know well from the myth of the new land or new world associated for three centuries with what is the contemporary United States). The problem with such projections, or parallel – if better – worlds is that they are static and outside history, since once perfection has been achieved, the implication is that time has stopped or must stop. It was only when historical process and the notion of progress were introduced into the form that utopia could be set in future time (Levitas 1993). A strong movement based on the analysis of a need for change effected through time and history has been associated in this century with inspirational moments in the women's movement, from Charlotte Perkins Gilman's *Herland* (1915) – one of many utopian feminist texts produced in the late nineteenth and early twentieth centuries (Kessler [ed] 1984) – to utopian fictions of the 1960s and 1970s by Ursula Le Guin, Marge Piercy and Joanna Russ. A later example of feminist science fiction in this mould, Margaret Atwood's *The Handmaid's Tale* (1985) is described by Fredric Jameson (1991: 160) as marking the end of the utopian hopes of contemporary FEMINISM. Where the earlier examples echoed and helped form the hopes of the earlier period, Atwood's novel is seen as a parable of the intentions of New Right regimes of the 1980s. Whether a persuasive reading or not, this suggests how utopian and dystopian fictions are now most commonly read: more as allegorical projections of the best and worst tendencies of their own times, than as detached visions of a better or nightmare future world.

An earlier contrast was drawn by Friedrich Engels (1880) between 'utopian' versions of a socialist future and those presented by 'scientific socialism' (i.e. MARXISM). The first, Engels argued, viewed socialism as a perfect social order; the achieved expression of absolute truth, reason and justice, which had only to be recognized as such, through the force of persuasion, propaganda or the concrete evidence of model communities, to conquer all doubts and resistance. For Marx and Engels, by contrast, the virtues of socialism were neither self-evident nor unopposed. Above all, they stressed the question and the role of social AGENCY (in classical Marxism, a revolutionary working CLASS) necessary to bring about social change. This emphasis and the accompanying sense of 'utopian' as a vague and empty optimism remain influential. Also, if the importance of agency (how you get from bad society A to good society B) is recognized, it means there can be no blueprint of a perfect future, socialist or otherwise, since the form of future society depends on history or, more precisely, historical events and actors, rather than on the force of opinion or inevitable natural or technological processes (termed 'technologism' or 'technological determinism').

A further influential position in Marxist Cultural Theory has associated an imagined better future, not with the working class, but with art. This view was advanced notably by Herbert Marcuse (1978) and to a lesser degree by his fellow members of the Frankfurt School (see CRITICAL THEORY). Marcuse saw the function of art as the CRITIQUE or ESTRANGEMENT of present society and as the bearer of a utopian impulse or vision. 'All authentic art,' he commented 'is negative' (Kearney 1995: 203). Its function is to 'negate present society; to anticipate the trends of future society… to suggest "images" of creative and unalienating zones' (1995: 205). Art's utopian effect is mediated rather than direct, said Marcuse, but is aided by the direct indictment of present society performed 'by theory and politics' (1995: 205).

An additional key text theorizing the relations of art and utopia is Ernst Bloch's *The Principle of Hope* (1990), written in the 1940s. Bloch claimed that emancipatory moments critical of CAPITALISM or state socialism occur in a range of kinds of text, from daydreams to literature, philosophy and religion. This view of the mixed and contradictory nature of literary and cultural texts, or systems of belief, as at once mystificatory or ideological and liberating is taken up, notably, in Fredric Jameson's essay 'Reification and utopia in mass culture' (1990c). Jameson sees the texts of MASS culture (his discussion is concerned chiefly with Hollywood films) as simultaneously a vehicle of ideological containment and the expression of a resistant collective ethos opposed to the dehumanizing systems of capitalism. This kind of analysis has commonly been adopted in a form of radical cultural criticism that seeks to read mass culture 'against the grain' of its intended ideological effects so as to reveal unconscious, suppressed or distorted needs and desires, and thus to open the possibility of alternative modes of fulfilment (Williamson 1978; Dyer 1993a).

It is often thought that POSTMODERNISM has cancelled the aspect of radical critique, whether in AVANT-GARDE or mass culture, and at the same time cancelled the idea of the future, having to replace history with a flat spatiality reminiscent of the early classical utopias (Harvey 1989). Ruth Levitas argues, by contrast, that the utopian imagination survives in the present and that the difficulty now lies elsewhere: in 'identifying points of intervention in an increasingly complex social and economic structure, and of identifying the agents and bearers of social transformation' (1993: 258).

VALUE

For Steven Connor, our 'orientation towards the better, and revulsion from the worse' (1992: 2) follows from the inescapable imperative of evaluation. For Barbara Herrnstein Smith, the experience of 'aesthetic value' is so fundamental that it can be understood as 'a function of species – wide mechanisms of perception and cognition' (1988: 15). What – both in EVERYDAY LIFE and AESTHETIC or Cultural Theory – has dogged this very human impulse has been the debate on the existence, possibility, or impossibility of objective standards or universal criteria of value. Raymond Williams reports in an essay of 1970 how the physical sciences provided Sociology with such a model of objective value-free research. This was, he argues, a false trail, because:

> the central business of social studies... because they must deal with men in social relationships and in history, must, whether they know it or not, deal with active values and with choices, including the values and choices of the observers.
> (1980b: 15)

Williams posits two centres of value: the object or material of study and the valuing observer. One way to investigate the question of value would be to ask how far this view has been accepted, in both its aspects, in not only the physical and social sciences, but in the various forms of cultural study.

Within Literary Studies, especially, value has traditionally been viewed as the intrinsic property of texts. Assessing this value (in terms of combined aesthetic, moral and ideological criteria) decided their place in a selective CANON or tradition. This approach and its results have been relevant to continuing debates on high and low CULTURE – where the terms of the original hierarchical distinction are evidently evaluative – and to the related study of POPULAR culture and MASS society. In these instances, the impulse to discriminate between 'better' and 'worse' is institutionalized or established as part of a cultural hegemony.

More recent theories of TEXTUALITY and READING are sceptical of the certainties of the canon or cultural orthodoxy. They have drawn attention accordingly to the instability of texts and to the active role of AUDIENCES and readers in producing meaning and value (as in the second part of Williams' formulation). This has highlighted the way viewers/readers negotiate with the 'preferred meanings' inscribed in texts and the positions from which they engage in this process. Both texts and their consumers are therefore understood as situated within the changing complex of institutions and ideologies governing the formation of GENDERed, CLASS or ethnically inflected identities. Value, in this view, can only accrue to texts in so far as they are valued in the contexts by which SUBJECTIVITY and social relations in general are constituted. This has been investigated, especially in relation to literary taste and value, by Barbara Herrnstein Smith (1988). Valuation, she argues, is 'always compromised, impure, contingent'; it is 'continuous and ongoing' and 'variable' (1988: 1). The student or theorist of value must therefore seek to account for this state of things in the conditions producing it, 'in relation to the total economy of our existence' (1988: 16). There might emerge equivalencies or constancies in the midst of variation, but there can be 'no transcendental guarantees… no objective truths' and 'no theoretical analysis' that can 'expose a state of affairs as objectively… unjust or wrong' (1988: 175). We can therefore only establish and defend values in a scrupulously relativistic manner within the contingent circumstances – of which, these values and a perspective on them are a product. Among other issues, this argument raises the question of the role of the valuing critic as arbiter on questions of value, and this has been brought into sharper focus in studies of POPULAR culture and 'fandom', where the 'critic as fan' is more evidently positioned both inside and outside the object of study (see Bennett 1990; Henry Jenkins 1992; Brooker 2000).

What might be termed the 'politics of value' involved in these positions has a further, though not often connected, point of reference in Marxist economic theory: specifically, in the key distinction made by Marx between 'use value' and 'exchange value'. Thus, an object produced for use by human labour is valued in the marketplace, says Marx, in terms of its exchange value. A saucepan, for example, might be worth a hammer in a system of barter, but will be valued in more advanced economies in money terms. In capitalist economies, the price of such an object is more than the cost of the labour, or more precisely what is paid for the labour of producing it. The difference between price and wages produces profit, or what Marx calls 'surplus value'. The priorities, or values, of the market therefore replace or repress another set of what are thought to be more human values. Terry Lovell (1980) gives Marx's sense of 'use value' a wider, positive relevance to consumer societies. It defines, she says, 'the ability of the commodity to satisfy some human want'. According to Marx, this may 'spring from the stomach or from the fancy' (1980: 57).

The question of ethical and political values, including those associated with the Marxist tradition, have been made especially problematic by the changed economies and cultures of contemporary societies. Common aesthetic, moral or political values (those of western MODERNITY, for example) appear less credible. This situation, and responses to it, are debated within the associated theories of POST-FORDISM, POST-MARXISM, POSTMODERNISM and POSTCOLONIALISM, which have been prompted by, and seek to explain, these changes. Sometimes the debate on ethical values, in particular, is associated with what is termed post-foundationalist thought.

The relation of these theoretical movements to questions of literary or cultural value is very usefully focused by Connor (1992), and by Squires (1993) and Frow (1995). Connor views the recurrent wish in debates on value to separate and hierarchize absolute and relative values, aesthetics and ethics, politics and pleasure, use and exchange value as untenable. A relativist position such as Smith's, above, betrays its own commitment to absolute value, he argues, in precisely and so categorically denying the validity of claims to universalist value. We are bound, therefore, to accept and try to think these paradoxical pairings together. The process of evaluation is nevertheless a reflexive one, argues Connor, committing us not only to an inescapable evaluative disposition, but also to a continuous critique of the terms of value. Such an activity, he believes, belongs to – is indeed the 'essence' of – 'a political discourse of emancipation' (1992: 5).

See also CONSUMERISM; ETHICS; FOUNDATIONALISM.

VIRTUAL REALITY

A term used to refer to computer-generated SIMULATIONS that either reproduce actual environments or invent new ones with no 'real-life' equivalent. Such simulations are put to practical use in the training of airline pilots and astronauts, in surgery, and in the world of design and architecture, but are associated, above all, with the world of media entertainment. In the increasingly prosaic sense that all computers produce 'virtual' experience (since word processors, spell-checks, calculators and games are not 'actually' there to point to in the machine memory or in software), computer technology has made the experience of virtual reality an everyday occurrence. Aided by modems, routers, programmes, apps and downloadable digital media files, such as MP3, access to the augmented experience of music, educational material, financial information, or multimedia HYPERTEXT is also possible through home computers, giving rise to terms such as 'Edutainment' and 'Infotainment'.

Primarily, however, virtual reality is associated with wearing a 'rig' of headset and data glove to experience a stereoscopic, out-of-body visual and audio environment. Some view this development as a symptom of the IMAGE-led character of POSTMODERNISM and the harbinger of a UTOPIAN world of uncomplicated, unrestricted PLEASURE. 'We are on the brink,' wrote Harvey Rheingold in his *Virtual Worlds,* 'of having the power of creating any experience we desire' (1991: 386). A more sceptical note is sounded by Benjamin Woolley (1993); present technology, he suggests, is cumbersome, limited and slow, if intellectually exciting. Chiefly, Woolley is concerned with the implications for conceptions of reality. 'Is the computer just a new creative medium?' he asks. 'Are fictional worlds the same as virtual worlds? Do computers create reality, or discover it?' (1993: 243). His answer is that 'Computers are virtual, not actual entities' where 'virtual', in the more prosaic sense above, means 'a mode of simulated existence resulting from computation' (1993: 68). Reality, meanwhile, contra some postmodern scenarios, is 'still there', says Wooley. This is not the independent physical universe understood by a naïve MATERIALISM, however, but the reality known to science and revealed 'in the formal, abstract domain' of 'mathematics and computation' (1993: 254). Virtual reality, that is to say, is the reality of mathematics.

In a further take on the concept, the social theorist Manuel Castells reverses its terms to argue for the experience of 'real virtuality'. By this, he means that the media technologies and global communication systems characterizing a changed information or NETWORK society have the power to produce an instant transcultural experience; to make the rap culture of American urban ghettos, in his example, a reality around the world. The familiar complaint is that reality has been lost to this media-generated virtual reality. But all CULTURE, Castells argues, is an interactive symbolic system, centred now in our contemporary audio-visual universe. Thus, the resulting 'virtuality, the coded representation in an interactive electronic system... is our reality'. Indeed, 'the culture of real virtuality is the dominant culture' (1997: 150–1). Robins and Webster (1999) trace the cultural impact of two centuries of technological innovation leading to this present situation.

See also DIGITAL; CYBERSPACE; HYPERREALITY.

WORLD LITERATURE

The concept of 'world literature' has been a part of debates in Literary Studies, and particularly of Comparative Literary Studies, since the nineteenth century. The idea has found a new vigour and pertinence, however, in the age of GLOBALIZATION and the INTERNET, prompted by widespread reservations, felt since the 1970s, concerning the limiting assumptions on genre, mode, gender and ethnicity maintained in the traditional Anglo-American or European CANON.

A leading figure in this new initiative is David Damrosch, the author of studies in both comparative and world literature. His *What is World Literature?* (2003) has been followed by *How to Read World Literature* (2009) as well as the edited volumes, *Teaching World Literature* (2009), *World Literature in Theory* (2014) and the six-volume, co-edited *Longman Anthology of World Literature* (2009). He is also Chair of the Institute of World Literature established at Harvard which organizes an annual month-long session at different venues around the world. This changed agenda can be witnessed at the same time in the increasing number of critical works and anthologies appearing in the 2010s (see D'haen, 2011; Wollaeger and Eatough [eds] 2012; Lane [ed] 2013, Tötösy de Zepetnek and Mukherjee [eds] 2013), in teaching programmes, publishers' lists, online websites and blogs, and the expanded scope of literary prizes.

However, the concept and project of world literature raises a series of questions, some long-standing, concerning: the enduring priority of English as a world language, the vagaries of translation, and the limited prospects, therefore, for a full comparative study of texts in their original and translated language and respective geo-historical contexts. A particular concern also in current debate is the power of western universities and the suspicion of complicity on the part of the academic world with the operations of the global market (see Apter, 2013). Proponents of world literature speak, on the other hand, of the heightened possibility of deeper cultural exchange and a challenge to dominant paradigms. A global approach, it is said, forestalls the projection of national values as universal; it calls for the adaptation of theoretical models, or the adoption of those from different traditions, promoting an awareness and knowledge of hybridity and difference, of networks not unities, of independence not assimilation (see Damrosch [ed] 2014 esp. Part Two).

Aware of such issues, Damrosch (2003) has called less for an expanded canon – and not at all for an 'airport literature' written-by-numbers for a world book market – than for a thoroughly open critical perspective upon multicultural literatures, past and present. He directs attention to how specific works are 'reframed' in circuits of translation, production, distribution and reception, at 'what is lost and what is gained in translation… the intertwined shifts of language, era, region, religion, social status and literary context that a work can incur as it moves from its point of origin out into a new cultural sphere' (2003: 34). But if this answers some questions, it sets out an extremely demanding agenda which risks making the study of world literature paradoxically more selective than ever. For would other than expert readers be able to meet the high level of linguistic and cultural fluency such a multinational comparative approach requires? And would more than a minority of readers have the depth of experience to offer considered judgements of literary VALUE? Indeed, is the idea of 'worldwide' criteria of value a deluded and distorting objective?

A related question concerns the sheer extent and quantity of world literature. Franco Morretti (2013) concludes that this spells an end to the traditional practice of 'close reading' and a necessary recourse instead to 'distant reading' provided by computer analyses of common features of form and plot across a mammoth database of works (say the world novel) that cannot be practically or meaningfully read in the old way.

For his part, Damrosch ([ed] 2014) responds that 'a world systems approach', such as Moretti's, needs to be counterbalanced with close attention to the particularity of cultures, languages and specific texts, avoiding both a reductive overview and atomistic short focus.

The study of world literature therefore presents a series of new issues, by turns, exhilarating and problematic. Of these, both Moretti and Damrosch point to perhaps the primary, underlying question: less the scale of production or rhythms of circulation, or 'what to read', so much as 'how to read' world literature. To this extent, Damrosch's guidance and illustrative case studies of pairs of texts, across modes and genres, times and cultures, and in translation, makes his *How to Read World Literature* (2009) a testing, but particularly impressive model.

See also DIASPORA, POSTCOLONIALISM; POST-THEORY.

WRITERLY

See READERLY.

BIBLIOGRAPHY

Abelove, Henry, Barale, Michèle Aina and Halperin, David M. (eds) (1993). *The Lesbian and Gay Studies Reader.* London: Routledge.

Ades, Dawn (1986). *Photomontage.* London: Thames and Hudson.

Adorno, Theodor W. (1955). *Prisms.* Cambridge MA: MIT Press.

Adorno, Theodor W. (1984 [1970]). *Aesthetic Theory.* Trans. C. Lenhart. London: Routledge.

Adorno, Theodor W. (1990). *Negative Dialectics.* Trans. E.B. Ashton. London: Routledge.

Adorno, Theodor W. (1991). *The Culture Industry: Selected Essays on Mass Culture.* Ed. J.M. Bernstein. London: Routledge.

Adorno, Theodor W. (1992 [1936]). 'Letter to Walter Benjamin'. In Brooker (ed) (1992).

Adorno, Theodor W. and Horkheimer, Max (1972). 'The culture industry: enlightenment as mass deception'. In Adorno and Horkheimer (1979). Included in During (ed) (1993).

Adorno, Theodor W. and Horkheimer, Max (1979 [1947]). *The Dialectic of Enlightenment.* London: Verso.

Adrian, Chris and Horowitz, Eli (2015). *The New World.* Atavist ebook and New York: Farrar, Straus and Giroux.

Agamben, Giorgio (1998 [1995]). *Homo Sacer: Sovereign Power and Bare Life.* Trans. Daniel Heller-Roazen. Stanford CA: Stanford University Press.

Agamben, Giorgio (2002 [1999]). *Remnants of Auschwitz: The Witness and the Archive.* Trans. Daniel Heller-Roazen. Cambridge MA: MIT Press.

Agamben, Giorgio (2005 [2003]). *State of Exception.* Trans. Kevin Attell. Chicago IL: University of Chicago Press.

Agamben, Giorgio (2004). Trans. Kevin Attell. *The Open*: *Man and Animal.* Stanford CA: Stanford University Press.

Ahmad, Aijaz (1992). *In Theory: Classes, Nations, Literatures.* London: Verso.

Ahmad, Aijaz (1994). 'Reconciling Derrida: "Spectres of Marx" and deconstructive politics'. *New Left Review,* 208, Nov/Dec, 88–119.

Ahmed, Akbar, S. (1992). *Postmodernism and Islam.* London: Routledge.

Alaimo, Stacy (2010). *Bodily Natures: Science, Environment and the Material Self.* Bloomington IN: Indiana University Press.

Alaimo, Stacy (2014). 'Thinking as the Stuff of the World', *O-Zone: A Journal of Object-Oriented Studies.* Object/Ecology, 1, 13–21.

Alaimo, Stacy and Hekman, S.J. (eds) 2008. *Material Feminisms.* Bloomington IN: Indiana University Press.

Althusser, Louis (1969 [1965]). 'The "Piccolo Teatro": Bertolazzi and Brecht'. In Althusser, Louis (1969).

Althusser, Louis (1969). *For Marx.* Trans. Ben Brewster. London: Allen Lane. Reprinted New Left Books, 1977.

Althusser, Louis (1971a [1970]). 'Ideology and ideological state apparatuses'. In *Lenin and Philosophy and Other Essays.* Trans. Ben Brewster. London: New Left Books.

Althusser, Louis (1971b). 'A letter on art in reply to André Daspre (April, 1966)'. In *Lenin and Philosophy and Other Essays.* Trans. Ben Brewster. London: New Left Books.

Althusser, Louis (1976). *Essays in Self-Criticism.* London: Verso.

Althusser, Louis (1979). 'Marxism is not an historicism'. In Althusser, Louis and Balibar, Étienne (1979).

Althusser, Louis and Balibar, Étienne (1979). *Reading 'Capital'.* Trans. Ben Brewster. London: Verso.

Altick, Richard, D. (1963). *The English Common Reader: A Social History of the Mass Reading Public 1800–1900.* Chicago IL: University of Chicago Press.

Altman, Dennis, Vance, Carole, Vicinus, Martha, Weeks, Jeffrey and others. (eds) (1989). *Homosexuality, Which Homosexuality?* London: Gay Men's Press.

Anderson, Benedict (1983). *Imagined Communities: Reflections on the Origin and Spread of Nationalism.* London: Verso.

Anderson, Perry (1979). *Considerations on Western Marxism.* London: Verso.

Anderson, Perry (1984). *In the Tracks of Historical Materialism.* London: Verso.

Anderson, Perry (1988). 'Modernity and revolution'. In Nelson and Grossberg (eds) (1988).

Ang, Ien (1985). *Watching 'Dallas': Soap Opera and the Melodramatic Imagination.* London: Methuen.

Ang, Ien (1988). 'Feminist desire and female pleasure: on Janice Radway's *Reading the Romance; Women, Patriarchy and Popular Literature*'. *Camera Obscura,* 16, 179–90.

Ang, Ien (1990). *Desperately Seeking the Audience.* London: Routledge.

Ang, Ien (1994). 'On not speaking Chinese: postmodern ethnicity and the politics of diaspora'. *New Formations,* 24, Winter, 1–19.

Anzaldúa, Gloria (ed) (1990). *Making Face, Making Soul, Haciendo Cams: Creative and Critical Perspectives by Women of Color.* San Francisco CA: Auntlute Foundation.

Appadurai, Arjun (ed) (1986). *The Social Life of Things: Commodities in Cultural Perspective.* Cambridge: Cambridge University Press.

Apter, Emily (2013). *Against World Literature.* London: Verso 2013.

Archibugi, Daniele (2000). 'Cosmopolitical democracy'. *New Left Review,* 4, Second Series, Jul–Aug, 137–150.

Archibugi, Daniele and Held David (eds) (1995). *Cosmopolitan Democracy. An Agenda for a New World Order.* Cambridge: Polity.

Aronowitz, Stanley (1981, rev. edn 1989). *The Crisis in Historical Materialism: Class, Politics and Culture in Marxist Theory.* London: Macmillan.

Ashcroft, Bill, Griffiths, Gareth and Tiffin, Helen (eds) (1995). *The Post-Colonial Studies Reader.* London: Routledge.

Atkins, Dawn (1998). *Looking Queer: Body Image and Identity in Lesbian, Bisexual, Gay, and Transgender Communities.* Hove: Psychology Press.

Attridge, Derek and Elliott, Jane (eds) (2011). *Theory after 'Theory'.* New York: Routledge.

Back, Les (1996). *New Ethnicities and Urban Culture: Racism and Multiculture in Young Lives.* London: UCL Press Ltd.

Badiou, Alain ([1988] 2006). *Being and Event,* trans. Oliver Feltham. London: Continuum.

Badiou, Alain ([2006] 2009). *Logics of Worlds.* Trans. Alberto Toscano, London: Continuum,

Badiou, Alain (2011). 'Tunisie, Egypte: quand un vent d'est balaie l'arrogance de l'Occident', *Le Monde,* 18 February.

Badiou, Alain, and Toscano, Alberti (2005). *Handbook of Inaesthetics.* Stanford CA: Stanford University Press.

Baker, Houston A. Jnr (1987). *Modernism and the Harlem Renaissance.* Chicago IL: University of Chicago Press.

Bakhtin, M.M. (1963 [1929]). *Problems of Dostoevsky's Poetics.* Ed. and trans. C. Emerson. Minneapolis MN: University of Minnesota Press.

Bakhtin, M.M. (1965). *Rabelais and His World.* Trans. H. Iswolsky. Bloomington: Indiana University Press.

Bakhtin, M.M. (1981 [1934–41]). *The Dialogic Imagination.* Ed. M. Holquist, trans. C. Emerson and M. Holquist. Austin TX: University of Texas Press.

Barad, Karen. (2007). *Meeting the Universe Halfway: Quantum Physics and the Entanglement of Matter and Meaning.* Durham NC: Duke University Press.

Barker, Francis, Hulme, Peter, Loxley, Diana and Iverson, Margaret (eds) (1986) *Literature, Politics, Theory: Papers from the Essex Conference 1976–84.* London: Routledge.

Barnsley, Michael, Pietgen, Heinz Otto and Saupen, Dietmar (eds) (1988). *The Science of Fractal Images.* New York and London: Springer Verlag.

Barrett, Michèle (1980, rev. edn 1988). *Women's Oppression Today: Problems in Marxist Feminist Analysis.* London: Verso.

Barrett, Michèle (1991). *The Politics of Truth: From Marx to Foucault.* Cambridge: Polity Press.

Barrett, Michèle, Corrigan, Philip, Kuhn, Annette and Wolff, Janet (eds) (1979) *Ideology and Cultural Production.* London: Croom Helm.

Barthes, Roland (1972a [1957]). *Mythologies.* Trans. Annette Lavers. London: Cape.

Barthes, Roland (1972b [1964]). *Critical Essays.* Evanston IL: Northwestern University Press.

Barthes, Roland (1975 [1970]) *S/Z.* Trans. Richard Miller. London: Jonathan Cape.

Barthes, Roland (1976 [1973]). *The Pleasure of the Text.* Trans. Richard Miller. London: Jonathan Cape.

Barthes, Roland (1977a [1968]). 'The death of the author'. In Barthes (1977b).

Barthes, Roland (1977b). *Image-Music-Text.* Ed. Stephen Heath. London: Collins.

Barthes, Roland ([1978], 2002. trans. 2005). *The Neutral.* New York: Columbia University Press.

Baudelaire, Charles (1982 [1863]). 'The painter of modem life'. In Frascina, Francis and Harrison, Charles (eds) (1982).

Baudrillard, Jean (1970). *La Société de Consommation.* Paris: Gallimard.

Baudrillard, Jean (1975). *The Mirror of Production.* Trans. Mark Poster. St Louis MO: Telos Press.

Baudrillard, Jean (1981). *For a Critique of the Political Economy of the Sign.* Trans. C. Levin. St Louis MO: Telos Press.

Baudrillard, Jean (1988). *Selected Writings.* Ed. and introduced by Mark Poster. Cambridge: Polity Press.

Baudrillard, Jean (1993 [1976]). 'The tactile and the digital'. In *Symbolic Exchange and Death.* Trans. Iain Hamilton Grant. London: Sage.

Baudrillard, Jean (1994 [1981]). *Simulacra and Simulation.* Trans. Sheila Faria Glaser. Ann Arbor MI: University of Michigan Press.

Baudrillard, Jean, ([2002] 2012). *The Spirit of Terrorism: And Requiem for the Twin Towers.* Trans. Chris Turner. London: Verso.

Bauman, Zygmunt (1987). *Legislators and Interpreters: On Modernity, Post-Modernity and Intellectuals.* Cambridge: Polity Press.

Bauman, Zygmunt (1993). *Postmodern Ethics.* Oxford: Blackwell.

Baxandall, Lee and Morawski, Stefan (1973). *Marx and Engels on Literature and Art.* St Louis MO: Telos Press.

302

Bayer-Berenbaum, Linda (1982). *The Gothic Imagination.* London and Toronto: Associated University Press.

Beck, Ulrich (1992 [1986]). *Risk Society: Towards a New Modernity.* London: Sage.

Beck, Ulrich, Giddens, Anthony and Lash, Scott (1994). *Reflexive Modernization: Politics, Tradition and Aesthetics in the Modern Social World.* Cambridge: Polity Press.

Bell, David (2001). *An Introduction to Cybercultures.* London: Routledge.

Bell, David and Kennedy, Barbara ([eds] 2000). *The Cybercultures Reader.* London: Routledge.

Belsey, Catherine (1980). *Critical Practice.* London: Routledge.

Benhabib, Seyla (1992). *Situating the Self: Gender, Community and Postmodernism in Contemporary Ethics.* Cambridge: Polity Press.

Benjamin, Walter (1923). 'Goethe's elective affinities'. In Tiedeman, Rolf and Schweppenhauser, Herman (eds). *Walter Benjamin. Gesammelte Schriften. Vol. 1* (1972) Frankfurt am Main: Surkamp Verlag.

Benjamin, Walter (1970a [1940]). 'Thesis on the philosophy of history'. In Benjamin (1970b). As 'On the Concept of History', trans. H. Zohn. In Eiland, H. and Jennings, M.W. (eds) *Walter Benjamin: Selected Writings* (vol. 4 1938–1940). Cambridge MA: Harvard University Press.

Benjamin, Walter (1970b). *Illuminations.* Ed. Hannah Arendt. London: Fontana.

Benjamin, Walter (1973a). 'The author as producer'. In Walter Benjamin (ed). *Understanding Brecht.* Introduced by Stanley Mitchell. London: New Left Books.

Benjamin, Walter (1973b). *Charles Baudelaire: A Lyric Poet in the Era of High Capitalism.* Trans. Harry Zohn. London: New Left Books.

Benko, Georges and Strohmayer, Ulf (eds) (1997). *Space and Social Theory: Interpreting Modernity and Postmodernity.* Oxford: Blackwell.

Bennett, Jane (2010). *Vibrant Matter. A Political Economy of* Things. Durham NC: Duke University Press.

Bennett, Tony (1979). *Formalism and Marxism.* London: Routledge.

Bennett, Tony (1990). *Outside Literature.* London: Routledge.

Bennett, Tony (1998). *Culture. A Reformer's Science.* London: Sage.

Benson, Sarah (1997). 'The body, health and eating disorders'. In Woodward (ed) (1997).

Berman, Marshall (1982). *All That Is Solid Melts Into Air: The Experience of Modernity.* London: Verso.

Bernstein, Richard, J. (1991). *The New Constellation: The Ethical and Political Horizons of Modernity/Postmodernity.* Cambridge: Polity Press.

Bertens, Hans (1995). *The Idea of the Postmodern: A History.* London: Routledge.

Best, Steven and Kellner, Douglas (1991). *Postmodern Theory: Critical Interrogations.* London: Macmillan.

Best, Steven and Marcus, Sharon (eds) (2009). 'Surface Reading: An Introduction', *Representations,* 108 (Fall), 1–21.

Bhabha, Homi (1990). 'Interview with Homi Bhabha. "The Third Space"'. In Rutherford (ed) (1990b).

Bhabha, Homi (1991). 'Conference presentation'. In Philomena, Mariani (ed) (1991).

Bhabha, Homi (1994). *The Location of Culture.* London: Routledge.

Billig, Michael, Condor, Susan, Edwards, Derek and Gane, Mike (1988). *Ideological Dilemmas: A Social Psychology of Everyday Thinking.* London: Sage.

Bird, Jon, Curtis, Barry, Putnam, Tim, Robertson, George and Tickner, Lisa (eds) (1993). *Mapping the Futures: Local Cultures, Global Chnge.* London: Routledge.

Blake, Charlie, Molly, Claire, and Shakespeare, Steven (2012). *Beyond Human: From Animality to Transhuman.* London: Continuum.

Bloch, Ernst (1990 [1959]). *The Principle of Hope.* Oxford: Blackwell.

Bloch, Ernst *et al.* (1977). *Aesthetics and Politics*. London: New Left Books.

Blonsky, Marshall (ed) (1985). *On Signs: A Semiotics Reader*. Oxford: Blackwell.

Bloom, Harold (1973). *The Anxiety of Influence: A Theory Of Poetry*. Oxford: Oxford University Press.

Bloom, Harold (1995). *The Western Canon*. London: Macmillan.

Bogost, Ian (2012). *Alien Phenomenology: Or What It's Like to Be a Thing*. Minneapolis MN: University of Minnesota Press.

Bogue, Roland (1989). *Deleuze and Guattari*. London: Routledge.

Bonneuil, Christophe and Fressoz, Jean-Baptiste (2015). *Shock of the Anthropocene: The Earth, History and Us*. London: Verso.

Boone, Joseph A. and Cadden, Michael (eds) (1990). *Engendering Men: The Question of Male Feminist Criticism*. London: Routledge.

Booth, Wayne (1988). *The Company We Keep: An Ethics of Fiction*. Berkeley CA: University of California Press.

Botting, Fred (1996). *Gothic*. London: Routledge.

Bourdieu, Pierre (1984). *Distinction: A Social Critique of the Judgement of Taste*. London: Routledge.

Bourdieu, Pierre (1990). *The Logic of Practice*. Cambridge: Polity Press.

Bourdieu, Pierre and Passeron, Jean-Claude (1977). *Reproduction in Education, Society and Culture*. London: Sage.

Bourdieu, Pierre, with L. Wacquant (1992). *An Invitation to Reflexive Sociology*. Cambridge: Polity Press.

Bowie, Malcolm (1987). *Freud, Proust and Lacan: Theory as Fiction*. Cambridge: Cambridge University Press.

Bowie, Malcolm (1991). *Lacan*. London: Collins.

Bowlby, Rachel (1985). *Just Looking: Consumer Culture in Dreiser, Gissing and Zola*. London: Routledge.

Bowlby, Rachel (1992). *Still Crazy After All These Years*. London: Routledge.

Bradbury, Malcolm and McFarlane, James (eds) (1976). *Modernism: 1890–1930*. Harmondsworth: Penguin.

Braidotti, Rosi (1994). *Nomadic Subjects: Embodiment and Sexual Difference in Contemporary Feminist Theory*. New York: Columbia University Press.

Brassier, Ray (2007). *Nihil Unbound: Enlightenment and Extinction*. London: Palgrave Macmillan.

Brennan Tim (1989). *Salman Rushdie and the Third World*. New York: St Martin's Press.

Brenner, Susan W. (2010). *Cybercrime: Criminal Threats from Cyberspace* (Crime, Media and Popular Culture). Westport CT: Praeger Publishers Inc.

Brewer, Anthony (1980). *Marxist Theories of Imperialism: A Critical Survey*. London: Routledge.

Bristow, Joseph and Wilson, Angela R. (eds) (1993). *Activating Theory: Lesbian, Gay, Bisexual Politics*. London: Lawrence and Wishart.

Bromley, Roger (2000). *Narratives for a New Belonging*. Edinburgh: Edinburgh University Press.

Brookeman, Christopher (1984). *American Culture and Society Since the 1930s*. London: Macmillan.

Brooker, Peter ([1988] 2016). *Bertolt Brecht: Dialectics, Poetry, Politics*. London: Routledge Revivals.

Brooker, Peter (ed) (1992). *Modernism/Postmodernism*. London: Longman.

Brooker, Peter (1999). 'The wandering *flâneur*, or, something lost in translation'. *Miscelánea*, Vol. 20, Zaragoza: Universidad de Zaragoza, 115–30.

Brooker, Peter (2002). *Modernity and Metropolis: Writing, Film and Urban Formations*. London: Palgrave.

Brooker, Peter (2005). 'Terrorism and Counter Narratives: Don DeLillo and the New York Imaginary'. *New Formations*, 57, 10–25.

Brooker, Peter and Brooker, Will (eds) (1997). *Postmodern After-Images: A Reader in Film, TV and Video*. London: Arnold.

Brooker, Peter, Gasiorek, Andrzej, Longworth, Deborah and Thacker, Andrew (eds) (2010). *The Oxford Handbook of Modernisms*. London: Oxford.

Brooker, Peter and Widdowson, Peter (eds) (1996). *A Practical Reader in Contemporary Literary Theory*. Hemel Hempstead: Prentice Hall.

Brooker, Will (2000). *Batman Unmasked. Analysing a Cultural Icon*. London: Continuum.

Brooker, Will (2002). *Using the Force. Creativity, Community and Star Wars Audiences*. London: Continuum.

Brooker, Will (2017). *Forever Stardust. David Bowie Across the Universe*. London: I.B. Tauris.

Brooker, Will and Jermyn, Deborah (eds) (2002). *The Audience Studies Reader*. London: Routledge.

Brooks, Adrian (2015). *The Right Side of History: 100 Years of LGBT Activism*. Berkeley CA: Cleis Press.

Brooks, Peter (1984). *Reading for the Plot: Design and Intention in Narrative*. Oxford: Clarendon Press.

Brooks, Peter (1994). *Psychoanalysis and Storytelling*. Oxford: Blackwell.

Brown, Bill, (1996). *The Material Unconscious. American Amusement. Stephen Crane & The Economies of Play*. Cambridge MA: Harvard University Press.

Brown, Bill (ed). (2001). *Things*. Special Issue of *Critical Inquiry* 28.1.

Brown, Bill (2003). *A Sense of Things: The Object Matter of American Literature*. Chicago IL: University of Chicago Press.

Brown, Roger, (1965). *Social Psychology*. London: Macmillan.

Brown, Roger, with Carasso, Helen (2013). *Everything for Sale? The Marketisation of UK Higher Education*. London: Routledge.

Bryant, Levi R. (2011). *The Democracy of Objects*. Ann Arbor MI: Open Humanities Press, imprint of Michigan Publishing, University of Michigan Library.

Bryant, Levi R, Srnicek, Nick and Harman Graham (eds) (2011). *The Speculative Turn. Continental Materialism and Realism*. Melbourne, VIC: re.press.

Buell, Lawrence (2005). *The Future of Environmental Criticism: Environmental Crisis and Literary Imagination*. Oxford: Wiley.

Burchell, Graham, Gordon, Colin and Miller, Peter (eds) (1991). *The Foucault Effect: Studies in Governmentality*. London: Harvester Wheatsheaf.

Bürger, Peter (1984). *The Theory of the Avant-Garde*. Trans. Michael Shaw, foreword by Jochen Schulte-Sasse. Manchester: Manchester University Press.

Burgin, Victor, Donald, James and Kaplan, Cora (eds) (1986). *Formations of Fantasy*. London: Routledge.

Burke, Edmund (1939). *The Works of Edmund Burke*. Vol. 5. Boston MA: Charles C. Little and James Brown.

Burke, Sean (1992). *The Death and Return of the Author*. Edinburgh: Edinburgh University Press.

Burke, Sean (ed) (1994) *Authorship from Plato to the Postmodern: A Reader*. Edinburgh: Edinburgh University Press.

Butler, Judith (1990). *Gender Trouble: Feminism and the Subversion of Identity*. London and New York: Routledge.

Butler, Judith (1993). *Bodies That Matter: On the Discursive Limits of Sex.* London: Routledge.

Butler, Judith (1994). 'Gender as performance: an interview with Judith Butler', *Radical Philosophy,* 67, Summer, 32–7.

Butler, Judith (1995). 'Desire'. In Lentricchia and McLaughlin (eds) (1995).

Butler, Judith, Guillory, John and Thomas, Kendall (eds) (2000). *What's Left of Theory.* London: Routledge.

Butler, Rex (ed) (2014). *The Žižek Dictionary.* Durham: Acumen.

Caldwell, Bruce, J. (1982, rev. edn 1994). *Beyond Positivism: Economic Methodology in the Twentieth Century.* London: Routledge.

Callari, Antonio, Cullenberg, Stephen and Biewener, Carole (eds) (1995). *Marxism in the Postmodern Age: Confronting the New World Order.* London and New York: The Guilford Press.

Callinicos, Alex (1989). *Against Postmodernism.* Cambridge: Polity Press.

Callon, Michel (1986). 'Some elements of a Sociology of Translation: Domestication of the Scallops and the Fishermen of St Brieuc Bay'. In John Law (ed) (1986), *Power, Action and Belief: A New Sociology of Knowledge.* London: Routledge & Kegan Paul.

Callon, Michel, Law, John and Rip, Arie (eds) (1986). *Mapping the Dynamics of Science and Technology, Sociology of Science in the Real World.* London: Macmillan.

Carby, Hazel (1987). *Reconstructing Womanhood: The Emergence of the Afro-American Woman Novelist.* New York: Oxford University Press.

Carey, James, W. (1992). *Communication as Culture.* London: Routledge.

Carter, Erica, Donald, James and Squires, Judith (eds) (1993). *Space and Place: Theories of Identity and Location.* London: Lawrence and Wishart.

Castells, Manuel (1989). *The Informational City.* Oxford: Blackwell.

Castells, Manuel (1996). *The Information Age: Economy, Society and Culture. Vol. 1: The Rise of the Network Society.* Oxford: Blackwell.

Castells, Manuel (1997). 'Citizen movements, information and analysis. An interview with Manuel Castells'. *City, 7, May,* 140–55.

Caughie, John (ed) (1981). *Theories of Authorship.* London: Routledge.

Centre for Contemporary Cultural Studies (1982). *The Empire Writes Back: Race and Racism in 70s Britain.* University of Birmingham and London: Hutchinson.

Chambers, Iain (1993). *Migrancy, Culture, Identity.* London: Comedia/Routledge.

Chambers, Iain (2001). *Culture After Humanism.* London: Routledge.

Champagne, Roland, A. (1995). *Jacques Derrida.* New York: Twayne.

Cheah Pheng and Robbins, Bruce (eds) (2000). *Cosmopolitics.* Minneapolis MN: University of Minnesota Press.

Childs, Peter and Williams, Patrick (1997). *An Introduction to Post-Colonial Theory.* London: Prentice Hall/Harvester.

Chodorow, Nancy (1978). *The Reproduction of Mothering: Psychoanalysis and the Sociology of Gender.* Berkeley CA: University of California Press.

Chomsky, Noam (1969). *American Power and the New Mandarins.* Harmondsworth: Penguin.

Chomsky, Noam (1991). *Deterring Democracy.* London: Verso.

Cixous, Hélène (1976). 'Fiction and its phantoms: a reading of Freud's Das Unheimliche ("the Uncanny")'. *New Literary History,* 7, 525–48.

Cixous, Hélène (1981a [1975]). 'Sorties'. In Cixous, Hélène and Clement, Catherine, *The Newly Born Woman* (1975). Trans. B. Wing. Manchester: Manchester University Press. Also in Marks and de Courtivron (eds) (1981).

Cixous, Hélène (1981b [1976]). 'The laugh of the Medusa'. Trans. K. Cohen and P. Cohen. In Marks and de Courtivron (eds) (1981).

Clarke, Jon, Critcher, Chas and Johnson, Richard (1979). *Working Class Culture: Studies in History and Theory.* London: Hutchinson.

Clarke, Paul Barry (1996). *Deep Citizenship.* London: Pluto.

Clifford, James (1980). 'Review essay of Edward Said's *Orientalism'. History and Theory,* 19, 2, 204–23.

Clifford, James (1988) *The Predicament of Culture: Twentieth Century Ethnography, Literature and Art.* Cambridge MA: Harvard University Press.

Clifford, James (1992). 'Traveling cultures'. In Grossberg, Nelson and Treicler (eds) (1992), 112–16.

Clifford, James and Marcus, George (eds) (1986). *Writing Culture: The Poetics and Politics of Ethnography.* Berkeley CA: University of California Press.

Cocker, Mark (2015). 'Death of a Naturalist', *New Statesman,* 12–18 June, 43–5.

Cohan, Steven and Shires, Linda M. (1988). *Telling Stories: A Theoretical Analysis of Narrative Fiction.* London: Routledge.

Cohen, Stanley (1987 rev. edn). *Folk Devils and Moral Panics: Mods and Rockers.* Oxford: Blackwell.

Cohen, Stanley and Young, Jock (eds) (1981 rev. edn). *The Manufacture of News: Deviance, Social Problems and the Media.* London: Constable.

Collier, Peter and Davies, Judith (eds) (1989). *Modernism and the European Unconscious.* Cambridge: Polity Press.

Collins, Jim (1993). 'Genericity in the nineties: eclectic irony and the new sincerity'. In Collins *et al.* (eds) (1993).

Collins, Jim, Racher, Hilary and Collins, Ava Preacher (eds) (1993). *Film Theory Goes to the Movies.* London: Routledge.

Collins, Richard (1990). *Television.* London: Unwin Hyman.

Colls, Robert and Dodd, Philip (eds) (1986, 2nd edn 2014). *Englishness. Politics and Culture 1880–1920.* Afterword by Will Self. London: Bloomsbury.

Connell, Rob (1987). *Gender and Power.* Cambridge: Polity Press.

Connell, Rob (1995). *Masculinities.* Cambridge: Polity Press.

Connor, Steven (1989, rev. edn 1997). *Postmodernist Culture.* Oxford: Basil Blackwell.

Connor, Steven (1992). *Theory and Cultural Value.* Oxford: Basil Blackwell.

Connor, Steven (2011). 'Doing Without Art', *New Literary History,* 42, 53–69.

Cook, Pam (ed) (1985). *The Cinema Book.* London: British Film Institute.

Coombs, Danielle Sarver and Collister, Simon (2015). *Debates for the Digital Age: The Good, the Bad, and the Ugly of Our Online World.* Santa Barbara CA: Praeger.

Coward, Rosalind (1983). *Patriarchal Precedents.* London: Routledge.

Coward, Rosalind (1992). *Our Treacherous Hearts: Why Women Let Men Get Their Way.* London: Faber.

Coward, Rosalind and Ellis, John (1977). *Language and Materialism.* London: Routledge.

Cranny-Francis, Anne (1990). *Feminist Fiction: Feminist Uses of Generic Fiction.* Cambridge: Polity Press.

Creed, Barbara (1993). *The Monstrous Feminine.* London: Routledge.

Creed, Barbara (1997 [1987]). 'From here to modernity', *Screen,* 28(2), 47–67. In Brooker and Brooker (eds) (1997).

Cresswell, Tim (1997). 'Imagining the nomad: mobility and the postmodern primitive'. In Benko, Georges and Strohmayer, Ulf (eds) (1997), 360–79.

Crews, Frederick *et al.* (1997). *The Memory Wars: Freud's Legacy in Dispute.* London: Granta.

Critchley, Simon (1992). *The Ethics of Deconstruction. Derrida and Lévinas.* Oxford: Blackwell.

Culler, Jonathan (1976). *Ferdinand de Saussure.* London: Collins.

Culler, Jonathan (1982). *The Pursuit of Signs: Semiotics, Literature, Deconstruction.* London: Routledge.

Culler, Jonathan (1997). *Literary Theory: A Very Short Introduction.* Oxford: Oxford University Press.

Cunningham, Valentine (2002). *Reading After Theory.* Oxford: Blackwell.

Curran, James and Seaton, Jane (1991, 4th edn). *Power Without Responsibility. The Press and Broadcasting in Britain.* London: Routledge.

Currie, Mark (2013). *The Invention of Deconstruction.* London: Palgrave Macmillan.

Cutting, Gary (ed) (1994). *The Cambridge Companion to Foucault.* Cambridge: Cambridge University Press.

Damrosch, David (2003). *What is World Literature?* Princeton NJ: Princeton University Press.

Damrosch, David (2009). *How to Read World Literature.* London: Blackwell.

Damrosch, David (ed) (2009). *Teaching World Literature.* New York: Modern Language Association.

Damrosch, David (ed) (2014). *World Literature in Theory.* Oxford: John Wiley and Sons, Ltd.

Damrosch, David, *et al.* (eds) (2009). *The Longman Anthology of World Literature.* 6 Vols. New York: Pearson Longman.

Dance, F. and Larson, C. (1976). *The Functions of Human Communication: A Theoretical Approach.* New York: Holt, Rinehart and Winston.

Darley, Andrew (2000). *Visual Digital Culture.* London: Routledge.

Davidoff, Sherri and Ham, Jonathan (2012). *Network Forensics: Tracking Hackers Through Cyberspace.* Upper Saddle River NJ: Prentice Hall.

Davis, Mike (1988). 'Urban renaissance and the spirit of postmodernism'. In Kaplan (ed) (1988).

Davis, Mike (1990, 2nd edn 2006). *City of Quartz.* London: Verso.

Davis, Todd F. and Womack, Kenneth (eds) (2001). *Mapping the Ethical Turn: A Reader in Ethics, Culture, and Literary Theory.* Charlottesville VA: University of Virginia.

de Certeau, Michel (1988). *The Practice of Everyday Life.* Trans. Steven Rendell. Berkeley CA: University of California Press.

Deacon, David, Pickering, Michael, Golding, Peter, Murdock, Graham (1999). *Researching Communications.* London: Arnold.

Dean, Mitchell (1999). *Governmentality. Power and Rule in Modern Society.* London: Sage.

Deane, Seamus (1995). 'Imperialism/nationalism'. In Lentricchia and McLaughlin (eds) (1995).

Debord, Guy (1970 [1967]). *Society of the Spectacle.* Detroit MI: Black and Red.

Debord, Guy (1998). *Comments on the Society of the Spectacle.* Trans. Malcolm Imrie. London: Verso.

del Rio, Elena (2008). *Deleuze and the Cinemas of Performance: Powers of Affection.* Edinburgh: University of Edinburgh Press.

Deleuze, Gilles and Guatarri, Felix (1984 [1972]). *Anti-Oedipus.* New York: Viking Press.

Deleuze, Gilles and Guattari, Félix (1987 [1980]). *A Thousand Plateaus.* Trans. Brian Massumi. London: Athlone Press.

Dentith, Simon (1994). *Bakhtinian Thought: An Introductory Reader.* London: Routledge.

Denzin, Norman K. and Lincoln, Yvonna, S. (eds) (1994). *Handbook of Qualitative Research.* London: Sage.

Derrida, Jacques (1976 [1967]). *Of Grammatology.* Trans. Gayatri Chakravorty Spivak. Baltimore MD and London: Johns Hopkins University Press.

Derrida, Jacques (1978 [1967]) *Writing and Difference*. Trans. Alan Bass. London: Routledge.

Derrida, Jacques (1981a [1972]). *Positions*. Trans. Alan Bass. Chicago IL: Chicago University Press.

Derrida, Jacques (1981b [1972]). *Dissemination*. Trans. Barbara Johnson. Chicago IL: Chicago University Press.

Derrida, Jacques (1992a). *Acts of Literature*. Ed. Derek Attridge. London: Routledge.

Derrida, Jacques (1992b). 'The law of genre'. In Derrida (1992a).

Derrida, Jacques (1993). 'Chora'. In Kipnis, J. (ed) (1993).

Derrida, Jacques (1994a). 'Spectres of Marx'. *New Left Review*, 205, 31–58.

Derrida, Jacques (1994b). *Spectres of Marx: The State of the Debt, The Work of Mourning and the New International*. Trans. Peggy Kamuf. London: Routledge.

Derrida, Jacques (1996). *Archive Fever*. Chicago IL: University of Chicago Press.

Derrida, Jacques (2001). *On Cosmopolitanism and Forgiveness*. London: Routledge.

Derrida, Jacques (2008). (ed Marie-Louise Mallet; trans. David Wills). *The Animal that Therefore I Am*. New York: Fordham University Press.

D'haen, Theo (2011). *The Routledge Concise History of World Literature*. London: Routledge.

Doane, Mary Ann (1987). *The Desire to Desire: Women's Film of the 1940s*. Bloomington IN: Indiana University Press.

Docherty, Thomas (1990, repr. 1996). *After Theory: Postmodernism/Postmarxism*. Edinburgh: Edinburgh University Press.

Docherty, Thomas (ed) (1993). *Postmodernism: A Reader*. Hemel Hempstead: Harvester.

Docherty, Thomas (1996). *Alterities: Criticism, History, Representation*. Oxford: Clarendon Press.

Docherty, Thomas (1997). *After Theory*. Edinburgh: Edinburgh University Press.

Docker, John (1994). *Postmodernism and Popular Culture: A Cultural History*. Cambridge: Cambridge University Press.

Dollimore, Jonathan (1991). *Sexual Dissidence: Augustine to Wilde, Freud to Foucault*. Oxford: Clarendon Press.

Donald, James (ed) (1989). *Fantasy and the Cinema*. London: British Film Institute.

Donald, James (ed) (1991). *Psychoanalysis and Cultural Theory*. London: Macmillan.

Donald, James (1992a). *Sentimental Education: Schooling, Popular Culture and the Regulation of Liberty*. London: Verso.

Donald, James (1992b). 'What's at stake in vampire films?' In Donald, James (1992a).

Donald, James (1993). 'How English is it? Popular literature and national culture'. In Carter *et al.* (eds) (1993).

Donald, James (1999). *Imagining the Modern City*. London: The Athlone Press.

Donald, James and Rattansi, Ali (eds) (1992). *'Race', Culture and Difference*. London, New York and New Delhi: Open University/Sage.

Dovey, Jon (ed) (1996). *Fractal Dreams: New Media in Social Context*. London: Lawrence and Wishart.

Drucker, Johanna, (2009). *Speclab: Digital Aesthetics and Projects in Speculative Computing*. Chicago IL: University of Chicago Press.

Du Bois, W.E.B. (1903). *The Souls of Black Folk*. Chicago IL: A.C. McClurg & Co.

Du Gay, Paul (ed) (1997) *Production of Culture/Cultures of Production*. London: Sage/Open University.

Du Gay, Paul, Hall, Stuart, Janes, Linda, Mackay, Hugh and Negus, Keith (1997). *Doing Cultural Studies: The Story of the Sony Walkman*. London: Sage/Open University.

During, Simon (ed) (1993, rev. edn 1999). *The Cultural Studies Reader*. London: Routledge.

Dworkin, Andrea (1981). *Pornography: Men Possessing Women.* London: The Women's Press.

Dyer, Richard (1977). *Gays and Film.* London: British Film Institute.

Dyer, Richard (1990). *Now You See It: Studies on Lesbian and Gay Film.* London: Routledge.

Dyer, Richard (1993a [1977]). 'Entertainment and utopia'. In During (ed) (1993).

Dyer, Richard (1993b). *The Matter of Images: Essays on Representation.* London: Routledge.

Eaglestone, Robert (1997). *Ethical Criticism. Reading After Lévinas.* Edinburgh: Edinburgh University Press.

Eagleton, Mary (ed) (1991). *Feminist Literary Theory: A Critical Reader.* London: Longman.

Eagleton, Terry (1976). *Criticism and Ideology.* London: Verso.

Eagleton, Terry (ed) (1983a) *Raymond Williams: Critical Perspectives.* Oxford: Blackwell.

Eagleton, Terry (1983b). 'Base and superstructure in Raymond Williams'. In Eagleton, Terry (ed) (1983a).

Eagleton, Terry (1984). *The Function of Criticism: From 'The Spectator' to Post-Structuralism.* London: Verso.

Eagleton, Terry (1986a). *Against the Grain.* London: Verso.

Eagleton, Terry (1986b). 'Capitalism, modernism and postmodernism'. In Eagleton (1986a).

Eagleton, Terry (1986c). 'Poetry, pleasure and politics'. In Eagleton (1986a).

Eagleton, Terry (1990). *The Ideology of the Aesthetic.* Oxford: Basil Blackwell.

Eagleton, Terry (1991). *Ideology: An Introduction.* London: Verso.

Eagleton, Terry (1996). *The Illusions of Postmodernism.* Oxford: Blackwell.

Eagleton, Terry (2003). *After Theory.* New York: Basic Books.

Eagleton, Terry (2005). *Holy Terror.* Oxford: Oxford University Press.

Eagleton, Terry (2013). *The Event of Literature.* New Haven CT: Yale University Press.

Eagleton Terry (2015). 'Dr Vlad', review of Edna O'Brien, *The Little Red Chairs, London Review of Books,* 37:30, 22 October, 37.

Eagleton, Terry, Jameson, Fredric, Said, Edward W. (1990). *Nationalism, Colonialism, Literature: A Field Day Company Book.* Minneapolis MN and London: University of Minnesota Press.

Easthope, Antony (1983). *Poetry as Discourse.* London: Routledge.

Easthope, Antony (1988). *British Post-Structuralism Since 1968.* London: Routledge.

Easthope, Antony (1989). *Poetry and Phantasy.* Cambridge: Cambridge University Press.

Easthope, Antony (1991). *Literary into Cultural Studies.* London: Routledge.

Easthope, Antony (ed) (1993). *Contemporary Film Theory.* London: Longman.

Easthope, Antony (1998). *Englishness and National Culture.* London: Routledge.

Easthope, Antony and Thompson, John, O. (eds) (1991). *Contemporary Poetry Meets Modern Theory.* Hemel Hempstead: Harvester.

Eco, Umberto (1979a). *A Theory of Semiotics.* Bloomington IN: Indiana University Press.

Eco, Umberto (1979b). *The Role of the Reader.* Bloomington IN: Indiana University Press.

Eco, Umberto (1986). *Travels in Hyperreality.* London: Picador.

Elias, Norbert (1978 [1939]). *The Civilising Process. Volume 1: The History of Manners.* New York: Pantheon Books.

Ellen, Roy and Fukui, Katsuyoshi (1996). *Redefining Nature: Ecology, Culture and Domestication.* Oxford: Berg.

Elliott, Anthony and Turner, Bryan, S. (eds) (2001). *Profiles in Contemporary Social Theory.* London: Sage.

Elliott, Gregory (ed) (1994). *Althusser: A Critical Reader.* Oxford: Blackwell.

Ellman, Maud (1990). 'Eliot's abjection'. In Fletcher and Benjamin (eds) (1990), 178–200.

Engels, Friedrich (1969 [1880]). 'Socialism: utopian and scientific'. In *Marx and Engels, Selected Works. Vol. 3.* Moscow: Progress Publishers.

Enzensberger, Hans Magnus (1970). 'Constituents of a theory of the media'. *New Left Review,* 64, 13–36.

Epstein, Julia and Straub, Kristina (eds) (1991). *Body Guards.* London: Routledge.

Fairlamb, Horace L. (1994). *Critical Conditions: Postmodernity and the Question of Foundations.* Cambridge: Cambridge University Press.

Faludi, Susan (1992). *Backlash: The Undeclared War Against Women.* London: Chatto and Windus.

Fanon, Frantz (1986 [1952]). *Black Skin, White Masks.* London: Pluto.

Fanon, Frantz (1988 [1961]). *The Wretched of the Earth.* New York: Grove Press.

Farley, Paul and Symmons, Michael (2012). *Edgelands: Journeys into England's True Wilderness*. London: Vintage.

Featherstone, Mike (ed) (1990). *Global Culture: Nationalism, Globalization and Modernity.* London: Sage.

Featherstone, Mike (1991). *Consumer Culture and Postmodernism.* London: Sage.

Featherstone, Mike and Burrows, Roger (eds) (1995). *Cyberspace/Cyberbodies/ Cyberpunk.* London: Sage.

Featherstone, Mike, Lash, Scott and Robertson, Roland (eds) (1995). *Global Modernities.* London: Sage.

Fee, Margery (1995). 'Who can write as other?' In Ashcroft *et al.* (eds) (1995).

Felman, Shoshana (ed) (1982). *Literature and Psychoanalysis: The Question of Reading: Otherwise.* Baltimore MD: Johns Hopkins University Press.

Felman, Shoshana (1987). *Jacques Lacan and the Adventure of Insight.* Cambridge MA and London: Harvard University Press.

Fetterly, Judith (1978). *The Resisting Reader: A Feminist Approach to American Fiction.* Bloomington IN: Indiana University Press.

Figes, Eva (1970). *Patriarchal Attitudes.* London: Virago.

Firestone, Shulamith (1970). *The Dialectic of Sex.* New York: Bantam.

Fish, Stanley (1980). *Is There a Text in This Class? The Authority of Interpretive Communities.* London: Harvard University Press.

Fiske, John (1987). *Television Culture.* London: Routledge.

Fiske, John (1989). *Understanding Popular Culture.* London: Unwin Hyman.

Fiske, John and Hartley, John (1978). *Reading Television.* London: Routledge.

Fletcher, John and Benjamin, Andrew (eds) (1990). *Abjection, Melancholia and Love: The Work of Julia Kristeva.* London: Routledge.

Ford, Martin (2015). *Rise of the Robots: Technology and the Threat of a Jobless Future*. New York: Basic Books.

Foster, Hal (ed) (1983). *The Anti-Aesthetic.* Seattle WA: Bay Press. Published *as Postmodern Culture.* London: Pluto.

Foucault, Michel (1972). *The Archaeology of Knowledge and the Discourse on Language.* Trans. A.M. Sheridan Smith. New York: Harper and Row.

Foucault, Michel (1977a). 'Intellectuals and power'. In *Language, Counter-Memory and Practice: Selected Essays and Interviews.* Ed. with an introduction by Donald F. Bouchard. Ithaca NY: Cornell University Press.

Foucault, Michel (1977b). 'The political function of the intellectual'. *Radical Philosophy,* 17, 12–14.

Foucault, Michel (1979). *The History of Sexuality, Vol. 1: An Introduction.* London: Allen Lane.

Foucault, Michel (1980a). *Power/Knowledge: Selected Interviews and Other Writings 1972–1977.* Ed. Colin Gordon. Trans. Gordon *et al.* Brighton: Harvester.

Foucault, Michel (1980b). 'Two lectures'. In Foucault (1980a).

Foucault, Michel (1980c). 'Questions of geography'. In Foucault (1980a).

Foucault, Michel (1980d). 'The eye of power'. In Foucault (1980a).

Foucault, Michel (1983). 'The subject of power'. In *Michel Foucault: Beyond Structuralism and Hermeneutics.* Ed. Dreyfus, Hubert L. and Rabinow, Paul. Chicago IL: University of Chicago Press.

Foucault, Michel (1986a). *The Foucault Reader.* Ed. Paul Rabinow. London: Peregrine.

Foucault, Michel (1986b [1969]). 'What is an author?' In Foucault (1986a).

Foucault, Michel (1986c). 'Space, power and knowledge'. In Foucault (1986a).

Foucault, Michel (1997 [1986]). 'Of other spaces; utopias and heterotopias'. In Leach, Neil (ed) (1997), 350–8.

Frascina, Francis and Harrison, Charles (eds) (1982). *Modern Art and Modernism: A Critical Anthology.* London: Harper and Row Ltd.

Frazer Elizabeth, Hornsby, Jennifer and Lovibond, Sabina (1992). *Ethics. A Feminist Reader.* Oxford: Blackwell.

Freud, Sigmund (1974a). *The Standard Edition of the Complete Psychological Works of Sigmund Freud.* 24 vols. Trans. James Stracey. London: Hogarth Press and the Institute of Psycho-Analysis.

Freud, Sigmund (1974b [1900]). 'The interpretation of dreams'. In *Standard Edition,* 4–5.

Freud, Sigmund (1974c [1905a]). 'Three essays on the theory of sexuality'. In *Standard Edition,* 7, 1–246.

Freud, Sigmund (1974d [1905b]). 'Fragment of an analysis of a case of hysteria'. In *Standard Edition,* 7, 1–122.

Freud, Sigmund (1974e [1912]). 'The dynamics of the transference'. In *Standard Edition,* 2, 97–100.

Freud, Sigmund (1974f [1914]). 'Remembering. Repeating and Working-Through'. In *Standard Edition,* 12, 145–56.

Freud, Sigmund (1974g [1915]). 'The unconscious'. In *Standard Edition,* 14, 159–256.

Freud, Sigmund (1974h [1918]). 'From the history of an infantile neurosis'. In *Standard Edition,* 17, 3–122.

Freud, Sigmund (1974i [1919]). 'The "uncanny"'. In *Standard Edition, 17,* 219–56.

Freud, Sigmund (1974j [1920]). 'Beyond the pleasure principle'. In *Standard Edition,* 18, 1–64.

Freud, Sigmund (with Josef Breuer), (1974k [1893]). 'On the Psychical Mechanism of Hysterical Phenomena'. In *Standard Edition,* 2, 1–18.

Freund, Elizabeth (1987). *The Return of the Reader: Reader-Response Criticism.* London: Routledge.

Frith, Simon (1996). *Performing Rites.* Oxford: Oxford University Press.

Frow, John (1995). *Cultural Studies and Cultural Value.* Oxford: Clarendon Press.

Gagnon, John and Simon, William (1973). *Sexual Conduct: The Social Sources of Human Sexuality.* Chicago IL: Aldine.

Gallop, Jane (1992). *Around 1981: Academic Feminist Theory.* London: Routledge.

Gamman, Lorraine and Marshment, Margaret (eds) (1988). *The Female Gaze: Women as Viewers of Popular Culture.* London: The Women's Press.

Garber, Marjorie (1992). *Vested Interests: Cross-Dressing and Cultural Anxiety.* London: Routledge.

Garber, Marjorie (1997). *Vice Versa: Bisexuality and the Eroticism of Everyday Life.* London: Hamish Hamilton.

Garber, Marjorie, Hanssen, Beatrice, Walkowitz, Rebecca L. (eds) (2000). *The Turn to Ethics*. New York and London: Routledge.

Gamham, Nicholas (1986). 'Extended review: Bourdieu's *Distinction'. Sociological Review,* Vol. 34, 423–33.

Gamham, Nicholas (1990). *Capitalism and Communication.* London: Sage.

Garrard, Greg (2012). *Ecocriticism.* London: Routledge.

Garrard, Greg (ed) (2014). *The Oxford Handbook of Ecocriticism.* Oxford: Oxford University Press.

Garreau, Joel (1992). *Edge City: Life on the New Frontier.* New York: Anchor Books.

Gates, Henry Louis (1988). *The Signifying Monkey. A Theory of Afro-American Criticism.* New York and Oxford: Oxford University Press.

Geertz, Clifford (1975). *The Interpretation of Cultures.* London: Hutchinson.

Gelder, Ken (1994). *Reading the Vampire.* London: Routledge.

Gellner, Ernest (1992). *Postmodernism, Reason and Religion.* London: Routledge.

Genette, Gérard (1980). *Narrative Discourse: An Essay in Method.* Trans. Jane E. Lewin. Oxford: Blackwell.

Genette, Gérard (1982). *Figures of Literary Discourse.* Trans. Alan Sheridan. Oxford: Blackwell.

Genocchio, Benjamin (1995) 'Discourse, discontinuity, difference: the question of "Other" spaces'. In Watson and Gibson (eds) (1995), 35–46.

George, Stephen, K. (ed) (2005. 2 ed.) *Ethics, Literature, and Theory: An Introductory Reader.* Lanham MD: Rowman and Littlefield.

Geras, Norman (1987). 'Post-Marxism?' *New Left Review,* 163, 40–82.

Geras, Norman (1988). 'Ex-Marxism without substance. Being a real reply to Laclau and Mouffe'. *New Left Review,* 169, 34–61.

Gere, Charlie (2015) 'Media'. *The Year's Work in Critical and Cultural Theory.* Oxford: Oxford University Press.

Giddens, Anthony (1987). *Social Theory and Modern Sociology.* Cambridge: Polity Press.

Giddens, Anthony (1990). *The Consequences of Modernity.* Cambridge: Polity Press.

Gillespie, Marie (1995). *Television, Ethnicity and Cultural Change.* London: Routledge.

Gilroy, Paul (1987). *There Ain't No Black in the Union Jack.* London: Hutchinson.

Gilroy, Paul (1993). *The Black Atlantic: Modernity and Double Consciousness.* London: Verso.

Gledhill, Christine (ed) (1987). *Home is Where the Heart is: Studies in Melodrama and the Woman's Film.* London: British Film Institute.

Gledhill, Christine (1994). 'Pleasurable negotiations'. In Storey (ed) (1994).

Gledhill, Christine (1997). 'Genre and gender: the case of soap opera'. In Hall (ed) (1997b).

Gleick, James (1988). *Chaos: Making a New Science.* London: Cardinal Books.

Glotfelty, Cheryll and Fromm, Harold (eds) (1996). *The Ecocriticism Reader. Landmarks in Literary Ecology.* Athens GA: University of Georgia Press.

Goldmann, Lucien (1975). *Towards a Sociology of the Novel.* London: Tavistock.

Gramsci, Antonio (1971a). *Selections from the Prison Notebooks.* Ed. Quintin Hoare and Geoffrey Nowell Smith. London: Lawrence and Wishart.

Gramsci, Antonio (1971b). The intellectuals'. In Gramsci (1971a), 3–23.

Grant, Iain Hamilton (2006). *On An Artificial Earth: Philosophies of Nature After Schelling* London: Continuum.

Granta (2008). *The New Nature Writing.* 102. London: Granta Publications.

Gratton, Peter (2014). *Speculative Realism. Problems and Prospects.* London: Bloomsbury.

Gray, Ann (1992). *Video Playtime: The Gendering of a Leisure Technology.* London: Routledge.

Gray, Ann and McGuigan, Jim (eds) (1997 rev. edn). *Studying Culture.* London: Arnold.

Gray, Chris Hables (2001). *Cyborg Citizen. Politics in the Posthuman Age.* London: Routledge.

Gray, Chris Hables, Mentor, Steven and Figueroa-Sarriera, Heidi (eds) (1995). *The Cyborg Handbook.* London: Routledge.

Green, Eileen and Adam Alison (eds) (2001). *Virtual Gender.* London: Routledge.

Greenberg, Clement (1939). 'Avant-garde and kitsch'. In Harrison, Charles and Wood, Paul (eds) (1995).

Greenblatt, Stephen (1988). *Shakespearean Negotiations: The Circulation of Social Energy in Renaissance England.* Berkeley CA: University of California Press.

Greenblatt, Stephen (1990). *Learning to Curse: Essays in Early Modern Culture.* London: Routledge.

Greer, Germaine (1971). *The Female Eunuch.* London: Paladin Books.

Gregg, Melissa and Seigworth, Gregory J. (eds) (2010). *The Affect Theory* Reader. Durham NC and London: Duke University Press.

Greimas, Algirdas Julien (1987). *On Meaning: Selected Writings in Semantic Theory.* London: Pinter.

Grossberg, Lawrence (1984). 'Another Boring Day in Paradise: Rock and Roll and the Empowerment of Everyday Life', *Popular Music.* 4, 'Performers and Audiences', 225–58.

Grossberg, Lawrence (1986). 'Is There Rock after Punk?' *Critical Studies in Mass Communication,* 3, 50–74.

Grossberg, Lawrence (1992) *We Gotta Get Out of This Place: Popular Conservatism and Postmodern Culture.* New York and London: Routledge.

Grossberg, Lawrence with Fry, T., Curthoys, A. and Patton, P. (1988). *It's a Sin: Essays on Postmodernism, Politics, and Culture.* Sydney: Power Publications.

Grossberg, Lawrence, Nelson, Cary and Treichler, Paula (eds) (1992). *Cultural Studies.* London and New York: Routledge.

Grosz, Elizabeth (1990). *Jacques Lacan: A Feminist Introduction.* London: Routledge.

Grosz, Elizabeth (1995). 'Woman, chora, dwelling'. In Watson and Gibson (eds) (1995).

Grosz, Elizabeth (1996). *Space, Time, Perversion.* London: Routledge.

Guha, Ranajit (ed) (1982–94). *Subaltern Studies: Writings on South Asian History and Society.* 8 vols. New Delhi: Oxford University Press.

Guillory, John (1995). 'Canon'. In Lentricchia and McLaughlin (eds) (1995).

Habermas, Jürgen (1975). *Legitimation Crisis.* Cambridge: Polity Press.

Habermas, Jürgen (1989 [1962]). *The Structural Transformation of the Public Sphere.* Trans. T. Burger and F. Lawrence. Cambridge MA: MIT Press.

Habermas, Jürgen (1992a [1985]). 'Modernity – an incomplete project'. In Brooker (ed) (1992).

Habermas, Jürgen (1992b rev. edn). *Autonomy and Solidarity: Interviews with Jürgen Habermas.* Ed. Peter Dews. London: Verso.

Halberstam, Judith and Livingstone, Ira (eds) (1995). *Posthuman Bodies.* Bloomington IN: Indiana University Press.

Hall, Stuart (1969). 'The hippies, an American moment'. In Nagel, J. (ed) (1969).

Hall, Stuart (1988). *The Hard Road to Renewal: Thatcherism and the Crisis of the Left.* London: Verso.

Hall, Stuart (1990). 'Cultural identity and diaspora'. In Rutherford (ed) (1990b), 222–37.

Hall, Stuart (1996a [1980]). 'Cultural studies: two paradigms'. In Storey (ed) (1996).

Hall, Stuart (1996b [1988]). 'New ethnicities'. In Morley and Chen (eds) (1996).

Hall, Stuart (1997a [1974]). 'The television discourse – encoding and decoding'. In Gray and McGuigan (eds) (1997).

Hall, Stuart (ed) (1997b). *Representation: Cultural Representations and Signifying Practices.* London and Milton Keynes: Sage and Open University.

Hall, Stuart (1997c). 'The spectacle of the "Other"'. In Hall (ed) (1997b).

Hall, Stuart and Jacques, Martin (1983). *The Politics of Thatcherism.* London: Lawrence and Wishart.

Hall, Stuart and Jefferson, Tony (eds) (1976). *Resistance Through Rituals: Youth Subcultures in Postwar Britain.* London: Hutchinson.

Hall, Stuart and Whannel, Paddy (1964). *The Popular Arts.* London: Hutchinson.

Hall, Stuart, Roberts, Brian, Clarke, John, Jefferson, Tony and Critcher, Chas (eds) (1979). *Policing the Crisis: Mugging, the State and Law and Order.* London: Macmillan.

Halliday, Fred (1996). *Islam and the Myth of Confrontation.* London: I.B. Tauris.

Hallward, Peter (2003). *Badiou. A Subject to Truth.* Foreword by Slavjo Žižek. Minneapolis MN and London: University of Minnesota Press.

Hamilton, Paul (1996). *Historicism.* London: Routledge.

Haraway, Donna (1990 [1985]). 'A manifesto for cyborgs: science, technology, and socialist feminism in the 1980s'. In Nicholson (ed) (1990).

Haraway, Donna (1991). *Simians, Cyborgs and Women: The Reinvention of Nature.* London: Free Association Books.

Harman, Graham (2002). *Tool-Being: Heidegger and the Metaphysics of Objects.* Chicago IL: Open Court.

Harman, Graham (2005). *Guerrilla Metaphysics: Phenomenology and the Carpentry of Things* Chicago IL: Open Court.

Harrison, Charles and Wood, Paul (eds) (1995). *Art in Theory 1900–1990.* Oxford: Blackwell.

Hartley, John (1982). *Understanding News.* London: Routledge.

Hartley, John (1992). *Tele-ology: Studies in Television.* London: Routledge.

Hartley, John (1996). *Popular Reality: Journalism, Modernity and Popular Culture.* London: Arnold.

Harvey, David (1989). *The Condition of Postmodernity.* Oxford: Blackwell.

Harvey, David (1993). 'Class relations, social justice and the politics of difference'. In Squires (ed) (1993), 85–120.

Harvey, David (1996) *Justice, Nature and the Geography of Difference.* Oxford: Blackwell.

Hawkes, David (1996). *Ideology.* London: Routledge.

Hawkins, Harriet (1990). *Classics and Trash: Tradition and Taboos in High Literature and Popular Modern Genres.* Hemel Hempstead: Harvester.

Hawkins, Harriet (1995). *Strange Attractors: Literature, Culture and Chaos Theory.* Hemel Hempstead: Prentice Hall/Harvester.

Hayles, Katherine, N. (1990). *Chaos Bound: Orderly Disorder in Contemporary Literature and Science.* Ithaca NY: Cornell University Press.

Hayles, Katherine, N. (ed) (1991). *Chaos and Order: Complex Dynamics in Literature and Science.* Chicago IL and London: University of Chicago Press.

Hayles, Katherine, N. (1999). *How We Became Posthuman: Virtual Bodies, Cybernetics, Literature and Informatics.* Chicago IL and London: University of Chicago Press.

Hayles, Katherine N. (2008). *Electronic Literature: New Horizons for the Literary.* South Bend IN: University of Notre Dame Press.

Hayles, Katherine N. (2012). *How We Think: Digital Media and Contemporary Technogenesis.* Chicago IL: The University of Chicago Press.

Hayles, Katherine, N. (2014). 'Speculative Aesthetics and Object-Oriented Inquiry (OOI)' in *Speculations: A Journal of Speculative Realism* V 158–179.

Heath, Stephen (1981). *Questions of Cinema.* London: Macmillan.

Hebdige, Dick (1979). *Subculture: The Meaning of Style.* London: Routledge.

Hebdige, Dick (1988). *Hiding in the Light.* London: Routledge/Comedia.

Hebdige, Dick (1989). 'New times. After the masses'. *Marxism Today,* Jan, 48–53.

Heilbrun, Carolyn (1964). *Toward A Recognition of Androgyny.* New York and London: Norton.

Held, David (2000) 'Regulating globalization?' In Held and McGrew (eds) (2000), 420–30.

Held, David and McGrew, Anthony (eds) (2000). *The Global Transformations Reader.* Cambridge: Polity.

Heller, Agnes (1984). 'Can cultures be compared?' *Dialectical Anthropology,* 8 (April), 269–74.

Hennessy, Peter (1986). *The Great and the Good: An Inquiry into the British Establishment.* London: Policy Studies Institute.

Hewitt, Roger (1986). *White Talk, Black Talk: Inter-Racial Friendship and Communication Amongst Adolescents.* London: Cambridge University Press.

Highmore, Ben (2001). *Everyday Life and Cultural Theory.* London: Routledge.

Hirschkop, Ken and Shepherd, David (1989). *Bakhtin and Cultural Theory.* Manchester and New York: Manchester University Press.

Hobsbawm, Eric (1996). 'Identity politics and the *Left'. New Left Review,* 217.

Hobson, Dorothy (1982). *'Crossroads': The Drama of a Soap Opera.* London: Methuen.

Hodge, Robert and Kress, Gunther (1988). *Social Semiotics.* Cambridge: Polity Press.

Hoggart, Richard (1970). *Speaking to Each Other: About Society.* London: Chatto and Windus.

Hoggart, Richard (1990 [1957]). *The Uses of Literacy.* Harmondsworth: Penguin.

Holderness, Graham (1988). *The Shakespeare Myth.* Manchester: Manchester University Press.

Holmes, David (1997). *Virtual Politics: Identity and Community in Cyberspace.* London: Sage.

Holub, Robert, C. (1984). *Reception Theory: A Critical Introduction.* London: Routledge.

Honneth, Axel (1994). 'History and interaction: on the structuralist interpretation of historical materialism'. In Elliott (ed) (1994).

Hood, Stuart (1972). 'The politics of television'. In McQuail, Denis (ed) (1972).

hooks, bell (1981). *Ain't I a Woman: Black Women and Feminism.* Boston MA: South End Press.

hooks, bell (1990a). *Yearning, Race, Gender and Cultural Politics.* Boston MA: South End Press.

hooks, bell (1990b). 'Postmodern blackness'. In hooks (1990a).

hooks, bell (1992). *Black Looks: Race and Representation.* Boston MA: South End Press.

hooks, bell (1994). *Outlaw Culture: Resisting Representation.* London: Routledge.

hooks, bell and West, Cornell (1991). *Breaking Bread: Insurgent Black Intellectual Life.* Boston MA: South End Press.

Horgan, John and Braddock, Kurt (2011). *Terrorism. A Reader.* London: Routledge.

Horowitz, Eli, Derby, Matthew, Moffett, Kevin, Quinn, Russell (2014). *The Silent History.* Cazadero CA: Sudden Oak.

Hoy, David Couzens (ed) (1986). *Foucault: A Critical Reader.* Oxford: Blackwell.

Huggan, Graham and Tiffin, Helen (2010). *Postcolonial Ecocriticism: Literature, Animals, Environment.* London: Routledge.

Humm, Maggie (1991). *Border Traffic: Strategies of Contemporary Women Writers.* Manchester: Manchester University Press.

Hutcheon, Linda (1980). *Narcissistic Narrative: The Metafictional Paradox.* London and New York: Methuen.

Hutcheon, Linda (1989). *The Politics of Postmodernism.* London: Routledge.

Huyssen, Andreas (1986). *After the Great Divide: Modernism, Mass Culture, Postmodernism.* London: Macmillan.

Irigaray, Luce (1985a [1974]). *Speculum of the Other Woman.* Trans. Gillian Gill. Ithaca NY: Cornell University Press.

Irigaray, Luce (1985b [1977]). *This Sex Which Is Not One.* Trans. Catherine Porter with Carolyn Burke. Ithaca NY: Cornell University Press.

Irigaray, Luce (1987 [1984]). 'Sexual difference'. In Moi, Toril (ed) (1987).

Iser, Wolfgang (1974). *The Implied Reader.* Baltimore MD: Johns Hopkins University Press.

Iser, Wolfgang (1978). *The Act of Reading: A Theory of Aesthetic Response.* Baltimore MD: Johns Hopkins University Press.

Jackson, Peter, Lowe, Michelle, Miller, Daniel and Mort, Frank (eds) (2000). *Commercial Cultures.* Oxford: Berg.

Jackson, Rosemary (1981). *Fantasy: The Literature of Subversion.* London: Routledge.

Jackson, Stevi and Scott, Sue (eds) (1996). *Feminism and Sexuality: A Reader.* Edinburgh: Edinburgh University Press.

Jakobson, Roman (1988). 'Concluding statement: linguistics and poetics'. In Lodge (ed) (1988).

Jameson, Fredric (1981). *The Political Unconscious. Narrative as a Socially Symbolic Act.* London: Methuen.

Jameson, Fredric (1984). 'Postmodernism, or the cultural logic of late capitalism'. *New Left Review,* 146, 53–92.

Jameson, Fredric (1988a). 'Ideology of the text'. In Jameson, Fredric (1988). *The Ideologies of Theory, Vol. 1.* London: Methuen.

Jameson, Fredric (1988b). 'Marxism and historicism'. In Jameson, Fredric (1988). *The Ideologies of Theory, Vol. 2.* London: Methuen.

Jameson, Fredric (1988c). 'Periodizing the 60s'. In Jameson, Fredric (1988). *The Ideologies of Theory, Vol. 2.* London: Methuen.

Jameson, Fredric (1990a). *Late Marxism: Adorno, or the Persistence of the Dialectic.* London: Verso.

Jameson, Fredric (1990b). *Signatures of the Visible.* London: Routledge.

Jameson, Fredric (1990c [1979]). 'Reification and utopia in mass culture'. In Jameson (1990b).

Jameson, Fredric (1991). *Postmodernism, or, the Cultural Logic of Late Capitalism.* Durham NC: Duke University Press.

Jameson, Fredric (1992). *The Geopolitical Aesthetic: Cinema and Space in the World System.* Bloomington IN: Indiana University Press.

Jameson, Fredric (1995). 'Marx's purloined letter'. *New Left Review,* 209, Jan/Feb, 75–109.

Jardine, Alice (1985). *Gynesis: Configurations of Women and Modernity.* Ithaca NY and London: Cornell University Press.

Jardine, Alice and Smith, Paul (eds) (1987). *Men in Feminism.* London: Methuen.

Jauss, Hans Robert (1982). *Toward an Aesthetic of Reception.* Trans. T. Bahti. Hemel Hempstead: Harvester.

Jencks, Charles (1993). *The Architecture of the Jumping Universe.* London: Academy Editions.

Jencks, Christopher, Peterson, Paul E. (eds) (1991). *The Urban Underclass.* Washington DC: The Brookings Institution.

Jenkins, Henry (1992). *Textual Poachers.* London: Routledge.

Jenkins, Henry (1998). 'The Poachers and the Stormtroopers: Cultural Convergence in the Digital Age', http://web.mit.edu/21fms/People/henry3/pub/stormtroopers.htm.

Jenkins, Henry and Tulloch, John (1995). *Science Fiction Audiences: Watching 'Star Trek' and 'Doctor Who'.* London: Routledge.

Jenkins, Richard (1992). *Pierre Bourdieu.* London: Routledge.

Johnson, Richard (1979a). 'Histories of culture/theories of ideology'. In Barrett, Michèle, Corrigan, Philip *et al.* (eds) (1979).

Johnson, Richard (1979b). 'Three problematics'. In Clarke *et al.* (1979).

Johnston, Claire (1976). Women's cinema as countercinema'. In Nicholls, B. (ed) (1976).

Jones, Owen (2014). *The Establishment – And How They Get Away With It.* London: Penguin.

Jones, Steven G. (1997). *Virtual Culture: Identity and Communications in Cybersociety.* London: Sage.

Jordan, Glenn and Weedon, Chris (1995). *Cultural Politics: Class, Gender, Race and the Postmodern World.* London: Routledge.

Kamuf, Peggy (ed) (1991). *A Derrida Reader: Between the Blinds.* Hemel Hempstead: Harvester.

Kaplan, E. Ann (ed) (1988). *Postmodernism and Its Discontents.* London: Verso.

Kaplan, E. Ann (ed) (1990). *Psychoanalysis and Cinema.* London: British Film Institute.

Kaplan, Jerry (2015). *Humans Need Not Apply. A Guide to Wealth and Work in the Age of Artificial Intelligence.* New Haven CT: Yale University Press.

Kearney, Richard (1995). *States of Mind.* Manchester: Manchester University Press.

Keith, Michael and Pile, Steve (eds) (1993). *Place and the Politics of Identity.* London: Routledge.

Kellner, Douglas (1984). *Herbert Marcuse and the Crisis of Marxism.* London: Macmillan.

Kellner, Douglas (1989a). *Critical Theory, Marxism, and Modernity.* Cambridge: Polity Press.

Kellner, Douglas (1989b). *Jean Baudrillard: From Marxism to Postmodernism and Beyond.* Cambridge: Polity Press.

Kelso, William Alton (1995). *Poverty and the Underclass.* New York: New York University Press.

Kennedy, Liam (2000). *Race and Urban Space in Contemporary America.* Edinburgh: Edinburgh University Press.

Kessler, Carol Farley (ed) (1984). *Daring to Dream: Utopian Stories by United States Women 1836–1919.* London: Pandora Press.

King, Anthony D. (ed) (1996). *Re-Presenting the City: Ethnicity, Capital and Culture in the 21st Century Metropolis.* London: Macmillan.

King, Nicola (2000). *Memory, Narrative, Identity. Remembering the Self.* Edinburgh: Edinburgh University Press.

Kipnis, J. (ed) (1993) *Choral Works: A Collaboration Between Peter Eisenman and Jacques Derrida.* New York: Rizzoli Architectural Press.

Kirkpatrick, Kathryn and Faragó, Bobala (eds) (2015). *Animals in Irish Literature and Culture*. London: Palgrave.

Klein, Naomi (2000). *No Logo.* London: Flamingo.

Knabb, Ken (ed) (1981). *Situationist International Anthology.* Berkeley CA: Bureau of Public Secrets.

Kosaku, Yoshino (1992). *Cultural Nationalism in Contemporary Japan.* London: Routledge.

Kracauer, Siegfried (1995 [1929]). *The Mass Ornament. Weimar Essays.* Cambridge MA: Harvard University Press.

Krauss, Rosalind (1985). *The Originality of the Avant-Garde and Other Modernist Myths.* Cambridge MA: MIT Press.

Kristeva, Julia (1982). *The Powers of Horror: An Essay in Abjection.* Trans. Leon S. Roudiez. Oxford: Blackwell.

Kristeva, Julia (1984a [1974]). *Revolution in Poetic Language.* Trans. Leon S. Roudiez. New York: Columbia University Press.

Kristeva, Julia (1984b [1980]). *Desire in Language: A Semiotic Approach to Literature and Art.* Ed. Leon S. Roudiez, trans. Thomas Gora *et al.* New York: Columbia University Press.

Kristeva, Julia (1986a [1966]). 'Word, dialogue and novel'. In Moi (ed) (1986).

Kristeva, Julia (1986b [1977]). 'A new type of intellectual: the dissident'. In Moi (ed) (1986).

Krupnick, Mark (ed) (1983). *Displacement: Derrida and After.* Bloomington IN: Indiana University Press.

Krutnik, Frank (1991). *In a Lonely Street: Film Noir, Genre, Masculinity.* London and New York: Routledge.

Kuberski, Philip (1994). *Chaosmos: Literature, Science and Theory.* Albany NY: State University of New York Press.

Lacan, Jacques (1977 [1966]). *Ecrits: A Selection.* Trans. Alan Sheridan. London: Tavistock.

Lacan, Jacques (1979). *The Four Fundamental Concepts of Psychoanalysis.* Trans. Alan Sheridan. London: Hogarth Press.

La Caze, Marguerite and Lloyd, Henry Martyn (eds) (2011). 'Philosophy and the Affective Turn'. *Parrhesia,* 13. Special issue on Affect, 1–13.

Laclau, Ernesto (1990). *New Reflections on the Revolution of Our Time.* London: Verso.

Laclau, Ernesto and Mouffe, Chantal (1985). *Hegemony and Socialist Strategy: Towards a Radical Democratic Politics.* London: Verso.

Lanchester, John (2013). *Capital.* London: Faber and Faber.

Landow, George P. (1992). *Hypertext: The Convergence of Contemporary Critical Theory and Technology.* Baltimore MD and London: Johns Hopkins University Press.

Lane, Richard, J. (ed) (2013). *Global Literary Theory*. London: Routledge.

Laplanche, Jean (1989). *New Foundations for Psychoanalysis.* Trans. David Macey. Oxford: Blackwell.

Laplanche, Jean and Pontalis, Jean-Bertrand (1988). *The Language of Psycho-Analysis* ([1967, 1973]; repr. London: H. Karnac (Books) Ltd.

Latour, Bruno (1987). *Science in Action: How to Follow Scientists and Engineers Through Society.* Milton Keynes: Open University Press.

Latour, Bruno (1993). *We Have Never Been Modern.* Hemel Hempstead: Harvester Wheatsheaf.

Latour, Bruno (1999). 'On *Recalling ANT'. The Sociological Review,* 47: S1, 15–25.

Latour, Bruno (2005). *Reassembling the Social. An Introduction to Actor-Network-Theory.* Oxford: Oxford University Press.

Lauretis, Teresa De (1987). *Technologies of Gender: Essays on Theory, Film and Fiction.* London: Macmillan.

Law, John (2014), 'Notes on the Theory of the Actor Network: Ordering, Strategy and Heterogeneity'. In Ewa Bińczyk and Aleksandra Derra (eds). *Science and Technology Studies: A Reader.* Wydawnictwo Naukowe UMK: The Nicolaus Copernicus University Press.

Law, John and Hassard, John (eds) (1999). *Actor Network Theory and After.* Oxford and Keele: Blackwell and the Sociological Review.

Law, Randall D. (2009). *Terrorism. A History.* Cambridge: Polity.

Leach, Neil (ed) (1997). *Rethinking Architecture. A Reader in Cultural Theory.* London: Routledge.

Le Doeuff, Michèle (1989). *'Long Hair and Short Ideas'. The Philosophical Imaginary.* London and Palo Alto CA: Athlone Press and Stanford University Press, 100–28.

Lefebvre, Henri (1991a). *Critique of Everyday Life, Vol. 1.* London: Verso.

Lefebvre, Henri (1991b [1974]). *The Production of Space.* Oxford: Blackwell.

Le Gates, Richard T. and Stout, Frederic (eds) (1996). *The City Reader.* London: Routledge.

Leitch, Thomas (2014). *Wikipedia U. Knowledge, Authority and Liberal Education in the Digital Age.* Baltimore MD: John Hopkins Press.

Lentricchia, Frank and McLaughlin, Thomas (eds) (1995). *Critical Terms for Literary Study.* Chicago IL: University of Chicago Press.

Lévinas, Emmanuel (1969). *Totality and Infinity.* Trans. Alphonso Lingis. Pittsburgh KS: Duquesne University Press.

Lévinas, Emmanuel (1989). *The Lévinas Reader.* Ed. Sean Hand. Oxford: Blackwell.

Lévi-Strauss, Claude (1966). *The Savage Mind.* London: Weidenfeld and Nicolson.

Levitas, Ruth (1993). 'The future of thinking about the future'. In Bird, Jon *et al.* (eds) (1993).

Leys, Ruth (2007). *From Guilt to Shame: Auschwitz and After.* Princeton NJ: Princeton University Press.

Leys, Ruth (2011). 'The Turn to Affect: A Critique'. *Critical Inquiry* 37 (Spring), 434–72.

Linklater, Andrew (1998). *The Transformation of Political Community.* Cambridge: Polity.

Lodge, David (ed) (1988). *Modern Criticism and Theory: A Reader.* London: Longman.

Lodge, David (1990). *After Bakhtin: Essays on Fiction and Criticism.* London: Routledge.

Love, Heather (2010). 'Close but not Deep: Literary Ethics and the Descriptive Turn'. *New Literary History,* 41, 371–91.

Lovell, Terry (1980). *Pictures of Reality: Aesthetics, Ideology and Pleasure.* London: British Film Institute.

Luckhurst, Roger (2008). *The Trauma Question.* London: Routledge.

Lukács, Georg (1963). *The Meaning of Contemporary Realism.* London: Merlin Press.

Lukács, Georg (1969 [1932]). *The Historical Novel.* Trans. Hannah Mitchell and Stanley Mitchell. Harmondsworth: Peregrine.

Lukács, Georg (1971 [1923]). *History and Class Consciousness.* Trans. Rodney Livingstone. London: Merlin Press.

Lunt, Peter K. and Livingstone, Sonia (1992). *Mass Consumption and Personal Identity.* Buckingham: Open University Press.

Lyon, David (1994). *Postmodernity.* Buckingham: Open University Press.

Lyotard, Jean-François (1983, 2nd edn 1988). *The Differend: Phrases in Dispute.* Manchester: Manchester University Press.

Lyotard, Jean-François (1984 [1979]). *The Postmodern Condition: A Report on Knowledge.* Trans. Geoff Bennington and Brian Massumi. Manchester: Manchester University Press.

Lyotard, Jean-François (1986). 'Defining the postmodern'. In Appignanesi, Lisa (ed) *Postmodernism: ICA Documents.* London: ICA. Reprinted in Docherty (ed) (1993).

Lyotard, Jean-François (1990 [1977]). *Duchamps Trans/Formers.* Venice CA: The Lapis Press.

McBeath, Graham and Webb, Stephen A. (1997). 'Cities, subjectivity and cyberspace'. In Westwood and Williams (eds) (1997).

MacCabe, Colin (1974). 'Realism and the cinema. Notes on some Brechtian theses'. *Screen,* 15(2), 7–27.

MacCabe, Colin (1993). "Preface" to Fredric Jameson'. *The Geopolitical Aesthetic.* London: British Film Institute, ix–xvi.

Macfarlane, Robert (2008). *Mountains of the Mind: A History of a Fascination.* London: Granta.

Macfarlane, Robert (2013). *The Old Ways: A Journey on Foot*. London: Penguin.

Macfarlane, Robert (2015a). *Landmarks*. London: Hamish Hamilton.

Macfarlane, Robert (2015b). 'Green shoots and silver buckshot', *New Statesman*, 4–10 September, 33–7.

Macfarlane, Robert (2016). 'What have we Done?' *Guardian, Saturday Review*, 2 April, 2–4.

McCaffery, Larry (ed) (1991). *Storming the Reality Studio: A Casebook of Cyberpunk and Postmodern Fiction*. London and Durham NC: Duke University Press.

MacCannell, Dean (1989). *The Tourist: A New Theory of the Leisure Class*. London: Macmillan.

Macdonell, Diane (1986). *Theories of Discourse: An Introduction*. Oxford: Blackwell.

Maher, Shiraz (2016). *Salafi-Jihadism: The History of an Idea*. London: C Hurst and Co.

Mason, Paul (2015). *Postcapitalism. A Guide to Our Future*. London: Allen Lane.

Massumi, Brian (1995, 2002). 'The Autonomy of Affect' in Massumi, Brian, *Parables for the Virtual: Movement, Affect, Sensation*. Durham NC and London: Duke University Press, 23–45.

McGuigan, Jim (1992). *Cultural Populism*. London: Routledge.

McGuigan, Jim (1996). *Culture and the Public Sphere*. London: Routledge.

McHale, Brian (1993). *Constructing Postmodernism*. London: Routledge.

McLuhan, Marshall and Fiore, Quentin (1967). *The Medium is the Massage*. London: Allen Lane.

McQuail, Denis (ed) (1972). *Sociology of Mass Communications*. London: Penguin.

McQuail, Denis (1987). *Mass Communication Theory: An Introduction*. London: Sage.

McQuillan, Martin, Macdonald, Graeme, Thomson, Stephen and Purves, Robin (eds) (1999). *Post-Theory: New Directions in Criticism*. Edinburgh: Edinburgh University Press.

McRobbie, Angela (1991). *Feminism and Youth Culture*. London: Macmillan.

McRobbie, Angela (1992). 'Post-Marxism and cultural studies: a postscript'. In Grossberg *et al.* (eds) (1992), 719–30.

McRobbie, Angela (1994). *Postmodernism and Popular Culture*. London: Routledge.

McRobbie, Angela (1999). *In the Culture Society: Art, Fashion and Popular Music*. London: Routledge.

Macey, David (1988). *Lacan in Contexts*. London: Verso.

Macherey, Pierre (1978 [1966]). *A Theory of Literary Production*. Trans. Geoffrey Wall. London: Routledge and Kegan Paul.

Macherey, Pierre and Balibar, Étienne (1993 [1974]). 'On literature as an ideological form'. In Mulhern (ed) (1993).

MacKinnon, Catharine (1987). *Feminism Unmodified*. London: Macmillan.

Mainzer, Klaus (1994). *Thinking in Complexity: The Complex Dynamics of Matter, Mind and Mankind*. Berlin: Springer Verlag.

Mann, Kirk (1992). *The Making of the English 'Underclass': The Social Divisions of Welfare and Labour*. Milton Keynes: Open University.

Marcuse, Herbert (1978). *The Aesthetic Dimension*. Boston MA: Beacon Press.

Marks, Elaine and de Courtivron, Isabelle (eds) (1981). *New French Feminisms: An Anthology*. Brighton: Harvester Press.

Marris, Paul and Thornham, Sue (eds) (1996). *Media Studies: A Reader*. Edinburgh: Edinburgh University Press.

Marshall, T.H. (1977). *Class, Citizenship and Social Development*. Chicago IL and London: University of Chicago Press.

Marshall, T.H. (1981). *The Right to Welfare and Other Essays*. London: Heinemann.

Marx, Karl and Engels, Friedrich (1968, 1969, 1970). *Selected Works*. 3 vols. Moscow: Progress Publishers.

Marx, Karl, Engels, Friedrich and Lenin, Vladimir Illich (1977). *On Dialectical Materialism*. London: Lawrence and Wishart.

Massey, Doreen (1993). 'A global sense of place'. In Gray and McGuigan (eds) (1997).

Massey, Doreen and Jess, Pat (eds) (1995). *A Place in the World*. Milton Keynes: Open University/Oxford University Press.

Masterman, Len (ed) (1983). *Television Mythologies: Stars, Shows and Signs*. London: Routledge.

Meillassoux, Quentin (2009). *After Finitude: An Essay on the Necessity of Contingency*. Trans. Ray Brassier. London: Continuum.

Melling, Phil (1999). *Fundamentalism and its Revisions: American Literature, Culture and Society in the 1990s*. Edinburgh: Edinburgh University Press.

Menand, Louis (1995). 'Diversity'. In Lentricchia and McLaughlin (eds) (1995).

Mercer, Kobena (1994). *Welcome to the Jungle*. London: Routledge.

Metcalfe, Andy and Humphries, Martin (1985). *The Sexuality of Men*. London: Pluto.

Metz, Christian (1974). *Film Language: A Semiotics of the Cinema*. Trans. M. Taylor. New York and Oxford: Oxford University Press.

Michael, Mike (2000). *Reconnecting Culture, Technology and Nature*. London: Routledge.

Miles, Robert (1982). *Racism and Migrant Labour*. London: Routledge. Miles, Robert (1989). *Racism*. London: Routledge.

Miller, Daniel (ed) (2001). *Consumption*. 4 vol. set. London: Routledge.

Miller, David (ed) (1995). *Acknowledging Consumption: A Review of New Studies*. London: Routledge.

Miller, J. Hillis (1989). *The Ethics of Reading: Kant, De Man, Eliot, Trollope, James and Benjamin*. New York: Columbia University Press.

Miller, Peter and Rose, Nikolas (1990). 'Governing economic life'. *Economy and Society*, 19(1), 1–31.

Millett, Kate (1970). *Sexual Politics*. New York: Avon Books.

Mitchell, Juliet (1974). *Psychoanalysis and Feminism*. London: Allen Lane.

Mitchell, Juliet (ed) (1986). *The Selected Melanie Klein*. London: Penguin.

Mitchell, Juliet and Rose, Jacqueline (eds) (1982). *Feminine Sexuality: Jacques Lacan and the École Freudienne*. London: Macmillan.

Moi, Toril (1985). *Sexual/Textual Politics: Feminist Literary Theory*. London and New York: Methuen.

Moi, Toril (ed) (1986). *The Kristeva Reader*. Oxford: Blackwell.

Moi, Toril (ed) (1987) *French Feminist Thought*. Oxford: Blackwell.

Moi, Toril (1991). 'Appropriating Bourdieu: feminist theory and Pierre Bourdieu's sociology of culture'. *New Literary History*, 22, 1017–49. In Lovell, T. (ed) (1995) *Feminist Cultural Studies*. 2 vols. Aldershot: Edward Elgar.

Monbiot, George (2013). *Feral: Searching for Enchantment on the Frontiers of Rewilding*. London: Penguin.

Morgan, Robin (ed) (1970). *Sisterhood is Powerful: An Anthology of Writings from the Women's Liberation Movement*. New York: Vintage.

Moretti, Franco (1998). *Atlas of the European Novel, 1800–1900*. London: Verso.

Moretti, Franco (2013). *Distant Reading*. London: Verso.

Moriarty, Michael (1994). 'Barthes on theatre'. In *The Polity Reader in Cultural Theory*. Cambridge: Polity Press.

Morley, David (1980). *The 'Nationwide' Audience: Structure and Decoding*. London: British Film Institute.

Morley, David (1986). *Family Television: Cultural Power and Domestic Leisure*. London: Comedia.

Morley, David (1995). 'Theories of consumption in media studies'. In Miller, David (ed) (1995), 296–328.

Morley, David (2000). *Home Territories. Media, Mobility and Identity.* London: Routledge.

Morley, David and Chen, Kuan-Hsing (eds) (1996). *Stuart Hall: Critical Dialogues in Cultural Studies.* London: Routledge.

Morris, Meaghan (1988). *The Pirate's Fiancée: Feminism, Reading, Postmodernism.* London: Verso.

Morris, Meaghan (1996). 'Banality in cultural studies'. In Storey (ed) (1996).

Morrison, Toni (1992). *Playing in the Dark: Whiteness and the Literary Imagination.* Cambridge MA: Harvard University Press.

Mort, Frank (1996). *Cultures of Consumption: Commerce, Masculinities and Social Space in Late Twentieth Century Britain.* London: Routledge.

Mouffe, Chantal (1993). 'Liberal socialism and pluralism: which citizenship?' In Squires (ed) (1993), 69–84.

Mouzelis, Nicos P. (1990). *Post-Marxist Alternatives: The Construction of Social Orders.* London: Macmillan.

Mulhern, Francis (ed) (1993). *Contemporary Marxist Literary Criticism.* London: Longman.

Mulhern, Francis (1995). 'Message in a bottle: Althusser in literary studies'. In Elliott (ed) (1994).

Mulhern, Francis (2000). *Culture/Metaculture.* London: Routledge.

Mulvey, Laura (1989a). *Visual and Other Pleasures.* London: Macmillan.

Mulvey, Laura (1989b [1975]). 'Visual pleasure and narrative cinema'. In Mulvey (1989a).

Mulvey, Laura (1989c [1981]). 'Afterthoughts on "Visual pleasure and narrative cinema" inspired by King Vidor's *Duel in the Sun* (1946)'. In Mulvey (1989a).

Nadal, Marita and Calvo Monica (eds) (2014). *Trauma in Contemporary Literature, Narrative and Representation.* London: Routledge.

Nagel, J. (ed) (1969). *Student Power.* London: Merlin.

Nancy, Jean-Luc (1991). *The Inoperative Community.* Ed. Peter Connor; Foreword by Christopher Fynsk. Minneapolis MN: University of Minnesota Press.

Nash, Christopher (ed) (1990). *Narrative in Culture.* London: Routledge.

Nava, Mica (1992). *Changing Cultures: Feminism, Youth and Consumerism.* London: Sage.

Negus, Keith (1999). *Music Genres and Corporate Cultures.* London: Routledge.

Nelson, Cary and Grossberg, Lawrence (eds) (1988). *Marxism and the Interpretation of Culture.* London: Macmillan.

Newman, Peter C. (1975, 1981, 1998). *The Canadian Establishment.* Three Volumes. Toronto: McClelland and Stewart.

Nicholls, B. (ed) (1976). *Movies and Methods.* Berkeley CA: University of California Press.

Nicholls, Peter (1995). *Modernisms: A Literary Guide.* London: Macmillan.

Nicholls, Peter (1996). 'The belated postmodern: history, phantoms and Toni Morrison'. In Brooker and Widdowson (eds) (1996), 441–56.

Nicholson, Linda (ed) (1990). *Feminism/Postmodernism.* London: Routledge.

Nicholson, Linda and Seidman, Steven (eds) (1995). *Social Postmodernism: Beyond Identity Politics.* Cambridge: Cambridge University Press.

Nixon, Sean (1997). 'Circulating culture'. In Du Gay, Paul (ed) (1997), 177–234.

Nixon, Sean (2000). 'In pursuit of the professional ideal: advertising and the construction of commercial expertise in Britain 1953–64'. In Jackson, Peter *et al.* (eds) *Commercial Cultures.* Oxford: Berg.

Nixon, Sean (2002). *Creative Cultures: Gender and Creativity at Work in Advertising.* London: Sage.

Norris, Christopher (1982). *Deconstruction: Theory and Practice.* London: Routledge.

Norris, Christopher (1985). *The Contest of Faculties: Philosophy and Theory after Deconstruction.* London: Methuen.

Norris, Christopher (1987). *Derrida.* London: Collins.

Norris, Christopher (1992). *Uncritical Theory: Postmodernism, Intellectuals and the Gulf War.* London: Lawrence and Wishart.

Norris, Christopher (2013). *Philosophy Outside-In. A Critique of Academic Realism.* Edinburgh: Edinburgh University Press.

Onega, Susana and Ganteau, Jean-Michel (eds) (2014). *Contemporary Trauma Narratives, Liminality and the Ethics of Form.* London: Routledge.

Ong, Walter, J. (1982). *Orality and Literacy: The Technologizing of the Word.* London: Methuen.

Orbach, Susie (1978). *Fat is a Feminist Issue.* London: Paddington Press.

Orbach, Susie (1993 rev. edn). *Hunger Strike: The Anorexic's Struggle as a Metaphor of our Age.* London: Penguin.

Owens, Craig (1980). 'The allegorical impulse: toward a theory of postmodernism', Parts I and II. In *October,* 12, 67–86, and *October,* 13, 59–80.

Pacione, Michael (ed) (2001). *The City.* 4 vol. set. London: Routledge.

Paglia, Camille (1992). *Sex, Art, and American Culture.* London: Penguin.

Papadakis, Andreas, C. (ed) (1989). *Deconstruction II.* London: Academy Editions.

Parma, Pratibha (1990). 'Black feminism: the politics of articulation'. In Rutherford (ed) (1990b), 101–26.

Parrinder, Patrick (1980). *Science Fiction: Its Criticism and Teaching.* London: Methuen.

Patton, Paul (1995). 'Imaginary cities: images of postmodernity'. In Watson and Gibson (eds) (1995).

Patton, Paul (2001). 'Gilles Deleuze and Felix Guattari'. In Elliott, Anthony and Turner, Bryan S. (eds) (2001), 205–15.

Payne, Michael and Shad, John (eds) (2003). *Life. After. Theory.* London: Continuum.

Pearce, Lynne (1994). *Reading Dialogics.* London: Arnold.

Pfeil, Fred (1988). 'Postmodernism as a "structure of feeling"'. In Nelson and Grossberg (eds) (1988), 381–402.

Philomena, Mariani (ed) (1991). *Critical Fictions: The Politics of Imaginative Writing.* Seattle WA: Bay Press.

Piketty, Thomas (2014). *Capital in the Twenty-First Century.* Cambridge MA: Harvard University Press.

Plant, Sadie (1995). 'The future looms: weaving, women and cybernetics'. *Body and Society,* 1(3–4), 45–64.

Plant, Sadie (1996). 'The virtual complexity of culture'. In Robertson, George *et al.* (eds) (1996).

Pollock, Griselda (1992). *Avant-Garde Gambits, 1888–1893: Gender and the Colour of Art History.* London: Thames and Hudson.

Poster, Mark (ed) (1988). *Jean Baudrillard: Selected Writings.* Cambridge: Polity Press.

Potts, Jason and Stout, Daniel (eds) (2014). *Theory Aside.* Bloomsbury.

Pribram, Deirdre, E. (ed) (1988). *Female Spectators: Looking at Film and Television.* London: Verso.

Prigogine, Ilya and Stengers, Isabelle (1985). *Order Out of Chaos: Man's New Dialogue with Nature.* London: Flamingo.

Probyn, Elspeth (1990). 'Travels in the postmodern: making sense of the local'. In Nicholson (ed) (1990).

Propp, Vladimir (1968 [1958]). *Morphology of the Folktale*. Trans. L. Scott. Austin TX: University of Texas Press.

Pullen, Christopher (ed) (2010). *LGBT Identity and Online New Media*. London: Routledge.

Punter, David (1997, 2nd edn). *The Literature of Terror*. 2 vols. London: Longman.

Rabaté, Jean-Michel (2002). *The Future of Theory*. Oxford: Blackwell.

Rabaté, Jean-Michel (2014). *Crimes of the Future: Theory and its Global Reproduction*. New York and London: Bloomsbury.

Rabinow, Paul (ed) (1986). *The Foucault Reader*. Harmondsworth: Penguin.

Radford, Jean (1997). *The Other Side of Modernity: Modernism Revisited*. Edinburgh: Edinburgh University Press.

Radway, Janice (1984, rev. edn 1987). *Reading the Romance: Women, Patriarchy and Popular Literature*. London: Verso.

Rancière, Jacques (2004). *The Politics of Aesthetics. The Distribution of the Sensible*. Trans. and Introduction by Gabriel Rockhill. London: Continuum.

Rancière, Jacques (2010). *Dissensus: On Politics and Aesthetics*. Trans. Steven Cocoran. London: Continuum.

Readings, Bill (1991). *Introducing Lyotard. Art and Politics*. London: Routledge.

Reiser, Julie (2009). *Trauma, 9/11, and the Limits of Affective Materialism*. Diss. Baltimore MD: John Hopkins University.

Reiser, Julie (2012). 'Blind Hope: A Review of Gregg and Seigworth's *The Affect Theory Reader*'. http://www.electronicbookreview.com/thread/endconstruction/affective.

Rex, John (1986). *Race and Ethnicity*. Buckingham: Open University Press.

Rheingold, Harvey (1991). *Virtual Reality*. London: Secker and Warburg.

Rhodes, Chris (2016). Tourism Statistics and Policy: Briefing Paper No. 06022, 20 June 2016. London: House of Commons Library.

Rich, Adrienne (1987 [1980]). 'Compulsory heterosexuality and lesbian existence'. In Rich, Adrienne, *Blood, Bread and Poetry. Selected Prose, 1979–1985*. London: Virago, 23–75.

Rimmon-Kenan, Shlomith (1983). *Narrative Fiction: Contemporary Poetics*. London: Routledge.

Riviere, Joan (1929). 'Womanliness as a masquerade'. *International Journal of Psycho-Analysis,* 10,303–13.

Robbins, *Bruce* (1992). 'Comparative cosmopolitanism'. *Social Text,* 31/32, 169–86. Reprinted in Cheah and Robbins (eds) (2000).

Robbins, Derek (1991). *The Work of Pierre Bourdieu*. Milton Keynes: Open University Press.

Robertson, George, Mash, Melinda, Tickner, Lisa, Bird, Jon, Curtis, Barry and Putnam, Tim (eds) (1996). *Future Natural: Nature, Science, Culture*. London: Routledge.

Robertson, Roland (1995). 'Glocalization: time-space and homogeneity–heterogeneity'. In Featherstone *et al.* (eds) (1995).

Robins, Keith and Webster, Frank (1999). *Times of the Technoculture from the Information Society to the Virtual Life*. London: Routledge.

Roche, Maurice (1992). *Rethinking Citizenship: Welfare Ideology and Change in Modern Society*. Cambridge: Polity Press.

Rodowick, D.N. (2014). *Elegy for Theory*. Cambridge MA: Harvard University Press.

Roiphe, Katie (1994). *The Morning After: Sex, Fear and Feminism*. London: Hamish Hamilton.

Rojek, Chris and Turner, Bryan (1993). *Forget Baudrillard?* London: Routledge.

Rorty, Richard (1980). *Philosophy and the Mirror of Nature*. Oxford: Blackwell.

Rorty, Richard (1982). *Consequences of Pragmatism: Essays 1972–1980*. Minneapolis MN: University of Minnesota Press.

Rorty, Richard (1989). *Contingency, Irony and Solidarity*. Cambridge: Cambridge University Press.

Rose, Jacqueline (1993). *Why War? Psychoanalysis, Politics and the Return to Melanie Klein*. Oxford: Blackwell.

Rose, Margaret, A. (1983). *Parody: Ancient, Modern and Post-Modern*. Cambridge: Cambridge University Press.

Ross, Andrew (1989). *No Respect: Intellectuals and Popular Culture*. London: Routledge.

Rouse, Joseph (1994). 'Power/knowledge'. In Cutting, Gary (ed) (1994).

Rushdie, Salman (1992). *Imaginary Homelands. Essays and Criticism, 1981–1991*. London: Granta.

Rutherford, Jonathan (1990a). 'A place called home: identity and the cultural politics of difference'. In Rutherford (ed) (1990b).

Rutherford, Jonathan (ed) (1990b). *Identity: Community, Culture, Difference*. London: Lawrence and Wishart.

Ryan, Michael (1982). *Marxism and Deconstruction: A Critical Articulation*. Baltimore MD: Johns Hopkins University Press.

Saddler, Simon (1998). *The Situationist City*. Boston MA: MIT Press.

Said, Edward (1978). *Orientalism*. London: Routledge.

Said, Edward (1986). 'Orientalism reconsidered'. In Barker, Francis, Hulme, Peter, Loxley, Diana and Iverson, Margaret (eds) (1986).

Said, Edward (1993a). *Culture and Imperialism*. London: Chatto and Windus.

Said, Edward (1993b). *Representations of the Intellectual*. Reith Lectures. London: Vintage.

Sakai, Naoki (1997). *Translation & Subjectivity. On 'Japan' and Cultural Nationalism*. Foreword by Meaghan Morris. Minneapolis MN: University of Minnesota Press.

Sandler, Blair and Diskin, Jonathan (1995). 'Post-Marxism and class'. In Callari *et al.* (eds) (1995), 178–87.

Sarup, Madan (1992). *Jacques Lacan*. Hemel Hempstead: Harvester.

Sarup, Madan (1993, 2nd edn). *An Introductory Guide to Post-Structuralism and Postmodernism*. Hemel Hempstead: Harvester.

Sarup, Madan (1996). *Identity, Culture and the Postmodern World*. Edinburgh: Edinburgh University Press.

Sassen, Saskia (1991). *The Global City: New York, London, Tokyo*. Princeton NJ: Princeton University Press.

Saussure, Ferdinand de (1966 [1915]). *A Course in General Linguistics*. Trans. W. Baskin. London: Collins.

Savage, Mike (2015). *Social Class in the 21st Century*. London: Pelican.

Schnapp, Jeffrey T. and Battles, Matthew (2014). *The Library Beyond the Book*. Cambridge MA: Harvard University Press.

Schreibman, Susan, Siemens, Ray, Unsworth, John (eds) (2004). *A Companion to Digital Humanities*. Oxford: Oxford Wiley.

Schreibman, Susan, Siemens, Ray, Unsworth, John (eds) (2016). *A New Companion to Digital Humanities*. Oxford: Oxford Wiley.

Scott, Laurence (2015). *The Four Dimensional Human: Ways of Being in the Digital World*, London: William Heinemann.

Seabrook, Jeremy (2007). *World Poverty*. Northampton: New Internationalist Publications Ltd.

Seabrook, Jeremy (2015). *Pauperland. Poverty and the Poor in Britain*. London: C Hurst & Co Ltd.

Sedgwick, Eve Kosofsky (1985). *Between Men: English Literature and Male Homosocial Desire*. New York: Columbia University Press.

Sedgwick, Eve and Frank, Adam (1995). 'Shame in the Cybernetic Fold. Reading Sylvan Tomkins'. *Critical Inquiry*, 21(2), 496–522.

Segal, Lynne (1987). *Is the Future Female? Troubled Thoughts on Contemporary Feminism.* London: Virago.

Segal, Lynne (1997). Sexualities'. In Woodward (ed) (1997).

Segal, Lynne and McIntosh, Mary (eds) (1992). *Sex Exposed: Sexuality and the Pornography Debate.* London: Virago.

Seidler, Victor J. (1989). *Rediscovering Masculinity.* London: Routledge.

Seidler, Victor J. (ed) (1992). *Men, Sex and Relationships: Writings* from *Achilles Heel.* London: Routledge.

Seiter, Ellen, Borchers, Hans, Kreutzner, Gabriele and Worth, Eva-Maria (ed) (1989). *Remote Control: Television, Audiences and Cultural Power.* London: Routledge.

Selden, Raman, Widdowson, Peter and Brooker, Peter (2017). *A Reader's Guide to Contemporary Literary Theory.* 6th edition. London: Routledge.

Sennett, Richard (ed) (1969). *Classic Essays on the Culture of Cities.* Upper Saddle River NJ: Prentice Hall.

Shaviro, Steven (2014). *The Universe of Things: On Speculative Realism.* Minneapolis MN: University of Minnesota Press.

Shaw, Debra Benita and Humm, Maggie (eds) (2016). *Radical Space: Exploring Politics and Practice.* London: Rowman and Littlefield International.

Shiach, Morag (1991). *Hélène Cixous: A Politics of Writing.* London: Routledge.

Shields, Rob (1999). *Lefebvre: Love and Struggle, Spatial Dialectics.* London: Routledge.

Shilling, Chris (1997). 'The body and difference'. In Woodward (ed) (1997), 63–120.

Showalter, Elaine (ed) (1986). *The New Feminist Criticism: Essays on Women, Literature and Theory.* London: Virago.

Siemens, Ray, Schreibman, Susan (eds) (2013*). A Companion to Digital Literary Studies.* Oxford: Wiley-Blackwell.

Silk, Leonard Solomon and Silk, Mark (1980). *American Establishment.* New York: Basic Books.

Sim, Stuart (1996). *Jean-François Lyotard.* London: Harvester Wheatsheaf.

Simmel, Georg (1969 [1903]). 'The metropolis and mental life'. In Sennett, Richard (ed) (1969), 47–60.

Sinfield, Alan (1992). *Faultlines: Cultural Materialism and the Politics of Dissident Reading.* Oxford: Oxford University Press.

Sinfield, Alan (1994a). *The Wilde Century.* London: Cassell.

Sinfield, Alan (1994b). *Cultural Politics: Queer Reading.* London: Routledge.

Slack, Jennifer Daryl (1996). 'The theory and method of articulation in cultural studies'. In Morley and Chen (eds) (1996), 112–27.

Smith, Neil (1996) 'The production of nature'. In Robertson, George *et al.* (eds).

Smith, Barbara Herrnstein (1998). *Contingencies of Value: Alternative Perspectives for Critical Theory.* Cambridge MA: Harvard University Press.

Soja, Edward W. (1989). *Postmodern Geographies: The Reassertion of Space in Critical Social Theory.* London: Verso.

Soja, Edward W. (1995). 'Heterotopologies: a remembrance of other spaces in the citadel-LA'. In Watson and Gibson (eds) (1995), 13–34.

Soja, Edward W. (1996). *Thirdspace.* Oxford: Blackwell.

Sollers, Werner (ed) (1996). *Theories of Ethnicity.* London: Macmillan.

Sontag, Susan (1966). 'Notes on camp'. In *Against Interpretation.* New York: Farrar, Straus and Giroux.

Sontag, Susan (1988). *AIDS and its Metaphors.* London: Allen Lane.

Soper, Kate (1996). 'Nature/"nature"'. In Robertson, George *et al.* (eds) (1996).

Sparks, Colin (1996). 'Stuart Hall, cultural studies and Marxism'. In Morley and Chen (eds) (1996), 71–101.

Spivak, Gayatri Chakravorty (1983). 'Displacement and the discourse of woman'. In Krupnick, Mark (ed) (1983).

Spivak, Gayatri Chakravorty (1987). *In Other Worlds: Essays in Cultural Politics.* London: Routledge.

Spivak, Gayatri Chakravorty (1988). 'Can the subaltern speak?' In Nelson and Grossberg (eds) (1988).

Spivak, Gayatri Chakravorty (1990). *The Post-Colonial Critic: Interviews, Strategies, Dialogues.* Ed. Sarah Harasym. London: Routledge.

Squires, Judith (ed) (1993). *Principled Positions: Postmodernism and the Recovery of Value.* London: Lawrence and Wishart.

Squires, Judith (1996). 'Fabulous feminist futures and the lure of cyberculture'. In Dovey (ed) (1996).

Stacey, Jackie (1994). *Star-Gazing: Hollywood Cinema and Female Spectatorship.* London: Routledge.

Stallybrass, Peter and White, Allon (1986). *The Politics and Poetics of Transgression.* London: Methuen.

Stam, Robert (1988). 'Bakhtin and Left cultural critique'. In Kaplan (ed) (1988).

Stam, Robert (1989). *Subversive Pleasures: Bakhtin, Cultural Criticism and Film.* Baltimore MD and London: Johns Hopkins University Press.

Stam, Robert and Shohat, Ella (1996). *UnThinking Eurocentricism.* London: Routledge.

Steinberg, Deborah Lynn and Kear, Adrian (eds) (1999). *Mourning Diana. Nation, Culture and the Performance of Grief.* London: Routledge.

Sterling, Bruce (1988). *Mirrorshades: The Cyberpunk Anthology.* London: Paladin.

Storey, John (1993). *An Introductory Guide to Cultural Theory and Popular Culture.* Hemel Hempstead: Prentice Hall/Harvester.

Storey, John (ed) (1994). *Cultural Theory and Popular Culture: A Reader.* Hemel Hempstead: Prentice Hall/Harvester.

Storey, John (ed) (1996). *What is Cultural Studies? A Reader.* London: Arnold.

Storey, John (1999). *Cultural Consumption and Everyday Life.* London: Arnold.

Storry, Mike and Childs, Peter (eds) (1997). *British Cultural Identities.* London: Routledge.

Strehle, Susan (1992). *Fiction in the Quantum Universe.* London and Chapel Hill NC: University of North Carolina Press.

Stryker, Susan (2008). *Transgender History.* Berkeley CA: Seal Press.

Strinati, Dominic (1995). *Introduction to Theories of Popular Culture.* London: Routledge.

Sturrock, John (ed) (1979). *Structuralism and Since.* Oxford: Oxford University Press.

Suleiman, Susan Rubin (1990). *Subversive Intent: Gender, Politics and the Avant-Garde.* Cambridge MA: Harvard University Press.

Sutherland, John (1978). *Fiction and the Fiction Industry.* London: Athlone Press.

Suvin, Darko (1979). *Metamorphoses of Science Fiction.* New Haven CT: Yale University Press.

Tallack, Douglas (ed) (1995). *Critical Theory: A Reader.* Hemel Hempstead: Prentice Hall/Harvester.

Tanguay, Liane (2013). *Hijacking History: American Culture and the War on Terror.* Montreal QC and Kingston ON: McGill Queens University Press.

Teitelbaum, Matthew (ed) (1992). *Montage and Modern Life, 1919–1942.* Cambridge MA: Institute of Contemporary Art/MIT Press.

Tester, Keith (ed) (1994). *The 'Flâneur'*. London: Routledge.

Thomas, Calvin (2013). *Ten Lessons in Theory: An Introduction to Theoretical Writing*. New York and London: Bloomsbury.

Thompson, E.P. (1961). 'Review of *The Long Revolution'*. *New Left Review*, 9, 24–33.

Thompson, E.P. (1963). *The Making of the English Working Class*. London: Penguin.

Thompson, E.P. (1978). *The Poverty of Theory and Other Essays*. London: Merlin.

Thompson, John (1994). 'The theory of the public sphere: a critical appraisal'. In *The Polity Reader in Cultural Theory*. Cambridge: Polity Press.

Thornton, Sarah and Gelder, Ken (eds) (1996). *The Subcultures Reader*. London: Routledge.

Tiedeman, Rolf and Schweppenhauser, Herman (eds) (1972). *Walter Benjamin. Gesammelte Schriften. Vol.* 1. Frankfurt am Main: Surkamp Verlag.

Timms, Edward and Kelley, David (eds) (1985). *Unreal City: Urban Experience in Modern European Literature and Art.* Manchester and New York: Manchester University Press and St Martin's Press.

Timpanaro, Sebastian (1973). *On Materialism*. London: NLB.

Todd, Jane Marie (1986). 'The veiled woman in Freud's Das Unheimliche'. *Signs,* 2/3, 519–28.

Todorov, Tzvetan (1973). *The Fantastic*. Ithaca NY: Cornell University Press.

Todorov, Tzvetan (1977 [1971]). *The Poetics of Prose*. Trans. Richard Howard. Ithaca NY: Cornell University Press.

Tötösy de Zepetnek, Steven, and Mukherjee, Tutun (eds) (2013). *Companion to Comparative Literature, World Literatures, and Comparative Cultural Studies.* New Delhi: Cambridge University Press.

Tower, Beeke Sell (ed) (1990). *Envisioning America: Prints, Drawings, and Photographs by George Grosz and his Contemporaries, 1915–1933.* Cambridge MA: Busch-Reisinger Museum, Harvard University.

Toynbee, Jason (2000). *Making Popular Music*. London: Arnold.

Trexler, Adam (2015). *Anthropocene Fictions. The Novel in a Time of Climate Change.* Charlottesville VA: University of Virginia Press.

Trinh, T. Minh-ha (1989). *Woman, Native, Other: Writing, Post-Coloniality and Feminism.* Bloomington IN: University of Indiana Press.

Tsing, Anna (2016). *The Mushroom at the End of the World. On the Possibility of Life in Capitalist Ruins.* Princeton NJ: Princeton University Press.

Turner, Bryan, S. (ed) (1993). *Citizenship and Social Theory*. London: Sage.

Turner, Victor (1969). *The Ritual Process*. London: Routledge and Kegan Paul.

Twine, Richard and Taylor, Tik (eds) (2014). *The Rise of Critical Animal Studies – From the Margins to the Centre*. London: Routledge.

Ungar, R. and Crawford, M. (1992). *Women and Gender: A Feminist Psychology.* New York: McGraw-Hill.

Urry, John (1981). *The Anatomy of Capitalist Societies: The Economy, Civil Society and the State*. London: Macmillan.

Urry, John (1990). *The Tourist Gaze: Leisure and Travel in Contemporary Societies.* London: Sage.

Urry, John (1995). *Consuming Places*. London: Routledge.

van Gennep, Arnold (1960). *The Rites of Passage*. London: Routledge and Kegan Paul.

Vance, C. (1989). 'Social construction theory: problems in the history of sexuality'. In Altman, D. *et al.* (eds) (1989).

Veeser, H. Aram (ed) (1989). *The New Historicism*. London: Routledge.

Vice, Sue (1995) (ed) *Psychoanalytic Criticism: A Reader*. Cambridge: Polity.

Vilar, P. (1994). 'Marxist history. A history in the making. Towards a dialogue with Althusser'. In Elliott (ed) (1994).

Vince, Gaia (2015). *Adventures in the Anthropocene. A Journey to the Heart of the Planet We Made.* London: Chatto and Windus.

Vološhinov, V.N. (1986 [1929]). *Marxism and the Philosophy of Language.* Trans. Ladislav Matejka and I.R. Titunik. Cambridge MA: Harvard University Press.

Wakeford, Nina (2000). *Networks of Desire.* London: Routledge.

Walsh, Martin (1981). *The Brechtian Aspect of Radical Cinema.* Ed. Keith M. Griffiths. London: British Film Institute.

Warner, Michael (ed) (1997). *Fear of a Queer Planet. Queer Politics and Social Theory.* Minneapolis MN: University of Minnesota Press.

Watson, Sophie and Gibson, Katherine (eds) (1995). *Postmodern Cities and Spaces.* Oxford: Blackwell.

Waugh, Patricia (1984). *Metafiction: The Theory and Practice of Self-Conscious Fiction.* London and New York: Routledge.

Webster, Duncan (1996). 'Pessimism, optimism, pleasure: the future of cultural studies.' In Storey (ed) (1996).

Weeks, Jeffrey (1985). *Sexuality and its Discontents: Meanings, Myths and Modern Homosexualities.* London: Routledge.

Weeks, Jeffrey and Holland, Janet (eds) (1996). *Sexual Cultures.* London: Macmillan.

West, Cornell (1988). 'Marxist theory and the specificity of Afro-American Oppression'. In Nelson and Grossberg (eds) (1988).

West, Cornell (1993). *Race Matters.* Boston MA: Beacon Press.

Westwood, Sallie and Williams, John (eds) (1997). *Imagining Cities: Scripts, Signs, Memory.* London: Routledge.

Whelehan, Imelda (1995). *Modern Feminist Thought: From the Second Wave to 'Post-Feminism'.* Edinburgh: Edinburgh University Press.

Whiteley, Sheila (2000). *Women and Popular Music.* London: Routledge.

Whitford, Margaret (ed) (1991). *The Irigaray Reader.* Oxford: Blackwell.

Willett, John (1978). *The New Sobriety: Art and Politics in the Weimar Period 1917–1933.* London: Thames and Hudson.

Williams, Patrick and Chrisman, Laura (eds) (1993). *Colonial Discourse and Postcolonial Theory: A Reader.* Hemel Hempstead: Prentice Hall/Harvester.

Williams, Raymond (1961). *The Long Revolution.* Harmondsworth: Penguin.

Williams, Raymond (1962). *Communications.* London: Penguin.

Williams, Raymond (1973). *The Country and the City.* London: Chatto and Windus.

Williams, Raymond (1974). *Television, Technology and Cultural Form.* London: Collins.

Williams, Raymond (1976a, 3rd edn 1962). *Communications.* London: Penguin.

Williams, Raymond (1976b). *Keywords.* London: Collins.

Williams, Raymond (1977). *Marxism and Literature.* Oxford: Oxford University Press.

Williams, Raymond (1979). *Politics and Letters.* London: Verso.

Williams, Raymond (1980a). *Problems in Materialism and Culture.* London: Verso.

Williams, Raymond (1980b). 'Literature and sociology: in memory of Lucien Goldmann'. In Williams (ed) (1980a).

Williams, Raymond (1981). *Culture.* London: Collins.

Williams, Raymond (1989a). *Resources of Hope.* London: Verso.

Williams, Raymond (1989b). *The Politics of Modernism.* London: Verso.

Williams, Raymond (1992 [1985]). 'The metropolis and the emergence of modernism'. In Brooker (ed) (1992).

Williamson, Judith (1978). *Decoding Advertisements: Ideology and Meaning in Advertisements.* London: Marion Boyars.

Willis, Paul (1979). *Learning to Labour.* London: Saxon House.

Willis, Paul (1990). *Common Culture.* Milton Keynes: Open University Press.

Wilson, Elizabeth (1991). *The Sphinx in the City.* London: Verso.

Wilson, Elizabeth (1993). 'Is transgression transgressive?' In Bristow, Joseph and Wilson, Angela R. (eds) (1993).

Wilson, Elizabeth (1995). 'The invisible flâneur'. In Watson and Gibson (eds) (1995), 58–79.

Wilson, Elizabeth (1997). 'Looking backward, nostalgia and the city'. In Westwood and Williams (eds) (1997), 127–39.

Wilson, Scott (ed) (1995). *Cultural Materialism: Theory and Practice.* Oxford: Blackwell.

Winner, Langdon (1993). 'Upon Opening the Black Box and Finding it Empty: Social Constructivism and the Philosophy of Technology'. *Science, Technology and Human Values*, 18:3, 362–78.

Winters, David (2015). 'Theory on Theory', *The Year's Work Critical and Cultural Theory*, 23 (1). Oxford: Oxford University Press, 40–59.

Wittig, Monique (1992). *The Straight Mind and Other Essays.* London: Harvester Wheatsheaf.

Wolf, Naomi (1990). *The Beauty Myth.* London: Chatto and Windus.

Wolf, Naomi (1993). *Fire Against Fire: The New Female Power and How it will Change the 21st Century.* London: Chatto and Windus.

Wolfe, Cary (2010). *What Is Posthumanism?* Minneapolis MN: University of Minnesota Press.

Wolff, Janet (1993). 'On the road again: metaphors of travel in cultural criticism', *Cultural Studies*, 7/2, May, 1993, 224–39.

Wolff, Janet (1994). 'The invisible flâneuse: women and the literature of modernity'. In *The Polity Reader of Cultural Theory.* Cambridge: Polity Press, 200–9.

Wolff, Robert Paul, Moore Jr., Barrington and Marcuse, Herbert (1965). *A Critique of Pure Tolerance.* Boston: Beacon Press.

Wollaeger. Mark with Eatough, Matt (eds) (2012). *The Oxford Handbook of Global Modernisms.* New York: Oxford University Press.

Wollen, Peter (1969, rev. edn 1972). *Signs and Meanings in the Cinema.* London: Secker and Warburg.

Wollen, Peter (1993). *Raiding the Icebox: Reflections on Twentieth-Century Culture.* London: Verso.

Wolmark, Jenny (ed) (1999). *Cybersexualities. A Reader on Feminist Theory, Cyborgs and Cyberspace.* Edinburgh: Edinburgh University Press.

Woman: A Cultural Review (1990). Ed. Isobel Armstrong and Helen Carr. 'Positioning Klein', 1/2.

Woodward, Kathryn (ed) (1997). *Identity and Difference.* London: Sage/Open University.

Woolley, Benjamin (1993). *Virtual Worlds: A Journey in Hype and Hyperreality.* London: Penguin.

Woolf, Virginia (1973 [1929]). *A Room of One's Own.* London: Penguin.

Wright, Elizabeth (1984). *Psychoanalytic Criticism: Theory in Practice.* London: Routledge.

Wright, Elizabeth (1989). 'The uncanny and surrealism'. In Collier, Peter and Davies, Judith (eds) (1989).

Wright, Elizabeth (ed) (1992). *Feminism and Psychoanalysis: A Critical Dictionary.* Oxford: Blackwell.

Wyatt, Sally, Henwood, Flis, Miller, Nod and Senker, Peter (eds) (2000). *Technology and In/equality: Questioning the information society.* London: Routledge.

Young, Iris Marion (1990). 'The ideal of community and the politics of difference'. In Nicholson (ed) (1990).

Young, Jock (1981). 'The myth of drugtakers in the mass media'. In Cohen and Young (eds) (1981).

Young, Lola (1995). *Fear of the Dark: 'Race', Gender and Sexuality in the Cinema.* London: Routledge.

Young, Robert (ed) (1981). *Untying the Text. A Post-Structuralist Reader.* Brighton: Harvester.

Young, Robert (1990). *White Mythologies: Writing, History and the West.* London: Routledge.

Žižek, Slavoj (1989). *The Sublime Object of Ideology.* London: Verso.

Žižek, Slavoj (1997). *The Plague of Fantasies.* London: Verso.

Žižek, Slavoj (2002). 'Are we in a war? Do we have an enemy?' *London Review of Books*, 24:10, May, 3–6.

Žižek, Slavoj (2004). 'The Lesson of Rancière'. 'Afterword' to Rancière, *The Politics of Aesthetics*. London: Continuum, 69–79.